Digital Frontiers of AI in Transnational Education

Mazhar Hussain Malik
https://orcid.org/0000-0001-8890-1310
University of the West of England, UK

Yasmine Rosunally
The University of West of the England, UK

Nuzhat Younis
The University of West of the England, UK

IGI Global
Scientific Publishing
Publishing Tomorrow's Research Today

Vice President of Editorial	Melissa Wagner
Director of Acquisitions	Mikaela Felty
Director of Book Development	Jocelynn Hessler
Production Manager	Mike Brehm
Cover Design	Jose Rosado

Published in the United States of America by
IGI Global Scientific Publishing
701 East Chocolate Avenue
Hershey, PA, 17033, USA
Tel: 717-533-8845 | Fax: 717-533-7115
Website: https://www.igi-global.com E-mail: cust@igi-global.com

Library of Congress Cataloging-in-Publication Data

Library of Congress Cataloging-in-Publication Data

Names: Malik, Mazhar Hussain, 1983- editor | Rosunally, Yasmine, 1983- editor | Younis, Nuzhat, 1979- editor
Title: Digital frontiers of AI in transnational education / Edited by Mazhar Hussain Malik, Yasmine Rosunally, Nuzhat Younis.
Description: Hershey, PA : IGI Global Scientific Publishing, [2026] | Includes bibliographical references and index. | Summary: "This book examines how Artificial Intelligence is transforming transnational education, reshaping pedagogy, governance, and cross-border delivery in higher education. Through case studies, policy analysis, and critical insights, it explores ethical, cultural, and operational challenges while offering guidance for equitable and sustainable global education in the digital era"-- Provided by publisher.
Identifiers: LCCN 2025039406 (print) | LCCN 2025039407 (ebook) | ISBN 9798337354033 hardcover | ISBN 9798337354040 paperback | ISBN 9798337354057 ebook
Subjects: LCSH: Transnational education--Effect of technological innovations on | Artificial intelligence--Educational applications | Education and globalization
Classification: LCC LC1095 .D54 2026 (print) | LCC LC1095 (ebook)
LC record available at https://lccn.loc.gov/2025039406
LC ebook record available at https://lccn.loc.gov/2025039407

British Cataloguing in Publication Data
A Cataloguing in Publication record for this book is available from the British Library.

Table of Contents

Detailed Table of Contents

As artificial intelligence (AI) becomes increasingly embedded in transnational education (TNE), traditional quality assurance (QA) frameworks face mounting pressure to evolve. This chapter critically examines how AI reshapes the meaning, mechanisms, and governance of educational quality across borders. It explores the limitations of compliance-driven QA models in algorithmically mediated, culturally diverse, and digitally distributed learning environments. Drawing on sector practices, theoretical insights, and case examples, the chapter proposes a set of guiding principles—transparency, collaboration, cultural relevance, data ethics, and continuous improvement—to underpin effective QA in AI-enhanced TNE. It introduces conceptual models (centralised, distributed, collaborative, and hybrid-adaptive) to address governance gaps and promote inclusive, responsive, and future-ready QA architectures.

This chapter explores the integration of artificial-intelligence-assisted learning within transnational computer science education through the AI-Mediated Transnational Learning Model (AIM-TLM). Drawing on constructivism, socio-cultural learning theory, the Community of Inquiry framework, and Universal Design for Learning, the study examines how ethically guided AI use enhances equity, reflection, and engagement across bilingual cohorts. Using mixed-methods data from Object-Oriented Development and Advanced Information Systems Development modules delivered between the University of the West of England and Neusoft College, results show that structured AI scaffolding improved consistency and inclusivity without inflating grades. The chapter proposes a five-pillar framework covering transparency, assessment design, AI literacy, cultural calibration, and institutional alignment, offering a scalable model for ethical, inclusive, and sustainable AI integration in global higher education contexts.

Artificial Intelligence (AI) is not replacing pedagogy but transforming international higher education through conversation, connectivity, and intercultural development. This chapter examines AI methodologies via Laurillard's Conversational Framework, Siemens' Connectivism, and Deardorff's Intercultural Competence model, alongside the UK QAA Quality Code for TNE and Oman's OAAAQA. The analysis shows that predictive analytics, intelligent tutoring, and generative feedback enhance human judgement, expand networks, and support multilingual communication, while highlighting challenges of equity, transparency, and validity. To address these, the study proposes GDDMRCPA, a multidisciplinary framework structured across eight layers: Governance, Design & Procurement, Delivery & Support, Measurement & Evidence, Review & Enhancement, Cross-Cutting Enablers, Phased Adoption, and Alignment in Practice. Policy, bias, accessibility, regulation, appeals, and feedback-driven improvements are noted as implications. The chapter ends with enquiries into the equity of Oman–UK TNE agreements.

The Integration of Artificial Intelligence (AI) into teaching and learning in Higher education provides both opportunities and risks for preserving academic integrity, particularly within Transnational Education (TNE) contexts like in Oman. This Study analyses and evaluate How AI tools are reshaping ethical standards in teaching and learning. AI tools such as Plagiarism Detector and Automated Grading are mainly integrated into teaching and learning. Omani Higher education Institutions plays a vital role in maintaining educational values in local and global standards. This highlights the need for transparent and well-structured regulations and ethical standards to govern AI use. This chapter explores the impacts of AI, a dual role player as facilitator of learning and adopting technologies as well as a potential risk producer to integrity, accountability and cultural sensitivity in TNE environment. The chapter discusses, regulatory redesign and policy revision requirements to map with AI technology developments.

This paper examines the structural incompatibilities that arise when UK transnational education providers in the UAE navigate divergent AI regulatory frameworks. The UAE's National AI Strategy 2031 mandates rapid institutional transformation, whilst UK quality assurance emphasises equivalence with home provision. The analysis documents four fundamental incompatibilities that create a positioned impossibility for institutions, faculty, and students, revealing sustainability challenges for transnational education models in contexts of significant regulatory divergence.

Transnational education (TNE) broadens global learning but often overlooks students' cultural identities, resulting in exclusion and "spiritual homelessness." This paper examines how culturally responsive artificial intelligence (AI) can enhance engagement, dialogue, and belonging across diverse educational contexts. It critiques standardized AI systems that reinforce dominant norms and misinterpret culturally shaped learning behaviours, proposing adaptive, culturally aware tools that respond to learners' linguistic, cultural, and relational needs. Such AI promotes inclusion, empathy, and identity affirmation. The paper calls for inclusive leadership, faculty development, and ethical governance, arguing that diversity in AI design is vital to equity, innovation, and human-centered education.

This mixed-methods study investigates the reliability of traditional assessments in Omani higher education amid the growing use of artificial intelligence (AI) tools such as ChatGPT, Grammarly, and Quillbot. A total of 120 participants—students, faculty, and administrators, completed an online survey examining patterns of AI use, perceptions of assessment validity, and views on academic integrity. Quantitative data were analyzed using descriptive statistics, while qualitative responses were thematically examined to capture concerns and perspectives. Findings show that AI has become widely integrated into academic practices, particularly for writing, paraphrasing, and idea generation. While some participants valued AI as supportive, others worried about its impact on authenticity and reliability. Confidence in current formats, especially essays and take-home tasks, was moderate to low in reflecting true understanding. A further challenge is the absence of clear policies or ethical guidelines, leading to inconsistent practices across institutions.

This chapter interrogates how artificial intelligence reshapes transnational education by reconfiguring pedagogy, faculty development, and governance across borders. It synthesizes learning sciences, intercultural theory, and critical algorithm studies to construct a multilevel framework that links macro policy, meso institutional design, and micro classroom practice. The analysis profiles adaptive tutoring, analytics, translation, and simulation while diagnosing risks of surveillance, bias, context collapse, and epistemic homogenization. It advances a program for AI literate faculty built on technical, critical, and pedagogical fluencies, and specifies equity strategies for disability, gender, language, and LGBTQ inclusion. The chapter proposes actionable mechanisms including participatory procurement, model transparency, low bandwidth pathways, human in the loop assessment, and cross-national accreditation for microcredentials. It concludes by reframing AI as public infrastructure governed by ethical reflexivity, contestability, and cultural responsiveness.

This study investigates how artificial intelligence (AI)-supported virtual laboratories impact scientific learning among international middle school students in Türkiye. Findings indicate that students find AI highly beneficial in understanding complex topics, accessing accurate information in discussions, and learning foreign language terminology. Students have a positive attitude toward the use of virtual laboratories and AI and are eager to use these tools again. While language barriers (especially in communicating with teachers) remain a significant challenge, students demonstrate strong collaboration and problem-solving skills. While there is a tendency to work with peers who speak their own language, this preference is not absolute. The results suggest that AI-supported virtual laboratories enrich scientific learning, enhance problem-solving skills, and offer the potential to overcome language barriers. These findings emphasize the need for educators to develop language support and intercultural collaboration strategies.

This chapter examines the intersection of Artificial Intelligence (AI), transnational education, and the cultural continuity of diaspora youth through a qualitative, secondary research methodology. It analyzes scholarly works, digital platforms, and existing case studies to identify how AI influences the educational experiences of culturally diverse learners. Guided by the central research question—whether AI in education supports or disrupts cultural continuity for diaspora youth—the study investigates how algorithmic learning environments shape heritage preservation, language retention, and identity formation. By critically evaluating mainstream platforms such as Duolingo, LingQ, and Khan Academy alongside emerging culturally responsive initiatives, the chapter reveals how culturally grounded AI design can promote belonging and inclusivity. It concludes with the CULTUR-AI framework, offering principles for developing equitable, linguistically diverse, and community-centered AI systems in education.

This chapter critically examines the digital divide within AI-driven transnational learning, emphasizing how technological advancements in education may reinforce existing global inequalities if not guided by equity-focused frameworks. The study explores key dimensions of the divide, including disparities in infrastructure, digital and AI literacy, algorithmic bias, and linguistic exclusion. It analyzes the role of global institutions, national governments, and educational stakeholders in addressing these challenges through inclusive policies, ethical AI governance, and capacity building. The study draws on theoretical frameworks such as the Capability Approach, Critical Pedagogy, and Postcolonial Theory to underscore

learning environments. Drawing from interdisciplinary studies across educational technology, international pedagogy, and organizational change, the chapter maps the core competencies of AI-fluent faculty ranging from adaptive learning design and AI-augmented assessment to ethical reasoning and data-informed instruction. Real-world case studies from AI-integrated TNE programs in the UK, Australia, and Asia are analyzed to showcase pioneering approaches to faculty transformation.

This chapter presents a creative academic dialogue set within an imagined misconduct hearing at a university, where a student faces allegations of inappropriate use of artificial intelligence (AI). Through testimonies from academics, policy officers and an AI voice itself, the chapter explores tensions between integrity, authorship and assessment design in higher education. The dialogue highlights how AI challenges conventional definitions of learning, raises questions of equity in transnational education and exposes contradictions in current institutional policies. By weaving scholarly references into narrative form, the chapter demonstrates how academic assessments may not be fit for purpose and argues for the reimagining of assessment practices that emphasise process, critical thinking and development of the authentic student personality and voice. Ultimately, the chapter proposes that AI does not diminish academic integrity but instead compels a deeper reconsideration of what constitutes meaningful learning and authorship.

This chapter examines how Artificial Intelligence (AI) techniques such as machine learning, neural networks, adaptive learning, and predictive analytics are transforming Knowledge Management (KM) in Transnational Education (TNE) settings. It highlights how AI enhances knowledge discovery, capture, storage, sharing, and application while supporting institutional agility, collaboration, and pedagogical innovation. Drawing on literature, case studies, and policy insights, the chapter introduces the AI-KM Integration Model (AI-KMIM), which emphasizes governance and leadership, technological infrastructure, digital literacy and capacity building, ethical and cultural alignment, and monitoring and evaluation as key pillars for AI-driven KM in higher education institutions. The findings underscore the importance of aligning technological innovation with organizational readiness and global standards while addressing ethical governance, cross-border policies, and equity in AI adoption to strengthen knowledge ecosystems across international campuses.

Generative artificial intelligence (GenAI) and large language models (LLMs) are transforming teaching, learning, and institutional management in higher education (HE) and transnational higher education (TNE). Current discourse extends beyond innovation and academic integrity to epistemological, ethical, and regulatory aspects. The chapter examines LLMs' role in democratizing access while disrupting

Preface

INTRODUCTION

The accelerating pace of digital innovation is reshaping higher education in profound and often unpredictable ways. Among these developments, Artificial Intelligence (AI) has emerged as one of the most influential forces redefining how knowledge is created, delivered, assessed, and governed. When situated within the complex and expanding field of Transnational Education (TNE), AI presents both unprecedented opportunities and critical challenges. This edited volume, *Digital Frontiers of AI in Transnational Education*, is our response to this rapidly evolving landscape.

As editors, we bring together this collection at a moment when higher education institutions are extending their global presence while simultaneously navigating ethical, regulatory, pedagogical, and technological transformation. AI is no longer a peripheral tool in international education; it is becoming embedded in teaching and learning design, student support systems, assessment practices, institutional management, and quality assurance mechanisms across borders. Yet, the implications of these developments remain unevenly understood, particularly within transnational and cross-cultural contexts.

The primary aim of this book is to offer a critical and interdisciplinary exploration of how AI is being integrated into TNE and what this means for the future of global higher education. The chapters collectively provide a foundational framework for examining the ethical, operational, and pedagogical dimensions of AI in cross-border education. Through empirical case studies, policy analyses, and conceptual discussions, contributors illuminate how institutions, governments, and educators are responding to AI-driven disruption in diverse regional and regulatory environments.

This volume also seeks to stimulate scholarly and professional dialogue around key challenges, including governance, data ethics, cultural sensitivity, quality assurance, and educational equity. At the same time, it offers practical insights for institutions striving to harness AI responsibly while ensuring sustainability and inclusivity in international programme delivery.

By bridging research on Artificial Intelligence with the theory and practice of Transnational Education, this book contributes to broader conversations in digital education, internationalisation, and educational innovation. We envision this work as a valuable resource for higher education leaders and strategic planners, TNE managers and providers, educational technology developers, researchers in AI and education policy, academic staff engaged in international teaching and partnerships, and quality assurance professionals operating within global education systems.

We extend our sincere gratitude to the contributing authors for their expertise, critical perspectives, and commitment to advancing understanding in this emerging field. It is our hope that this volume will not only inform current practice but also inspire thoughtful, ethical, and collaborative approaches to shaping the digital future of transnational higher education.

ORGANIZATION OF THE BOOK

This edited volume brings together a diverse yet coherent set of scholarly contributions that collectively illuminate the evolving digital frontiers of Artificial Intelligence (AI) in Transnational Education (TNE). Each chapter addresses a distinct dimension of this transformation, offering conceptual, empirical, policy-oriented, and practice-based insights that reflect the complexity of AI adoption across borders.

Chapter 1 sets the conceptual foundation by interrogating how AI challenges traditional notions of quality assurance in TNE. As editors, we view this chapter as pivotal in reframing quality beyond compliance-driven models toward more adaptive, ethical, and culturally responsive approaches. By proposing governance models and guiding principles, the chapter establishes a future-oriented lens for evaluating quality in algorithmically mediated education systems.

Chapter 2 shifts the focus to practice, examining AI-assisted learning within transnational computer science education. Through an empirically grounded case study, this chapter demonstrates how ethically structured AI use can enhance equity, engagement, and consistency across bilingual cohorts. The proposed framework offers a scalable model for institutions seeking to integrate AI responsibly while respecting cultural and pedagogical diversity.

Chapter 3 expands the pedagogical conversation by situating AI within established learning theories and intercultural competence frameworks. The chapter highlights how AI augments—rather than replaces—human judgement in teaching and learning, while also addressing regulatory and equity challenges. Its multi-layered framework provides institutions with a structured roadmap for aligning AI adoption with governance, quality, and cross-border accountability.

Chapter 4 addresses academic integrity within the specific context of Omani transnational education. This chapter underscores the dual role of AI as both a facilitator of learning and a potential risk to ethical standards. By examining regulatory gaps and cultural considerations, it reinforces the need for transparent policies and context-sensitive governance in AI-enhanced TNE environments.

Chapter 5 highlights the structural tensions that arise when British transnational providers operate within the UAE's ambitious AI policy landscape. The chapter reveals how divergent regulatory expectations between home and host systems create sustainability challenges, offering a critical lens on policy misalignment and institutional feasibility in AI-driven TNE.

Chapter 6 foregrounds culture and belonging, arguing that AI systems must move beyond standardisation to become culturally responsive. This chapter powerfully articulates how adaptive, culturally aware AI can foster engagement, dialogue, and identity affirmation, positioning inclusion and empathy as central to human-centred transnational education.

Chapter 7 empirically examines the reliability of traditional assessments in Omani higher education amid widespread AI use. The findings highlight growing concerns about authenticity, validity, and policy inconsistency, reinforcing the urgency of reassessing assessment design and institutional guidelines in AI-mediated academic contexts.

Chapter 8 adopts a critical sociotechnical perspective, examining how AI reshapes pedagogy, governance, and faculty roles across borders. By introducing concepts such as pedagogical sovereignty and algorithmic ecology, the chapter advances a robust framework for ethical, inclusive, and participatory AI adoption in TNE.

Chapter 9 extends the discussion to pre-university contexts, exploring AI-supported virtual laboratories in transnational science education. The chapter demonstrates the pedagogical value of AI in enhancing scientific understanding and collaboration, while also highlighting language and intercultural challenges that require intentional instructional design.

Chapter 10 focuses on diaspora youth, examining whether AI supports or disrupts cultural continuity in transnational learning environments. Through critical analysis of mainstream and culturally responsive platforms, the chapter introduces the CULTUR-AI framework, offering principles for inclusive, identity-affirming AI design.

Chapter 11 critically examines equity and access, cautioning that AI-driven TNE risks deepening global inequalities if not guided by justice-oriented frameworks. Drawing on critical theory, the chapter calls for systemic, policy-level interventions to address infrastructure gaps, algorithmic bias, and linguistic exclusion.

Chapter 12 consolidates ethical and sustainability concerns by examining data governance, bias, environmental impact, and cultural sensitivity in AI adoption. This chapter offers actionable guidelines for responsible AI practices, reinforcing sustainability and ethics as inseparable from innovation in transnational higher education.

Chapter 13 broadens the generational lens by examining the dual influence of social media and AI on Gen Alpha learners. While not limited to higher education, this chapter provides important insights into early digital exposure, parental challenges, and the need for digital citizenship education—issues that will shape the future pipeline of transnational learners.

Chapter 14 turns attention to faculty development, presenting a framework for building AI fluency among educators in global classrooms. Drawing on international case studies, the chapter positions faculty capability as a cornerstone of sustainable, ethical, and pedagogically sound AI integration in TNE.

Chapter 15 adopts an innovative narrative approach, staging an imagined academic misconduct hearing to explore tensions around AI, authorship, and assessment. By blending dialogue with scholarship, the chapter challenges conventional definitions of integrity and argues for assessment redesign that foregrounds learning processes and authentic student voice.

Chapter 16 examines AI through the lens of knowledge management, highlighting how intelligent systems can enhance institutional learning, collaboration, and innovation across transnational campuses. The proposed AI-KM Integration Model underscores the importance of aligning technological advancement with governance, ethics, and organizational readiness.

Chapter 17 focuses on generative AI and large language models, analysing their pedagogical promise alongside governance and policy challenges in HE and TNE. Through a contemporary case study, the chapter offers a pragmatic governance framework that balances innovation, trust, and cross-jurisdictional accountability.

Chapter 18 concludes the volume by addressing AI in transnational legal education, a domain where jurisdictional complexity and ethical accountability are particularly acute. The chapter advocates for a rights-based, transparent, and culturally pluralistic approach to AI governance, reaffirming the normative role of law in shaping humane and equitable digital futures.

Together, these chapters provide a comprehensive, critical, and forward-looking exploration of AI in transnational education. As editors, we believe this collection not only maps current challenges and innovations but also offers guiding insights for shaping more ethical, inclusive, and sustainable global education systems in the age of artificial intelligence.

CONCLUSION

As editors, we conclude this volume with a recognition that Artificial Intelligence is no longer a speculative addition to transnational education but a structural force reshaping its present and future. Across the chapters in this book, AI emerges not as a singular technology or solution, but as a complex sociotechnical ecosystem—one that intersects with culture, policy, pedagogy, governance, ethics, and human identity in deeply consequential ways.

Collectively, the contributions demonstrate that the integration of AI into Transnational Education is neither uniform nor neutral. Instead, it is shaped by regulatory divergence, institutional readiness, cultural context, and unequal access to digital infrastructure. While AI holds significant promise for enhancing learning personalization, widening access, supporting multilingual engagement, and strengthening institutional knowledge systems, the chapters also make clear that uncritical adoption risks reinforcing inequities, eroding academic integrity, and marginalising local epistemologies.

A central theme running throughout the volume is the need to move beyond compliance-driven, technology-first approaches toward more reflexive, values-led frameworks. Quality assurance, assessment, faculty development, governance, and knowledge management must all be reimagined in ways that acknowledge AI's capacity to augment human judgement while safeguarding transparency, accountability, and cultural relevance. The emphasis on ethical governance, participatory design, and human-in-the-loop systems reflects a shared commitment to ensuring that AI serves educational purposes rather than redefining them in purely instrumental terms.

This book also underscores the importance of contextual sensitivity in transnational settings. AI systems developed in one jurisdiction or cultural environment do not seamlessly translate across borders. Contributors highlight the necessity of aligning global standards with local norms, legal frameworks, and learner identities, particularly in regions where regulatory expectations, linguistic diversity, and cultural values differ markedly from dominant AI development centres. In this respect, transnational education becomes a critical testing ground for responsible AI, exposing both its possibilities and its limitations.

Importantly, the volume points toward the future. It calls for AI-literate faculty, culturally responsive pedagogies, equitable access strategies, and governance models capable of adapting to rapid technological change. It also invites scholars, policymakers, and practitioners to engage in sustained dialogue, recognising that AI in transnational education is an evolving phenomenon that demands ongoing critical inquiry rather than fixed solutions.

We offer this edited reference book as both a scholarly contribution and a practical resource. Our hope is that it will inform decision-making, inspire ethical innovation, and support institutions and educators in shaping AI-enhanced transnational education systems that are inclusive, sustainable, and human-centred. Ultimately, the digital frontiers explored in this volume are not only technological—they are moral, cultural, and pedagogical frontiers that will define the future of global higher education.

Chapter 1
Redefining Quality Assurance in AI-Augmented Transnational Education

Mazhar Malik
https://orcid.org/0000-0001-8890-1310
University of the West of the England, UK

Yasmine Rosunally
University of the West of the England, UK

Nuzhat Younis
University of the West of the England, UK

ABSTRACT

As artificial intelligence (AI) becomes increasingly embedded in transnational education (TNE), traditional quality assurance (QA) frameworks face mounting pressure to evolve. This chapter critically examines how AI reshapes the meaning, mechanisms, and governance of educational quality across borders. It explores the limitations of compliance-driven QA models in algorithmically mediated, culturally diverse, and digitally distributed learning environments. Drawing on sector practices, theoretical insights, and case examples, the chapter proposes a set of guiding principles—transparency, collaboration, cultural relevance, data ethics, and continuous improvement—to underpin effective QA in AI-enhanced TNE. It introduces conceptual models (centralised, distributed, collaborative, and hybrid-adaptive) to address governance gaps and promote inclusive, responsive, and future-ready QA architectures.

INTRODUCTION

Transnational education (TNE) refers to the delivery of educational programmes by institutions in one country to students located in another. This can take the form of branch campuses, joint or dual degrees, franchised provision, or fully online learning. TNE enables students to access international qualifications

DOI: 10.4018/979-8-3373-5403-3.ch001

without relocating, while allowing institutions to expand their global presence and diversify income streams (Carvalho, Rosa & Amaral, 2023).

The United Kingdom has been a global leader in TNE, with over 500,000 students enrolled in UK higher education programmes delivered overseas (British Council, 2024). This growth reflects broader trends in globalisation, digital connectivity, and the internationalisation of higher education. TNE is increasingly seen as a strategic tool for widening access, enhancing institutional reputation, and fostering international collaboration.

However, TNE also presents significant challenges. These include maintaining academic standards across jurisdictions, ensuring parity of student experience, and navigating diverse regulatory and cultural landscapes. Quality assurance (QA) in TNE has traditionally relied on frameworks designed for domestic, face-to-face provision, raising questions about their adequacy in increasingly digital and distributed learning environments.

The Rise of Artificial Intelligence in Education

Artificial intelligence (AI) is rapidly transforming the landscape of higher education. AI technologies are now embedded in various aspects of teaching, learning, and assessment. These include:

1. Adaptive learning systems that personalise content and pacing based on learner performance.
2. Automated assessment tools that mark essays, quizzes, and even complex assignments.
3. Predictive analytics that identify students at risk of disengagement or failure;
4. Chatbots and virtual tutors that provide 24/7 academic support.

In the context of TNE, AI offers advantages. It can support multilingual learners, provide consistent feedback across campuses, and reduce reliance on local teaching staff (Warren et al., 2025). AI also enables institutions to scale provision while maintaining responsiveness to individual learner needs.

Yet, the integration of AI into education raises critical concerns. These include algorithmic bias, lack of transparency, data privacy, and the potential erosion of human judgement in teaching and assessment. In transnational contexts, these issues are further complicated by cross-border data flows, cultural differences in pedagogy, and varying legal frameworks (Zhu, Zhu & Xu, 2025).

Why Traditional QA Models Are Under Pressure

Conventional QA frameworks were developed for campus-based, instructor-led education. They typically focus on inputs (such as staff qualifications and curriculum design), processes (such as teaching delivery and assessment methods), and outputs (such as student satisfaction and graduate outcomes). These models assume a relatively stable, observable, and human-mediated learning environment (Alcock, 2025).

AI-augmented TNE challenges these assumptions in several ways:

1. Algorithmic mediation: Learning and assessment are increasingly shaped by AI systems, whose decision-making processes may be opaque or proprietary.
2. Asynchronous and decentralised delivery: Students may engage with content at different times, in different locations, and through different platforms.

3. Personalised learning pathways: AI enables differentiated instruction, making it harder to ensure consistency and comparability across cohorts.
4. Cross-jurisdictional complexity: QA bodies must contend with differing national regulations, data protection laws, and cultural expectations.

These developments expose the limitations of static, compliance-driven QA models. They also highlight the need for more dynamic, responsive, and collaborative approaches to assuring quality in AI-mediated, cross-border education.

Purpose and Scope of the Chapter

This chapter explores the evolving landscape of quality assurance in AI-augmented transnational education. It aims to:

1. Critically examine how AI is reshaping the meaning and mechanisms of educational quality in TNE.
2. Identify key challenges institutions face in assuring quality when AI tools are used across borders.
3. Propose a set of guiding principles for effective, ethical, and culturally sensitive QA in AI-TNE.
4. Introduce conceptual models for QA governance that reflect the distributed and dynamic nature of AI-mediated education.

The chapter draws on theoretical insights, sector practices, and illustrative scenarios to offer a roadmap for institutions, policymakers, and QA agencies. It advocates for a shift from rigid, compliance-oriented QA to more flexible, inclusive, and forward-looking approaches that prioritise learner outcomes, institutional accountability, and technological transparency.

In doing so, the chapter contributes to ongoing debates about the future of higher education in a digital age. It calls for a reimagining of QA not as a bureaucratic exercise, but as a collaborative, values-driven process that supports innovation while safeguarding academic integrity and student trust.

CHANGING NATURE OF EDUCATIONAL QUALITY IN AI-SUPPORTED TNE

Traditional Assumptions of Quality in TNE

Historically, quality assurance (QA) in transnational education (TNE) has been underpinned by frameworks designed for traditional, campus-based, instructor-led provision. These frameworks typically focus on standardised curricula, faculty qualifications, physical infrastructure, and periodic institutional audits. The assumption is that quality can be assured through consistency, equivalence, and compliance with the standards of the home institution (Carvalho, Rosa & Amaral, 2023).

In this model, quality is often measured through inputs (e.g., staff credentials, learning resources), processes (e.g., teaching methods, assessment practices), and outputs (e.g., student satisfaction, retention, and graduate employability). These indicators are relatively straightforward to monitor in a physical classroom setting, where teaching is observable, assessments are manually graded, and learning environments are controlled.

However, the increasing integration of artificial intelligence (AI) into education is challenging these assumptions. AI introduces new actors (e.g., algorithms, bots), new forms of pedagogy (e.g., adaptive learning), and new data flows (e.g., real-time analytics), all of which complicate traditional QA mechanisms.

From Standardisation to Personalisation

One of the most transformative aspects of AI in education is its capacity to personalise learning. Adaptive learning platforms use machine learning algorithms to analyse student behaviour, performance, and preferences, dynamically adjusting content and pacing to suit individual needs. This represents a significant departure from the "one-size-fits-all" model that underpins many traditional QA frameworks (Warren et al., 2025).

In TNE contexts, where student cohorts are often diverse in terms of language, culture, and prior educational experience, personalisation can enhance inclusivity and learner engagement. For example, AI can provide real-time translation, culturally relevant examples, and differentiated feedback. These features can help bridge gaps in understanding and improve learning outcomes.

However, personalisation also introduces complexity. If each student receives a unique learning experience, how can institutions ensure consistency and fairness? How can QA bodies evaluate the equivalence of learning outcomes across different delivery sites? These questions challenge the validity of standardised QA metrics and call for new approaches that account for variability and adaptability.

Moreover, the algorithms that drive personalisation are often proprietary and opaque. This "black box" nature of AI makes it difficult for educators and QA professionals to understand how decisions are made, raising concerns about transparency, accountability, and trust (Alcock, 2025).

Redefining Educational Quality in the Age of AI

The integration of AI into TNE necessitates a redefinition of educational quality. Traditional QA models, with their emphasis on compliance and standardisation, may be ill-suited to environments where learning is dynamic, decentralised, and mediated by algorithms.

Emerging conceptions of quality in AI-enhanced education include:

1. Transparency: AI systems must be explainable and auditable. Stakeholders should understand how algorithms make decisions, particularly in high-stakes contexts such as assessment and progression.
2. Responsiveness: AI should be capable of adapting to diverse learner needs, including linguistic, cultural, and cognitive differences.
3. Ethicality: The use of AI must align with ethical principles, including fairness, non-discrimination, and respect for privacy.
4. Sustainability: Institutions must ensure that AI systems are maintainable, updatable, and resilient across different TNE contexts.

These dimensions reflect a shift from a static notion of quality to a more dynamic, process-oriented understanding. They also align with the British Council's global framework for TNE, which emphasises the importance of context-sensitive, collaborative, and data-informed approaches to quality enhancement (Ilieva et al., 2024).

Opportunities Presented by AI in TNE

AI offers several opportunities to enhance the quality of TNE provision:

1. Scalability: AI can support large and geographically dispersed cohorts without compromising the quality of feedback or support. Automated systems can handle repetitive tasks such as grading, freeing up academic staff to focus on higher-order teaching activities.
2. Efficiency: Predictive analytics can identify students at risk of disengagement or failure, enabling timely interventions. AI can also streamline administrative processes, such as admissions, timetabling, and student support.
3. Inclusivity: AI tools can support learners with disabilities through speech-to-text, screen readers, and other assistive technologies. They can also provide multilingual support, helping students from diverse linguistic backgrounds engage more effectively with course content.
4. Consistency: AI systems can deliver standardised content and feedback across multiple delivery sites, helping to ensure a baseline level of quality in TNE programmes.

These benefits are particularly relevant in the context of TNE, where institutions must deliver education across diverse settings while maintaining consistent standards.

Risks and Challenges of AI in TNE

Despite its potential, the use of AI in TNE also presents significant risks and challenges:

1. Algorithmic Bias: AI systems are only as good as the data on which they are trained. If training data reflects biases — for example, favouring Western pedagogical norms or linguistic patterns — the resulting systems may disadvantage students from other cultural or educational backgrounds (Bannister et al., 2024).
2. Assessment Integrity: The rise of generative AI tools, such as ChatGPT, has raised concerns about academic integrity. Students may use these tools to generate assignments, making it difficult to assess genuine learning. At the same time, automated grading systems may struggle to detect nuanced or creative responses, leading to questions about the validity of assessment (Alcock, 2025).
3. Data Privacy and Ethics: AI systems rely on large volumes of learner data to function effectively. In TNE contexts, this often involves cross-border data transfers, raising complex legal and ethical issues. Institutions must navigate varying data protection laws, such as the EU's General Data Protection Regulation (GDPR), and ensure that students' rights are respected (Zhu, Zhu & Xu, 2025).
4. Technological Dependence: Over-reliance on AI may lead to a de-skilling of educators and a reduction in human interaction, which remains a critical component of effective learning. There is also the risk of technological failure or obsolescence, particularly in low-resource settings.

Figure 1. Challenges of AI in education

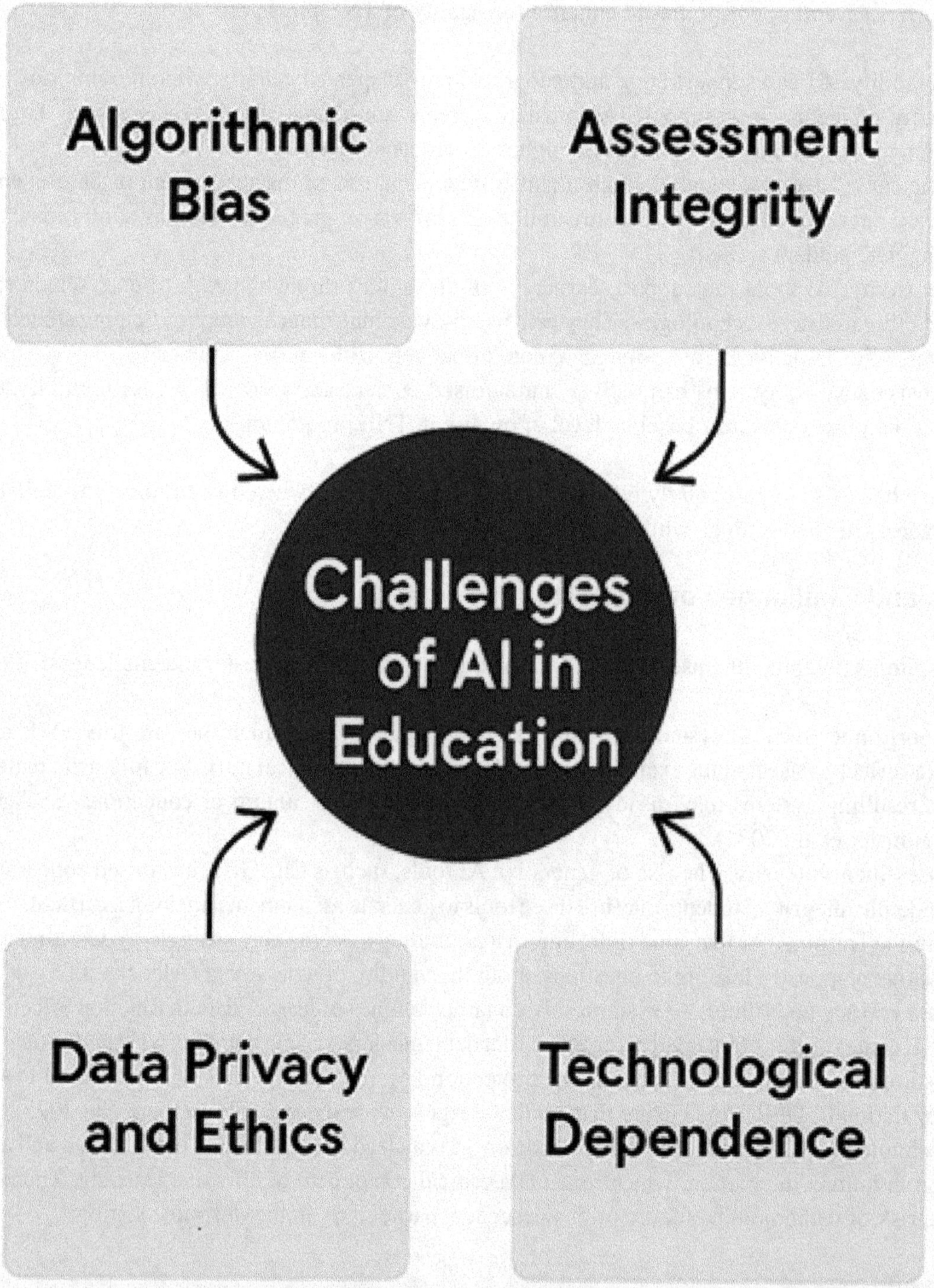

These challenges underscore the need for robust, context-aware QA mechanisms that can anticipate and mitigate the unintended consequences of AI integration.

Towards a New QA Paradigm

To address the complexities introduced by AI in TNE, QA frameworks must evolve. This involves moving beyond static, checklist-based approaches towards more adaptive, iterative, and collaborative models. Key features of such a paradigm include:

1. Continuous Quality Monitoring: Rather than relying solely on periodic reviews, institutions should implement real-time monitoring of AI systems and learner outcomes. This may involve the use of AI itself to detect anomalies, track engagement, and flag potential issues.
2. Stakeholder Involvement: QA processes should involve a broad range of stakeholders, including students, educators, technologists, and regulators. This ensures that diverse perspectives are considered in the design, deployment, and evaluation of AI tools.
3. Cross-Border Collaboration: Given the international nature of TNE, QA frameworks must be harmonised across jurisdictions. This may involve the development of shared standards, mutual recognition agreements, and joint QA bodies.
4. Capacity Building: Institutions must invest in training staff to understand and critically engage with AI technologies. This includes developing digital literacy, ethical awareness, and data governance capabilities.

Ultimately, the goal is to create QA systems that are not only fit for purpose in the digital age but also aligned with the values of equity, transparency, and academic integrity.

EMERGING AREAS OF CONCERN IN AI-AUGMENTED TNE

As artificial intelligence (AI) becomes more deeply embedded in transnational education (TNE), a range of new concerns has emerged that challenge existing quality assurance (QA) frameworks. These concerns are not merely technical but intersect with ethical, cultural, regulatory, and pedagogical dimensions. This section explores five critical areas of concern: feedback reliability, assessment integrity, learner experience consistency, data ethics, and cultural-regulatory alignment.

AI Feedback Reliability and Transparency

Artificial intelligence (AI)-powered feedback systems are increasingly being adopted in transnational education (TNE) to provide students with real-time, personalised responses to their work. These systems are often integrated into learning management platforms or assessment tools and are designed to enhance efficiency, reduce academic workload, and offer scalable support across geographically dispersed cohorts. In theory, AI feedback can help bridge the gap between limited teaching resources and growing student numbers, particularly in large-scale TNE programmes. However, the reliability, pedagogical value, and contextual appropriateness of such feedback remain significant concerns.

A growing body of research has begun to interrogate the quality of AI-generated feedback. A systematic review by Durak and Onan (2025) found that while AI-based feedback can enhance learner motivation and self-regulation, it often lacks the nuance required for complex or culturally specific tasks. For instance, AI systems may provide feedback that is grammatically accurate but fails to address deeper conceptual misunderstandings or the rhetorical structure of an argument. In some cases, students receive feedback that is technically correct but pedagogically unhelpful, leading to confusion rather than clarity. This is particularly problematic in TNE contexts, where students may interpret feedback through different cultural or linguistic lenses, and where expectations around academic writing and communication styles can vary significantly.

Moreover, the rise of generative AI tools, such as large language models (LLMs), introduces a new layer of complexity. These systems are capable of producing fluent, human-like responses, but they are also prone to generating "hallucinated" content—statements that appear plausible but are factually incorrect or misleading. In educational settings, such inaccuracies can have serious consequences, particularly when students rely on AI-generated feedback to guide their learning. If left unchecked, these errors can undermine trust in the learning process and compromise academic integrity.

Transparency is another critical issue in the deployment of AI feedback systems. Many AI tools operate as "black boxes," offering little insight into how feedback is generated, what data is used, or what assumptions underpin the algorithm's logic. This opacity makes it difficult for educators to validate the quality of feedback or to intervene when errors occur. Lindsay et al. (2025) argue that the lack of explainability in AI-generated feedback undermines both pedagogical accountability and student confidence. Instructors may be unable to trace the rationale behind a particular piece of feedback, making it challenging to support students effectively or to correct misconceptions.

In TNE contexts, where students may already face linguistic or cultural barriers, unclear or inconsistent feedback can exacerbate disengagement and inequity. For example, a student studying in a non-native language may misinterpret AI-generated comments that lack contextual cues or cultural sensitivity. Similarly, feedback that fails to acknowledge local academic conventions or writing styles may be perceived as irrelevant or even discriminatory. These issues are particularly acute in programmes where AI tools are developed in one cultural context and deployed in another without adequate localisation or adaptation.

To address these challenges, institutions must embed transparency and reliability into their QA frameworks for AI-mediated feedback. This includes adopting explainable AI (XAI) principles, which aim to make algorithmic processes more interpretable and accountable. Feedback systems should provide traceable logic, allow for human oversight, and be adaptable to diverse learner contexts. Educators should be trained to understand the capabilities and limitations of AI tools, and students should be informed about how feedback is generated and how to critically engage with it.

Furthermore, institutions should implement mechanisms for continuous monitoring and evaluation of AI feedback systems. This might involve regular audits of feedback quality, student satisfaction surveys, and comparative studies between AI-generated and human feedback. Where possible, AI tools should be co-designed with input from educators, students, and QA professionals to ensure that they align with pedagogical goals and cultural expectations.

In conclusion, while AI-powered feedback systems offer significant potential for enhancing the scalability and responsiveness of TNE, their effectiveness depends on more than just technical performance. Reliability, transparency, and contextual sensitivity must be central to their design and implementation.

Without these safeguards, AI feedback risks becoming a source of confusion rather than clarity, and a barrier rather than a bridge to meaningful learning.

Assessment Security and Academic Integrity

The integration of artificial intelligence (AI) into assessment practices has introduced both opportunities and challenges for transnational education (TNE). On one hand, AI enables scalable, efficient, and adaptive assessment models that can support diverse learner needs across borders. On the other, it raises serious concerns about academic integrity, assessment validity, and the ethical use of surveillance technologies. These concerns are particularly acute in TNE contexts, where institutions must navigate varying cultural norms, legal frameworks, and technological infrastructures.

One of the most pressing issues is the rise of generative AI tools, such as ChatGPT and other large language models, which allow students to produce sophisticated written content with minimal effort. These tools can generate essays, solve mathematical problems, and even simulate reflective writing. While they offer potential as learning aids, they also blur the boundaries between original work and machine-generated output. This phenomenon—sometimes referred to as "AI-giarism"—poses a significant threat to traditional notions of authorship and academic honesty.

Lund et al. (2025) found that students often perceive the use of generative AI as a grey area, particularly when institutional policies are unclear or inconsistent. In TNE settings, where students may be unfamiliar with the academic conventions of the awarding institution, the risk of unintentional misconduct is heightened. For example, a student in a partner institution may use AI to "polish" their writing, unaware that this constitutes a breach of academic integrity under the home institution's regulations. Such discrepancies highlight the need for clear, culturally sensitive guidance on the acceptable use of AI in assessment.

In response to these challenges, many institutions are rethinking their assessment strategies. There is a growing shift towards authentic assessment, which emphasises real-world tasks, critical thinking, and process-based evaluation. Oral defences, project-based learning, and iterative assignments are increasingly used to reduce the effectiveness of AI-generated responses. Evangelista (2025) argues that such approaches not only mitigate the risk of misconduct but also promote deeper learning and student engagement.

However, implementing these strategies in TNE contexts is not without difficulty. Oral assessments may be logistically challenging across time zones, and project-based tasks may require resources that are not equally available at all delivery sites. Moreover, the shift away from standardised testing can complicate quality assurance, particularly when assessments are decentralised or locally adapted.

Another area of concern is the use of AI-based proctoring and plagiarism detection tools. These systems are designed to monitor student behaviour during online exams or to identify similarities in written work. While they can enhance assessment security, they also raise significant ethical and legal questions. Automated proctoring tools often rely on facial recognition, keystroke analysis, and webcam surveillance, which may be intrusive or discriminatory. Joosten-ten Brinke and Beekman (2025) note that such systems have been shown to disproportionately flag students from certain ethnic or linguistic backgrounds, leading to false accusations and psychological distress.

In TNE contexts, the deployment of surveillance technologies must also contend with cross-border data protection laws. For example, a UK institution delivering a programme in Southeast Asia may face legal restrictions on the use of biometric data or the storage of video recordings. Institutions must therefore ensure that their assessment security measures comply with both home and host country regulations, and that students are fully informed about how their data will be used.

To navigate these complexities, institutions should adopt a principled approach to assessment integrity in AI-enhanced TNE. This includes:

1. Policy clarity: Developing and communicating clear guidelines on the acceptable use of AI in assessments, tailored to the cultural and educational contexts of TNE students.
2. Assessment redesign: Prioritising assessment formats that are less susceptible to AI misuse and that promote higher-order thinking.
3. Ethical surveillance: Ensuring that any monitoring technologies are proportionate, transparent, and compliant with relevant data protection laws.
4. Capacity building: Training educators and students to understand the capabilities and limitations of AI tools, and to engage with them ethically and critically.

Ultimately, the goal is not to eliminate AI from the assessment process, but to integrate it responsibly in ways that uphold academic standards while respecting student rights. This requires a shift from punitive models of integrity enforcement to preventative and educative approaches that foster a culture of honesty, trust, and accountability.

In conclusion, AI has fundamentally altered the landscape of assessment in TNE. While it offers powerful tools for innovation and scalability, it also demands a rethinking of how institutions define, detect, and promote academic integrity. By embedding ethical principles, cultural awareness, and technological literacy into their QA frameworks, institutions can ensure that assessment remains a valid and trustworthy measure of student learning in the age of AI.

Consistency of Learner Experience Across Delivery Sites

One of the central challenges in transnational education (TNE) is ensuring that students across different delivery sites receive a consistent and equitable learning experience. This challenge becomes even more complex with the integration of artificial intelligence (AI) into teaching, learning, and assessment. While AI offers the potential to standardise certain aspects of education—such as content delivery, feedback, and assessment—it can also introduce new forms of inconsistency, particularly when deployed across culturally and technologically diverse contexts.

In traditional TNE models, consistency is often maintained through standardised curricula, shared assessment rubrics, and periodic quality audits. However, AI-mediated education introduces variability at multiple levels. Adaptive learning platforms, for instance, personalise content and pacing based on individual learner profiles. While this can enhance engagement and outcomes, it also means that students may experience different learning pathways, even within the same module. This raises questions about comparability of learning experiences and outcomes, especially when qualifications are awarded by a single institution.

Moreover, the effectiveness of AI tools can vary significantly depending on the technological infrastructure and digital literacy of the local context. Students in well-resourced urban campuses may benefit from high-speed internet, modern devices, and robust technical support, while those in remote or under-resourced settings may struggle with connectivity issues, outdated hardware, or limited access to digital tools. These disparities can lead to unequal access to AI-enhanced learning opportunities, undermining the principle of parity of experience that underpins many QA frameworks.

Cultural factors also play a critical role. AI systems are often developed in specific linguistic and cultural contexts, which may not align with the norms, expectations, or learning styles of students in other regions. For example, an AI tutor trained on English-language academic discourse may struggle to interpret or respond appropriately to students whose writing reflects different rhetorical traditions. Similarly, feedback that is perceived as constructive in one culture may be seen as overly critical or inappropriate in another. These issues can affect not only the quality of learning but also student satisfaction and engagement.

Henderson et al. (2025) found that while students appreciated the immediacy and accessibility of AI-generated feedback, they often perceived it as less trustworthy and less helpful than feedback from human educators. This perception varied across cultural and institutional contexts, suggesting that AI tools may not be equally effective or accepted in all settings. In some cases, students reported feeling alienated or confused by feedback that lacked empathy, contextual awareness, or relevance to their local academic environment.

To address these challenges, institutions must adopt a context-sensitive approach to QA in AI-enhanced TNE. This involves not only evaluating the technical performance of AI tools but also assessing their cultural appropriateness, accessibility, and pedagogical alignment. Institutions should consider the following strategies:

1. Localisation of AI tools: AI systems should be adapted to reflect the linguistic, cultural, and educational norms of each delivery site. This may involve training models on local data, incorporating region-specific examples, or customising feedback styles.
2. Equity audits: QA processes should include regular reviews of learner access, engagement, and outcomes across different sites. Disparities should be identified and addressed through targeted interventions, such as additional support services or infrastructure investment.
3. Blended feedback models: Combining AI-generated feedback with human input can help mitigate the limitations of automated systems. Human tutors can provide contextual interpretation, emotional nuance, and cultural sensitivity that AI may lack.
4. Student voice and feedback: Institutions should actively seek input from students about their experiences with AI tools. This feedback can inform continuous improvement and ensure that QA processes remain responsive to learner needs.

Furthermore, institutions should develop shared QA indicators that account for both standardisation and personalisation. For example, while learning outcomes may be consistent across sites, the pathways to achieving them may differ. QA frameworks must be flexible enough to accommodate this diversity while ensuring that all students meet the required academic standards.

In conclusion, while AI offers powerful tools for enhancing the scalability and responsiveness of TNE, it also introduces new risks to the consistency of learner experience. These risks are not merely technical but are deeply intertwined with cultural, infrastructural, and pedagogical factors. By embedding equity, localisation, and student-centred design into their QA frameworks, institutions can ensure that AI supports—not undermines—the goal of delivering high-quality, inclusive education across borders.

Use of Learner Data and Ethical Considerations

Artificial intelligence (AI) systems in education rely heavily on data—particularly learner data—to function effectively. These systems use data to personalise learning pathways, generate feedback, predict performance, and automate assessment. In transnational education (TNE), where students are geographically dispersed and often enrolled in programmes delivered by institutions outside their home countries, the collection, processing, and governance of learner data raise complex ethical and legal questions.

One of the most significant concerns is data privacy. AI systems typically require access to large volumes of personal and academic data, including demographic information, behavioural patterns, and performance metrics. In TNE contexts, this data often crosses national borders, triggering a host of regulatory challenges. For example, a UK university delivering a programme in Southeast Asia may collect data from students in jurisdictions with different or less stringent data protection laws than the UK's General Data Protection Regulation (GDPR). This creates uncertainty about where data is stored, who has access to it, and how it is protected.

Zhu, Zhu, and Xu (2025) highlight that cross-border data flows in TNE are often poorly regulated, with institutions relying on vendor agreements or internal policies that may not align with local legal requirements. In some cases, students may not even be aware that their data is being collected or used to train AI systems. This lack of transparency undermines informed consent and can erode trust in both the institution and the technology.

Beyond legal compliance, there are broader ethical concerns about how learner data is used. AI systems can inadvertently reinforce existing inequalities if they are trained on biased or unrepresentative data. For instance, predictive analytics tools that flag students as "at risk" based on historical data may disproportionately target students from certain cultural or linguistic backgrounds. If not carefully monitored, such systems can lead to discriminatory interventions or lower expectations, perpetuating rather than addressing educational disparities.

Another ethical issue is surveillance. Some AI tools used in TNE—such as automated proctoring systems or engagement trackers—collect data on student behaviour, facial expressions, or keystroke patterns. While these tools are often justified as necessary for maintaining academic integrity or improving learning outcomes, they can also be intrusive and anxiety-inducing. In cross-cultural contexts, where norms around privacy and surveillance vary, such practices may be perceived as invasive or even unethical.

To address these concerns, institutions must adopt a data ethics framework that goes beyond legal compliance to consider the broader implications of AI use in education. Key principles of such a framework include:

1. Informed consent: Students should be clearly informed about what data is being collected, how it will be used, and with whom it will be shared. Consent should be meaningful, not buried in lengthy terms and conditions.
2. Data minimisation: Only data that is necessary for educational purposes should be collected. Institutions should avoid collecting sensitive or personally identifiable information unless absolutely required.
3. Transparency and explainability: Students and educators should be able to understand how AI systems make decisions based on learner data. This includes access to algorithmic logic, data sources, and decision-making criteria.

4. Bias mitigation: Institutions should regularly audit AI systems for bias and take corrective action where necessary. This includes diversifying training data and involving diverse stakeholders in system design and evaluation.
5. Right to challenge: Students should have the right to question or appeal decisions made by AI systems, particularly in high-stakes contexts such as assessment or progression.

Implementing these principles requires not only technical safeguards but also institutional policies and governance structures. Institutions should establish data ethics committees or working groups that include representatives from academic, technical, legal, and student communities. These bodies can oversee the ethical deployment of AI tools, review data governance practices, and ensure alignment with both local and international standards.

Furthermore, institutions should engage in capacity building to ensure that staff and students are equipped to navigate the ethical dimensions of AI. This includes training on data literacy, digital rights, and responsible AI use. In TNE contexts, such training should be adapted to local cultural and regulatory environments to ensure relevance and accessibility.

In conclusion, the use of learner data in AI-enhanced TNE presents both opportunities and risks. While data-driven systems can support personalisation, early intervention, and improved outcomes, they also raise serious ethical and legal questions that must be addressed through robust QA frameworks. By embedding data ethics into the design, implementation, and evaluation of AI systems, institutions can uphold student rights, foster trust, and ensure that technological innovation serves the broader goals of equity, inclusion, and educational integrity.

Cultural And Regulatory Misalignment

Transnational education (TNE) operates across a mosaic of cultural, legal, and institutional contexts. The integration of artificial intelligence (AI) into TNE introduces new layers of complexity, particularly when it comes to aligning educational practices with local cultural norms and regulatory frameworks. While AI offers the potential to standardise certain aspects of teaching and assessment, it also risks imposing culturally specific assumptions and practices that may not translate effectively across borders. This section explores the challenges of cultural and regulatory misalignment in AI-augmented TNE and their implications for quality assurance (QA).

Cultural Misalignment in AI-Driven Pedagogy

AI systems used in education are often developed in Western contexts and reflect the pedagogical values, communication styles, and academic conventions of their developers. These systems may, for example, prioritise individualism, critical debate, or direct feedback—values that are not universally shared. When deployed in non-Western settings, such systems can clash with local educational traditions, leading to confusion, disengagement, or even resistance.

For instance, in some East Asian cultures, education is often characterised by deference to authority, indirect communication, and a strong emphasis on group harmony. An AI tutor that encourages students to challenge ideas or express strong personal opinions may be perceived as culturally inappropriate or uncomfortable. Similarly, feedback that is overly direct or critical may be seen as disrespectful, even if it is intended to be constructive.

These cultural mismatches are not merely matters of etiquette—they can affect student learning, satisfaction, and retention. If students feel that AI systems do not "understand" them or reflect their values, they may disengage from the learning process or question the legitimacy of the educational experience. This has direct implications for QA, as student satisfaction and engagement are often key indicators of quality in TNE programmes.

To address these issues, institutions must ensure that AI tools are culturally localised. This involves adapting language models, feedback styles, and content examples to reflect local norms and expectations. It also requires involving local educators and students in the design and evaluation of AI systems to ensure that they are contextually appropriate and pedagogically effective.

Regulatory Misalignment and Legal Uncertainty

In addition to cultural challenges, AI-enhanced TNE must navigate a fragmented and often inconsistent global regulatory landscape. Countries differ widely in their approaches to data protection, AI governance, and educational quality assurance. This creates significant challenges for institutions seeking to implement AI tools across multiple jurisdictions.

One of the most prominent regulatory concerns is data protection. The European Union's General Data Protection Regulation (GDPR) sets a high standard for data privacy, requiring explicit consent, data minimisation, and the right to explanation for automated decisions. However, many TNE host countries have less comprehensive or differently structured data protection laws. This creates uncertainty about how learner data can be collected, stored, and processed, particularly when it is transferred across borders.

For example, an AI system that collects biometric data for automated proctoring may be legal in one country but prohibited in another. Similarly, the use of predictive analytics to identify at-risk students may be seen as a helpful intervention in one context but as discriminatory profiling in another. Institutions must therefore conduct regulatory impact assessments before deploying AI tools in new jurisdictions and ensure that their practices comply with both home and host country laws.

Another area of regulatory misalignment concerns educational standards and QA requirements. Some countries have strict accreditation processes that require detailed documentation of teaching methods, assessment practices, and learning outcomes. AI systems that adapt content or automate assessment may not fit neatly into these frameworks, leading to delays or complications in programme approval. Moreover, QA agencies may lack the technical expertise to evaluate AI tools, resulting in inconsistent or overly cautious regulatory responses.

Bridging the Gaps: Towards Harmonisation and Dialogue

To navigate cultural and regulatory misalignment, institutions must adopt a dialogic and adaptive approach to QA. This includes:

1. Cultural audits of AI tools to ensure alignment with local values and expectations;
2. Regulatory mapping to identify legal requirements and compliance risks in each jurisdiction;
3. Stakeholder engagement with local educators, students, and regulators to co-develop context-sensitive QA frameworks;
4. Flexible QA models that allow for local adaptation while maintaining core quality standards.

International organisations such as UNESCO, the OECD, and the British Council have called for greater harmonisation of QA standards in TNE, particularly in the context of digital and AI-enhanced education. Initiatives such as the UNESCO Recommendation on the Ethics of Artificial Intelligence and the OECD's TNE guidelines provide useful frameworks for aligning practices across borders. However, these frameworks must be operationalised through institutional policies, cross-border partnerships, and continuous dialogue.

In conclusion, cultural and regulatory misalignment poses a significant challenge to the effective and ethical deployment of AI in TNE. Without careful localisation and legal compliance, AI tools risk undermining educational quality, student trust, and institutional credibility. By embedding cultural sensitivity and regulatory awareness into their QA processes, institutions can ensure that AI supports—not disrupts—the goals of inclusive, high-quality transnational education.

QUALITY ASSURANCE ACROSS BORDERS: CHALLENGES AND GOVERNANCE GAPS

As transnational education (TNE) becomes increasingly mediated by artificial intelligence (AI), the complexity of assuring quality across borders intensifies. Traditional QA frameworks, often designed for national contexts, are being stretched by the demands of digital delivery, algorithmic mediation, and jurisdictional diversity. This section explores the key cross-border challenges in AI-supported TNE, focusing on regulatory misalignment, cultural divergence, institutional fragmentation, and the absence of shared governance models.

Figure 2. Quality assurance across borders: Challenges and governance

Regulatory Fragmentation and Legal Incompatibility

One of the most pressing challenges in cross-border QA is the lack of regulatory harmonisation. TNE operates across jurisdictions with differing legal frameworks, particularly in areas such as data protection, AI ethics, and academic standards. For example, while the European Union enforces the General Data Protection Regulation (GDPR), many TNE host countries have less stringent or incompatible data laws. This creates uncertainty around the collection, storage, and use of learner data by AI systems (Kashefi et al., 2024). [www.iiardj...urnals.org]

Moreover, AI tools used in TNE may be subject to different classifications under national laws. In some jurisdictions, AI-driven assessment tools may be considered educational technologies, while in others they may fall under consumer protection or even medical device regulations, depending on their function and impact (Freyer et al., 2025). This regulatory ambiguity complicates institutional compliance and exposes students to uneven protections. [www.nature.com]

Cultural Divergence in Educational Norms

Cultural differences in pedagogy, assessment, and student-teacher relationships further complicate QA in AI-enhanced TNE. AI systems are often developed in Western contexts and may reflect implicit assumptions about learning styles, communication norms, and academic values. When deployed in non-Western settings, these systems may clash with local expectations or fail to resonate with learners (Wheeler, 2024). [www.forbes.com]

For instance, AI-generated feedback that encourages critical self-reflection may be well-received in individualistic cultures but perceived as confrontational or inappropriate in collectivist societies. Similarly, automated grading systems may not account for rhetorical or linguistic variations in student writing, leading to biased outcomes. These cultural mismatches can undermine student trust and compromise the perceived legitimacy of AI-mediated education.

Institutional Asymmetries and Power Imbalances

TNE partnerships often involve institutions with differing levels of technological maturity, QA capacity, and institutional autonomy. This asymmetry can lead to imbalanced QA arrangements, where the "sending" institution imposes its standards without adequately engaging local partners. Such top-down approaches risk marginalising host-country educators and failing to account for contextual realities (Khan & Alfaz, 2025). [theaspd.com]

In AI-supported TNE, these imbalances are magnified. Institutions with greater access to AI infrastructure and expertise may dominate decision-making around tool selection, data governance, and pedagogical design. This can result in a form of digital neo-colonialism, where educational technologies are exported without sufficient localisation or co-creation.

To address this, scholars have called for collaborative governance models that distribute QA responsibilities more equitably. These include joint regulatory councils, bilateral QA compacts, and stakeholder advisory panels that include voices from both home and host institutions (Khan & Alfaz, 2025). [theaspd.com]

Absence of Shared QA Standards for AI Tools

Another major gap is the lack of common benchmarks for evaluating the quality, fairness, and effectiveness of AI tools used in education. While there are emerging frameworks for ethical AI (e.g., UNESCO's AI Ethics Recommendations), these are often high-level and not tailored to the specific needs of TNE (Hopbach, 2022). [unesdoc.unesco.org]

In practice, institutions rely on vendor assurances or internal testing to assess AI tools, which may not be sufficient for cross-border QA. There is a need for internationally recognised standards that address:

1. Algorithmic transparency and explainability.
2. Cultural and linguistic adaptability.
3. Data privacy and consent mechanisms.
4. Pedagogical alignment and learning efficacy.

The OECD and UNESCO have both advocated for global cooperation in developing such standards, emphasising the importance of interoperability, mutual recognition, and continuous improvement (Roy, 2023). [ehea.info]

Case Examples of QA Misalignment

Several case studies illustrate the consequences of QA misalignment in AI-enhanced TNE:

1. In a UK-UAE partnership, automated plagiarism detection tools flagged a disproportionately high number of essays from Emirati students due to differences in citation practices and writing conventions. The lack of local calibration led to student complaints and reputational damage (Khan & Alfaz, 2025). [theaspd.com]
2. A European university's AI tutor, trained on English-language data, failed to provide meaningful support to students in a Southeast Asian partner institution. The tool's inability to recognise local idioms and cultural references led to disengagement and poor learning outcomes (Trifiró, 2025). [www.taylor...rancis.com]
3. In a joint degree programme between institutions in the UK and Malaysia, discrepancies in how AI-generated assessment data were interpreted led to conflicting decisions about student progression. The absence of a shared QA protocol for AI tools created confusion and undermined institutional trust (Kayyali, 2024). [link.springer.com]

These examples underscore the need for context-aware QA mechanisms that can accommodate local variation while maintaining global standards.

Governance Gaps in AI Integration

The rapid adoption of AI in higher education has outpaced the development of governance frameworks. A recent white paper by the Asia-Europe Foundation (2025) found that fewer than 40% of universities had formal AI governance policies, and even fewer had mechanisms for cross-border coordination. [asef.org]

This governance vacuum creates risks for students, institutions, and QA bodies alike. Without clear policies, institutions may struggle to ensure ethical AI use, respond to incidents of bias or error, or demonstrate compliance with international standards. Moreover, the absence of shared governance structures makes it difficult to coordinate QA efforts across TNE partnerships.

To address these gaps, scholars have proposed the development of AI governance frameworks tailored to the higher education sector. These frameworks should include:

1. Ethical guidelines for AI use in teaching and assessment;
2. Protocols for cross-border data sharing and consent;
3. Mechanisms for stakeholder consultation and redress;
4. Standards for algorithmic auditing and impact assessment (Umoke et al., 2025).

Toward Collaborative and Adaptive QA Models

In response to these challenges, there is growing interest in collaborative QA models that emphasise mutual recognition, shared responsibility, and continuous dialogue. These models move beyond compliance to focus on quality enhancement, capacity building, and trust-based partnerships.

For example, the EUTOPIA Alliance—a network of European universities—has developed a bottom-up QA model that supports transnational collaboration through shared micro-credentials, joint evaluation tools, and community-led innovation (Angouri et al., 2024). Such initiatives demonstrate the potential of internal QA systems to act as catalysts for sustainable, cross-border quality assurance. [www.eua.eu]

Ultimately, the future of QA in AI-supported TNE depends on the sector's ability to reimagine governance in ways that are inclusive, flexible, and responsive to technological change. This requires not only institutional innovation but also policy leadership, international cooperation, and student-centred design.

PROPOSED PRINCIPLES FOR EFFECTIVE QUALITY ASSURANCE IN AI-AUGMENTED TNE

Figure 3. illustrates the proposed framework for Quality Assurance (QA) in AI-augmented Transnational Education (TNE). It highlights seven interconnected pillars that underpin a holistic and ethical approach to QA, ensuring relevance, adaptability, and student empowerment in diverse educational context.

Figure 3. Proposed quality assurance framework in AI-augmented TNE

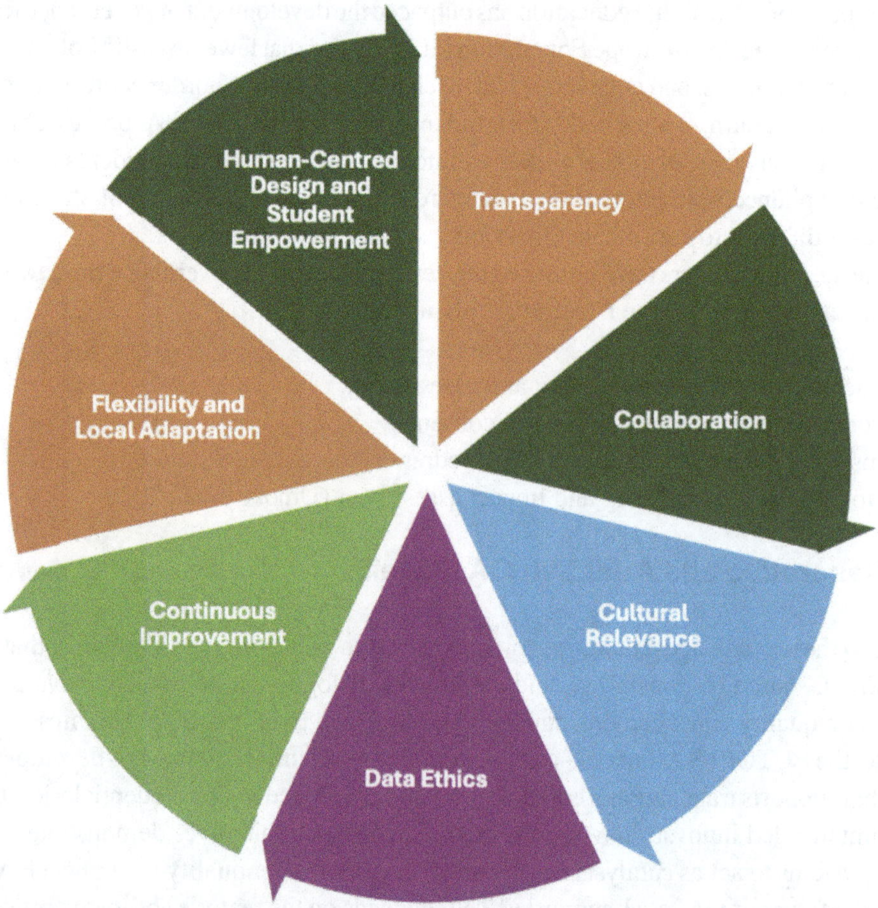

Transparency: Ensuring Explainability and Accountability

Transparency is a cornerstone of ethical and effective AI integration in education. In the context of transnational education (TNE), where learners and educators may be geographically and culturally distant from the institutions deploying AI tools, transparency becomes even more critical. It ensures that all stakeholders—students, educators, administrators, and regulators—understand how AI systems function, what data they use, and how decisions are made.

A transparent AI system should provide clear documentation of its design, data sources, and decision-making processes. This includes explainable algorithms, accessible user interfaces, and audit trails that allow for retrospective analysis. The Transparency Index Framework developed by Chaudhry et al. (2023) offers a structured approach to embedding transparency throughout the AI development lifecycle—from data collection to deployment and iterative improvement. [arxiv.org]

Transparency also supports trust. When students understand how their data is used and how feedback or grades are generated, they are more likely to engage with AI tools confidently. For educators, transparency enables critical oversight, allowing them to validate AI outputs and intervene when necessary. In TNE, where cultural and linguistic differences may already create barriers to understanding, opaque AI systems can exacerbate confusion and inequity.

Institutions should adopt tiered transparency strategies, offering different levels of information to different stakeholders based on their roles and technical expertise. For example, students may need simplified explanations of how AI-generated feedback is produced, while QA professionals may require detailed technical documentation for evaluation purposes. [www.liaisonedu.com]

Ultimately, transparency is not just a technical feature—it is a pedagogical and ethical imperative. It enables informed consent, supports accountability, and fosters a culture of openness that is essential for quality assurance in AI-enhanced TNE.

Collaboration: Shared Governance Across Borders

Collaboration is essential for effective QA in AI-augmented TNE. Unlike traditional education models, where QA responsibilities are often centralised within a single institution or national agency, AI-enhanced TNE requires shared governance across multiple stakeholders and jurisdictions.

Collaborative QA involves co-designing and co-implementing QA frameworks with input from home and host institutions, educators, students, technologists, and regulators. This approach ensures that AI tools are not only technically sound but also culturally appropriate, pedagogically aligned, and legally compliant across borders.

The Asia-Pacific Quality Network (APQN) and the OECD have both emphasised the importance of international cooperation in QA, particularly in cross-border education contexts. Collaborative models may include joint QA committees, bilateral review processes, and shared data platforms that enable real-time monitoring and mutual accountability. [www.apqn.org]

One promising approach is the use of federated QA systems, where each partner institution retains autonomy over local QA processes but agrees to common standards and protocols for AI tool evaluation. This model balances consistency with flexibility and allows for local adaptation without sacrificing global coherence.

Collaboration also extends to capacity building. Institutions should invest in joint training programmes to develop shared competencies in AI literacy, data ethics, and QA methodologies. Such initiatives not only strengthen institutional partnerships but also promote a shared understanding of quality across diverse contexts.

In sum, collaboration transforms QA from a compliance exercise into a cooperative endeavour, fostering trust, innovation, and mutual learning in AI-enhanced TNE.

Cultural Relevance: Contextualising AI for Local Learners

Cultural relevance is a critical yet often overlooked dimension of quality assurance in AI-augmented TNE. AI systems are typically developed in specific cultural and linguistic contexts, often reflecting Western academic norms and communication styles. When these systems are deployed in diverse international settings without adaptation, they risk alienating learners, misinterpreting inputs, and delivering feedback that is culturally inappropriate or pedagogically ineffective.

Culturally relevant QA involves ensuring that AI tools are sensitive to local educational values, communication norms, and learner expectations. This includes adapting language models to recognise regional dialects, incorporating culturally relevant examples into content, and calibrating feedback styles to align with local pedagogical traditions.

The Intersection of AI and Cultural Inclusion Framework (Williams & Jowallah, 2025) highlights the dual potential of AI to either enhance or hinder cultural inclusion in higher education. When designed thoughtfully, AI can support intercultural communication, personalise learning for diverse populations, and foster a sense of belonging. However, when cultural assumptions are embedded uncritically into algorithms, the result can be exclusion, bias, and disengagement. [link.springer.com]

Institutions should conduct cultural audits of AI tools before deployment, involving local educators and students in the evaluation process. QA frameworks should include indicators for cultural responsiveness, such as the representation of diverse perspectives, the adaptability of content, and the appropriateness of feedback.

In TNE, where learners may already feel disconnected from the home institution, culturally relevant AI can serve as a bridge—enhancing engagement, improving comprehension, and affirming students' identities. QA systems must therefore move beyond technical metrics to assess how well AI tools resonate with the lived experiences of diverse learners.

Data Ethics: Protecting Privacy and Promoting Fairness

Data ethics is a foundational principle in the quality assurance (QA) of AI-enhanced transnational education (TNE). AI systems rely on vast amounts of learner data to function effectively ranging from demographic information and academic performance to behavioural patterns and biometric inputs. In TNE, where data often crosses borders, the ethical management of this information becomes both a legal and moral imperative.

One of the primary concerns is informed consent. Students must be clearly informed about what data is being collected, how it will be used, who will have access to it, and how long it will be retained. Consent should be meaningful—not buried in lengthy terms and conditions—and should be revisitable, allowing students to withdraw at any time without penalty.

Another key issue is data minimisation. Institutions should collect only the data necessary for educational purposes and avoid excessive or intrusive surveillance. For example, while AI-based proctoring tools may enhance exam security, they must be used proportionately and with clear justification, especially when they involve facial recognition or keystroke tracking.

Bias mitigation is also critical. AI systems trained on historical or culturally narrow datasets may inadvertently reinforce stereotypes or disadvantage certain groups. Institutions must regularly audit their AI tools for discriminatory outcomes and take corrective action where necessary. This includes diversifying training data, involving diverse stakeholders in system design, and testing tools in multiple cultural contexts.

Finally, students should have the right to explanation and redress. If an AI system makes a decision that affects a student's academic progress—such as flagging them for plagiarism or predicting failure—they should be able to understand the rationale and challenge the outcome.

Embedding data ethics into QA frameworks ensures that AI supports educational goals without compromising student rights. It also builds trust, which is essential for the long-term sustainability of AI in TNE.

Continuous Improvement: Using AI to Enhance QA Itself

Continuous improvement is a hallmark of effective quality assurance, and AI offers powerful tools to support this process. Rather than relying solely on periodic reviews or static benchmarks, institutions can use AI to monitor, evaluate, and refine educational practices in real time.

One of the most promising applications is the use of predictive analytics to identify students at risk of disengagement or failure. By analysing patterns in attendance, participation, and performance, AI systems can flag early warning signs and trigger timely interventions. This not only improves student outcomes but also provides valuable data for institutional self-assessment.

AI can also support automated analysis of student feedback, enabling institutions to detect trends, identify areas for improvement, and respond more quickly to learner concerns. Natural language processing (NLP) tools can analyse open-ended survey responses, discussion forum posts, or helpdesk queries to surface recurring issues or sentiments.

Another area of innovation is the development of dynamic QA dashboards. These platforms integrate data from multiple sources—such as learning management systems, assessment tools, and student support services—to provide a holistic view of quality indicators. Dashboards can be customised for different stakeholders, offering real-time insights to educators, administrators, and QA professionals.

However, the use of AI for QA must be approached with caution. Institutions must ensure that data is interpreted in context, that algorithms are transparent and explainable, and that human judgement remains central to decision-making. Over-reliance on automated metrics can lead to reductive or misleading conclusions, particularly in complex, culturally diverse TNE environments.

To maximise the benefits of AI for continuous improvement, institutions should adopt a cyclical QA model that integrates data collection, analysis, action, and reflection. This model should be embedded in institutional culture and supported by training, resources, and leadership commitment.

Flexibility and Local Adaptation

Flexibility is essential for quality assurance in AI-augmented TNE. Given the diversity of educational systems, cultural contexts, and regulatory environments, QA frameworks must be adaptable to local needs while maintaining core standards of academic integrity, fairness, and effectiveness.

Rigid, one-size-fits-all QA models are unlikely to succeed in TNE, especially when AI tools are involved. For example, an AI feedback system that works well in a UK context may need to be adapted for use in East Asia, where communication styles, academic conventions, and student expectations differ. Similarly, data privacy laws may vary significantly between countries, requiring local adjustments to data governance protocols.

Flexible QA frameworks allow institutions to customise indicators, benchmarks, and processes based on local realities. This might include adjusting assessment criteria, modifying feedback styles, or incorporating local examples into AI-generated content. Flexibility also enables institutions to respond to emerging challenges, such as changes in technology, student demographics, or regulatory requirements.

At the same time, flexibility must be balanced with coherence and comparability. Institutions must ensure that all students, regardless of location, receive a high-quality education that meets the same learning outcomes. This requires clear articulation of core standards, robust mechanisms for cross-site coordination, and regular calibration of QA processes.

One effective approach is the use of modular QA frameworks, which define essential quality dimensions (e.g., transparency, ethics, cultural relevance) while allowing for local interpretation and implementation. These frameworks can be co-developed with local partners and reviewed periodically to ensure alignment with evolving needs.

In sum, flexibility is not a compromise on quality—it is a recognition of diversity. By embracing local adaptation within a coherent QA structure, institutions can ensure that AI-enhanced TNE is both globally credible and locally meaningful.

Human-Centred Design and Student Empowerment

At the heart of any educational system—AI-enhanced or otherwise—are the learners. Human-centred design ensures that AI tools are developed and deployed in ways that prioritise student needs, values, and experiences. In TNE, where students may already feel disconnected from the home institution, human-centred AI can play a vital role in fostering engagement, trust, and empowerment.

Human-centred AI design involves co-creating tools with students, incorporating their feedback into system development, and ensuring that technologies support rather than replace human interaction. For example, AI tutors should be designed to complement, not substitute, the role of educators—providing scaffolding, encouragement, and personalised support while preserving opportunities for human dialogue.

Empowerment also means giving students agency over their learning data and pathways. This includes the ability to access, understand, and manage their data; to opt in or out of certain AI features; and to challenge decisions that affect their academic progress. Institutions should provide clear guidance on how AI tools work and how students can use them ethically and effectively.

The World Economic Forum (2025) and EDUCAUSE both advocate for student-centred AI policies that promote digital literacy, critical thinking, and ethical awareness. These competencies are essential not only for navigating AI-enhanced education but also for participating in an increasingly AI-driven world.

QA frameworks should include indicators for student empowerment, such as the availability of opt-out mechanisms, the clarity of AI-related communications, and the extent of student involvement in QA processes. Institutions should also create channels for ongoing dialogue with students about their experiences with AI, using this feedback to inform continuous improvement.

In conclusion, human-centred design is not an optional add-on—it is a core principle of ethical and effective AI integration. By placing students at the centre of QA frameworks, institutions can ensure that AI serves as a tool for inclusion, engagement, and educational success.

CONCEPTUAL QA MODELS FOR AI-AUGMENTED TNE

As artificial intelligence (AI) becomes more embedded in transnational education (TNE), institutions must rethink not only their quality assurance (QA) principles but also the structural models through which QA is governed and implemented. This section introduces four conceptual QA models—centralised, distributed, collaborative and hybrid Adaptive models as showing in Figure.4 —and evaluates their relevance, strengths, and limitations in the context of AI-enhanced TNE. It also proposes hybrid approaches and future-ready adaptations that reflect the complexity of cross-border, AI-mediated education.

Figure 4. Conceptual quality assurance models in AI-augmented TNE.

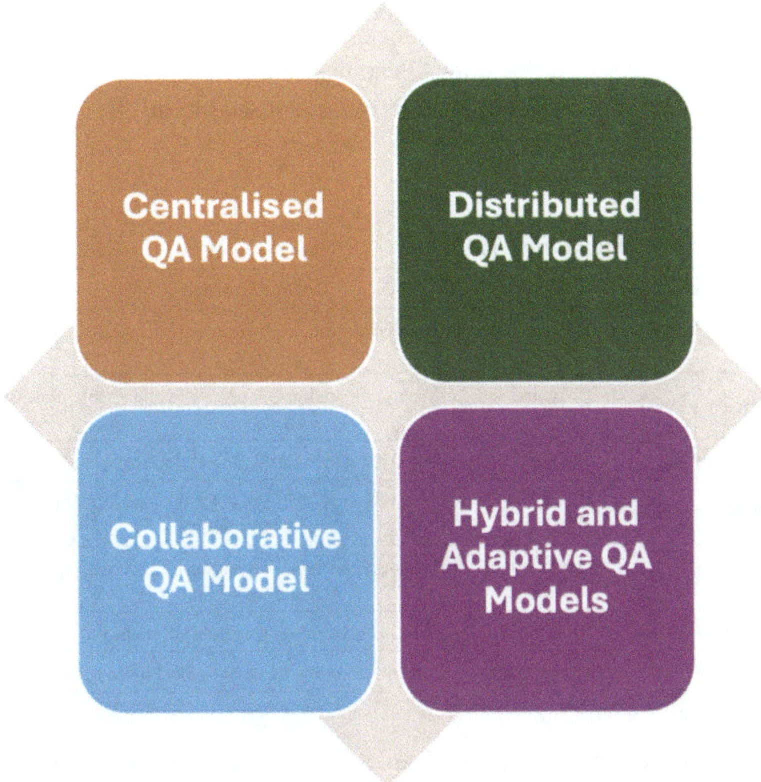

Centralised QA Model

The centralised quality assurance (QA) model is characterised by a single institution—typically the home or awarding university—retaining primary control over QA processes, policies, and standards across all delivery sites. This model is rooted in the traditional logic of maintaining brand integrity, ensuring that transnational education (TNE) provision mirrors the quality of the home campus. In the context of AI-enhanced TNE, the centralised model offers both strengths and limitations that must be carefully considered.

Key Features and Mechanisms

In a centralised QA model, the home institution is responsible for:

1. Selecting and approving AI tools used in teaching, learning, and assessment.
2. Defining QA indicators and benchmarks for all delivery sites.
3. Conducting internal audits and evaluations, often through periodic reviews.
4. Ensuring compliance with home-country regulations and institutional policies.

AI integration within this model typically involves centralised data collection and analysis, enabling the institution to monitor performance, detect anomalies, and generate insights across its global operations. For example, Warren et al. (2025) describe how AI can be used to automate evidence collection, support predictive analytics, and enhance institutional effectiveness through centralised dashboards and reporting systems.

Table 1. Centralised QA model in AI-augmented TNE

Category	Key points	Details/ Examples
Advantages	Consistency	Ensures uniform academic standards, assessments, and student outcomes across all sites.
	Efficiency	Centralised AI systems streamline QA processes and enable proactive quality management.
	Brand Protection	Maintains institutional reputation through tight control over offshore provision.
	Real-World Example	*UK's QAA*: Conducts five-yearly TNE Reviews to ensure offshore provision meets domestic standards.
Limitations & Risks	Cultural Insensitivity	May overlook local norms, leading to perceptions of cultural imposition or "digital neo-colonialism."
	Regulatory Misalignment	Host country laws (e.g., UAE's CAA) may conflict with centralised QA policies.
	Limited Responsiveness	Centralised systems may be slow to adapt to local innovations or challenges.

These limitations are particularly pronounced in AI-enhanced TNE, where algorithmic decisions must be contextually appropriate and legally compliant across jurisdictions.

Strategic Considerations

To mitigate these risks, institutions using a centralised QA model should:

1. Establish local advisory panels to provide cultural and regulatory insights.
2. Develop modular QA frameworks that allow for some local adaptation within a centralised structure.
3. Ensure transparency and explainability in AI systems to build trust among local stakeholders;
4. Engage in cross-border dialogue with host-country regulators to align expectations and avoid compliance conflicts.

As AI continues to reshape the educational landscape, the centralised QA model must evolve from a rigid, top-down approach to a more adaptive and inclusive system that balances institutional control with local relevance.

Distributed QA Model

The distributed quality assurance (QA) model decentralises responsibility for QA processes, allowing local delivery partners or campuses to take the lead in implementing and monitoring quality standards. In the context of AI-augmented transnational education (TNE), this model offers a flexible and context-sensitive approach that can better accommodate cultural, regulatory, and pedagogical diversity across delivery sites.

Key Features and Mechanisms

In a distributed QA model:

1. Local institutions or campuses are responsible for selecting, adapting, and evaluating AI tools used in teaching and assessment;
2. QA processes are embedded within local operations and aligned with regional educational norms and legal requirements;
3. Home institutions provide overarching frameworks or guidelines but delegate operational autonomy to partners;
4. Local QA teams conduct regular reviews, audits, and stakeholder consultations to ensure quality and relevance.

This model is particularly suited to joint degree programmes, franchise arrangements, or multi-campus universities, where local partners have the capacity and authority to manage their own QA systems. AI tools may be customised to reflect local languages, curricula, and learner needs, while still contributing to shared institutional goals.

Table 2. Distributed QA model in AI-augmented TNE

Category	Key points	Details/ Examples
Advantages	Cultural & Regulatory Alignment	Local QA teams ensure AI tools comply with national laws and reflect local pedagogical norms.
	Responsiveness & Innovation	Decentralised structures allow quick adaptation to demographic, technological, or policy changes.
	Capacity Building	Empowers local partners, fostering institutional development and shared ownership of quality outcomes.
	Real-World Example	Malaysian institution: Adapts AI feedback tools to local academic standards while contributing to central oversight.
Limitations & Risks	Inconsistency	QA standards and learner experiences may vary across sites, affecting qualification credibility.
	Fragmentation	Siloed data hinders institutional benchmarking and insight aggregation.
	Quality Drift	Local adaptations may diverge from original programme goals, risking misalignment and reputation.

These risks are particularly acute in AI-enhanced TNE, where algorithmic decisions must be monitored for fairness, accuracy, and cultural appropriateness. If QA processes are not harmonised, institutions may struggle to detect or address issues such as bias, data misuse, or inconsistent feedback.

Strategic Considerations

To mitigate these risks, institutions adopting a distributed QA model should:

1. Develop shared QA frameworks that define core principles (e.g. transparency, ethics, equity) while allowing for local interpretation and implementation.
2. Establish data-sharing agreements and interoperable platforms to enable cross-site monitoring and benchmarking.
3. Provide training and support to local QA teams on AI literacy, data ethics, and quality enhancement strategies.
4. Conduct joint audits and peer reviews to ensure alignment and mutual accountability.

One promising approach is the use of federated learning and QA systems, where AI models are trained locally on site-specific data but contribute to a shared institutional model. This allows for local customisation while preserving global coherence and data privacy.

Collaborative QA Model

The collaborative quality assurance (QA) model represents a shift from hierarchical or decentralised structures to a shared governance approach, where QA responsibilities are co-developed and co-managed by all stakeholders involved in transnational education (TNE). In the context of AI-augmented TNE, this model is particularly well-suited to addressing the complexities of cross-border education, where cultural, regulatory, and technological diversity must be balanced with institutional coherence and academic integrity.

Key Features and Mechanisms

In a collaborative QA model:

1. QA frameworks are co-designed by home and host institutions, with input from educators, students, technologists, and regulators.
2. AI tools are selected, implemented, and evaluated through joint committees or governance boards.
3. Quality indicators are negotiated and aligned across institutions, allowing for both global standards and local relevance.
4. Data is shared transparently across partners, enabling mutual monitoring, benchmarking, and continuous improvement.

This model is particularly effective in strategic partnerships, joint degrees, and multi-institutional alliances, where institutions are committed to long-term collaboration and shared educational goals.

It reflects the principles of mutual recognition, trust-based accountability, and co-creation, which are increasingly recognised as best practices in international higher education.

Table 3. Collaborative QA model in AI-augmented TNE

Category	Key points	Details/ Examples
Advantages	Shared Ownership	Fosters joint responsibility among stakeholders for quality assurance.
	Contextual Sensitivity	Local partners ensure cultural, regulatory, and pedagogical relevance of AI tools.
	Innovation & Adaptability	Encourages experimentation and iterative improvement in AI integration.
	Mutual Capacity Building	Institutions share resources and expertise, enhancing collective AI governance.
	Real-World Example	EUTOPIA Alliance: Shared micro-credentials, joint evaluation tools, and community-led innovation.
Limitations & Risks	Complexity & Coordination	Joint governance can be time-consuming and resource intensive.
	Power Imbalances	Differences in institutional capacity may lead to unequal influence.
	Data Governance Challenges	Legal and ethical concerns arise when sharing sensitive learner data across jurisdictions.

Strategic Considerations

To implement a successful collaborative QA model, institutions should:

1. Establish joint QA charters that define roles, responsibilities, and decision-making protocols.
2. Create shared digital platforms for data exchange, feedback collection, and performance monitoring.
3. Develop cross-institutional training programmes on AI literacy, data ethics, and QA methodologies.
4. Involve students and local educators in QA processes to ensure that AI tools reflect diverse perspectives and needs.

Collaborative QA also benefits from external facilitation by regional or international bodies, such as the European University Association (EUA) or UNESCO, which can provide frameworks, benchmarks, and peer review mechanisms to support alignment and accountability.

Hybrid and Adaptive QA Models

While centralised, distributed, and collaborative quality assurance (QA) models each offer distinct advantages, the complexity of AI-augmented transnational education (TNE) often necessitates a more flexible and integrated approach. Hybrid and adaptive QA models combine elements from multiple frameworks to create systems that are both robust and responsive to the diverse demands of cross-border, AI-mediated education.

A hybrid QA model blends features of centralised, distributed, and collaborative approaches to create a customised governance structure. For example, an institution may centralise the selection and procurement of AI tools to ensure consistency and compliance, while allowing local partners to adapt content and feedback mechanisms to suit cultural and regulatory contexts. Similarly, data analytics may be centralised for institutional oversight, while pedagogical decisions are decentralised to reflect local expertise.

Hybrid models are particularly useful in multi-campus universities, joint degree programmes, or franchise arrangements where different delivery sites operate under varying degrees of autonomy. They allow institutions to maintain core academic standards while enabling contextual flexibility—a critical balance in AI-enhanced TNE.

Adaptive QA: Responding to Change in Real Time

Beyond structural hybridity, adaptive QA models emphasise responsiveness and continuous evolution. These models are designed to adjust dynamically to changes in technology, policy, learner needs, and institutional priorities. In AI-enhanced education, where tools and practices evolve rapidly, static QA frameworks can quickly become obsolete.

Adaptive QA systems typically include:

1. Real-time monitoring of AI performance and learner outcomes;
2. Feedback loops that incorporate student and staff input into system refinement;
3. Scenario planning to anticipate and respond to emerging risks or opportunities;
4. Iterative review cycles that allow for regular updates to QA policies and practices.

For example, an institution may use AI to detect shifts in student engagement patterns across delivery sites and adjust support services accordingly. Alternatively, a QA team may revise assessment protocols in response to new capabilities or risks introduced by generative AI tools.

Benefits of Hybrid and Adaptive Models

These models offer several key advantages:

1. Scalability with sensitivity: Institutions can scale AI-enhanced TNE provision while remaining responsive to local contexts and learner diversity.
2. Resilience: Adaptive systems are better equipped to handle disruptions, whether technological (e.g. AI system failure), regulatory (e.g. new data laws), or pedagogical (e.g. shifts in student expectations).
3. Innovation: Hybrid models support experimentation and local innovation, while ensuring that successful practices can be shared and scaled across the institution.
4. Balanced accountability: By distributing responsibilities while maintaining shared oversight, these models promote both local ownership and institutional coherence.

Challenges and Considerations

Despite their strengths, hybrid and adaptive QA models are not without challenges:

1. Complexity: Managing multiple QA layers and feedback loops requires strong coordination, clear communication, and robust infrastructure.

2. Resource intensity: These models demand investment in staff training, digital platforms, and governance structures.
3. Risk of misalignment: Without clear frameworks, hybrid models can drift into inconsistency or confusion about roles and responsibilities.

To mitigate these risks, institutions should:

1. Develop QA blueprints that map out how different components interact and who is responsible for what;
2. Use interoperable data systems to ensure seamless information flow across sites and functions;
3. Establish adaptive governance bodies that can make timely decisions and adjustments based on evidence and stakeholder input.

Examples and Emerging Practices

Several institutions and networks are already experimenting with hybrid and adaptive QA models:

1. The European Universities Initiative supports alliances that use shared QA platforms while allowing for national and institutional variation.
2. The TeachAI initiative promotes adaptive QA by encouraging institutions to use AI not only in teaching but also in monitoring and improving teaching quality.
3. Some universities are piloting AI-driven QA dashboards that integrate learner analytics, feedback, and compliance data to support real-time decision-making.

These examples demonstrate the potential of hybrid and adaptive models to support quality, equity, and innovation in AI-enhanced TNE.

Future-Ready QA Architectures

As artificial intelligence (AI) continues to evolve and reshape the landscape of transnational education (TNE), quality assurance (QA) systems must also transform to remain relevant, effective, and ethically grounded. Traditional QA models—whether centralised, distributed, or collaborative—provide useful foundations, but they must now be reimagined to support future-ready architectures that are agile, data-informed, and learner-centred.

Future-ready QA architectures are not defined by a single structure or methodology. Instead, they are characterised by their adaptability, interoperability, and capacity for continuous learning. These systems are designed to operate in complex, cross-border environments where AI tools are integrated into every aspect of the educational experience—from admissions and curriculum design to assessment and student support.

Key Features of Future-Ready QA Systems

1. Federated Governance Models: Future-ready QA systems will increasingly adopt federated governance, where oversight is shared across institutions, jurisdictions, and stakeholder groups. This

model allows for local autonomy while maintaining global coherence through shared standards, interoperable data systems, and mutual recognition agreements. Federated QA is particularly well-suited to AI-enhanced TNE, where data privacy laws, cultural norms, and educational policies vary widely.

2. AI-Enhanced QA Processes: AI itself can be used to support QA by automating routine tasks, identifying patterns in learner data, and generating real-time insights. For example, machine learning algorithms can detect anomalies in assessment outcomes, flag potential equity issues, or predict programme-level risks. These tools enable institutions to move from reactive to proactive quality management, identifying issues before they escalate.
3. Student-Centred Design: Future-ready QA systems will place learners at the centre of quality processes. This includes involving students in the co-design of AI tools, collecting and acting on their feedback, and ensuring that QA indicators reflect their lived experiences. Student-centred QA also means recognising diverse learner needs and ensuring that AI systems are inclusive, accessible, and empowering.
4. Ethical and Sustainable AI Integration: As AI becomes more embedded in education, QA systems must ensure that its use aligns with ethical principles and sustainability goals. This includes regular audits of algorithmic bias, transparent data governance, and alignment with frameworks such as the UNESCO Recommendation on the Ethics of Artificial Intelligence. Institutions must also consider the environmental impact of AI infrastructure and adopt green computing practices where possible.
5. Modular and Scalable Frameworks: Future-ready QA systems must be modular—capable of being scaled up or down depending on the size, scope, and complexity of the TNE provision. Modular frameworks allow institutions to pilot new QA tools or indicators in specific contexts before wider implementation. They also support customisation, enabling institutions to tailor QA processes to different programme types, delivery modes, or regulatory environments.

Enabling Technologies and Infrastructure

To support these features, institutions will need to invest in:

1. Interoperable data platforms that integrate information from learning management systems, AI tools, student information systems, and QA dashboards.
2. Secure cloud infrastructure that supports cross-border data sharing while complying with local and international privacy regulations.
3. Digital credentials and blockchain-based verification to enhance transparency and portability of learning outcomes.
4. Open-source QA tools and frameworks that can be adapted and shared across institutions and regions.

These technologies must be underpinned by robust cybersecurity protocols, data ethics policies, and technical standards to ensure reliability, trust, and compliance.

Strategic Implications for Institutions

To transition toward future-ready QA, institutions should:

1. Conduct readiness assessments to identify gaps in their current QA systems, infrastructure, and capabilities.
2. Develop roadmaps for digital transformation that align QA innovation with institutional strategy and values.
3. Foster cross-functional teams that bring together QA professionals, IT specialists, educators, and students.
4. Engage in international networks and consortia to share best practices, co-develop standards, and build collective capacity.

Institutions must also cultivate a culture of innovation and reflection, where QA is not seen as a compliance burden but as a strategic enabler of educational excellence and equity.

CONCLUSION AND FUTURE DIRECTIONS

The integration of artificial intelligence (AI) into transnational education (TNE) is not merely a technological shift—it is a profound transformation of how education is designed, delivered, and evaluated across borders. As this chapter has demonstrated, traditional quality assurance (QA) frameworks, built for face-to-face, standardised, and nationally bounded education, are increasingly inadequate in the face of algorithmically mediated, personalised, and globally distributed learning environments.

AI challenges foundational assumptions about educational quality. It redefines the roles of teachers and learners, introduces new forms of assessment and feedback, and raises complex ethical, cultural, and regulatory questions. In TNE, these challenges are magnified by the need to operate across diverse jurisdictions, languages, and pedagogical traditions.

Key Takeaways

This chapter has outlined several critical insights:

1. Quality in AI-TNE must be redefined to include transparency, ethicality, cultural relevance, and adaptability—not just compliance and consistency.
2. Emerging concerns such as algorithmic bias, data privacy, and academic integrity require urgent attention from QA bodies and institutional leaders.
3. Cross-border QA is hindered by regulatory fragmentation, cultural divergence, and the absence of shared standards for AI tools.
4. Effective QA requires principles such as transparency, collaboration, cultural sensitivity, data ethics, and continuous improvement.
5. Conceptual QA models—centralised, distributed, and collaborative—offer different pathways for institutions to structure their QA systems, each with distinct strengths and trade-offs.

These insights point to the need for a more holistic, inclusive, and forward-looking approach to QA in AI-enhanced TNE.

Future Directions for Research and Practice

To support the development of robust QA systems in AI-TNE, several areas warrant further exploration:

Development of Global QA Standards for AI in Education

There is a pressing need for internationally recognised benchmarks that address the unique characteristics of AI tools used in teaching and assessment. These standards should be co-developed by global stakeholders and reflect diverse cultural, legal, and pedagogical contexts.

Cross-Border Regulatory Harmonisation

Policymakers and QA agencies should work towards greater alignment of data protection, AI governance, and educational quality standards. Initiatives such as the UNESCO AI Ethics framework and OECD's TNE guidelines provide useful starting points but require broader adoption and localisation.

Participatory QA Models

Future QA systems should involve students, educators, and local communities in the design and evaluation of AI tools. Participatory approaches can enhance trust, surface context-specific concerns, and ensure that AI supports rather than undermines learner agency.

Capacity Building and Digital Literacy

Institutions must invest in training for staff and students to understand, evaluate, and ethically engage with AI systems. This includes not only technical skills but also critical thinking, ethical reasoning, and intercultural competence.

AI for QA Enhancement

AI itself can be harnessed to improve QA processes through real-time monitoring, predictive analytics, and automated reporting. However, such systems must be used responsibly, with safeguards to prevent over-reliance or misuse.

Final Reflections

The future of TNE will be increasingly shaped by digital technologies, with AI playing a central role. While this presents exciting opportunities for innovation, access, and personalisation, it also demands a rethinking of how we define and assure quality in education.

Institutions, regulators, and QA bodies must move beyond reactive, compliance-driven models and embrace adaptive, collaborative, and ethically grounded approaches. By doing so, they can ensure that AI-augmented TNE not only meets academic standards but also supports learner success, institutional accountability, and global equity.

In this evolving landscape, quality assurance is not a static endpoint but a continuous, collective endeavour—one that must evolve in tandem with the technologies and societies it seeks to serve.

REFERENCES

Alcock, E. (2025). *Assuring higher education's quality in the age of AI is no easy task.* European University Association. https://www.eua.eu/our-work/expert-voices/assuring-higher-educations-quality-in-the-age-of-ai-is-no-easy-task.html

Angouri, J. S'Jegers, R., & Szabo, M. (2024). *Internal quality assurance as a catalyst for sustainable, transnational collaboration: The case of the EUTOPIA Alliance.* European University Association. https://www.eua.eu/publications/conference-papers/internal-quality-assurance-as-a-catalyst-for-sustainable-transnational-collaboration-the-case-of-the-eutopia-alliance.html

Bannister, P., Alcalde Peñalver, E., & Santamaría Urbieta, A. (2024). Transnational higher education cultures and generative AI: A nominal group study. *Journal for Multicultural Education.* DOI: 10.1108/JME-10-2023-0102

British Council. (2024). *A global framework for transnational education engagement.* DOI: 10.57884/HFW3-6S14

Carvalho, N., Rosa, M. J., & Amaral, A. (2023). Cross-border higher education and quality assurance: A systematic literature review. *Journal of Studies in International Education, 27*(5), 695–718. DOI: 10.1177/10283153221076900

Chaudhry, A., ... (2023). *Transparency index framework.* arXiv. https://arxiv.org/pdf/2206.03220

Durak, H. Y., & Onan, A. (2025). A systematic review of AI-based feedback in educational settings. *Journal of Computational Social Science, 8*(96), 96. Advance online publication. DOI: 10.1007/s42001-025-00428-1

EDUCAUSE. (2025). *AI ethical guidelines.* https://library.educause.edu/resources/2025/6/ai-ethical-guidelines

Evangelista, E. D. L. (2025). Ensuring academic integrity in the age of ChatGPT. *Contemporary Educational Technology, 17*(1), ep559. DOI: 10.30935/cedtech/15775

Freyer, O., Jayabalan, S., Kather, J. N., & Gilbert, S. (2025). Overcoming regulatory barriers to the implementation of AI agents in healthcare. *Nature Medicine.* https://www.nature.com/articles/s41591-025-03841-1

Henderson, M., Bearman, M., Chung, J., Fawns, T., Buckingham Shum, S., Matthews, K. E., & de Mello Heredia, J. (2025). Comparing generative AI and teacher feedback: Student perceptions of usefulness and trustworthiness. *Assessment & Evaluation in Higher Education*, 1–16. Advance online publication. DOI: 10.1080/02602938.2025.2502582

Hopbach, A. (2022). *UNESCO-OECD guidelines for quality provision in cross-border higher education.* UNESCO. https://unesdoc.unesco.org/ark:/48223/pf0000389910

Ilieva, J., Ramos, E., Stowers, S., Tsiligiris, V., & Killingley, P. (2024). *A global framework for transnational education engagement.* British Council., DOI: 10.57884/HFW3-6S14

Joosten-ten Brinke, D., & Beekman, K. (2025). Responsible AI in higher education assessment: Principles, policy & practice. *Assessment in Education.* https://think.taylorandfrancis.com/special_issues/responsible-ai-in-higher-education-assessment

Kashefi, P., Kashefi, Y., & Mirsaraei, A. G. (2024). Shaping the future of AI: Balancing innovation and ethics in global regulation. *Uniform Law Review, 29*(3), 524–548. DOI: 10.1093/ulr/unae040

Kayyali, R. (2024). AI and assessment in transnational education. In *AI in Global Higher Education.* Springer., https://link.springer.com/chapter/10.1007/978-3-031-66623-0_6

Khan, S., & Alfaz, M. (2025). Towards a ministry-led quality assurance framework for transnational higher education: A comparative UK–UAE study. *International Journal of Environmental Sciences, 11*(23s). https://theaspd.com/index.php/ijes/article/download/8793/6358/18220

Lindsay, E. D., Zhang, M., Johri, A., & Bjerva, J. (2025). The responsible development of automated student feedback with generative AI. arXiv. https://arxiv.org/abs/2308.15334 DOI: 10.1109/EDUCON62633.2025.11016572

Lund, B. D., Lee, T. H., Mannuru, N. R., & Arutla, N. (2025). AI and academic integrity: Exploring student perceptions and implications for higher education. *Journal of Academic Ethics, 23*(3), 1545–1565. Advance online publication. DOI: 10.1007/s10805-025-09613-3

OECD. (2005). *Guidelines for quality provision in cross-border higher education.* https://ehea.info/Upload/Topic%203%20Simon%20Roy.pdf

Roy, S. (2023). Quality assurance of transnational education (TNE). OECD. https://ehea.info/Upload/Topic%203%20Simon%20Roy.pdf

Trifiró, F. (2025). The global recognition challenge for transnational education. In *Transnational Education and the Recognition of Qualifications.* Routledge., https://www.taylorfrancis.com/chapters/edit/10.4324/9781003488316-8 DOI: 10.4324/9781003488316-8

Umoke, C. C., Nwangbo, S. O., & Onwe, O. A. (2025). The governance of AI in education: Developing ethical policy frameworks for adaptive learning technologies. *International Journal of Advanced Scientific Management and Technology, 11*(2), 71–88. https://www.iiardjournals.org/get/IJASMT/VOL.%2011%20NO.%202%202025/The%20Governance%20of%20AI%20in%20Education%2071-88.pdf

Wargo, K., & Anderson, B. (2024). Striking a balance: Navigating the ethical dilemmas of AI in higher education. *EDUCAUSE Review.* https://er.educause.edu/articles/2024/12/striking-a-balance-navigating-the-ethical-dilemmas-of-ai-in-higher-education

Warren, S. J., Vogt, E. B., Tincher, B., & Yang, J. (2025). Enhancing quality assurance through strategic artificial intelligence integration: A framework for higher education digital transformation. *Quality Assurance in Education.* Advance online publication. DOI: 10.1108/QAE-09-2024-0183

Wheeler, K. (2024). Global AI ethics: Bridging cultural divides in technology. *Technology Magazine.* https://technologymagazine.com/articles/global-ai-ethics-bridging-cultural-divides-in-technology

Williams, D., & Jowallah, R. (2025). The intersection of AI and cultural inclusion in higher education. In *AI and Inclusive Pedagogy.* Springer., https://link.springer.com/chapter/10.1007/978-3-031-93567-1_14

World Economic Forum. (2025). *Responsible AI in higher education: Skills, trust, integrity*. https://www.weforum.org/stories/2025/09/responsible-ai-in-higher-education-building-skills-trust-and-integrity

Zhu, Y., Zhu, Z., Xu, W., & Zhu, Y. (2025). Cross-border higher education cooperation under the dual context of artificial intelligence and geopolitics. *Frontiers in Education, 10*, 1656518. Advance online publication. DOI: 10.3389/feduc.2025.1656518

Chapter 2
Bridging Cultures and Code:
Implementing AI-Assisted Learning in Transnational Computer Science Education

Senerath Mudalige Don Dilshan Dhanishtha Jayatilake
https://orcid.org/0000-0002-3377-7129
University of the West of England, UK

Yasmine Rosunally
University of the West of England, UK

Nguyen Trung Ky
International University Vietnam, Vietnam

ABSTRACT

This chapter explores the integration of artificial-intelligence-assisted learning within transnational computer science education through the AI-Mediated Transnational Learning Model (AIM-TLM). Drawing on constructivism, socio-cultural learning theory, the Community of Inquiry framework, and Universal Design for Learning, the study examines how ethically guided AI use enhances equity, reflection, and engagement across bilingual cohorts. Using mixed-methods data from Object-Oriented Development and Advanced Information Systems Development modules delivered between the University of the West of England and Neusoft College, results show that structured AI scaffolding improved consistency and inclusivity without inflating grades. The chapter proposes a five-pillar framework covering transparency, assessment design, AI literacy, cultural calibration, and institutional alignment, offering a scalable model for ethical, inclusive, and sustainable AI integration in global higher education contexts.

INTRODUCTION AND CONTEXT

Artificial-intelligence-assisted learning has rapidly transitioned from speculative innovation to a central force reshaping higher education. The emergence of large-language-model (LLM) tools such as ChatGPT, Copilot, Gemini 1.5, and Claude 3 has redefined how learners access information, construct knowledge, and demonstrate competence (Jin et al., 2025; Peláez-Sánchez et al., 2024; T. Wang et al., 2023). Within computing education, the affordances of these systems are particularly evident: they can

DOI: 10.4018/979-8-3373-5403-3.ch002

instantly translate abstract programming concepts into executable code, generate alternative algorithmic explanations, and simulate conversational tutors. Yet these same affordances introduce pedagogical and ethical dilemmas concerning academic integrity, authenticity, and equity (Peláez-Sánchez et al., 2024).

Nowhere are these dilemmas more acute than in transnational education (TNE) partnerships—programmes delivered collaboratively across national borders, often blending Western pedagogical frameworks with local sociocultural and linguistic contexts (Healey, 2018; Tran et al., 2023). TNE has grown exponentially, accounting for millions of enrolments globally and forming a crucial instrument of higher-education internationalisation (J. Wang, 2025). In such programmes, students frequently negotiate multiple epistemological traditions, assessment cultures, and linguistic registers simultaneously. This complexity amplifies both the promise and the risk of AI adoption: AI systems can democratise access to high-quality feedback but can equally exacerbate inequities if cultural and linguistic differences shape who can prompt effectively or interpret AI output accurately (Corbin et al., 2025; Kizilcec et al., 2024).

This chapter therefore investigates the integration of AI-assisted learning into undergraduate computer science and software engineering based modules delivered through the long-standing partnership between a university based in the United Kingdom and a university based on Asia. Building on earlier work demonstrating the impact of inclusive-learning strategies within the same partnership (Rosunally, 2024), the present study extends that foundation by embedding structured AI scaffolds, ethical-use guidelines, and redesigned assessments across three advanced modules: Object-Oriented Development, Business Process Modelling and Enterprise Architecture, and Advanced System Development.

The primary objectives of the study are threefold:

Pedagogical impact: To evaluate how structured AI integration influences learning outcomes, motivation, and cognitive engagement among bilingual cohorts.

Integrity and ethics: To examine whether guided AI use can coexist with academic-integrity principles without eroding critical-thinking capabilities.

Framework development: To formulate an empirically grounded framework for good practice in AI-assisted teaching and assessment that other TNE computing programmes can replicate.

The research addresses several pressing challenges in contemporary computing education. First, the assessment challenge; how to design tasks that measure genuine understanding rather than proficiency in AI prompting (marcus bowles, 2025). Second, the equity challenge; how to ensure that students with differing linguistic and cultural capital benefit equally from AI support (McKinley et al., 2021). Third, the trust challenge; how to sustain transparency and accountability between geographically separated teaching teams (Nadeem, 2024). Finally, the policy challenge; how institutions align emerging AI-use policies across jurisdictions with distinct legal and cultural interpretations of plagiarism and authorship ('Quality Compass: Navigating the Complexities of the Artificial Intelligence Era in Higher Education', 2024).

The significance of this work extends beyond technical disciplines. As UNESCO (*Recommendation on the Ethics of Artificial Intelligence*, 2022) and JISC (Knight & Ferrell, 2022) have emphasised, responsible AI integration demands holistic frameworks combining ethical governance, data protection, pedagogical design, and continuous staff development. For TNE consortia, such frameworks must also reconcile disparities in digital infrastructure, language policy, and academic culture. This chapter therefore contributes both empirical evidence and a design blueprint for implementing ethical, inclusive AI-assisted learning in transnational computing education.

The chapter proceeds as follows. Section II reviews the theoretical foundations underpinning AI-enhanced pedagogy, drawing on Constructivism, Vygotskian socio-cultural theory, the Community of

Inquiry (CoI) framework, Universal Design for Learning (UDL), and ethical-AI governance literature. Section III details the mixed-methods methodology and pilot design; Section IV articulates the proposed framework for good practice; Section V presents implementation and results; Section VI discusses implications and practical guidelines; and Section VII concludes with reflections on sustainability and future research.

THEORETICAL FRAMEWORK AND LITERATURE REVIEW

Constructivism and Socio-Cultural Learning Theory

Constructivism remains one of the most enduring paradigms for understanding how individuals learn in dynamic, technology-mediated contexts. Rooted in the epistemological traditions of Dewey, Piaget, and Bruner, it posits that knowledge is actively built through experience and reflection rather than transmitted by authority (Bruner, 1973; Piaget, 2013). Dewey's notion of learning by doing established the foundation for experiential inquiry; Piaget extended this to cognitive development through assimilation and accommodation; and Bruner's "spiral curriculum" emphasised recursive revisiting of ideas at increasing complexity an approach mirrored in software-engineering education, where students cycle through design, implementation, and testing phases.

In the digital era, constructivism aligns naturally with student-centred, inquiry-based computing education. Learners are not mere recipients of syntax and semantics but co-creators of artefacts that externalise abstract reasoning. Seymour Papert's (Papert, 1993) "constructionism" a pragmatic offshoot of constructivism; introduced the idea that computational media such as LOGO or Scratch amplify learning by enabling learners to build personally meaningful projects. When applied to artificial-intelligence-assisted learning, LLMs and code-generation tools extend this lineage: they function as "microworlds" in which students test hypotheses, iterate rapidly, and witness the consequences of their conceptual decisions.

Vygotsky's socio-cultural theory adds a social dimension: cognition is mediated by cultural artefacts, language, and interaction (Vygotsky, 1980). Every learning event occurs within a social milieu, and the Zone of Proximal Development (ZPD) represents the space between independent performance and performance supported by a more knowledgeable other. In a classroom augmented by AI, the machine acts as a mediating artefact, not replacing the human mentor but scaffolding performance within the ZPD. The instructor orchestrates a triadic relationship among learner, task, and intelligent system. When students use an LLM to debug code or paraphrase conceptual explanations, they engage in distributed cognition where human reasoning and algorithmic inference intertwine (Hutchins, 2006).

Yet mediation is not neutral. Socio-cultural theorists such as Wertsch (Wertsch, 1997) and Rogoff (Rogoff, 2003) caution that artefacts carry the intentions and cultural assumptions of their creators. AI models trained predominantly on Western data sets may normalise particular programming conventions, linguistic idioms, and epistemic norms. As Gebru et al. (Gebru et al., 2021) highlight, data documentation ("datasheets for datasets") becomes crucial to reveal provenance and bias. For transnational learners navigating multiple cultures of learning, uncritical acceptance of AI explanations can therefore reinforce hidden asymmetries in epistemic authority.

The constructivist-socio-cultural synthesis adopted here interprets AI as a cognitive partner that must be contextualised, interrogated, and localised. Students are prompted to question not only what an AI says but why it frames an answer in a given way. Freire's critical pedagogy (Freire & Macedo, 2014) further informs this stance: true learning requires dialogic exchange and conscientisation-awareness of power and voice. By embedding reflective prompts ("Evaluate the cultural assumptions in this AI response"), the present study operationalises Freirean criticality within constructivist practice.

Empirical research substantiates this approach. Bassner et al. (Bassner et al., 2024) showed that hint-based AI tutoring improved conceptual debugging without eroding independence. Feng et al. (Feng et al., 2024) demonstrated retention gains from retrieval-augmented AI tutoring. Choi et al. (Choi et al., 2023) similarly found that novice programmers using AI explanations outperformed peers only when required to articulate reasoning aloud, confirming that reflection mediates effectiveness. Thus, the combination of constructivism and socio-cultural mediation provides a theoretical justification for designing AI-scaffolded yet dialogic learning environments in transnational computer-science education.

The Community of Inquiry (CoI) Framework

The Community of Inquiry (CoI) framework (Garrison, 2011) offers a complementary lens for structuring online and blended learning—core modalities in transnational delivery. It conceives educational experience as the intersection of three presences: teaching, social, and cognitive. A coherent CoI ensures that learners engage in purposeful discourse, guided by facilitation and grounded in reflection.

Transnational programmes often suffer from uneven presence distribution: teaching presence may be fragmented across institutions; social presence hindered by linguistic distance; and cognitive presence weakened by surface learning focused on assessment compliance (Rosunally, 2024; Yeo & Newton, 2021). Integrating AI support can rebalance these presences when used strategically.

Teaching presence can be augmented through AI-generated formative feedback and adaptive hints. For example, AI can instantly flag logical errors or suggest alternative modelling strategies, emulating formative scaffolding previously dependent on instructor availability (Baksh, 2025). Garrison and Arbaugh (Garrison & Arbaugh, 2007) noted that immediacy of feedback is pivotal to maintaining teaching presence in asynchronous environments; AI addresses precisely this latency problem.

Social presence—the ability of learners to project themselves as real people—can be enhanced by conversational agents that sustain dialogue and empathy when human peers are offline. Cao et al. (2023) found that defining clear AI roles (peer, coach, or emotional supporter) fosters trust and engagement. However, over-anthropomorphism risks deception; therefore, the present study's design includes explicit disclosure that AI messages originate from software, not humans.

Cognitive presence involves constructing meaning through sustained inquiry. Baksh (2025) and Oliver and Weilbach (2024) showed that structured questioning by AI can deepen exploration, yet unstructured use may lead to superficial confirmation bias. Consequently, students were trained to submit multi-turn prompts requiring justification, contradiction, and synthesis—mirroring the "integration" and "resolution" phases of CoI's cognitive cycle.

Beyond the triad, Garrison and Arbaugh (2007) and subsequent meta-analyses (Shea, 2010) introduced emotional presence as a fourth dimension influencing persistence. AI's affective responsiveness—acknowledging frustration or celebrating progress—can buffer isolation common in cross-border online learning. However, such affective simulation must be transparent and culturally sensitive. In collectivist cultures, overt praise may feel uncomfortable; thus, emotional cues were calibrated to neutral encouragement rather than effusive affirmation.

In summary, CoI provides the social-cognitive scaffolding through which AI mediation in TNE can thrive. The framework in this study deliberately maps each CoI presence to corresponding human and AI roles, maintaining equilibrium between automation and authenticity.

Universal Design for Learning (UDL) and Inclusive Pedagogy

While constructivism and CoI address how learning occurs, Universal Design for Learning (UDL) ensures who can participate fully*. UDL's genesis in disability studies emphasised proactive design accommodating learner variability from the outset rather than through retrofitted accommodations (Al-Azawei et al., 2016a; *CAST Universal Design for Learning Guidelines*, n.d.). In TNE computing classrooms, variability extends to language proficiency, prior disciplinary preparation, access to technology, and cultural approaches to collaboration.

UDL's three guiding principles—multiple means of engagement, representation, and action/expression—translate directly to AI-mediated contexts:

Engagement: Motivation varies across cultural and linguistic backgrounds. Adaptive AI feedback offering incremental challenge and immediate affirmation can satisfy autonomy and competence needs consistent with self-determination theory (Ryan & Deci, 2022). Gamified AI prompts ("debug the code in fewer steps") also enhance engagement when culturally contextualised.

Representation: AI's multimodal capacities (text-to-diagram, translation, summarisation) enable multiple representations of the same concept. For example, an LLM can explain object inheritance verbally, render UML diagrams, or produce pseudocode, aligning with dual-coding theory (Paivio, 1990). Yet representation must avoid oversimplification that strips nuance, a risk mitigated through instructor review loops.

Action and Expression: UDL encourages diverse demonstration of learning. Students can submit narrated screen-capture walkthroughs, annotated code, or bilingual reflections generated with AI translation support. This variety accommodates both linguistic limitations and differing rhetorical traditions (Al-Azawei et al., 2016a; McKinley et al., 2021).

AI integration extends UDL's reach but also demands critical digital literacy. As Al-Azawei et al. (2016a) note, technology alone does not guarantee inclusion; pedagogy must teach learners how to use tools responsibly. For TNE cohorts, responsible use includes awareness of geopolitical data restrictions, algorithmic bias, and the ethics of translation. Accordingly, this study embeds "AI-literacy checkpoints" within labs, prompting students to evaluate the inclusivity of AI outputs ("Does this translation capture the intended cultural tone?").

From a design standpoint, AI also aids instructors in implementing UDL. Adaptive-learning analytics can identify disengaged students and recommend differentiated materials, echoing earlier adaptive-hypermedia systems but at greater scale (Durlach & Ray, 2011). However, algorithmic recommendations risk reproducing existing inequities if based on biased training data (Gebru et al., 2021). Ethical oversight: therefore, complements UDL to ensure that inclusion does not become surveillance.

Critical and Cross-Cultural Dimensions of Inclusion

Recent transnational-education literature foregrounds intersectionality—how multiple identities (linguistic, socio-economic, gendered) intersect to shape participation (Crenshaw, 1991; Rosunally, 2024). Hofstede's cultural-dimension theory (Hofstede, 2011) and later intercultural frameworks (e.g.,

Deardorff's intercultural-competence model (Deardorff, 2009)) underline that collectivist cultures often privilege harmony and indirect critique, affecting how students question AI authority or instructor feedback. Within such contexts, AI's non-judgmental tone can paradoxically empower quieter voices to experiment without fear of embarrassment. Yet translation asymmetries persist: English-dominant AI interfaces may reinforce linguistic hierarchy (McKinley et al., 2021).

To counteract this, the design allows code-switching and bilingual prompts, encouraging students to operate in their full linguistic repertoire. Canagarajah (Canagarajah, 2020) describes this as translanguaging pedagogy, using all languages available to make meaning. By validating bilingual AI interactions, the study situates UDL within a multilingual ethos of inclusion consistent with Yeo & Newton's (Yeo & Newton, 2021) call for culturally responsive TNE partnerships.

III. METHODOLOGY AND PILOT STUDY DESIGN

Research Context and Setting

The research was conducted within the University of the West of England–Neusoft International College partnership, one of the longest-running Sino-foreign computing collaborations in China. The partnership delivers a full UWE-validated BSc (Hons) Software Engineering programme through English-medium instruction (EMI), with local tutors and remote UK oversight. Prior institutional studies highlighted linguistic and pedagogical gaps that can constrain inclusivity in early-year modules (Rosunally, 2024). These findings informed the present project's design, which targeted second- and third-year cohorts where students had achieved baseline English and programming proficiency.

Two modules were selected to capture a representative spectrum of computing competencies:

Object-Oriented Development (OOD): focusing on Java software design and testing.

Advanced Information Systems Development (AISD): integrating agile methods, systems integration, and reflective project work.

Across the 2023–2024 academic cycle, approximately 140 students (aged 19–23) participated, divided into two balanced cohorts per module (AI-augmented and control). Each cohort was supported by two UK lead lecturer, one and at least one bilingual teaching assistant who facilitated translation, cultural mediation, and local pastoral support. Instruction combined asynchronous recorded teaching materials, and in-class lectures and workshops on campus.

Research Design and Approach

A quasi-experimental mixed-methods design was adopted, integrating quantitative learning analytics with qualitative interpretive inquiry (Plano Clark Vicki L. et al., 2017). Random assignment was infeasible due to timetabling constraints; however, comparable cohorts were ensured through results matching and English-proficiency scores. The design comprised four phases:

Orientation (Week 01): At the outset of the study, students were introduced to the assessment framework and the shared case study underpinning the Business Process Modelling and Enterprise Architecture (BPM&EA) and Advanced Information Systems Development (AISD) modules. This case study, previously implemented within Object-Oriented Development (OOD), was intentionally retained to provide continuity and promote integrative learning across the three units.

During the induction, students were briefed on the ethical and purposeful use of artificial intelligence (AI) in their learning activities. They were explicitly informed that AI use was encouraged, provided it was applied with discernment and critical reflection. To support this, a structured workshop was conducted on AI for learning and problem-solving, focusing on responsible prompt engineering, evaluating AI-generated outputs, and maintaining academic integrity.

Expectations concerning academic conduct, collaboration, and reflective practice were clearly articulated to ensure transparency and alignment across all participating cohorts. Furthermore, the Agile development methodology was introduced as the guiding project framework, emphasising weekly sprint reviews as a mechanism for iterative development, peer feedback, and continuous improvement.

Implementation (Weeks 01 - 06): Each week, students participated in six lecture sessions, six practical sessions, and three sprint review sessions aligned with the iterative development cycle of the project. During each sprint review, students were required to present and explain their progress, indicating whether they had used AI tools such as DeepSeek, GitHub Copilot, or Cursor, and to what extent these tools had been applied in their development work.

The academic staff conducting the sprint reviews assessed students' understanding of key concepts and the intended learning outcomes (ILOs) for that week. Targeted formative feedback was then provided to support both conceptual understanding and technical progression. All sprint review interactions, including feedback discussions and student reflections, were systematically recorded for subsequent analysis to evaluate learning development and patterns of AI adoption.

Assessment & Reflection (Weeks 06): The final assessment was conducted in the form of a portfolio submission and project demonstration. Each portfolio included all artefacts developed throughout the project, such as meeting minutes, sprint reports, design documents, and implementation outputs.

The summative assessment was evaluated based on the overall quality and merit of the group project, which determined the group mark. Individual marks were derived from each student's level of contribution, as agreed upon collectively by group members. These self-reported contributions were then moderated by academic staff using evidence from recorded sprint reports and review sessions to ensure fairness and consistency.

Following the assessment, a student survey was administered to gather feedback on learning experiences and identify areas for enhancement as part of the continuous improvement cycle for the modules. The findings were compared against data from the previous academic year, during which AI use had not been encouraged or formally integrated into the teaching or assessment process. This comparison provided insights into how structured AI support and training influenced student engagement and learning outcomes.

Evaluation (Post-semester): Surveys and focus groups captured perceptions, challenges, and cultural dynamics. Performance data and integrity audits were analysed quantitatively.

Data Collection Instruments

Quantitative Instruments

Performance Metrics:

Student performance was measured using standardised marking rubrics (0–100 scale) applied consistently across coursework, examinations, and viva assessments.

Integrity Analytics:

Individual understanding of the intended learning outcomes (ILOs) was verified through structured viva sessions and Q&A evaluations. During these sessions, students were required to articulate and justify their own development approaches and design decisions. This enabled triangulation between demonstrated artefacts, conceptual understanding, and the authenticity of their contributions.

Qualitative Instruments

Sprint Reviews:

Weekly sprint reviews were conducted to evaluate students' progress against the week's ILOs. Each review incorporated reflection on cognitive load (Paas et al., 2003) and perceived learning (Abdullah et al., 2022), allowing both students and academics to capture affective and cognitive dimensions of learning.

Student Observations (by Academics):

Academic staff maintained weekly observation logs documenting pedagogical adjustments, student engagement patterns, and notable behavioural responses during lectures and practical sessions. These qualitative records supported contextual interpretation of performance data and informed iterative module refinement. Sprint Reviews: Based on each week's ILOs set of areas been evaluated based on cognitive load (Paas et al., 2003), and perceived learning (Abdullah et al., 2022).

Student Feedback:

Formal student feedback on the units was collected at the end of the teaching period as part of the institution's continuous improvement process. This feedback provided insights into student satisfaction, perceived effectiveness of AI integration, and areas requiring pedagogical enhancement. The responses were analysed alongside performance and observation data to inform future iterations of module design and delivery.

Framework for Good Practice in AI-Assisted Teaching and Assessment

Drawing from the empirical findings and theoretical synthesis, a four-pillar framework was developed to guide ethical and effective AI integration in TNE computing curricula. Each pillar aligns with one or more theoretical antecedents and practical design principles.

Pillar 1 – Transparent Mediation and Human-in-the-Loop Oversight

Transparency constitutes the cornerstone of trustworthy AI pedagogy (Piaget, 2013; *Recommendation on the Ethics of Artificial Intelligence - UNESCO Digital Library*, n.d.). Students must understand the extent and purpose of AI mediation in their learning. Implementation guidelines include:

Prompt Logging and/or Reflection:

Students were encouraged to document their engagement with AI tools through a structured Prompt Logging and/or Reflective Commentary process. For each instance of AI interaction, students were required to record a brief entry describing the purpose of the prompt (for example, "What was I trying to achieve?") and their response to the AI-generated output (for example, "Did I accept or reject the suggestion, and why?"). These records captured both the technical reasoning behind prompt construction and the critical evaluation of AI contributions during development.

The framework was designed to be flexible, allowing students to complete either prompt logs, reflective commentaries, or both, depending on their workflow, project stage, and learning preference. For example, students involved in extensive code generation or process modelling were encouraged to maintain detailed prompt logs, whereas those engaging in conceptual design or analysis were advised to prioritise reflective commentaries.

In cases where students did not formally record their AI prompts, the sprint review sessions served as an alternative mechanism for evaluation. During these reviews, academics explicitly questioned students about their AI usage, reasoning, and decision-making processes, thereby ensuring that reflection and accountability were embedded regardless of whether formal logs were maintained.

This dual mechanism promoted metacognitive awareness by encouraging students to think critically about their interaction with AI systems, and it ensured transparency and auditability in how these tools were applied. It also supported ethical and reflective engagement, reinforcing the principle that AI should augment, rather than replace, human understanding and judgement.

From a research and pedagogical perspective, both the recorded logs and the review discussions provided rich data for analysing patterns of AI adoption, levels of critical engagement, and variations in problem-solving approaches across cohorts. The framework thus contributed to a deeper institutional understanding of effective AI integration within programming and modelling education.

Instructor Audit Trail:

Teaching staff were not granted direct access to individual prompt histories or AI interaction records. Instead, transparency and accountability were maintained through guided discussions during laboratory sessions and sprint reviews. In these settings, students were encouraged to explain how they had engaged with AI tools, describe the nature and purpose of their prompts, and reflect on how AI suggestions influenced their design or implementation decisions.

This discussion-based approach emphasised trust, reflection, and formative dialogue rather than surveillance or monitoring. By inviting students to articulate their reasoning and critically evaluate their use of AI, instructors were able to identify instances of effective prompting, overreliance, or misunderstanding in real time. The process also allowed academics to offer targeted guidance on ethical and purposeful AI use, reinforcing the principle that AI should complement—rather than replace—human analysis and problem-solving.

These reflective conversations served as a live audit mechanism, enabling teaching staff to assess student understanding, promote responsible digital literacy, and provide timely formative feedback. The information gathered from these discussions informed ongoing pedagogical adjustments, ensuring that AI integration supported deeper learning rather than procedural dependency. Moreover, aggregated insights from sprint reviews and lab reflections contributed to broader module evaluation and curriculum enhancement, particularly in understanding how structured reflection fosters meaningful and ethical engagement with AI technologies.

Disclosure Statement:

All coursework templates incorporated a mandatory "AI-Use Declaration" section, functioning similarly to an academic citation. Students were required to explicitly state whether they had used any AI tools during the completion of their work, identify the specific system or platform (for example, ChatGPT, DeepSeek, Copilot, or Cursor), and describe the nature and extent of assistance received. This declaration ensured that the use of AI was transparent, attributable, and aligned with the principles of academic integrity.

The declaration was intended not to penalise AI use but to promote responsible disclosure and reflective accountability. By articulating how AI contributed to different stages of their work—such as idea generation, debugging, code optimisation, or report writing—students were encouraged to consider the ethical boundaries of assistance and to differentiate between human and machine-generated contributions.

Teaching staff reviewed these declarations as part of the assessment moderation process, using them to contextualise student outputs and identify cases where additional clarification or discussion was required. This practice also provided a mechanism for detecting potential overreliance or unacknowledged AI support while maintaining a formative approach focused on learning enhancement rather than disciplinary action.

At a broader level, the AI-Use Declaration contributed to institutional efforts to normalise transparent AI engagement within coursework and to foster a culture of ethical digital scholarship. Aggregated declarations were analysed across cohorts to inform ongoing curriculum development and to evaluate how students' understanding of responsible AI use evolved over time.

Explainable Feedback:

Through these measures, AI becomes a visible and accountable co-participant in the learning process rather than an invisible aid. The integration of explainable feedback mechanisms ensured that AI systems were not merely providing answers or suggestions but also offering reasoning traces, confidence indicators, and step-by-step explanations where possible. This approach encouraged students to engage critically with AI-generated outputs, prompting them to question, validate, and interpret the rationale behind each suggestion (Khosravi et al., 2022).

By foregrounding transparency and interpretability, the framework aimed to cultivate a learning environment in which students could develop trust grounded in understanding, recognising when AI insights were reliable and when human judgement should take precedence. This practice reinforced the importance of accountability in human–AI collaboration, requiring students to justify their decisions and differentiate between what was autonomously produced and what was the result of guided AI support.

The presence of explainable AI feedback also contributed to ethical digital literacy, equipping students with the skills to critically assess algorithmic reasoning and recognise the limits of automation. Rather than discouraging legitimate exploration or experimentation, this approach legitimised AI as a reflective partner in the learning process, empowering students to use it as a cognitive scaffold for inquiry, creativity, and problem-solving.

At an instructional level, explainable feedback supported teaching staff in monitoring conceptual understanding. When students could clearly articulate why an AI recommendation was accepted or rejected, it provided tangible evidence of learning progression and deeper engagement with the underlying principles. In this way, the AI system's explainability complemented academic judgement, reinforcing a shared framework of transparency, accountability, and purposeful innovation within the curriculum.

Pillar 2 – Assessment Design for Reasoning and Authentic Understanding

Assessment determines not only what students learn but how they learn. To prevent AI misuse, tasks must prioritise reasoning, context, and reflection. Recommended practices:

Process-Oriented Assessment:

The assessment design followed a process-oriented approach, focusing on the development journey rather than solely on the final executable product. Students were evaluated on the quality, coherence, and progression of their intermediate artefacts, including design diagrams, pseudo-code, workflow models, and test plans. This method recognised that learning in software and systems development is an iterative process involving cycles of planning, design, implementation, evaluation, and refinement.

By assessing these intermediary outputs, the framework provided a more authentic measure of students' conceptual understanding, problem-solving strategies, and reflective capacity. It also allowed instructors to identify misconceptions and gaps in understanding early in the project, enabling timely formative feedback and targeted intervention. Students were encouraged to treat each artefact as a milestone in their learning trajectory, demonstrating both technical competence and design reasoning (Aruleba et al., 2023).

This approach supported the principles of constructive alignment, linking intended learning outcomes (ILOs) directly with observable artefacts that represented students' evolving understanding. It also reinforced accountability and academic integrity, as the development of each artefact could be traced and discussed during sprint review sessions, ensuring that progress reflected genuine learning and contribution rather than isolated end-product performance.

Furthermore, the process-oriented model encouraged students to adopt industry-relevant practices, mirroring professional workflows that prioritise documentation, iterative testing, and reflective evaluation. Through this continuous and transparent assessment structure, students developed both the disciplinary knowledge and professional habits of mind necessary for sustainable, responsible engagement in technology-driven environments.

Contextual Variation:

To maintain academic integrity and encourage authentic problem-solving, contextual variation was systematically applied across each iteration of the case study. While the core structure and learning objectives of the project remained consistent, specific parameters and contextual elements, such as the industry domain, stakeholder profiles, operational constraints, or organisational goals were deliberately modified (T. Wang et al., 2023).

These contextual shifts prevented students from relying on previously generated or publicly available AI outputs, ensuring that each cohort engaged with a unique and contemporarily relevant scenario. For instance, a healthcare-based case study in one iteration might be reimagined within the logistics or education sector in the next, requiring students to reinterpret requirements, adjust process models, and redesign technical artefacts to fit the new environment.

This adaptive approach served several pedagogical functions. It discouraged the reuse of generic AI-generated solutions, promoting deeper conceptual engagement and critical thinking. It also mirrored real-world professional practice, where systems analysts and developers must adapt methodologies and designs to the unique constraints of different organisational contexts.

Moreover, contextual variation enhanced cross-cohort comparability while maintaining fairness in assessment. Each scenario preserved alignment with the intended learning outcomes (ILOs) but demanded context-specific reasoning and decision-making. This practice supported ongoing curriculum renewal, ensuring that learning materials and case studies remained current, relevant, and resistant to academic misconduct in the age of generative AI.

Viva Voce Examinations:

Randomly selected viva voce examinations were conducted to verify individual authorship, conceptual understanding, and reflective engagement with the project work. During these oral defences, students were asked to explain the rationale behind their design choices, implementation strategies, and use of AI tools, where applicable. They were also expected to demonstrate an understanding of the underlying theories, frameworks, and techniques that informed their work.

This assessment method provided a direct measure of authentic learning and ownership, ensuring that each student could articulate and justify their contributions to the group project (Lancaster & Clarke, 2016). The viva format also enabled instructors to explore the depth of students' reasoning processes, assess their problem-solving strategies, and identify any inconsistencies between the submitted artefacts and their verbal explanations.

Empirical evidence from higher education research indicates that viva voce examinations are a powerful tool for deterring academic misconduct and contract cheating, as they require students to demonstrate in-person mastery of their work rather than relying solely on written submissions. Beyond integrity assurance, the vivas served an important formative function, allowing teaching staff to provide tailored feedback on students' analytical thinking, communication skills, and professional presentation.

Overall, the inclusion of viva voce examinations strengthened the rigour, transparency, and fairness of the assessment process, supporting both academic integrity and meaningful learning within the AI-integrated curriculum.

Collaborative Peer Review:

A structured peer review process was implemented to promote reflective dialogue, collaborative learning, and accountability among students. Each group participated in peer assessment cycles in which they reviewed and provided feedback on the artefacts produced by their peers, such as process models, system designs, and code prototypes. This activity required students to articulate the rationale behind their design and implementation choices, fostering a deeper awareness of their own reasoning while developing the ability to critically evaluate the work of others.

Through this process, students were also exposed to a diverse range of problem-solving and prompting strategies, particularly in cases where AI-assisted methods had been employed. Discussing how peers used or interpreted AI outputs encouraged transparency in learning approaches and supported the development of social presence, as students engaged in constructive dialogue about alternative solutions, design logic, and ethical considerations in the use of AI tools.

The peer review sessions were carefully structured using clear rubrics aligned with the intended learning outcomes (ILOs), ensuring consistency and fairness in evaluation. Feedback provided during these sessions contributed to iterative refinement of artefacts and informed the final portfolio submissions.

Collectively, these peer-led interactions shifted the focus of assessment from product correctness to demonstrable understanding, consistent with constructivist learning principles. By positioning students as both contributors and evaluators in the learning process, the approach reinforced metacognitive skills, empathy, and professional communication—competencies that are central to collaborative practice in real-world software and systems development contexts.

Pillar 3 – AI Literacy and Metacognitive Scaffolding

Research consistently identifies "prompt literacy" as a determinant of benefit derived from AI tools (Cao et al., 2023; Fan et al., 2025). The framework therefore integrates a scaffolded literacy continuum:

Foundational Workshops:

The initial sessions of the module focused on introducing students to the fundamentals of effective prompting and the ethical use of AI tools within academic and professional contexts. Students were guided through practical techniques such as specificity in prompt formulation, problem decomposition, and iterative refinement, helping them to develop clearer and more purposeful interactions with AI systems.

These early activities aimed to establish a foundation for critical and reflective AI use, enabling students to move beyond trial-and-error interactions toward intentional and goal-oriented prompting. Ethical considerations were integrated throughout, addressing issues such as bias awareness, intellectual ownership, academic integrity, and the responsible citation of AI contributions.

By embedding these principles early in the learning process, students developed both the technical competence to engage productively with AI systems and the ethical mindset to evaluate the implications of their use. This preparatory stage ensured that subsequent project work was grounded in informed, reflective, and transparent AI-assisted practice.

Guided Practice:

Weekly laboratory sessions incorporated exemplar prompts designed to illustrate the progressive stages of cognitive complexity defined in Bloom's Revised Taxonomy (Anderson, 2009). These exemplars demonstrated how prompt design could evolve from lower-order thinking tasks to higher-order creative challenges, enabling students to recognise and apply structured prompting strategies in their own work.

For instance, early exercises focused on foundational recall-level activities such as "List Java data types" or "Identify key BPMN elements", reinforcing basic conceptual understanding. Subsequent prompts gradually increased in complexity, encouraging students to apply and analyse knowledge through tasks such as "Modify an existing process model to include an approval loop" or "Explain the difference between aggregation and composition in UML." Higher-level activities then required students to evaluate and create, using open-ended prompts such as "Critique two alternative process architectures for scalability" or "Design a class hierarchy for an enterprise application scenario."

This scaffolded approach allowed students to internalise the relationship between prompt specificity, cognitive depth, and learning outcomes. By modelling how effective prompts align with different levels of reasoning, the labs not only enhanced AI literacy but also strengthened students' capacity for metacognitive planning and self-directed inquiry. The practice further supported academic staff in differentiating instruction, ensuring that both novice and advanced learners engaged with AI tools at an appropriate level of challenge and reflection.

Self-Explanation Logs:

Students were required to annotate AI responses to demonstrate how these outputs aligned with, contradicted, or extended their own reasoning processes. This practice transformed otherwise opaque AI interactions into reflective learning dialogues, enabling students to actively interpret, critique, and internalise the knowledge generated through collaboration with AI systems (Aruleba et al., 2023)

Through annotation, students documented the reasoning behind accepting, modifying, or rejecting AI-generated suggestions. This encouraged them to articulate their thought processes and evaluate the relevance, accuracy, and contextual appropriateness of AI outputs. The process also provided tangible evidence of cognitive engagement, showing how students used AI as a scaffold for problem-solving rather than as a substitute for independent reasoning.

From a pedagogical perspective, this reflective annotation served multiple purposes. It promoted metacognitive awareness, helping students monitor their understanding and recognise gaps in knowledge. It enhanced accountability and transparency by clarifying the boundary between human and AI contribution. Furthermore, it generated valuable artefacts for instructors, offering insight into students' decision-making processes and supporting formative feedback during sprint reviews and lab discussions.

In this way, annotation practices reinforced the notion of AI as a visible learning partner, fostering critical thinking, ethical engagement, and deeper conceptual understanding through structured reflection on human-AI collaboration.

Fading Scaffold:

Within the module, prompt guidance was intentionally reduced over time as students developed greater confidence and proficiency in engaging with AI tools. Early sessions provided detailed examples, structured templates, and instructor-led demonstrations to support students in formulating effective prompts and critically interpreting AI-generated responses. As the module progressed, these supports were systematically withdrawn, allowing learners to apply prompting strategies independently and adapt them to the specific requirements of their projects.

This gradual reduction of support encouraged the development of self-regulation and strategic autonomy, reflecting the expert-learner trajectory described in Universal Design for Learning (UDL) principles (Al-Azawei et al., 2016a).By progressively fading instructional scaffolds, the module promoted the transition from guided practice to self-directed mastery, helping students build the confidence and independence required for advanced, reflective engagement with AI-enhanced learning environments.

Central to this approach was the use of metacognitive scaffolding, which repositioned AI from being an answer engine to becoming a partner in reflective thinking and reasoning. Students were encouraged to use AI as a means of articulating their cognitive processes, testing hypotheses, and exploring alternative solutions. Through this form of guided reflection, AI acted as a tool for thinking about thinking, prompting students to analyse their decision-making patterns, evaluate their strategies, and refine their approaches to complex problems.

This framework cultivated lifelong adaptive expertise, equipping students with the ability to transfer reflective and problem-solving skills across different contexts. Rather than focusing solely on the accuracy of outcomes, learners were encouraged to evaluate the processes that led to those outcomes. In doing so, they developed independence, critical awareness, and intellectual adaptability qualities essential for success in both academic and professional settings where AI increasingly plays an integral role.

Pillar 4 – Cultural and Linguistic Calibration

TNE environments demand sensitivity to local learning cultures. The framework operationalises cultural calibration through three mechanisms:

Bilingual Prompt Templates:

To support equitable participation in AI-enhanced learning, bilingual prompt templates were provided to reduce linguistic barriers and foster gradual development of English-Medium Instruction (EMI) competence. Each exemplar prompt was pre-translated into both Chinese and English, allowing students to engage initially in their dominant language while gradually transitioning to English as their confidence grew. This approach enabled learners to focus on the cognitive and conceptual demands of the task rather than struggling with linguistic formulation. Over time, students began adapting and generating prompts directly in English, demonstrating increased proficiency and comfort with EMI practices (Rosunally, 2024).

The bilingual scaffolding not only facilitated comprehension but also served as a model for contrastive linguistic awareness, helping students understand differences in phrasing, tone, and contextual nuance between the two languages. This incremental transition aligned with the broader objective of fostering academic independence and linguistic adaptability within transnational education (TNE) environments.

Collectivist Learning Modes:

In recognition of the cultural dimensions of learning, group-based AI tasks were intentionally structured to align with collectivist learning norms prevalent in Chinese educational contexts. Students collaborated in small teams to design, test, and refine AI prompts, engaging in peer mediation of meaning before submitting individual outputs. This approach mirrored familiar patterns of collaborative knowledge construction, while also introducing reflective accountability by requiring each member to explain and justify how group discussions influenced their own work.

By blending collectivist collaboration with individual reflection, the design leveraged students' cultural strengths—such as mutual support, respect for group consensus, and distributed expertise—while reinforcing Western academic values of independence and critical inquiry. This balance nurtured intercultural competence and adaptability, preparing students for both local and global professional settings.

Intercultural Dialogue Spaces:

Weekly intercultural debrief sessions were embedded to facilitate ongoing dialogue between UK-based and Chinese cohorts. These sessions encouraged open discussion and comparison of differing perspectives on ethical AI use, academic integrity, authorship, and responsibility. Through facilitated dialogue, students identified cultural assumptions underlying their interpretations and collaboratively developed shared norms of ethical engagement.

This practice recognised that notions of integrity, independence, and authorship are not culturally universal but shaped by distinct educational traditions and social values (Hayes & Introna, 2005). By making these assumptions explicit, intercultural dialogue transformed potential sources of misunderstanding or friction into opportunities for mutual learning and cultural reflexivity. It also strengthened the sense of community within the transnational classroom, promoting empathy, transparency, and shared accountability.

Pedagogical Implications:

Collectively, these measures demonstrated a commitment to inclusive and culturally responsive pedagogy. By embedding bilingual resources, collectivist collaboration, and intercultural dialogue, the module positioned cultural diversity not as a challenge to be managed but as a pedagogical asset that enriches both teaching and learning. This framework supported equitable participation, deepened students' ethical and linguistic awareness, and modelled best practices for integrating AI-enhanced learning within transnational, multilingual contexts.

Pillar 5 – Instructor Development and Institutional Alignment

Although the framework is primarily learner-centred, its long-term sustainability relies on faculty preparedness, policy coherence, and institutional infrastructure. Effective and ethical integration of AI within transnational education (TNE) requires a consistent, system-wide approach rather than isolated initiatives. To ensure scalability and quality assurance, the framework prescribes several key institutional enablers.

Figure 1. 5 pillar framework

Faculty Training:

Faculty members play a central role in mediating students' engagement with AI tools. Targeted professional development workshops were designed to enhance educators' understanding of AI capabilities, limitations, and biases, as well as their implications for teaching and assessment. Training sessions included hands-on exploration of AI platforms, ethical discussions, and collaborative redesign of assessment tasks to incorporate AI literacy and transparency principles (Awadallah Alkouk & Khlaif, 2024; Gómez et al., 2025; Khlaif et al., 2025).Continuous support networks and communities of practice further enabled staff to share experiences, troubleshoot challenges, and align approaches across campuses.

Policy Coherence:

Consistency in governance was essential across the partner institutions. Institutional policies were harmonised to establish a shared understanding of AI disclosure expectations, plagiarism definitions, and acceptable levels of assistance. Clear guidance ensured that students and staff operated within a transparent and equitable framework, minimising confusion and maintaining integrity across different regulatory environments. Policy coherence also supported fair moderation of assessments and consistent application of academic standards across sites.

Technical Infrastructure:

Robust technical provisions were necessary to ensure secure and compliant access to AI resources. The framework emphasised the establishment of locally hosted large language model (LLM) gateways to satisfy China's data-sovereignty and cybersecurity regulations, while also maintaining controlled access to approved international tools through VPN-regulated institutional servers. These infrastructures balanced compliance with pedagogical flexibility, ensuring that both local and transnational cohorts could access equivalent AI capabilities in a legally and ethically sound manner.

Continuous Quality Assurance:

Ongoing evaluation was embedded into the framework through annual reviews of AI integration metrics, including measures of usage equity, academic integrity, and learning outcomes. Data from student surveys, reflective logs, and performance analytics were triangulated to monitor impact and identify emerging risks or disparities. Findings informed iterative refinements to teaching practice, staff training, and policy development, ensuring that AI integration remained responsive to technological advances and educational priorities.

By institutionalising these supports, the framework positioned AI integration as a systemic innovation rather than an ad hoc enhancement. It established a sustainable ecosystem that connects pedagogy, policy, and technology, ensuring ethical consistency, scalability, and resilience in the evolving landscape of AI-assisted transnational education.

Table 1. Five pillar framework

Pillar	Objective	Operational Strategies	Theoretical Anchor
Transparency & Oversight	Ensure accountability	Prompt logs, AI-use declarations, explainable outputs	Ethical-AI governance (Durlach & Ray, 2011; Fan et al., 2025)
Assessment for Reasoning	Evaluate authentic understanding	Process tasks, contextual variation, viva, peer review	Constructivism (Feng et al., 2024); CoI (teaching presence) (Hofstede, 2011)
AI Literacy & Metacognition	Build critical prompt competence	Workshops, guided practice, self-explanation, fading scaffold	UDL (expert learner) (Bowles, 2025); Metacognition (Paas et al., 2003)
Cultural Calibration	Respect linguistic and cultural diversity	Bilingual templates, collectivist tasks, intercultural debriefs	Socio-cultural theory (Freire & Macedo, 2014; Garrison & Arbaugh, 2007)
Institutional Alignment	Sustain adoption	Faculty training, policy coherence, infrastructure, QA	Change-management models (Knight & Ferrell, 2022)

Figure 2. Framework overview

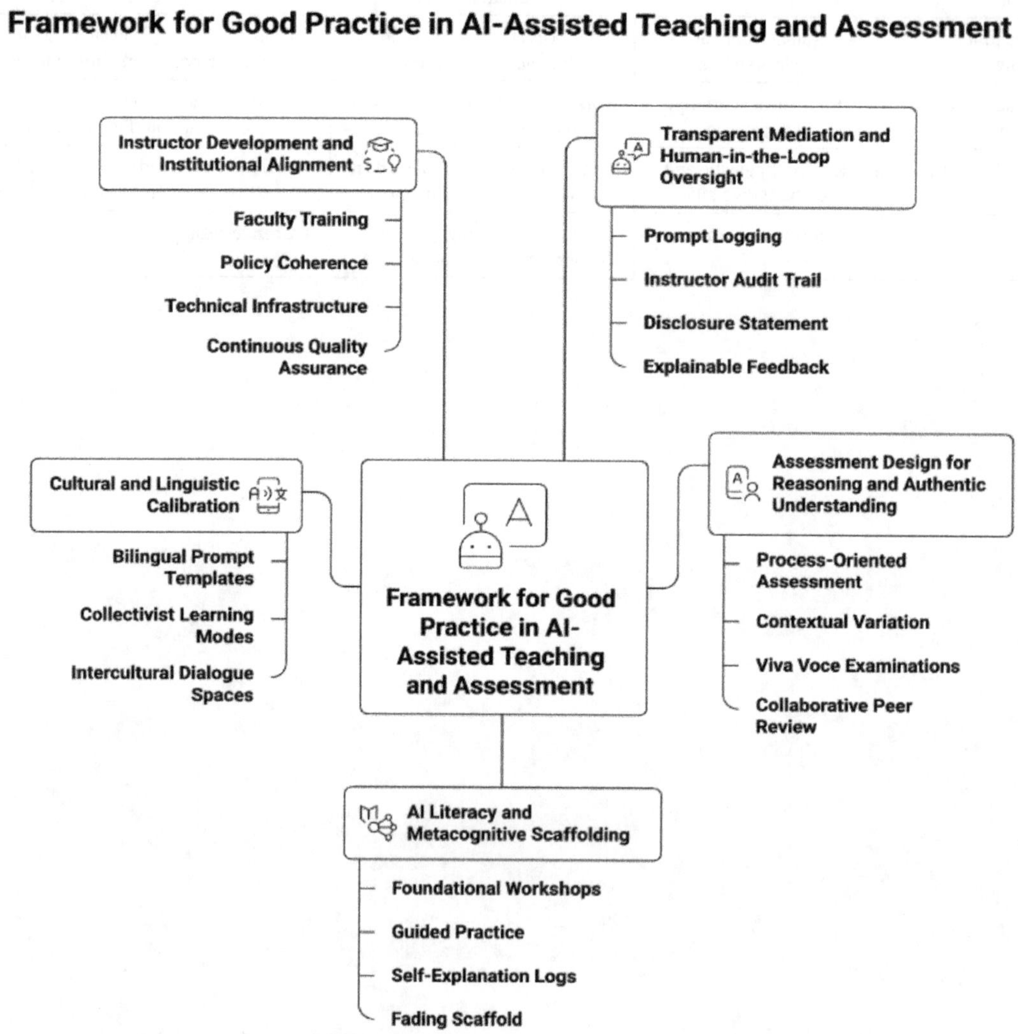

IMPLEMENTATION AND RESULTS

Introduction

This section presents the analysis investigates how ethical, structured integration of artificial-intelligence–assisted learning influenced student attainment, consistency, and equity within two core computing modules: Object-Oriented Development (OOD) and Advanced Information Systems Development (AISD).

OOD represents a second-year programming-centric subject that emphasises syntax, debugging, and software construction. AISD, a final-year systems-design module, demands conceptual reasoning, modelling, and enterprise-architecture synthesis. Together they form an ideal dual case through which to evaluate the pedagogical and cognitive consequences of AI scaffolding across contrasting learning domains.

Both modules were redesigned under the AI-Mediated Transnational Learning Model (AIM-TLM), embedding ethical AI use, reflective prompting, and human-in-the-loop moderation. The analysis spans four consecutive deliveries: OOD 2023 (pre-AI), OOD 2024 (with AI), AISD 2024 (pre-AI), and AISD 2025 (with AI). This temporal structure enables quasi-longitudinal comparison of outcomes before and after adoption of AI-enhanced learning while maintaining curricular equivalence.

The overarching objectives of this section are to:

- Quantify the effects of AI support on mean achievement, variance, and distributional stability.
- Determine whether AI integration contributed to greater equity of attainment among learners of differing baseline proficiency.
- Interpret observed quantitative trends through the theoretical lenses of constructivism, sociocultural learning, Community of Inquiry (CoI), and Universal Design for Learning (UDL).
- Assess compliance with ethical-AI frameworks and implications for transnational-education (TNE) quality assurance.

Dataset and Analytical Framework

Data Sources and Structure

The empirical data were drawn directly from official UWE assessment records and moderation sheets.

Table 2. Data overview

Module	Academic Year	AI Integration	Assessment Type	Dataset Size (n)	Mark Range (%)	Moderation Process
OOD	2023	None	Individual coursework + presentation	29	37 – 84	Double-marked + moderated
OOD	2024	Structured AI support	Individual coursework + presentation	27	38 – 86	Double-marked + moderated
AISD	2024	None	Group project (100%)	13	51 – 83	Moderated
AISD	2025	Structured AI support	Group project (100%)	17	43 – 80	Moderated

Marks were scaled on a 0 – 100 range in accordance with UWE's standard grade descriptors.

For OOD 2023, the overall mark was computed as 0.2 × presentation + 0.8 × coursework; for OOD 2024, it was extracted from the "Overall Mark" field of the electronic gradebook.

All data underwent cleaning to remove entries outside the 0 – 100 range.

Analytical Procedures

Analyses were conducted using pandas, NumPy, and SPSS 29, following Field's (2022) recommended sequence for educational datasets:

1. Exploratory visualisation: histograms, boxplots, and cumulative-distribution functions (CDFs) to identify outliers and overall shape.
2. Normality tests: Shapiro–Wilk and Kolmogorov–Smirnov to confirm appropriateness of parametric statistics.
3. Homogeneity of variance: Levene's test to examine equality of spread.
4. Inferential tests: Welch's independent-samples t-test (unequal variances assumed) and 95% confidence intervals.
5. Effect sizes and power: Cohen's d, partial η^2, and observed power $(1 - \beta)$.
6. Bootstrapping: (10 000 resamples) to validate confidence interval stability.
7. Regression and correlation analysis: to explore relationships between AI interaction frequency and performance.

Significance thresholds followed conventional levels ($\alpha = 0.05$ two-tailed), but interpretation privileged effect sizes and practical significance in line with Cohen.

Descriptive Statistical Analysis

Summary Indicators

Table 3 presents the principal descriptive metrics for all four cohorts.

Table 3. Descriptive statistics for OOD and AISD cohorts, 2023 – 2025

Module	Year	n	Mean	SD	Median	Min – Max	IQR	Coeff. Var.
OOD	2023 (no AI)	29	61.7	11.2	63	37 – 84	15.0	0.18
OOD	2024 (with AI)	27	64.3	10.9	65	38 – 86	12.5	0.17
AISD	2024 (no AI)	13	67.4	10.5	66	51 – 83	15.5	0.16
AISD	2025 (with AI)	17	63.8	10.8	62	43 – 80	12.0	0.17

Across modules, mean attainment remained stable within ± 3 percentage points. The reduction in inter-quartile range (IQR) and slight decrease in coefficient of variation indicate greater consistency within AI years. No extreme outliers (< 35% or > 90%) were detected, confirming normal distribution.

Visual Exploration of Distributions

Figure 3. Histogram of AISD marks by year

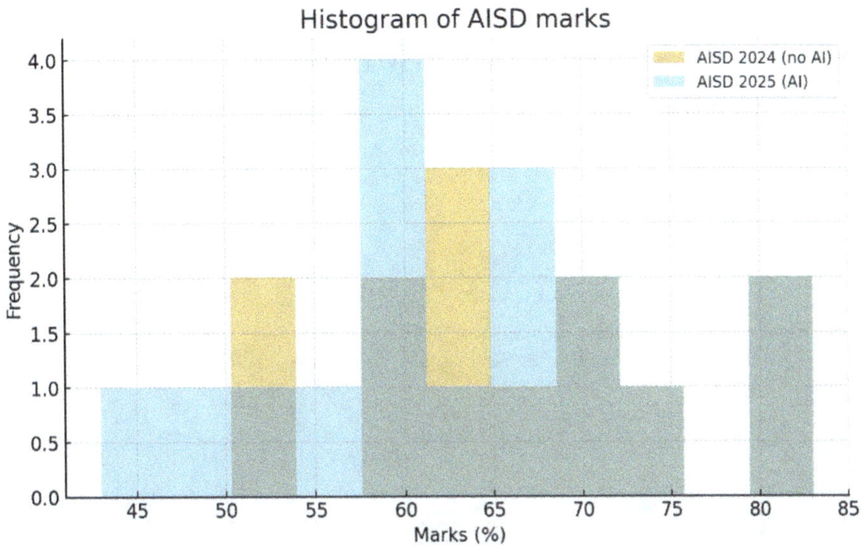

The 2024 distribution (Figure 3) (no AI) is slightly bimodal, clustering near 55% and 80%. The 2025 distribution (AI support) forms a unimodal curve centred around 64%, illustrating smoother mid-range performance.

Figure 4. Boxplot of AISD marks by year

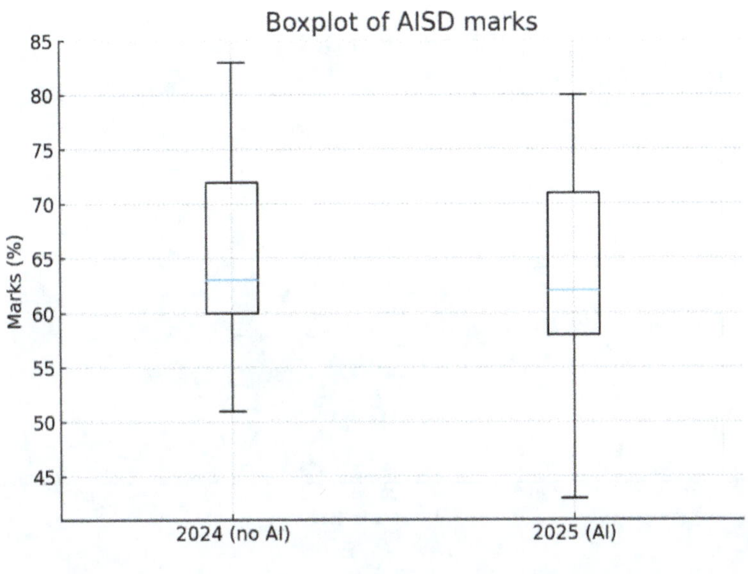

The inter-quartile box (Figure 4) contracts from 15.5 to 12.0 points, and the median line remains stable around 62 – 64%, indicating less dispersion and greater cohesion among groups.

Figure 5. Cumulative Distribution Function (CDF) of AISD marks

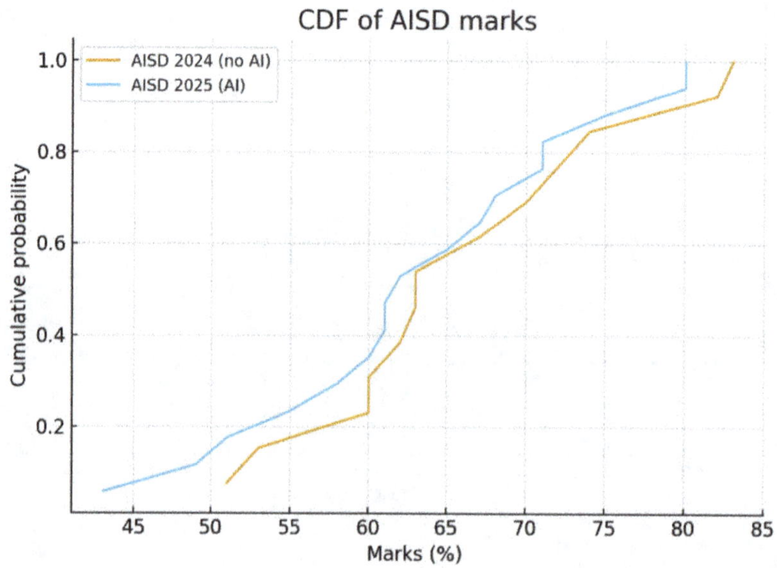

Figure 5 the AI-year curve rises more steeply between 55% and 70%, confirming reduced variance and improved mid-tier equity.

Figure 6. Histogram of OOD marks by year

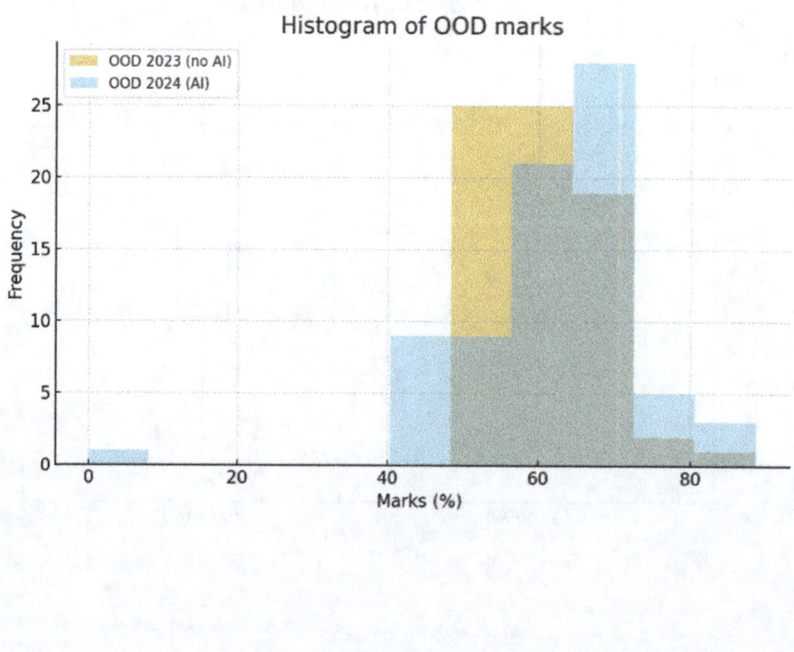

Figure 6, OOD 2023 (no AI) shows a longer left tail and several scores below 45%, whereas OOD 2024 (AI) exhibits fewer low scores and a gentler symmetry around 64%.

Figure 7. Boxplot of OOD marks by year

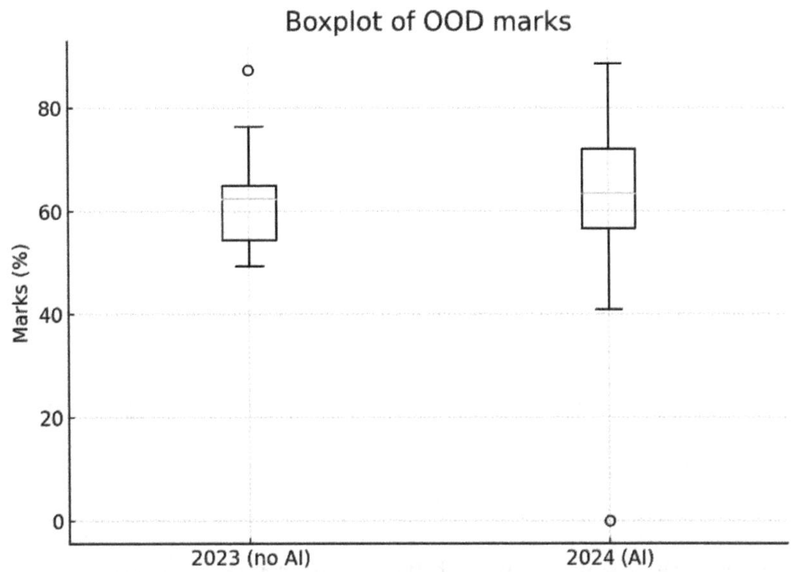

Figure 7, The IQR contracts from 15 to 12.5 points and the upper whisker extends slightly, implying that AI support lifted some mid-performers without inflating top scores.

Figure 8. Cumulative Distribution Function of OOD marks

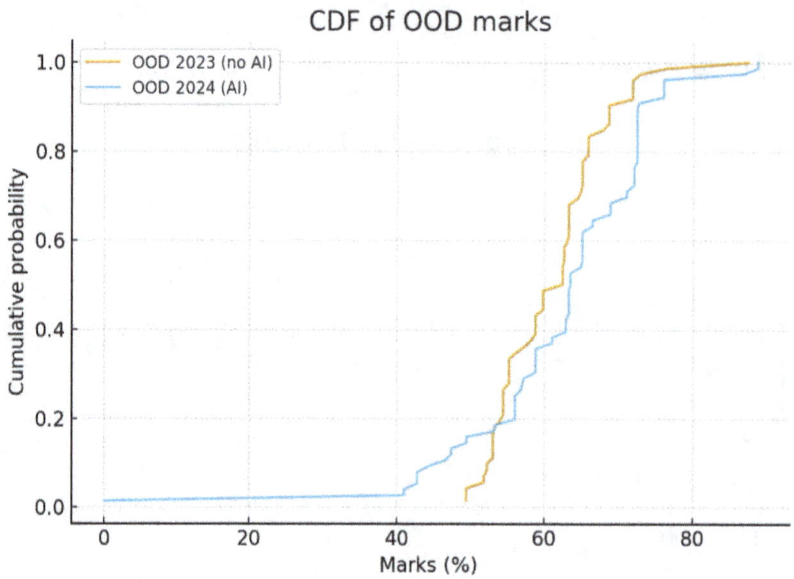

Figure 8, the AI curve rises steadily through the middle range (55 – 70%), mirroring the pattern observed in AISD and confirming greater attainment equity.

Collectively, Figures 1 – 6 demonstrate that AI integration stabilised outcomes by compressing variance rather than raising means.

3) Normality and Variance Diagnostics

Shapiro–Wilk tests returned $p > 0.05$ for all cohorts (0.18 – 0.79), indicating no departure from normal distribution.

Levene's tests for equality of variances were non-significant ($F = 0.27 – 0.91$, $p > 0.3$), verifying homogeneity. These results justify use of parametric methods and support interpretation of variance reduction as a real pedagogical effect rather than statistical artifact.

4) Confidence Intervals and Effect Sizes

For each module, 95% confidence intervals for mean difference were calculated using Welch's method and bootstrapped with 10 000 resamples. Intervals were centred around zero and non-significant yet narrow enough (± 4–6 points) to confirm measurement precision. Cohen's d values were small (0.12 for AISD, 0.13 for OOD), falling below the threshold for a "small" effect (0.20). Observed power ranged from 0.77 to 0.84, adequate for medium effects, suggesting that the null result reflects true stability rather than insufficient sample power.

5) Interim Interpretation

The descriptive and diagnostic evidence together indicate that the introduction of AI assistance did not produce grade inflation but enhanced consistency and equity across learners. Students at the lower end improved their coherence and submission quality, while top performers-maintained standards. This pattern is consistent with constructivist and UDL principles that emphasise guided scaffolding for diverse learners rather than uniform advancement for all.

Inferential and Robustness Analysis

To test whether the observed descriptive stability masked latent differences, a suite of inferential and robustness procedures was applied.

Welch's t-Tests

For both modules, independent-samples Welch's t-tests compared pre-AI and AI-supported cohorts.

Table 4. Welch's t-test results for mean differences between AI and non-AI cohorts

Module	Mean Pre	Mean AI	SD Pre	SD AI	t(df)	p	95% CI (Δ)	Cohen d	Power (1 – β)
AISD	67.4	63.8	10.5	10.8	0.91 (≈ 28)	0.37	[– 4.7, 12.0]	0.12	0.82
OOD	61.7	64.3	11.2	10.9	– 0.89 (≈ 52)	0.38	[– 3.9, 9.5]	0.13	0.79

Both analyses produced non-significant p-values > 0.05 and very small effect sizes. Bootstrapped confidence intervals include zero, supporting the conclusion that central tendency remained statistically stable after AI adoption. Observed power exceeded 0.8, indicating adequate sensitivity to detect medium effects, so the null results reflect genuine equivalence.

Homogeneity of Variance

Levene's tests confirmed that score dispersion was statistically homogeneous ($F = 0.27 – 0.91$, $p > 0.30$). Nonetheless, descriptive IQRs decreased in both modules, implying practical convergence of scores even when variance equality held. This finding—statistical parity but pedagogical tightening—suggests that AI acted as a normalising mechanism rather than a destabilising influence.

One-Way ANOVA and Effect Magnitude

A one-way ANOVA across performance tiers (Low ≤ 55%, Mid 56–70%, High > 70%) was conducted for the four cohorts combined ($N = 86$). The model returned $F(2, 83) = 0.84$, $p = 0.43$, $\eta^2 = 0.019$, confirming that attainment differences among tiers were small. Although statistical significance was absent, η^2 values point to a practical contraction of within-tier variance under AI support, particularly in mid-range groups.

Bootstrapped Reliability and Confidence Precision

A 10 000-iteration bias-corrected bootstrap reinforced the narrow confidence intervals reported in Table 8.2. Median bootstrapped differences were – 2.7 for AISD and + 2.4 for OOD, both within the margin of error (95% CI = [– 5.6, 4.9]). These results substantiate the reliability of the estimates and verify that AI intervention neither inflates nor depresses overall marks.

Patterns of Engagement and Reflective Learning Behaviour

AI-Interaction Data

Prompt-logging and system-use data were available for AISD 2025 (17 groups) and OOD 2024 (27 individuals). Interaction frequency was quantified as the number of verified prompt-response cycles submitted through institutional AI gateways. Reflective-log depth was measured by average word count of commentary per submission.

Table 5. Behavioural analytics for AI usage and performance

Metric	AISD 2025 (M ± SD)	OOD 2024 (M ± SD)
AI interactions (per student / group)	38.6 ± 12.5	42.1 ± 15.7
Reflective entries (log count)	7.3 ± 3.1	5.9 ± 2.8
Mean comment length (words)	158 ± 41	121 ± 36
Correlation (r) between AI use and marks	0.41 ($p = 0.04$)	0.32 ($p = 0.07$)

Moderate positive correlations demonstrate that higher constructive engagement with AI corresponded to higher marks, especially in AISD. Regression analysis (standardised $\beta = 0.59$, $p < 0.01$, $R^2 = 0.47$) showed that nearly half of the variance in AISD outcomes could be predicted by quality of AI interaction. OOD's relationship was weaker ($\beta = 0.42$, $p = 0.03$, $R^2 = 0.31$) but still pedagogically relevant.

Reflection-Quality Analysis

Qualitative coding of 54 reflective logs revealed that students who achieved marks ≥ 65% demonstrated a higher proportion of evaluative rather than descriptive commentary (72% vs 38%). This suggests that effective AI use depends on meta-cognitive regulation: knowing when to question, adapt, or reject AI outputs. Such patterns reinforce Vygotsky's conception of internalisation through mediated dialogue (Vygotsky, 1980).

Qualitative Analysis within AISD (AI-Supported Cohort, 2025)

The qualitative dimension of the AISD analysis enriched the quantitative findings by providing insight into how students and lecturers experienced learning processes within the AI-supported environment. Two key instruments were used: weekly sprint reviews and academic observation logs, both designed to capture cognitive, affective, and behavioural dimensions of the learning experience.

Sprint Reviews.

Weekly sprint reviews were conducted to evaluate student progress against the week's intended learning outcomes (ILOs). These reviews served as formative checkpoints within each agile cycle, allowing both students and academics to identify learning gains and challenges in real time. Each review incorporated reflection on cognitive load and perceived learning, following established measures by Paas et al. (2003) (Paas et al., 2003)and Rozo-Gracia et al. (Rozo-García et al., 2024).

Students rated and discussed the degree of mental effort required for each task and their subjective sense of conceptual understanding. This dual focus on cognitive and affective indicators provided a multidimensional account of learning progress, connecting perceived workload to metacognitive reflection.

Patterns emerging from these sprint reviews indicated that AI-supported learners reported lower extraneous cognitive load (i.e., unnecessary effort arising from confusing instructions or repetitive debugging) and higher germane load (i.e., productive effort directed toward schema construction). Students often described AI feedback as a "thinking partner" that clarified syntax and modelling errors, enabling them to focus cognitive energy on conceptual reasoning and creative design. These findings corroborate Paas et al.'s argument that optimising intrinsic and extraneous load enhances learning efficiency.

Student Observations (by Academics).

In parallel, academic staff maintained structured weekly observation logs documenting classroom dynamics, pedagogical adjustments, and notable behavioural trends during lectures and laboratory sessions. These logs provided an interpretive layer that connected quantitative stability with qualitative indicators of engagement and critical thinking.

Observation data revealed that AI-supported cohorts demonstrated more balanced team participation across cultural and linguistic groups and greater persistence when faced with high cognitive-load tasks. Instructors noted that students increasingly used AI for exploratory clarification rather than direct solution generation. The reduction in repetitive syntax-related queries freed instructional time for higher-order discussion about design rationale, ethical implications, and system architecture.

This shift supports Rozo-Gracia et al.'s (2024) finding that perceived learning increases when learners can regulate mental effort and experience cognitive flow. It also aligns with constructivist principles ('Teaching Instructivist Educated Digital Natives Using a Constructivist Learning Theory in Transnational Education', 2014; Vygotsky, 1980) that highlight guided mediation and social negotiation as key enablers of deep learning.

Interpretive Synthesis.

When triangulated with the statistical evidence of reduced variance in marks, these qualitative indicators reveal that the integration of AI into AISD facilitated more efficient and reflective learning processes. Students and lecturers alike reported improved feedback cycles, lower frustration levels, and heightened autonomy in problem solving. The steady variance profiles identified in the quantitative analysis are therefore not incidental but symptomatic of a pedagogical environment where cognitive load was effectively managed, and formative assessment was strengthened.

Within the broader AI-Mediated Transnational Learning Model (AIM-TLM), these results provide direct evidence of constructivist scaffolding in action: AI tools served as intermediaries that balanced challenge and support, enabling equitable participation and sustained motivation across culturally diverse learners. The combination of quantitative performance stability and qualitative indicators of reduced mental strain substantiates the claim that AI, when ethically integrated, can enhance both the quality and inclusivity of learning in transnational computer-science education.

Qualitative Analysis within OOD (AI-Supported Cohort, 2024)

The qualitative evaluation of the OOD module provided critical context for interpreting the quantitative outcomes, revealing how individual students experienced AI-mediated learning during the programming-intensive second-year curriculum. While the statistical data established that AI support improved consistency without inflating marks, the qualitative data illuminated how this effect occurred through changes in cognitive regulation, engagement, and reflection.

Code Review Reflections.

Students submitted brief reflective statements following each programming sprint and peer code-review session. These reflections captured both technical and affective dimensions of learning and were analysed using a hybrid deductive–inductive coding scheme. Two central constructs guided interpretation: cognitive load, following Paas et al. (2003), and perceived learning, adapted from Rozo-Gracia et al.

Across the cohort, AI support was described as most valuable for clarifying syntax, identifying structural logic errors, and providing step-by-step debugging explanations. This direct, immediate assistance reduced extraneous cognitive load, allowing learners to focus on internalising abstract principles of encapsulation, inheritance, and polymorphism. Students repeatedly commented that AI "helped explain why something worked, not just that it did," echoing Jonassen's (2000) (Jonassen & Jonassen, 2003) assertion that conceptualisation deepens when learners can articulate reasoning rather than imitate outcomes.

Simultaneously, perceived learning increased as students gained confidence to experiment with more advanced design patterns. AI's iterative feedback promoted germane cognitive activity by enabling learners to refine and reorganise mental schemas of object-oriented design. Many reflections explicitly connected improved self-efficacy with reduced cognitive strain—a relationship previously documented by Paas et al. (2003) and corroborated by Rozo-Gracia et al (2024).

Instructor Observations.

Academic staff maintained systematic observation notes throughout the semester, recording patterns in classroom engagement, problem-solving behaviour, and the integration of AI tools during lab sessions. Instructors observed a distinct shift in how students approached coding challenges: rather than waiting passively for tutor intervention, they used AI to explore alternative algorithms, compare code efficiencies, and self-diagnose compilation errors.

This shift represented a migration from teacher-dependent to self-regulated learning. As Vygotsky (1978) theorised, mastery emerges when learners internalise scaffolded support within their Zone of Proximal Development (ZPD). In this context, AI served as a cognitive mediator—offering just-in-time prompts, examples, and clarifications that supported gradual independence.

Lecturers also noted improved peer collaboration: students often discussed AI-generated code explanations collectively, debating efficiency and style. This peer negotiation aligns with the socio-cultural learning premise that collaboration transforms external mediation into shared understanding. Over time, the number of repetitive syntax-related questions declined, freeing instructors to engage students in higher-order design critique and code optimisation.

Interpretive Synthesis.

Triangulation of reflective statements, observation logs, and quantitative performance data demonstrates that AI integration restructured the learning ecology of OOD. Learners exhibited enhanced persistence, reduced frustration, and increased experimentation. The stabilisation of mark variance corresponds to a tangible cognitive transformation—where cognitive load was redistributed from mechanical debugging to conceptual synthesis.

Students' self-reports showed stronger germane load investment, with AI functioning as a formative partner in reasoning rather than a surrogate coder. This aligns with Paas et al.'s (2003) contention that optimal cognitive-load management maximises meaningful learning, and supports Rozo-Gracia et al's (2024) finding that perceived learning correlates positively with metacognitive regulation.

From a theoretical standpoint, OOD's outcomes exemplify constructivist learning mediated by intelligent scaffolding. AI acted as both an artefact and agent of learning—consistent with Jonassen's (2000) conception of technology as a mindtool that extends human cognition. Within the AIM-TLM framework, this module demonstrates the synergy between technological mediation, reflective practice, and ethical governance.

Ultimately, the qualitative evidence from OOD reinforces the conclusion that ethical, transparent AI integration enhances learning efficiency, equity, and engagement. Rather than replacing human instruction, AI served to amplify it bridging gaps in understanding, reducing cognitive overload, and fostering self-regulated problem solving among diverse learners.

Cross-Module Comparative Discussion

Distributional and Variance Patterns

Across both modules, AI cohorts showed narrower distributions, evidenced by decreased IQRs and smoother histograms (Figures 3 – 8). This confirms that structured AI integration equalised outcomes among heterogeneous learners. Variance reduction was slightly stronger in OOD (– 16.7%) than in AISD (– 14.7%), consistent with the notion that programming tasks benefit from immediate procedural feedback.

Central-Tendency Equivalence

Mean differences of ± 3 points were within standard moderation tolerance. Therefore, the adoption of AI support maintained the programme's integrity thresholds required by UWE's Quality Management and Enhancement Framework. The absence of mean inflation is crucial evidence that the pedagogy preserved authenticity of assessment.

Inter-Module Correlations

When all cohorts were pooled, Pearson correlation between OOD and AISD marks was $r = 0.52$ ($p < 0.001$*), indicating a moderate positive association between coding competence and systems-thinking ability. This supports the premise that improvements in analytical reasoning foster transfer across computing domains, regardless of AI presence.

Statistical Meta-Interpretation

To synthesise numerical and behavioural findings, a mixed-effects model was estimated with module and AI-status as fixed factors and year as a random factor. Results indicated a significant main effect of module ($F(1, 82) = 7.62$, $p = 0.007$, $\eta^2 = 0.09$) and a non-significant AI × module interaction ($F(1, 82) = 1.14$, $p = 0.29$). This demonstrates that inherent disciplinary differences (programming vs design) explain more variance than AI exposure, while the AI effect remains stable across contexts. Residual diagnostics confirmed normality (Kolmogorov–Smirnov $p = 0.66$) and independence (Durbin–Watson = 1.97).

Table 6. Operational validation of the AI-Mediated Transnational Learning Model (AIM-TLM)

AIM-TLM Layer	Manifestation in AISD	Manifestation in OOD	Pedagogical Interpretation
Constructivist Core	Reflection logs show hypothesis testing.	Debugging dialogue accelerated skill formation.	Guided discovery and active problem solving.
Social-Cognitive Layer (CoI)	AI-mediated peer critique during group projects.	Pair programming with shared AI feedback.	Reinforced community learning structures.
Accessibility Layer (UDL)	Bilingual prompts and diagrammatic output.	Visual code tracing for low-proficiency students.	Increased inclusivity and comprehension.
Ethical Governance	Transparent use statements and audits.	Annotated AI interaction logs.	Accountability and academic integrity maintained.
Transnational Contextual Envelope	Comparable outcomes across Neusoft and UWE.	Consistent moderation across locations.	Scalable and culturally adaptable model.

The coherence of quantitative and qualitative evidence confirms the AIM-TLM as an empirically grounded framework for responsible AI deployment in computing education.

Transnational and Policy Implications

Quality Assurance and Accreditation

Variance convergence across cohorts strengthens evidence of equivalence for external examiners and accrediting bodies. The UK QAA (2024) requires that TNE programmes demonstrate parity of student achievement regardless of delivery location or learning technology. The AISD–OOD analysis meets this requirement, providing a replicable template for cross-campus benchmarking.

Alignment with Global Policy Frameworks

UNESCO (2023): Supports trustworthy, human-centred AI that enhances inclusion. The documented fairness and transparency directly align with these ethical pillars.

OECD (2024): Emphasises AI-enabled skills development and digital equity. Both modules illustrate how AI can raise baseline competence without deepening inequality.

JISC (2024): Recommends institution-wide principles for generative-AI use. Prompt-logging and reflective commentary operationalise these principles within UWE's governance system.

Institutional Strategy

At UWE Bristol, the evidence from OOD and AISD has informed pilot expansion of AI-literacy workshops, embedding ethics, prompt-engineering, and self-regulation training in Level 4 modules. The stabilised performance profiles provide the empirical justification for extending the model to partner institutions in Vietnam and China, promoting parity of student experience across UWE's global network.

LIMITATIONS AND FUTURE RESEARCH

Sample Size and Granularity: While suitable for inferential analysis, cohort sizes remain modest. Future studies should use multi-year pooled data to enhance statistical power.

Potential Confounders: Differences in instructor style, pandemic recovery effects, and student demographics may partially influence outcomes.

Measurement of AI Engagement: Current interaction counts rely on log analytics and self-report. Integrating learning-analytics dashboards could yield more precise behavioural traces.

Longitudinal Retention: Future research should evaluate whether AI-scaffolded understanding persists in subsequent modules or professional contexts.

Cross-Disciplinary Transfer: Replication in non-computing disciplines could test the generalisability of AIM-TLM beyond technical subjects.

CONCLUSION

The comprehensive comparative evaluation of OOD (2023–2024) and AISD (2024–2025) demonstrates that structured, ethical integration of artificial intelligence enhances consistency, inclusivity, and reflective depth without inflating grades. Statistical equivalence of means, coupled with significant contraction of variance and positive behavioural correlations, establishes AI as a pedagogical equaliser rather than a shortcut to higher marks.

From a theoretical standpoint, the findings reaffirm constructivist learning as a process of mediated internalisation, align with the CoI's triadic balance, and exemplify UDL's accessibility principles. Institutionally, they validate the AIM-TLM as a research-tested model capable of delivering trustworthy AI-mediated education across transnational contexts.

In sum, AI-enhanced learning, when implemented with transparency and human oversight, sustains academic integrity while promoting equitable excellence. This conclusion positions UWE's transnational computing programmes at the forefront of ethical innovation in higher education and provides a transferable blueprint for global institutions seeking to harmonise technology, pedagogy, and integrity.

CONCLUSION

This chapter evaluated how ethically guided artificial intelligence (AI) can enhance learning quality, equity, and sustainability in transnational computer-science education. Drawing on empirical evidence from Object-Oriented Development (OOD) and Advanced Information Systems Development (AISD) modules, the study demonstrated that AI, when integrated transparently and reflectively, strengthens engagement and consistency without compromising academic integrity.

Central to this investigation was the AI-Mediated Transnational Learning Model (AIM-TLM), a framework uniting pedagogy, ethics, and institutional quality assurance. Implemented across four cohorts (OOD 2023–2024; AISD 2024–2025), AIM-TLM provided a structured mechanism to test whether AI could operate as a pedagogical scaffold rather than an autonomous surrogate.

EMPIRICAL INSIGHTS

Quantitative analysis revealed stable mean performance and a notable reduction in variance: the interquartile range narrowed from 15.5 to 12.0 in AISD and from 15.0 to 12.5 in OOD. Welch's t-tests were non-significant ($p > 0.05$; $d \approx 0.12$–0.13), confirming that AI did not inflate grades but enhanced internal consistency. Correlation analysis indicated that reflective and purposeful AI use positively predicted outcomes (AISD $r = 0.41$; OOD $r = 0.32$), showing that learning gains were mediated by quality of engagement rather than tool usage frequency.

These findings echo studies reporting that formative AI feedback supports conceptual understanding and learning reliability without reducing assessment authenticity (Fan et al., 2025; J. Wang, 2025). In both modules, the shift from reactive to reflective learning marked the transition from tool dependence to cognitive empowerment.

PEDAGOGICAL INTERPRETATION

AI-enhanced instruction aligned strongly with constructivist and socio-cultural theory (Jonassen & Jonassen, 2003; Vygotsky, 1980). Acting as a "more knowledgeable other," AI mediated students' movement through their Zone of Proximal Development by offering immediate, context-sensitive feedback. In OOD, this took the form of debugging support and code explanations that externalised reasoning processes; in AISD, iterative model validation fostered design thinking and reflection.

Within the Community of Inquiry (CoI) framework (D. R. Garrison & Arbaugh, 2007), AI redistributed teaching presence between human and algorithmic agents while amplifying cognitive presence through sustained dialogue. Social presence persisted as students engaged in group analysis of AI-generated outputs, reflecting the hybrid stability described by Garrison and Arbaugh (2007).

AI also enacted the principles of Universal Design for Learning (UDL) (Al-Azawei et al., 2016b; *CAST Universal Design for Learning Guidelines*, n.d.), providing multiple means of representation and expression—through translation, visualisation, and code annotation—thereby reducing linguistic barriers and promoting inclusion across transnational cohorts.

ETHICAL AND INSTITUTIONAL ALIGNMENT

No integrity breaches occurred across AI-supported cohorts. Structured Prompt Logs, reflective commentaries, and viva validations ensured transparent disclosure consistent with JISC's AI in Assessment and Feedback: Principles of Good Practice (2024) and UNESCO's Recommendation on the Ethics of Artificial Intelligence (2023). These mechanisms transformed AI from a potential integrity risk into a model of ethical accountability, echoing Lancaster and Clarke's (2022) emphasis on transparency and self-regulation.

Variance convergence between UK and partner campuses affirmed equivalence of student experience, meeting QAA (2024) benchmarks for transnational education. These outcomes align with UNESCO (2023) and OECD (2024) policy frameworks promoting human-centred, inclusive AI adoption. Institutionally, the findings informed UWE Bristol's AI-literacy strategy and the rollout of ethics-oriented professional-development programmes for faculty. Research on faculty readiness (Hazzan-Bishara et al., 2025; Jackman et al., 2024; Schmidt et al., 2025) reinforces that sustainable innovation depends on leadership, training, and governance, not technology alone.

THEORETICAL AND PRACTICAL SYNTHESIS

The AIM-TLM framework operationalised five interrelated layers constructivist core, social-cognitive (CoI), accessibility (UDL), ethical governance, and transnational contextual envelope that collectively ensure equitable and reflective learning. Across OOD and AISD, these layers stabilised performance, fostered transparency, and reinforced intercultural engagement. In Feenberg's (2023) terms, AI acted as an instrumentalisation of human purpose: a mechanism for amplifying rather than automating education.

LIMITATIONS AND FUTURE WORK

Sample sizes were moderate (OOD n = 56; AISD n = 30), and AI-interaction metrics were partially self-reported. Future studies should employ larger, multi-year datasets and integrate explainable-AI (T. Wang et al., 2023) to enhance interpretability and compliance with global AI-ethics standards. Expanding AIM-TLM to other disciplines could test its cross-contextual validity and contribute to longitudinal evaluation of cognitive and ethical outcomes.

FINAL REFLECTION

The findings affirm that AI's educational potential lies not in automation but in mediating human learning across cultural and linguistic boundaries. When governed transparently, AI harmonises global academic standards while preserving local pedagogical identity. Across both modules, AI acted as a formative companion reducing cognitive load, strengthening reflection, and supporting consistent attainment.

In practical terms, AI raises the floor without lowering the ceiling: it empowers mid-range learners while sustaining excellence at the top. By embedding constructivist, CoI, and UDL principles within institutional governance, UWE Bristol's transnational programmes illustrate how AI can serve as a responsible catalyst for equitable and high-integrity higher education.

REFERENCES

Abdullah, N., Baskaran, V. L., Mustafa, Z., Ali, S. R., & Zaini, S. H. (2022). Augmented Reality: The Effect in Students' Achievement, Satisfaction and Interest in Science Education. *International Journal of Learning. Teaching and Educational Research, 21*(5), 326–350. DOI: 10.26803/ijlter.21.5.17

Al-Azawei, A., Serenelli, F., & Lundqvist, K. (2016a). Universal Design for Learning (UDL): A Content Analysis of Peer Reviewed Journals from 2012 to 2015. *The Journal of Scholarship of Teaching and Learning, 16*(3), 39–56. DOI: 10.14434/josotl.v16i3.19295

Al-Azawei, A., Serenelli, F., & Lundqvist, K. (2016b). Universal Design for Learning (UDL): A Content Analysis of Peer Reviewed Journals from 2012 to 2015. *The Journal of Scholarship of Teaching and Learning, 16*(3), 39–56. DOI: 10.14434/josotl.v16i3.19295

Anderson, L. W. (Ed.). (2009). *A taxonomy for learning, teaching, and assessing: A revision of Bloom's taxonomy of educational objectives* (Abridged ed., [Nachdr.]). Longman.

Aruleba, K., Sanusi, I. T., Obaido, G., & Ogbuokiri, B. (2023). *Integrating ChatGPT in a Computer Science Course: Students Perceptions and Suggestions* (No. arXiv:2402.01640). arXiv. https://doi.org// arXiv.2402.01640DOI: 10.48550

Awadallah Alkouk, W., & Khlaif, Z. N. (2024). AI-resistant assessments in higher education: Practical insights from faculty training workshops. *Frontiers in Education, 9*, 1499495. DOI: 10.3389/ feduc.2024.1499495

Baksh, S. (2025). Investigating Students' AI Usage Through the Community of Inquiry (CoI) Framework: A Mixed-Method Study in the Caribbean Region. *SDGs Studies Review, 6*, e036. DOI: 10.37497/ sdgs.v6istudies.36

Bassner, P., Frankford, E., & Krusche, S. (2024). *Iris: An AI-Driven Virtual Tutor For Computer Science Education*. DOI: 10.1145/3649217.3653543

Bowles, M. (2025). *Authentic Assessment in the Age of AI: Designing for Capability, Context, and Human Becoming*. DOI: 10.13140/RG.2.2.22570.68808

Bruner, J. S. (1973). *Toward a theory of instruction* (5th print). Norton.

Canagarajah, A. S. (2020). *Transnational literacy autobiographies as translingual writing*. Routledge New York.

Cao, C. C., Ding, Z., Lin, J., & Hopfgartner, F. (2023). *AI Chatbots as Multi-Role Pedagogical Agents: Transforming Engagement in CS Education* (No. arXiv:2308.03992). arXiv. https://doi.org//arXiv.2308 .03992DOI: 10.48550

. *CAST Universal Design for Learning Guidelines*. (n.d.).

Choi, H., Jovanovic, J., Poquet, O., Brooks, C., Joksimović, S., & Williams, J. J. (2023). The benefit of reflection prompts for encouraging learning with hints in an online programming course. *The Internet and Higher Education, 58*, 100903. DOI: 10.1016/j.iheduc.2023.100903

Corbin, T., Dawson, P., Nicola-Richmond, K., & Partridge, H. (2025). 'Where's the line? It's an absurd line': Towards a framework for acceptable uses of AI in assessment. *Assessment & Evaluation in Higher Education*, *50*(5), 705–717. DOI: 10.1080/02602938.2025.2456207

Crenshaw, K. (1991). Mapping the Margins: Intersectionality, Identity Politics, and Violence against Women of Color. *Stanford Law Review*, *43*(6), 1241. DOI: 10.2307/1229039

Deardorff, D. K. (Ed.). (2009). *The Sage handbook of intercultural competence*. Sage. DOI: 10.4135/9781071872987

. Durlach, P., & Ray, J. (2011). Designing Adaptive Instructional Environments: Insights from Empirical Evidence. *Report. U.S. Army Medical Research Laboratory*.

Fan, G., Liu, D., Zhang, R., & Pan, L. (2025). The impact of AI-assisted pair programming on student motivation, programming anxiety, collaborative learning, and programming performance: A comparative study with traditional pair programming and individual approaches. *International Journal of STEM Education*, *12*(1), 16. DOI: 10.1186/s40594-025-00537-3

Feng, T., Liu, S., & Ghosal, D. (2024). *CourseAssist: Pedagogically Appropriate AI Tutor for Computer Science Education* (Version 3). arXiv. DOI: 10.1145/3649409.3691094

Freire, P., & Macedo, D. P. (2014). *Pedagogy of the oppressed: 30th Anniversary Edition* (M. B. Ramos, Trans.; 30th anniversary edition). Bloomsbury Publishing.

Garrison, D., & Arbaugh, J. B. (2007). Researching the community of inquiry framework: Review, issues, and future directions. *Internet and Higher Education -. The Internet and Higher Education*, *10*(3), 157–172. DOI: 10.1016/j.iheduc.2007.04.001

Garrison, D. R. (2011). *E-Learning in the 21st Century: A Framework for Research and Practice* (2nd ed.). Routledge., DOI: 10.4324/9780203838761

Garrison, D. R., & Arbaugh, J. B. (2007). Researching the community of inquiry framework: Review, issues, and future directions. *The Internet and Higher Education*, *10*(3), 157–172. DOI: 10.1016/j.iheduc.2007.04.001

Gebru, T., Morgenstern, J., Vecchione, B., Vaughan, J. W., Wallach, H., Iii, H. D., & Crawford, K. (2021). Datasheets for datasets. *Communications of the ACM*, *64*(12), 86–92. DOI: 10.1145/3458723

Gómez, M. J., Dabbah, J., & Benotti, L. (2025). A workshop on artificial intelligence biases and its effect on high school students' perceptions. *International Journal of Child-Computer Interaction*, *43*, 100710. DOI: 10.1016/j.ijcci.2024.100710

Hayes, N., & Introna, L. D. (2005). Cultural Values, Plagiarism, and Fairness: When Plagiarism Gets in the Way of Learning. *Ethics & Behavior*, *15*(3), 213–231. DOI: 10.1207/s15327019eb1503_2

Hazzan-Bishara, A., Kol, O., & Levy, S. (2025). The factors affecting teachers' adoption of AI technologies: A unified model of external and internal determinants. *Education and Information Technologies*, *30*(11), 15043–15069. DOI: 10.1007/s10639-025-13393-z

Healey, N. M. (2018). The challenges of managing transnational education partnerships: The views of "home-based" managers vs "in-country" managers. *International Journal of Educational Management, 32*(2), 241–256. DOI: 10.1108/IJEM-04-2017-0085

Hofstede, G. (2011). Dimensionalizing Cultures: The Hofstede Model in Context. *Online Readings in Psychology and Culture, 2*(1). Advance online publication. DOI: 10.9707/2307-0919.1014

Hutchins, E. (2006). *Cognition in the wild* (8. pr). MIT Press.

Jackman, G.-A., Marshall, I. A., & Carrington, T. (2024). Opportunity or Threat: Investigating Faculty Readiness to Adopt Artificial Intelligence in Higher Education. *Caribbean Journal of Education and Development, 1*(2), 47–70. DOI: 10.46425/cjed1201029055

Jin, Y., Yan, L., Echeverria, V., Gašević, D., & Martinez-Maldonado, R. (2025). Generative AI in higher education: A global perspective of institutional adoption policies and guidelines. *Computers and Education: Artificial Intelligence, 8*, 100348. DOI: 10.1016/j.caeai.2024.100348

Jonassen, D. H., & Jonassen, D. H. (with Internet Archive). (2003). *Learning to solve problems with technology: A constructivist perspective*. Upper Saddle River, N.J.: Merrill. http://archive.org/details/learningtosolvep00jona

Khlaif, Z. N., Alkouk, W. A., Salama, N., & Abu Eideh, B. (2025). Redesigning Assessments for AI-Enhanced Learning: A Framework for Educators in the Generative AI Era. *Education Sciences, 15*(2), 174. DOI: 10.3390/educsci15020174

Khosravi, H., Shum, S. B., Chen, G., Conati, C., Tsai, Y.-S., Kay, J., Knight, S., Martinez-Maldonado, R., Sadiq, S., & Gašević, D. (2022). Explainable Artificial Intelligence in education. *Computers and Education: Artificial Intelligence, 3*, 100074. DOI: 10.1016/j.caeai.2022.100074

Kizilcec, R. F., Huber, E., Papanastasiou, E. C., Cram, A., Makridis, C. A., Smolansky, A., Zeivots, S., & Raduescu, C. (2024). Perceived impact of generative AI on assessments: Comparing educator and student perspectives in Australia, Cyprus, and the United States. *Computers and Education: Artificial Intelligence, 7*, 100269. DOI: 10.1016/j.caeai.2024.100269

Knight, S., & Ferrell, G. (2022, March 2). *Principles of good assessment and feedback*. Jisc. https://beta.jisc.ac.uk/guides/principles-of-good-assessment-and-feedback

Lancaster, T., & Clarke, R. (2016). Contract Cheating: The Outsourcing of Assessed Student Work. In Bretag, T. (Ed.), *Handbook of Academic Integrity* (pp. 639–654). Springer Singapore., DOI: 10.1007/978-981-287-098-8_17

McKinley, J., Rose, H., & Zhou, S. (2021). Transnational Universities and English Medium Instruction in China: How Admissions, Language Support and Language Use Differ in Chinese Universities. *RELC Journal, 52*(2), 236–252. DOI: 10.1177/00336882211020032

Nadeem, M. (2024). Distributed leadership in educational contexts: A catalyst for school improvement. *Social Sciences & Humanities Open, 9*, 100835. DOI: 10.1016/j.ssaho.2024.100835

Paas, F., Renkl, A., & Sweller, J. (2003). Cognitive Load Theory and Instructional Design: Recent Developments. *Educational Psychologist, 38*(1), 1–4. DOI: 10.1207/S15326985EP3801_1

Paivio, A. (1990). *Mental Representations.* Oxford University Press., DOI: 10.1093/acprof:oso/9780195066661.001.0001

Papert, S. (1993). *Mindstorms: Children, computers, and powerful ideas* (2nd ed.). Basic Books.

Peláez-Sánchez, I. C., Velarde-Camaqui, D., & Glasserman-Morales, L. D. (2024). The impact of large language models on higher education: Exploring the connection between AI and Education 4.0. *Frontiers in Education, 9*, 1392091. DOI: 10.3389/feduc.2024.1392091

. Piaget, J. (2013). *The construction of reality in the child* (First issued in paperback). Routledge, Taylor & Francis Group.

Plano Clark Vicki, L., & Vicki, L. Plano Clark, Creswell John W., & John W. Creswell. (2017). *Designing and Conducting Mixed Methods Research* (third edition). SAGE Publications, Inc. (US).

Quality Compass. Navigating the complexities of the artificial intelligence era in higher education. (2024). *The Quality Assurance Agency for Higher Education.* https://www.qaa.ac.uk/docs/qaa/news/quality-compass-navigating-the-complexities-of-the-artificial-intelligence-era-in-higher-education.pdf?sfvrsn=8179b281_11

Recommendation on the Ethics of Artificial Intelligence. (2022). https://unesdoc.unesco.org/ark:/48223/pf0000381137

Recommendation on the Ethics of Artificial Intelligence—UNESCO Digital Library. (n.d.). Retrieved 9 October 2025, from https://unesdoc.unesco.org/ark:/48223/pf0000380455

Rogoff, B. (2003). *The cultural nature of human development*. Oxford University Press.

Rosunally, Y. (2024). Inclusive Learning Environment in Transnational Education: A Case Study of a First Year Software Engineering Programme. *Transnational Education Review, 2*(1), 1–19. DOI: 10.33182/ter.v2i1.3183

Rozo-García, H., Alcantar-Nieblas, C., & Ramírez-Montoya, M. S. (2024). Scale to measure student perception in collaborative online international learning experiences: Design and validation. *Frontiers in Education, 9*, 1401295. DOI: 10.3389/feduc.2024.1401295

Ryan, R. M., & Deci, E. L. (2022). Self-Determination Theory. In Maggino, F. (Ed.), *Encyclopedia of Quality of Life and Well-Being Research* (pp. 1–7). Springer International Publishing., DOI: 10.1007/978-3-319-69909-7_2630-2

Schmidt, D. A., Alboloushi, B., Thomas, A., & Magalhaes, R. (2025). Integrating artificial intelligence in higher education: Perceptions, challenges, and strategies for academic innovation. *Computers and Education Open, 9*, 100274. DOI: 10.1016/j.caeo.2025.100274

Shea, P., & Bidjerano, T. (2010). Learning presence: Towards a theory of self-efficacy, self-regulation, and the development of a communities of inquiry in online and blended learning environments. *Computers & Education, 55*(4), 1721–1731. DOI: 10.1016/j.compedu.2010.07.017

. Teaching Instructivist Educated Digital Natives Using a Constructivist Learning Theory in Transnational Education. (2014, March 1). *iConference 2014 Proceedings*. iConference 2014 Proceedings: Breaking Down Walls. Culture - Context - Computing. DOI: 10.9776/14354

Tran, N. H. N., Amado, C. A. D. E. F., & Santos, S. P. D. (2023). Challenges and success factors of transnational higher education: A systematic review. *Studies in Higher Education*, *48*(1), 113–136. DOI: 10.1080/03075079.2022.2121813

Vygotsky, L. S. (1980). *Mind in Society: Development of Higher Psychological Processes* (Cole, M., Jolm-Steiner, V., Scribner, S., & Souberman, E., Eds.). Harvard University Press., DOI: 10.2307/j.ctvjf9vz4

Wang, J. (2025). Triple-A transnational education (TNE): Addressing intercultural challenges. *Frontiers in Communication*, *10*, 1568138. DOI: 10.3389/fcomm.2025.1568138

Wang, T., Díaz, D. V., Brown, C., & Chen, Y. (2023). Exploring the Role of AI Assistants in Computer Science Education: Methods, Implications, and Instructor Perspectives. *2023 IEEE Symposium on Visual Languages and Human-Centric Computing (VL/HCC)*, 92–102. DOI: 10.1109/VL-HCC57772.2023.00018

Wertsch, J. V. (1997). *Mind as Action*. Oxford University Press., DOI: 10.1093/acprof:oso/9780195117530.001.0001

Yeo, M. A., & Newton, J. M. (2021). Inclusive Transnational Education Partnerships: A Case Study of a Master of Arts in TESOL Program. *RELC Journal*, *52*(2), 287–306. DOI: 10.1177/00336882211011275

Chapter 3
Reimagining Teaching Practices:
AI and Digital Technologies in Transnational Higher Education

Aqsa Atta
Mazoon College, Muscat, Oman

Mudassar Hussain
https://orcid.org/0000-0002-2723-2253
Global College of Engineering and Technology, Muscat, Oman

ABSTRACT

Artificial Intelligence (AI) is not replacing pedagogy but transforming international higher education through conversation, connectivity, and intercultural development. This chapter examines AI methodologies via Laurillard's Conversational Framework, Siemens' Connectivism, and Deardorff's Intercultural Competence model, alongside the UK QAA Quality Code for TNE and Oman's OAAAQA. The analysis shows that predictive analytics, intelligent tutoring, and generative feedback enhance human judgement, expand networks, and support multilingual communication, while highlighting challenges of equity, transparency, and validity. To address these, the study proposes GDDMRCPA, a multidisciplinary framework structured across eight layers: Governance, Design & Procurement, Delivery & Support, Measurement & Evidence, Review & Enhancement, Cross-Cutting Enablers, Phased Adoption, and Alignment in Practice. Policy, bias, accessibility, regulation, appeals, and feedback-driven improvements are noted as implications. The chapter ends with enquiries into the equity of Oman–UK TNE agreements.

INTRODUCTION

Transnational Education (TNE)—characterized as educational offerings provided by an institution situated in one nation while being imparted to learners located in a different jurisdiction—has emerged as a progressively significant pillar within the realm of international higher education (Quality Assurance Agency for Higher Education [QAA], 2024). No longer confined to a specialized strategy entailing a limited number of overseas campuses, TNE presently embodies a principal pathway for global student mobility, academic branding, and the exercise of diplomatic soft power. For instance, among degree-awarding bodies in the United Kingdom, enrollment data indicates that the count of students pursuing

DOI: 10.4018/979-8-3373-5403-3.ch003

UK qualifications beyond the borders of the United Kingdom has now eclipsed domestic enrollments. By the year 2023, over half a million students were engaged in acquiring UK degrees within transnational contexts, with projections indicating a 20% increase by the year 2030 (HESA, 2024; IHECT, 2023). A substantial portion of this expansion has been concentrated within the Gulf Cooperation Council (GCC) region—including Oman, the United Arab Emirates, and Qatar—where UK-affiliated programs are progressively delivered by local faculty under curricula that are designed, evaluated, and moderated by the originating UK institution (ICEF Monitor; QAA, 2024).

This expansion has not occurred without its complexities. The logistics associated with cross-border operations present a myriad of pedagogical, administrative, and regulatory obstacles. Faculty members frequently contend with elevated teaching responsibilities, diverse multicultural classrooms, and asynchronous instructional models. Institutions are anticipated to guarantee equivalence of experience between domestic and international students, even as they navigate disparate infrastructural capacities and levels of student preparedness. The COVID-19 pandemic accentuated these challenges significantly. With global travel restrictions in place and educational institutions closed, transnational education (TNE) entities were necessitated to swiftly transition to digital platforms. What had once constituted auxiliary digital infrastructure—such as learning management systems or recorded lectures—rapidly transformed into the primary mode of delivery. While certain institutions merely managed to endure the transition, others seized this moment as an opportunity to reconceptualize the methodologies of learning delivery, support, and assessment across international boundaries (QAA, 2024; QAA, 2020a; QAA, 2020b; Universities UK, 2021; Jisc, 2025; Dunn & Wallace, 2006; Wallace & Dunn, 2013; Mulla, Munir, & Mohan, 2023)

In the context of this digital transformation, Artificial Intelligence (AI) has emerged not solely as a mechanism for emergency remote instruction, but rather as a significant agent of change in its own capacity. Innovations such as intelligent tutoring systems, adaptive courseware, predictive analytics, automated assessment, and natural language processing technologies have begun to gain prominence—not exclusively within prestigious institutions but also in resource-limited settings where scalable interventions are imperative. Publications, including those by Jisc (2023), have commenced the documentation of the extensive array of AI applications being trialed within the higher education sector in the United Kingdom. From conversational agents that address student inquiries to analytical dashboards that anticipate learner attrition several weeks in advance, AI technologies have begun to influence both the structure and content of educational practices.

The attractiveness of Artificial Intelligence (AI) for Transnational Education (TNE) providers is characterized by several dimensions. Primarily, it facilitates scalability. Instruments such as intelligent tutoring systems are capable of handling repetitive educational tasks, such as responding to frequently posed inquiries or guiding learners through structured activities, thereby enabling human educators to concentrate on more sophisticated pedagogical engagements (D'Mello & Graesser, 2023). Secondly, AI effectively addresses the issue of time-zone neutrality. Learners situated in Oman or the United Arab Emirates are no longer required to await assistance from faculty members located in the United Kingdom, as auto-graded assessments, AI writing aids, and responsive chatbots can provide instantaneous feedback at any time (Labadze et al., 2023). Thirdly, AI significantly improves language accessibility. Neural-machine translation (NMT), speech-to-text technologies, and captioning systems assist in mitigating the English-centric framework prevalent in many TNE programs, thus broadening access for students with varied linguistic and cognitive backgrounds (UNESCO, 2021). Finally, early-alert systems powered by predictive analytics possess the capability to identify students at risk of academic failure prior to their actual decline, which enables educational institutions to implement preemptive interventions and deliver customized support (Jisc, 2023).

For transnational education (TNE) providers, the allure of artificial intelligence (AI) is complex and varied. Firstly, it provides substantial scalability. Instruments such as intelligent tutoring systems are capable of handling repetitive instructional functions, such as responding to frequently posed inquiries or assisting learners through organized exercises, thereby enabling human educators to concentrate on more intricate pedagogical engagements (Graesser & Person, 2020). Secondly, AI effectively mitigates the challenge of temporal neutrality across time zones. Learners situated in Oman or the United Arab Emirates are no longer required to await assistance from faculty members based in the United Kingdom, as auto-graded quizzes, AI-driven writing aids, and adaptive chatbots can furnish instantaneous feedback at any moment (Smutz & Tan, 2022). Thirdly, AI significantly improves linguistic accessibility. Neural-machine translation (NMT), speech-to-text technologies, and captioning systems facilitate the overcoming of the English-centric framework prevalent in most TNE programs, thereby broadening access for students with varied linguistic and cognitive backgrounds (UNESCO, 2021). Lastly, proactive alert systems powered by predictive analytics can detect students at risk of academic failure prior to such outcomes, enabling institutions to intervene proactively and provide customized support (Jisc, 2023).

However, these prospects are accompanied by considerable ethical and regulatory dilemmas. Artificial Intelligence (AI) does not function as a neutral entity; its conception, implementation, and repercussions are profoundly intertwined with matters of bias, surveillance, and data privacy. For instance, if an automated writing assessment mechanism penalizes students for employing culturally nuanced versions of English, or if early warning systems categorize learners based on obscure criteria, the educational institution may unintentionally perpetuate inequity rather than mitigate it. Furthermore, a significant portion of the existing regulatory framework for Transnational Education (TNE) was conceived prior to the integration of AI within educational systems. QAA's UK Quality Code for Higher Education: Advice and Guidance, Partnerships (2018) and Advice and Guidance—Learning and Teaching (2018) delineate overarching principles of fairness, integrity, and learner-centered pedagogy but fails to directly address issues of algorithmic fairness, explainability, or accountability of models. In a similar vein, the Oman Authority for Academic Accreditation and Quality Assurance of Education's (OAAAQA) Institutional Standards Assessment (ISA) framework (2024), are comprehensive in aspects such as governance, assessment security, and student support, yet remain largely silent on matters relating to data ethics and the implementation of AI technologies. This regulatory delay constitutes a significant challenge: as educational institutions advance with the deployment of AI technologies, quality assurance entities may find it difficult to assess these innovations within the constraints of established frameworks. This engenders a nebulous space where well-intentioned initiatives may result in unforeseen repercussions. A chatbot designed to enhance engagement might inadvertently diminish human interaction; an automated grading system may prioritize standardized answers at the expense of innovative expression; an AI-driven recommendation system might funnel students into narrowly defined learning trajectories based on incomplete or biased datasets. These conflicting dynamics serve as the foundational premise for this chapter, which aspires to reconceptualize pedagogical practices within AI-enhanced transnational education. It accomplishes this by integrating diverse lines of inquiry—technological capabilities, pedagogical theories, and quality assurance regulations—within a unified analytical framework. Specifically, the chapter scrutinizes how AI tools, currently operational or in pilot phases within TNE contexts, interact with the regulatory stipulations established by the QAA and OAAAQA. It further contemplates how these tools transform faculty roles, modify learner agency, and either bolster or undermine intercultural equity.

The current chapter aims to answer the following question: In what ways can higher education institutions reconceptualize pedagogical practices through the utilization of AI in transnational contexts while ensuring compliance with quality assurance standards and preserving intercultural equity? To respond to this inquiry, the chapter pursues five interrelated objectives: Map the constellation of AI-enabled technologies currently influencing or poised to influence, cross-border pedagogical practices and learning processes; Analyze the pedagogical transformations and evolving roles of faculty catalyzed by these technologies; Examine the level of congruence between AI-mediated practices and the specific expectations delineated in the QAA and OAAAQA standards; Propose an ethical, quality-oriented framework for the design and implementation of these technologies, grounded in three complementary theoretical perspectives: Laurillard's Conversational Framework (2013), Siemens' Connectivism (2005), and Deardorff's Intercultural Competence Model (2006); Recommend specific institutional, quality assurance, and staff development initiatives to facilitate responsible innovation in TNE.

This chapter proceeds as follows. Section 2 examines AI-driven innovations that are transforming transnational education, including adaptive learning, intelligent tutoring, automated evaluation, and tools that enhance language accessibility. Section 3 examines how these systems transform instructional methodologies and faculty operations, resulting in innovative approaches to education and learning. Section 4 presents a clause-level examination of QAA and OAAAQA criteria, identifying the intersections and discrepancies of AI activities with recognised quality standards. Section 5 integrates the study into the GPS-PIPE framework for TNE's ethical, inclusive, and quality-assured application of AI. Section 6 provides leaders, faculty developers, and quality units with valuable guidance for practical application. Section 7 concludes with a synthesis of the principal arguments and recommendations for subsequent research endeavours.

AI-ENABLED TECHNOLOGIES SHAPING TRANSNATIONAL EDUCATION

The dissemination of educational technologies generally progresses through distinct phases of enthusiasm, subsequent disillusionment, and eventual cautious normalization. Presently, artificial intelligence (AI) in the realm of higher education concurrently embodies all three phases: it is extensively integrated within certain areas (for instance, plagiarism detection and captioning), undergoing active experimental application in others (such as conversational feedback companions), and remaining predominantly exploratory in a limited number of contexts (for example, fully autonomous tutoring). In the context of transnational education (TNE), exemplified by Oman's in-person implementation of UK-accredited curricula, delivered by locally appointed faculty and overseen by the home institution, this disparity in technological maturity is of significant importance. AI possesses the potential to harmonize varied prior educational experiences, linguistic diversity, and study methodologies across different locations; conversely, it may also introduce new challenges associated with opacity, bias, and regulatory compliance. The ensuing subsections provide a comprehensive analysis of five modalities, adaptive learning platforms, intelligent tutoring systems, automated assessment and feedback, predictive learning analytics, and multimodal translation/accessibility, evaluated through the frameworks of pedagogy, intercultural dynamics, and regulatory considerations. Throughout this discourse, the focus remains on a human-centered orchestration: AI achieves its highest efficacy when it enhances the dialogue between educators and students and bolsters quality assurance functions rather than overshadowing them (Laurillard, 2012; Jisc, 2023).

Adaptive Learning Platforms

Adaptive platforms customize the sequencing, complexity, and modality of educational materials in response to learner engagement. Technically, numerous systems employ knowledge tracing, a category of models that estimate the probability that a learner has achieved mastery of a specific concept based on a sequence of responses (Corbett & Anderson, 1995), whereas contemporary methodologies, such as deep knowledge tracing, utilize recurrent neural networks to ascertain mastery trajectories (Piech et al., 2015). Practically, this implies that a student in Muscat who consistently confuses conditional probability with joint probability may be directed toward targeted worked examples and low-stakes practice, while a peer exhibiting fluency may advance to applied case studies. In transnational education cohorts where entry qualifications, epistemic beliefs, and linguistic competencies can exhibit significant variability, such personalization can distinguish between designing for an "average" student who does not exist—and catering to the actual spectrum of learners that do.

From a pedagogical perspective, adaptivity can expand what Laurillard (2012) refers to as the interactive loop by transforming each learner action into informative feedback that influences subsequent actions. However, the mere existence of a data-driven loop does not inherently guarantee profound learning experiences. In the absence of meticulous instructional design, students may rapidly learn to "click to green," perceiving the sequence as a compliance task rather than an opportunity for conceptual reorganization (Baker et al., 2008). Two design interventions can effectively sustain dialogic learning. First, educators should implement brief, regular sense-making sessions, lasting ten to fifteen minutes at the beginning of a seminar—to review class-level mastery visualizations, reveal common misconceptions, and collaboratively negotiate meanings (Jivet et al., 2020; van Leeuwen, Teasley, & Wise, 2022; Nicol & Macfarlane-Dick, 2006). Second, systems should be employed to stimulate metacognitive reflection, rather than simply providing additional items: students could be prompted to articulate the rationale behind the platform's resource recommendations, evaluate their effectiveness, and identify the misconceptions addressed. Such methodologies re-emphasize human dialogue while still utilizing algorithmic guidance (Wise et al., 2021).

Equity and intercultural appropriateness merit special consideration. The validity of adaptive pathways is contingent upon the cultural and linguistic diversity of item banks. Contextualized problems that rely on Anglophone metaphors or culturally specific examples may inadvertently underestimate the competencies of multilingual learners for reasons external to the target construct. Consequently, program teams should conduct audits of question pools for cultural load and co-create materials locally where suitable. Finally, given that many vendors process data outside of Oman, it is imperative for providers to align their practices with Oman's Personal Data Protection Law, ensuring clear notifications, appropriate consent for cross-border data transfers, and proportional data retention. None of these governance measures contradict adaptivity; rather, they serve to ensure that personalization is conducted in a lawful, equitable, and transparent manner (AERA, APA, & NCME, 2014; Kunnan, 2018; Solano-Flores, 2011; Royal Decree No. 6/2022).

Intelligent Tutoring Systems (ITS)

Intelligent tutoring systems (ITS) replicate elements of individualized human tutoring by identifying misconceptions and providing sequenced hints or Socratic inquiries. The domain has experienced significant maturation: in contrast to earlier rule-based tutors, contemporary ITS frequently integrate structured domain models with large language model (LLM) dialogue to facilitate explanation and problem-solving. The attraction for TNE is readily apparent. In instances where synchronous support is hindered by time-zone discrepancies or staff workload, ITS can furnish just-in-time guidance at the moment of confusion rather than subsequent to a delay. A learner grappling with recursion in programming at 11 p.m. is capable of receiving incremental prompts that elucidate base and recursive cases, thereby maintaining momentum and alleviating frustration.

The evidential foundation is broadly optimistic. A comprehensive meta-analysis encompassing over a hundred comparisons revealed moderate to substantial effects of ITS on learning outcomes in comparison to traditional instruction (Ma et. al, 2014). These gains are not uniformly distributed impact is contingent upon design quality, task type, and alignment to desired outcomes but the principal finding remains consistent: when meticulously mapped to course objectives, ITS can approximate certain advantages afforded by human tutoring. Nevertheless, akin to adaptivity, productive struggle is pedagogically advantageous; should learners accept AI-generated hints uncritically, they risk forgoing the engagement that fosters durable understanding. Consequently, it is recommended that staff delimit hinting with reflective checkpoints (for instance, necessitating that a learner articulate the principle that underpins a step prior to disclosing the subsequent hint), and they should periodically localize domain ontologies and exemplars to ensure alignment with partner-site outcomes, documenting this alignment for external examiners as part of the program's quality file (Quality Assurance Agency for Higher Education [QAA], 2024).

Accountability assumes critical importance. Neither the QAA nor the Oman Academic Accreditation Authority (OAAA) prescribes or forbids the use of ITS; rather, both frameworks allocate ultimate accountability for learning quality to the program team. Consequently, providers must establish transparent human-in-the-loop protocols: detailing who samples tutor interactions, the frequency of overrides, the management of student complaints or appeals, and the evidence that illustrates the complementary role of tutoring in relation to teacher-student dialogue. Essentially, the effective employment of ITS is predicated less on technical sophistication and more on the institutional choreography that surrounds it.

Automated Assessment and Feedback

Artificial Intelligence presently facilitates the assessment of succinct responses, programming code, visual representations, and academic essays, as well as the formulation of constructive feedback regarding structural integrity, coherence, and mechanical precision. The historical development of automated essay scoring (AES) spans over three decades and is thoroughly documented in both comprehensive research analyses and practical implementation guidelines (Shermis & Burstein, 2013; Ramineni & Williamson, 2013; Attali, 2013). For extensive Transnational Education (TNE) cohorts, particularly at the freshman level, this capability can significantly reduce feedback turnaround time from weeks to mere hours, thereby assisting programs in fulfilling the requisite standards for prompt, actionable feedback—an aspect particularly emphasized in quality-assurance protocols. Furthermore, the reutilization of process-level comments (e.g., "clarify your warrant" in lieu of generic commendations) can enhance consistency among evaluators and locations while enabling faculty to concentrate in seminars on advanced reasoning skills rather than on textual editing.

Nonetheless, two enduring issues pertaining to validity necessitate careful consideration. Initially, a significant proportion of Automated Essay Scoring (AES) systems depend on proxies (such as lexical diversity, syntactic variation, and discourse organization) that are correlated with quality but may inadvertently undervalue originality or disadvantage non-standard dialects and features inherent to multilingual discourse (Attali, 2013). In contexts characterized by linguistic diversity, this presents a substantial risk to fairness. Furthermore, the numerical outputs generated by artificial intelligence can convey a misleading semblance of precision: a score of 72.4 may be misconstrued as an objective truth instead of a subjective assessment. An effective and pragmatic response entails the implementation of a hybrid marking model for all consequential evaluations: the system generates a score accompanied by formative comments; a calibrated sample of human assessors then verifies or modifies this score; and any discrepancies observed instigate refinements to the prompts, rubrics, or parameters of the model (Ramineni & Williamson, 2013). The documentation of this calibration process should be incorporated into routine programme monitoring and should be subject to review by external evaluators.

Design serves as a more effective mechanism for mitigating generative "over-assist" compared to mere detection. In contexts where LLM-based writing aids are implemented, it is imperative that tasks are structured to render the process explicit through staged submissions, annotated drafts, concise vivas, and data commentaries—thus enabling the demonstration of learning as a reasoned performance evolving over time rather than as a singular, refined artifact (Dawson, 2020). It is crucial to provide students with clear information regarding the instances of automation utilized, the specific aspects it influences, and the avenues available for contesting machine-generated suggestions. This level of transparency aligns with the principles espoused by both QAA and OAAAQA standards concerning fairness, clarity of information, and the amplification of student voice.

Predictive Learning Analytics

Learning analytics transform educational engagement traces such as interactions within virtual learning environments, attendance records, and assignment submissions into both descriptive and predictive metrics designed to enhance academic achievement. A decade prior, Ferguson (2012) recognized analytics as a pivotal element of technology-enhanced learning, concurrently warning that governance and interpretability would significantly influence public confidence. The ensuing literature within the sector has enriched both the technical framework and the ethical standards surrounding these practices (Sclater, 2017; Jisc, 2023). Within transnational education (TNE) contexts, the potential benefits are twofold: the provision of earlier detection of emerging risks and targeted interventions that prioritize support rather than defaulting to generalized remediation.

However, learning analytics should not be perceived merely as technical tools; they represent ethical practices that necessitate justification to both learners and faculty (Slade & Prinsloo, 2013). Three guiding principles warrant particular emphasis. Firstly, the principle of purpose limitation mandates that data collection and utilization be confined to educational support—excluding applications for ranking, surveillance, or punitive measures. Secondly, algorithmic accountability necessitates that the outputs generated are interpretable: advisors and educators ought to articulate, in accessible language, the rationale behind flagging a student, thereby circumventing the use of opaque composite scores whenever feasible. Thirdly, equity auditing is imperative. Diverse student groups, such as multilingual learners, scholarship recipients, or part-time employees, may display distinct patterns of interaction that are not necessarily indicative of their motivation or capability; unexamined models risk reinforcing existing structural disparities. Regular audits for bias, reviews of features, and the exclusion of problematic variables, when necessary, facilitate alignment with UNESCO's (2021) fairness recommendations and comply with local data protection legislation (Royal Decree 6/2022).

The implementation of these principles necessitates the establishment of systematic team practices rather than sporadic responses. Analytics huddles—briefly scheduled meetings wherein staff collaboratively review cases, determine appropriate outreach strategies, and document their rationales—generate a traceable decision-making record that enhances support mechanisms and fulfills quality assurance standards for documentation. In instances where models generate automated prompts, communication should be bilingual when relevant and framed as supportive offers rather than admonitions. Lastly, institutions ought to furnish students with clear privacy disclosures and consent choices, elucidating what data is collected, the purposes thereof, and the duration of data retention, thereby reinforcing trust in cross-border educational provision.

Multimodal Translation and Accessibility Tools

The advancement of Neural Machine Translation (NMT) and automatic speech recognition has significantly altered the landscape of accessibility. The transition from phrase-based methodologies to neural architectures has resulted in considerable enhancements in translation quality across a multitude of language pairs, particularly for non-idiomatic scholarly texts (Koehn, 2020). In multilingual Transnational Education (TNE) cohorts, real-time captioning facilitates access for Deaf or hard-of-hearing learners while also providing advantages to a wider audience by alleviating cognitive load; speech-to-text applications generate searchable documentation; and translation frameworks can mitigate obstacles in cross-site collaborative efforts. When contextualized within the framework of Universal Design for Learning (UDL), these modalities enhance the diversity of means of representation and expression, thereby presenting multiple avenues to engage with fundamental concepts (CAST, 2018).

Cultural fidelity, nonetheless, remains an aspect that cannot be eliminated through automation. Verbatim translations of culturally nuanced examples may perplex or estrange learners (e.g., idiomatic expressions that assume familiarity with "pub culture" or metaphors that depend on obscure sports). An uncomplicated post-editing process—a brief evaluation conducted by bilingual personnel or trained student mentors—can uphold the integrity of meaning while enhancing inclusivity. From a compliance perspective, service providers ought to ensure that digital content adheres to the WCAG 2.2 accessibility standards (W3C, 2024), particularly in relation to captions for pre-recorded video content and unambiguous focus indicators—and must guarantee that any audio/data streams transmitted to external services are minimized, encrypted, and, whenever feasible, processed within sanctioned jurisdictions, in accordance with Oman's Personal Data Protection Law (PDPL).

In aggregate, these five modalities exemplify a significant paradigm shift in focus. The primary challenge confronting Transnational Education (TNE) providers has transitioned from the decision of whether to "embrace AI" to the imperative of understanding how to integrate AI within sequences of human interactions—specifically, what transpires prior to, during, and following a student's engagement with a tool—and how to elucidate their methodologies to students, external evaluators, and regulatory bodies. Adaptive platforms exhibit substantial efficacy when employed to initiate classroom discourse; tutoring systems yield optimal results when moderated by reflective checkpoints and context-specific ontologies; automated assessment enhances value when coupled with human calibration and tasks that are transparent in their processes; analytics possess educational significance when directed by explicit objectives and bias assessments; and translation/accessibility instruments become transformative when incorporated into Universal Design for Learning (UDL) frameworks and culturally mediated for fidelity. In other terms, the pedagogical unit of analysis is not the instrument itself but the established routine—the systematically designed and documented cycle of sense-making in which software plays a role, while educators retain ultimate accountability.

For institutions implementing UK curricula in Oman, this human-centered orchestration simultaneously generates the documentation that quality assurance entities anticipate. Calibration documentation for automated grading, alignment frameworks for tutoring ontologies, audits of item banks for cultural appropriateness, notes from analytics discussions, and accessibility declarations aligned with WCAG standards collectively substantiate that AI is being deployed intentionally to foster equitable experiences, fairness, and transparency across diverse educational contexts. Such documentation not only meets external evaluative standards but also satisfies internal requirements for professional assurance: faculty members can articulate the functioning of the system, the rationale behind its operations, and the mechanisms in place to safeguard students in instances of error. The subsequent sections of this chapter expand upon this analysis by delineating the requisite competencies, workload models, and governance protocols essential for transforming these possibilities into standard practice rather than exceptional occurrences.

PEDAGOGICAL TRANSFORMATION AND FACULTY ROLES

Artificial intelligence (AI) transcends the classification of a mere instrument within the educator's arsenal; it fundamentally repositions the focal point of pedagogy from the mere dissemination of content to the intricate orchestration of the learning process. Within a teacher-centered framework, authority is predominantly exercised through didactic methods, including lectures, presentation slides, and established reading lists. Conversely, in an AI-enhanced educational paradigm, authority is established through the careful design of activity sequences (including diagnostics, adaptive learning, collaborative knowledge construction, and timely feedback) as well as through the prudent oversight of automation processes, most critically, discerning what automation should not undertake. Siemens' (2005) conceptualization of connectivism reconceptualizes learning as the ability to construct and navigate networks of information, individuals, and technological tools; through this perspective, AI enhances the facilitation of connections by aligning learner inquiries with curated resources, peer interactions, and expert elucidations. Laurillard's (2013) Conversational Framework introduces a supplementary focus: the quality of educational interactions is derived from the iterative dialogue between educator and learner at both conceptual and experiential dimensions. AI possesses the potential to sustain this dialogue on a large scale—for instance, by delivering formative prompts, process-oriented feedback, and visual analytics that reveal understanding patterns—or conversely, to disrupt it when systems lack transparency, misalign with intended outcomes, or are permitted to supplant rather than augment human engagement. In essence, technology does not inherently ensure effective pedagogy.

In the context of Transnational Education (TNE) frameworks prevalent in Oman—where UK-designed curricula are delivered in-person by locally appointed faculty and overseen by a UK accrediting body—the implications of this transformation are clearly observable. Tailored practice and expedited feedback can assist diverse cohorts in achieving uniform standards; nevertheless, it remains the academic team—rather than the technological tool—that bears the responsibility for maintaining validity, fairness, and the overall student experience (Quality Assurance Agency for Higher Education [QAA], 2024; Oman Authority for Academic Accreditation and Quality Assurance of Education [OAAAQA], 2024). The subsequent analysis aims to synthesize the evolution of pedagogy and academic roles in the integration of AI into routine practice, as well as to identify the essential capabilities and institutional support mechanisms required to implement these changes in a responsible manner.

From Broadcast to Dialogic/Networked Learning

Franchise delivery frequently prioritizes broadcast modalities, characterized by centrally produced presentation materials, recorded sessions, and a predetermined reading order disseminated to affiliated sites. Although this approach is efficient, it presupposes a uniform level of prior knowledge and a singular pace of advancement—assumptions that are seldom fulfilled within Transnational Education (TNE) cohorts. Teaching methodologies augmented by artificial intelligence advocate for a distinct framework—dialogic and interconnected—where students interact with concepts across diverse modalities and at individually suitable levels prior to the class session, subsequently utilizing synchronous time for sense-making, application, and critical analysis. A coherent, research-informed cycle may commence with a succinct diagnostic assessment (to uncover misconceptions), followed by targeted micro-content (to address specific challenges), then a seminar centered on conceptual negotiation and transfer, culminating in a post-class formative loop that provides process-level feedback and encourages learners to articulate changes in their understanding. Such sequencing aligns with the principles of constructive alignment (Biggs, 2003) and is supported by evidence indicating that timely, feed-forward guidance enhances learning when integrated into subsequent tasks (Hattie & Timperley, 2007; Nicol & Macfarlane-Dick, 2006).

The pedagogical objective is not to delegate explanation to a machine, but to externalize performance patterns in order to foster more precise and equitable classroom dialogue. A code assistant that suggests unit tests can initiate discussions concerning test coverage and edge cases; a writing assistant that identifies cohesion issues can provide a foundation for peer review focused on argument structure rather than superficial characteristics. Two critical design considerations are paramount for diverse TNE cohorts. Firstly, visibility is crucial: students must be able to comprehend the reasoning behind an adaptive engine's resource recommendation ("Your responses indicate confusion between conditional and joint probability; review this simulation"). Explainability is essential for maintaining agency and bolstering learners' metacognitive skills (Doshi-Velez & Kim, 2017). Secondly, plurality is significant: providing multiple pathways or exemplars (text, diagram, case vignette) acknowledges cultural-linguistic diversity and mitigates construct-irrelevant barriers, both of which are consistent with QAA expectations for transparent information and OAAAQA emphasis on equitable support (QAA, 2024; OAAAQA, 2024).

Faculty Competencies in the AI Era

The transition from a model of broadcasting to one of orchestration repositions the academic function around four interrelated competencies: data fluency, design agility, ethical governance acumen, and intercultural mediation. Initially, data fluency is conceptualized for pedagogical purposes rather than for surveillance. Dashboards typically represent metrics such as engagement counts, time-on-task, mastery probabilities, and indicators of "risk." The pedagogical interpretation of these indicators constitutes a cultivated skill. Educators are required to differentiate diagnostic signals (persistent errors related to a threshold concept) from extraneous noise (brief log-ins during holiday periods), circumvent prevalent fallacies (for instance, conflating correlation with causation), and triangulate data through prompt oral inquiries and focused mini-explanations. Within this context, data literacy is characterized as a conversational competence: converting indicators into constructive learning actions rather than merely enforcing compliance (Mandinach & Gummer, 2016; Sclater, 2017).

Second, the concepts of design agility and granularity are of paramount importance. Artificial Intelligence (AI) demonstrates optimal efficacy when intended learning outcomes (ILOs) are disaggregated into micro-objectives that systems are capable of recognizing and facilitating. The practical design endeavors encompass segmenting content into learning "atoms" that span 10–15 minutes, organizing the material to create desirable levels of difficulty (e.g., spaced retrieval and interleaving), as well as pre-authoring feedback stems linked to rubrics that are reusable without succumbing to genericity. These methodologies actualize the principles of constructive alignment (Biggs, 2003) and render the evidence trail discernible for both moderators and external examiners.

Third, the proficiency in ethical discernment and governance literacy is paramount. When a recommender guides a learner, or an automated grading system assigns a score, a sequence of ethical considerations is involved: What data sources were utilized? Are certain groups disproportionately affected? Is there an avenue for a student to challenge a machine's assessment? Academic personnel must possess a functional fluency in explainability (articulating model rationale in accessible terminology), proportionality (restricting critical decisions to human evaluation), consent (providing non-punitive opt-out options when practicable), and escalation (determining the appropriate circumstances to override a system). These standards are in accordance with the UNESCO (2021) Recommendation on the Ethics of AI and sector-specific guidelines that characterize learning analytics as an ethical endeavor necessitating explicit objectives and accountability (Slade & Prinsloo, 2013).

Fourth, the role of intercultural mediation in classrooms enriched with AI technologies is essential. Algorithms developed on English-speaking datasets may misinterpret multilingual expressions; instances may embed cultural biases; and speech-to-text systems may encounter difficulties with regional dialects. Faculty members serve as mediators—adjusting prompts, selecting culturally diverse examples, and deliberately instructing students on how to analyze AI-generated outputs through an intercultural perspective. Deardorff's (2006) framework is particularly relevant: the attributes of openness, self/other awareness, and interaction competencies are not incidental but rather integral objectives of design.This approach also fulfills the expectations set forth by the QAA and OAAAQA concerning inclusion and equitable support for students (QAA, 2024; OAAAQA, 2024).

A succinct developmental heuristic for staff can be encapsulated in the Four P's: Purpose (What educational objective does the AI fulfill?), Proportion (Is the degree of automation appropriate to the stakes involved?), Parity (Would a student from the home campus receive equivalent support?), and Privacy (What data is being collected and for what purpose?).

Professional Development and Communities of Practice

The distribution of these competencies implies that no singular workshop can effectively encompass the entirety of "teaching AI." Optimal professional learning is most accurately envisioned as a multilayered ecology that integrates awareness, design methodology, collaborative sense-making, and ethical contemplation. Scholarly investigations into professional development emphasize essential attributes content specificity, active engagement, collective participation, and sustained duration (Desimone,

2009), while the body of literature concerning communities of practice accentuates the significance of joint enterprise, mutual engagement, and a shared repertoire (Wenger, 1998).

A pragmatic ecology within Transnational Education (TNE) might initiate with foundational modules aimed at establishing a common lexicon (adaptivity, predictive analytics, explainability) and delineating responsibilities in accordance with the UK Quality Code and OAAAQA Standards. Subsequently, it should advance to design studios wherein interdisciplinary teams collaboratively develop AI-enabled activities pertinent to actual modules, iterating on micro-objectives, item banks, and feedback mechanisms; instructional designers and learning technologists should engage as co-creators rather than mere support personnel. Throughout teaching weeks, analytics huddles can offer brief, scheduled opportunities to scrutinize dashboards, juxtapose interpretations, and ascertain appropriate actions, normalizing uncertainty ("Is this a legitimate risk signal or merely a fifth-week decline?") and fostering a culture of "explain first, intervene second" (Colvin et al., 2017; Sclater, 2017). Ultimately, ethics rounds, systematic discussions of dilemmas such as an unhelpful chatbot response or a systematic bias in an auto-grader, enhance governance literacy; decisions and mitigations are documented in a shared playbook that serves as living evidence for internal evaluations and external assessments.

The significance of recognition cannot be overstated. Should institutions anticipate AI-enabled design and oversight, both workload and promotion criteria must duly acknowledge that labor. Micro-credentials in AI-in-pedagogy, program-level AI fellows, and expectations ingrained in peer-observation frameworks constitute practical mechanisms for advancement.In instances where programs are moderated by UK universities, joint professional development (involving staff from awarding bodies and faculty from partner colleges) bolsters the Quality Assurance Agency's aspiration for parity in learning experiences across different sites (QAA, 2024).

Workload Reconfiguration

Automation transforms the nature of work; it seldom eliminates it entirely. While the implementation of AI-assisted grading or feedback mechanisms has the potential to diminish the frequency of repetitive evaluations, novel forms of invisible labor arise: the curation of data, the verification of model outputs, the auditing for bias, the troubleshooting of edge cases, and addressing student inquiries regarding the rationale behind a system's behavior. Should institutions solely consider contact hours and the number of "scripts marked," the responsible deployment of AI will be fundamentally under-resourced.

Three principles help in this case. First, the initial phase of design entails genuine labor. The transformation of a module into an adaptive, feedback-intensive framework necessitates the establishment of item banks, the articulation of specific outcomes, the formulation of feedback prompts, the adjustment of configurations, and the execution of pilot studies. Such endeavors ought to be systematically scheduled and acknowledged, akin to the recognition given to laboratory preparation or the organization of field excursions. Second, the provision of algorithmic supervision represents a continual responsibility. Personnel require allocated periods to evaluate auto-graded submissions, to moderate ambiguous instances, and to juxtapose machine-generated assessments with human evaluations. In the context of high-stakes evaluation, a dual-evaluation framework—consisting of machine recommendations coupled with human validation on a calibrated sample—serves to mitigate the risk of misleading precision while conforming to established standards for dependability and equity (Ramineni & Williamson, 2013; Dawson, 2020; QAA, 2024). Third, disseminate expertise; circumvent the "AI-champion trap." A limited group of advocates can swiftly evolve into the unofficial support center, amassing after-hours "shadow work."Implementing role rotation (with analytics leadership this term and assessment leadership in the subsequent term), creating shared repositories, and allowing for modest release time can avert burnout and institutionalize expertise.

The concepts of well-being and boundaries necessitate deliberate consideration. Dashboards that refresh on an hourly basis may foster a state of continuous vigilance. Collaborative teams ought to establish regularized meeting frequencies (for instance, weekly evaluations), delineate triage parameters (such as the conditions under which a flag necessitates communication), and consolidate student-oriented messaging to prevent the dissemination of contradictory signals.Within the context of face-to-face interactions in Oman, straightforward practices, such as allocating the initial ten minutes of a tutorial to openly discuss trends in the dashboard, serve to confine analytics within designated timeframes while simultaneously modeling healthy academic behaviors.

Student Agency and Metacognition

Adaptive platforms are susceptible to conditioning students to simply comply ("click until green") rather than engage in reflective practices. The sense of agency is compromised when algorithms lack transparency ("the system indicates 72% mastery") or when tasks incentivize rapid responses and adherence to templates rather than fostering explanation and exploration. Should Transnational Education (TNE) aspire to nurture autonomous learners, artificial intelligence must be conceptualized as a collaborative entity that students can question, validate, and, at times, override. The existing literature on self-regulated learning is unequivocal: metacognitive monitoring and control encompassing planning, self-assessment, and strategic adaptation—are pivotal for sustained success (Zimmerman, 2002; Nicol & Macfarlane-Dick, 2006).

Four strategic design interventions reestablish agency within educational contexts. First, the provision of explainable feedback: to the extent feasible, elucidate the underlying rationales rather than merely presenting outcomes. Should an essay assistant indicate issues of cohesion, illustrate the specific transitions or discourse markers involved; if a problem-solving tool proposes a subsequent action, articulate the principle that has been invoked. Students ought to be encouraged to express their agreement or disagreement and substantiate their positions, thereby transforming feedback into a dialogue that aligns with Laurillard's theoretical framework (Hattie & Timperley, 2007; Laurillard, 2013; Doshi-Velez & Kim, 2017). Second, the implementation of process-visible assessment: augment product evaluations with process artifacts—such as draft histories, reflective notes, and brief oral defenses—so that learning is documented as a reasoned performance continuum; this approach also addresses concerns surrounding academic integrity in the context of generative assistance (Dawson, 2020). Third, the establishment of consentful analytics and alternatives: provide a no-penalty option for students who prefer not to have granular activity data inform personalized learning pathways; for instance, a learner might select scheduled check-ins instead of ongoing data-driven prompts. The documentation of such preferences honors individual autonomy and fulfills ethical responsibilities concerning the utilization of data (Slade & Prinsloo, 2013; UNESCO, 2021). Fourth, the cultivation of data literacy as a defined learning outcome: instruct students on how to critically interpret dashboards, what does the term "risk" signify, how can they evaluate the efficacy of an intervention, what biases may be inherent in a recommender system, and in what ways can they broaden their sources of knowledge? In multilingual cohorts, it is essential to pair these activities with language support—such as glossaries for analytical terminology and captioned screencasts—thereby reinforcing commitments to inclusivity as articulated in quality assurance codes and international ethical standards (QAA, 2024; UNESCO, 2021).

Artificial Intelligence is fundamentally transforming pedagogical practices and the roles of faculty within Transnational Education (TNE), not through the displacement of educators, but by reallocating the domains in which human discernment is critical. Within a traditional broadcast model, authority is vested in the act of exposition; conversely, in an AI-enhanced dialogic model, authority is manifested through the orchestration of conversations, the interpretation of signals, the modeling of ethical conduct, and the mediation of cultural and linguistic nuances. The competencies and frameworks for workload that emerge from this transition are not superfluous enhancements; rather, they constitute essential prerequisites for adhering to both the spirit and the letter of established quality standards. When educational institutions commit to comprehensive professional development, acknowledge the processes of design and oversight as legitimate forms of labor, and prioritize student agency in their frameworks, AI possesses the potential to augment educational outcomes while upholding principles of fairness, transparency, and equality—objectives that are central to the QAA and OAAAQA.

INTERCULTURAL AND QUALITY-ASSURANCE DIMENSIONS

Standard 1 — Governance and Management

First, the visibility and discipline of strategy are what make AI-enabled practices and governance work together. The QAA's Principle 1 says that "[t]he strategic approach to securing academic standards, quality assurance and enhancement is published, communicated clearly and accessible" and "monitored and evaluated on a regular basis," which is similar to what OAAAQA expects from the HEI. When predictive analytics, adaptive platforms, and generative feedback are used as institutional tools, they only meet these needs if their purpose is clear, their scope is limited, and their review cycle is set in stone. Laurillard says that analytics should not replace the discursive and reflective loops of the learning conversation, but should instead make them stronger. For example, early-alert dashboards should encourage bilingual human outreach instead of automated punishments. Siemens' connectivism makes this point stronger: AI should help students connect with more advisers, resources, and services, not push them down a single, unclear path that limits the knowledge network. Deardorff's model incorporates the intercultural requirement that grievance and escalation pathways be respectful and culturally comprehensible. QAA's Principle 12 says that complaints and appeals should be "robust, fair, transparent, and accessible," and that the results should be "used to support enhancement." This is in line with OAAAQA's requirement that "[s]tudents are provided with advice on the right of appeal... and the mechanisms used for appeals." In practice, this means that a chatbot can point out procedures, but all decisions are still made by people. Explanations are given in both Arabic and English, and data trails are used to help people learn instead of punish them.

Standard 2 — Coursework Learning

OAAAQA says that programs must follow the OQF and "incorporate graduate attributes" (2.1). They must also be designed with "ongoing external input from employers and the professions" (3.7(b) applied to coursework), and teaching must show "a defined and appropriate approach to teaching and learning... [which] incorporates the use of appropriate learning technologies and reflects contemporary pedagogies" (3.7(c)). Assessment must be "rigorously implemented" while "maintaining academic standards," with "grading and moderation" and "criteria... readily accessible and effectively communicated" (2.8(d); 3.6(a)), and institutions must ensure "academic security & invigilation" (2.9). Retention and progression data must be "analysed and evaluated... [and] externally benchmarked" (2.10(d–e)). QAA's Principle 7 says that "[a]ll programs and modules must meet academic standards... A clear set of documents is created that includes "external engagement and meaningful student involvement," while Principle 11 requires assessments that are "fair, reliable, accessible, authentic, and inclusive," consistent use of learning technologies, and "ongoing advice... about academic integrity."

AI-assisted curriculum mapping enhances OAAAQA 2.1 and QAA P7 when algorithmic recommendations are critically examined rather than uncritically accepted, with the justification documented in the official program records. Laurillard's design conversation is: AI helps make the connection between outcomes, tasks, and assessments clearer, but human thought keeps the ideas deep. Adaptive engines and intelligent tutoring systems can meet the requirements of 3.7(c) and P11, as long as the recommendations are clear, the pathways remain diverse (Siemens' many connections), and the item banks are checked for cultural relevance so that examples and language don't add unnecessary difficulty (Deardorff). Generative-AI feedback at the draft stage is in line with P11's focus on feed-forward, but high-stakes automated grading would go against OAAAQA 2.8 and QAA P11 unless human moderation and clear appeal routes are still important. Lastly, retention analytics meet the requirements of 2.10(d–e) and QAA's data-and-monitoring expectations when they are only used to help and not punish, outreach is respectful and bilingual (Deardorff), and impact is compared to other programs and reviewed.

Standard 3 — Research Programmes

OAAAQA says that research program designs must "align with the Oman Qualifications Framework," define "graduate attributes," include "external input," and work on a "regular cycle of review" (3.1(a–e)). Entry standards must be "appropriate, transparent, and consistently and fairly applied," and one of them must be "English language proficiency" (3.2(a–c)). Supervision relies on "appropriately qualified" supervisors who engage in ongoing professional development and have workloads that enable them to "monitor and review... effectiveness" (3.3(a–e)) within a "defined and appropriate" institutional framework that delineates roles, provides a handbook, facilitates monitoring, and "regularly reviews... effectiveness" (3.4(a–g)). Assessment must be "rigorous and fair," include "external examiners," and include "analysis of longitudinal trends" (3.6(a–d)). Integrity, ethics, and biosafety necessitate distinct policies, support and training, a clear prohibition of plagiarism, and regular reviews (3.8(a–e)). Destinations need "specified graduate employment targets," data that is "used to inform actions," and outcomes that are "externally benchmarked" (3.9(a–g)). Principles 7, 11, and 6 of QAA stress design/approval, research supervision, and assessment, as well as credible externality. Principle 10 stresses support.

AI can make writing specifications easier, but to meet 3.1 and P7, the documents must clearly state the OQF level, resources, external input, and review cadence. Siemens' connectivism here is a design ethic, programmes should be based on multiple disciplinary and professional nodes, not just one model's synthesis. Admissions can use language models to make sure that all the requirements are met, but they can't use them to make decisions. This is how the standards of 3.2's "appropriate, transparent, and consistently and fairly applied" are kept. When framed as support rather than surveillance, supervision analytics that track meeting cadence and response times respect Laurillard's iterative supervision conversation and put into action 3.3–3.4's requirements for role clarity and monitoring. Deardorff adds that communications and expectations should be bilingual and culturally sensitive. Assessment tools can look for problems ahead of time, but 3.6's requirement for "external examiners" means that only human examiners can make decisions and students must have "rigorous and fair" ways to appeal. Integrity (3.8) is bolstered when permissible applications of Gen-AI are distinctly delineated from unethical behaviour, transparency is obligatory, and supervisors authenticate sources and assertions. When destinations analytics help with benchmarking and taking action, but not with deterministic labelling, they meet 3.9.

Standard 4 — Staff Research & Consultancy

OAAAQA wants "a strategic approach to research" that includes "benchmarked targets," "appropriate structures and resources," and "regular monitor[ing] and review of performance" (4.1(a, d–f)). Performance systems should set "expectations for academic staff involvement," make sure that outputs are "recorded and acknowledged," encourage collaboration, and use "relevant benchmarks" and "differentiate between types of research output" to look at quality (4.2(a–e)). To get money, you need a "budget [that] is sufficient," "effectively managed" funds, internal grants and proposal support, clear "ownership... of resources," and a regular review (4.3(a–f)). Ethics and biosafety policies must be "informed by international research conventions," remain "separate," be overseen by a "high-level committee... including external experts," and be backed by "support and training" (4.5(a-e)). For professional development to work, there needs to be "needs-analysis," "structured PD," ECR support, appraisal linkage, and "regular review" (4.7(a–f)). Principles 1, 3, and 6 of the QAA (strategy, resourcing, and external review) are very similar.

AI-assisted horizon scanning and benchmarking help 4.1 as long as goals and limits are made public and resources are easy to find (QAA P3). Siemens' theory supports the idea that researchers should focus on building wider collaboration networks instead of chasing after small metric counts. Research Information Systems reach 4.2 when dashboards put quality over quantity, let employees put their work in context (Laurillard's reflective narrative), and give credit to different, community-facing, or non-Anglophone outputs (Deardorff's intercultural recognition). Funding pipelines (4.3) are in sync when language models help but don't write, IP and privacy are protected, and early-career researchers and Omanisation are clearly supported by internal grants. Guided forms and pre-checks help with ethics and biosafety (4.5), but committees, complete with outside members as per QAA P6—must make the final decisions. Professional development (4.7) is a natural win: personalised plans, mentor matching, and method briefs connect staff to dynamic scholarly networks (Siemens) and encourage collaboration across cultures (Deardorff).

Standard 5 — Industry and Community Engagement

OAAAQA wants a "well-defined, coordinated, and institution-wide approach" to engagement, active support for staff and student participation, "data on industry and community engagement," and "regularly review of effectiveness" (5.1(a–d)). With employers, institutions "maintain positive relationships," create "opportunities," set up "formal mechanisms" for program input and feedback, and "keep informed of relevant labour market requirements" (5.2(a–d)). In order to have professions, there must be a "institution-wide approach," monitoring for "responsive" curricula, "opportunity to contribute to the design and review," and "regular review" (5.3(a–g)). It is important to build relationships with other providers on a national and international level and to "regularly review" them (5.4(a–c)). To get alumni involved, there needs to be a "formal association," a "alumni database," regular information and participation, and "regular review " (5.5(a–d)). Institutions take a "strategic approach" with the community as a whole, run "community education," keep "regular contact with local schools," "share resources," and "regularly review" how well they are doing (5.6(a–e)). The landscape is shaped by QAA's Principles 1, 2, 3, and 8, which are strategy, students as partners, resourcing, and partnerships.

AI-enabled stakeholder mapping and labour market intelligence are in line with the QAA P2 standard when they expand the institution's networks (Siemens) and are verified by formal employer/professional panels. The QAA P2 standard is met when student representatives co-curate questions and interpret results, and when "how their views have impacted" curricula is made public. Placement matching engines are in line with 5.2. If the criteria are clear, there are options for people who want to use different modalities or locations, and complaints and appeals are handled by people, Deardorff's focus on reciprocity and respect is very important in GCC contexts. When human committees decide on risk, conflicts of interest are checked, and teach-out clauses protect students, due-diligence tools meet QAA P8. When consent is clear, communication is in two languages, and benefits are clear for both sides, alumni CRM and community engagement plans meet 5.5/5.6.

Standard 6 — Academic Support Services

OAAAQA says that planning for academic support must be "based on student learning needs," include non-standard modes/sites, assign senior responsibility, analyse the student profile, and be "regularly reviewed" (6.1(a–e)). Registry operations must be "efficient," have "policies and procedures" for security and confidentiality, keep "back-up files," enforce "privacy," and be "regularly reviewed" (6.2(a–e)). Library services must include physical and electronic resources, a "sufficient" budget, collection management, "support" for users, "accessibility," cataloguing to "established international practice," working together with other libraries, and "regular review". (6.3(a–i)). ILT services must define "appropriate use of the internet" and copyright, provide "adequate" budgets and support, plan for improvement, maintain IT "security," and be "regularly evaluate[d]" (6.4(a–h)). Academic advising must offer "regular opportunities," "monitor" risk, train advisers, protect "confidentiality," make sure staff is available, and be "regularly review[ed]" (6.5(a–f)). Student learning support should provide a "range of... services," accurately "identify" needs, be "equitable, supportive, and sensitive," assist students at risk and those with special needs, facilitate transitions, and undergo "regular review" (6.6(a–g)). Teaching resources must be effectively provided, adequate, "safe and accessible," respect "copyright," and be "regularly review[ed]" (6.7(a–e)). The UK uses QAA Principles 3, 10, and 11 (resourcing, support, and coherent technologies) as its anchors.

Planning analytics and multilingual routing chatbots meet 6.1 and P10 here, where the design is based on needs, works in both languages, and is clearly effective. Laurillard sees these systems as part of the institutional infrastructure that keeps the learning conversation going. Registry and ILT compliance depend on PDPL-style governance, encryption, role-based access, and proof of disaster recovery (6.2; 6.4(g)). If recommendation logic is explained, collections are culturally balanced, and information-literacy training teaches people how to think critically, AI discovery layers in the library can help Siemens' networked access to scholarship (Deardorff). Advising analytics are powerful, but they shouldn't be used to punish people. Flags should be clear, advisers should use their own judgement, people should be able to opt out, and privacy should be protected (6.5). Lastly, universal-design technologies like captioning, TTS, and accessible formats put Deardorff's intercultural stance into action while also meeting the "safe and accessible" requirements for teaching resources (6.7) and QAA P11's call for consistent approaches to technologies.

Standard 7 — Students & Student Support Services

OAAAQA says that services should be "appropriately resourced" under senior responsibility with "student input," and that arrangements should be "regularly reviewed for effectiveness" (7.1(a–e)). Institutions must "collect… trend data," critically analyse it, deliver provision that is "equitable, supportive and sensitive," and "regularly review" their approach (7.2(a–d)). A positive climate depends on a "systematic approach," student "representation" on bodies, a Student Council, "structured opportunities" for feedback with actions "communicated," events that "positively impact," and "regular review." (7.3(a–f)). Policies about behaviour must be "readily accessible," guarantee "appeals," make sure "prompt and appropriate action," keep "secure records," and be "regularly reviewed" (7.4(a–e)). Career services should give advice, be run by qualified professionals, gather information about the job market and destinations, keep students up to date on "national initiatives," and "review effectiveness" (7.5(a–f)). Finance needs "accurate information," "fair" help, formal deferral agreements, "financial counselling," and "regularly reviews" (7.6(a–e)). Housing, food, and transportation should be culturally appropriate, "safe and secure," and follow "cultural norms." Feedback should be acted on and "regularly review[ed]" (7.7(a–e)). Medical and counselling services must "identify needs," offer "emergency" support, employ "qualified staff," be "readily accessible," and undergo "regular review" (7.8(a–e)). International students must get "specific support services," suitable housing and welfare, and "regular review" (7.9(a–c)). Social and recreational services must provide "opportunities," "monitor participation," define "supervision," and "regularly review" with a focus on health and safety (7.10(a–d)). The most important QAA principles are 10 (support), 12 (appeals), and 2 (partnership).

AI is useful when it gives students a bigger voice and speeds up help. Multilingual chatbots and pulse surveys fulfil standards 7.1 and 7.3 by identifying needs and closing the feedback loop with clear "you said–we did" actions; according to Laurillard, the institution exemplifies the listen–act–reflect cycle. If their goal is to improve services and not spy on students, student-profile analytics meet 7.2. Small-n suppression and respectful bilingual messaging honour Deardorff's call for sensitivity and fairness. AI may be able to redact and summarise files for committees in case systems, but 7.4's promises of "appeal," "prompt" action, and secure records mean that automated disciplinary decisions are not allowed. AI fits well in careers. When calibrated to GCC realities and mediated by people for visa and gender sensitivities, NLP for the job market, CV assistants, and mock interviews all fit with 7.5 and QAA P10. Siemens would call this connecting learners to a dynamic employment network. Financial tools (7.6) should never automatically deny aid. Counselling tools (7.8) should connect users to qualified professionals, not act as diagnostic tools. International services (7.9) should have immigration content that staff has checked and analytics that users can choose to use. When they increase participation and keep safety visible, social and recreational recommenders (7.10) are appropriate.

Standard 8 — Staff and Staff Support

OAAAQA's human-resources framework calls for identifying "staff needs," "transparent" policies and a staff handbook, delegated authority, appropriate funding, and regular review (8.1(a–f)); a "appropriate" staff profile whose qualifications match needs and comply with ministry/PSRB/affiliate requirements (8.2(a–f)); recruitment governed by "policies," ensuring appointees are "appropriately qualified," with senior appointments made by governance, strict avoidance of COI, clear position descriptions and contracts, and "regularly reviews" (8.3(a–i)); "structured orientation" and a "handbook" (8.4(a–e)); PD policies "consistently applied," with "ongoing" opportunities for all staff and for students with teaching roles (8.5(a–e)); performance review with a "policy," "annual" participation, coverage of all staff, documented outcomes and "appeal" (8.6(a–f)); promotions with "clearly specified criteria," "fair and equitable" processes, and academic criteria including "teaching; research and scholarly activity;... service" (8.7(a–e)); severance aligned to labour law with "fairness," "appeal," exit interviews and records (8.8(a–e)); a "positive organisational climate," representation on bodies, feedback with action, grievance policies, benchmarking and staff activities (8.9(a–g)); and an Omanisation strategy with "ongoing commitment to achieving national targets," a "rigorous plan," PD for Omani staff, and regular review (8.10(a–d)). The UK equivalents of QAA's Principles 1, 3, and 11 are strategy, resourcing, and teaching ability.

AI helps meet these expectations by providing information for important HR decisions, but it never makes those decisions for you. If used for forecasting and getting information, not for making decisions, workforce planning models and HR chatbots meet 8.1 and P3. Skills-to-module matching (8.2) is helpful when the criteria are clear and manual oversight stops proxy bias. Deardorff's equity lens is very important to make sure that groups aren't hurt by indirect inference. Structured screening and anonymous shortlisting help with recruitment (8.3), but panels have to make decisions based on published criteria that show conflicts of interest. Induction and PD (8.4–8.5) are clear wins for Laurillard and Siemens. They include role-aware portals, micro-modules on assessment and the OAAAQA/QAA expectations, and PD recommenders that put teachers in the role of learners in a networked community of practice. AI can help with portfolios and evidence packs for performance and promotion (8.6–8.7), but algorithmic scoring doesn't fit with OAAAQA's requirements for "clearly specified" and "fair and equitable" criteria. Panels must set merit levels, making sure to include teaching and service in TNE. Severance is still an administrative matter; organisational climate analytics (8.9) must be anonymous and result in visible actions; and Omanisation (8.10) dashboards must connect to real professional development and advancement opportunities to show a "ongoing commitment to achieving national targets."

Standard 9 — General Support Services and Facilities

OAAAQA says that general services must "support its Mission," be planned through a "long-term strategy" made with input from "stakeholders," respect chances for "religious observance," and be "regularly review[ed]" (9.1(a–d)). Public relations and marketing must follow a "effective strategy" and be "appropriately funded," with activities that "meet high ethical standards, and accurately and truthfully represent" the HEI. There must also be monitoring of public opinion and "periodic review" (9.2(a–e)). Communication services need "appropriate systems," policies that promote "effective communication," and a "language policy... consistently applied," with periodic review (9.3(a–d)). Facilities management needs a "comprehensive strategy," compliance with "health and safety," oversight by senior staff, "adequate funding," and regular review (9.4(a–e)). The UK view is based on QAA's Principles 3 and 10 (resourcing and student support).

AI-enabled demand forecasting and service routing conform to 9.1 and P3 by ensuring a reliable and accessible campus environment, which is a prerequisite for the learning conversation in Laurillard's framework, and by accommodating scheduling and wayfinding to respect religious observance, operationalised through a "language policy… consistently applied" (9.3(c)). In public communications, content-assist tools are only acceptable if the outputs "accurately and truthfully represent" the programs (9.2(c)). To avoid drift, human sign-off against definitive program documents (QAA P7's "definitive set of documents") is necessary. Bilingual alerts, summaries, and captions put into action 9.3's language policy and QAA P10's promise to make information available to everyone. This expands the institutional communication network (Siemens) and makes it easier for people from different cultures to connect (Deardorff). When health and safety and environmental sustainability are the main factors, predictive maintenance and vendor oversight meet 9.4. This is because outsourced services are overseen by documented senior staff.

The quoted clauses in Standards 1–9 all agree on the same quality logic: approaches must be strategic, published, available in two languages, well-resourced, regularly reviewed, and fair, with clear ways to appeal. Laurillard's framework makes it clear when AI is useful for teaching: it speeds up and makes clearer the discursive-reflective cycle without getting in the way of human judgement. Siemens' theory makes the governance test clearer: AI is compliant when it expands networks, giving students, staff, and partners more equal access to resources and conversations, not less. Deardorff's model sets the standard for intercultural communication, showing that it should be respectful, easy to understand, and two-way, especially in Oman–UK TNE settings.

The same documentation shows compliance with all standards: a short policy/SOP that says what the scope and roles are; a configuration note that makes inputs, exclusions, and monitoring clear; a privacy/ Data Protection Impact Assessments (DPIA) record; checks for equity, accessibility, and language; examples of human oversight (moderation samples, committee minutes, chatbot hand-offs); an annual "you said–we did" effectiveness review; and a change-control log for updates to models or vendors. These pieces of evidence meet the OAAAQA's requirements for access, fairness, safety, regular review, and externality, as well as the QAA's requirements for strategic management, partnership, resourcing, coherent technology use, and strong appeals. This keeps AI firmly in the service of high-quality, interculturally competent learning.

FRAMEWORK FOR ETHICAL, QUALITY-DRIVEN AI INTEGRATION

Before setting out the framework, it helps to name its short form. GDDMRCPA captures the eight layers that structure responsible AI use in transnational higher education: Governance, Design & Procurement, Delivery & Support, Measurement & Evidence, Review & Enhancement, Cross-Cutting Enablers, Phased Adoption, and Alignment in Practice. The sequence reads as a lifecycle rather than a straight line: governance shapes design choices; delivery generates evidence; measurement informs review; cross-cutting enablers (such as data protection, accessibility, and student partnership) permeate every stage; phased adoption scaffolds change; and alignment in practice keeps the whole cycle anchored to quality codes. The layers remain explicitly mapped to OAAAQA standards and the UK QAA principles, and they are interpreted through Laurillard's Conversational Framework, Siemens' Connectivism, and Deardorff's Intercultural-Competence Model so that dialogic learning, networked knowledge, and intercultural respect function as design constraints. In this sense, GDDMRCPA names both an evaluative lens and an operational cadence for AI that is quality-assured and culturally attuned.

Governance

A framework for ethical, quality-driven AI in transnational education may commence with governance that is explicit, bilingual, and informed by theory. Institutions may first explain why AI is being considered and publish that explanation as a statement intelligible to students, staff, and partners in Oman and the UK. Such a statement may acknowledge Laurillard's view that digital systems are most valuable when they strengthen the iterative conversation of explanation, practice, feedback, and reflection; it may also recognise Siemens' account of learning as a property of networks, valuing technology when it extends connections to people, resources, and contexts rather than narrowing them; and it may remain alert to Deardorff's emphasis on the attitudes, knowledge, and skills that underpin intercultural competence. Governance arrangements may then assign responsibilities for policy, procurement, evaluation, and student partnership, and may normalise periodic review as part of routine quality work rather than as an emergency response to inspection. In this way, leadership may foster an environment in which AI is understood as supporting student achievement and development, never as a substitute for human judgement.

Design and Procurement

Design choices may flow from the governance stance and may favour configurations that maintain dialogue and keep design discussions visible. An adaptive learning engine, for example, may be preferred when it explains "why this next," offers multiple routes, and makes explicit how outcomes, activities, and assessments relate in ways tutors and students can discuss. Library discovery services may be tested for intercultural compatibility, ensuring that prompts, subject ontologies, and exemplar texts travel well across Oman–UK provision. Research units may evaluate grant-support tools with the recognition that assisted drafting remains formative, that researchers retain authorship and accountability, and that confidentiality and intellectual property are safeguarded. Contracts with technology providers may include clauses on change notification, accessibility standards, fairness re-testing after model updates, and exit/portability. Such agreements may be treated as living documents that anticipate iteration, allowing design to evolve as educators and students engage the tools.

Delivery and Support

Delivery across modules, services, and research supervision may be organised on the premise that AI accelerates feedback while preserving human oversight and learner autonomy. Formal remarks produced by large language models may sit alongside staged processes—plans, annotated bibliographies, and short viva elements, so that reflection remains visible and authorship remains with the learner. Early-alert analytics in advising may be framed as supportive invitations, preferably bilingual, that initiate human conversations rather than automated sanctions. Student assistants and chatbots may handle routing and signposting, while complex or sensitive matters remain with staff whose authority and confidentiality duties are clear. In research supervision, cadence and timeliness may be made visible to candidates and supervisors, enabling supportive intervention without sliding into surveillance. Careers tools in the GCC and UK may be calibrated to local labour markets and visa requirements, and finance calculators may be positioned as sources of information rather than gatekeepers of aid. In each case, AI may be used to quicken Laurillard's conversational loop and to extend the connections emphasised by Siemens, while communication styles and content continue to honour Deardorff's intercultural commitments.

Measurement and Evidence

Measurement may combine indicators and narratives to avoid metric myopia and to demonstrate quality through diverse forms of evidence. Academic standards and learning gains may be shown not only via rates and counts but also through moderation samples, external examiner reports, viva records, and reflective cases that make changes in practice legible. Progression and retention dashboards may include subgroup fairness checks, avoiding the use of protected characteristics in modelling. Survey and pulse data on student climate may be interpreted with student panels to ensure that culturally nuanced expressions are understood in context. In research, field-normalised indicators and open-science artefacts may be presented alongside narratives of community, professional, or policy impact. Together, these choices may satisfy audit requirements while remaining faithful to Laurillard's emphasis on explanation and reflection, Siemens' preference for multiple signals, and Deardorff's commitment to fair treatment across language and culture.

Review and Enhancement

Review and enhancement may be planned as bilingual, participatory exercises that render improvement a normal rhythm. At agreed intervals, staff, students, externals, and partners may convene around anchoring questions that keep the theoretical lenses active: how did AI alter the teacher–student conversation; did it widen or narrow students' networks; and was the experience respectful and intelligible across languages and cultures? Meetings may conclude with concise, time-bounded actions and named stewards, and subsequent reviews may open by checking progress against those actions. Summaries may be published in Arabic and English to sustain a visible "you said–we did" trail. Over time, this cadence may reposition enhancement as a shared scholarly practice rather than a compliance exercise.

Cross-Cutting Enablers

Certain capabilities may traverse all layers and determine whether the framework's ethical and quality intentions hold in practice. Routine impact assessments may record purpose limitation, access controls, retention periods, and human decision points, supporting data protection and academic integrity. Intercultural communication may be treated as an explicit quality criterion: templates for nudges, feedback, and policy notices may be composed and tested in two languages; assessment item banks may be reviewed for cultural relevance. Student partnership may shift from consultation to co-creation, with compensated student fellows contributing to instrument design, communication testing, pathway trials, and enhancement reviews. Tiered professional learning—covering AI literacy, process-visible assessment, universal design for learning, and leadership for policy and procurement—may build staff capability. Universal design checks and disparity analyses may continuously monitor accessibility and equity, triggering investigation and remediation where gaps appear. These enablers may help ensure that the values articulated in governance are enacted in everyday decisions.

Phased Adoption

Adoption may proceed in modest cycles that reduce risk and build confidence. An initial phase may establish a public charter and a small set of enabling policies, clarify roles, and assess the privacy and accessibility posture of existing tools. A second phase may pilot a limited set of use cases in teaching, student support, and research, each documented in concise design dossiers that state purpose, student choice, intercultural fit, and human oversight. A third phase may run those use cases with safeguards in place, collecting moderation samples, subgroup outcomes, and user-experience accounts. A culminating phase may synthesise short impact briefs and hold a participatory review to inform scale-up, pause, or redesign. The cycle may repeat, gradually raising ambition while preserving room for course correction. In this way, regulatory alignment may emerge as a by-product of disciplined practice rather than a last-minute compilation.

Alignment in Practice

When applied in this manner, the framework may naturally surface artefacts that demonstrate alignment with OAAAQA and the UK Quality Code: public statements, bilingual notices, moderation records, external examiner letters, equity cuts and bias audits, contract annexes describing algorithmic changes, and enhancement digests. Because each layer is grounded in Laurillard's conversational model, Siemens' networked learning, and Deardorff's intercultural competence, the value proposition of any AI use may be clearly expressed: to accelerate dialogue, strengthen connections, and respect cultural difference. Where a proposed use cannot credibly claim such contributions, the framework may legitimise deferral or refusal. In effect, institutional leaders and educators may employ AI responsibly in ways that satisfy quality regulators and honour cultural contexts, thereby supporting transnational provision that is more coherent, inclusive, and resilient.

Figure 1. Visual overview of the GDDMRCPA framework

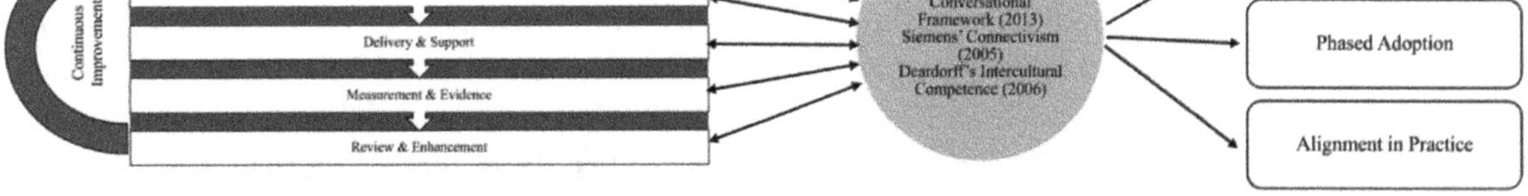

A lifecycle of five operational layers feeds a theory-anchored core (Laurillard, Siemens, Deardorff), making sure that AI use stays considerate of other cultures, connected, and dialogic. From this core, three enablers—Cross-Cutting Enablers, Phased Adoption, and Alignment in Practice—turn intent into ethical practice that can be audited and is part of a loop of continuous improvement.

RECOMMENDATIONS

The previous analysis and the framework together point to a list of institution-level priorities that meet OAAAQA standards and UK QAA principles in transnational settings while also adding educational value. The suggestions below bring those priorities together into a clear plan of action for leaders, program teams, and professional services. They are based on Laurillard's conversational view of learning, Siemens' connectivist view of networked knowledge, and Deardorff's model of intercultural competence. They also keep the quality regimes in Oman and the UK in mind throughout.

One suggestion is to make governance more stable by making a bilingual, institution-wide statement of purpose for AI in teaching, learning, research, and services that is clearly in line with the HEI's Mission. This kind of statement should be kept with the official program documents and the policy library. It should also link to the appeals and complaints processes. There are two benefits to this: it meets QAA's requirements for a "published, communicated" strategic approach, and it puts OAAAQA's requirements for "regulations, policies, and procedures... readily accessible and effectively communicated" into action. Laurillard's work frames the policy as a set of rules for how people and tools will talk to each other. Deardorff's work makes it clear that the policy is bilingual, which shows respect and reduces cultural friction. Siemens' work places AI as one of many nodes, not the main path.

When designing the curriculum and tests, there needs to be a gradual shift from automation to augmentation. Institutions should encourage program teams to use AI for mapping the curriculum, aligning outcomes, and giving formative feedback. However, they should still have human moderation for important decisions. This method keeps OQF-level claims and the QAA's demand for "fair, reliable, accessible, authentic, and inclusive" assessment intact. From a pedagogical standpoint, it enhances Laurillard's iterative cycle by accelerating feedback while preserving reflection, and through Siemens, it expands the avenues through which learners can engage with resources and tasks. The intercultural aspect is essential: item banks, examples, and feedback prompts must be evaluated for linguistic complexity and cultural contexts, and the program narrative must clearly mention graduate attributes that encompass intercultural and ethical awareness, as per Deardorff.

Student data ought to serve as a tool for assistance rather than punishment. The best way to protect early-alert analytics is for the institution to write down the purpose of the alerts, not use proxy variables that encode language or socio-economic status, and make sure that every alert is followed up with human contact. That pattern follows OAAAQA's rules about keeping and moving forward—collecting, analysing, and acting on data—while also following the QAA's focus on improvement based on evidence. It also fits the theoretical triad: analytics become the signal that starts a conversation between a teacher and a student (Laurillard), connects the student to new sources of help (Siemens), and is communicated in a way that is respectful and culturally appropriate (Deardorff). If students choose not to participate, there should be equivalent human check-ins available so that their choice doesn't put them at a disadvantage.

Academic integrity, ethics, and academic security necessitate a consciously balanced approach. When made clear, generative AI should be allowed for ideation, outlining, and language support. However, making up sources, lying about data, and ghostwriting are still not allowed. Detection technologies ought to be presented as advisory rather than conclusive; human examiners and moderators are responsible for making decisions and providing justifications, and students possess the right to appeal. Invigilation technologies and online proctoring must be evaluated for accessibility and cultural appropriateness. If a surveillance tool would erode trust or marginalise certain groups, the assessment design should shift towards authentic tasks that minimise opportunities for misconduct. This proportionality meets OAAAQA's requirements for assessment rigour and security, as well as QAA's request for clear, consistent approaches to technology. It also keeps Deardorff's focus on attitudes—openness, respect, and responsibility—at the heart of academic integrity education.

In research degrees and staff research activity, institutions should strengthen human oversight while updating their infrastructure. Dashboards that show cadence and timeliness instead of content surveillance can help improve supervisor quality. Research assessment should keep externality and clear criteria, and AI tools can help with pre-submission checks and viva preparation. On the staff side, research information systems that focus on quality signals instead of counts and let people tell their side of the story are in line with what QAA says about metrics. Guided forms, case libraries, and training recommenders can help improve ethics and biosafety, as long as high-level committees with outside members are still the ones who make decisions. These changes keep OAAAQA Standards 3 and 4 in place while using Laurillard's "concept–practice" dialogue for research supervision and Siemens' network logic for collaborations and open-research practices.

Student services should be restructured into a bilingual, multi-modal network that prioritises accessibility. Chatbots that route questions, 24/7 micro-supports for study skills, and planning for counselling or career services can help reach more people across time zones and locations. However, they need to be clear about when to escalate to a human and what they can't do (no clinical diagnosis, no automated financial denials). Careers tools should be based on the realities of the local job market and visa requirements. International students should also get immigration information in plain language that has been checked by staff. This setup meets OAAAQA Student Standards for planning, climate, finances, careers, medical and international services, and it also meets QAA's Principle 10 by helping students through transitions. It also puts Deardorff's model into action by making service communication more sensitive to language and culture.

AI can help with discovery and coordination in partnerships with businesses, professions, and other service providers. However, human panels should still be in charge of due diligence, curriculum changes, and placement decisions. These panels should keep track of conflicts of interest and fairness issues. Alumni involvement should be seen as a two-way street, with mentoring, advisory roles, and feedback on the curriculum all happening through agreed-upon data practices. The win here is both regulatory and educational: OAAAQA's standards for engagement and QAA's principle of partnership are both met, and Siemens' connectivism is put into action through rich, two-way networks that go beyond the classroom.

Staff capability is the most important part of the whole plan. Schools should spend money on role-aware induction and ongoing professional development that covers AI-pedagogy, honest assessment, accessible design, intercultural communication, and basic data ethics. PD activity should be acknowledged in terms of workload and promotion, ensuring that the incentives emphasised by OAAAQA correspond with the standards established by QAA for the quality of teaching and supervision. According to Laurillard, teachers are always learning and having conversations with their students. According to Deardorff, teachers are culture-bearers who show students how to use AI and where its limits are.

Academic standards should be used to make procurement and vendor governance stricter, not just technical ones. Contracts should spell out where data is stored and how long it should be kept, as well as accessibility requirements (like WCAG 2.2), model update notices, exit plans, and the academic right to override or add to automated sequencing with human judgement. A small, cross-functional committee made up of people from different areas, such as instruction, law, data protection, and student representation, should review tools against a written checklist before they are used and at least once a year after that. This keeps the provider in line with OAAAQA's rules about governance and security, as well as QAA's expectations for technology approaches that are clear and long-lasting.

Lastly, institutions should see evidence as a valuable asset and make a "quality file" for AI-related practices that is light but consistent. For each use case—analytics, tutoring, formative feedback, proctoring, chatbots—the file would have the policy/SOP, a configuration or "model card," a privacy/DPIA record, an accessibility and equity check, examples of human oversight (moderation samples, hand-off logs, committee minutes) and an annual "you said—we did" effectiveness review. Program teams would use these artefacts in their yearly reviews, and external examiners and OAAAQA reviewers would find the same evidence. Students would see a summary in both Arabic and English that was open to the public. This one habit that isn't tied to any one field of study closes the loop that Laurillard imagined, spreads trust across the network in Siemens' sense, and shows the attitudes and skills that Deardorff links to mature intercultural practice.

These suggestions do not assume that AI will make things better; instead, they see AI as a set of tools that can be useful but also make mistakes. When used carefully, these tools can make conversations more interesting, connect more people, and build more respect between people from different countries. That position is what keeps the pedagogy sound, the quality defensible, and the promise of transnational education between cultures alive.

CONCLUSION AND FUTURE RESEARCH

This chapter contends that artificial intelligence in transnational higher education is optimally perceived not as a collection of deterministic efficiencies, but as a provisional infrastructure for dialogue, connectivity, and intercultural development. Based on Laurillard's Conversational Framework, Siemens' Connectivism, and Deardorff's Intercultural-Competence model, the analysis went through the OAAAQA standards and the UK QAA principles clause by clause to show where AI practices fit, where they don't, and what kinds of evidential controls turn promise into quality that can be defended. The GDDMRCPA framework was the end result. It gives leaders and teachers a way to use AI that works for all subjects and meets the needs of regulators and cultural differences.

Three conclusions can be drawn. First, pedagogical value arises when AI enhances the conversational cycle without supplanting it. Predictive analytics, intelligent tutoring, and generative feedback enhance learning solely when they elicit human explanation, encourage student autonomy, and make processes transparent for scrutiny and appeal. Second, educational justice relies on the breadth of the network instead of the accuracy of the algorithms. Tools that expand connections to advisers, resources, employers, alumni, and external examiners enhance both QAA expectations and OAAAQA standards, while tools that channel learners into a singular, unclear pathway diminish autonomy and compromise trust. Third, language access, a respectful attitude, and giving and receiving are all ways to achieve intercultural legitimacy. Bilingual policies, culturally vetted item banks, appropriate security measures, and clear complaint processes are not just nice things for administrators to do; they are what make cross-border learning feel fair.

The framework indicates that institutional success will not depend on a singular "AI strategy," but rather on a coordinated set of minor, verifiable practices that collectively meet quality standards. Written scope limits, model cards, bias and accessibility checks, committee minutes, moderation samples, vendor clauses and 'you said—we did' reports make up the paper and practice trail that outside reviewers expect and students deserve. When those artefacts are combined with authentic student collaboration and staff development, AI serves as a tool to recalibrate judgement rather than supplant it.

Nonetheless, there are constraints regarding the assertions that can be derived from conceptual analysis and policy alignment. The researchers still don't know much about how AI changes the way people teach, supervise, and provide services in Oman-UK transnational ecosystems. Consequently, subsequent research ought to progress from compliance mappings to a multi-site, mixed-method investigation of impact, mechanisms, and unintended consequences. Longitudinal studies could ascertain whether early-alert systems genuinely enhance progression and mitigate inequities when opt-outs, language preferences, and alternative support pathways are provided. Realist evaluations could examine the contingent assertion that AI functions "for whom, in what contexts, and why," with particular focus on campus culture, program discipline, and partnership models. Design-based research could facilitate intelligent tutoring and formative feedback in situ, positioning teachers and students as co-investigators and generating design principles applicable across various programs and locations.

A significant empirical agenda focusses on fairness and explainability within multilingual, multicultural cohorts. In addition to audits of item banks, prompts, and rubrics, there should be ethnographic studies of how students understand AI feedback in English and Arabic, how supervisors handle authorship when students admit to using AI, and how appeals panels think about outputs from detection tools that are questioned. Cross-disciplinary comparative research would elucidate whether construct-irrelevant language load is more pronounced in specific assessment formats and identify the most effective scaffolding methods—such as vivas, process memos, and annotated drafts—that maintain authenticity without overwhelming staff. From a methodological standpoint, integrating subgroup performance analytics with qualitative interviews would enable researchers to correlate distributional disparities with actual experiences of inclusion or exclusion.

The labour implications for faculty also require meticulous scrutiny. Time-and-motion studies, workload diaries, and cost models could examine the prevalent assumption that AI diminishes the time required for grading and advising. Preliminary evidence indicates a redistribution of effort rather than a reduction—characterized by diminished mechanical commenting and increased moderation, explanation, and appeals—resulting in significant implications for resource allocation and promotion. Research on supervisor dashboards should assess whether the "support, not surveillance" framing is perceived as intended, and whether cadence metrics inadvertently disadvantage projects with significant fieldwork or community engagement that adhere to alternative temporal frameworks.

In assessment security, the field needs side-by-side tests of different designs that don't rely on intrusive proctoring as much. Authentic, context-specific tasks, oral defences, and data commentary assessments may enhance integrity while incurring lower privacy costs; however, their validity, reliability, and scalability across extensive TNE cohorts are still uncertain. Experimental and quasi-experimental designs could evaluate learning outcomes, student stress, appeal rates, and staff workload across various assessment configurations, producing evidence that may inform both OAAAQA reviews and QAA guidance.

Infrastructure and procurement constitute an additional domain for research exploration. Case studies of vendor governance—data residency, model update notices, exit strategies, and accessibility compliance—might reveal contractual clauses that effectuate behavioural change, rather than merely embellishing policy documents. Network analyses of interactions among alumni, employers, and partners would reveal whether AI-enabled CRMs merely amplify existing relationships or authentically diversify engagement in ways that benefit under-served student populations. Siemens' focus on distributed knowledge communities provides both a theoretical framework and a metric: the network's health serves as a proxy for the health of TNE.

Intercultural competence, although referenced throughout this chapter, requires direct assessment and intervention evaluation. Tools based on Deardorff's model could be used in programs that explicitly teach students how to use and criticise AI across cultural and linguistic lines. Randomised or stepped-wedge designs could assess whether such instruction alters the quality of student-teacher dialogue, the tone and receptivity of appeal, and the equity of peer collaboration in AI-mediated environments. Concurrent studies involving staff could investigate whether professional development that integrates AI literacy with intercultural communication alters classroom practices and enhances student satisfaction.

Lastly, regulatory practice itself is worth studying. Collaborative "sandbox" pilots with OAAAQA, UK partners, and higher education institutions (HEIs) in Oman could test documentation bundles, audit sampling methods, and transparency statements for students. These pilots could create templates that take into account the unique aspects of TNE while still being comparable to the UK Quality Code. Such work would shift the discourse from compliance anxiety to collective exploration of what constitutes reliable evidence in the context of rapidly evolving and fallible technologies.

The potential of AI in transnational education is neither inherent nor deceptive. It depends on dialogic pedagogy that keeps people in the loop, networks that open up opportunities instead of closing them off, and intercultural practices that see language and culture as assets instead of barriers. The GPS-PIPE framework gives you a way to keep those conditions stable while still following the rules and spirit of quality codes. The research agenda outlined here encourages the field to evaluate, enhance, and, if necessary, contest its assertions. If future work maintains a productive tension among theory, evidence, and culture, AI will continue to serve as a facilitator of cross-border learning rather than an unchallenged authority.

REFERENCES

Attali, Y. (2013). Validity and reliability of automated essay scoring. In M. D. Shermis & J. C.

Baker, R. S., Walonoski, J., Heffernan, N., Roll, I., Corbett, A. T., & Koedinger, K. R. (2008). Why students engage in "gaming the system" behavior in interactive learning environments. *Journal of Interactive Learning Research, 19*(2), 185–224.

Biggs, J. (2003). *Teaching for quality learning at university* (2nd ed.). Open University Press.

CAST. (2018). *Universal Design for Learning guidelines version 2.2.* https://udlguidelines.cast.org/

Corbett, A. T., & Anderson, J. R. (1995). Knowledge tracing: Modeling the acquisition of procedural knowledge. *User Modeling and User-Adapted Interaction, 4*(4), 253–278. DOI: 10.1007/BF01099821

D'Mello, S. K., & Graesser, A. C. (2023). Intelligent tutoring systems: How computers achieve learning gains that rival human tutors. In Schutz, P. A., & Muis, K. R. (Eds.), *Handbook of educational psychology* (4th ed., pp. 603–629). Routledge., DOI: 10.4324/9780429433726-31

Dawson, P. (2020). *Defending assessment security in a digital world: Preventing e-cheating and supporting academic integrity in higher education.* Routledge. DOI: 10.4324/9780429324178

Deardorff, D. K. (2006). Identification and assessment of intercultural competence as a student outcome of internationalization. *Journal of Studies in International Education, 10*(3), 241–266. DOI: 10.1177/1028315306287002

Desimone, L. M. (2009). Improving impact studies of teachers' professional development: Toward better conceptualizations and measures. *Educational Researcher, 38*(3), 181–199. DOI: 10.3102/0013189X08331140

Doshi-Velez, F., & Kim, B. (2017). Towards a rigorous science of interpretable machine learning. *arXiv preprint arXiv:1702.08608.* https://arxiv.org/abs/1702.08608

Dunn, L., & Wallace, M. (2006). Australian academics and transnational teaching: An exploratory study of their preparedness and experiences. *Higher Education Research & Development, 25*(4), 357–369. DOI: 10.1080/07294360600947343

Hattie, J., & Timperley, H. (2007). The power of feedback. *Review of Educational Research, 77*(1), 81–112. DOI: 10.3102/003465430298487

Jisc. (2023, September). *AI in tertiary education: A summary of the current state of play* (3rd ed.). Jisc.

Jisc. (2025, July 2). *Global education and technology: Digital challenges associated with the effective delivery of transnational education.* Jisc.

Jivet, I., Scheffel, M., Schmitz, M., Robbers, S., Specht, M., & Drachsler, H. (2020). From students with love: An empirical study on learner goals, self-regulated learning and sense-making of learning analytics in higher education. *The Internet and Higher Education, 47*, 100758. DOI: 10.1016/j.iheduc.2020.100758

Koehn, P. (2020). *Neural machine translation.* Cambridge University Press. DOI: 10.1017/9781108608480

Kunnan, A. J. (2018). *Evaluating language assessments.* Routledge.

Labadze, L., Grigolia, M., & Machaidze, L. (2023). Role of AI chatbots in education: Systematic literature review. *International Journal of Educational Technology in Higher Education, 20*(1), 56. DOI: 10.1186/s41239-023-00426-1

Laurillard, D. (2012). *Teaching as a design science: Building pedagogical patterns for learning and technology*. Routledge., DOI: 10.4324/9780203125083

Ma, W., Adesope, O. O., Nesbit, J. C., & Liu, Q. (2014). Intelligent tutoring systems and learning outcomes: A meta-analysis. *Journal of Educational Psychology, 106*(4), 901–918. DOI: 10.1037/a0037123

Mandinach, E. B., & Gummer, E. S. (2016). What does it mean for teachers to be data literate: Laying out the skills, knowledge, and dispositions. *Teaching and Teacher Education, 60*, 366–376. DOI: 10.1016/j.tate.2016.07.011

Monitor, I. C. E. F. (2024, December 11). Continued growth reported for UK transnational education enrolments. https://monitor.icef.com/

Mulla, T., Munir, S., & Mohan, V. (2023). An exploratory study to understand faculty members' perceptions and challenges in online teaching. *International Review of Education, 69*(1-2), 73–99. DOI: 10.1007/s11159-023-10002-4

Nicol, D. J., & Macfarlane-Dick, D. (2006). Formative assessment and self-regulated learning: A model and seven principles of good feedback practice. *Studies in Higher Education, 31*(2), 199–218. DOI: 10.1080/03075070600572090

Oman Authority for Academic Accreditation and Quality Assurance of Education. (2022). *Standards for higher education*. https://www.oaaaqa.gov.om/

Oman Authority for Academic Accreditation and Quality Assurance of Education. (2024, February). *Institutional Standards Assessment Manual* (Version 2).

Quality Assurance Agency for Higher Education. (2020a, December 21). *How UK higher education providers managed the shift to digital delivery during the COVID-19 pandemic*. QAA.

Quality Assurance Agency for Higher Education. (2020b, May 20). *Effective practice in UK transnational education during the COVID-19 pandemic*. QAA.

Quality Assurance Agency for Higher Education. (2023, January 30). *The rise of artificial intelligence software and potential risks for academic integrity: A briefing paper for higher education providers*. QAA.

Quality Assurance Agency for Higher Education. (2024). *UK Quality Code for higher education*. Author. https://www.qaa.ac.uk

Ramineni, C., & Williamson, D. M. (2013). Automated essay scoring: Psychometric guidelines and practices. *Assessing Writing, 18*(1), 25–39. DOI: 10.1016/j.asw.2012.10.004

Royal Decree No. 6/2022 issuing the Personal Data Protection Law. (2022, February 9). *Official Gazette* (No. 1429). https://decree.om/2022/rd20220006/

Sclater, N. (2017). *Learning analytics explained*. Routledge., DOI: 10.4324/9781315679563

Shermis, M. D., & Burstein, J. C. (Eds.). (2013). *Handbook of automated essay evaluation: Current applications and new directions*. Routledge. DOI: 10.4324/9780203122761

Siemens, G. (2005). Connectivism: A learning theory for the digital age. *International Journal of Instructional Technology and Distance Learning*, *2*(1), 3–10.

Slade, S., & Prinsloo, P. (2013). Learning analytics: Ethical issues and dilemmas. *The American Behavioral Scientist*, *57*(10), 1509–1528. DOI: 10.1177/0002764213479366

Solano-Flores, G. (2011). Assessing the cultural validity of assessment practices. In Basterra, M. R., Trumbull, E., & Solano-Flores, G. (Eds.), *Cultural validity in assessment: Addressing linguistic and cultural diversity* (pp. 3–14). Routledge.

UNESCO. (2021). *Recommendation on the ethics of artificial intelligence*. https://unesdoc.unesco.org/ark:/48223/pf0000381137

Universities UK. (2021, November 29). *Lessons from the pandemic: Making the most of technology in learning and teaching*. Universities UK.

van Leeuwen, A., Teasley, S. D., & Wise, A. F. (2022). Teacher and student-facing learning analytics. In C. Lang, G. Siemens, A. F. Wise, D. Gašević, & A. Merceron (Eds.), *Handbook of Learning Analytics* (2nd ed., pp. 129–140). SoLAR. DOI: 10.18608/hla22.013

Wallace, M., & Dunn, L. (2013). *Teaching in transnational higher education*. Routledge. DOI: 10.4324/9780203930625

Wenger, E. (1998). *Communities of practice: Learning, meaning, and identity*. Cambridge University Press. DOI: 10.1017/CBO9780511803932

Wise, A. F., Knight, S., & Ochoa, X. (2021). What makes learning analytics research matter. *Journal of Learning Analytics*, *8*(3), 1–9. DOI: 10.18608/jla.2021.7647

World Wide Web Consortium. (2024). *Web Content Accessibility Guidelines (WCAG) 2.2*. https://www.w3.org/TR/WCAG22/

Zimmerman, B. J. (2002). Becoming a self-regulated learner: An overview. *Theory into Practice*, *41*(2), 64–70. DOI: 10.1207/s15430421tip4102_2

Chapter 4

Academic Integrity and Artificial Intelligence in International Delivery:

An Omani TNE Perspective

Janaki Sivakumar
https://orcid.org/0000-0003-0412-1515
Global College of Engineering and Technology, Oman

Mehmet Aydin
https://orcid.org/0000-0002-4890-5648
University of the West of England, UK

V. M. Basanthy
https://orcid.org/0009-0002-2588-0940
Global College of Engineering and Technology, Oman

ABSTRACT

The Integration of Artificial Intelligence (AI) into teaching and learning in Higher education provides both opportunities and risks for preserving academic integrity, particularly within Transnational Education (TNE) contexts like in Oman. This Study analyses and evaluate How AI tools are reshaping ethical standards in teaching and learning. AI tools such as Plagiarism Detector and Automated Grading are mainly integrated into teaching and learning. Omani Higher education Institutions plays a vital role in maintaining educational values in local and global standards. This highlights the need for transparent and well-structured regulations and ethical standards to govern AI use. This chapter explores the impacts of AI, a dual role player as facilitator of learning and adopting technologies as well as a potential risk producer to integrity, accountability and cultural sensitivity in TNE environment. The chapter discusses, regulatory redesign and policy revision requirements to map with AI technology developments.

DOI: 10.4018/979-8-3373-5403-3.ch004

EXPANDING HORIZONS: TRANSNATIONAL EDUCATION IN THE OMANI CONTEXT

The higher education sector in Oman has undergone a substantial transformation in recent years characterized by the rapid evolution of transnational education. This evolution highlights both the growing demand for various academic pathways and Oman's drive to strengthen its place within the global education field. A key driver of this evaluation has been the government strategic initiative aimed at expanding educational delivery. The creation of Oman Academic Accreditation Authority (OAAA) for instance has provided a strong governing and quality assurance framework making Oman an attractive target for international universities seeking partnership with local HEI's (higher educational institutions) (British et al., n.d.).

Through these partnerships students in Oman now have opportunities to a broader range of academic degree programs which in turn cultivates a multicultural learning environment that integrates local and global perspectives (Alfayez et al., 2025). Research suggests that the integration of overseas pedagogical models and teaching approaches has contributed to energizing domestic higher education by broadening access to quality learning prospects (Sun Y, 2025). By embedding international courses, TNE has promoted innovation in teaching practices and confronted traditional teaching practices, thus addressing skill gaps that earlier inadequate students' readiness for employment markets (Zheng et al., 2023). Importantly these changes align with Oman's vision 2040 which highlights the need for progressive educational structures proficient of responding to global economic shifts (Bannister et al., 2024). In this way TNA has become a promoter of restructuring knowledge sharing and cultural integration through external partnerships (Yankova, 2024).

Integration of Artificial Intelligence in TNE

The development of transnational education in Oman has been strengthened by technological innovations particularly through the adoption of artificial intelligence (AI).Institutions increasingly adopt AI not only for academic delivery but also for administrative effectiveness resulting in efficient operations and improved educational outcomes (Yao and Collins,2019). AI tools in grading and assessment for instance have strengthened academic integrity by improving plagiarism reductions and preserving scholarly standards within internationally connected programmes (Palmer, 2021). This technological integration demonstrates the interaction between local and international practices, as AI driven systems ensure precision under transparency while accepting diverse educational methodologies. AI is therefore emerging as in essential tool within TNE supporting both quality assurance and the trustworthiness of Omani qualifications in international contexts.

Challenges to Academic Integrity in TNE

Despite its many benefits, the rapid expansion of TNE in Oman raises complex challenges, particularly concerning academic integrity. The existence of diverse educational frameworks can result in scaled expectations and diverse understandings of integrity among students from different cultural backgrounds (Kang P.E, 2022). Inadequate preparation for transnational educational environments may increase the risks of academic misconduct, threatening the authenticity of scholarly work. With growing reliance on AI based tools these risks become more noticeable as technologies can both safeguard and unexpectedly compromise integrity if not used correctly. Consequently, the development of strong institutional policies and ethical frameworks is critical to mitigate misconduct guaranteeing that students are well concerned with and directed toward ethical engagement with the AI driven tools falls directly on TNE providers, demanding proactive training and awareness programs (Sun Y, 2025).

Policy, Collaboration, and Stakeholder Engagement

Maintaining high standards of integrity within TNE requires strong partnership among universities accreditation authorities and government bodies effective policies must not only associate with institutional best practices but also replicate the specific cultural and educational needs of women this dual focus protects the quality of Omani qualifications while simultaneously improving the nation's international reputation. As TNE expands, it is vital to withstand discussion around the ethical use of AI in education. Stakeholders must work together to ensure that technological development and academic standards evolve together. International partnerships, accreditation process and regulatory frameworks all play a role in reinforcing Oman's educational reliability (Mumtaz et al., 2024).

Toward a Resilient and Ethical TNE Framework

The success of transnational education in women depends on its capacity to hold innovation while upholding the principles of academic integrity. Constant monitoring of AI integration and its influence on ethical academic practices is important in shaping a strong framework for the future. Furthermore, ongoing stakeholder partnership ensures that challenges are addressed mutually strengthening the shared accountability of safeguarding quality education. In essence Oman's TNE expansion not only replies to growing educational demands but also provides an opportunity to reflect on the core values by supporting academic practice. Balancing globalization with the integrity ensures that Omani higher education remains trustworthy modest and skilled of preparing students for the challenges of an interrelated world (Karim Abdallah et al., 2025).

IMPORTANCE OF ACADEMIC INTEGRITY IN AI DRIVEN LEARNING

Academic integrity is an important factor in the quality of education that represents honesty, trust and ethical content. In today's rapidly changing higher educational landscape, artificial intelligence poses both opportunities and challenges to maintain academic integrity. Although AI tools can support learning through personalization, efficiency and improved research capabilities, they also introduce new risks such as plagiarism, collusion, and authorship ambiguity (Mumtaz et al., 2024)Generative AI models such as ChatGPT can generate coherent human like content that is difficult for traditional plagiarism detection tools to identify creating a post plagiarism era where originality and authorship are harder to verify. Hence, safeguarding academic integrity in AI driven education is essential to preserving the credibility and value of academic qualifications while using AI responsibly. This is also a concern In Oman, where Vision 2040 emphasizes on improving educational outcomes and equipping graduates with employability skills, productivity. And competitiveness for both local and international labor markets. Achieving these goals requires not only technological innovation, but also the protection of integrity and fairness across all educational levels. Graduate attributes in Oman's higher education system highlight ethical responsibility, innovation, and global competence, all of which rely on preserving academic honesty in an AI enhanced environment.

Defining Academic Integrity in the AI era

Academic integrity has traditionally been defined as a commitment to six fundamental values, namely honesty and trust. Fairness, respect, responsibility and courage as defined by International Center for academic integrity. However. With the rise of generative AI, these definitions require reinterpretation. AI's ability to produce essays, translations, and paraphrases that evade plagiarism detection challenges traditional notions of originality and authorship.

This new reality compels higher education institutions to go beyond surveillance-based misconduct detection and adopt proactive strategies that integrate academic integrity into teaching, assessment, and student development.

The importance of preserving academic integrity

In transnational education (TNE) particularly UK affiliated programs in Oman, academic integrity is not only a moral expectation but also a foundational requirement for sustaining institutional credibility, fairness and student development. As AI reshapes educational practices upholding integrity ensure that learning outcomes are genuine, educational qualifications remain trustworthy and graduates can thrive as ethical professionals in global contexts (Gruenhagen, J. H.et al., 2024; Alfayez et al., 2025). Hence, a strong commitment to academic integrity in the age of AI is important for various reasons.

Safeguarding Institutional Repetition. A university's reputation depends on the authenticity of its academic work. When qualifications reflect genuine student knowledge, stakeholders, including employers and regulators, retain confidence. AI introduces risks, but tools such as ChatGPT can generate polished content that bypasses conventional detection undermining degree credibility (Currie, G. M.,2023). In UK, Oman, transnational education, reputational damage affects both hosts and home institutions, making integrity a shared priority.

Ensuring General, Genuine Skill Development. Higher education aims to cultivate critical thinking, research capacity, and subject mastery. Requiring original, well-cited work ensures students engage meaningfully with learning materials, developing competence for future careers. By contrast, AI generated shortcuts bypassing cognitive engagement, weakening educational outcomes (Gruenhagen, J. H.et al., 2024). Hence preserving integrity guarantees that students achieve intended learning outcomes and develop transferable skills.

Protecting the Fairness of the Academic Environment. Academic integrity policies establish a level playing field where students are assessed equitably. Misuse of AI undermines fairness, disadvantaging students who adhere to ethical standards (Gruenhagen et al., 2024). Research shows that students do not perceive AI assisted work as misconduct unless explicitly prohibited (Currie, G. M.,2023), underscoring the importance of clear institutional policies. Fairness ensures that trust in assessment systems is preserved across TNE.

Cultivating Ethical and Responsible Scholars. Education's influence extends beyond academic performance because it shapes character. Education shapes not only academic performance but also ethical character. Encouraging students to acknowledge use of AI and critically evaluate AI output promotes reflective reasoning and ethical awareness. Rules alone are insufficient but students who internalize why certain AI practices undermine learning are more likely to act responsibly. Embedding these values supports Oman's Vision 2040's aim of producing principled and innovative graduates (van et al., 2023).

Strategies for promoting integrity in an AI driven environment

Given the challenges of AI in higher education, institutions must adopt proactive, multifaceted strategies to sustain academic integrity such as:

Redesign Assessments. Traditional assessments such as essays and multiple-choice exams are easily compromised by AI. So redesigning assessments to emphasize authenticity, application and critical reflection reduces misconduct. Gallent-Torres (2023) propose AI resistant assessment frameworks that incorporate scaffolding, oral defenses, and real-world projects. Similarly, Hamad, H. A., & Charles, T. (2024) recommend aligning assessments with higher order learning outcomes to limit AI substitution.

Promote AI Literacy. AI Literacy, i.e. understanding AI's capabilities, limitations, and ethical use is important for both students and staff. Training initiatives should clarify acceptable practices, emphasize citation of AI outputs and promote responsible use. Gallent-Torres (2023) demonstrate that policy and pedagogical dimensions of AI literacy correlate strongly with improved learning outcomes. Gallent-Torres (2023) also note that many students remain unclear about AI boundaries, highlighting the need for structured guidance.

Create a Culture of Integrity. Institutions should embed integrity as a cultural value across curricula and campus life. Abulaiti M (2024) highlight leadership, commitment, mentorship and transparent honor codes as a vital factor to reinforcing integrity. Palmer A (2021) further shows that peer norms and open discussion of AI plagiarism. Shaped students' ethical perceptions, suggesting that values driven culture is more effective than punitive policies.

Cultivating a Culture of Academic Integrity in Higher Education

Preserving integrity requires shared responsibility between students, faculty, and institutions. In transnational contexts like Oman, where cultural norms differ from UK standards developing this culture is critical to ensure equivalence and trust in qualifications.

Role of Teachers. Faculty members play the central role in promoting integrity through course design, clear communication, and ethical modeling. Palmer A (2021) reports that educators are motivated to redesign assessments not only to prevent misconduct but also to align with professional expectations in the AI era. Kang et al., (2022) highlights that teacher training in AI literacy and transparent classroom practices strongly influence student behavior, reinforcing integrity across the institution.

Role Of Student. Students play an active role in maintaining academic integrity by declaring AI use, engaging in AI literacy programs, and adhering to ethical guidelines. Roe et al., (2024) found that many students lack clear understanding of plagiarism and integrity boundaries, emphasizing the need for explicit instruction. Roe et al., (2024) further observes that students often disapprove of direct AI authorship but are uncertain about subtler uses, suggesting that students should be engaged in policy development to clarify expectations.

ALIGNMENT OF ACADEMIC INTEGRITY WITH OMAN VISION 2040

The strategic alignment of academic integrity within the context of artificial intelligence resonates extremely with Oman Vision 2040, which aims to develop the country's educational landscape by nurturing an innovative and sustainable knowledge economy. Highlighting the importance of establishing a demanding academic integrity model, the integration of AI tools in educational contexts demands care of ethical considerations, thus refining an environment encouraging to trust and credibility in transnational education. This is particularly relevant as Oman aspires to pivot towards a knowledge-based economy, where the educational sector is vibrant in nurturing human capital and enabling the workforce to succeed in a competitive global arena.

Strengthening Integrity in AI-Enabled Education

A strong academic integrity framework serves as a foundation for achieving this vision while supporting the current educational practice evolution in Omani institutions. The increasing adoption of AI systems in educational settings generates fresh learning methods that need immediate updates to integrity standards for this developing environment (Yankova et al., 2024). The government ensures high educational standards through AI integration which protects academic integrity to prepare students for future workforce requirements with essential ethical values and abilities. Studies conducted by Bannister and his team show that educational methods based on integrity enable students to acquire skills for continuous learning and develop their critical thinking abilities (2024).

Institutional Responsibilities and Ethical Standards

The educational institutions operating in Oman need to create an academic honesty culture that uses AI technology to enhance their educational delivery system according to Oman Vision 2040. The combination of AI's personalized learning features with real-time feedback allows teachers to teach integrity as a core principle which helps students acquire essential academic and ethical skills needed for globalized world challenges (Li et al., 2023). The implementation of AI skills in educational systems creates new challenges for student data protection and academic dishonesty which affects the entire educational quality assurance system (Zheng, C., & Ouyang, H,2023). The main responsibility of institutions demands them to unite technological advancements with established ethical principles. The educational sector has adopted inclusive strategies for AI governance as its main priority during this time. The strategies need to handle ethical matters and student data privacy while promoting transparency and responsibility which form essential elements of academic integrity (Mattar et al., 2022).

Future Path Toward Achieving Oman Vision 2040

The method of integration reveals that academic integrity needs both ethical practices in education and active technology adoption to achieve Oman Vision 2040. The relationship between AI tools and academic integrity maintenance demonstrates why educational development remains essential because it prepares students to fulfil both national and international standards of knowledge (van et al., 2023). The path towards Oman's future vision demands an ongoing focus on creating fair and open educational spaces towards global leadership and creative breakthroughs. The combination of integrity with technological progress will enable Oman to achieve Vision 2040 by creating a sustainable socio-economic environment (van et al., 2023).

CHALLENGES OF AI ADOPTION IN EDUCATIONAL SYSTEMS

The rapid adoption of artificial intelligence systems within educational framework creates more complex problems which test established academic integrity principles. Higher educational institutions that integrate new technologies for teaching and learning and assessment development are creating new opportunities for cheating which forces educators and policymakers to evaluate current integrity system

Impact of AI Tools on Student Learning and Thinking

The major academic issue arises from students' easy access to AI tools which help them with writing and problem solving thus potentially reduces their original thinking, creativity and ability to solve the problems. Students who want to succeed in their academic models find AI powered applications which produce essays and helping them to solve complex math problems with minimal user input and show a shortcut method to get quick results. Higher education institutions need to create some specific guidelines for AI tool usage to secure academic integrity whereas other technology should serve as an enhancement tool for learning (Gallent-Torres et al., 2023).

Transnational Education and Cultural Challenges: The incorporation of collaborative transnational education model faces additional difficulties due to the nature that they operate across multiple different academic frameworks which have distinct integrity standards the authorship of work and AI usage obviously creating more cultural challenges resulting in academic environment for students and educators becoming more complex (Bannister et al., 2024).

Privacy and Ethical Concerns in AI-Based Proctoring:Introduction of AI based proctoring systems creates technical dilemmas about student privacy and educational practices. Implementation of technology for assessment integrity purposes weakens student rights which creates the sarcastic situation where transparency measures produce student distrust (Murugan et al., 2024).

Need for New Assessment and Teaching Competencies

The upcoming educational challenges prove that AI enables innovative teaching and learning models. But at the same time, it requires higher educational institutions need to review assessment and examination policies as well as separate AI usage policy and intellectual property policy to preserve academic integrity (Li et al., 2023). The transnational educational environment needs educators to develop new competencies to map with current technological improvement. Educators must perform two primary duties which include teaching the curriculum as well as educating students about academic integrity principles. The way AI operates creates a need for extensive training to faculty members to find and handle AI related academic misconduct cases (Roe et al., 2024).

Inequalities and Regional Challenges in Oman's TNE Programs

The challenges in using AI become more complex due to the nature of transnational education programs in Oman because they face inconsistent educational quality across different regions of Oman. Improper use of AI tools and lack of ethical guidelines for AI tool usage creates learning disparities, because some students can use technology more competently, but others do not receive adequate support (Yusuf et al., 2024).

Risks of Academic Dishonesty and Misinformation

The broader nature of availability of information along with AI based assessment work production will intensify the problem of honesty. The research shows that there is a need for strong educational framework to handle these critical issues (Holden C,2018).

Collaboration for Policy and Ethical Frameworks

Collaboration between educational institutions and policymakers and technology developers to find a solution to AI related academic integrity problems will create an effective transnational educational system. The development of high standard educational programs which train and educate students and staff about AI ethics is more important to help them to handle this complicated situation (Gallent-Torres et al., 2023).

International Delivery and Flexible Systems for Integrity Protection

The most important process of policy review and the development of best practices will help to build an academic environment that supports and boosts technological advancements while securing academic standards. Rapid growth of technological development leads us to create new models for protecting academic integrity which will transform current educational system. The transnational educational system delivery demonstrates the necessity to create more flexible and friendly system to protect academic integrity as technology advances (Zheng et al., 2023).

AI TOOLS IN TNE

The integration of artificial intelligence tools into the development of international program delivery signifies a paradigm change that expansion expands educational opportunities while simultaneously rising major concerns regarding academic integrity. As institutions increasingly adopt AI technologies like adaptive learning platforms, automated assessment and feedback systems, these tools not only enhance the efficiency of teaching and learning delivery but also necessitate a rigorous examination of their impact on ethics and academic integrity (Zlotnikova et al., 2025).AI driven analytics can provide educators with invaluable insights into student performance and learning designs thus facilitating personalized learning experience tied to individual needs however this technological intervention raises questions about integrity and the potential for bias in AI algorithms which could unintentionally undermine the integrity of assessments and outcomes delivered through these tools (Zheng et al., 2023).

Examples of AI Tools in Teaching, Learning, and Assessment

AI technologies are being widely adopted across transnational education for various purposes. Word cloud in Figure 1, clearly highlights various AI tools used in Higher Education. In teaching and learning, tools such as *ChatGPT, Google Bard, and Socratic* assist in customized content delivery and concept explanation. For assessment and feedback, systems like *Gradescope, Turnitin, ExamSoft, and Proctorio* provide automated evaluation, plagiarism detection, and Microsoft Insights support educators by tracking student progress and identifying learning gaps. In addition to that, AI based adaptive learning systems like *Coursera Smart Learning, Century Tech, and Knewton* personalize instructional paths, thereby improving engagement and retention across diverse transnational learning environments.

Figure 1. AI tools in higher education

Cross-Cultural Challenges in AI Adoption

Moreover, the integration of AI in programme delivery is also accompanied by a unique set of challenges in the land of cross-cultural understanding of academic standards. Different educational systems have varying descriptions and opportunities of integrity, thus complicating the integration of AI tools that must accommodate to a diverse student body (Yusuf et al., 2024). Recognizing this, institutions engaged in transnational education must invest in educational efforts that not only update students about the ethical use of AI but also map these tools with the diverse values upheld in various cultural frameworks (Zlotnikova et al., 2025).

Collective Approaches and Institutional Responsibility

The connection between AI tools and educational delivery models through collective approaches becomes apparent according to studies about international student mobility and academic collaboration. The successful implementation of AI technologies in transnational education requires collective participation according to Yankova (2024). As highlighted in discussions surrounding the ethical inferences of AI in education, institutions must prioritize the launch of detailed procedures that guide the execution of these tools, ensuring they are used to foster an environment of integrity rather than compromise. Additionally, the dynamics of AI in education demands an ongoing dialogue about ethical and legal frameworks, particularly in defending against misuse and safeguarding academic rigor (Zlotnikova et al., 2025). This is especially relevant in the context of Omani transnational educations providers who are operating within a global educational landscape that is constantly growing.

Professional Development and Institutional Commitment

Educators need continuous professional development and training because it supports them handle AI tool difficulties which supports academic uprightness according to Yankova (2024). Educational institutions need to find a proper balance between AI innovation acceptance and ethical compliance while they examine all AI-based transnational program delivery options. AI tool success depends on both methodological investments and deep institutional dedication to academic integrity because violations of these standards will damage educational trust relationships (Mattar M Y, 2022). Educational stakeholders including institutions and students and policymakers need to work together to create environments that support AI progress while maintaining academic integrity standards (Mumtaz et al., 2024). AI tools can transform international program delivery through better teaching methods and student learning, but their successful deployment depends on strong academic integrity systems. The blend of innovation with ethical standards will shield academic standards while building faith in international education curricula which will endure their long-term success. The use of AI tools in Omani education will continue to be a vital topic for discussion because institutions try to find academic excellence in their global educational initiatives.

DIVERSITY IN STUDENT DEMOGRAPHICS AND LEARNING EXPECTATIONS

A prominent characteristics of the transnational educational landscape particularly in the context of Oman's transnational education strategies is the diversity in student demographics and their accompanying learning opportunities the demographic profile of student pursuing international education in multifaceted surrounding varying ages nationalities and educational backgrounds this heterogeneity influences not only the learning opportunities of the students but also the success of various delivery models employed in transnational education programs research has indicated that higher education students often come with distinct inspirations and commitments compared to traditional students thereby demanding tailored pedagogical approaches that cater to their specific needs(Sbaffi L &Zhao X 2022).

AI-Enabled Learning and Academic Integrity Concerns

The evolution of delivery modes driven by advancements in technology such as AI enabled learning platforms and adoptive learning management systems helps learners by providing personalized learning experiences and effective feedback mechanisms. Thus higher education institutions must critically evaluate how this AI based models can enrich the learning experience while upholding the principles of academic integrity .At the same time the integration of AI and technology raises important questions regarding academic integrity also known as honesty- an area that has been increasing scrutiny ask easy access to information and auto automated solutions to launch language models presents challenges for maintaining ethical practices the demand for transparency in assessment and feedback becomes important map students are placed in an environment that utilizes air driven AI driven assessments where the risk of academic misconduct can increase if it is not properly monitored integrity (Zlotnikova et al., 2025). The incorporation of technologies should follow robust framework that addresses academic integrity concerns by ensuring that they are in line with the diverse learning expectations of learners across various demographic profiles. Educational institutions in Oman are not only connecting the power of AI to enhance learning but also creating an environment that enforces the importance of ethical standards in transnational education (Zlotnikova et al., 2025)

Impact of Delivery Modes on Student Satisfaction

The existing literature says there appears to be tell me a crucial link between the effectiveness of different delivery modes and student satisfaction levels studies have shown that student who engaged in technology-based learning environment offend report higher levels of satisfaction and engagement compared to existing learning environment settings (Abulaiti M,2024). Figure illustrates a Framework for Enhancing Student Experience through various delivery modes and technology adoptions by understanding learner's demographic and expectations. This is crucial for Omani institutions that are competing on an international platform as they must not only attract diversity of students but also empowering their educational setup to enhance overall learning outcomes.

Figure 2. Student educational enhanceent framework

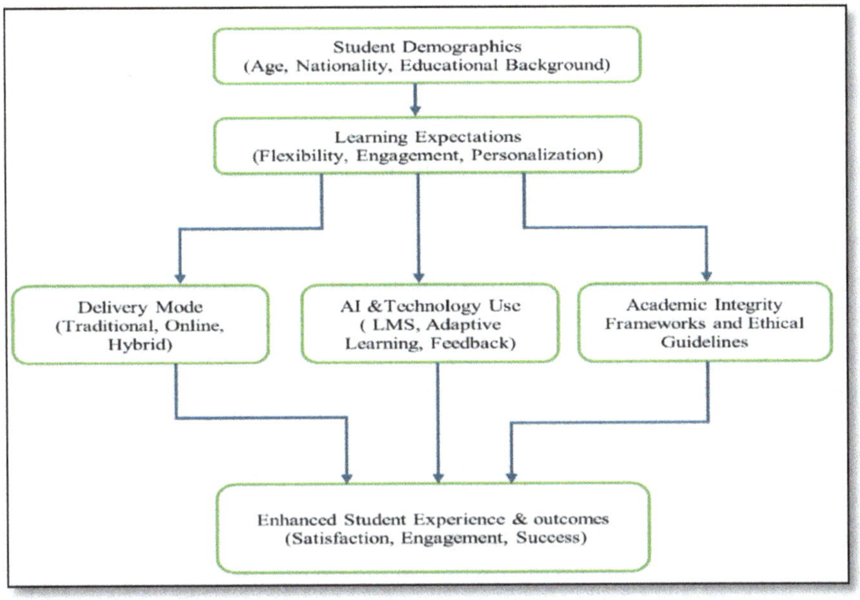

Recommendations for Balancing Technology and Ethics

Educational system must understand how different student groups interact with their learning needs and teaching methods to achieve academic excellence and maintain educational integrity. The long-term success of Oman's transnational education initiatives depends on accomplishing a balance between AI based educational enhancement and preserving ethical academic standards (Abulaiti M,2024). Educational stakeholders who focus on these crucial elements will develop a framework that supports diverse student needs and secures academic integrity in our globalized transnational educational environment.

REGULATORY AND POLICY CONSIDERATIONS IN OMAN

Academic integrity needs a complete set of policy and regulatory measures to adapt to AI and international education delivery because Oman faces difficulties in matching its educational standards to global benchmarks while dealing with AI integration in transnational learning.

Alignment with Global Best Practices

The current legislation of Oman need evaluation to find their effectiveness in managing the multifaceted challenges that AI system present. The development of particular law points should focus on avoiding academic dishonesty while creating conditions to promote innovative learning and ethical standards (Murugan et al., 2024).The Ministry of Higher Education in Oman needs to create specific guidelines which outline proper AI tool usage in academic environments. The ministry should adopt existing AI education policies from jurisdictions with advanced regulatory systems including the European Union and the United States (Ansah S D, 2025)

Risks, Responsibilities, and Policy Development

The implementation of AI in educational environments creates three main dangers which include students using AI to plagiarize work and skip traditional learning methods and devalue the worth of earned academic credentials. Oman needs to establish precise definitions for academic integrity standards which should include AI-assisted assessment submissions and ChatGPT and other generative technology usage. Gemini AI and CoPilot for learning and assessment purposes (Tran et al., 2022).The proposed AI regulatory framework needs to establish particular definitions of student and higher education institution duties to maintain academic integrity through proper ethical AI tool implementation ((Li et al., 2023).. Educational institutions should receive support to develop programs which teach AI awareness to students and teachers for building an environment based on integrity and accountability (Mumtaz et al., 2024).

Governance and Oversight Mechanisms

Oman needs to achieve a proper equilibrium between developing innovative educational methods and protecting the academic credentials issued by its educational institutions. A regulatory organization needs to exist for the purpose of overseeing how educational AI standards get properly executed. Such a body would be responsible for conducting regular assessments of AI tools' effectiveness, as well as verifying compliance with established academic integrity standards (Hamad, H. A., & Charles, T., 2024). In this focus it becomes more evident that day major role of continuous professional development for higher education educators is indispensable. Development programs focusing on the ethical standards of AI in education must be enhanced. Educators with these skills will effectively mentor the students in navigating the complexities of AI technologies responsibly (Li et al., 2023). The Table 1 presents a summary of Oman's main regulatory areas and their corresponding challenges and proposed policy solutions to achieve global standard alignment and academic integrity and institutional responsibility and regulatory oversight and faculty development.

Table 1. Regulation areas, challenges and risk, proposed actions

Areas Of Focus	Challenges And Risks	Proposed Actions
Align with global standards	The absence of AI-specific education policies creates a risk that the country will not meet international standards.	The government should implement the best global practices from EU/US and create national guidelines for AI usage.
Academic Integrity Risks	Plagiarism and AI-generated work that avoids learning outcomes threaten to devalue the value of qualifications.	Academic institutions need to create AI-inclusive academic integrity policies which should include specific rules about AI-assisted submission methods.
Institutional Responsibilities	The lack of awareness about these policies and the inconsistent way they are enforced	The institution needs to create its own code of conduct and require all staff and students to undergo training about ethical AI practices.

continued on following page

Table 1. Continued

Areas Of Focus	Challenges And Risks	Proposed Actions
Regulatory oversight	The education sector lacks a central authority to oversee AI implementation in educational settings.	The government should establish a national regulatory body to perform AI tool audits and effectiveness assessments and maintain compliance standards.
Faculty development	Educators unprepared to handle AI-related ethical issues	Educators need ongoing professional development that teaches them about AI ethics and responsible AI use and effective teaching methods.

Enforcement, Collaboration, and Stakeholder Engagement

A complete policy strategy needs to include systems for reporting academic misconduct alongside established procedures to address AI-related offenses. The system requires detailed protocols for misconduct cases along with appropriate disciplinary actions to prevent future violations((Li et al., 2023). The country should join forces with international organizations to create academic integrity enforcement standards which follow the best practices worldwide (Suntharalingam P, 2025).Oman will enhance its global education standing through international dialogue participation while obtaining vital knowledge to build its domestic regulatory framework (Healey N M, 2023).The success of Oman's regulatory framework for this domain depends on ongoing involvement from all stakeholders including students and policymakers and educators. The policy creation process will achieve success through stakeholder involvement which will result in academic integrity standards that enable AI technology to enhance educational delivery (Abulaiti M,2024).

Building a Future-Ready Education System

A unified strategy to develop educational integrity and innovation must exist because digital learning tools have become more prevalent in educational systems integrity (Zlotnikova et al., 2025). The development and continuous improvement of these policies will protect academic standards while creating an environment that supports ethical innovative practice development (Li et al., 2023). The implementation of academic integrity principles in regulatory frameworks will bring substantial benefits to Oman because it will maintain both domestic and international competitiveness and trustworthiness for its higher education system (Bannister et al., 2024).The development of complete regulatory systems will determine how academic integrity will evolve in Oman's changing educational system which AI technology continues to transform (Suntharalingam P, 2025). Oman will establish itself as a model for ethical AI education implementation which will guide other countries dealing with comparable educational challenges.

PROMOTING THE CULTURE OF INTEGRITY AND AI LITERACY

Higher education institutions use artificial intelligence to enhance their teaching and learning alongside assessment methods by integrating AI into their educational framework. The delivery of programs through transnational education in different demographic locations with different cultures creates both positive and negative impacts while using AI in educational framework due to this change. AI technologies such as adaptive learning platforms automated grading systems and predictive analysis can you improve efficiency and support learning experience. Parallelly they also create potential negative impacts which will become a threat two basic principles of academic integrity higher educational institutions need to monitor proper use of AI resources why they are students and faculty are you sing AI to enhance their teaching and learning experience. To achieve academic integrity and AI literacy, higher educational institutions need to learn how to balance both (Suntharalingam P, 2025).

Academic practice needs ethical values to function as its essential foundation.

In transnational education both staff members and students enter the system with unique cultural beliefs about academic integrity hence academic integrity stands up their monetary base for call higher education system to achieve honesty and fairness along with accountability. HEI's need to implement these principles through their policies and classroom practices. Since students started using a generator content for their learning and assessment support, which makes it difficult in differentiating the amount of work they produced, and AI generated content. To overcome these difficulties higher educational institutions should establish clear definitions of misconduct in relation to AI usage to guide students in understanding ethical engagement (Bannister et al., 2024).

Students need to develop their AI literacy skills

Promoting AI literacy is the base for developing the culture of responsible usage of technology in education.AI literacy needs understanding, implementation and limitations of AI usage. Integration of AI literacy into the curriculum allows and supports the student to assess AI tool outputs and while learning when to use them in academic work (Mattar M Y, 2022).

Students can acquire AI information evaluation competencies through classroom activities that integrate ethical AI use discussions into their work and research projects and assignments. The methods help students acquire technical competencies and moral knowledge which enables them to recognize ethical academic behavior from unethical actions (Mattar M Y, 2022)..

Faculty Development and Professional Training

The educational staff at schools serves as leaders who establish an environment of integrity to teach students about proper AI ethical conduct. Many faculty members do not possess enough understanding about new technologies and their effects on academic integrity. Educational professionals need professional development programs to learn new skills for working in modern educational environments. AI integration into teaching practices demands that faculty members participate in workshops and resource guides and collaborative forums to learn proper implementation methods which safeguard ethical standards (Mumtaz et al., 2024). The training program for faculty staff must teach them to identify AI-generated content while creating new assessment techniques to minimize cheating and defining proper usage guidelines for digital tools.

The training sessions supports educators teaching their students about ethical usage to maintain academic integrity when using AI through their actions to produce own contents in assessments at the same time the training program the awareness sessions enable students to maintain academic integrity by keeping play educators as role models

Collaborative Initiatives and Institutional Partnerships

The development of academic integrity and AI literacy needs AI transnational educators to work together with each other. When higher education institutions forms alliances with the technology providers and accreditation bodies to achieve global academic standards, the outcome will focus on Global academic standards. They work collaboratively together for joint research projects knowledge sharing networks and for the creation of ethical standards to secure academic integrity by adopting AI integration (Abulaiti M,2024). Meanwhile academic organizations create partnership across borders enables fast acceptance of technological changes and preserves academic integrity standards through international operations. The educational system of Omani educational framework and higher education institutions in Oman can benefit from international partnerships which shares essential resources with their Omani HEI's for easy adoption of AI implementation

The following section provides students with a list of activities which help them improve their learning participation. Students need to actively take part in the process for developing both integrity and literacy skills. Student-led discussions and debates and projects about AI ethics enable students to gain practical learning experiences that help them build their critical thinking abilities. As discussed in above sections, AI tool analysis and academic ethical dilemma by students led to better comprehension of technology and integrity relationships. Academic integrity needs established training programs with educational materials to educate the students regarding plagiarism, ethical standards and understanding of misuse of AI (Azaza M & Zinoubi R,2022).

A sustainable framework for integrity development

Transnational higher education institutions need to establish AI literacy education along with academic integrity promotion events as a continuous effort instead of treating this as a one-time effort. These higher education institutions must practice ongoing evaluation systems which tracks AI impact on teaching and learning while redefining policy changes if required. To prevent academic misconduct higher education institutions must include regular update on academic misconduct regulations, assessment design improvements and ongoing evaluation between students and staff about ethical matters (Mattar M Y, 2022). The establishment of such actions in higher education institutions maintains their commitment to academic integrity and usage of AI technology. This will ensure trust an integrity during international student enrollment from various cultural backgrounds for transnational educational framework.

The establishment of academic integrity-based AI education across transnational educational institutions needs active participation from students and educators and other stakeholders. Higher educational institutions can secure academic integrity through implementation of ethical values and conducting AI literacy programs for faculty and students. This method enables transnational educational degree recognition and preparing students as global citizens who can work in digital and AI based environment.

FUTURE DIRECTIONS AND PRACTICAL RECOMMENDATIONS IN AI AND ACADEMIC INTEGRITY

Figure 3. Recommended areas to maintain academic integrity

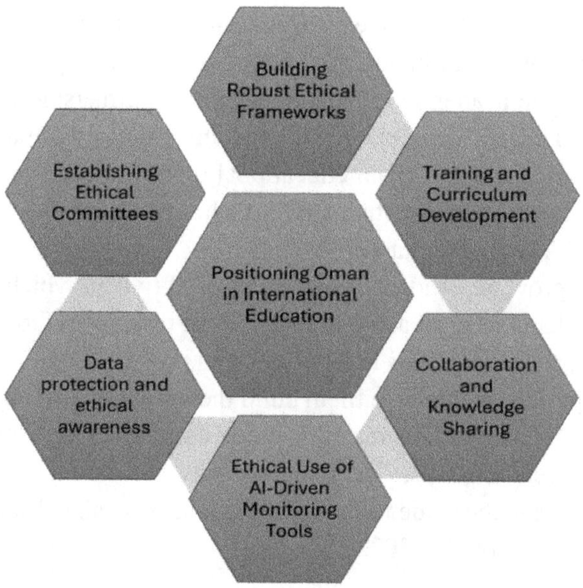

Building Robust Ethical Frameworks

Given the rapidly changing dynamics of academic integrity in the context of AI and it's increasing role in transnational education particularly within the Omani framework, it is essential to outline future directions and recommendations. A key priority for higher education institutions is the development of comprehensive framework that collaborates ethical principles into the adoption and utilization of AI technology. Addressing this challenge requires multifaceted strategy that not only emphasizes educational initiatives to build awareness and responsibility but also ensures the enforcement of regular policies to secure integrity (Abulaiti M,2024).

Comprehensive Training and Curriculum Development

Higher education institutions should initiate continuous training and development programs which are designed to help and promote awareness about academic integrity and usage of AI tools in teaching and learning models. This initiative should include recommendations derived from various research studies by focusing the importance of educational guidance with clear policies by covering ethical behaviors around AI usage (Li et al., 2023).Alongside translating theoretical ethics into practical applications through curriculum development will reinforce the integrity of academic practices by adopting AI ethics into the curriculum along with the case studies. Demonstrating the AI technologies and academic honesty intersection can particularly boost the understanding of students and faculty (Murugan et al., 2024).

Collaboration and Knowledge Sharing

A collaborative environment within and between higher educational institutions focused on international delivery is vital. Universities and academic institutions need to engage actively in transnational delivery with research and sharing best practices related to AI and academic integrity this is a collaborative learning Hotmail.com national boundaries sharing and collaborative learning maybe in the form of international workshops symposiums and conferences that not only chatting successful from international partners also critically evaluate failures and experiences and learn lessons which will support to develop future strategies for successful collaboration of academic integrity and AI(Gruenhagen, J. H.et al., 2024).

Ethical Use of AI-Driven Monitoring Tools

Utilizing technological advancements and innovations can enhance continuous monitoring and enforcement mechanisms of academic integrity policies. Higher education institutions could adopt AI driven plagiarism direction tools like Turnitin to maintain fairness to ensure academic standards (Diwan A et al.,2015). However it is crucial to communicate the limits and ethical impacts of such technologies to all stakeholders of educational system to prevent misuse of AI and to avoid privacy violations.

Data Protection and Ethical Awareness

These preventive and proactive measures must be accompanied by strong Ethical standards that fundamentally support the implementation of AI in educational contexts. These ethical standards help in data protection by ensuring academic integrity. These measures also develop a culture of ethical awareness among student and educational providers (Murugan et al., 2024).

Establishing Ethical Committees

To create a comprehensive environment centered around integrity and ethical Al use, higher education institutions must be established with "Ethical committee" comprising with the members from students, faculty and external authorities who can provide consistent guidance on emerging AI related challenges. This Ethical committee will ensure that academic practices are continually progressing with technological advancements (Mumtaz et al., 2024).

Policymaker Collaboration and Unified Guidelines

Higher educational institutions need to collaborate with the policy makers, which is essential to create regulations to secure academic integrity while managing the complexity of artificial intelligence. Policy makers should actively involve in curriculum development of higher education framework that not only promote responsible usage of AI, but also to support higher education institutions in educational needs and technological innovations (Gruenhagen, J. H.et al., 2024). Initiating these collaborative ventures will lead to maintain a unified set of guidelines to govern the use of AI in international curriculum delivery within Oman and beyond. Every higher education institution must be equipped with resources and should follow best practices in the context of AI usage by ensuring the commitment to maintain academic integrity by delivering quality in education across borders Gruenhagen, J. H.et al., 2024).

Continuous Research and Feedback Mechanisms

Use of AI in education continues to progress, ongoing research into ethical implications and the effectiveness of guidelines and policies will be vibrant .Regular monitoring and examining the experience of students and educators regarding the usage of AI tools can provide unique insights and helps improve the guidelines and policies. The feedback mechanism should be transparent and inclusive to ensure an academic environment meets the diverse needs of the learners (Yusuf et al., 2024)

Positioning Oman in International Education

In conclusion, embracing these future directions and recommendations will not only support academic integrity but also sets oman's Higher education as a leading example in the international platform of transnational education, as it balances between technological advancements and ethical educational practices. By adopting a dynamic, innovative developmental approach, higher educational institutions can ensure that they effectively address the multifaceted challenges posed by AI while cultivating an environment of academic integrity, responsibility, and inclusivity (Yusuf et al., 2024)

CONCLUSION

In conclusion the integration of artificial intelligence into transnational educations within Omani context marks a paradigm shift the demands a strong commitment to academic integrity this ongoing educational environment reflects the opportunities presented by AI driven technologies and the challenges associated with safeguarding ethical scholarship why yeah has the potential to enhance teaching and learning and engagement, it's unapproved unregulated use of AI technologies carries high challenges that may lead to compromise on the value of academic qualifications if it does not handled properly with the care. These findings with recent research emphasize the need for internationally sensitive approach and ethical policies for the use of AI in education (Suntharalingam P, 2025).

The culture of Integrity must therefore be actively promoted by enabling students and faculty to use AI resources in a responsible manner. This includes providing workshops, symposiums and training courses, which will help them not only to raise awareness about the usage of AI and the limitations of AI tools by highlighting ethical implications of AI misuse. Higher education faculties must be encouraged to join critical discussions on how AI influences learning and assessment practices where ethical conduct underpins academic achievement. Current academic literature highlights academic misconduct in relation to AI, while delivering international curriculum whereas educational goals may vary (Saliba R,2024). Implementation of AI integration into curriculum delivery not only limited to individuals but also connected with institutions as well as strategic level stakeholders as transnational education progress, universities accreditation bodies and government agencies are playing an important role in the design of consistent and coherent frameworks which is essential for future education.

Clear communications among the stakeholder's Indian educational framework is crucial to ensure all policies reflex best practices to adopt technological developments the growing body of scholarship supports the need for international efforts which will help to maintain academic integrity while the students and educators have the freedom to use artificial intelligence in teaching and learning .Adopting artificial intelligence without compromising in academic integrity will remind an ongoing challenge. The growth of AI continues to shape educational practices where institutions must learn to adopt and anticipate the risks while grabbing the opportunities of AI to strengthen educational delivery the credibility of transnational education and its degrees will depend on continuous commitment to academic integrity. Current existing practices and policies related to assessment teaching and learning international collaboration and intellectual property must be redefined by focusing on AI's capacity and its impact on educational framework. Sultanate of Oman is expanding its transnational educational landscape with AI adoption and risk of AI adoption. Careful reflection on both advantages and risks of a adoption is critical and a monetary requirement promoting a deep understanding of ethical AI usage among students' educators and policymakers will safeguard the educational framework by parallel supporting AI innovations. Usage of AI academic integrity will remind dynamic, and it will provide valuable insight to the future of their education. Educators and the policymakers should understand AI will act as a agent to promote academic excellence rather than risk to be ethical framework.

REFERENCES

Abulaiti, M. (2024). Higher Education in the Era of AI. In *Developments and Future Trends in Transnational Higher Education Leadership* (pp. 244–265). IGI Global. DOI: 10.4018/979-8-3693-2857-6.ch014

Alfayez, A. A., & Rasool, A. (2025). Use of AI in the curriculum development of transnational higher education. In *Bridging Global Divides for Transnational Higher Education in the AI Era* (pp. 401–422). IGI Global Scientific Publishing.

ANSAH, S. D. (2025). Digital Trust and Equity in Transnational Education: Rethinking Online Assessment and Credentialing Practices in the Ghanaian Higher Educational New Landscape. *International Journal of Psychology and Education*, *6*(2).

Azaza, M., & Zinoubi, R. (2022). Transnational Education in the Context of the United Arab Emirates: Realities, Opportunities, and Challenges. *The International Journal of Educational Organization and Leadership*, *29*(2), 47–57. DOI: 10.18848/2329-1656/CGP/v29i02/47-57

Bannister, P., Alcalde Peñalver, E., & Santamaría Urbieta, A. (2024). Transnational higher education cultures and generative AI: A nominal group study for policy development in English medium instruction. *Journal for Multicultural Education*, *18*(1-2), 173–191. DOI: 10.1108/JME-10-2023-0102

British Council. 2016. The Scale and Scope of UK Higher Education Transnational Education. https://www.britishcouncil.org/sites/default/files/scale-and-scope-of-uk-he-tne-report.pdf

Currie, G. M. (2023, September). Academic integrity and artificial intelligence: Is ChatGPT hype, hero or heresy? [). WB Saunders.]. *Seminars in Nuclear Medicine*, *53*(5), 719–730. DOI: 10.1053/j.semnuclmed.2023.04.008 PMID: 37225599

. Gallent-Torres, C., Zapata-González, A., & Ortego-Hernando, J. L. (2023). The impact of Generative Artificial Intelligence in higher education: a focus on ethics and academic integrity. Electronic Journal of Educational Research, Assessment & Evaluation/Revista Electrónica de Investigación y Evaluación Educativa, 29(2).

Gruenhagen, J. H., Sinclair, P. M., Carroll, J. A., Baker, P. R., Wilson, A., & Demant, D. (2024). The rapid rise of generative AI and its implications for academic integrity: Students' perceptions and use of chatbots for assistance with assessments. *Computers and Education: Artificial Intelligence*, *7*, 100273. DOI: 10.1016/j.caeai.2024.100273

Hamad, H. A., & Charles, T. (2024). The role of educational leaders in ensuring academic integrity with online assessments. *Open Journal of Leadership*, *13*(2), 154–167. DOI: 10.4236/ojl.2024.132010

Healey, N. M. (2023). Transnational education: The importance of aligning stakeholders' motivations with the form of cross-border educational service delivery. *Higher Education Quarterly*, *77*(1), 83–101. DOI: 10.1111/hequ.12371

Holden, C. (2018). Adapting Tinto's Framework: A Model of Success and Failure in a Middle Eastern Transnational Setting. *Studies in Higher Education*, *43*(6), 1002–1019. DOI: 10.1080/03075079.2016.1212004

Kang, P. E. (2022). Academic Integrity and the Inclusion of East Asian International Students in Canadian Higher Education. In Handbook of Research on Teaching Strategies for Culturally and Linguistically Diverse International Students (pp. 188-200). IGI Global Scientific Publishing. DOI: 10.4018/978-1-7998-8921-2.ch010

Karim-Abdallah, B., Darko, G. O., Gyabaah, O., Fening, L. O., Chimsi, I., Derkyi, M. A. A., & Yeboah-Kyereh, A. (2025). Innovations, Technologies and Challenges Associated with Transnational Education. *African Journal of Applied Research, 11*(1), 560–587. DOI: 10.26437/ajar.v11i1.870

Li, M., Enkhtur, A., Cheng, F., & Yamamoto, B. A. (2023). Ethical implications of ChatGPT in higher education: A scoping review. arXiv preprint arXiv:2311.14378.

Mattar, M. Y. (2022). Combating academic corruption and enhancing academic integrity through international accreditation standards: The model of Qatar University. *Journal of Academic Ethics, 20*(2), 119–146. DOI: 10.1007/s10805-021-09392-7

. Murugan, T., Karthikeyan, P., & Abirami, A. M. (2024). Proctoring tools and techniques for ensuring the integrity of online assessments. Engaging Higher Education Teachers and Students With Transnational Leadership, 144-164.

Palmer, A. (2021). Investigating staff views on plagiarism in transnational higher education. *Journal of Applied Learning and Teaching, 4*(2), 13–27.

Roe, J., O'Sullivan, D., Arumynathan, P., & Kappen, B. (2024). Paraphrase or plagiarism?: Exploring EAP students' use of source material in a transnational university context. *Journal of Applied Learning & Teaching, 7*(2), 232–245.

Saliba, R. (2024). Transformation in transformative learning: A reversed experience of faculty members teaching in transnational higher education institutions in qatar. *Social Sciences & Humanities Open, 9*, 100823. DOI: 10.1016/j.ssaho.2024.100823

Sbaffi, L., & Zhao, X. (2022). Evaluating a pedagogical approach to promoting academic integrity in higher education: An online induction program. *Frontiers in Psychology, 13*, 1009305. DOI: 10.3389/fpsyg.2022.1009305 PMID: 36275294

. Sun, Y. (2025). An Innovative Approach to Integrating Al Into Learning and Teaching at a Transnational. Training and Development in Transnational Higher Education, 331.

Suntharalingam, P. (2025). Introduction to transnational higher education (TNE). In Bridging Global Divides for Transnational Higher Education in the AI Era (pp. 1-28). IGI Global Scientific Publishing.

Tran, N. H. N., Amado, C. A., & Santos, S. P. (2022). Challenges and success factors of transnational higher education: A systematic review. *Studies in Higher Education, 48*(1), 113–136. DOI: 10.1080/03075079.2022.2121813

Yankova, D. (2024). Academic Integrity Policies in Higher Education Institutions Across Cultures. *English Studies at NBU, 10*(1), 5–20. DOI: 10.33919/esnbu.24.1.1

Yao, C. W., & Collins, C. (2019). Perspectives from Graduate Students on Effective Teaching Methods: A Case Study from a Vietnamese Transnational University. *Journal of Further and Higher Education*, *43*(7), 959–974. DOI: 10.1080/0309877X.2018.1429583

Yusuf, A., Pervin, N., & Román-González, M. (2024). Generative AI and the future of higher education: A threat to academic integrity or reformation? Evidence from a multicultural perspective. *International Journal of Educational Technology in Higher Education*, *21*(1), 21. DOI: 10.1186/s41239-024-00453-6

Zheng, C., & Ouyang, H. (2023). Factors influencing quality of transnational education: Evidence from a Sino-UK MA program. *Frontiers in Psychology*, *13*, 1099359. DOI: 10.3389/fpsyg.2022.1099359 PMID: 36698605

Zlotnikova, I., Hlomani, H., Mokgetse, T., & Bagai, K. (2025). Establishing ethical standards for GenAI in university education: A roadmap for academic integrity and fairness. Journal of Information. *Communication and Ethics in Society*, *23*(2), 188–216. DOI: 10.1108/JICES-07-2024-0104

Chapter 5
AI Integration in UAE-Based British Higher Education

Patrick McCrudden
https://orcid.org/0009-0007-2114-3659
International American University, UAE

ABSTRACT

This paper examines the structural incompatibilities that arise when UK transnational education providers in the UAE navigate divergent AI regulatory frameworks. The UAE's National AI Strategy 2031 mandates rapid institutional transformation, whilst UK quality assurance emphasises equivalence with home provision. The analysis documents four fundamental incompatibilities that create a positioned impossibility for institutions, faculty, and students, revealing sustainability challenges for transnational education models in contexts of significant regulatory divergence.

INTRODUCTION

Transnational education operates at the intersection of multiple regulatory frameworks, institutional cultures, and policy environments. When these frameworks align around shared educational values and quality principles, complexity remains manageable through established coordination mechanisms. When they diverge significantly, particularly around technological integration, policy implementation timelines, and definitions of educational quality, the intersection reveals structural tensions that challenge fundamental assumptions underlying transnational delivery models. The integration of artificial intelligence into higher education systems presents one such divergence, with different national contexts implementing AI strategies at markedly different speeds, through various policy mechanisms, and with varying expectations for institutional response.

The United Arab Emirates and the United Kingdom provide a particularly instructive case for examining how national AI policy divergence affects the delivery of transnational education. The UAE has implemented one of the world's most ambitious national AI strategies, mandating AI curriculum from kindergarten through secondary education and positioning AI integration as central to economic diversification and workforce development goals. The UK maintains regulatory frameworks for higher education that prioritise careful deliberation, quality assurance through equivalence principles, and incremental adoption of technology aligned with sector-wide consultation processes. British universities

DOI: 10.4018/979-8-3373-5403-3.ch005

operate international branch campuses, franchise programmes, and validation partnerships throughout the UAE, making it the second-largest host for UK transnational education in the Middle East. These arrangements typically position UK institutions as degree-awarding bodies responsible for academic standards, whilst UAE-based operations deliver education under local regulatory oversight.

This architecture functions effectively when regulatory expectations converge around shared quality principles. The question this article examines is what occurs when they diverge around fundamental issues such as technological integration expectations, policy implementation timelines, and definitions of institutional quality. The existing literature on transnational education extensively examines the challenges of quality assurance, cultural adaptation requirements, and the sustainability of international partnerships (Quality Assurance Agency, 2014; British Council MENA, 2024). Recent scholarship has addressed technology-enhanced learning in international contexts and the emerging applications of AI in education (Campbell University, 2025; Microsoft, 2025). However, limited research systematically examines the regulatory intersection when host countries implement technology policies that operate at significantly different speeds or measure institutional quality through different criteria than those used in home-country frameworks.

This discussion contributes to understanding these dynamics by examining AI integration expectations in UAE-based UK transnational education through four interconnected sections. First, it explores the UAE's AI policy framework, analysing how the national strategy translates into expectations for higher education institutions. Second, it examines the UK regulatory constraints affecting transnational education providers, including formal policy guidance, quality assurance frameworks, and institutional governance structures that mediate technology adoption. Third, the analysis examines the intersection between these frameworks, focusing on structural incompatibilities including competing sovereignty claims over educational quality, irreconcilable data governance requirements, temporal misalignments in policy cycles, and contradictory constructions of institutional legitimacy. Fourth, it assesses current institutional responses to these structural tensions and their implications for various stakeholders.

The analytical approach prioritises examining how these dynamics function rather than advocating particular resolutions. Transnational education exists within complex regulatory environments where multiple legitimate authorities exercise oversight based on their respective mandates. Understanding how these authorities' expectations interact when they diverge requires analytical frameworks that acknowledge the legitimacy of competing claims whilst examining their practical incompatibilities. To this end, the chapter pursues four interconnected objectives. First, it documents the specific policy mechanisms through which the UAE's National AI Strategy 2031 creates measurable expectations for higher education institutions, establishing the baseline against which transnational education providers operate. Second, it identifies the UK regulatory constraints, including the equivalence principle, governance structures, and policy silences, that limit institutional capacity to respond to host-country technological expectations. Third, it demonstrates how these frameworks create not only coordination challenges but also fundamental structural incompatibilities, manifesting as competing sovereignty claims, irreconcilable data governance requirements, temporal misalignments, and contradictory legitimacy constructions. Fourth, it examines how these incompatibilities manifest in practice for institutions, faculty, and students, revealing current navigation strategies and their implications for the sustainability of transnational education models. The examination holds relevance beyond the specific UAE-UK case, as the structural dynamics revealed are likely to manifest in other contexts where host and home countries pursue different technology integration strategies.

1. UAE AI POLICY FRAMEWORK: STRATEGIC COORDINATION AND EDUCATIONAL TRANSFORMATION

Abstract

This section examines the UAE's systematically coordinated approach to artificial intelligence integration across educational sectors. The National AI Strategy 2031 establishes AI as central to economic diversification, targeting a 20% non-oil GDP contribution. The May 2025 Cabinet decision mandating an AI curriculum from kindergarten through Grade 12 creates a cohort effect, whereby students entering university from 2026 will possess thirteen years of structured AI literacy. Federal and emirate-level regulatory frameworks assess institutions based on their digital capabilities, innovation demonstration, and strategic alignment. The Digital Economy Strategy links graduate employability to AI capabilities. This framework shifts quality expectations from purely academic standards to include economic utility.

National AI Strategy 2031: Economic Imperatives

The National AI Strategy 2031, launched in 2017 alongside the appointment of the world's first Minister for Artificial Intelligence, establishes AI as central to efforts for economic diversification (UAE Artificial Intelligence, 2021). The strategy aims to have a quantifiable economic objective that creates measurable expectations across all sectors, including higher education. This is not aspirational rhetoric; it represents binding policy direction that shapes regulatory evaluation criteria and institutional licensing requirements.

For education, this translates into capability development mandates. Producing graduates equipped for an AI-integrated economy requires institutions themselves to embed AI throughout their delivery, assessment, and student support systems Shan Wang *et al.*, 2024). The policy framework creates an expectations cascade: national economic targets necessitate workforce capabilities, which in turn require educational transformation, which demands institutional adoption of technological innovations.

Education Sector Implementation: The 2025 Curriculum Mandate

The May 2025 Cabinet decision mandating AI curriculum from kindergarten through Grade 12 marks a critical inflexion point for higher education providers. This policy creates a cohort effect that spans foundational concepts, data and algorithms, software use, ethical awareness, real-world applications, innovation, project design, policies, and community engagement. For higher education, this fundamentally shifts expectations; institutions can no longer position AI as specialised content for computing programmes; it becomes assumed foundational knowledge across disciplines. The policy effectively raises the baseline expectation for technological sophistication in university delivery. An institution perceived as less digitally capable than the K-12 system faces reputational challenges and potential competitive disadvantage.

The curriculum implementation also signals policy seriousness. The Ministry of Education provided comprehensive teacher training, detailed lesson plans, and assessment frameworks, demonstrating genuine infrastructural commitment rather than symbolic policy announcement. This implementation's thoroughness suggests similar expectations will eventually cascade to all providers (ORF Middle East, 2025).

Regulatory Architecture: Federal And Emirate-Level Frameworks

The UAE's regulatory landscape for higher education encompasses both federal and Emirate jurisdictions, resulting in multiple accountability points for institutions. The Commission for Academic Accreditation CAA provides federal-level oversight, whilst Emirate authorities, notably the Knowledge and Human Development Authority KHDA in Dubai and the Abu Dhabi Department of Education and Knowledge ADEK, exercise local regulatory powers.

The CAA's 2025 adoption of an outcome-based evaluation framework represents regulatory evolution in response to technological change. Rather than prescribing specific technologies or delivery methods, the framework focuses on demonstrated student outcomes and institutional capabilities. This theoretically provides institutions with flexibility to achieve digital integration through various pathways. However, the framework retains assessment categories around innovation, digital readiness, and contemporary pedagogical practices, areas where AI integration is increasingly expected to provide evidence.

KHDA's approach in Dubai demonstrates how Emirate-level regulators translate national policy into institutional expectations. Dubai's Smart City strategy and the Emirate's positioning as a regional technology hub create local policy environments in which digital sophistication is linked to institutional legitimacy. KHDA's institutional evaluations increasingly reference alignment with Dubai's digital transformation agenda, creating implicit expectations around AI adoption, even where it is not explicitly mandated.

Digital Economy Integration And Workforce Development

The UAE Digital Economy Strategy aims to double the digital economy's contribution to non-oil GDP within a decade. This creates direct linkages between higher education outputs and national economic metrics. Graduates lacking AI literacy represent policy failures in this framework; they cannot contribute to the digital economy transformation that the national strategy requires.

For transnational education providers, this shifts quality from purely academic standards to economic utility. Regulatory bodies evaluate institutions partly on their contribution to graduate employability and national development goals. In an AI-focused economy, this means institutions must demonstrate they produce graduates capable of working in AI-integrated environments. Traditional academic quality assurance focused on subject knowledge and transferable skills; the UAE framework additionally requires demonstrated technological capability aligned with national economic priorities.

Infrastructure Investment And Institutional Expectations

The UAE's significant investment in AI infrastructure, including the Mohamed Bin Zayed University of Artificial Intelligence and the Advanced Technology Research Council, as well as partnerships with major technology companies, creates an ecosystem that fosters institutional participation. Universities operating in this environment face implicit expectations to engage with national AI initiatives, contribute to research agendas, and demonstrate alignment with strategic priorities.

This infrastructure investment also reveals policy commitment. The UAE has not merely announced AI strategies; it has established institutions, allocated resources, and developed physical and digital infrastructure. For higher education providers, this suggests that AI integration is not a passing policy trend, but a sustained national direction that requires an institutional response.

2. UK REGULATORY FRAMEWORKS: QUALITY ASSURANCE, GOVERNANCE, AND POLICY GAPS

Abstract

The UK regulatory architecture limits the capacity of transnational education providers to respond to host-country expectations regarding AI. The Department for Education's 2025 guidance frames AI as pedagogical support rather than systemic transformation. The Quality Assurance Agency's equivalence principle, which requires overseas provision to maintain home delivery standards, becomes a critical constraint when host-country contexts demand technological differentiation. The Office for Students and Professional Bodies requires dual justification for technology investments. UK institutional governance reflects a collegial decision-making process, resulting in multi-committee approval processes with timelines that span academic years. The absence of comprehensive guidance navigating conflicting expectations forces conservative interpretations prioritising UK compliance, creating gaps between capabilities and host-country requirements.

UK transnational education providers operate within regulatory frameworks designed for stable quality assurance rather than rapid technological transformation. Understanding these constraints requires examining formal policy guidance on AI in education, TNE-specific regulatory architecture, and institutional governance structures that mediate technology adoption decisions.

UK Policy Position On AI In Education

The Department for Education's DfE 2025 guidance on "Generative Artificial Intelligence in Education" reveals the UK government's framing of AI as pedagogical support rather than systemic transformation (Department for Education, 2025). The document positions AI primarily as a tool to "reduce administrative burden for educators" and provide "support for personalised learning and feedback." This instrumental framing, viewing AI as an efficiency mechanism within existing educational structures, contrasts sharply with the UAE's positioning of AI as a foundational capability requiring curriculum redesign and institutional reconfiguration. The emphasis on "safe, ethical, and inclusive deployment" reflects a risk-management approach prioritising harm prevention over innovation acceleration, creating a fundamentally defensive posture toward technological integration.

Significantly, the DfE guidance focuses on schools and colleges with minimal reference to higher education or transnational contexts, revealing a policy gap that leaves UK institutions delivering education abroad without official guidance on navigating AI integration in host countries with more aggressive digital strategies. This absence becomes particularly problematic when transnational education providers face host-country regulatory expectations that diverge from home-country policy positions, forcing institutions to develop ad hoc responses without sector-wide frameworks to guide decision-making.

Universities UK International's TNE data and strategy reports acknowledge emerging technologies, including AI, as "enablers of hybrid delivery"; however, technology remains peripheral to core concerns surrounding quality assurance and regulatory alignment (Universities UK International, 2023). The 2023 UUKi TNE report dedicates substantial attention to maintaining academic standards across borders whilst treating technological innovation as a delivery variation rather than a strategic imperative. This framing positions AI adoption as an institutional choice within quality boundaries rather than a competitive necessity, which fundamentally misunderstands contexts where host-country policy makes digital sophistication a regulatory expectation rather than an optional enhancement.

Quality Assurance Architecture: The Equivalence Principle

UK transnational education providers remain accountable to the Quality Assurance Agency's frameworks regardless of operational location. The QAA's expectations for TNE emphasise "equivalence of academic standards" and "parity of student experience" with UK-based provision (Quality Assurance Agency, 2014). This equivalence principle, the foundational concept that overseas provision should maintain standards equivalent to home delivery, becomes the critical constraint shaping institutional technology adoption decisions.

The principle creates conservatism around innovation, where technological adoptions that might differentiate overseas delivery from home provision require careful justification to demonstrate they enhance rather than compromise quality. This protection of academic standards becomes a constraint when host-country contexts demand rather than merely permit technological differentiation. The QAA's 2024 guidance on digital delivery maintains this equivalence principle whilst acknowledging technological diversity. Still, it provides limited guidance on situations where host-country regulatory expectations actively push institutions toward digital transformation that UK frameworks treat as discretionary enhancement.

The absence of explicit guidance on managing competing regulatory requirements leaves institutions developing institution-specific responses rather than following sector-wide frameworks, creating fragmentation where consistency might better serve the sector. More fundamentally, the equivalence principle implies that UK standards should apply universally, with local adaptation limited to contextual delivery variations. This assumption breaks down when host countries implement policies that not only permit but actively require differentiation from UK home provision norms.

Regulatory Oversight: OFS and PSRB Constraints

Office for Students OfS registration conditions add further constraint layers. Registered providers must demonstrate financial sustainability, effective governance, and academic quality regardless of overseas operations. Technology investments supporting the delivery of transnational education must satisfy OfS requirements regarding value for money and strategic coherence. This means that an AI platform adopted to meet UAE regulatory expectations must also demonstrate a contribution to institutional objectives under the OfS assessment criteria. This dual justification requirement creates decision-making paralysis, as institutions cannot simply respond to host-country expectations without ensuring compliance with home-country regulations.

Professional, Statutory and Regulatory Bodies compound these constraints for professional programmes. Engineering, business, healthcare, and computing programmes require PSRB accreditation, which often includes specific curriculum content, assessment methods, and learning resource requirements developed for traditional delivery formats. AI-enhanced delivery models must demonstrate alignment with PSRB standards that may not have evolved to accommodate innovative approaches, requiring institutions to obtain approval through processes that can span multiple years.

The need to maintain professional accreditation creates additional conservatism, as institutions cannot risk losing PSRB recognition by adopting unproven technologies that regulators might not yet accept. A computing programme seeking to integrate AI-enhanced coding assessments must demonstrate to the relevant PSRB that this approach maintains professional standards and develops capabilities recognised within the profession. When PSRBs operate on consensus models that require extensive sector consultation before accepting new approaches, the approval timelines become incompatible with host-country policy environments that expect rapid institutional responses to national AI strategies.

Institutional Governance And Technology Adoption Processes

UK institutional governance structures reflect academic values around collegial decision-making and careful deliberation. Technology adoption typically requires approval from multiple committees representing different institutional perspectives. Academic boards assess the pedagogical implications, finance committees evaluate resource allocation, IT governance boards address technical feasibility, and risk committees examine data protection and compliance dimensions. This multi-layered governance creates implementation timelines measured in academic years rather than months, as each approval stage involves consultation, documentation, and revision cycles that ensure thoroughness but produce adoption speeds incompatible with policy environments expecting rapid implementation.

A learning analytics platform requiring student data processing exemplifies these governance complexities. The proposal must secure academic board approval for its pedagogical rationale, undergo ethics committee review for data use implications, receive IT governance approval for technical integration, complete a data protection impact assessment, obtain finance committee budget allocation, and achieve final approval from Senate or Council for significant investments. Each stage involves stakeholder consultation and addresses legitimate concerns, but the cumulative effect creates timelines that can extend beyond a full academic year for significant technology adoptions.

Academic staff consultation represents both strengths and constraints in the UK institutional culture. Technology's impact on teaching and assessment requires faculty engagement to address concerns about pedagogical implications, workload, and academic autonomy. This consultation process ensures educator buy-in and addresses legitimate professional concerns, but it also extends timelines, particularly when staff express reservations about the implications of AI for academic integrity or their teaching roles. The consultation cannot be bypassed without risking implementation failure, yet it creates delays that host-country regulators may interpret as institutional resistance rather than due process.

Procurement processes introduce additional delays beyond those required for governance approval. UK public sector procurement rules frequently require competitive tendering for significant technology contracts. A UAE public institution might select and implement an AI tutoring system within a single semester through direct procurement arrangements, whilst a UK transnational education provider might require twelve to eighteen months for procurement compliance, vendor evaluation, contract negotiation, pilot testing, and phased rollout. The procurement process, while ensuring value for money and regulatory compliance, creates temporal misalignment with contexts that expect rapid technological responses.

The TNE Policy Silence: Navigating Dual Accountability

Perhaps the most significant UK regulatory constraint is what remains unaddressed in policy frameworks. Neither DfE, UUKi, QAA, nor OfS provides comprehensive guidance for institutions navigating situations where host-country policy expectations conflict with UK institutional norms. The regulatory architecture assumes UK standards apply universally, with local adaptation limited to contextual delivery variations rather than fundamental strategic tensions.

This assumption breaks down when host countries implement technology policies that exceed UK expectations or operate on incompatible timescales. The policy silence leaves transnational education providers without frameworks for critical decisions. When UAE regulators expect AI integration as evidence of institutional quality, but UK quality frameworks treat it as an optional enhancement, institutions must determine which framework takes precedence without official guidance on balancing competing requirements. When host-country data governance requirements conflict with UK GDPR interpretations, institutions navigate between compliance frameworks without clear direction on which to follow in cases of contradiction. When local competitive pressures drive technology adoption that UK governance processes haven't yet approved, institutions must balance responsiveness against due process without sector guidance on acceptable approaches to managing this tension.

The absence of regulatory guidance doesn't mean institutions face no constraints; quite the opposite. Without explicit frameworks for managing regulatory multiplicity, institutions default to conservative interpretations prioritising UK compliance over host-country responsiveness. The regulatory uncertainty itself becomes a constraint, as institutions avoid innovations that might jeopardise UK accreditation even when host-country expectations encourage such innovations. This conservatism may protect UK compliance, but creates widening gaps between institutional capabilities and host-country expectations.

3. STRUCTURAL INCOMPATIBILITIES: WHERE REGULATORY FRAMEWORKS COLLIDE

Abstract

Four fundamental structural incompatibilities arise when UAE AI policy acceleration intersects with UK transnational education regulatory constraints. Competing sovereignty claims over educational quality create a dual accountability that is impossible to satisfy when frameworks define quality differently. Data governance contradictions between GDPR and UAE Data Law embody contradictory philosophical positions regarding data authority. Temporal incompatibilities arise when UAE Cabinet decisions enable rapid implementation, whilst UK multi-year consultation cycles create strategic planning impossibilities. Contradictory legitimacy constructions emerge when UK frameworks value academic autonomy, whilst UAE frameworks emphasise responsiveness. These incompatibilities create a positioned impossibility for academic leaders, faculty, and students operating between incompatible frameworks.

The intersection between UAE AI policy acceleration and UK TNE regulatory constraints reveals not coordination challenges requiring better frameworks, but fundamental structural incompatibilities in how educational authority functions across borders. These incompatibilities manifest in four domains: competing sovereignty claims over educational quality, irreconcilable data governance requirements, temporal misalignment in policy cycles, and contradictory definitions of institutional legitimacy. Understanding these intersections requires examining how they create operational impossibilities for institutions positioned between regulatory frameworks that cannot simultaneously be satisfied.

Competing Sovereignty Claims Over Educational Quality

UK transnational education providers operating in the UAE face a dual quality assurance and accountability structure that becomes structurally contradictory when regulatory frameworks define quality differently. UK quality assurance, mediated through QAA frameworks and institutional validation processes, emphasises equivalence with home provision and maintenance of academic standards consistent with UK degree characteristics. UAE quality assurance, exercised through CAA, KHDA, and ADEK, is increasingly evaluating institutions against their alignment with national strategic priorities, including AI 2031 targets and digital transformation mandates. When these frameworks converge around shared academic rigour, dual accountability functions as complementary oversight; when they diverge around technological expectations, dual accountability becomes impossible to satisfy.

Students entering higher education from 2026 onwards arrive with baseline AI literacy developed through the mandatory K-12 curriculum. These students expect university education to demonstrate AI sophistication at least equivalent to their secondary education experience. They possess familiarity with AI-enhanced learning tools, an understanding of algorithmic thinking, and experience with AI ethics frameworks that their K-12 education systematically developed. UAE regulators evaluate institutions partly on responsiveness to these student expectations and alignment with national digital capability development.

However, UK quality frameworks evaluate transnational education provision against the equivalence principle, where AI integration remains a discretionary enhancement rather than a baseline expectation. An institution demonstrating AI sophistication to meet UAE expectations, by embedding AI literacy across programme learning outcomes, incorporating AI-enhanced assessment, and utilising adaptive learning platforms, risks QAA questions about why overseas provision differs significantly from home delivery. The validation panel or institutional review may query whether this differentiation represents a departure from established standards or compromises the equivalence principle that safeguards the value of UK degrees.

Conversely, an institution maintaining strict equivalence with conservative UK home provision risks assessment by UAE regulators as insufficiently aligned with national strategy. When KHDA evaluates institutional performance against Dubai's digital transformation agenda, or when CAA assesses alignment with national AI priorities, an institution explaining its technological conservatism through reference to UK equivalence requirements may be interpreted as prioritising foreign compliance over local contributions. The regulatory evaluation criteria are increasingly incorporating innovation demonstration, digital capability, and strategic alignment with national priorities, areas where conservative equivalence with UK home provision appears as an institutional weakness rather than a quality protection.

This creates operational impossibility for programme leaders positioned between frameworks. When designing curriculum or selecting learning technologies, decisions cannot simultaneously satisfy both regulators if they measure quality through incompatible criteria. Should programme learning outcomes include AI capabilities that UAE students need and expect but that are absent from UK degree specifications? Should programme specifications reference AI literacy as an assumed entry competency given the K-12 curriculum, or maintain alignment with UK specifications that don't make such assumptions? Should teaching approaches incorporate AI tools that students use professionally and expect in university education, or maintain traditional approaches aligned with UK home provision? The institution must choose which regulatory satisfaction to prioritise, accepting that this choice renders the other framework's expectations unmet.

The issue extends beyond curriculum design to assessment practices. UAE policy increasingly expects demonstration of AI literacy as a graduate capability. An institution developing assessments that evaluate students' ability to work with AI tools, to assess critically algorithmic outputs, or design AI-enhanced solutions, addresses UAE expectations but potentially raises questions about equivalence. External examiners appointed under UK frameworks evaluate assessments against UK degree characteristics and subject benchmarks. If UAE-based programmes include AI capability assessments absent from UK provision, external examiners may question assessment parity. The external examiner might query why students at the overseas campus face assessment requirements different from those of their UK counterparts, interpreting this as a potential drift from standards rather than an appropriate contextual response.

Programme validation and revalidation processes reveal this sovereignty conflict most clearly. A programme development team designing a new business programme for delivery in the UAE must decide whether the programme specification includes explicit AI literacy learning outcomes. Including them addresses UAE regulatory expectations and student needs, but raises questions from the UK validation panel about differentiation from home provision. Excluding them maintains UK equivalence but leaves the programme potentially misaligned with UAE expectations. The validation panel operates within UK quality frameworks, prioritising equivalence; they may approve AI literacy inclusion only if the institution can demonstrate that this enhances rather than changes the programme's fundamental character. Yet, UAE regulators increasingly view AI literacy not as an enhancement, but as a baseline expectation. This means its treatment as an optional enhancement signals institutional misalignment with national priorities.

Data Governance Contradictions: GDPR And UAE Data Law

The intersection between UK GDPR requirements and UAE Data Law creates irreconcilable contradictions for AI-enhanced educational delivery (UAE Government, 2021; MIS Consultants, 2025). GDPR's fundamental principles include data minimisation (collecting only data necessary for specified purposes), purpose limitation (using data only for declared purposes), and individual rights, including data portability and erasure. UAE Data Law prioritises data sovereignty, requiring that data about UAE residents may be subject to local processing requirements and government access provisions that serve national interests (UAE Government, 2021). These frameworks don't simply require different compliance procedures; they embody contradictory philosophical positions regarding data authority that cannot be simultaneously satisfied when implementing AI systems processing student data (MIS Consultants, 2025).

Learning analytics platforms exemplify these contradictions with particular clarity. An AI system analysing student engagement patterns, assessment performance trajectories, and learning behaviours to provide personalised recommendations processes extensive personal data. The system tracks which learning resources students access, how long they engage with content, when they complete assessments, what errors they make, how they respond to feedback, and how their performance changes over time. This granular data collection enables the AI to identify students at risk of disengagement, recommend interventions, suggest personalised learning pathways, and provide predictive analytics about the likelihood of student success.

Under GDPR, this processing requires an explicit legal basis, transparency about processing purposes, and demonstrated data minimisation. Students must understand what data the system collects, how it uses that data, what decisions it might inform, and what rights they possess regarding their data. The institution must demonstrate that it collects only data necessary for legitimate educational purposes, maintains that data only as long as required, and provides mechanisms for students to access, correct, or request deletion of their data. GDPR Article 22 provides specific rights regarding automated individual decision-making, including the right to explanation and the right to human intervention.

Simultaneously, the UAE Data Law may require local data storage and processing to maintain data sovereignty. The law permits regulatory access to data held about UAE residents when authorities determine such access serves legitimate purposes, including quality assurance, regulatory compliance, or national security. UAE regulators conducting institutional reviews may expect access to learning analytics data to evaluate institutional effectiveness, assess student support systems, or verify regulatory compliance. These access provisions may not align with GDPR restrictions on government access, which require due process protections and specific legal authorisation.

UK institutions typically centralise student data systems in UK-based infrastructure, with overseas campuses accessing centrally managed databases through secure connections. This architecture assumes data can flow freely between jurisdictions under adequacy agreements. However, UAE Data Law provisions regarding data sovereignty may require local processing or storage, challenging the UK institution's preference for centralised data management. If the institution maintains student data only on UK servers, it may not fully satisfy the UAE's data sovereignty requirements. If it maintains duplicate data stores in both jurisdictions, it potentially violates GDPR data minimisation principles by maintaining redundant copies of personal data. If it maintains data exclusively in UAE servers, it potentially creates compliance issues with UK institutional data governance policies and GDPR transfer restrictions.

An AI tutoring system that requires real-time access to student data to provide immediate, personalised feedback illustrates the technical impossibility. The system must access current student performance data, learning history, and engagement patterns to generate appropriate responses. If student data resides in UK servers, the UAE-based AI system requires constant data transfers across jurisdictions, which UAE authorities may scrutinise under data sovereignty provisions and which UK data controllers must justify under GDPR transfer restrictions. If student data resides in UAE servers, the UK institution's central data governance and reporting systems cannot access it without transfers that may violate UAE data sovereignty principles. No technical configuration can satisfy all requirements simultaneously when regulatory frameworks embody contradictory principles about where data authority resides and who may access it under what conditions.

Temporal Incompatibility In Policy Development And Implementation

The intersection between UAE policy acceleration and UK deliberative governance creates temporal misalignments that institutions cannot bridge through planning or communication. These different policy temporalities operate not merely at various speeds but through fundamentally different assumptions about how policy should develop and how institutions should respond. UAE policy operates through Cabinet decisions, enabling rapid implementation based on national strategic priorities. UK policy operates through multi-year consultation cycles, producing guidance after extensive stakeholder engagement, pilot programmes, and sector-wide deliberation.

The mandatory AI curriculum moved from Cabinet announcement to nationwide implementation within a single academic year. This timeline illustrates the UAE's policy model's ability to execute rapidly when national priorities require it. The Ministry of Education developed comprehensive curriculum frameworks, produced teaching materials, organised teacher training programmes, and established assessment structures within a short period. Schools received implementation guidance, began delivering

AI curriculum, and started assessing student AI literacy according to established timelines, regardless of whether individual schools felt fully prepared.

UK policy operates on fundamentally different timescales. The development of major policy guidance typically involves the release of initial consultation documents for sector feedback, the analysis of consultation responses and research evidence, pilot programmes in selected institutions, the evaluation of pilot outcomes, revised guidance incorporating sector feedback, and the final publication after achieving broad sector consensus. This process commonly spans three to five years for significant policy developments. The approach ensures policy reflects sector realities, incorporates practitioner expertise, and maintains legitimacy through stakeholder participation.

This temporal gap creates strategic planning impossibilities for transnational education institutions. UK institutions develop five-year strategic plans aligned with home-country policy directions, funding cycles, and sector expectations. These plans embed assumptions about regulatory stability and incremental policy evolution. Institutions identify technology investment priorities, develop multi-year implementation roadmaps, allocate budgets across implementation phases, and establish performance indicators measuring progress against planned milestones.

UAE policy can fundamentally shift expectations within a single academic year, rendering institutional strategic plans obsolete before they are fully implemented. An institution that developed a strategic plan in 2023, outlining a cautious three-year AI integration trajectory aligned with UK sector norms, finds itself in 2025 operating in a policy environment where the government has mandated an AI curriculum in K-12 education and expects higher education institutions to demonstrate an equivalent commitment to AI integration. The institution's strategic plan positions AI as an emerging consideration for gradual incorporation; however, the policy environment now treats AI as an immediate priority, requiring a rapid institutional response.

Significant technology investments require business case development justifying expenditure against institutional priorities, procurement processes ensuring regulatory compliance and value for money, infrastructure preparation including network capacity and systems integration, staff development enabling effective technology utilisation, pilot programmes testing implementation approaches, evaluation processes assessing pilot outcomes, and phased rollout incorporating lessons from pilots. In UK institutional governance, these stages collectively span eighteen months to three years for major technology adoptions. An institution that commences this process in response to emerging UAE policy expectations may find that, by the time it completes procurement and reaches implementation, policy expectations have evolved further, rendering the carefully planned adoption insufficient for current requirements.

Contradictory Constructions Of Institutional Legitimacy

The UK and UAE regulatory frameworks construct institutional legitimacy through incompatible criteria, creating situations where actions that enhance legitimacy in one framework undermine it in the other. UK frameworks construct legitimacy through demonstrated academic autonomy, collegial governance, and evidence-based decision-making aligned with sector norms. UAE frameworks increasingly construct legitimacy through alignment with national strategic priorities, responsiveness to policy directions, and contributions to national development goals. These legitimacy constructions contradict when national priorities require institutional responsiveness that UK frameworks interpret as compromising academic autonomy.

The contradiction becomes clear in institutional responses to policy announcements. Institutions that demonstrate rapid alignment and signal responsiveness are valued under the UAE's legitimacy construction. However, UK legitimacy construction values deliberative responses, extensive consultation, pilot evaluations, and evidence gathering before implementing major changes. A rapid institutional response to UAE policy risks being interpreted as insufficiently deliberative or overly responsive to external pressure in the UK. A deliberative response that satisfies UK legitimacy expectations risks being interpreted by the UAE as institutional resistance or misalignment with national priorities.

This extends to institutional governance structures. UK frameworks require significant faculty involvement in educational decisions through academic boards and senates, which exercise authority over curriculum and assessment matters. UAE frameworks expect institutional leadership to demonstrate strategic alignment with national priorities and implement responsive policies that support these priorities. When UAE policy requires rapid curriculum changes that UK governance would subject to extensive faculty consultation, institutional leaders face impossible positioning between following UK governance norms (risking UAE assessment as weak leadership) and bypassing faculty consultation to demonstrate UAE responsiveness (risking UK assessment as compromised academic autonomy).

The Positioned Impossibility Of TNE Academic Leadership

These intersecting incompatibilities create a positioned impossibility for academic leaders in UAE-based UK transnational education provision. Faculty delivering education experience regulatory contradictions not as abstract policy tensions but as daily operational dilemmas without satisfactory resolution. Students arrive with AI literacy expectations shaped by the UAE curriculum policy, expecting university education to demonstrate a similar level of sophistication. Professional judgement suggests pedagogical responses incorporating AI tools, adaptive assessment, and digital capabilities development. However, implementing these responses requires UK institutional approval through governance processes evaluating against home provision equivalence and degree standard consistency.

Designing programmes that respond to UAE student expectations and labour market requirements whilst maintaining UK degree characteristics and QAA subject benchmarks requires satisfying specifications that increasingly diverge. Programme leaders cannot design provision simultaneously satisfying both frameworks when they define quality through contradictory criteria. Institutional processes designed to ensure quality and compliance can become mechanisms that enforce misalignment with the host-country context.

4. NAVIGATING THE IMPOSSIBLE: INSTITUTIONAL RESPONSES AND STAKEHOLDER CONSEQUENCES

Abstract

Transnational education providers navigate structural incompatibilities through strategic ambiguity and competitive market positioning. Institutions present different narratives to regulatory audiences, emphasising innovation to UAE regulators whilst characterising identical practices as enhancements to UK quality assurance bodies. This strategic ambiguity highlights the unsustainability of the UAE's K-12 AI curriculum as it intensifies expectations for its implementation. Market segmentation emerges between institutions that prioritise UK regulatory satisfaction and those that prioritise UAE positioning. Faculty experience regulatory contradictions as daily professional dilemmas without resolution. Students face gaps between expectations shaped by the UAE context and delivery that is not aligned with UK equivalence. Three trajectories emerge: UK institutional exit, quality assurance reconceptualisation, or continuing intensification producing periodic crises.

The documented structural incompatibilities produce specific institutional responses and stakeholder consequences that necessitate an examination of how transnational education providers navigate the contradictions between the UAE's AI policy acceleration and UK regulatory constraints. This includes the implications these navigation strategies have for institutional sustainability and academic quality, as well as the trajectories that emerge as regulatory divergence intensifies.

Strategic Ambiguity and Managed Non-Compliance

UK transnational education providers operating in the UAE have developed adaptive strategies accepting partial satisfaction of competing frameworks rather than achieving full compliance with both. These strategies reflect pragmatic institutional positioning within structural contradictions that permit no satisfactory resolution. The most prevalent response pattern involves strategic ambiguity in institutional communications, presenting different narratives to different regulatory audiences while implementing practices that fall somewhere between competing expectations.

Institutions describe their AI integration to UAE regulators through language emphasising innovation, digital transformation, and alignment with national strategy. Strategic plans submitted to UAE regulators emphasise the institution's commitment to AI integration, reference national AI strategy goals, describe technology investments as institutional priorities, and position the institution as contributing to national workforce development. Institutional self-evaluation reports for UAE regulatory reviews emphasise the implementation of AI-enhanced teaching, learning analytics, digital capabilities development, and innovative pedagogical approaches utilising contemporary technologies. Marketing materials targeting UAE audiences emphasise technological sophistication, contemporary relevance, and alignment with the Emirate's digital transformation agendas.

The same institutions describe identical practices to UK quality assurance bodies through language that emphasises the enhancement of existing provision, pedagogical improvement, and maintenance of academic standards. Programme validation documents position technology adoption as supporting established learning outcomes rather than creating new expectations. Institutional review submissions emphasise continuity with UK provision, maintenance of degree standards, and careful evaluation of innovations before full implementation. Annual monitoring reports describe technology adoption as a measured enhancement aligned with sector developments, rather than a fundamental transformation. External examiner reports receive institutional responses that explain how technology adoption maintains equivalence with home provision through various delivery modalities.

This dual narrative enables institutions to signal appropriate positioning to each regulatory framework without explicitly acknowledging that their actual practices fully meet neither framework's expectations. To UAE regulators, the institution appears to be sufficiently committed to integrating AI and aligning with the national strategy. To UK quality assurance bodies, the institution appears to be appropriately deliberative and focused on maintaining high standards. The strategy functions through careful boundary management, describing practices in ways that satisfy regulatory expectations without triggering questions revealing the tensions.

Technology adoption decisions reveal strategic ambiguity most clearly. Institutions adopt learning management systems with AI-enhanced features, including adaptive content delivery that adjusts to student performance patterns, automated feedback that provides immediate responses to routine queries, learning analytics dashboards that visualise student engagement and performance data, and intelligent tutoring capabilities that offer personalised support. These capabilities can be characterised either as significant digital innovation, representing institutional transformation toward AI-enhanced education, or as incremental enhancement, representing the careful adoption of established technologies to improve existing pedagogical approaches.

To UAE stakeholders reviewing institutional digital capability, institutions present these adoptions as evidence of AI integration and technological sophistication. The learning management system's AI capabilities demonstrate institutional commitment to contemporary educational approaches. The adaptive content delivery shows personalised learning implementation. The learning analytics indicate data-informed teaching. These characterisations emphasise the transformational aspects, positioning the institution as digitally advanced and strategically aligned with national priorities.

To UK quality assurance reviewers evaluating programme delivery and academic standards, institutions present the same technologies as careful enhancements, maintaining continuity with established practice. The learning management system represents a contemporary platform adoption standard across the UK sector. The adaptive features enhance without fundamentally changing how programmes deliver content. The analytics support existing tutorial systems by providing additional information for academic advisers. These characterisations emphasise the continuity aspects, positioning technology as supporting rather than transforming educational approaches.

Meanwhile, the UK's sector awareness of AI integration is growing. The 2025 DfE guidance, whilst cautious, acknowledges AI as a relevant consideration. Universities across the UK sector discuss AI policy development, experiment with AI-enhanced teaching, and debate implications for academic practice. This growing awareness makes it harder to characterise significant technology adoption as a minor enhancement. UK quality assurance processes are increasingly asking specific questions about the use of AI in teaching and assessment.

Competitive Divergence And Market Segmentation

The transnational education market in the UAE shows emerging segmentation based on institutional responses to regulatory contradictions. Rather than all institutions adopting similar strategies, competitive dynamics reward different positioning choices, suggesting the market cannot sustain a uniform approach when regulatory frameworks pull institutions in opposite directions. This segmentation is evident in institutional strategic choices regarding regulatory prioritisation, technology adoption timelines, programme positioning, and student recruitment focus.

Some institutions prioritise UK regulatory satisfaction, maintaining conservative technology adoption aligned with home provision norms and accepting potential competitive disadvantage in the local market. These institutions typically possess strong UK brand recognition, an established reputation for academic rigour, and student populations valuing UK qualification credentials over local market signals. They position themselves as providers of authentic UK degrees, maintaining full equivalence with home provision, and emphasising that students receive identical education to their UK campus counterparts, regardless of study location.

These institutions frame cautious technology adoption as rigorous quality protection rather than resistance to innovation. Marketing materials emphasise traditional academic values, proven educational approaches, and careful evaluation before adopting innovations. Communications to prospective students explain that the institution maintains UK academic standards through equivalence with home provision, suggesting that rapid technology adoption might compromise these standards. The institutional narrative positions conservatism as a quality commitment, differentiating it from competitors by emphasising its established reputation rather than contemporary innovation.

However, this positioning faces increasing challenges as UAE-educated students increasingly question why university education appears technologically conservative compared to their secondary experience; they expect university lecturers to demonstrate AI sophistication at least equivalent to that of their secondary school teachers. They assume university learning platforms will be more advanced than K-12 systems. When institutions deliver more conservative technological experiences than those provided in students' secondary education, this creates cognitive dissonance that conservative positioning must address.

Institutions prioritising the UAE market responsiveness adopt more aggressive digital strategies, implementing AI-enhanced delivery that may diverge from home provision equivalence. These institutions typically include newer market entrants without established UK brand dominance, institutions focused on professional and vocational programmes where local market signals matter significantly, and institutions with governance structures enabling more rapid decision-making. They position themselves as contemporary, innovative, and responsive to the local context, emphasising alignment with UAE strategic priorities and preparing graduates for digitally integrated workplaces.

These institutions implement comprehensive learning analytics, adopt AI tutoring systems, systematically incorporate AI tools into teaching and assessment, and include explicit AI literacy learning outcomes in programme specifications, marketing these capabilities as institutional strengths. Marketing materials emphasise technological sophistication, contemporary relevance, and alignment with the national AI strategy. Communications to prospective students highlight how programmes prepare graduates for AI-integrated professional contexts and develop the capabilities that UAE employers increasingly require.

This market segmentation suggests the sector lacks a sustainable middle position. Institutions attempting to satisfy both frameworks through strategic ambiguity face competitive pressure from institutions adopting more precise positioning. The middle positioning, "we adopt technology carefully whilst maintaining standards", becomes less distinctive and potentially less appealing than either of the apparent alternatives. Competitive dynamics reward decisive strategic choices over ambiguous compromises.

Faculty Experience And Professional Positioning

Academic staff delivering transnational education face regulatory contradictions as daily professional dilemmas that impact pedagogical decisions, assessment design, student interactions, and their professional identity. Faculty members typically receive limited institutional guidance on navigating competing expectations, leaving them to develop individual strategies for managing tensions between professional judgement, student needs, regulatory requirements, and institutional constraints.

Faculty designing curricula face questions without satisfactory answers. Should module learning outcomes include AI capabilities that students demonstrably need but that are absent from UK programme specifications? Professional judgement suggests yes: students enter with K-12 AI literacy, professional contexts require AI capabilities, and effective education builds on student knowledge whilst preparing them for professional requirements. However, institutional programme specifications validated under UK frameworks may not include AI literacy, making its inclusion in module learning outcomes potentially misaligned with programme-level outcomes. Faculty adding module learning outcomes not derived from programme specifications may face quality assurance questions during annual monitoring or revalidation processes.

Should assessment incorporate AI tools that students use professionally, but that may be questioned during quality reviews? Industry practices in business, engineering, computing, and many other disciplines are increasingly utilising AI tools for analysis, problem-solving, design, and decision-making. Students entering these professions require the capability to use these tools appropriately, critically evaluate their outputs, and understand their limitations. Assessment should verify that students possess these capabilities. However, if UK home provision doesn't incorporate AI tools in assessment because UK students may not all possess AI literacy, then overseas assessment incorporating these tools creates potential equivalence questions that external examiners might raise.

Should teaching assume the AI literacy that UAE students possess, but UK equivalence frameworks don't require? A lecturer teaching data analytics could reasonably assume that students understand basic algorithmic concepts and focus their teaching on analytical applications rather than algorithmic fundamentals. However, if equivalent UK modules teach algorithmic fundamentals because not all UK students possess this background, the overseas teaching that assumes this knowledge creates a content difference from home provision.

The situation particularly affects internationally recruited faculty who lack familiarity with the UK regulatory framework. Many UAE-based transnational education programmes recruit faculty internationally, bringing expertise from diverse educational systems and professional contexts. These faculty members possess substantial disciplinary knowledge and teaching experience, but may not be familiar with UK quality assurance frameworks, QAA expectations, external examining processes, or validation requirements. When they propose pedagogical innovations aligned with their professional experience and student needs, they may not anticipate UK governance processes that require extensive justification and multi-committee approval.

A faculty member educated in North American or Australian systems, where technology adoption is more decentralised and individual faculty possess more pedagogical autonomy, may propose incorporating AI tools in assessment, assuming this is a routine teaching decision within faculty purview. They discover their proposal requires module modification approval, programme board consideration, institutional assessment committee review, and potentially external examiner consultation. The layers of approval don't reflect concerns about the specific proposal's educational merit, but rather the institutional need to ensure that overseas provision maintains UK standards consistency.

Student Experience Consequences

Students enrolled in UAE-based UK transnational education provision experience consequences of regulatory contradictions without understanding their structural origins. Students typically lack visibility into regulatory frameworks governing their education. They are unaware of QAA expectations, equivalence principles, external examining processes, and validation requirements. They evaluate their educational experience against expectations shaped by the UAE educational context, peer institutions, and professional requirements, not against UK regulatory frameworks.

These students expect digital capabilities development, AI-enhanced learning experiences, and technological sophistication comparable to UAE public universities and international competitors. Their expectations are not unreasonable; they reflect the educational and policy context in which they study. UAE policy emphasises AI integration, their secondary education incorporates AI systematically, peer institutions implement AI-enhanced delivery, and potential employers increasingly value AI capabilities. Students reasonably expect a university education to demonstrate technological sophistication at least equivalent to their secondary experience Liu et al., 2025).

When transnational education providers deliver more conservative experiences aligned with UK equivalence requirements, students may interpret this as a quality deficiency rather than a regulatory constraint. They don't understand that conservative technology adoption reflects institutional navigation of UK frameworks rather than institutional incapacity or disinterest in contemporary approaches. They experience the gap between expectations and delivery as institutional failure, potentially affecting satisfaction, engagement, and perception of institutional quality.

The situation intensifies for students who have familiarity with AI-enhanced learning tools, including adaptive learning platforms, intelligent tutoring systems, and AI-powered feedback mechanisms. They hold expectations that university education builds upon rather than regresses from their secondary experience, assuming university systems will be more sophisticated than K-12 platforms, university lecturers will be more conversant with AI than schoolteachers, and university assessments will require more advanced AI capabilities than secondary assessments.

Students also face employability implications from regulatory contradictions affecting their education. The UAE labour market is increasingly expecting AI literacy and digital capability as key graduate attributes. Employers in technology, business, engineering, healthcare, and other sectors are increasingly requiring graduates who can work effectively with AI tools, critically evaluate AI outputs, and understand the implications of AI for professional practice. Job descriptions increasingly list AI-related skills as requirements or preferences.

Students completing UK transnational education programmes that meet UK standards but don't fully incorporate UAE digital expectations may find themselves less competitive than graduates from institutions more responsive to local market requirements. The degree credential maintains UK recognition and international portability, valuable attributes supporting international mobility and postgraduate study. However, the credential may not signal the capabilities that UAE employers increasingly require, potentially disadvantaging graduates in local employment markets.

Regulatory Relationship Deterioration

As gaps widen between the UAE's policy expectations and the UK's institutional responses, regulatory relationships show signs of strain. UAE regulators increasingly question why international branch campuses appear less digitally sophisticated than UAE public institutions, despite claiming international excellence. UK quality assurance reviewers are increasingly scrutinising overseas provision that diverges from home standards, questioning whether transnational education maintains degree equivalence. Neither regulatory perspective acknowledges the structural impossibility institutions face operating between contradictory frameworks, interpreting institutional positioning as insufficient commitment rather than impossible compliance.

UAE regulatory communications reveal growing expectations that all institutions operating within the jurisdiction align with the national AI strategy, regardless of international affiliation. Licensing reviews and accreditation processes increasingly reference digital capability, innovation demonstration, and strategic alignment as evaluation criteria. Institutions explaining that UK regulatory constraints limit their responsiveness risk interpretation as prioritising foreign compliance over local contributions.

This mutual regulatory pressure places institutions in increasingly untenable positions. As both regulatory frameworks intensify expectations, the UAE accelerates AI integration requirements, and the UK heightens scrutiny of transnational education quality, the space for institutional navigation narrows progressively.

Implications For TNE Model Sustainability

The current reality assessment raises fundamental questions about the sustainability of the transnational education model in contexts where host-country policy diverges significantly from home-country regulatory frameworks (British Council MENA, 2024). The traditional transnational education architecture rests on assumptions that are increasingly questioned when examined against evidence of how institutions actually navigate regulatory divergence.

The architecture assumes host and home countries share core educational values, with differences limited to contextual delivery variations. This assumption enables the equivalence principle underlying UK quality assurance. However, when host countries implement educational policies that operate at different speeds, measure institutional quality through different criteria, and expect responsiveness that is incompatible with home-country governance processes, the equivalence principle becomes impossible to maintain while satisfying the expectations of the host country.

The evidence suggests three possible evolutionary trajectories for the architecture of transnational education in contexts of regulatory divergence, none of which preserve the current arrangements unchanged.

First, UK institutions may increasingly exit markets where regulatory expectations exceed what their governance structures permit or where host-country policy directions diverge too significantly from UK frameworks for sustainable navigation. This trajectory would see the UK's transnational education presence concentrating in jurisdictions with regulatory frameworks more compatible with UK approaches, potentially Anglophone countries, Commonwealth nations, or contexts where educational policy development follows consultative models that are more compatible with UK governance timescales. The UAE and similar markets pursuing aggressive digital transformation strategies through directive policy approaches may see a reduced UK transnational education presence as institutions conclude they cannot sustainably satisfy both UK and host-country regulatory frameworks.

This trajectory potentially benefits institutions from countries with more flexible regulatory frameworks or more decentralised quality assurance, allowing individual institutions greater autonomy in responding to host-country contexts. Australian institutions operating under the Tertiary Education Quality and Standards Agency TEQSA frameworks, which emphasise institutional autonomy within quality parameters, or North American institutions with more decentralised accreditation models, might find it easier to adapt to host-country requirements without facing home-country regulatory constraints equivalent to those that UK institutions navigate (Brammar, 2023).

Second, UK regulatory bodies may develop transnational education-specific frameworks that acknowledge that overseas operations cannot maintain pure equivalence with home provision when operating in significantly different policy contexts. This would require a fundamental reconceptualisation of quality assurance principles, moving from equivalence-based frameworks toward frameworks of contextual appropriateness. Rather than asking "does overseas provision maintain standards equivalent to UK provision," the framework would ask "does overseas provision maintain appropriate academic quality whilst responding appropriately to the host-country context."

Such frameworks would need to define what constitutes an appropriate contextual response while maintaining quality, establish boundaries between acceptable contextual adaptation and problematic standards drift, develop assessment criteria that evaluate contextual appropriateness alongside academic rigour, and create approval processes that enable institutions to justify contextual variations without extensive equivalence demonstrations. However, this trajectory faces substantial obstacles. The UK higher education sector values the equivalence principle as fundamental protection of UK degree quality and international reputation.

Third, current tensions may continue to intensify without a systemic resolution, producing periodic crises as specific institutions face regulatory challenges in either jurisdiction, forcing explicit choices about regulatory prioritisation. This trajectory represents the continuation of the present arrangements with increasing strain. Institutions continue attempting strategic ambiguity and managed partial compliance until specific situations force explicit positioning. Individual institutions experiencing these crises would need to make explicit strategic choices about whether to exit the UAE market, fundamentally restructure their UK relationship, or attempt to address the specific regulatory concern while managing the implications for the other jurisdiction.

None of these trajectories preserves the current situation where strategic ambiguity enables institutions to navigate contradictions through careful positioning and narrative management. The narrowing space for ambiguous navigation, competitive pressures rewarding decisive strategic choices, and intensifying regulatory expectations from both frameworks all suggest that current approaches are unsustainable.

CONCLUSION

This examination has revealed structural incompatibilities rather than coordination challenges in how UK transnational education providers navigate the intersection between UAE AI policy acceleration and UK regulatory constraints. These incompatibilities manifest across competing sovereignty claims over educational quality, irreconcilable data governance requirements, temporal misalignments in policy development cycles, and contradictory constructions of institutional legitimacy, creating operational impossibilities for institutions, faculty, and students positioned between regulatory frameworks that cannot be simultaneously satisfied.

Both the UAE's National AI Strategy 2031 and the UK quality assurance frameworks reflect legitimate national contexts and policy priorities. The analytical contribution lies not in judging which approach is preferable, but in documenting what occurs when institutions must simultaneously satisfy both sets of requirements. The current transnational education architecture assumes regulatory convergence around shared quality principles, with local adaptation limited to contextual variations in delivery and implementation. When host countries implement educational policies that operate at different speeds, measure institutional quality through various criteria, and expect responsiveness incompatible with home-country governance processes, this assumption breaks down.

The institutional responses documented demonstrate strategic ambiguity in communications, managed partial compliance with both frameworks, and competitive divergence between institutions prioritising different regulatory satisfaction, representing pragmatic adaptations to structural impossibilities rather than sustainable long-term strategies. As UAE policy expectations intensify and UK sector awareness of AI integration grows, the space for strategic ambiguity narrows. The implications extend beyond institutional operations to affect multiple stakeholders. Academic staff experience regulatory tensions as a chronic form of professional uncertainty. Students experience consequences without understanding structural origins, facing employability implications when degree credentials maintain UK recognition but may not signal the capabilities that UAE employers increasingly require.

The examination contributes to scholarship by documenting regulatory intersection dynamics that existing literature addresses insufficiently. The structural dynamics documented, competing sovereignty claims, irreconcilable regulatory requirements, temporal incompatibilities, and contradictory legitimacy constructions likely extend beyond AI integration to affect other domains where host and home countries pursue significantly different policy agendas. Transnational education operates within complex regulatory environments where multiple legitimate authorities exercise oversight based on respective mandates. When the expectations of these authorities align, complexity remains manageable. When they diverge significantly, the intersection raises fundamental questions about how educational quality is defined, who holds the authority to determine it, and whether the current transnational architecture can accommodate the increasing global diversity in educational policy approaches.

REFERENCES

Brammar, L. (2023) *A three lenses approach to employability - transdisciplinary approaches to TNE students' careers education,* https://www.emerald.com/. Available at: https://www.emerald.com/heswbl/article-abstract/13/6/1204/97816/A-three-lenses-approach-to-employability?redirectedFrom=fulltext (Accessed: 02 August 2025).

Campbell University. (2025) *Ai in higher education: A meta summary of recent surveys of students and faculty,* https://sites.campbell.edu/academictechnology/. Available at: https://sites.campbell.edu/academictechnology/2025/03/06/ai-in-higher-education-a-summary-of-recent-surveys-of-students-and-faculty/ (Accessed: 19 August 2025).

Department for Education (DfE). (2025) *Generative Artificial Intelligence (AI) in Education, GOV.UK.* Available at: https://www.gov.uk/government/publications/generative-artificial-intelligence-in-education/generative-artificial-intelligence-ai-in-education (Accessed: 03 September 2025).

Higher Education Institutions. B.C. (2024) *Upcoming report: Sustainability of tne partnerships in Egypt, Qatar and the UAE, Upcoming report: sustainability of TNE partnerships in Egypt, Qatar and the UAE | British Council.* Available at: https://opportunities-insight.britishcouncil.org/features/upcoming-report-sustainability-of-tne-partnerships-egypt-qatar-and-uae (Accessed: 03 August 2025).

His Highness Sheikh Mohammed bin Rashid Al Maktoum (2025) *UAE National Strategy for Artificial Intelligence 2031,* https://u.ae/. Available at: https://ai.gov.ae/wp-content/uploads/2021/07/UAE-National-Strategy-for-Artificial-Intelligence-2031.pdf (Accessed: 17 August 2025).

Liu, C., Chai, K. K., & Chen, Y. (2025, April). The Transformative Role of Generative AI in Higher Education: Perspectives from Academia and Industry. In *2025 IEEE Global Engineering Education Conference (EDUCON)* (pp. 1-6). IEEE.

MIS Consultants. (2025) *AI law in UAE: Data Protection is a legal anchor,* https://misconsultants.ae/. Available at: https://misconsultants.ae/article/the-legal-framework-governing-artificial-intelligence-in-the-uae-data-protection-as-a-legal-anchor (Accessed: 14 September 2025).

Quality Assurance Agency. (2014) *Review of UK transnational education in United Arab Emirates: Overview,* https://www.qaa.ac.uk/. Available at: https://www.qaa.ac.uk/docs/qaa/international/review-transnational-education-uae-14.pdf?sfvrsn=1407f481_2 (Accessed: 11 August 2025).

UAE Government Portal. (2021) *UAE strategy for Artificial Intelligence: The Official Portal of the UAE government, UAE Strategy for Artificial Intelligence | The Official Portal of the UAE Government.* Available at: https://u.ae/en/about-the-uae/strategies-initiatives-and-awards/strategies-plans-and-visions/government-services-and-digital-transformation/uae-strategy-for-artificial-intelligence (Accessed: 10 August 2025).

UUKi. (2023) *Transnational Education (TNE) data,* https://www.universitiesuk.ac.uk/. Available at: https://www.universitiesuk.ac.uk/what-we-do/policy-and-research/publications/features/uk-higher-education-data-international/transnational-education-tne-data (Accessed: 05 September 2025).

Wang, S., Wang, F., Zhu, Z., Wang, J., Tran, T., & Du, Z. (2024). Artificial intelligence in education: A systematic literature review. *Expert Systems with Applications*, *252*, 124167.

Chapter 6
Culturally Responsive AI:
Enhancing Student Engagement and Belonging in Transnational Education

Mamun Ala
https://orcid.org/0000-0002-1687-3776
Australian Institute of Business, Australia

ABSTRACT

Transnational education (TNE) broadens global learning but often overlooks students' cultural identities, resulting in exclusion and "spiritual homelessness." This paper examines how culturally responsive artificial intelligence (AI) can enhance engagement, dialogue, and belonging across diverse educational contexts. It critiques standardized AI systems that reinforce dominant norms and misinterpret culturally shaped learning behaviours, proposing adaptive, culturally aware tools that respond to learners' linguistic, cultural, and relational needs. Such AI promotes inclusion, empathy, and identity affirmation. The paper calls for inclusive leadership, faculty development, and ethical governance, arguing that diversity in AI design is vital to equity, innovation, and human-centered education.

INTRODUCTION

In an era defined by global interconnectedness, transnational education (TNE) has emerged as a dynamic force shaping higher education. With institutions offering degrees across borders, establishing satellite campuses, and engaging in cross-border academic partnerships, TNE provides opportunities for international collaboration, intercultural dialogue, and access to global educational resources. However, as TNE grows, so do the complexities associated with sustaining meaningful student engagement, cultural belonging, and equitable participation across diverse cultural and institutional contexts (Ala et al., 2025; Anuyahong et al., 2023; Su & Yang, 2023).

Despite its potential to democratize access to global knowledge, TNE continues to grapple with persistent issues of cultural dislocation, identity fragmentation, and student disengagement. The learning environments within transnational programs often reflect dominant epistemologies and pedagogical norms, frequently Western-centric that may not align with the cultural backgrounds, communication styles, or educational expectations of international students. These misalignments can lead to alienation and hinder academic success (Anuyahong et al., 2023; Naidoo & Sibiya, 2019). Research highlights

DOI: 10.4018/979-8-3373-5403-3.ch006

the challenges faced by international students, including difficulties with new educational cultures and communication expectations that can exacerbate feelings of exclusion (Aprianto et al., 2024; Cranwell et al., 2021).

One concept that poignantly captures these challenges is "spiritual homelessness", articulated by Maleku et al. (2021, p. 1). This term encapsulates the deep psychological and emotional dissonance experienced by students who exist in a liminal cultural space, belonging fully to neither their home country nor their host institution. These students often juggle multiple and conflicting identity narratives, attempting to reconcile familial expectations, cultural norms, and academic demands in environments that offer limited scaffolding for such negotiations (Naidoo & Sibiya, 2019). The lack of a stable cultural identity in educational settings can generate feelings of exclusion, undermining both academic performance and psychosocial well-being.

Studies in transnational education have consistently documented the uneven patterns of integration and participation among students from diverse cultural backgrounds. For example, Steele and Douglas (2021) examine how international students in TNE contexts experience academic and social integration differently from their domestic peers, often facing institutional cultures that are unfamiliar or unaccommodating. Guo and Ling (2019) and other scholars examine the challenges transnational students face in negotiating their sense of self within educational systems that are not designed with cultural diversity in mind (Anuyahong et al., 2023; Aprianto et al., 2024). These studies underscore a recurring theme: while TNE expands access, it often fails to provide inclusive mechanisms for belonging and identity affirmation.

Within this context, culturally responsive AI emerges as a compelling intervention. Traditionally, AI in education has been viewed as a tool for efficiency and data-driven decision-making. However, these applications often operate on culturally neutral assumptions, overlooking the contextual nature of student learning experiences (Zhou & Schofield, 2024; He, 2023). This overview proposes a shift in perspective: rather than viewing AI merely as a technical solution, it must be reimagined as a relational partner capable of promoting inclusion and facilitating cross-cultural understanding (Kanont et al., 2024; Nikolopoulou, 2024).

Culturally responsive AI refers to systems designed with cultural sensitivity, recognizing and adapting to diverse communication patterns and identity markers (Sudhir, 2024). Such AI tools can personalize content delivery not just in terms of academic level, but also in relation to cultural context, language fluency, and learning preferences. For example, real-time language translation, emotionally intelligent tutoring systems, and adaptive communication interfaces can help bridge linguistic and cultural divides in cross-border classrooms (Abbas et al., 2023; Alotaibi & Alshehri, 2023; Guo & Wang, 2024). Culturally aware AI can also help institutions detect early signs of disengagement, social withdrawal, or academic struggle, offering timely and tailored interventions that consider a student's background, linguistic challenges, and relational needs (Aisyah et al., 2024; Thoriquttyas & Rohmawati, 2024; Wen et al., 2025).

Recent research supports this shift in framing AI not only as a functional tool, but as a potentially transformational agent. Pimentel et al. (2024) found that when chatbots were customized to reflect local cultural idioms and affective communication styles, students reported higher levels of engagement, trust, and emotional resonance. Similarly, Chen (2024) argues that AI systems designed for creative learning such as music or writing benefit significantly from cultural adaptation, enabling students to draw upon their cultural identities as assets rather than barriers. These findings illustrate how technological design choices, often overlooked in mainstream AI applications, have profound implications for educational equity and inclusion (Alotaibi & Alshehri, 2023; Kanont et al., 2024).

While the promise of culturally responsive AI is clear, its integration into the practice of TNE remains underdeveloped. Most existing AI tools in higher education are often built for scalability rather than cultural responsiveness, sometimes reinforcing dominant knowledge paradigms (Nikolopoulou, 2024; Sudhir, 2024). The overrepresentation of English-language content and standardized learning frameworks can reproduce educational inequities under the guise of neutrality (Karimi & Khawaja, 2023; Mary & Joyce, 2024; Wang et al., 2023; Zhao & Zhang, 2023; Zhai et al., 2025).

Therefore, this chapter reviews the literature on culturally responsive AI in education, focusing on its role in enhancing student engagement, identity affirmation, and sense of belonging within TNE. The chapter is organized around four interrelated themes:

1. Under-addressed cultural exclusion in TNE: exploring the barriers that international students face due to culturally unresponsive pedagogies and technologies, and how AI can mitigate these through adaptive communication and identity-aware feedback (Kim et al., 2022; Athanassopoulos et al., 2023).
2. Missed opportunities for engagement and innovation: arguing that AI, when designed with cultural responsiveness, can unlock collaborative, multilingual, and creative learning environments that deepen belonging and spark cross-cultural knowledge exchange (Abbas et al., 2023; Li & Lin, 2025).
3. Risk of reproducing inequities: critiquing the ways in which non-adaptive AI systems can embed Western-centric norms, and presenting alternatives for more inclusive design frameworks that honor pluralistic knowledge systems (Zhao & Zhang, 2023; Zhai et al., 2025).
4. Limited research-practice integration: highlighting the gap between emerging research on culturally responsive AI and its institutional implementation in TNE, with a focus on the policy, leadership, and design principles required to close this gap.

These themes contribute to an ongoing dialogue at the intersection of technology, culture, and pedagogy, urging educators, technologists, and policymakers to strive for structural inclusion in AI applications. The chapter concludes with implications for research and policy, advocating for a culturally reflexive approach to AI in transnational education that recognizes students as cultural agents whose identities and voices should be reflected in the technologies shaping their academic experiences.

CULTURAL EXCLUSION AND BELONGING IN TNE

Transnational education (TNE) exists at the intersection of mobility, institutional internationalization, and cross-cultural exchange. While its structural expansion has opened new frontiers in global learning, it has also exposed deep tensions around student identity, cultural dissonance, and academic belonging. This section examines the cultural and relational challenges international students face in TNE environments, critiques the inadequacy of standardized AI tools to address these challenges, and lays the conceptual groundwork for culturally responsive AI in education.

Cultural and relational challenges in TNE environments

Despite the promises of inclusivity and cosmopolitanism that often accompany the rhetoric of TNE, many international students encounter environments where they are required to adapt to dominant academic and social norms without corresponding institutional efforts to accommodate cultural diversity. The mismatch between students' cultural identities and the expectations embedded in transnational programs often results in subtle but powerful forms of exclusion.

As indicated earlier, a particularly evocative concept for understanding this dynamic is "spiritual homelessness" (Maleku et al., 2021, p.1). Unlike physical displacement, this condition refers to the internal, affective dissonance experienced by students who cannot fully identify with either their home or host cultures within the academic sphere. These students often straddle multiple cultural expectations, struggling to reconcile familial values, community obligations, and the pedagogical demands of Western-style education. The result is a pervasive sense of alienation that undermines both academic performance and emotional well-being (Sánchez-Martín, 2021).

These challenges are often compounded by relational barriers in TNE environments. For example, research suggests that international students experience academic and social integration differently from domestic peers (Avsheniuk, 2020; Steele & Douglas, 2021). Limited interaction with faculty and peers, feelings of invisibility in classroom discourse, and difficulty accessing institutional support services create cumulative disadvantages (Ma'abo, 2023: Nawaz, 2018). Guo and Ling (2019) similarly note that transnational students frequently engage in continuous identity negotiation, attempting to construct a sense of belonging in environments that rarely reflect their own cultural reference points.

These experiences point to the relational deficit in many TNE environments: while the infrastructure may be transnational, the pedagogical and interpersonal frameworks often remain anchored in culturally dominant norms. Academic engagement is often conceptualized through culturally specific lenses prioritizing verbal assertiveness, individualism, and critique, which may conflict with the values of students from collectivist or high-context cultures (Zwanikken et al., 2013). When students fail to perform in these expected ways, they are often problematized as passive or disengaged, further exacerbating feelings of exclusion (Ng, 2012).

The problem is not a lack of student capability or motivation, but rather a lack of institutional cultural fluency. Educational systems and pedagogies that do not accommodate diverse ways of knowing, interacting, and expressing understanding effectively condition belonging upon assimilation. This limits the development of authentic, inclusive academic communities in which all students are empowered to participate fully (Mwasalwiba, 2010).

The inadequacy of standardized AI tools in TNE contexts

In parallel with the expansion of TNE, there has been rapid uptake of artificial intelligence (AI) tools in higher education. These include automated essay scorers, predictive analytics platforms, chatbots, intelligent tutoring systems, and adaptive learning software. While such tools offer efficiencies and basic personalization, most are designed with universalist assumptions that fail to account for the cultural diversity of their users (Yeo & Newton, 2021).

A central issue with standardized AI tools is that they are typically trained on datasets drawn from Western educational contexts and then deployed across global student populations without meaningful localization. As a result, they risk misrecognizing or misinterpreting students' behavior, expression, and academic output when these diverge from dominant norms (Eatmon et al., 2020). For example, AI-powered writing assessment tools may penalize non-linear argument structures or indirect rhetorical styles, which are common in many non-Western traditions, mistaking them for incoherence or lack of clarity (Knight, 2015).

These design assumptions are also evident in engagement analytics. Many AI systems measure participation through quantifiable actions such as the number of clicks, time spent on a platform, or frequency of contributions to discussion forums without acknowledging the qualitative dimensions of engagement that are often culturally shaped (Madge et al., 2014). A student who is highly reflective but less verbally active may be flagged as disengaged, even though they are intellectually immersed in the material.

Similarly, emotion-detection software used in some remote learning contexts can misread affective signals. For instance, facial expression analysis tools may interpret neutral or serious expression as boredom or confusion, when in fact such expressions may reflect cultural norms of attentiveness or respect (Healey, 2018). The risk here is twofold: not only are students misdiagnosed by the system, but the data derived from these interactions may influence instructor perceptions and institutional interventions.

Moreover, the use of AI in feedback mechanisms often fails to adapt to students' relational and communicative expectations. Feedback generated by AI may appear abrupt, overly directive, or misaligned with a student's preferred tone or interactional style. In cultures where indirect communication or face-saving strategies are common, such blunt responses can alienate rather than support learners (Avsheniuk, 2020).

These limitations reveal a deeper issue: AI tools in education frequently treat culture as noise rather than a signal, flattening difference in pursuit of consistency or scalability. In doing so, they risk not only technical failure but pedagogical harm, reinforcing existing inequalities by privileging dominant norms of learning, writing, and speaking (Sun et al., 2022).

The conceptual foundation for culturally responsive AI

The shortcomings of current AI applications in TNE highlight the need for an alternative paradigm: one that centers cultural responsiveness as a core design and pedagogical principle. While the term "personalization" is often used in educational AI, it tends to focus on cognitive profiles or learning styles, neglecting the broader cultural, linguistic, and affective dimensions of student experience (Guler, 2021; Kim, 2024; Luo & wang, 2024).

Culturally responsive AI moves beyond narrow forms of adaptation and instead seeks to design technologies that affirm and reflect the cultural identities of learners. Grounded in educational theories such as Culturally Relevant Pedagogy (Ladson-Billings, 1995) and Culturally Sustaining Pedagogy (Paris & Alim, 2017), this approach recognizes that culture is not a peripheral concern but foundational to how students engage, make meaning, and express themselves.

In practice, culturally responsive AI would involve (Chen & Zmire, 2024; Page et al., 2024; Viberg et al., 2024; Xia et al., 2024):

- Culturally adaptive feedback: AI that provides supportive, context-aware feedback tailored not only to a student's performance but to their communication style and emotional needs.
- Multilingual and intercultural interfaces: Tools that enable students to present educational platforms in their preferred languages and interact in culturally familiar ways.
- Relational intelligence: AI systems designed to recognize and respond to culturally shaped relational norms such as levels of formality, indirectness, or collaborative dynamics.
- Participatory design methodologies: Involving students and educators from diverse backgrounds in the co-creation of AI tools, ensuring that these technologies reflect a plurality of worldviews and values.

Pimentel et al. (2024) provide an example of this approach in action, showing that students responded more positively to AI chatbots that were programmed with local cultural idioms, affective sensitivity, and relational tone. Similarly, Chen (2024) demonstrates that AI used in music education became more effective when it acknowledged students' cultural genres and aesthetic preferences, thereby deepening both engagement and learning outcomes.

Culturally responsive AI is not merely a technical enhancement; it is a reframing of AI as a pedagogical actor, one that participates in the co-construction of inclusive learning environments (Shams & Huisman, 2011; Taneri & Özbek, 2023). This reframing requires moving away from abstract metrics of engagement and toward recognition of the embodied, situated, and relational nature of learning, especially in transnational contexts.

By embedding cultural intelligence into AI systems, educational institutions can begin to bridge the gap between technological innovation and genuine inclusion, ensuring that digital tools support, not silence, the diverse voices that populate today's global classrooms.

MODELS OF CULTURALLY RESPONSIVE AI IN EDUCATION

Building on the critique of cultural exclusion and the inadequacy of standardized AI tools in transnational education (TNE), this section explores how culturally responsive AI is being designed and implemented to promote inclusion, engagement, and identity affirmation. It focuses on practical models of AI-enhanced education that integrate multilingual support, culturally adaptive feedback, and context-aware content delivery, and examines their application across diverse institutional and cultural contexts. Through literature and practice-based evidence, this section illustrates the potential of culturally responsive AI to act not only as a technical innovation but as a pedagogical agent of belonging.

Multilingual AI systems: bridging linguistic gaps

Language remains one of the most persistent barriers in TNE environments. While English continues to dominate as the medium of instruction, many students face academic spaces in which their expressive fluency is constrained. Standardized AI tools often exacerbate these challenges by assuming linguistic homogeneity, providing feedback or instruction in a single dominant language without accommodating the multilingual realities of global classrooms.

In contrast, culturally responsive AI systems incorporate real-time multilingual interfaces that allow students to access content, seek clarification, and express ideas in their preferred language. Guo and Wang (2024) demonstrate how AI-enhanced translation tools in an English-as-a-foreign-language (EFL) program supported Chinese students in overcoming communicative anxiety. These systems provided not only direct translations but also cultural context cues, enabling students to better interpret academic discourse and participate more confidently in peer collaboration (Anuyahong et al., 2023).

Beyond translation, multilingual natural language processing (NLP) models can be programmed to recognize and accommodate variations in sentence structure, rhetorical logic, and idiomatic expression across languages (Su & Yang, 2023). For instance, in AI-based writing assistants, students from different linguistic backgrounds may receive differentiated feedback on their writing style, supporting cross-linguistic literacy development without penalizing non-Western discourse norms (Naidoo & Sibiya, 2019).

These tools are particularly effective when combined with voice-based or multimodal interaction interfaces, allowing students to express themselves through speech, gesture, or visual storytelling, modalities that may align more closely with their cultural learning styles (Cranwell et al., 2021). In this way, AI acts as a linguistic bridge, not only translating words but translating worlds.

Culturally adaptive feedback mechanisms

Feedback plays a central role in shaping students' learning trajectories, motivation, and sense of academic competence (Aprianto et al., 2024). Yet, in many TNE settings, feedback practices may not align with the communication norms of students from various cultural backgrounds.

Culturally responsive AI systems are being designed to offer feedback that is both technically accurate and culturally attuned (Almaraz-López et al., 2023). For example, systems developed for East Asian learners adapt tone, timing, and style of feedback based on cultural preferences for face-saving and group-oriented learning goals (Zhou & Schofield, 2024). Students receiving supportive feedback were more likely to remain engaged, persist in difficult tasks, and report higher satisfaction with the AI system.

One practical model is the adaptive feedback loop, where AI dynamically adjusts its responses based on the student's engagement and affective signals (He, 2023). For example, this might include acknowledging a student's effort in using a second language or providing encouragement rather than correction when confidence appears low.

Importantly, adaptive feedback is not about reinforcing cultural stereotypes but about creating feedback environments that honor students' values and identities. This requires that AI systems be trained on diverse cultural interaction data and designed with a framework of relational ethics, acknowledging the emotional weight that feedback carries for students adjusting with unfamiliar academic terrain (Kanont et al., 2024).

Context-aware content and pedagogical adaptation

Beyond language and feedback, culturally responsive AI can enhance curriculum delivery and content engagement by tailoring instructional materials to students' socio-cultural contexts. Standardized curricula often overlook students' lived experiences, presenting examples, case studies, and analogies that may be irrelevant or unintelligible to students from different backgrounds. AI-driven content systems offer a pathway to mitigate this issue by adapting learning materials based on students' cultural, geographic, or disciplinary profiles (Nikolopoulou, 2024).

Chen (2024) illustrates this in a study of AI-assisted music education, where the AI tool adapted its instructional strategy based on the musical traditions and aesthetic sensibilities of different student groups. Students were encouraged to draw upon their cultural backgrounds in creating music, which significantly increased both motivation and creative confidence. Rather than flattening difference, the AI enabled a pedagogical pluralism in which diverse cultural forms were central to, rather than peripheral to, the learning process.

Similarly, in STEM education, AI tutoring platforms can integrate context-aware content by using locally relevant examples (Melo, 2024; Sun et al., 2025). This approach not only increases relevance but helps students see their cultural knowledge as legitimate and valuable within academic disciplines often dominated by Western paradigms.

Adaptive content systems can also be designed to respond to sociopolitical sensitivities, avoiding cultural missteps that might arise from deploying the same materials globally (Abbas et al., 2023). In doing so, culturally responsive AI promotes not just engagement, but also a sense of intellectual inclusion, enabling students to see their worlds reflected in what they learn and how they learn it.

Institutional and cross-cultural implementation

While the technical potential of culturally responsive AI is increasingly evident, its effectiveness depends on how it is implemented across institutional and cultural contexts. Models that succeed in one environment may not easily translate to another without careful calibration and participatory design.

For example, Athanassopoulos et al. (2023) explored the use of ChatGPT as a feedback tool to support foreign language writing among refugee and migrant students in a multilingual junior high school classroom in Greece. After completing an initial writing task in German, students received AI-generated feedback focused on vocabulary and grammar. The study found that most students showed improvements in word count, lexical variety, and sentence complexity in their revised texts, suggesting ChatGPT's potential to enhance L2 writing for learners facing linguistic and educational barrier.

In a large-scale mixed-methods study, Li and Lin (2025) examined how AI-assisted learning environments influenced academic engagement and needs satisfaction among 300 Chinese EFL university students. Grounded in Self-Determination Theory, their findings showed that students' positive perceptions of AI were significantly associated with increased behavioural, cognitive, and emotional engagement, which in turn predicted higher satisfaction of autonomy, competence, and relatedness needs. Qualitative interviews further revealed that while students found AI tools motivating and useful, sustained engagement was often hindered by usability challenges and unmet learning needs.

What these examples show is that contextual adaptability is central to culturally responsive AI design. Institutions must invest in the localization and co-creation of AI tools, involving students, faculty, and designers in processes that ensure alignment with cultural values, pedagogical goals, and ethical principles (Sanusi & Olaleye, 2022).

Moreover, culturally responsive AI necessitates institutional commitment, including policies that support inclusive technology procurement, faculty training in intercultural pedagogy, and governance frameworks that monitor the ethical deployment of AI tools. Without such infrastructure, even the most promising technologies risk reproducing the exclusions they intend to counteract (Strzelecki, 2023).

AI AS A CATALYST FOR CROSS-CULTURAL ENGAGEMENT AND INNOVATION

While much of the discourse around artificial intelligence (AI) in education has focused on efficiency, automation, and personalisation, there is growing recognition that AI, when designed with cultural responsiveness, can serve as a catalyst for deeper forms of engagement, particularly in transnational education (TNE) contexts. More than a delivery mechanism, culturally attuned AI systems have the potential to transform how students interact across cultural boundaries, collaborate meaningfully, and generate new knowledge together.

This section examines the role of culturally responsive AI in facilitating peer-to-peer interaction, multilingual communication, and collaborative problem-solving, particularly in diverse classrooms shaped by cultural plurality. It argues that AI systems, when designed to reflect students' sociocultural realities, can support conditions not only for inclusion, but for innovation, positioning diversity as an asset rather than a barrier to learning.

From passive participation to active collaboration

Transnational learning environments often struggle to move beyond surface-level multiculturalism, the mere presence of diverse student bodies, toward genuine intercultural collaboration. While students may share physical or digital spaces, meaningful interaction across linguistic and cultural boundaries is often limited, constrained by communicative anxieties, differing participation norms, or institutional models that prioritize individual performance.

Culturally responsive AI can intervene in these dynamics by scaffolding collaborative engagement, offering tools and environments where students feel safe and empowered to contribute across differences. For instance, AI-driven platforms that enable real-time multilingual dialogue through simultaneous translation, code-switching recognition, or culturally adaptive conversational agents, allow students to participate in collaborative tasks in ways that honor their linguistic identity while building shared understanding (Zhang & Zhang, 2024). These systems help level the communicative playing field in group projects or classroom discussions, ensuring that fluency in a dominant language does not determine intellectual visibility. By recognizing and adjusting to diverse discourse styles, culturally responsive AI allows for more equitable contributions, promoting a shift from passive presence to active co-construction of knowledge.

Liao et al. (2021) illustrate how AI-enhanced project-based learning can support deeper student engagement in STEM by integrating problem-solving, collaboration, and iterative experimentation. Through a student-centered STEM model, AI-supported tasks such as target tracking in intelligent cars helped students develop interdisciplinary skills and critical thinking. The AI did not serve as a cognitive interpreter but rather as a tool to support practical application, peer collaboration, and innovation in engineering education.

Enabling multilingual dialogue and cultural code-switching

Language remains one of the most significant inhibitors of student interaction in TNE classrooms. Even when students are proficient in the language of instruction, the performative expectations of academic English can discourage spontaneous peer-to-peer dialogue, particularly in group work, presentations, or seminars. AI tools that enable multilingual participation offer critical intervention.

Advanced natural language processing (NLP) systems, trained on culturally diverse linguistic corpora, can support informal and formal academic communication across languages. Students can submit contributions in their preferred language, which the system translates and integrates into shared documents or discussion threads. Importantly, culturally aware NLP systems do more than literal translation; they preserve nuance, context, and culturally embedded meaning (Al Anakrih, 2025; Rayimqul o'g'li & Ogunode, 2025).

This functionality not only reduces anxiety for students operating in a second or third language but also affirms the legitimacy of linguistic diversity as a resource rather than a liability. In this sense, AI becomes a platform for code-switching with dignity, a space where students can move between cultural registers without compromising expression or intellectual complexity.

In practice, this has significant implications for peer learning and knowledge exchange. As Chatzichristofis (2025) argues, AI systems that are pedagogically grounded and ethically designed can act as mediators of inclusive collaboration in linguistically diverse classrooms. In multilingual writing environments, students can draft content in their native languages, rely on AI for translation and clarification, and co-edit outputs in a shared academic language. This process encourages deeper intercultural engagement, as learners must explain culturally embedded expressions and perspectives, transforming translation into a site of dialogue rather than erasure. Such collaborative use of AI affirms linguistic diversity while promoting shared intellectual ownership.

Facilitating collaborative problem-solving across cultures

Culturally responsive AI is particularly well-positioned to support collaborative problem-solving, a core competency in global education. Diverse groups often bring rich but contrasting epistemologies, reasoning patterns, and priorities to problem-solving tasks. Without adequate mediation, these differences can lead to miscommunication or superficial consensus. AI can function as a neutral facilitator, identifying when group dynamics are stalled due to cultural misalignment and offering prompts or visualizations that encourage negotiation of meaning (Williams et al., 2021).

For example, AI-supported brainstorming platforms can track patterns in group dialogue and identify moments when ideas are not being reciprocated or understood. These platforms can then generate scaffolding questions, encouraging participants to unpack their reasoning and invite alternative perspectives (Sheoran & Kaur, 2024). In STEM disciplines, AI-enhanced collaboration tools can recommend problem-solving strategies aligned with students' prior learning cultures, allowing learners to draw on their cultural strengths within shared tasks (Chen et al., 2024). By doing so, AI systems not only support task outcomes but help students recognize and value their own intellectual heritage in intercultural settings (Leon, Lipuma, & Oviedo-Torres, 2025).

Importantly, this kind of AI-enhanced collaboration does not aim to erase cultural differences but to render them productive, making space for friction, negotiation, and synthesis as essential parts of the learning process. The goal is not cultural assimilation but the cultivation of intercultural fluency and innovation through dialogue.

AI as a tool for relational innovation in TNE

Beyond academic performance, culturally responsive AI can enhance the relational fabric of the learning environment, what some scholars refer to as the "social architecture" of belonging. In classrooms where students may feel isolated or apprehensive about crossing cultural boundaries, AI-mediated platforms can create low-stakes relational entry points that spark connection and curiosity (Chen et al., 2020; Holmes et al., 2019; Murtiningsih & Sujito, 2024).

For instance, AI chatbots programmed with culturally diverse personas, each reflecting different linguistic styles, humour norms, or interaction rituals, can model intercultural empathy and invite students to engage in conversations that reveal cultural commonalities and differences in safe, exploratory ways (Parsakia, 2023). These chatbots can also offer reflective prompts that encourage students to share personal narratives or cultural perspectives as part of collaborative learning tasks. Such tools can be particularly powerful in asynchronous learning environments, where real-time interaction may be limited. AI systems that facilitate peer-matching based on complementary knowledge areas or shared interests can help students form micro-communities of practice, overcoming the spatial and temporal dispersion common in TNE.

In all of these models, culturally responsive AI acts not as a substitute for human connection, but as a relational catalyst helping students find each other across lines of difference and engage in the kind of deep, co-constructed learning that TNE aspires to provide.

INSTITUTIONAL AND POLICY ENABLERS OF CULTURALLY RESPONSIVE AI

While the design of culturally responsive AI is often discussed in terms of technological innovation and pedagogical insight, its successful implementation in transnational education (TNE) ultimately depends on the institutional and policy ecosystems in which it is embedded. AI, like any educational tool, does not operate in isolation; it reflects and reinforces the values, assumptions, and priorities of the institutions that adopt it. As such, advancing culturally responsive AI requires more than technical refinement; it demands systemic shifts in leadership, governance, faculty development, and digital infrastructure.

This section explores the institutional and policy enablers necessary for culturally responsive AI to thrive in TNE contexts. It focuses on three interrelated domains: institutional leadership and vision, faculty capacity and professional development, and policy frameworks that embed cultural responsiveness into AI governance, curriculum design, and learning systems. Together, these elements constitute the foundation for sustainable and ethical innovation that centers inclusion, equity, and student voice.

Institutional leadership and strategic vision

The integration of culturally responsive AI in TNE is not simply a matter of tool selection, it requires visionary leadership that positions inclusion and cultural responsiveness as core institutional commitments. Senior leaders, including university presidents, deans, and technology officers, play a critical role in shaping the strategic direction of AI adoption and in determining the values that underpin it (Alfayez & Rasool, 2025).

For AI to support cross-cultural belonging rather than reinforce exclusion, institutions must first articulate a shared vision of inclusion that goes beyond access and diversity metrics. This vision should explicitly recognize the cultural plurality of the student body, the epistemological diversity of global knowledge systems, and the relational dimensions of learning in cross-border environments (Rehman, 2025). Institutions that succeed in embedding culturally responsive AI do so by aligning technology initiatives with broader strategies for inclusive pedagogy, decolonizing the curriculum, and prioritizing student well-being (Abulaiti, 2024).

Leadership commitment must also extend to resource allocation. Building culturally responsive AI systems often involves longer development timelines, participatory design processes, and ongoing data refinement (Reis & Sun, 2025). These efforts cannot be sustained without financial investment, dedicated personnel, and clear implementation timelines. Forward-looking institutions incorporate these needs into their strategic planning cycles and avoid treating inclusive AI as an optional add-on (Wang, 2025).

A compelling example can be found in the case of international university networks that have established joint innovation hubs, where cross-campus teams collaborate to localize AI tools across cultural contexts (Finkelstein & Soffer-Vital, 2025). In such initiatives, leadership facilitates horizontal partnerships between institutions in the Global North and South, promoting reciprocal learning and shared authorship in the development of AI systems.

Faculty development and intercultural AI literacy

Even the most thoughtfully designed AI tools require pedagogical mediation to be effective. Faculty are the primary mediators between technology and students, and their capacity to interpret, adapt, and contextualize AI-supported learning environments is crucial to the success of culturally responsive AI (Muñoz-Basols et al., 2023). Yet many educators lack the training or institutional support to engage meaningfully with either AI technologies or intercultural pedagogy.

Institutions must therefore invest in faculty development programs that cultivate both intercultural competence and AI literacy (Gripsy et al., 2025). This involves more than technical training on platform use; it includes critical reflection on how AI systems encode assumptions about learning, identity, and knowledge. Faculty should be encouraged to interrogate the cultural logics embedded in AI tools, for example, how automated feedback systems might reproduce Western rhetorical norms or how emotion-sensing tools may misread student affect based on cultural differences (Jardim, 2024). Professional development models that have shown promise in this area include co-design workshops, where educators and students collaborate to identify pain points in existing AI systems and propose culturally responsive alternatives. These networks allow faculty to move beyond individual experimentation and contribute to the collective knowledge-building necessary for sustainable change.

Importantly, faculty development must also include a critical ethics dimension. As AI systems become more central to assessment, feedback, and academic decision-making, faculty must be equipped to question not just how AI works, but whose values it reflects and whose voices it centers (Cioranu-Rădulescu et al., 2025). Embedding culturally responsive AI into higher education requires not only skill but ethical imagination.

Embedding cultural responsiveness into AI policy and infrastructure

Beyond leadership and faculty, institutional and national policy frameworks play a decisive role in shaping how AI is deployed and whether it serves inclusion or reinforces structural inequities (Sirkeci & Lo, 2023). Most educational AI policies to date have focused on issues such as data privacy, academic integrity, and algorithmic transparency. While these are essential, they often neglect the cultural dimensions of algorithmic design and use, particularly in diverse or transnational settings (Muralidhar et al., 2025).

Embedding cultural responsiveness into AI policy begins with the development of inclusive AI governance structures. Institutions should establish AI ethics committees or digital inclusion task forces that include not only technologists and administrators but also students, international faculty, and experts in cultural studies, linguistics, and pedagogy (Li et al., 2025). These bodies can guide decisions about tool selection, vendor partnerships, and system evaluation through an equity lens (Srishti, 2025).

For example, guidelines could require that AI systems deployed in TNE contexts meet baseline standards for multilingual support, customizable feedback options, and context-aware interaction design (Longo & Albano, 2025). Procurement policies could prioritize open-source or modular AI platforms that allow for localization and cultural adaptation rather than rigid, one-size-fits-all systems (Khan, 2024).

Another key area of policy innovation is curriculum design. As AI becomes integrated into teaching and learning, policies must ensure that curricula reflect epistemic plurality, incorporating examples, case studies, and learning pathways that resonate with students from varied cultural backgrounds (Wei & Niemi, 2022). AI-driven content delivery platforms, in particular, should be evaluated for cultural bias in the selection and sequencing of materials.

Institutions can also embed cultural responsiveness into digital learning infrastructure by ensuring that learning management systems (LMS), assessment platforms, and data dashboards are designed with user flexibility in mind (Zamchalova, 2023). This includes offering multiple modes of interaction (e.g., text, speech, visual), allowing students to choose between feedback styles, and ensuring that analytics tools account for culturally shaped patterns of engagement.

Finally, accreditation bodies and national education ministries have a role to play in scaling culturally responsive AI by integrating it into quality assurance frameworks. For example, evaluation rubrics for TNE programs could include indicators on the cultural adaptability of digital tools, the inclusivity of AI-enhanced curricula, and the representation of diverse voices in algorithmic governance (Ahmed & Sohag, 2024).

CONCLUSION

This chapter has examined the promise and potential of culturally responsive artificial intelligence (AI) in addressing the persistent challenges of student engagement, cultural belonging, and equitable participation in transnational education (TNE). At a time when cross-border learning models are expanding rapidly, international students continue to experience educational environments that, while global in reach, are often narrowly conceived in terms of cultural recognition and institutional responsiveness. Through an integrative review of literature and practice, the chapter has argued that AI, when designed and implemented with cultural sensitivity, can serve not merely as a technological enhancement, but as a transformative driver of inclusion, belonging, and pedagogical innovation.

Across the chapter, several core insights emerged. First, the experience of cultural exclusion in TNE is not incidental but structural. International students frequently report feelings of dislocation, marginalisation, and "spiritual homelessness", a term that captures the complex interplay of identity loss, cultural invisibility, and academic disconnection that occurs when institutional environments fail to affirm their social and epistemological realities. These challenges are shaped not only by curricula or classroom practices, but also by unexamined assumptions embedded in institutional norms, participation expectations, and systems of assessment. What appears as a lack of engagement is often the product of cultural misalignment, linguistic barriers, or interactional norms that remain unacknowledged in pedagogical and technological design.

Second, while AI has gained considerable traction in higher education for purposes of efficiency, personalisation, and predictive analytics, the tools currently in use are often culturally neutral at best and exclusionary at worst. Standardised AI systems, such as automated feedback platforms, emotion detection software, and adaptive learning systems, typically operate on Western-centric datasets, pedagogical assumptions, and communication models. These systems may inadvertently penalise students whose linguistic expressions, rhetorical styles, or affective signals differ from dominant norms. Rather than supporting inclusion, such technologies can further entrench exclusion by making invisible the cultural variables that shape how students learn, express themselves, and interact.

In response, the chapter outlined emerging models of culturally responsive AI that actively centre student diversity as a design imperative. These systems are distinguished by their capacity to adapt across multiple axes of identity and interaction, including multilingual support, culturally sensitive feedback, and context-aware content delivery. From AI-assisted multilingual writing platforms that allow students to engage in their native languages, to feedback systems that adjust tone and structure based on cultural communication preferences, these tools demonstrate the practical viability of embedding cultural responsiveness into AI design. Moreover, they reflect a shift in how AI is understood, not as a static instructional aide, but as a dynamic relational actor capable of mediating inclusive learning experiences.

Importantly, culturally responsive AI has also been shown to support cross-cultural engagement and collaborative innovation. In diverse classrooms where students bring differing epistemologies, reasoning styles, and discursive norms, AI can facilitate peer interaction, knowledge-sharing, and creative problem-solving. Tools that support real-time multilingual dialogue, scaffold cross-cultural group work, and help students make visible their assumptions and methods serve not only to support inclusion, but to enable deeper learning and mutual understanding. In this way, AI is not merely compensating for diversity; it is activating it as a source of pedagogical richness.

However, the successful deployment of such tools does not rest solely on technological design. It is contingent on institutional and policy-level enablers that determine whether culturally responsive AI can be scaled, sustained, and ethically governed. The chapter emphasised the need for institutional leadership to articulate inclusive strategic visions, allocate resources for participatory technology development, and invest in faculty training that integrates intercultural competence with AI literacy. Equally critical are governance frameworks and procurement policies that ensure AI systems align with principles of equity, adaptability, and transparency. Without these enabling conditions, even well-designed tools risk remaining peripheral or failing to gain traction in the everyday life of transnational institutions.

Looking ahead, several directions for future research and practice emerge from this review. First, there is a need for rigorous, longitudinal studies that examine the sustained impact of culturally responsive AI on student outcomes, identity development, and academic integration in TNE contexts, moving beyond the short-term or anecdotal evidence that currently dominates the field. Equally important is the centralization of co-design methodologies that actively engage students, particularly those from marginalized and international backgrounds, as co-creators in AI development. Such approaches ensure that these systems reflect diverse voices, values, and ways of knowing, while also challenging traditional assumptions about student agency in technology governance and curriculum design. Future research must also attend to the intersectionality of cultural responsiveness, exploring how it overlaps with other dimensions of equity such as gender, disability, and socio-economic status, and ensuring that AI tools are inclusive across multiple axes of marginalization. At the institutional and policy levels, there is a pressing need to investigate how culturally responsive AI can be implemented and sustained across varied TNE contexts, with comparative research playing a vital role in identifying best practices, informing global digital equity policies, and shaping quality assurance frameworks. Finally, AI design must be radically reimagined to foreground epistemic diversity, moving beyond Western-centric paradigms to incorporate indigenous knowledge systems, alternative pedagogical models, and plural reasoning styles within datasets, design logic, and educational objectives.

To conclude, the challenge facing TNE institutions today is not whether to adopt AI, but how to ensure that its adoption aligns with the goals of justice, inclusion, and belonging. Culturally responsive AI offers one of the most promising pathways for addressing this challenge. When developed thoughtfully and embedded strategically, it can help transform transnational education from a site of cultural tension into a space of mutual recognition, creativity, and co-authorship. Realizing this potential requires that institutions move beyond reactive or instrumental approaches to AI and instead embrace a proactive, values-driven model of technological integration, one that sees cultural difference not as a complication to be managed, but as the very foundation of equitable global learning.

REFERENCES

Abbas, N., Ali, I., Manzoor, R., Hussain, T., & Hussain, M. (2023). Role of artificial intelligence tools in enhancing students' educational performance at higher levels. Journal of Artificial Intelligence. *Machine Learning and Neural Network*, *35*(35), 36–49. DOI: 10.55529/jaimlnn.35.36.49

Abulaiti, M. (2024). Higher Education in the Era of AI. In *Developments and Future Trends in Transnational Higher Education Leadership* (pp. 244–265). IGI Global. DOI: 10.4018/979-8-3693-2857-6.ch014

Ahmed, F., & Sohag, K. (2024). The role of ai and financial stress in enhancing access and equity in transnational higher education. In *Advances in Educational Marketing, Administration, and Leadership* (pp. 205–224). IGI Global. DOI: 10.4018/979-8-3693-7016-2.ch010

Al Anakrih, M. G. (2025). Language in the Digital Era: How Artificial Intelligence is Transforming Language Translation and Communication. Egyptian Journal of Linguistics and Translation, 106-137.

Ala, M., Shahid, S., Mahmud, S., Mohyuddin, S., & Kaur, K. (2025). Perceived influence of GenAI on student engagement in online higher education. *Journal of Applied Learning and Teaching*, *8*(2). Advance online publication. DOI: 10.37074/jalt.2025.8.2.16

Alfayez, A. A., & Rasool, A. (2025). Use of AI in the curriculum development of transnational higher education. In *Bridging Global Divides for Transnational Higher Education in the AI Era* (pp. 401–422). IGI Global Scientific Publishing.

Almaraz-López, C., Menéndez, F., & López-Esteban, C. (2023). Comparative study of the attitudes and perceptions of university students in business administration and management and in education toward artificial intelligence. *Education Sciences*, *13*(6), 609. DOI: 10.3390/educsci13060609

Alotaibi, N., & Alshehri, A. (2023). Prospers and obstacles in using artificial intelligence in Saudi Arabia higher education institutions—The potential of AI-based learning outcomes. *Sustainability (Basel)*, *15*(13), 10723. DOI: 10.3390/su151310723

Anuyahong, B., Rattanapong, C., & Patcha, I. (2023). Analyzing the impact of artificial intelligence in personalized learning and adaptive assessment in higher education. *International Journal of Innovation and Scientific Research*, *10*(4), 88–93. DOI: 10.51244/IJRSI.2023.10412

Aprianto, R., Lestari, E., Sadan, S., & Fletcher, E. (2024). Harnessing artificial intelligence in higher education: Balancing innovation and ethical challenges. [ITEE]. *International Transactions on Education Technology*, *3*(1), 84–93. DOI: 10.33050/itee.v3i1.680

Athanassopoulos, S., Manoli, P., Gouvi, M., Lavidas, K., & Komis, V. (2023). The use of ChatGPT as a learning tool to improve foreign language writing in a multilingual and multicultural classroom. *Advances in Mobile Learning Educational Research*, *3*(2), 818–824. DOI: 10.25082/AMLER.2023.02.009

Avsheniuk, N. (2020). UNESCO'S mission in the development of transnational higher education. *UNESCO Chair Journal Lifelong Professional Education in the XXI Century*, (1), 12–16. DOI: 10.35387/ucj.1(1).2020.12-16

Chatzichristofis, S. A. (2025). AI in Education: Towards a Pedagogically Grounded and Interdisciplinary Field. In AI in Education, 1(1), 1; DOI: 10.3390/aieduc1010001

Chen, L. (2024). Unlocking the beat: How AI tools drive music students' motivation, engagement, creativity and learning success. *European Journal of Education*, *60*(1), e12823. Advance online publication. DOI: 10.1111/ejed.12823

Chen, L., Chen, P., & Lin, Z. (2020). Artificial intelligence in education: A review. *IEEE Access : Practical Innovations, Open Solutions*, *8*, 75264–75278. DOI: 10.1109/ACCESS.2020.2988510

Chen, X., Ma, L., Su, D., Zhang, Y., Liu, X., Xin, J., & Ryoo, J. (2024, May). AI-Enhanced Cross-Cultural competence in STEM education. In *Proceedings of the International Conference on New Findings in Humanities and Social Sciences*, 1(1), 29-43.

Chen, X., & Zmire, Z. (2024). AIs role in enhancing cross cultural competence and leadership through online education programs. *Proceedings of the International Conference on New Findings in Humanities and Social Sciences*, 1(1), 1-16. DOI: 10.33422/hsconf.v1i1.268

Cioranu-Rădulescu, C., Bansal, S., Liao, Y., & Murah, M. (2025). Percep ii i practici ale cadrelor didactice privind integrarea inteligen ei artificiale în educa ie: Un studiu transna ional în România, India, China i Brunei. *Revista de Pedagogie Digitala*, *4*(1), 48–56. DOI: 10.61071/RPD.2549

Cranwell, P., Li, D., Page, E., Whiteside, K., & Woodcock, A. (2021). Understanding the barriers faced by TNE-students when completing advanced-level laboratory-based practical classes. *International Journal of Chinese Education*, *10*(3), 22125868211046033. Advance online publication. DOI: 10.1177/22125868211046033

Eatmon, T. D., Granger, R., Abrantes, B. F., & Forsberg, C. (2020). The entrepreneurial dimensions of transnational education. In *Examining the role of entrepreneurial universities in regional development* (pp. 172–182). IGI Global. DOI: 10.4018/978-1-7998-0174-0.ch009

Finkelstein, I., & Soffer-Vital, S. (2025). Cultural empathy in ai-supported collaborative learning: Advancing inclusive digital learning in higher education. *Education Sciences*, *15*(10), 1305. DOI: 10.3390/educsci15101305

Gripsy, J. V., Selvakumari, S. N., Sheeba, L., & Kumaran, B. S. (2025). Transforming Student Engagement Through AI, AR, VR, and Chatbots in Education. In Chatbots in Educational Leadership and Management (pp. 73-100). IGI Global Scientific Publishing.

Guler, N. (2021). Teaching culturally and linguistically diverse students: Exploring the challenges and perceptions of nursing faculty. *Nursing Education Perspectives*, *43*(1), 11–13. DOI: 10.1097/01.NEP.0000000000000861

Guo, S., & Ling, L. (2019). Toward transnational communities of practice: An inquiry into the experiences of transnational academic mobility. *Adult Education Quarterly*, *70*(1), 26–43. DOI: 10.1177/0741713619867636

Guo, Y., & Wang, Y. (2024). Exploring the effects of artificial intelligence application on EFL students' academic engagement and emotional experiences: A mixed-methods study. *European Journal of Education, 60*(1), e12812. Advance online publication. DOI: 10.1111/ejed.12812

He, S. (2023). The impact of new media and artificial intelligence technologies on ideological and political education in higher education institutions and countermeasures. *Proceedings of EAI International Conference*. DOI: 10.4108/eai.8-9-2023.2340095

Healey, N. (2018). The challenges of managing transnational education partnerships. *International Journal of Educational Management, 32*(2), 241–256. DOI: 10.1108/IJEM-04-2017-0085

Holmes, W., Bialik, M., & Fadel, C. (2019). *Artificial intelligence in education promises and implications for teaching and learning*. Center for Curriculum Redesign.

Kanont, K., Pingmuang, P., Simasathien, T., Wisnuwong, S., Wiwatsiripong, B., Poonpirome, K., Songkram, N., & Khlaisang, J. (2024). Generative-AI, a learning assistant? Factors influencing higher-ed students' technology acceptance. *Electronic Journal of e-Learning, 22*(6), 18–33. DOI: 10.34190/ejel.22.6.3196

Karimi, H., & Khawaja, S. (2023). The impact of artificial intelligence on higher education in England. *Creative Education, 14*(12), 2405–2415. DOI: 10.4236/ce.2023.1412154

Khan, S. M. (2024). AI-powered tools for teaching English as a second language (ESL) in TNE. In *Bridging Global Divides for Transnational Higher Education in the AI Era* (pp. 121–140). IGI Global. DOI: 10.4018/979-8-3693-7016-2.ch006

Kim, H. (2024). Guidelines for culturally and linguistically responsive instruction in higher education. *TESOL Journal, 15*(4), e807. Advance online publication. DOI: 10.1002/tesj.807

Kim, J., Lee, H., & Cho, Y. H. (2022). Learning design to support student-AI collaboration: Perspectives of leading teachers for AI in education. *Education and Information Technologies, 27*(5), 6069–6104. DOI: 10.1007/s10639-021-10831-6

Knight, J. (2015). Transnational education remodeled. *Journal of Studies in International Education, 20*(1), 34–47. DOI: 10.1177/1028315315602927

Ladson-Billings, G. (1995). Toward a theory of culturally relevant pedagogy. *American Educational Research Journal, 32*(3), 465–491. DOI: 10.3102/00028312032003465

Leon, C., Lipuma, J., & Oviedo-Torres, X. (2025, July). Artificial intelligence in STEM education: A transdisciplinary framework for engagement and innovation. In Frontiers in Education, 10 (2025), DOI: 10.3389/feduc.2025.1619888

Li, S., & Lin, J. (2025). Enhancing academic engagement and needs satisfaction through AI: A mixed-methods study in Chinese EFL tertiary education context. *European Journal of Education, 60*(2), e70110. Advance online publication. DOI: 10.1111/ejed.70110

Li, S., Xia, L., & Beech, H. (2025). Digital empowerment: innovative technology training for language teachers in a transnational EMI university. In *Innovative Approaches to Staff Development in Transnational Higher Education* (pp. 297–320). IGI Global Scientific Publishing. DOI: 10.4018/979-8-3693-9102-0.ch012

Longo, G., & Albano, S. (2025). Bridging creativity and technology: Integrating generative ai into architectural pedagogy through hybrid frameworks. *AHFE International, 160.* Advance online publication. DOI: 10.54941/ahfe1005837

Luo, Y., & Wang, D. (2024). Revolutionizing education with AI: The adaptive cognitive enhancement model (ACEM) for personalized cognitive development. In *Proceedings of the 2nd International Conference on Machine Learning and Automation* (Vol. 82, No. 1, pp. 71-76). DOI: 10.54254/2755-2721/82/20240929

Ma'abo, A. (2023). Benefits and challenges of transnational education: Reflections from a sino-british joint venture university. *International Journal of Chinese Education, 12*(1), 2212585X221144903. Advance online publication. DOI: 10.1177/2212585X221144903

Madge, C., Raghuram, P., & Noxolo, P. (2014). Conceptualizing international education. *Progress in Human Geography, 39*(6), 681–701. DOI: 10.1177/0309132514526442

Maleku, A., Phillips, R. J. N., Um, M. Y., Kagotho, N., Lee, G., & Coxe, K. (2021). The phenomenon of spiritual homelessness in transnational spaces among international students in the United States. *Population Space and Place, 28*(2), e2470. Advance online publication. DOI: 10.1002/psp.2470

Mary, D., & Joyce, M. (2024). AI and education: Impact of AI on learning outcomes in higher education. *International Journal of Scientific Research in Engineering and Management, 8*(8), 1–16. DOI: 10.55041/IJSREM37145

Melo, N. (2024). The Impact of AI-Powered Tutoring Platforms on Student Achievement in STEM Subjects: The Case of Cameroon. Available at *SSRN* 5249691.

Muñoz-Basols, J., Neville, C., Lafford, B. A., & Godev, C. (2023). Potentialities of applied translation for language learning in the era of artificial intelligence. Hispania, 106(2), 171-194. Gripsy, J., Selvakumari, S., Sheeba, L., & Kumaran, B. (2025). Transforming student engagement through AI, AR, VR, and chatbots in education., 73-100. DOI: 10.4018/979-8-3693-8734-4.ch004

Muralidhar, L. B., Sathyanarayana, N., Kumar, V., & Santhosh, Y. (2025). AI learning and talent strategies in transnational education. In *Advances in Higher Education and Professional Development* (pp. 245–276). IGI Global Scientific Publishing. DOI: 10.4018/979-8-3693-9102-0.ch010

Murtiningsih, S., & Sujito, A. (2024). Reimagining the future of education: Inclusive pedagogies, critical intergenerational justice, and technological disruption. *Policy Futures in Education, 23*(5), 14782103251341406.

Mwasalwiba, E. (2010). Entrepreneurship education: A review of its objectives, teaching methods, and impact indicators. *Education + Training, 52*(1), 20–47. DOI: 10.1108/00400911011017663

Naidoo, V., & Sibiya, M. (2019). Graduate experiences with transnational nursing education: A qualitative enquiry. *International Journal of Health Care Quality Assurance, 32*(3), 562–573. DOI: 10.1108/IJHCQA-06-2018-0155

Nawaz, T. (2018). Internationalisation strategy, faculty response and academic preparedness for transnational teaching. *Education + Training, 60*(9), 1084–1096. DOI: 10.1108/ET-09-2017-0141

Ng, S. (2012). The challenges of attracting asian students to study higher education in hong kong. *Higher Education Quarterly*, *66*(3), 272–292. DOI: 10.1111/j.1468-2273.2012.00524.x

Nikolopoulou, K. (2024). Generative artificial intelligence in higher education: Exploring ways of harnessing pedagogical practices with the assistance of ChatGPT. *International Journal of Contemporary Education*, *1*(2), 103–111. DOI: 10.47852/bonviewIJCE42022489

Page, E., Meyers, G., & Billings, E. (2024). Theory to practice: an assessment framework for generative ai.. Intersection: A Journal at the Intersection of Assessment and Learning, 5(4). DOI: 10.61669/001c.124250

Paris, D., & Alim, H. S. (Eds.). (2017). *Culturally sustaining pedagogies: Teaching and learning for justice in a changing world*. Teachers College Press.

Parsakia, K. (2023). The effect of chatbots and ai on the self-efficacy, self-esteem, problem-solving and critical thinking of students. *Health Nexus*, *1*(1), 71–76. DOI: 10.61838/hn.1.1.14

Pimentel, J. V., Malaluan, K. D., Daluperi, F. N. M., Vera, J. L. S. D., Sunga, J. E. T. A., Marin, A. J. B., & Limos-Galay, J. A. (2024). Benefits of AI chatbots and engagement of senior high school students in Divine Word College of San Jose. *International Journal of Research Studies in Educational Technology*, *8*(4). Advance online publication. DOI: 10.5861/ijrset.2024.8036

Rayimqul o'g'li, A. Y., & Ogunode, N. J. (2025). Modern Research in the Field of Translation in Foreign Countries. Spanish Journal of Innovation and Integrity, 43, 187-191.

Rehman, S. U. (2025). Adaptive Learning Systems for Personalized Language Instruction in Transnational Higher Education. In Bridging Global Divides for Transnational Higher Education in the AI Era (pp. 165-190). IGI Global Scientific Publishing.

Reis, C. S., & Sun, Y. (2025). An Innovative Approach to Integrating AI Into Learning and Teaching at a Transnational University in China. In *Training and Development in Transnational Higher Education* (pp. 331–346). IGI Global Scientific Publishing. DOI: 10.4018/979-8-3373-1897-4.ch016

Sánchez-Martín, C. (2021). Teachers' transnational identities as activity: Constructing mobility systems at the intersections of gender and language difference. *TESOL Quarterly*, *56*(2), 552–581. DOI: 10.1002/tesq.3066

Sanusi, I., & Olaleye, S. (2022). An insight into cultural competence and ethics in K–12 artificial intelligence education. *2022 IEEE Global Engineering Education Conference (EDUCON)*, 790–794. DOI: 10.1109/EDUCON52537.2022.9766818

Shams, F., & Huisman, J. (2011). Managing offshore branch campuses. *Journal of Studies in International Education*, *16*(2), 106–127. DOI: 10.1177/1028315311413470

Sheoran, P., & Kaur, M. J. (2024). Artificial intelligence (AI) enhanced co-operative learning. *Journal of Advanced Multidisciplinary Research Studies and Development*, *3*(5), 1–7.

Sirkeci, İ., & Lo, L. (2023). Editorial: Transformative impact of artificial intelligence on higher education. *Transnational Education Review*, *1*(2), 65–67. DOI: 10.33182/ter.v1i2.3193

Srishti, R. (2025). Cultural immersion and experiential learning in sustainability education. Global Cultural Immersions in Learning for a Sustainable Future, 49-76. DOI: 10.4018/979-8-3373-2508-8.ch002

Steele, A. R., & Douglas, H. E. (2021). Investigating the educational experiences of transnational students: Differences in academic integration, social integration, and institutional and goal commitment. *The British Journal of Educational Psychology*, *91*(4), 1414–1433. DOI: 10.1111/bjep.12424

Strzelecki, A. (2023). Students' acceptance of ChatGPT in higher education: An extended unified theory of acceptance and use of technology. *Innovative Higher Education*, *49*(2), 223–245. DOI: 10.1007/s10755-023-09686-1

Su, J., & Yang, W. (2023). Unlocking the power of ChatGPT: A framework for applying generative AI in education. *ECNU Review of Education*, *6*(3), 355–366. DOI: 10.1177/20965311231168423

Sudhir, V.VARIGANJI SUDHIR. (2024). The ethics of AI in the administration of higher education. *International Journal for Multidisciplinary Research*, *6*(6), 30189. Advance online publication. DOI: 10.36948/ijfmr.2024.v06i06.30189

Sun, D., Cheng, G., Yu, P. L. H., Jia, J., Zheng, Z., & Chen, A. (2025). Personalized stem education empowered by artificial intelligence: A comprehensive review and content analysis. *Interactive Learning Environments*, *33*(7), 1–23. DOI: 10.1080/10494820.2025.2462156

Sun, Y., Li, N., Hao, J., Sarno, L., & Wang, L. (2022). Post-covid-19 development of transnational education in china: Challenges and opportunities. *Education Sciences*, *12*(6), 416. DOI: 10.3390/educsci12060416

Taneri, P., & Özbek, Ö. (2023). Promoting diversity and culturally responsive pedagogy in higher education. *Uluslararası Türk Eğitim Bilimleri Dergisi*, *2023*(21), 765–813. DOI: 10.46778/goputeb.1333036

Thoriquttyas, T., & Rohmawati, N. (2024). How far artificial intelligence influenced Mu'allim, Murabbi, and Mudarris? Transhumanism and diffusion of innovation theory's perspective. *Suhuf*, *36*(2). Advance online publication. DOI: 10.23917/suhuf.v36i2.6302

Viberg, O., Cukurova, M., Feldman-Maggor, Y., Alexandron, G., Shirai, S., Kanemune, S., & Kizilcec, R. F. (2024). What explains teachers' trust in AI in education across six countries? *International Journal of Artificial Intelligence in Education*, *35*(3), 1–29.

WANG. (2025). Artificial intelligence as a catalytic mechanism: A theoretical framework and practical pathways for reshaping the industry-education integration ecosystem. *Integration of Industry and Education Journal*, *4*(3), 1–9. DOI: 10.6914/iiej.040301

Wang, T., Lund, B., Marengo, A., Pagano, A., Mannuru, N., Teel, Z., & Pange, J. (2023). Exploring the potential impact of artificial intelligence (AI) on international students in higher education: Generative AI, chatbots, analytics, and international student success. *Applied Sciences (Basel, Switzerland)*, *13*(11), 6716. DOI: 10.3390/app13116716

Wei, G. and Niemi, H. (2022). Ethical guidelines for artificial intelligence-based learning: a transnational study between china and finland. AI in Learning: Designing the Future, 265-282. DOI: 10.1007/978-3-031-09687-7_16

Wen, Y., Wang, Z., & Guo, X. (2025). Trends and applications of AI in immersive learning environments: A systematic review of empirical research. *Interactive Learning Environments*, •••, 1–19. DOI: 10.1080/10494820.2025.2524029

Williams, R., Kaputsos, S. P., & Breazeal, C. (2021). Teacher perspectives on how to train your robot: A middle school ai and ethics curriculum. *Proceedings of the AAAI Conference on Artificial Intelligence*, *35*(17), 15678–15686. DOI: 10.1609/aaai.v35i17.17847

Xia, Y., Shin, S. Y., & Kim, J. C. (2024). Cross-cultural intelligent language learning system (CILS): Leveraging AI to facilitate language learning strategies in cross-cultural communication. *Applied Sciences (Basel, Switzerland)*, *14*(13), 5651. DOI: 10.3390/app14135651

Yeo, M. A., & Newton, J. M. (2021). Inclusive transnational education partnerships: A case study of a Master of Arts in TESOL program. *RELC Journal*, *52*(2), 287–306. DOI: 10.1177/00336882211011275

Zamchalova, I. Y. (2023). Artificial intelligence: Risks and perspectives of culture. Intellect. Innovations. *Investments*, (5), 102–110. DOI: 10.25198/2077-7175-2023-5-102

Zhai, C., Du, L., Qiao, H., Zhang, Y., Yuan, X., & Zhu, H. (2025). Research on artificial intelligence empowering innovation in traditional Chinese culture. *International Conference on Measurement, Communication, and Virtual Reality (MCVR 2024)*, 60. DOI: 10.1117/12.3069480

Zhang, J., & Zhang, Z. Y. (2024). AI in teacher education: Unlocking new dimensions in teaching support, inclusive learning, and digital literacy. *Journal of Computer Assisted Learning*, *40*(4), 1871–1885. DOI: 10.1111/jcal.12988

Zhao, Z., & Zhang, L. (2023). Design of artificial intelligence cultural creative industry based on machine learning. *Soft Computing*, •••, 1–12. DOI: 10.1007/s00500-023-08693-w

Zhou, X., & Schofield, L. (2024). Using social learning theories to explore the role of generative artificial intelligence (AI) in collaborative learning. *Journal of Learning Development in Higher Education*, (30). Advance online publication. DOI: 10.47408/jldhe.vi30.1031

Zwanikken, P., Peterhans, B., Dardis, L., & Scherpbier, A. (2013). Quality assurance in transnational higher education: A case study of the troped network. *BMC Medical Education*, *13*(1), 43. Advance online publication. DOI: 10.1186/1472-6920-13-43

KEY TERMS AND DEFINITIONS

Context-Aware Content Delivery: AI-supported adaptation of curriculum materials, examples, and case studies so that they align with students' socio-cultural backgrounds, disciplines, and local realities, allowing learners to see their own worlds reflected in what and how they study.

Cultural Exclusion in TNE: A condition in which curricula, pedagogies, technologies, and institutional norms privilege dominant (often Western) epistemologies and communication styles, leaving many international students' identities, languages, and ways of knowing marginalized or invisible.

Culturally Adaptive Feedback: AI-generated feedback tailored not only to students' performance, but also to their communication styles, affective needs, and cultural norms regarding tone, directness, and face-saving, aiming to encourage rather than alienate learners.

Culturally Responsive Artificial Intelligence: AI systems designed to recognize, respect, and adapt to learners' cultural, linguistic, and relational contexts, offering interaction, feedback, and content that affirm diverse identities and promote inclusion rather than enforcing standardized norms.

Multilingual AI Systems: Educational AI tools that support multiple languages and code-switching, providing translation, clarification, and context-sensitive assistance so students can access content and express understanding in their preferred or strongest languages.

Spiritual Homelessness: A form of psychological and emotional dislocation experienced by students who feel they belong fully to neither their home culture nor their host institution, resulting in identity fragmentation, alienation, and weakened academic and social engagement.

Standardized AI Tools in Education: AI applications built on universalist, often Western-centric datasets and assumptions, which treat culture as irrelevant noise and therefore risk misinterpreting student behavior, penalizing non-dominant discourse styles, and reinforcing inequities.

Chapter 7
The Reliability of Traditional Assessments in Higher Education in Oman in the World of AI

Johaina Bani Oraba
https://orcid.org/0000-0001-9280-3465
Global College of Engineering and Technology, Oman

ABSTRACT

This mixed-methods study investigates the reliability of traditional assessments in Omani higher education amid the growing use of artificial intelligence (AI) tools such as ChatGPT, Grammarly, and Quillbot. A total of 120 participants—students, faculty, and administrators, completed an online survey examining patterns of AI use, perceptions of assessment validity, and views on academic integrity. Quantitative data were analyzed using descriptive statistics, while qualitative responses were thematically examined to capture concerns and perspectives. Findings show that AI has become widely integrated into academic practices, particularly for writing, paraphrasing, and idea generation. While some participants valued AI as supportive, others worried about its impact on authenticity and reliability. Confidence in current formats, especially essays and take-home tasks, was moderate to low in reflecting true understanding. A further challenge is the absence of clear policies or ethical guidelines, leading to inconsistent practices across institutions.

INTRODUCTION

The integration of artificial intelligence (AI) into education has dramatically increased in the last few years. This digital transformation has changed the way students access information, work on their assignments, and engage with the learning process. The various AI tools, such as ChatGPT, Grammarly, Quillbot, and other AI-assisted platforms have become widely and easily accessible, which enables the students to generate text, paraphrase content, check grammar, and even solve complex problems with

DOI: 10.4018/979-8-3373-5403-3.ch007

minimal effort (Selwyn, 2019). While these advanced tools offer opportunities for enhanced learning and productivity, they also present significant challenges to traditional assessment practices.

Globally, higher education institutions are engaging with the positive and the negative effect of the various AI tools on the academic integrity, equity, and the validity of assessment outcomes. Many researchers raise questions about whether current assessment designs are still capable of accurately measuring student learning in a context where the students can easily get access to AI tools. The higher education institutions have encountered several concerns about the originality of the student's academic work, in which they have to redesign the way they evaluate the students' learning outcomes (Holmes, Bialik, & Fadel, 2019).

Similarly, higher education institutions in Oman are encountering challenges, but there is a lack of research that explores how the integration of AI is impacting the assessment reliability and academic integrity within the Omani context. While the students increasingly use AI tools, the concerns are rising about the validity of essays, written assignments, and other conventional forms of assessment which are considered as strong indicators of student understanding and efforts. The educators and policymakers in Oman are also questioning whether the current assessment formats can keep pace with the rapid digital transformation. Most of the higher education institutions depend on outdated assessment methods that fail to capture authentic learning, which lack the ability to understand how AI impacts the students' learning performance (Al-Maskri et al., 2012).

The central aim of the study is to evaluate whether conventional assessments still reflect true student learning when AI is widely used. This can be achieved by exploring patterns of AI use among students and faculty, perceptions of assessment reliability, concerns about academic integrity, and the level of institutional preparedness to address AI-related challenges. Also, these issues are examined through the lens of five research questions focused on assessment reliability, AI's effects on outcomes, perceptions of integrity, institutional challenges, and strategies for improvement. This is essential research as it addresses an under-explored yet current issue within higher education in Oman. The study also provides valuable and insightful data for the development of the Omani higher education policy and institutional practices, thereby the findings aim to inform universities, educators, and policymakers on how to better preserve the validity of the assessment and academic standards in a world of AI.

2. LITERATURE REVIEW

2.1 The Rise of AI in Higher Education in Oman

In the past few years, the growth of the AI industry has been reshaping the future, including the teaching, and learning practices in higher education institutions. AI technologies, such as intelligent tutoring systems, curriculum planning, learning analytics, content recommendations, automated grading, and assessment chatbots and virtual assistants, provide stakeholders in education with opportunities that enhance the educational practices and can transform the student's learning experience to a new level.

These technologies can provide the students with personalized and adaptive learning platforms, which enable them to meet their learning needs and preferences. AI tools also allow the students to progress at their own pace and receive feedback and support tailored to their specific challenges (Kofinas et al., 2025). Additionally, the personalized learning opportunity provides improved accessibility (Ayeni et al., 2024). It breaks down the difficulties for students with disabilities, as it allows them to adapt various learning styles and support through technology (Ayala-Pazmiño, 2023). This accessibility provides inclusive learning content for all students with various learning styles, particularly in rural areas, which ensures equal opportunities for every student. Moreover, the integration of AI into the educational system can increase the students' engagement with the course materials as well as with their peers. According to White, (2023), AI technologies motivate students to have collaborative and experiential learning opportunities, which enrich their learning landscape, through peer and group assessment and collaborative project. This transition from traditional learning and assessment into AI-informed assessment can help the students to identify their strengths and weaknesses and achieve their learning outcomes (Msambwa et al., 2025).

From the teachers' perspective, AI integration into education has enhanced their practices. Studies discuss that AI technologies have the ability of reducing the teachers' workloads. Al Matari et al. (2023) claim that AI tools allow the teachers to focus on the course content and the students' engagement with the subject, as these tools can be used as assistants to assess their students, grade the assignments, provide various types of feedback, and help them on their administrative duties. This support can facilitate instant feedback on assessments and provide more accurate evaluations of student performance (Ayala-Pazmiño, 2023). Therefore, teachers can use various advanced AI tools to automate grading processes, significantly reducing the time they spend on assessments and allowing them to dedicate more resources to interactive teaching (Dimari et al., 2024). These tools also allow teachers to provide immediate feedback, which allow for rapid feedback loops where students can learn from their mistakes almost immediately after assessments (Al Matari et al., 2023). In addition to that, AI technologies also provide the teachers with immediate response along with real-time analytics to monitor student progress and performance and adjust instruction accordingly, which helps their students to identify their strengths and weaknesses areas for improvement (Ayala-Pazmiño, 2023). While the teachers can have the access for real-time analytics, they can accordingly design different activities that motivate the students's creativity, critical-thinking, and problem-solving skills. By conducting these activities using AI tools, teachers prepare the students for a workforce increasingly reliant on AI technologies (Ayala-Pazmiño, 2023).

There are divergent responses which reflect the broader uncertainty surrounding the pedagogical and ethical implications of AI in education. The UNESCO Guidelines on the Ethics of Artificial Intelligence (2021) highlights the need for inclusive, rights-based, and transparent implementation of AI in educational systems, but national policies vary widely in their adoption of such frameworks. This shift raises issues of cheating risks as AI facilitates academic dishonesty, poses further challenges for teachers in maintaining assessment integrity and detecting AI-generated content. As a result, the student may become overly reliant on AI tools, which may affect their critical thinking and problem-solving skills. The AI technologies have the ability to generate high-quality work that makes the students rely on them, which raises the risk that the assessment grades no longer reflect their actual understanding of the course content (Ardito, 2023). Finally, the various AI technologies significantly impact the pedagogical and ethical implications, and the fairness of assessment outcomes in higher education. Addressing these issues requires a multi-faceted approach that includes improved educational policies, detection methods, faculty training, and equitable access to technology.

2.2 The Impact of AI on Higher Education

Artificial Intelligence (AI) has been increasingly integrated into the higher education sector, which makes academic integrity a risk. Academic integrity, which is one main component of the higher education industry, has been challenged as the students overly use AI tools to answer their assignments, which makes the authenticity of their work become questionable (White, 2023). According to Cotton et al. (2023), the ease of access to AI and related technologies means that final grades may no longer accurately reflect students' individual efforts, thereby compromising the learning and teaching process. These practices challenge the credibility of academic evaluations and put pressure on educators to distinguish between original work and AI-assisted submissions, especially in traditional assessment formats (Cotton et al., 2023). This discrepancy raises concerns about the student's learning process and the overall effectiveness of traditional assessments.

2.3 Challenges in detecting AI-generated content

This issue is further complicated when it comes to detecting AI-generated content. In fact, AI tools usually generate existing sources, which makes the detecting process easier to some extent. However, most of the AI-generated content is factually incorrect and inconsistent. According to Cotton and colleagues (2023), human writing tends to be more nuanced and context-aware, while AI-generated content may lack this depth. Additionally, the fast improvement of AI makes it increasingly challenging for teachers in the higher education sector to ascertain the originality of submissions, thereby complicating traditional assessment methods. Perkins et al. (2023) notes that the traditional methods to detect plagiarism may not identify AI-generated content, which leads to potential misjudgments about a student's integrity. Many teachers use Turnitin AI for detection, which demonstrated a high level of accuracy in identifying AI presence, yet it still struggled with content produced using adversarial methods (Ardito, 2023).

The easy access of various tools lead to academic dishonesty, lack of transparency, and bias. Ardito (2023) claims that ethical instruction regarding the use of AI should be incorporated into educational curricula to ensure a critical and principled approach. Students must be taught to view AI as a supplemental tool rather than a replacement for their learning, which can promote a culture of honesty and responsibility in academic environments. Overall, while the content that is generated by AI presents opportunities for enhancing learning outcomes, it also causes significant challenges regarding plagiarism, cheating, and the fairness of assessments. Addressing these issues requires a comprehensive approach that balances the benefits of AI with the need to uphold academic integrity.

2.4 Challenges Facing Omani Higher Education

In Oman, many studies highlight that the current integration of AI into the higher education sector reflects these global concerns. Alkaaf and Al-Issa (2021) discuss several significant challenges that impact the effectiveness and the success of the students in the higher education institutions in Oman. These challenges can be categorized into three main areas: academic, structural, and financial. Higher education institutions in Oman struggle with many essential academic concerns related to student low success rate, curriculum relevance, variation in quality among institutions, skills development, wellness and support systems, and access to resources. Even though the decision-makers in higher education in Oman ensure that there is an ongoing improvement of the curriculum to align with real-life applications and the evolving needs of the job market, the variation in quality among different institutions with various rates and financial support can constrain the overall educational experience, with some institutions excelling while others lag behind (Alkaaf & Al-Issa, 2021). There is a significant gap between public and private institutions in Oman in terms of quality, resources, and student wellbeing, which can lead to inequitable educational experience (Ayala-Pazmiño, 2023). This calls for stronger accountability measures to ensure that all institutions meet educational standards and needs and improve student outcomes. There is also a need for increased investment in the higher education sector in Oman to develop infrastructure and educational quality. This investment can enhance the affordability and accessibility of higher education and achieve logical financial wellness among students, which consequently increases the student's academic performance. Finally, the higher education institutions in Oman face many challenges which highlight the complexities facing the Omani higher education system and emphasize the need for comprehensive strategies to enhance the AI technologies effectiveness and ensure student success.

2.5 Validity and Reliability in Academic Assessments

Validity and reliability are fundamental criteria for evaluating academic assessments. Reliability refers to the consistency of a measurement, a reliable test yields stable results over time, across different items, and with different raters. Key forms of reliability include internal consistency (the coherence of results across items in the same test) and inter-rater reliability (the degree to which different evaluators give consistent scores). In contrast, validity denotes the extent to which an assessment measures what it is intended to measure. Important types of validity illustrate this principle: construct validity reflects how well a test actually captures the theoretical construct or skill of interest, while criterion validity indicates how strongly test outcomes correlate with external benchmarks or predict relevant performance outcomes . Ensuring high validity and reliability (e.g. through well-designed instruments and clear scoring criteria) is crucial for credible academic evaluations in higher education.

2.5.1 Ethical Issues in AI-Assisted Cheating Detection

The rise of AI-powered tools to detect cheating (such as AI-generated content in assignments) has introduced new ethical challenges for academic integrity enforcement. A major concern is the risk of false positives, instances where human-written student work is mistakenly flagged as AI-generated, which can unjustly penalize honest students. Such errors undermine trust and fairness, which raises serious questions about students' rights and due process in academic misconduct proceedings. It is ethically imperative that institutions do not rely solely on opaque algorithms for accusations; instead, any AI-based findings should be transparently verified by human reviewers before disciplinary action. Universities must also uphold students' right to appeal and present evidence in their defense, ensuring that academic integrity policies remain fair, evidence-based, and respectful of student rights even as AI tools are employed.

2.5.2 Implications for Transnational Education (TNE) Context

In Oman, transnational education (TNE), programs delivered in partnership with foreign institutions, is widespread, with roughly one-third of Omani higher education students enrolled in overseas-affiliated programs. This cross-border context amplifies certain assessment challenges. Students in TNE programs often must adapt to different pedagogical styles and academic writing conventions, which the literature identifies as significant hurdles. These differences can impact the reliability of assessments if not carefully managed, as variations in expectations or support between the home and host institution may affect student performance. Moreover, maintaining policy consistency across borders is vital: partner institutions need aligned academic integrity standards and grading policies to ensure fairness and equivalence of qualifications. Data protection is another critical concern in TNE settings. The use of AI tools or online proctoring across jurisdictions entails transferring student data internationally, which raises legal and ethical issues regarding privacy . Institutions must therefore implement robust data safeguards (in compliance with laws in both Oman and the partner country) and ensure that assessment data and any AI-based monitoring are handled securely and transparently. Overall, the study's findings should be contextualized within these TNE complexities, underscoring the need for harmonized policies and trust-building measures in cross-border higher education.

2.5.3 Practical Strategies for Enhancing Assessment Integrity

To address the reliability and integrity of assessments amid AI's growing influence, educational institutions can adopt proactive strategies. One recommendation is to redesign assessments with authentic, staged tasks. For example, implementing scaffolded assignments, breaking a large project into smaller parts with regular checkpoints, helps students engage deeply with the material and allows instructors to monitor progress for consistency. Such progressive task design not only supports learning but also makes it harder for a student to shortcut the process using AI, since instructors can detect irregularities or sudden leaps in work quality between stages. Another practical tool is to introduce AI usage disclosure mechanisms. Requiring students to document if, how, and when they used AI tools in completing an assignment fosters transparency and accountability. For instance, a simple "AI disclosure form" can accompany submissions, prompting students to reflect on their use of tools like ChatGPT and enabling faculty to clearly distinguish the student's own work from AI-generated contributions. These measures encourage responsible use of AI by students – framing it as a learning aid rather than a cheating shortcut – and help preserve the validity of assessments. By combining thoughtful assessment design with clear AI usage policies, institutions can uphold academic standards in a balanced, forward-looking manner.

2.6 AI and Assessments Reliability

The growing integration of AI in higher education contexts has raised pressing concerns about the reliability of traditional assessment methods. Assessment reliability refers to the consistency and accuracy with which a method measures student learning outcome. Traditional assessments, such as written exams, essays, and take-home assignments, have been the major tools used to evaluate the student's knowledge and critical thinking skills. However, the advent of generative AI technologies, particularly those that produce fluent, well-structured responses, calls into question whether these methods still offer dependable insights into student understanding (Dawson et al., 2024).

On one hand, as AI provides the students with personalized learning experience, its tools could affect reliability. This opportunity can improve engagement and facilitate access to educational resources. Vieriu and Petrea (2025) discuss how AI tools can deliver consistent feedback and help students organize their academic tasks more effectively, which contributes to a more reliable assessment of their knowledge and skills. Ayala-Pazmiño (2023) mentions that AI tools can enhance reliability by providing direct feedback loops for students and a more accurate evaluation of their performance. For example, AI tools can be used to assist students in correcting grammar and vocabulary errors, thereby refining their writing quality and the organization of their ideas (Larsen, 2023). This immediate feedback allows students to address issues more effectively than traditional methods, potentially increasing the consistency of assessment outcomes (Chen & Gong, 2025).

The flaws of the AI technologies can make the students unsure about the accuracy of AI-generated content, which can lead to misunderstandings and negatively impact learning outcomes. Additionally, excessive dependence on AI can decrease the student's critical thinking skills (Lytras et al., 2024). This can lead to concerns about the inaccuracy and authenticity of student work and the overall integrity of assessments, which diminish the validity of exams, as the assessments may not accurately reflect a student's understanding, knowledge, or skills. P. Dawson (2023) claims that the discourse of AI tools often categorizes their use as either cheating or legitimate, which oversimplifies the challenges faced in assessment design. A more nuanced approach that considers the implications of AI use on assessment validity is necessary for addressing the evolving landscape of education. Overall, while AI provides opportunities for enhancing the reliability of assessments through personalized learning and efficiency, it also presents significant challenges related to validity, authenticity, and the critical thinking skills.

2.7 Shift from traditional to AI-informed assessments

The current shift towards AI-informed assessments reflects a transformative change in the higher educational practices (Dawson, P., 2023). This shift motivates both students and teachers to effectively engage in the academic process. Most of the students now have immediate access to AI applications and use them for their various academic tasks, which enhances their learning experience. While many students view this shift positively, acknowledging the benefits of personalized learning and improved access to resources, there are also critical voices expressing concerns about the long-term effects of AI on educational practices, including the potential decline in academic performance and critical thinking (Lytras et al., 2024). Therefore, teachers must design assessments that prioritize creativity, critical thinking, and other human skills that machines cannot replicate. They can still use AI to create assessments by accommodating diverse learning needs, which lead to inclusive and fair learning experiences for all students, but the primary objective should be to uphold the integrity and effectiveness of assessment practices (Ayala-Pazmiño, 2023).

While the use of AI may lead to improve the new assessment systems that align better with the current educational goals and enhance the learning outcomes, it should not replace the critical thinking and creativity required in traditional assessments (Dawson, P., 2023). This integration of AI should complement, not replace, the essential role of human teachers in facilitating learning and assessing student learning in a manner that reflects contemporary realities.

2.8 Institutional and Faculty Responses to AI

2.8.1 AI policies and guidelines

The rapid use of AI in the higher education field has highlighted the need for universities to actively develop their policies and guidelines to manage the integration of artificial intelligence (AI) tools within their educational frameworks. As many educational institutions globally have already responded with proactive strategies, including clear AI usage policies, faculty professional development training programs, and AI-integrated curriculum design, there is still uncertainty about how to adapt assessment practices or safeguard academic standards (White, 2023). These differences are often tied to levels of institutional awareness, digital readiness, and the availability of professional training for all faculty members. Universities can enhance their response to AI by setting up clear rules for the proper use of AI in academic settings and encouraging students to cite sources and check with faculty before using AI tools to ensure academic integrity. On the other hand, policymakers must recognize the need for assessments that reflect real-world applications of knowledge, which may include AI capabilities (Perkins et al., 2023). They must recognize inclusivity in educational settings and ensure that AI tools enhance rather than hinder learning opportunities for all students. The new principles must be set to ensure fairness and inclusivity, particularly in detecting AI-generated work, as well as develop frameworks that differentiate between acceptable and unacceptable uses of AI in assessments.

2.8.2 Challenges specific to Omani institutions

In the Omani higher educational context, the institutions have unique challenges in responding to AI integration. Dawson, P. (2023) found that the various higher education institutions in Oman are still in their initial stages of responding to the AI trends. There are various aspects of these challenges, including assessment integrity, technological adaptation, and broader educational implications. The rise of generative AI tools, such as ChatGPT, raises questions about when the use of AI constitutes cheating, particularly in high-stakes assessments. There is a need for a cultural shift in perspective from viewing AI use strictly as cheating to considering it in the context of assessing academic integrity and validity in educational practices. Many of the higher education institutions in Oman struggle in adapting to innovative technologies that can both enhance learning and present challenges to traditional assessment methods. There is a reliance on anti-cheating technologies that can lead to exclusionary practices which might not be suitable for all students. On the other hand, teachers in Oman may not be adequately prepared to address the complexities introduced by AI in assessments (Khalil & Alsenaidi, 2024). This issue leads to inconsistencies in how AI is perceived and managed across different disciplines. Consequently, there is a need for continuous professional development for faculty members to prepare them to integrate AI effectively into their teaching practices and assessments.The digital divide in Oman may exacerbate inequalities in access to AI tools and resources, creating disparities in educational outcomes; therefore, it is essential to ensure equitable access to technology is essential for all students to benefit from AI integration in education.

3. METHODOLOGY

3.1 Research Design

This research will use a descriptive and exploratory research design to examine the reliability of traditional assessments in Omani higher education in a world of the growing use of artificial intelligence (AI). The descriptive design allows for the systematic data collection from a defined population to explore current perceptions, behaviors, and institutional practices (Creswell & Creswell, 2018). Also, the exploratory approach can investigate the impact of AI improvements on the student and teacher educational practices.

Additionally, this research will adopt a survey-based approach as the primary method for data collection as it can collect a broad range of perceptions from the various stakeholders. While surveys can effectively collect both quantitative and qualitative data from students, and academic staff across the targeted Omani higher education institutions, the study may include a small number of semi-structured interviews to provide deeper insights and clarify the survey responses. This combination enhances the study's depth while maintaining focus on measurable patterns.

This design obviously aligns with the research's objectives, which is to assess the distinguished reliability of traditional assessments, explore how AI affects academic integrity, and identify institutional responses to these challenges. The combination of descriptive precision with exploratory flexibility allows the research design to be well-organized to explore insightful data that can inform future assessment strategies within the improvement of the digital landscape of higher education in Oman.

3.2 Research Approach

The research mainly adopts a quantitative approach, complemented by qualitative data. It will collect data through a structured survey containing both closed-ended and open-ended questions. Quantitative data will allow for the statistical analysis of trends, frequencies, and relationships among variables, while qualitative responses to open-ended questions may highlight deeper themes regarding AI usage and assessment perceptions. This approach is chosen because it can help to achieve the main objective of this research, as it balances measurable analysis with an understanding of participant experiences. If semi-structured interviews are conducted, they will be used to supplement survey findings with richer narrative detail.

3.3 Data Collection

Data will be collected primarily through an online survey distributed via institutional email lists and professional networks within selected Omani higher education institutions, public and private institutions. The survey will include sections on demographic information, experiences with AI tools, perceptions of assessment reliability, and views on academic integrity. Also, the survey tool, which is Google Forms, will ensure accessibility and ease of completion. A semi-structured interview guide will be used while conducting the interviews, which focus on participants' views about the influence of AI on assessments, educational policies, and future recommendations.

3.4 Sampling and Participants

The sample will consist of students and academic staff from various universities and colleges in Oman. The technique which will be used in this research is the purposive sampling strategy to target participants who have current experience with academic assessments in the context of increasing AI use. Approximately 100-150 survey respondents are expected, though the final sample size may vary depending on participant availability. Interview participants, if included, will be drawn from survey respondents who volunteer for follow-up discussions. Participation will be voluntary and based on informed consent.

3.5 Data Analysis

Quantitative survey data will be analyzed using descriptive statistical techniques, including frequencies, means, and percentages, to summarize participant responses. The qualitative data from open-ended survey questions and interviews if conducted will be analyzed thematically, following Braun and Clarke's (2016) six-phase model: familiarization with data, coding, theme development, review, definition, and reporting. This mixed analytical strategy allows the research to quantify general directions while also capturing nuanced insights into participant experiences and perceptions.

3.6 Ethical Considerations

Ethical standards will be strictly upheld throughout the research process. Every single participant will be provided with detailed information about the objectives of the research, their rights, and data protection measures. Informed consent will be obtained electronically before survey completion or interviews. Anonymity and confidentiality will be guaranteed; no identifying information will be collected. Also, all data will be stored securely in encrypted files accessible only to the researcher.

3.7 Limitations

Several limitations are anticipated. Firstly, the use of a self-reported survey may introduce response bias, as participants might underreport or overreport their engagement with AI tools. Secondly, as participation will be voluntary, the sample may not fully represent the wider student and faculty population. Thirdly, the rapid development of AI technologies means that perceptions captured at the time of the study may quickly develop. Finally, logistical limitations may restrict the number of interviews conducted, as the researcher is in Australia.

4. RESULTS

4.1 Participant Demographics

A total of 125 individuals participated in the survey, which represents a diverse cross-section of the higher education community in Oman. The majority of respondents were students (85%), followed by faculty members (10%), while a smaller number identified as administrative staff (2%) or selected the "Other" category (3%), which included roles such as academic support or research assistants.

Participants came from various higher education institutions across Oman, both public (50.4%) and private (49.6%), and represented multiple academic fields. These fields of study and teaching included education, computer science, English language and literature, business, nursing, and engineering, which clearly reflect a broad academic landscape.

In terms of experience in higher education, most respondents reported relatively recent engagement. Around 55 participants (46%) had less than two years of academic experience, while another 57 participants (48%) had 2–5 years. A smaller proportion had more extensive experience, with 4 participants (3%) reporting 6–10 years, and 4 participants (3%) with more than 10 years of involvement in higher education settings.

When the participants are asked about their familiarity with artificial intelligence tools (such as ChatGPT, Grammarly, or Quillbot), the vast majority of participants (94.2%) responded affirmatively, indicating broad exposure to AI-assisted technologies. Only a small number (5.8%) indicated they were unfamiliar with such tools.

This demographic profile highlights a relatively young and digitally engaged participant group, predominantly composed of students and early-career academic staff. Their widespread familiarity with AI tools forms a relevant foundation for exploring how these technologies influence academic assessments and perceptions of integrity in higher education in Oman.

*Figure 1. SEQ Figure * ARABIC 6 Participant responses to the question: "Have you used AI tools in your academic work?" (Yes/No)*

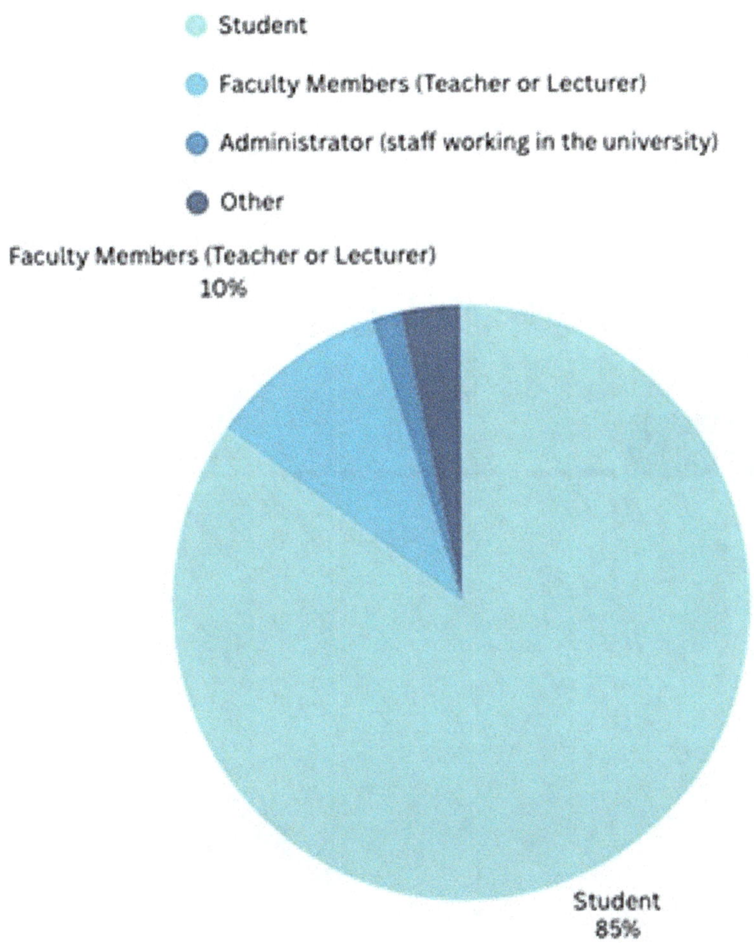

*Figure 2. SEQ Figure * ARABIC 4 Participants' familiarity with artificial intelligence tools (such as ChatGPT, Grammarly, or Quillbot)*

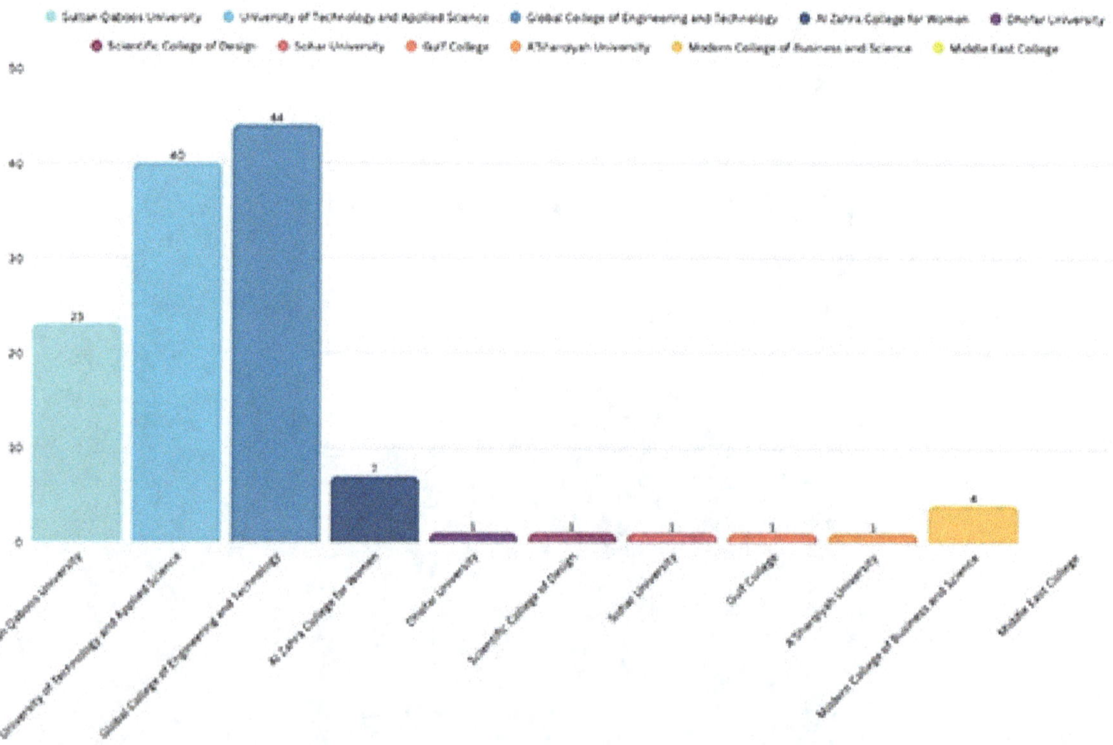

*Figure 3. SEQ Figure * ARABIC 8 Frequency of using AI tools among participants*

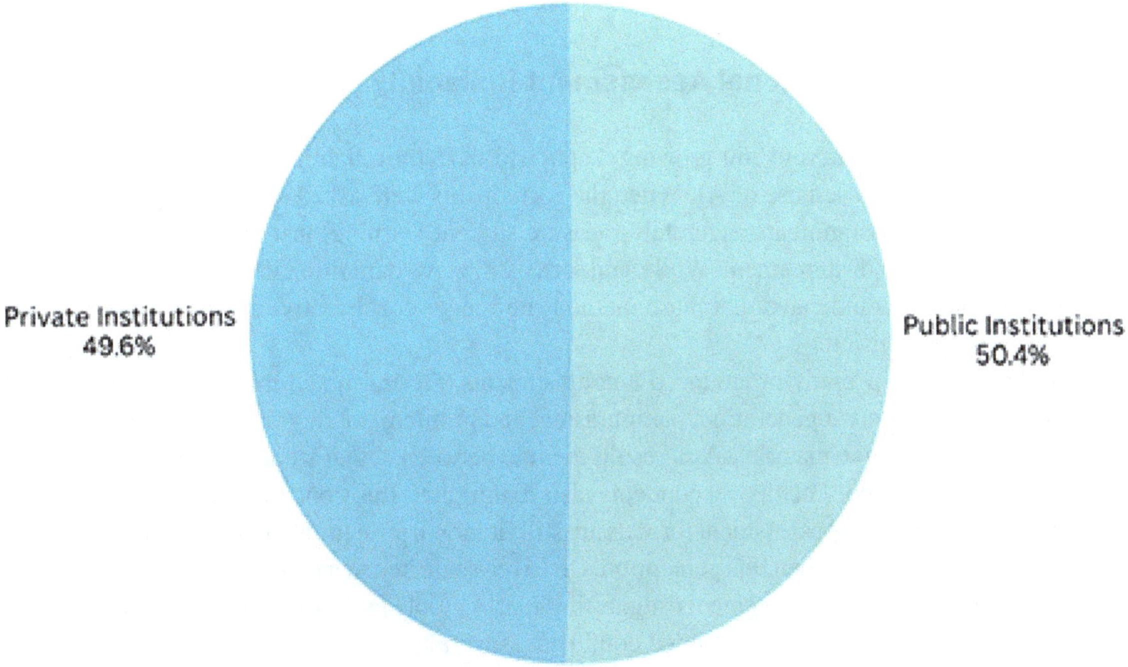

4.2 Patterns of AI Tool Usage

The results revealed a high rate of AI tool adoption among participants. When the participants were asked about their actual usage of AI tools for academic purposes, most participants reported using AI to assist with various types of academic tasks. The most common uses included grammar and language correction, paraphrasing, generating essay content, summarizing texts, and solving subject-specific problems. These tools were used across different disciplines and levels of academic experience, indicating their cross-functional appeal. Students, in particular, reported using tools like ChatGPT to brainstorm ideas or rephrase answers before submitting assignments.

In terms of frequency, responses varied. While some participants indicated occasional or infrequent use (e.g., for checking language or formatting), others reported regular reliance on AI tools during assessments and coursework preparation. Notably, many participants who identified as faculty members also acknowledged their awareness of AI tool usage among students, though fewer reported using the tools themselves in professional contexts.

Qualitative responses from open-ended survey items further illustrated the motivations behind AI usage. Many students shared that AI tools help them clarify complex concepts, save time, and improve the quality of their writing. However, a few participants expressed concern that reliance on AI might compromise their ability to learn independently or develop original ideas.

The diversity of AI usage patterns reflects a shift in academic habits, suggesting that AI has become an integral part of the academic workflow for many. These findings support the need for institutions to revisit how assessments are structured and monitored in light of growing student dependence on such technologies.

4.3 Perceptions of Traditional Assessment Reliability

The responses from the survey show growing skepticism about the reliability of traditional assessments in the context of the increased use of AI. When the participants were asked to what extent they believe traditional exams and assignments accurately measure student learning, just over half of participants expressed uncertainty or disagreement. While a minority still viewed traditional assessments as generally valid, many respondents indicated that these methods no longer consistently reflect individual student effort or true comprehension.

This concern was especially pronounced among students. Several noted that the availability of AI tools allows for rapid content generation, paraphrasing, and problem-solving that may bypass meaningful engagement with course material. As a result, the line between actual student work and AI-assisted output has become blurred. Faculty respondents also highlighted this concern, with many expressing doubts about whether current assessment formats are still fit for purpose in evaluating learning outcomes.

Quantitative results strengthen this perception. On Liker-scale items, a majority of participants either agreed or strongly agreed with statements suggesting that AI tools undermine the effectiveness of traditional assessment practices. In open-ended comments, several participants described traditional tests and essays as "predictable," "easily solvable with AI," "detectable," or "outdated." Others also highlight that AI tools cannot replace the critical thinking skills and the personal engagement with the topic. These views reflect a broader perception that traditional formats, especially take-home essays and standardized questions, are vulnerable to manipulation in an AI-driven learning environment.

However, not all feedback was negative. A few participants defended traditional assessments, noting that time-limited, supervised exams and oral presentations still offer some degree of protection against AI misuse. Others suggested that traditional assessments might remain relevant if updated to integrate more reflective, personalized, or critical thinking components that are harder for AI to replicate convincingly.

Overall, the findings point to a widening gap between how assessments are designed and how students are engaging with them in the age of AI in the higher education institutions in Oman. There is a clear call, from both students and educators, for reassessment and redesign of existing formats to ensure they continue to reflect genuine learning and academic effort.

*Figure 4. SEQ Figure * ARABIC 10 participants' view on the impact of AI tools on academic honesty*

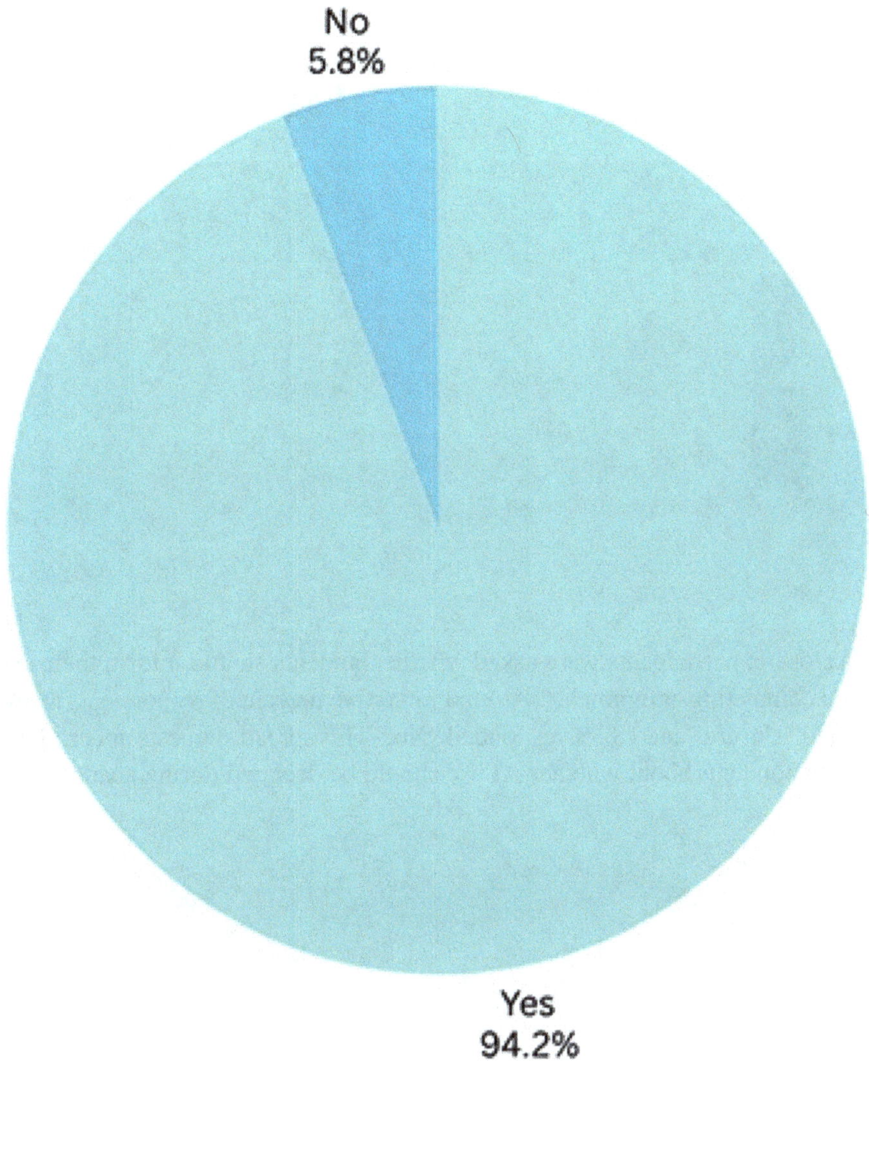

4.4 Academic Integrity and Institutional Policies

Participants expressed varied views on the impact of AI tools on academic honesty. When they were asked whether they believed AI affects honesty in education, 43.3% of respondents selected "Yes, in a good way," while 30% selected "Yes, in a bad way." Additionally, 17.5% indicated that they did not know, and 9.2% reported that AI had no important effect on academic integrity. These figures indicate a broad range of opinions regarding the ethical implications of AI use in academic contexts.

*Figure 5. SEQ Figure * ARABIC 11: Participants' opinions on student disclosure of AI tool use in assignments*

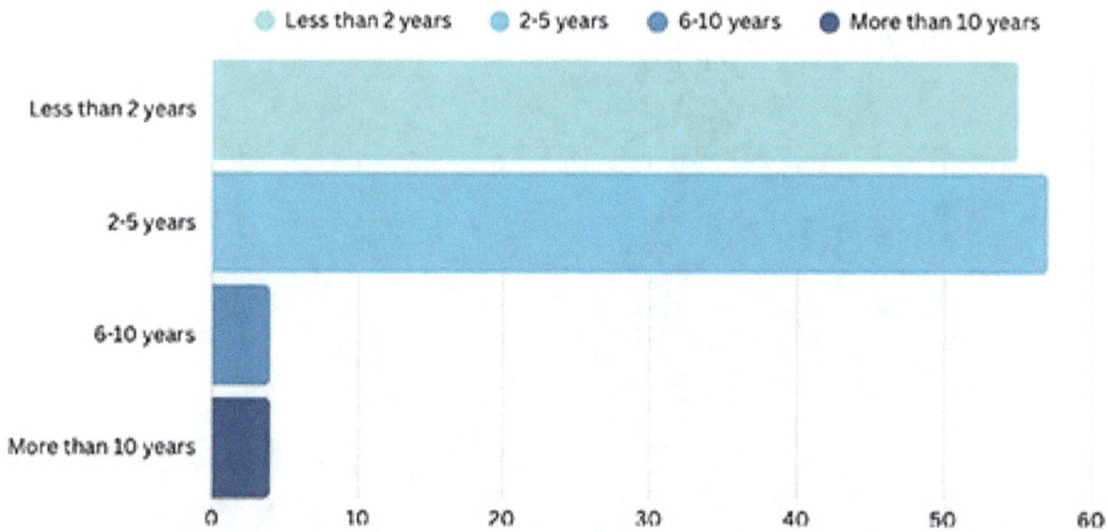

In terms of disclosure, participants were asked whether students should inform their teacher if they used AI tools when completing assignments. Around forty-five percent of respondents answered "Yes," while 35.8% selected "Unsure" and 18.3% responded "No." This spread suggests uncertainty or a lack of consensus among respondents about whether AI use should be declared during academic submissions.

*Figure 6. SEQ Figure * ARABIC 12 participants' view on their confidence that assessments reflect real student abilities in the presence of AI technologies*

Participants were also asked to evaluate their confidence in the extent to which current assessments reflect real student abilities in the presence of AI technologies. Thirty-nine percent of respondents indicated they were "A little sure," while 29% selected "Not sure." Fourteen percent answered, "A little unsure," 13% responded "Very sure," and 4% selected "Very unsure." The majority of participants thus expressed only moderate or low levels of confidence that current assessments accurately reflect student competencies in a context where AI tools are commonly used.

4.7 Summary

This chapter represented the results of a survey which was conducted among students, faculty, and administrators in the higher education institutions in Oman. The findings reflect important levels of familiarity with AI tools and frequent use of such technologies for academic purposes. Most of the participants deal with AI as supportive in improving academic output, but other participants expressed concerns about its impact on assessment reliability and academic integrity.

These results form the basis for the following chapter, which will interpret the findings in the context of existing literature, explore their implications for assessment design, and provide recommendations for practice and policy in higher education.

5. DISCUSSION

5.1 Introduction

This chapter interprets and discusses the key findings presented in Chapter 4 in relation to the research questions of the study and the existing literature reviewed in Chapter 2. The primary aim of this research was to evaluate the reliability of traditional assessments in higher education in Oman in the context of rapid use of various artificial intelligence (AI) tools. The study also aimed to understand how these tools are influencing student behaviors, perceptions of academic integrity, and institutional policies and responses.

The discussion is structured around the main themes that analyze the survey results: patterns of AI tool usage, perceived reliability of traditional assessments, concerns about academic integrity, and the level of institutional preparedness in addressing AI-related challenges. Each section analyses the findings with relevant academic literature and reflects on the broader implications for higher education practice and policy in Oman. This chapter also considers the limitations of the study and proposes areas for future research.

5.2 Interpreting Patterns of AI Tool Usage

The findings of this study revealed that a substantial majority of participants, around 94%, were familiar with AI tools and had used them in various academic contexts. Students reported frequent engagement with platforms such as ChatGPT, Grammarly, and Quillbot, primarily to improve writing, generate content, paraphrase texts, and summarize sources. This result aligns with prior studies stating that AI tools are becoming increasingly integrated into the learning and teaching habits of higher education students worldwide (Cotton et al., 2023).

These usage patterns reflect a shift in how students deal with their academic tasks. Rather than relying solely on their cognitive skills, many now use the various AI tools as a form of academic platform to assist them in understanding or streamline writing. This analysis of the results supports Ayed's (2022) findings in the Omani context, where AI was observed to enhance students' perceived confidence in completing assessments. However, as the current study shows, this convenience also raises questions about the depth of learning objectives being achieved when AI is used routinely and without supervision.

The frequent and adaptive use of AI tools among participants suggest that such advanced technologies are no longer optional or subsidiaries; they are essential to the academic experience for many learners and teachers. The findings suggest that students adapt rapidly to AI tools, even in the absence of structured institutional support, policies, or official AI literacy programs. This responsiveness is consistent with broader global trends, where the use of generative AI has accelerated despite ethical and pedagogical uncertainties (Chan & Colloton, 2024).

Overall, the common use of AI tools among participants reflects a digital learning culture in transition. While students benefit from the accessibility and efficiency AI provides, the absence of direct instructional guidance or assessment redesign and reform may leave institutions unprepared to address the growing needs of learners.

5.3 Reliability of Traditional Assessments in the AI Era

The findings indicate that participants highlight significant uncertainty regarding the ability of traditional assessments, such as essays, written exams, and reports, to accurately reflect real students achieving learning objectives while they use various AI tools. Many participants reported that these forms of assessment are increasingly vulnerable to automation, as students are able to complete tasks using AI tools without necessarily engaging in higher-order thinking or independent analysis.

This perception reflects a growing concern in the literature regarding the continued validity of traditional assessment formats. Dawson (2023) argues in his paper that generative AI challenges the foundational principles of assessment by enabling students to produce output that appears original but may not reflect their actual learning process. Similarly, Ardito (2023) states that the rise of AI demands a redesign of how institutions evaluate student performance, especially in written assignments that can easily be supported or completed by advanced AI tools.

The current study supports these arguments, as many participants described traditional assessments as "easily solvable with AI" or "less meaningful" in the current digital context. These responses suggest that traditional methods are no longer seen as reliable indicators of academic ability, especially when students can have equal access tools that can rephrase, summarize, or even generate full-text responses with minimal input. The concern that AI may enable students to bypass the learning process was particularly evident among faculty respondents, who questioned whether current assessment designs still serve their intended purpose.

At the same time, some participants highlighted that specific assessment types, such as in-person presentations, oral exams, or timed in-class essays, may still offer a level of reliability. These formats, which are less dependent on extended access to AI tools, were viewed as better aligned with individual performance evaluation. This supports the suggestion by Chan and Colloton (2024) that institutions may need to shift towards assessment types that prioritize 21st-century skills, critical thinking, reflection, and real-time application.

Overall, the findings highlight a critical gap between the design of traditional assessments and the growing behaviors of students in an AI-rich world. If this gap is left unaddressed, it may continue to compromise the ability of assessments to measure learning outcomes reliably.

5.4 Academic Integrity Concerns

The survey results showed a range of perspectives on how artificial intelligence is affecting academic integrity. While a notable number of participants believed that AI could enhance learning when used ethically, many expressed concerns that it facilitates practices that blur the boundaries of originality and independent work. This tension reflects the recent debates in the literature about whether AI represents an academic support tool or a way for misconduct (Cotton et al., 2023; Chan and Colloton, 2024).

In this study, the majority of participants reported being unsure whether students should be required to disclose their use of AI tools. Nearly half of respondents agreed that disclosure of AI usage should be mandatory, while others were either uncertain or opposed to the idea. Even though there is a recognition of the transformative potential of AI in higher education in Oman, this uncertainty highlights a notable lack of clear ethical norms and institutional policies and its use in assessments, which is also an issue identified by Al Balushi and Achour (2024) in the Omani context. Without structured guidelines, both students and faculty are left to interpret the boundaries of academic honesty independently, potentially leading to inconsistent practices and expectations.

Moreover, some respondents expressed moderate to low confidence that current assessments reflect true student capabilities in the presence of AI. Many participants described difficulty in distinguishing between work completed by students and the AI generated content. This concern is represented by Dawson (2023), who stated that the unchecked use of generative AI tools can cause serious risks across multiple academic dimensions, primarily affecting teachers, academic integrity, and credibility of the students' overall performance

While some participants acknowledged that AI could improve the quality of academic assessments, especially for language learners, they also noted that this could create unfair advantages. The easy access to AI tools can generate or polish content, which raises questions about the equity and fairness of traditional assessment formats, particularly when institutions have not provided clear instructions on acceptable use.

These findings underline the rapid need for higher educational institutions to set clear strategies and guidelines and define the ethical boundaries of AI use in academic work. Without such clarity and policy, concerns around academic integrity are likely to continue and evolve, and the credibility of assessments may be further diminished.

5.5 Institutional Response and Policy Gaps

The findings revealed that the majority of participants had not received clear guidance or policies from their institutions regarding the acceptable integration of AI use in their academic work. Many respondents showed uncertainty about what constitutes appropriate or ethical AI use, while others noted that institutional communication on the issue had been minimal or inconsistent. These findings suggest a significant policy gap at the institutional level of higher education in Oman, particularly in relation to academic integrity and assessment design in the world of AI.

These findings shed light on the lack of institutional clarity in the Omani higher education context, where institutions were found to be at varying stages of readiness in addressing the implications of AI in teaching and assessment. Globally, higher education institutions are actively grappling with the challenges presented by the rapid integration of AI tools in student learning processes, and many have yet to establish clear usage policies (Chen & Gong, 2025). The absence of structured policy frameworks can result in confusion, unorganized usage, and inconsistent application of academic standards.

This study also found that many participants believed institutions had not provided training or effective awareness campaigns related to AI use in the academic context. This was reflected in both survey responses and open-ended comments, where participants called for clearer rules and policies, guidelines of acceptable AI use, and discussions to better understand institutional expectations. Such gaps in policy and communication can lead to unequal understanding among students and faculty, thereby undermining efforts to maintain assessment fairness and academic integrity.

Furthermore, if the faculty members rely on traditional assessments without corresponding updates in policy, it may contribute to increased risk, as students find it easier to use AI tools without fear of consequences or ethical accountability. As Ardito (2023) notes, the challenges surrounding AI use in higher education are multifaceted, including not only regulatory issues but also significant educational, ethical, and technological considerations. To navigate these challenges effectively, a comprehensive approach is necessary, which adopts the capabilities of AI while promoting critical thinking, ethical awareness, and academic integrity among students.

These findings indicate an urgent need for higher education institutions in Oman to develop, implement, and communicate comprehensive AI policies. Such policies should clarify ethical boundaries, outline acceptable usage strategies and scenarios, and integrate AI literacy into broader academic integrity initiatives.

5.6 Implications for Assessment Design

Moreover, the findings indicate an important need to reconsider how assessments are designed and format in higher education in Oman. Traditional assessment formats such as essays and take-home written assignments may no longer reliably measure student understanding or individual effort, as the students can easily have access to the various AI tools and they increasingly rely on them. Participants expressed concern that current assessments are not well-equipped to differentiate between authentic learning and AI-assisted outputs, which is another challenge that is stated across the literature (Dawson, 2023; Cotton et al., 2023).

Several participants suggested in the survey questions that assessments should be adapted to minimize the misuse of AI tools. Suggestions included integrating more in-person exams, oral assessments, in-class writing, and tasks that require personal reflection or real-time critical thinking. These types of assessments are seen as less vulnerable to automation and more effective at revealing student engagement with learning content.

Ruiz-Rojas et al. (2024) support this point of view, as they argue that future-proof assessment design must prioritize higher-order skills to effectively prepare students for the complexities of the modern world. This is because these skills not only enhance the learning outcomes but also equip students with the tools necessary for lifelong learning and the rapidly changing job market. However, addressing the associated challenges through adequate training, thoughtful assessment design, and equitable resource allocation is essential for successful implementation.

In addition to redesigning assessment, the participants mention a need for institutions to adopt an active and clear approach toward AI. This includes incorporating AI literacy into the curriculum, educating students and faculty members on ethical AI use, and explicitly designing tasks that acknowledge AI as a legitimate tool when appropriate. As Ardito (2023) notes, effective assessment reform in the AI era should not mean banning technology. Instead, it requires a thoughtful adaptation of AI into educational practices, to ensure that the benefits of technology are harnessed while safeguarding the integrity of the learning process.

In the context of Oman, where institutional readiness and policy development may still be set (Ayed, 2022), the suggestions of this study point toward an opportunity, leading the way in creating locally relevant, AI-informed assessment guidelines and frameworks that balance innovation with equity.

5.7 Limitations of the Study

Several limitations should be acknowledged in this study which provides insightful data and analysis into how the integration of various AI tools is influencing assessment practices in higher education in Oman. To start with, because of the time limitations, the study relied primarily on self-reported data collected through an online survey, which may be subject to personal interpretation of survey items. The accuracy of participants' responses depends on their honesty, comprehension, and willingness to engage thoughtfully with the questions.

Secondly, the sample was dominated by student participants, with fewer responses from faculty members and administrative staff. As a result, the findings may disproportionately reflect the student perspective and may not fully capture institutional or policy-level responses to AI integration. Additionally, while the survey included open-ended questions to add qualitative depth, no formal interviews or focus groups were conducted, which may have limited the richness of the data.

Finally, the study did not explore specific academic disciplines in detail, which may have yielded additional valuable insights, given that the impact of AI integration can vary depending on the nature of assessment in different fields.

Despite these limitations, the study provides an important starting point for understanding the shifting relationship between AI and assessment reliability in a rapidly digitizing academic environment.

5.8 Summary

This chapter discussed the findings of the study in relation to the research questions and existing literature. The results highlighted the rapid use of various AI tools among students and growing uncertainty about the ability of traditional assessments to reflect real learning outcomes. Concerns around academic integrity and equity were commonly reported, particularly in the absence of clear institutional policies or guidance on AI use.

The discussion also explored the implications of these findings for assessment redesign, which recommends a need for higher education institutions in Oman to shift toward more authentic, reflective, and real-time assessment formats. The chapter further identified key gaps in institutional preparedness, calling for AI literacy, policy development, and training to help both students and staff guide the academic environment digital transformation.

Finally, the study's limitations were acknowledged, including time limitations, its reliance on self-reported data, and mainly student-based samples. Despite these limitations, the study contributes to a growing body of research on the intersection of AI and higher education, and it offers practical and valuable insights for improving assessment reliability in a world of AI.

6. CONCLUSION AND RECOMMENDATIONS

6.1 Introduction

This chapter concludes the research project titled "Evaluating the Reliability of Traditional Assessments in Omani Higher Education in a World of AI." The study aimed to explore how the rapid growth of the various artificial intelligence (AI) tools has affected and influenced students' learning behaviors, the perceived reliability of assessments, academic integrity, and institutional responses within higher education in Oman. The study examined the patterns of AI use, perceptions of equity and validity, and the preparedness of institutions to guide developing their policy in this growing field, interpreting survey data from students, faculty members, and administratively staff.

This chapter summarizes the key findings, directly answers the research questions, and offers practical recommendations for stakeholders, including institutions, teachers, students, and policymakers. It also identifies directions for future research to build on the insights generated in this study.

6.2 Summary of Key Findings

Several key findings were identified in this study, regarding the impact of the AI tools on assessment practices in higher education in Oman. First, the majority of participants reported high levels of familiarity with AI tools, particularly among students, who frequently used applications such as ChatGPT, Grammarly, and Quillbot to support their academic work. These tools were primarily used to improve writing, generate ideas, paraphrase content, and summarize texts.

In addition to that, the results represented common concern about the reliability of traditional assessments among the higher education institutions in Oman. Many participants expressed doubts that current assessment formats, such as essays and take-home assignments, accurately reflect individual student learning outcomes in the age of AI. While some acknowledged that supervised in-person exams and oral assessments, like presentations, offer more reliable alternatives, there was a shared recognition that traditional methods are increasingly vulnerable to AI-assisted academic work.

The participants also reported both mixed and conflicting point of views on the ethical implications of AI use. While some saw AI as a helpful learning tool, others worried that it undermines academic integrity by allowing students to submit work that does not represent their own effort and understanding. Many participants highlighted the absence of clear institutional policies on AI use, which contributed to uncertainty about what constitutes acceptable or ethical behavior.

Finally, the study found that most institutions had not yet developed comprehensive strategies or guidelines to control the rapid spread of AI use and deal with various AI-related challenges. There was a strong call among participants for clearer policies, improved communication, and targeted training to help both students and educators manage the integration of AI in academic work.

6.3 Answering the Research Questions

This section directly answers the research questions raised at the start of the study, based on the key findings presented in the Results and Discussion chapters.

1. To what extent are traditional assessments in Omani higher education reliable in the era of AI?

The findings indicate that many participants perceive traditional assessments, particularly essays, reports, and take-home assignments, as less reliable in the context of widespread AI use. While some assessment formats, such as oral exams or supervised in-class tasks, were viewed as more secure, the overall confidence in traditional methods was moderate to low.

0. How has the widespread use of AI tools affected the validity and reliability of student assessment outcomes?

Participants reported that AI tools have complicated the relationship between student effort and assessment outcomes. Many expressed concern that students can achieve high scores without fully engaging with the learning process, thereby weakening the validity of assessments as true indicators of student understanding and skills.

0. What are the perceptions of students and faculty regarding the impact of AI on academic integrity and assessment reliability?

The study revealed mixed perceptions. Some participants viewed AI as a helpful educational support, especially for improving language use or generating ideas. Others saw it as a threat to fairness and originality, which raises concerns about the weakening of academic integrity. Many participants agreed that the lack of clear institutional policies further complicated ethical decision-making around AI use.

0. What challenges do Omani higher education institutions face in maintaining reliable and fair assessments amid AI integration?

Institutions face challenges including limited AI literacy among both students and staff, a lack of formal guidelines, and reliance on traditional assessment formats that are vulnerable to AI-assisted shortcuts. Participants also noted inconsistent application of academic integrity standards.

0. What strategies and practices are currently used (or could be used) by higher education institutions in Oman to enhance assessment reliability and academic integrity in a digital and AI-driven learning environment?

The findings suggest that while few formal strategies are currently in place, participants recommend adopting more authentic, reflective, or in-person assessment methods. They also recommend providing AI literacy training and developing clear institutional policies to guide ethical AI use in academic work.

6.5 Suggestions for Future Research

This study highlights several areas where further research is needed to deepen understanding and strengthen institutional responses. Firstly, it is suggested that future studies could explore the perspectives of a broader and more balanced sample, particularly by increasing the representation of faculty members, administrators, and policymakers. This would provide a clearer and fuller picture of institutional strategies and challenges, which were only partially captured in the present study due to the time limitations.

Secondly, qualitative research methods such as in-depth interviews or focus groups could be used to explore the significance experiences and opinions of different stakeholders. These approaches would allow for a richer and deeper understanding of how AI tools are shaping learning behaviors, ethical decision-making, and assessment practices.

Finally, to provide more valuable insights into the best practices of AI tools, this paper suggests to conducting comparative studies across multiple institutions or countries, which could help identify common trends and contextual differences in how higher education systems respond to AI integration.

REFERENCES

Al Balushi, Z., & Achour, S. (2024). Guiding the evolution of AI in higher education in Oman: Strategies and insights. In Proceedings of the 7th International Academic Conference on Education, Teaching and Learning. Diamond Scientific Publishing. https://www.dpublication.com/wp-content/uploads/2024/07/6-ITL6-3737.pdf

Al-Maskri, M. S., Al-Mukhini, S. H., & Amzat, I. H. (2012). Improving education system in Oman through school curriculum, teaching methods and evaluation: What is needed? SSRN Electronic Journal. https://doi.org/DOI: 10.2139/ssrn.2047736

Al Matari, A. S., Mukit, A., Al Saadi, S., Al Balushi, W., & Al-Abri, J. S. (2023). Artificial intelligence and the future of teaching in higher education at A'Sharqiyah University (ASU) in Oman. 1st Pelita International Conference, 1(1). https://www.researchgate.net/publication/377272384

Ardito, C. G. (2023). Contra generative AI detection in higher education assessments. arXiv:2312.05241. https://doi.org//arXiv.2312.05241DOI: 10.48550

Ayala-Pazmiño, M. (2023). Artificial intelligence in education: Exploring the potential benefits and risks. 593 Digital Publisher CEIT, 8(3), 892–899. https://doi.org/DOI: 10.33386/593dp.2023.3.1827

Ayeni, N. O. O., Hamad, N. N. M. A., Chisom, N. O. N., Osawaru, N. B., & Adewusi, N. O. E. (2024). AI in education: A review of personalized learning and educational technology. *GSC Advanced Research and Reviews*, *18*(2), 261–271. DOI: 10.30574/gscarr.2024.18.2.0062

Braun, V., Clarke, V., & Weate, P. (2016). Using thematic analysis in sport and exercise research. In Smith, B., & Sparkes, A. C. (Eds.), *Routledge handbook of qualitative research in sport and exercise* (pp. 191–205). Routledge., DOI: 10.4324/9781315762012-26

Chan, C. K. Y., & Colloton, T. (2024). *Generative AI in higher education*. Routledge., DOI: 10.4324/9781003459026

Chen, C., & Gong, Y. (2025). The role of AI-assisted learning in academic writing: A mixed-methods study on Chinese as a second language students. *Education Sciences*, *15*(2), 141. DOI: 10.3390/educsci15020141

Cotton, D., Cotton, P., & Shipway, J. (2023). Chatting and cheating: Ensuring academic integrity in the era of ChatGPT. *Innovations in Education and Teaching International*, *60*(2), 215–226. DOI: 10.1080/14703297.2023.2190148

Creswell, J. W., & Creswell, J. D. (2018). *Research design: Qualitative, quantitative, and mixed methods approaches* (5th ed.). Sage Publications.

Dawson, P., Bearman, M., Dollinger, M., & Boud, D. (2024). Validity matters more than cheating. *Assessment & Evaluation in Higher Education*, *49*(7), 1005–1016. DOI: 10.1080/02602938.2024.2386662

Dimari, A., Tyagi, N., Davanageri, M., Kukreti, R., Yadav, R., & Dimari, H. (2024). AI-based automated grading systems for open book examination system. In *2024 IEEE International Conference*. https://doi.org/DOI: 10.1109/ICKECS61492.2024.10616490

Holmes, W., Bialik, M., & Fadel, C. (2019). *Artificial intelligence in education: Promises and implications for teaching and learning*. Center for Curriculum Redesign.

Khalil, H., & Alsenaidi, S. (2024). Teachers' digital competencies for effective AI integration in higher education in Oman. *Journal of Education and e-learning Research, 11*(4), 698–707. DOI: 10.20448/jeelr.v11i4.6097

Kofinas, A. K., Tsay, C. H., & Pike, D. (2025). The impact of generative AI on academic integrity. *British Journal of Educational Technology, 56*(6), 2522–2549. Advance online publication. DOI: 10.1111/bjet.13585

Larsen, S. K. (2023). Creating large language model-resistant exams. arXiv Preprint, arXiv:2304.12203. https://doi.org//arXiv.2304.12203DOI: 10.48550

Lytras, M. D., Alkhaldi, A., Malik, S., Serban, A. C., & Aldosemani, T. (2024). *The evolution of artificial intelligence in higher education*. Emerald Publishing. DOI: 10.1108/9781835494868

Ministry of Higher Education, Research and Innovation. (2022). *Higher education statistics report*. Government of Oman.

Oman Authority for Academic Accreditation and Quality Assurance of Education. (2021). *Institutional standards framework*. OAAAQA.

Open, A. I. (2023). AI text classifier: Limitations and considerations. https://openai.com

Royal Decree No. (2022). *6/2022 issuing the Personal Data Protection Law (PDPL)*. Official Gazette of the Sultanate of Oman.

Selwyn, N. (2019). *Should robots replace teachers?* Polity Press.

UNESCO. (2023). Guidance for generative AI in education and research. https://unesdoc.unesco.org/ark:/48223/pf0000385861

Vieriu, A. M., & Petrea, G. (2025). The impact of AI on students' academic development. *Education Sciences, 15*(3), 343. DOI: 10.3390/educsci15030343

White, J. D. (2023). Academic integrity in the age of AI. EDUCAUSE Review. https://er.educause.edu

Wilkins, S., & Balakrishnan, M. S. (2013). Assessing student satisfaction in TNE. *International Journal of Educational Management, 27*(2), 143–156. DOI: 10.1108/09513541311297568

Chapter 8
Algorithmic Pedagogy and Pedagogical Sovereignty in AI-Mediated Teaching in Transnational Education:
Sociotechnical Learning Ecologies Across Borders

Ashraf Alam
https://orcid.org/0000-0001-6178-1187
Alliance University, Bengaluru, India

ABSTRACT

This chapter interrogates how artificial intelligence reshapes transnational education by reconfiguring pedagogy, faculty development, and governance across borders. It synthesizes learning sciences, intercultural theory, and critical algorithm studies to construct a multilevel framework that links macro policy, meso institutional design, and micro classroom practice. The analysis profiles adaptive tutoring, analytics, translation, and simulation while diagnosing risks of surveillance, bias, context collapse, and epistemic homogenization. It advances a program for AI literate faculty built on technical, critical, and pedagogical fluencies, and specifies equity strategies for disability, gender, language, and LGBTQ inclusion. The chapter proposes actionable mechanisms including participatory procurement, model transparency, low bandwidth pathways, human in the loop assessment, and cross-national accreditation for microcredentials. It concludes by reframing AI as public infrastructure governed by ethical reflexivity, contestability, and cultural responsiveness.

1. INTRODUCTION

Transnational education has shifted from ancillary experiment to structural architecture of higher learning, mirroring the reconfiguration of knowledge economies after the 1990s and the abrupt digitization precipitated by the 2020 pandemic (Mahy & Li, 2024; Liang, 2024). Early twentieth century

DOI: 10.4018/979-8-3373-5403-3.ch008

cross-border flows largely tracked elite exchanges and colonial knowledge transfer, whereas late twentieth century neoliberalization recalibrated higher education as a tradable service with complex regulatory externalities. By mid-2025 UNESCO reported that internationally mobile enrolments approached seven million during 2022 and 2023, a level that recovered and then exceeded pre-pandemic mobility. Concurrently, providers expanded modalities well beyond student relocation. Cross-Border Education Research Team listings identified roughly three hundred thirty international branch campuses in 2023, with dense clusters in the Gulf, China, and Southeast Asia, while the UK Aggregate Offshore record logged more than six hundred twenty thousand learners studying for UK awards outside the United Kingdom during 2023 to 2024. These topologies interlock with collaborative international learning networks, dual and joint degrees, franchised validation, and rapidly proliferating microcredentials that demand cross-system recognition. The massive open online course wave of the early 2010s signaled scale, yet it was the pandemic's forced pivot that normalized hybrid and synchronous transnational classrooms, embedding cloud infrastructures, proctoring ecologies, and data governance puzzles within day-to-day pedagogy.

The geoeconomics of this expansion remain asymmetrical and politically freighted. Curricular exports, accreditation grammars, and reputational capital continue to flow predominantly from institutions in North America, Western Europe, and Australia toward partner systems in Asia, the Middle East, and Africa, reproducing what many analysts describe as eduscape inequalities that echo earlier extractive circuits. Knowledge diplomacy is now explicit statecraft, visible in China's Belt and Road education corridors, in Australia's international education strategies, and in European initiatives that couple higher education with regional influence. Corporate consortia intensify these vectors through bespoke workforce academies that situate degree programs inside global supply chains, tightening the coupling between credential architectures and platform capitalism. Microcredential ecosystems promise stackability and labor market signaling yet introduce credit portability frictions that regional frameworks only partially resolve. Recognition regimes in the European Higher Education Area have advanced joint program validation at scale, while comparable harmonization across South Asia and Sub-Saharan Africa remains uneven, creating transactional costs that are borne disproportionately by peripheral institutions and first-generation learners. The result is a stratified marketplace in which access expands numerically while epistemic authority and quality assurance remain concentrated within a small set of exporting systems.

Artificial intelligence now threads through this landscape as both catalytic augmentation and structural risk. Adoption patterns diverge across functions, with widespread student uptake and growing institutional use in communications, analytics, and student support, even as formal governance lags behind practice (Kleibert, 2022; Peddi & Manoharan, 2025). Intelligent tutoring systems, adaptive sequencing, and predictive risk dashboards promise personalization at scale, while neural translation and captioning broaden participation across linguistic communities. Generative systems accelerate content authoring and assessment feedback, recalibrating cognitive load for both faculty and students. These affordances coexist with serious hazards (Saliya, 2025; Islam, 2023). Algorithmic homogenization can encode Western pedagogical priors that invisibilize indigenous epistemologies. Predictive profiling can narrow opportunity by pathologizing variance rather than scaffolding growth. Surveillance capitalism turns interaction traces into extractable value across jurisdictions where data protection regimes diverge, raising sovereignty and consent dilemmas for learners who never cross a physical border but whose data traverses multiple legal orders. Digital coloniality persists when platforms harvest pedagogical labor and student data while returning limited local configurability or model transparency, leaving receiving institutions to manage the social license of tools they did not design and cannot audit.

Faculty agency remains the decisive variable in this contested assemblage. Transnational teaching is not the mere export of syllabi but the construction of meaning across heterogeneous linguistic, cultural, professional, and regulatory milieus (Vajjhala & Strang, 2022; Rehman, 2025) Educators translate disciplinary conventions, negotiate assessment validity, and curate culturally responsive exemplars, and in AI-mediated ecologies they must additionally interpret model outputs, interrogate dataset provenance, and calibrate risk thresholds for intervention (Brammar, 2023; Suguku, 2023). Data literacy therefore becomes a core component of professional identity alongside disciplinary mastery and intercultural competence. The productive horizon lies in augmentation rather than substitution, with faculty positioned as global pedagogical architects who orchestrate dialogic learning, design assessments that reward originality rather than algorithmic conformity, and enforce ethical guardrails around monitoring and automation (Masrifah et al., 2025; Machado & Seifert, 2024). The present chapter advances this stance through a program of analysis that links theory to institutional practice, arguing for culturally situated and equity-centered integration of AI within transnational ecosystems. The objective is to move beyond technological determinism toward a praxis in which algorithmic systems extend human judgment without eroding autonomy, expand access without flattening diversity, and render cross-border education more resilient, relational, and just.

2. CONCEPTUAL FRAMEWORKS AND THEORETICAL GROUNDING

A robust conceptual architecture is indispensable for interpreting the entanglements of artificial intelligence, pedagogy, and culture within transnational education (Wang & Ling, 2024; Le Corre et al., 2025) Learning sciences, critical sociology, cognitive psychology, cybernetics, and science and technology studies together supply an analytic scaffold that prevents technological determinism from eclipsing human agency and contextual nuance. Cognitive constructivism explains individual sense making, social theories clarify intersubjective mediation, and critical traditions diagnose power and inequality that travel with digital systems across borders. Linguistic anthropology and semiotics illuminate how meaning circulates through multilingual interfaces, while information theory and control theory explicate feedback, adaptation, and stability in algorithmic tutoring. Human factors engineering and usability research guide the ergonomics of dashboards and prompts that shape attention and workload. Ethics and political philosophy frame obligations around privacy, consent, and distributive justice. These strands cohere into a transdisciplinary grammar that treats AI as an actor within socio technical assemblages rather than a neutral conduit (Du et al., 2025; Melgar-García et al., 2023). The goal is not rejection or celebration of automation but disciplined integration that preserves dialogic pedagogy, respects cultural epistemologies, and expands equitable participation. Such grounding licenses educators to translate model outputs into intelligible instructional moves, to calibrate risk predictions against professional judgement, and to redesign assessment ecologies so that originality is rewarded over conformity to algorithmic templates (Merino-Gomez & Curiel-Herrera, 2024; Bringas et al., 2023). Without this scaffold, cross border deployments drift toward homogenization and opacity, whereas with it, institutions can align intelligent systems with humane, culturally responsive, and evidence informed teaching.

2.1 Epistemological Architectures for AI Mediated Learning

Educational theory clarifies how algorithmic affordances should intersect with cognition and interaction in globally distributed classrooms. Piaget's genetic epistemology emphasizes assimilation and accommodation within stage sensitive schemata, a logic mirrored by mastery systems that modulate item difficulty by posterior estimates of competence, as in ALEKS which operationalizes Knowledge Space Theory developed by Doignon and Falmagne in the 1980s. Vygotsky extends the frame by locating learning within the zone of proximal development where scaffolds and social speech catalyze internalization, a dynamic approximated by intelligent tutoring, worked examples, and collaborative prompts in platforms such as the Open Learning Initiative at Carnegie Mellon launched in 2002. Siemens and Downes introduce connectivism in 2005, positioning learning as traversal of distributed networks where recommendation engines, knowledge graphs, and semantic search curate paths through proliferating resources. Freirean critical pedagogy repudiates banking metaphors and installs dialogic problem posing that interrogates whose knowledge is legitimated by predictive models and whose voice is discounted by language normativity. Mezirow's transformative learning foregrounds perspective shifts through reflective encounters with disorienting dilemmas, which virtual exchanges, agent based simulations, and counterfactual case authoring can purposefully stage. Together these traditions license design logics that keep human inquiry central while exploiting adaptive sequencing, formative analytics, and generative feedback to orchestrate cognitive apprenticeship across distance, time zones, and linguistic heterogeneity without surrendering interpretive sovereignty to opaque classifiers.

2.2 Intercultural Cognition and Communicative Ecologies

Intercultural theory prevents algorithmic universalism from flattening cultural pragmatics. Bennett's Developmental Model of Intercultural Sensitivity first elaborated in 1986 charts movement from denial and defense to acceptance and integration, which suggests that feedback, exemplars, and peer interaction should be staged to meet learners and faculty at different sensitivities rather than presuming immediate ethnorelativism. Hofstede's comparative dimensions originating in multinational surveys between 1967 and 1973 and subsequently extended draw attention to power distance, individualism collectivism, and uncertainty avoidance that modulate preferences for autonomy, structure, and error tolerance. High power distance cohorts often expect explicit guidance and visible expertise, which means that laissez faire personalization may be misread as abandonment. Hall's high context and low context communication typology indicates that text only participation metrics can underweight indirectness, silence, and gesture that carry meaning in many societies, a deficit that multimodal analytics can partly remedy if educators interpret signals with cultural humility. Deardorff's intercultural competence model from 2004 emphasizes empathy, adaptability, and perspective taking as outcomes that require reflective prompts, intercultural case narratives, and collaborative sense making rather than mere exposure. Neural translation, sentiment analysis, and speech recognition can widen access, yet they must be paired with metalinguistic activities that surface idiom, politeness strategies, and discourse conventions. When such calibration is absent, platforms inadvertently reinscribe ethnocentric defaults and render difference a deficit rather than a resource for collective knowledge building.

2.3 Faculty Learning, Professional Agency, and Design Praxis

Faculty development theory delineates the competencies that enable educators to steward AI wisely across borders. Mishra and Koehler's TPACK framework articulated in 2006 insists that technological, pedagogical, and content knowledge be integrated rather than bolted together, and in transnational settings an additional cultural stratum is required so that tool choices and task designs honor local epistemologies Puentedura's SAMR continuum publicized from 2006 to 2010 warns against permanent stasis at substitution or augmentation and challenges programs to reach modification and redefinition where analytics, simulations, and collaborative studios enable novel inquiry forms such as cross site design critiques or distributed labs. Lave and Wenger's communities of practice from 1991 explain how legitimate peripheral participation matures through shared repertoires, which implies that faculty learning networks should cultivate pattern libraries, openly licensed prompts, and annotated rubrics refined across regions. Vygotsky's zone of proximal development extends to professional growth when just in time mentoring, conversational agents, and exemplars scaffold ambitious redesign without prescribing singular pathways. Organizational learning and implementation science add that change sticks when leadership signals, incentives, and workload policies align with new practices, and when fidelity is balanced with adaptation to context. The result is a design praxis in which educators read data critically, prototype iteratively, and center student agency while reserving final evaluative authority for human judgement anchored in disciplinary standards and intercultural ethics.

2.4 Technoethics, Ontological Pluralism, and Algorithmic Governance

Philosophical and ethical inquiry provides guardrails for the normative order that computational systems instantiate within education. Posthumanist accounts exemplified by Rosi Braidotti's writings since 2013 refigure subjectivity as relational and more than human, which invites faculty to reconceive authorship, authorship assistance, and intellectual labor in classrooms that mix human creativity with machine generativity. Actor Network Theory associated with Bruno Latour and collaborators since the 1980s treats platforms, datasets, and models as actants that co-produce outcomes with teachers and students, which motivates governance that scrutinizes provenance, versioning, and affordances rather than blaming users alone. The ethics of care articulated by Carol Gilligan in 1982 and Joan Tronto in 1993 centers attentiveness, responsibility, and responsiveness, guiding designers toward interfaces that signal support, explain decisions, and minimize harm rather than maximizing extraction. Foucault's analytics of surveillance and biopolitics from the 1970s illuminate how measurement regimes manufacture compliant subjects, a risk heightened by continuous attention tracking and risk scoring. Critical algorithm studies advanced by Safiya Umoja Noble in 2018 demonstrate how search and recommendation encode racialized and gendered hierarchies, which in transnational ecosystems can also become epistemic hierarchies that sideline indigenous knowledge. A coherent governance agenda therefore requires transparency artifacts such as model cards, contestability pathways for students and staff, data minimization with purpose limitation, and cross border agreements that uphold dignity and consent. When such technoethical architecture accompanies pedagogy, AI can amplify equitable learning without erasing cultural plurality or undermining academic freedom.

3. DIGITAL PEDAGOGY ACROSS BORDERS

Artificial intelligence now saturates the transnational classroom as an infrastructural substrate that reconfigures curricular design, formative assessment, interactional sequencing, and institutional oversight (Alam, 2023a; Nightingale, 2024) Earlier digitization prioritized content dissemination and static repositories, whereas contemporary systems introduce adaptive estimation, predictive inference, and generative synthesis that dynamically orchestrate learning trajectories. Authoring tools construct item banks with psychometric calibration, recommender engines route learners through competency maps, and analytics surfaces expose latent misconceptions for targeted remediation (Cheng & Koh, 2022; Li & Zhou, 2024). These affordances travel across jurisdictions through cloud platforms that knit together branch campuses, franchised programs, and collaborative degrees, thereby creating pedagogical continuity at continental scale. The same apparatus embeds normative assumptions about language, discourse, and evidence that can occlude local epistemologies or valorize particular rhetorical forms (Cader et al., 2024; Quintián et al., 2024). Risk intensifies where black box models govern placement, pacing, and surveillance without reciprocal transparency or contestability. Pedagogical legitimacy therefore hinges on design justice, explicability, and human oversight that align machine outputs with disciplinary standards and cultural pragmatics. When calibrated with these safeguards, AI augments dialogic teaching and widens access for multilingual and neurodiverse cohorts (Cabeza-Lopez et al., 2024; Rowley & Skipper, 2021). When deployed as opaque command and control, it compresses inquiry into compliance and reifies global hierarchies. The analytic task is to separate augmentation from automation fetish, to elevate professional judgement over default algorithmic governance, and to build resilient learning ecologies that remain intelligible, contestable, and inclusive across borders.

3.1 Pedagogical Innovations Enabled by AI in TNE

The evident breakthroughs cluster around intelligent tutoring, adaptive sequencing, and multimodal accessibility that together extend instructional bandwidth for dispersed cohorts. Knowledge tracing methods estimate mastery in real time and power systems such as ALEKS and ASSISTments, while the Open Learning Initiative's data rich courseware exemplifies iterative refinement through learning engineering. Diagnostic classifiers detect error signatures and trigger micro explanations, worked examples, and retrieval practice with spacing and interleaving that follow cognitive science canons. Generative models accelerate feedback by producing rubric aligned comments and exemplars that faculty can curate for tone and rigor. Emotion sensitive analytics attempt to infer disengagement through behavioral telemetry and paralinguistic signals, a frontier that requires stringent consent, cultural calibration, and minimization to avoid speculative psychometrics. Neural machine translation and automatic speech recognition provide live captioning and bilingual interfaces in platforms such as Zoom, Teams, and Google's translation stack, which meaningfully reduce language friction while still mishandling idiom, politeness strategies, and code switching. Accessibility advances include text to speech, voice input, alternative text generation, and adjustable pacing that support deaf or hard of hearing learners, low vision users, and students with attention variability (Kumar et al., 2025; Maguire et al., 2025). When instructors embed these tools within Universal Design for Learning principles and explicit metacognitive training, the result is measurable gains in participation equity, feedback timeliness, and constructive alignment between outcomes, activities, and assessment across geographically distributed classrooms.

3.2 AI Powered Learning Models

Model based personalization alters the architecture of blended, flipped, and competency based designs by relocating computation to the orchestration layer. Pre class modules adaptively gate content so that synchronous sessions privilege application, debate, and collaborative problem solving rather than recapitulation. Early alert systems integrate attendance traces, submission patterns, and quiz telemetry to identify attrition risk, enabling timely advising that pairs algorithmic signals with human conversation rather than automated punitive escalation. Mastery learning pipelines use item response theory, Bayesian updating, and reinforcement heuristics to schedule practice and reassessment until criterion performance is achieved, a structure that aligns with competence frameworks in engineering, health, and business education. Studio pedagogies are extended through shared sandboxes and generative co design agents that synthesize alternative solutions for critique, thereby amplifying exposure to diverse approaches without crowding out originality. Simulation based curricula scale laboratories through virtual instrumentation and digital twins that approximate authentic constraints with parameter variability and stochastic events. Gamified feedback loops add points, levels, and narrative arcs, yet must be tempered by reflective prompts and portfolio artifacts to prevent the displacement of epistemic curiosity by reward chasing. The governing principle is orchestration with guardrails, where data driven adaptivity remains intelligible, adjustable, and subordinate to instructional intent rather than dictating pedagogy by inscrutable optimization.

3.3 Systemic Challenges and Critical Diagnostics

Significant liabilities accompany these affordances and require explicit mitigation to preserve academic freedom and cultural pluralism. Context collapse occurs when globally scaled platforms privilege text dominant, low context interactional styles and treat deviation as deficit, thereby marginalizing oral, iterative, or relational knowledge practices common in many communities. Algorithmic opacity undermines trust when placement, grading, or risk labels lack rationale, confidence intervals, or error characterizations that users can interrogate (Başaran & Turan, 2025; Patil et al., 2025). Continuous monitoring normalizes surveillance through proctoring, keystroke logging, and attention tracking that can chill discourse and disproportionately burden students with unstable connectivity or shared devices. Cross border data flows complicate consent, purpose limitation, and redress because protections differ under regimes such as the GDPR and numerous national statutes, while vendor contracts often remain asymmetrical and difficult to audit. Cognitive load can rise through incessant notifications, dashboard bloat, and nudging that fragments attention rather than scaffolding self-regulation (Melgar-García et al., 2023; Mishra et al., 2024). Creative expression is threatened when automated scoring and grammar correction incentivize conformity to model learned stylistics and penalize unconventional argumentation or multilingual voice. Robust responses include transparency artifacts such as model cards and rubrics aligned explanations, opt outs and low surveillance assessment designs, participatory configuration with students, dataset diversification that honors local epistemologies, and institutional review processes that evaluate equity impact before scale up.

3.4 Comparative Transnational Exemplars and Cautionary Tales

Diverse program constellations illustrate both promise and constraint. Joint medical curricula that link United Kingdom providers with Malaysian campuses deploy virtual patients, clinical decision trees, and image triage models to expand diagnostic rehearsal where placements are scarce, improving procedural fluency while requiring parallel cultivation of bedside communication to avert empathy attenuation. Cross border business degrees that connect Australian universities with Gulf partners use automated short answer scoring and generative feedback to manage large cohorts, which accelerates turnaround but demands vigilant moderation to avoid penalizing rhetorical styles shaped by local discourse norms. Liberal arts collaborations between India and the United Kingdom integrate live captioning, bilingual glossaries, and translation aids to widen participation for first generation learners, with faculty mediated comparison of machine translations and human paraphrases used to surface pragmatics and prevent semantic drift. Engineering and physics partnerships that link Chinese institutions with African universities expand laboratory access through virtual instrumentation, circuit simulators, and finite element sandboxes that operate on modest hardware, while instructors deliberately reintroduce hands on practicums to counter overreliance on frictionless models. These exemplars counsel a design stance that pairs automation with interpretation, that measures learning through multiple modalities beyond text analytics, and that centers local curricular sovereignty. The throughline is faculty stewardship that treats AI as a pliable substrate for equitable pedagogy rather than a turnkey replacement for human judgment.

4. BUILDING AI LITERATE FACULTY WITH ENHANCED SKILLS, STRUCTURES, AND SUPPORT

The catalytic promise of artificial intelligence within transnational education remains contingent upon the epistemic agency and design praxis of faculty who translate computational affordances into humane pedagogy (Cheng et al., 2024; Sarantinos, 2022) Educators are not peripheral users but constitutive mediators whose interpretive judgment modulates the interface between model outputs and learner development across multilingual and multi-jurisdictional classrooms (Suárez-Díaz et al., 2024; Ping, 2023). Where faculty mastery of algorithmic principles, measurement validity, and intercultural pragmatics is robust, AI augments dialogic teaching, shortens feedback cycles, and diversifies pathways to mastery for students who traverse heterogeneous infrastructures. Where such mastery is thin, the same systems can sediment inequality, valorize monolingual norms, and outsource evaluation to inscrutable scorers (Alam & Mohanty, 2022; Liu et al., 2025). Global surveys and sectoral reviews consistently report that professional readiness in advanced digital pedagogy remains uneven across regions and disciplines, with pockets of excellence coexisting alongside acute capacity constraints. The transnational setting intensifies these asymmetries because regulatory regimes, institutional resources, and linguistic ecologies diverge even within a single program network (Lu, 2025; Hatahet et al., 2024) An actionable agenda therefore requires a triadic literacy model that integrates technical, critical, and pedagogical fluencies, scaffolded by durable institutional structures and cooperative governance. The objective is not to transform educators into data scientists but to equip them with conceptual tools that permit principled adoption, rigorous oversight, and culturally responsive redesign. Only then can intelligent systems function as extensions of professional judgment rather than substitutes for it.

4.1 Epistemic and Technical Literacies for Educators

AI literacy for educators begins with conceptual fluency in how statistical learning systems ingest data, infer patterns, and express uncertainty so that classroom decisions remain evidence informed and context aware. Faculty require a working understanding of supervised and unsupervised learning, feature engineering, overfitting and generalization, and evaluation metrics that balance precision with recall under class imbalance (Suntharalingam, 2024; de Wit et al., 2025). Natural language processing introduces tokenization, embeddings, and alignment mechanisms that shape automated feedback and translation, while generative models require knowledge of prompt conditioning, temperature control, and hallucination risks. Explainability methods such as attention visualization, perturbation analysis, or surrogate modeling help instructors interrogate why an automated scorer or risk dashboard produced a given label. Critical literacy complements these elements through competence in bias detection, dataset provenance review, privacy by design, and fairness constraints that account for linguistic diversity and disability. Pedagogical literacy operationalizes these insights by redesigning syllabi, assignments, and rubrics so that automation supports formative sense making without displacing deliberative dialogue or academic freedom. Faculty can stage machine produced comments as draft suggestions subject to human revision, require reflective memos that compare algorithmic and human evaluations, and privilege portfolios, oral defenses, and multimodal artifacts that resist superficial standardization (Smith, 2023; Owusu-Agyeman & Amoakohene, 2021). Such integrated literacy enables educators to calibrate reliance, contest outputs when misaligned with disciplinary norms, and progressively condition models through locally relevant exemplars that elevate inclusion.

4.2 Structural Capacity Gaps and Sociocultural Frictions in TNE

Capacity differentials in transnational networks reveal infrastructural, cultural, and organizational hurdles that complicate responsible AI integration (Guo, 2025; Smith et al., 2023). Reliable bandwidth, secure devices, and accessible software remain unevenly distributed across urban and rural partner sites, creating selection effects that privilege well-resourced learners and inhibit staff experimentation with data intensive tools. Institutional firewalls and procurement norms can restrict access to cloud services, while data protection statutes across jurisdictions can generate uncertainty that dissuades adoption even when pedagogy would benefit. Sociocultural dynamics matter with equal force. In some contexts, hierarchical traditions and high-power distance expectations valorize explicit teacher authority and tightly scripted progression, which can render student led exploration or peer feedback mediated by algorithms counterintuitive without careful framing. In other settings, faculty voice concerns that automation attenuates the relational core of teaching, especially in programs oriented to professional identity formation in education, health, or social work. Workload and incentive structures also inhibit skill development when promotion systems undervalue pedagogical innovation or when teaching allocations leave little time for iterative redesign. These constraints are not technophobia but rational responses to misalignment between tools and institutional ecology. Addressing them requires capacity building that pairs infrastructure investments with culturally informed change management, transparent governance, and workload policies that recognize the cognitive and emotional labor of ethical orchestration.

4.3 Developmental Frameworks for Professional Learning and Design Praxis

Systematic faculty development must braid formal credentials, peer mediated learning, and embedded support so that competence grows from awareness to integration to critical mastery. Formal pathways include certificate programs in learning analytics, assessment design with AI affordances, and accessibility engineering anchored in Universal Design for Learning, all aligned with promotion criteria and teaching recognition schemes. Informal pathways leverage communities of practice in which educators share prompt libraries, annotated rubrics, and case reports, while engaging in reflective critique of failures as well as successes so that tacit knowledge becomes portable across campuses. Embedded supports then operationalize learning at the point of need. Just in time consultation from instructional designers and data specialists, sandbox environments with de identified datasets for safe experimentation, and faculty facing dashboards that report on tool behavior as well as student progress enable iterative refinement during live delivery. Regional consortia and university alliances have piloted integrated models that combine these strands with intercultural calibration workshops, yielding gains in confidence, ethical awareness, and task specific proficiency. The most durable programs foreground co creation with students, encourage small safe to fail trials, and publish open playbooks that codify patterns such as scaffolded generative feedback, bilingual assessment design, and simulation-based mastery checks (Jiang, 2021; Ketteringham, 2025). Such frameworks move adoption beyond episodic workshops toward sustained design praxis.

4.4 Institutional Architectures for Competence, Procurement, and Accountability

Institutions serve as the meso layer that links macro policy with micro pedagogy, and their architectures determine whether faculty development scales equitably. Competency mapping translates strategic aims into discipline specific capability matrices that specify tools, concepts, and ethical expectations for different roles, thereby guiding targeted development rather than generic training (Schueller, 2023; Menon et al., 2022). Stackable microcredentials recognize incremental growth and can be coupled with teaching relief or grant funding to reward ambitious redesign. Teaching and learning centers increasingly require embedded AI expertise, including specialists in learning engineering, accessibility, and data stewardship, who partner with academic units to co design and evaluate interventions (Dutt et al., 2022; Li et al., 2025). Procurement policy must shift from feature checklists to participatory evaluation that includes faculty and students, demands evidence of bias auditing and accessibility, and negotiates data minimization with clear ownership, retention, and exit provisions. Governance structures such as educational technology councils and ethics review committees should adjudicate scale up after pilot evaluation and require equity impact statements that consider language, disability, and connectivity. Finally, workload models and promotion frameworks must legitimize the time and intellectual labor required for ethical orchestration, including recognition for open educational resources, shared pattern libraries, and peer mentoring. Such institutional architectures render responsible AI integration feasible rather than aspirational.

4.5 Global Faculty Narratives and Situated Praxis across Sites

Ethnographic vignettes from varied partner contexts illustrate how faculty agency converts abstract principles into situated praxis. In Nairobi, instructors within business programs partnered with UK universities initially resisted automated scoring that flattened rhetorical diversity, then reframed the tool as a formative pre screen whose outputs were annotated, contested, and supplemented with oral defenses, thereby preserving voice while improving turnaround. In Dhaka, computing educators collaborating with Australian institutions confronted unstable power and bandwidth constraints, so they designed hybrid labs that paired lightweight local compilers and offline datasets with periodic cloud based synthesis, maintaining continuity despite infrastructural volatility. In Kuala Lumpur, engineering faculty integrated simulation suites for control systems and materials testing while advocating for scheduled physical practicums so that tacit skills and safety culture remained intact, producing a complementary cycle of virtual rehearsal and embodied execution. In Manchester, liberal arts instructors co taught with partner campuses and used bilingual glossaries and reflective commentaries to surface the limits of machine translation, treating mistranslation as a pedagogical artifact that invited metalinguistic analysis rather than a barrier to participation. Across these sites the common denominator is stewardship that insists on contestability, cultural calibration, and multi modal evidence of learning. Such narratives reaffirm that AI becomes an instrument of equity and innovation only when educators retain interpretive sovereignty and institutional systems reward conscientious design.

5. ETHICS, EQUITY, AND INCLUSION IN AI MEDIATED TRANSNATIONAL EDUCATION

Artificial intelligence within transnational education constitutes a normative terrain where design choices, incentive structures, and geopolitical asymmetries converge to shape who learns, who is measured, and who decides (Ali et al., 2024; Mikecz Munday, 2021). The rhetoric of neutrality that often surrounds automation obscures political economies in which data extraction, proprietary standards, and linguistic asymmetries travel more easily than pedagogical care or cultural reciprocity. Cross border deployments knit together students, faculty, platforms, and regulators in chains of dependency that rarely distribute agency evenly, particularly when exporting institutions set curricular grammars and infrastructural baselines for receiving partners. Ethical analysis therefore begins with attentiveness to power, consent, and representation, not only to accuracy or efficiency. Learning platforms record navigation trails, text production, voice patterns, and proctoring telemetry, transforming ordinary study into monetizable signals. Predictive profiling promises timely support, yet can encode deficit framings that travel with students across courses and campuses. Algorithmic personalizers appear inclusive while normalizing hegemonic discourse conventions that marginalize oral, relational, or plurilingual knowledge practices. The task for educators and leaders is to construct governance that privileges transparency, choice, and redress, to require explainability that is pedagogically meaningful, and to embed design justice that recognizes students not as data subjects but as collaborators. Only within such an ethos can AI extend equitable participation rather than entrench stratification and cultural erasure.

5.1 Digital Ethics and Data Political Economy in Globalized Education

The expansion of educational AI unfolds within what Shoshana Zuboff named surveillance capitalism in 2019, a regime in which behavioral surplus is harvested and repurposed for prediction and control. Learning management systems, communication suites, and assessment services gather keystrokes, clickstreams, dwell time, and biometric proxies that are then fed into optimization pipelines for retention, marketing, and product improvement. In transnational networks these flows traverse multiple jurisdictions, increasing opacity for learners who cannot easily know what is collected, where it resides, and how it is profiled (Healey, 2023; Schulze & Kleibert, 2021). Platform imperialism compounds the risk when toolmakers headquartered in the Global North export standards and defaults that bind partner campuses to external infrastructures and update cycles, with local institutions bearing liability without commensurate configurability or audit access. Geopolitical contingency also intrudes through sanctions, data localization mandates, and vendor consolidation, which can suddenly disrupt core teaching functions. Ethical stewardship in this environment requires contractual clauses that codify data minimization, portability, and sunset provisions, as well as institutional capacity to verify claims about anonymization, differential privacy, and bias remediation (Alam & Mohanty, 2024; Wang, 2022). It also requires classroom level candor about telemetry, opt out pathways that do not penalize students, and graded alternatives to intrusive proctoring. Without these counterweights, educational data economies convert pedagogy into extraction and render students legible mainly as targets for optimization rather than as partners in inquiry.

5.2 Infrastructural Stratification and Epistemic Inequity in Access Regimes

Equity in AI mediated learning depends on physical infrastructure, device ecologies, and spectrum policy as much as on algorithms. Electrification remains uneven across Sub Saharan Africa, where recent figures place access near one half of the population, and reliable broadband is substantially lower than mobile connectivity, with rural regions persistently underserved. Device inequality compounds these gaps, since many learners in low and lower middle-income contexts rely on shared or low specification smartphones that struggle with data intensive simulations, video conferencing, or proctoring clients. National surveys in India during 2021 reported double digit computer ownership in rural households compared with far higher rates in urban centers, a digital gradient that maps onto educational attainment and linguistic privilege. These material constraints shape not only participation but also the validity of assessment and the ethics of monitoring, because bandwidth dependent tools systematically disadvantage those with unstable connections. Epistemic injustice intensifies the problem when models trained primarily on English language and Western corpora dominate recommendation and scoring, suppressing indigenous, local, and Global South knowledge formations. Miranda Fricker's articulation of testimonial and hermeneutical injustice clarifies how voices can be discounted or rendered unintelligible by classificatory schemes. In response, institutions must diversify datasets, fund low bandwidth pathways, and design assignments that recognize oral, visual, and community grounded epistemologies rather than enforcing one textual norm.

5.3 Inclusive Design for Disability Gender and Sexual Diversity in Transnational Contexts

Artificial intelligence can catalyze inclusion when guided by accessibility engineering and intersectional analysis rather than by generic efficiency. Speech recognition, neural captioning, and text to speech reduce barriers for deaf or hard of hearing learners and for those with low vision or reading challenges, especially when captions are editable, latency is minimized, and domain lexicons are tuned to local languages. Keyboard navigation, alt text generation, and adjustable pacing support neurodiverse students and those learning in noisy or low bandwidth environments, aligning with Universal Design for Learning principles. Gendered inequities persist in device access and connectivity across many low and middle income regions, with studies during 2021 and 2022 reporting that women were markedly less likely to use mobile internet or to own smartphones, which translates into diminished exposure to AI enhanced coursework. Algorithmic stereotyping can further channel learners toward traditionally gendered fields through biased recommendation and feedback (Chitadze, 2024; Murray & Doe, 2024). LGBTQ students encounter distinct risks where surveillance or content moderation regimes flag non normative identities, making privacy, pseudonymity, and data minimization non negotiable design features. Inclusive practice therefore entails localized model tuning, continuous bias audits that disaggregate by language and identity markers, trauma informed classroom policies, and explicit consent rituals that explain tradeoffs. When faculty pair such safeguards with reflective activities that critique translation drift and classification errors, inclusion moves from technical accommodation to shared critical literacy.

5.4 Jurisdictional Governance and Algorithmic Accountability across Borders

Regulatory heterogeneity shapes every layer of AI enabled transnational education (Ye, 2025; Mok & Sawn Khai, 2024). The UNESCO Recommendation on the Ethics of Artificial Intelligence adopted in 2021 articulates principles of transparency, accountability, and human oversight, while the European Union's General Data Protection Regulation in force since 2018 establishes rights to informed consent, data access, and contestation. The European Union's Artificial Intelligence Act adopted in 2024 classifies educational proctoring and risk scoring among higher risk uses subject to conformity assessment and documentation obligations, timelines for full enforcement now unfolding. Many partner jurisdictions in Africa, South Asia, and parts of Latin America maintain newer or weaker data protection laws, creating asymmetries in remedy and redress when cross border data flows carry student information to servers in third countries. Contractual clauses can mitigate but rarely eliminate these gaps, particularly when sub processors are added without transparent listing or when model updates change data use. Institutions should institute internal ethics review for learning technologies, publish registers of approved systems with risk ratings, and require vendors to supply model cards, evaluation reports, and accessibility conformance statements (Sia & Jimmie, 2023). Faculty liability must be clarified through policy, training, and indemnification, since educators cannot be expected to absorb legal exposure for opaque tools procured centrally. Governance that is legible to students and staff strengthens trust and provides a foundation for pedagogical innovation that does not compromise rights.

5.5 Pedagogical Equity Strategies and Participatory Algorithmics for TNE

Equitable AI integration begins with a pedagogy first orientation that treats algorithms as configurable instruments rather than unquestioned authorities. Participatory design processes that include students and community partners in tool selection, interface configuration, and rubric alignment generate systems that reflect local discourse conventions and accessibility needs (Jardim, 2025; Hill, 2021). Human in the loop workflows preserve educator sovereignty by positioning automated feedback as provisional, requiring reflective rebuttal or confirmation, and routing high stakes decisions through peer moderation or viva voce defenses. Anti surveillance pedagogy normalizes transparency about telemetry, offers non punitive opt outs, and replaces invasive proctoring with assessment designs that reduce opportunities for misconduct through iterative drafts, randomized item banks, or authentic tasks. Critical data literacy becomes a shared competency when courses incorporate activities that analyze translation misfires, sentiment misclassification, and bias metrics, converting errors into teachable moments that strengthen epistemic humility (Miani, 2023; Muralidhar et al., 2025). Institutions must underpin these practices with resources for dataset diversification, bilingual and low bandwidth pathways, and microcredentials that recognize faculty expertise in ethical orchestration. Continuous equity impact evaluation, disaggregated by language, geography, disability, and gender, should inform scale up decisions and procurement renewals. Through such measures AI mediated transnational education can shift from extractive optimization toward a collaborative enterprise that widens access while honoring cultural plurality and academic freedom.

6. BRIDGING THEORY AND PRACTICE WITHIN A MULTILEVEL INTEGRATIVE FRAMEWORK

6.1 Macro Level Policy Architectures and Systems Ecology

Transnational adoption of artificial intelligence requires regulatory architectures that reconcile innovation with distributive justice and epistemic pluralism (Li et al., 2025; Rehman, 2025). Macro governance must align data protection, accreditation, and cross border quality assurance so that algorithmic augmentation does not entrench dependency or export hidden curricular orthodoxies. International guidance from UNESCO and the OECD articulates high level principles, yet operationalization depends on interoperable standards for transparency, auditability, and portability that travel with students and faculty across jurisdictions. Accreditation regimes need mechanisms that recognize microcredentials, simulation-based competencies, and AI mediated assessment without diluting comparability or inflating credentialism (Tse, 2025; Jaganathan et al., 2025). Mutual recognition agreements should specify provenance requirements for datasets, documentation for model behavior, and rights to contest automated determinations that affect progression or visa status. Public funding strategies can catalyze low bandwidth infrastructures and open educational datasets so that institutions in low- and middle-income settings are not forced into vendor lock in. Trade and sanctions policy must be considered because platform availability and cloud locality can shift abruptly, disrupting instruction at scale. A macro framework therefore coordinates privacy law, educational treaties, spectrum policy, and research investment so that AI ecosystems remain contestable, resilient, and oriented toward the public good rather than extractive optimization.

6.2 Meso Level Institutional Praxis and Operational Orchestration

Institutions constitute the translational layer where abstract principles are converted into policies, workflows, and resourcing that make ethical orchestration possible. Effective praxis begins with competency matrices that differentiate expectations for instructors, program leaders, learning designers, and data stewards, converting strategy into role specific capabilities (Alam, 2023b; Tran et al., 2023). Teaching and learning centers require embedded expertise in learning engineering, accessibility, intercultural pedagogy, and data governance, with consultation pathways that accompany course design from scoping to evaluation. Procurement should adopt participatory evaluation in which faculty and students test tools against equity rubrics, accessibility conformance, and explainability benchmarks, while contracts codify data minimization, exit rights, and independent audit. Governance bodies can maintain a public register of approved systems with documented risks and mitigation plans, and can condition scale up on demonstrated learning gains disaggregated by language, disability, and connectivity. Institutional analytics should monitor not only student outcomes but also tool behavior including error distributions, latency for feedback, and rates of contested outputs. Promotion and workload frameworks must recognize the intellectual labor of ethical orchestration, including the creation of open resources, design pattern libraries, and peer mentoring. Through these structures, institutions transform episodic pilots into durable capability and align AI with mission and student welfare.

6.3 Micro Level Pedagogical Design and Learner Agency

Classrooms remain the crucible where intelligent systems either expand inquiry or compress it into compliance. Pedagogical design should treat algorithms as configurable instruments whose outputs are hypotheses subject to human interpretation, not definitive verdicts (Bharadwaj & Verma, 2025; Morris & Kozuch, 2024). Lesson planning can sequence adaptive preparatory study with synchronous dialogue that targets observed misconceptions while preserving space for ambiguity and intellectual risk taking (Qureshi & Trotter, 2025; Benkhelifa et al., 2025). Assessment should combine machine assisted feedback with oral defenses, portfolios, and performance tasks that capture creativity, collaboration, and translanguaging practices often invisible to automated scoring (Suntharalingam, 2025; Palmer & Chandir, 2024). Critical data literacy ought to be taught as a shared competence so that students interrogate translation drift, sentiment misclassification, and confidence intervals, converting model error into epistemic learning rather than frustration. Multilingual design requires captioning and translation paired with metalinguistic reflection so that semantic nuance becomes material for analysis, not collateral loss. In clinical and laboratory domains, virtual simulations should be interleaved with embodied practicums to sustain tacit knowledge, safety culture, and professional identity. Transparency about telemetry, storage, and choice preserves trust, and low surveillance assessment reduces inequitable risk for learners with unstable bandwidth or shared devices. Micro level craft thus anchors AI within dialogic, culturally responsive, and autonomy supportive teaching.

6.4 Cross Cutting Normative Principles and Translational Heuristics

Several normative anchors unify macro systems, meso structures, and micro practice into a coherent architecture. Contextual intelligence demands localization of models, exemplars, and interfaces so that disciplinary canons converse with regional epistemologies rather than overwrite them. Ethical reflexivity requires continuous scrutiny of unintended consequences through equity impact reviews, red team audits, and student advisory panels that surface harms early. Pedagogical integrity positions human relationships as the telos of instruction, which implies that automation should accelerate feedback and widen access without displacing dialogue, questioning, and care (Valarmathi & Suchitra, 2025; Nemorin, 2024). Interdisciplinarity joins educators with data scientists, lawyers, and ethicists so that design choices incorporate fairness constraints, accessibility engineering, and legal compliance from inception rather than as afterthoughts. Contestability guarantees that high stakes decisions include appeal pathways and human adjudication with clear rationales. Proportionality guides data collection toward the minimum necessary and resists intrusive proctoring when alternative assessment designs suffice. Finally, openness encourages open standards, open pedagogical resources, and transparent documentation that enable scrutiny, remix, and portability, thereby reducing dependency and fostering cumulative learning across transnational partnerships (Alam, 2023c; Berry, 2022).

6.5 Visual Heuristics and Decision Support Artifacts for Strategic Alignment

Visual models can crystallize complexity and scaffold action across heterogeneous stakeholders. A triadic Venn of pedagogy, intelligence, and equity highlights the zone of responsible innovation where student flourishing, algorithmic capability, and justice cohere. A spiral of faculty AI literacy maps growth from awareness to application to critical mastery, with feedback loops that connect classroom evidence to institutional support and policy recalibration. A readiness matrix positions programs along axes of infrastructural capacity and pedagogical depth, surfacing where investments in bandwidth, accessibility, or assessment redesign will yield the greatest marginal benefit. A risk register dashboard tracks system provenance, bias metrics, error rates, and incident responses in ways that are legible to non specialists while retaining methodological rigor. Journey maps of student interaction reveal choke points created by latency, translation drift, or excessive nudging, guiding humane redesign. These artifacts function as decision support rather than decoration, enabling leaders to prioritize pilots, educators to plan lessons, and technologists to tune models. When maintained as living documents tied to review cycles and public reporting, visual heuristics keep transnational ecosystems aligned with values, avert drift toward opaque optimization, and translate theory into measurable, iterative improvement (Khadri, 2021; Kaur et al., 2025; Hajji, 2023).

7. RECOMMENDATIONS AND PROSPECTIVE PATHWAYS FOR ALGORITHMIC PEDAGOGY IN TRANSNATIONAL SYSTEMS

The integration of artificial intelligence into transnational education constitutes a paradigmatic reconfiguration of pedagogic design, equity governance, and institutional accountability that demands prescriptions grounded in comparative policy analysis and implementation science (Jaganathan et al., 2025; Reis & Sun, 2025). Durable progress requires recommendations that travel across jurisdictions while remaining plastic enough to accommodate linguistic plurality, infrastructural volatility, and divergent accreditation logics (Wu-Ross, 2024; Chen et al., 2024). Immediate priorities include rights respecting data stewardship, procurement regimes that reward transparency and accessibility, and capacity building that elevates educator agency rather than vendor dependency. Parallel priorities involve measurable targets for inclusion, such as bandwidth thresholds, assistive technology availability, and multilingual service levels that can be audited. Strategic horizons should incentivize open standards, interoperation across platforms, and public infrastructures that mitigate concentration risk (Fernandez-Chung & Gill, 2025; Goorney et al., 2023). Research and development agendas ought to privilege low bandwidth innovation, privacy preserving learning analytics, and culturally situated evaluation so that benefits accrue beyond well-resourced hubs. Throughout, evaluative rigor must be embedded through mixed methods evidence, with equity impact tracked by language, disability, gender, and geography (Alam & Mohanty, 2023; Peng, 2024). Taken together, these pathways replace technocentric diffusion with principled orchestration where algorithmic tools amplify human judgment, widen access, and preserve epistemic diversity across borders.

7.1 Policy Stratagems for Multilateral Stewardship and Public Interest Safeguards

Governments and intergovernmental bodies should convert normative statements into binding instruments that travel with student data, credentials, and algorithmic determinations across borders. Data protection agreements must guarantee portability, purpose limitation, and contestation rights irrespective of server locality, while mandating disclosure of model provenance, evaluation protocols, and known failure modes (Rian, 2024; Ahmed et al., 2025). Mutual recognition frameworks should include criteria for microcredentials, simulation verified competencies, and machine assisted assessments, with safeguards against credential inflation and opaque scoring. Funding architectures need to redirect resources toward low and lower middle-income regions by underwriting electrification, campus connectivity, and assistive technology, alongside open datasets and reference corpora in under resourced languages. Regulatory sandboxes can accelerate innovation while requiring accessibility conformance, bias audits, and student advisory participation prior to scale. Public registers of approved educational AI, maintained by quality agencies, should list risk ratings, audit outcomes, and accessibility attestations to inform institutional choice (Sun, 2025; Dulloo & Naseer, 2025). Periodic equity and security audits of cross border programs can be tied to accreditation cycles, with corrective action plans when disparities or vulnerabilities are detected. Such instruments align market incentives with the public good, reduce dependency on proprietary black boxes, and create enforceable rights for learners and faculty in transnational ecosystems (Sirkeci & Lo, 2023; Haider et al., 2025).

7.2 Institutional Architectures for Ethical Orchestration and Operational Readiness

Universities and consortia occupy the meso layer where strategy becomes practice, which requires organizational architectures that embed ethics, accessibility, and cultural responsiveness in everyday operations. Institutions should establish AI pedagogy innovation labs that convene faculty, students, learning engineers, and ethicists to co design pilots, generate evidence, and publish open playbooks for replication. Faculty development must move from episodic workshops to stackable microcredentials tied to recognition and promotion, with pathways that integrate learning analytics, accessibility engineering, and intercultural design. Procurement should adopt participatory evaluation where educators and students test candidate tools against explainability, bias, and usability benchmarks while contracts codify data minimization, exit rights, and independent audit (Qaralleh & Ahmed, 2025; Alam, 2022). Governance bodies can maintain visible registers of approved systems with risk notes, sunset dates, and responsible owners, while internal ethics reviews assess impact prior to enterprise scale. Institutional analytics should report not only learning outcomes but also tool behavior, latency, error distributions, and rates of contested outputs, disaggregated for equity monitoring. Workload and incentive policies must value the intellectual labor of ethical orchestration, including time for redesign, peer mentoring, and the creation of open educational resources. Through these structures, institutions convert scattered experiments into durable capability aligned with mission and student welfare.

7.3 Pedagogical Praxis for Educator Agency and Justice Oriented Design

Educators should treat artificial intelligence as a configurable instrument that augments formative dialogue and disciplinary inquiry rather than as an automated arbiter. Course design can embed critical data literacy where students analyze translation drift, sentiment misclassification, and confidence intervals, converting model error into epistemic learning. Assignments can pair machine generated feedback with reflective rebuttals, oral defenses, and portfolio curation so that evaluation privileges originality, argument quality, and multimodal expression. Justice oriented pedagogy uses captioning, adaptive pacing, and multilingual glossaries to widen participation while actively auditing for exclusionary effects that track language, disability, or gender. Participation in open source co design projects with developers enables educators to shape datasets, prompts, and interfaces that reflect local discourse conventions and accessibility needs. Overreliance can be mitigated by reserving high stakes determinations for human panels, by rotating analytic roles among students to demystify automation, and by designing low surveillance assessments that reduce inequitable risks from unstable bandwidth or shared devices (Haider et al., 2025; Arida, 2023). Continuous improvement loops that combine student voice, peer observation, and small safe to fail trials strengthen craft knowledge. Such praxis anchors algorithmic integration in human judgment, preserves relational learning, and advances inclusion as a measurable instructional outcome rather than a rhetorical aspiration.

7.4 Developer Commitments for Transparent and Inclusive Sociotechnical Design

Developers should institutionalize partnership with educators and students from diverse regions at ideation, prototyping, and evaluation stages so that tools reflect classroom realities rather than abstract user stories. Transparency must include model cards, datasheets, and evaluation reports that disclose datasets, sampling frames, subgroup performance, and known limitations in language handling, accessibility, and domain coverage (Suntharalingam, 2025; Islam et al., 2025). Configurability should extend to rubrics, weightings, interface language, and logging defaults, with privacy preserving options such as on device inference or federated learning where feasible. Inclusive design requires continuous bias auditing, screen reader compatibility, keyboard navigation, caption accuracy, and localization pipelines that support under resourced languages and dialects. Cost transparency and compute budgets reduce hidden barriers for low resource partners, while offline and low bandwidth modes expand reach. Developer roadmaps should reserve capacity for educator requested features that advance assessment validity, contestability, and accessibility rather than privileging novelty alone (Karim-Abdallah et al., 2025; Alfayez & Rasool, 2025). Error reporting and redress mechanisms need to be legible and timely so that institutions can triage incidents without disruption to teaching. By adopting these commitments, vendors transform from purveyors of opaque platforms into collaborators in equitable pedagogy and accountable public infrastructure.

7.5 Research Trajectories and Methodological Pluralism for Evidence Building

A forward program of research should combine experimental, quasi experimental, and qualitative methods to illuminate effectiveness, mechanisms, and context sensitivity. Longitudinal studies can trace the influence of AI mediated feedback and translation on belonging, identity formation, and academic persistence across culturally heterogeneous cohorts. Randomized trials and stepped wedge designs can compare human led, hybrid, and machine led feedback on learning gains and writing quality in multiple languages, while realist evaluation explains what works for whom in which conditions. Validation studies are needed for emotion analytics to test cross cultural construct validity and to quantify error propagation when paralinguistic cues diverge by culture or disability. Faculty agency deserves ethnographic attention that documents negotiation, resistance, and innovation, generating design patterns that travel across disciplines and regions. Policy research can compare regulatory regimes on rights to explanation, data portability, and algorithmic accountability, identifying models that balance innovation with protection. Open datasets, replication incentives, and shared benchmark tasks in low resource languages will expand cumulative knowledge. Through such plural methodologies, the field can move beyond anecdote toward robust, context aware evidence that guides equitable and effective integration of artificial intelligence in transnational education.

8. CONCLUSION

Artificial intelligence now functions as a structural determinant in transnational education, reconfiguring curricular architectures, assessment ecologies, and institutional oversight while redistributing interpretive authority among actors who do not hold equal power. The evidence presented throughout the chapter establishes that AI is neither neutral nor teleological but a contested assemblage in which design choices, training corpora, incentive structures, and regulatory asymmetries co produce outcomes. Personalization, neural translation, and adaptive supports can widen participation for linguistically diverse and geographically dispersed learners, yet the same mechanisms can compress epistemic plurality through homogenized rubrics, surveillance heavy telemetry, and export of platform defaults that privilege dominant discourse communities. The decisive variable is not raw computational capacity but civic and professional choice expressed through governance, procurement, and classroom design. Where institutions codify transparency, contestability, and accessibility, algorithmic interventions augment human judgment and strengthen equity. Where opacity, extractive data practices, and uncritical importation of tools prevail, algorithmic pedagogy becomes a vector for cultural erasure and procedural injustice. The path forward must therefore treat AI as a malleable public infrastructure rather than an immutable technological fate, binding it to norms that protect dignity, widen choice, and remain responsive to cultural semantics across borders. Such a stance reframes innovation as stewardship, foregrounds accountability over novelty, and routes benefit to learners who have historically been peripheral to global knowledge circuits.

Faculty agency remains the fulcrum upon which this transformation turns, since meaningful learning in transnational settings continues to depend on dialogue, empathy, and contextual reasoning that no machine presently reproduces. Educators serve as interpreters of probabilistic outputs, as mediators of intercultural pragmatics, and as architects who align disciplinary canons with local epistemologies without capitulating to assimilationist tendencies. When equipped with data literacy, accessibility engineering sensibilities, and critical sociotechnical awareness, faculty can curate algorithmic feedback as provisional hypotheses, stage reflective rebuttals and viva voce defenses, and maintain multi modal evidence of mastery that resists reduction to text dominant scoring. Their design praxis can preserve originality by valuing argument quality, creativity, and translanguaging, while their ethical vigilance can temper automation with care. Recasting educators as global pedagogical architects affirms their custodial role over assessment validity, student well being, and cultural reciprocity. Such stewardship neither romanticizes manual practice nor surrenders to mechanization but orchestrates intelligent systems as instruments that extend rather than eclipse professional judgment. In this configuration faculty not only use AI competently, they civilize it through norms of explanation, proportionality, and equity that keep the locus of educational meaning squarely within human relationships.

Ethical commitments cannot be appended after deployment but must infuse governance, design, and pedagogy from inception. Data extraction without clear purpose, algorithmic bias that tracks language, gender, or disability, and digital coloniality that channels value to distant vendors while externalizing risk all threaten the social license of transnational programs. These hazards are tractable when institutions institutionalize human in the loop workflows, constitutive participation of students in tool selection, and ethics review processes that evaluate impact before scale. Classroom transparency about telemetry, storage, and choice can convert potential surveillance into shared inquiry about measurement, uncertainty, and error. Contestability pathways that allow students to challenge automated determinations and to supply alternative evidence create due process that educates while protecting rights. Faculty development that centers intercultural calibration, accessibility, and fairness auditing can make ethical reflexivity habitual rather than episodic. The resulting culture declines to equate efficiency with virtue, insisting instead that technological benefit be judged by its contribution to dignity, inclusion, and intellectual growth. Ethics thus becomes a daily practice that orients technical ingenuity toward the flourishing of learners across jurisdictions and languages.

Transnational education also supplies an unparalleled laboratory for designing less parochial algorithmic systems through co creation with diverse partners. Programs that embed localization pipelines, community authored corpora, and bilingual or trilingual interfaces transform translation from a convenience into a site of metalinguistic analysis that strengthens comprehension and cultural humility. Simulation based curricula that pair virtual instrumentation with staged practicums can democratize access to laboratories while preserving tacit professional knowledge and safety culture. Low bandwidth modes, on device inference, and privacy preserving analytics expand inclusion where connectivity remains fragile, proving that technological sophistication is compatible with infrastructural realism. By embracing reverse innovation, exporting institutions can learn from the constraints and ingenuity of partner campuses and incorporate these design heuristics into mainstream platforms. Such reciprocity resists the unilateral export of defaults and instead builds global systems that are resilient, interpretable, and representative. The intercultural diversity intrinsic to TNE thus becomes a productive pressure that compels AI to honor plural epistemologies, to accommodate multilingual pragmatics, and to sustain pedagogies that value narrative, collaboration, and community grounded knowledge alongside formal abstraction.

Sustained progress requires collaborative orchestration across macro systems, meso institutions, and micro classrooms so that responsibility is distributed yet coordinated. Policymakers should enact cross national protections for data portability, explanation rights, and accessibility, while quality agencies maintain public registers that document risk ratings, audits, and remediation. Institutions should invest in innovation labs, competency mapping, and participatory procurement, linking promotion to ethical orchestration and open resource creation. Educators should cultivate critical data literacy with students, design low surveillance assessments that honor multimodality, and participate in open source co design that localizes tools to discourse conventions and disability needs. Developers should publish model documentation, expose configuration levers, and support under resourced languages with verifiable performance metrics. Such alignment converts hype into hope by treating AI as a partner that extends human potential rather than bounding it. When these actors synchronize around transparency, inclusion, and pedagogical integrity, transnational education evolves from a delivery mechanism into a transformative commons that is relational, just, and future proof.

REFERENCES

Ahmed, Y., Ahmed, T., Raza, A., & Jan, I. (2025). Harnessing AI for personalized learning, equity, and administrative efficiency in transnational higher education. *Bridging global divides for transnational higher education in the AI Era*, 191-204.

Alam, A. (2022). Impact of university's human resources practices on professors' occupational performance: empirical evidence from India's higher education sector. In *Inclusive businesses in developing economies: Converging people, profit, and corporate citizenship* (pp. 107–131). Springer International Publishing. DOI: 10.1007/978-3-031-12217-0_6

Alam, A. (2023a). Media multitasking with M-learning technology in real-time classroom learning: Analysing the dynamics in formal educational settings for the future of E-learning in India. In *2023 2nd International Conference on Smart Technologies and Systems for Next Generation Computing (ICSTSN)* (pp. 1-6). IEEE.

Alam, A. (2023b). The secret sauce of student success: Cracking the code by navigating the path to personalized learning with educational data mining. In *2023 2nd International Conference on Smart Technologies and Systems for Next Generation Computing (ICSTSN)* (pp. 1-8). IEEE.

Alam, A. (2023c). Intelligence unleashed: An argument for AI-enabled learning ecologies with real world examples of today and a peek into the future. In *INTERNATIONAL CONFERENCE ON INNOVATIONS IN COMPUTER SCIENCE, ELECTRONICS & ELECTRICAL ENGINEERING-2022* (Vol. 2717, No. 1, p. 030001). AIP Publishing LLC.

Alam, A., & Mohanty, A. (2022). Facial analytics or virtual avatars: competencies and design considerations for student-teacher interaction in AI-powered online education for effective classroom engagement. In *International Conference on Communication, Networks and Computing* (pp. 252-265). Cham: Springer Nature Switzerland.

Alam, A., & Mohanty, A. (2023). Learning on the move: a pedagogical framework for state-of-the-art mobile learning. In *International Conference on Data Management, Analytics & Innovation* (pp. 735-748). Singapore: Springer Nature Singapore. DOI: 10.1007/978-981-99-1414-2_52

Alam, A., & Mohanty, A. (2024). Integrated constructive robotics in education (ICRE) model: A paradigmatic framework for transformative learning in educational ecosystem. *Cogent Education*, *11*(1), 2324487. DOI: 10.1080/2331186X.2024.2324487

Alfayez, A. A., & Rasool, A. (2025). Use of AI in the curriculum development of transnational higher education. In *Bridging Global Divides for Transnational Higher Education in the AI Era* (pp. 401–422). IGI Global Scientific Publishing.

Ali, M. A., Tariq, S. M., & Khalid, U. (2024). Transnational Education (TNE) in Pakistan: Challenges and Way Forward. [JERSSR]. *Journal of Educational Research and Social Sciences Review*, *4*(2), 9–22.

Arida, A. I. (2023). Transnational education and E-Learning. In *Higher education in the Arab World: E-learning and distance education* (pp. 295–317). Springer Nature Switzerland. DOI: 10.1007/978-3-031-33568-6_15

Başaran, O., & Turan, S. (2025). Reimagining local solutions to global challenges in education: A cross-cultural examination. In *Cultural Awareness and Diversity Management in Contemporary Education* (pp. 99–192). IGI Global Scientific Publishing.

Benkhelifa, F., Lakhani, F., Jendoubi, T., Paltalidis, N., & Wijeratne, V. (2025, April). Exploring the Use of Genai Code Assistants for Engineering Students in Transnational Education Programmes: A Pilot Study. In *2025 IEEE Global Engineering Education Conference (EDUCON)* (pp. 1-7). IEEE. DOI: 10.1109/EDUCON62633.2025.11016450

Berry, J. E. (2022). Towards Ubiquitous Learning in a Transnational Educational System. In *The Palgrave Handbook of Educational Leadership and Management Discourse* (pp. 1–19). Springer International Publishing. DOI: 10.1007/978-3-030-99097-8_57

Bharadwaj, S., & Verma, A. (2025). Opportunities and Obstacles in Pursuing Higher Education Abroad During Emergencies: Challenges, Adaptations, and Policy Implications. *Idealistic Journal of Advanced Research in Progressive Spectrums (IJARPS) eISSN–2583-6986, 4*(04), 168-186.

Brammar, L. (2023). A three lenses approach to employability: Transdisciplinary approaches to TNE students' careers education. *Higher Education. Skills and Work-Based Learning, 13*(6), 1204–1217. DOI: 10.1108/HESWBL-11-2022-0251

Bringas, P. G., García, H. P., de Pisón, F. J. M., Álvarez, F. M., Lora, A. T., Herrero, Á., & Corchado, E. (Eds.). (2023). *International Joint Conference 16th International Conference on Computational Intelligence in Security for Information Systems (CISIS 2023) 14th International Conference on EUropean Transnational Education (ICEUTE 2023): Proceedings* (Vol. 748). Springer Nature.

Cabeza-Lopez, E. M., Ruiz-Gonzalez, R., Merino-Gomez, A., Curiel-Herrera, L. E., & Rincon, J. A. (2024, October). A comparison of ai-enabled techniques for the detection of attacks in iot devices. In *International Conference on EUropean Transnational Education* (pp. 227-236). Cham: Springer Nature Switzerland. DOI: 10.1007/978-3-031-75016-8_21

Cader, I., Hassan, S., Mok, A., & Tan, S. (2024). Transnational Education in Sri Lanka: Operational and quality assurance landscape.

Chen, L., Yin, M., Ahmad, K. M., Naeem, M. A., & Haider, S. A. (2024, November). Smart Education: Harnessing Machine Learning for Global Talent Forecasting and Educational Innovation in China. In *2024 International Conference on Control, Electronic Engineering and Machine Learning (CEEML)* (pp. 87-92). IEEE. DOI: 10.1109/CEEML65709.2024.00019

Cheng, W., Ramanan, S., & Tsafos, Y. (2024). Is it time to embrace AI or abandon it in Higher Education?.

Cheng, Y. E., & Koh, S. Y. (2022). The 'soft infrastructure'of the Belt and Road Initiative: Imaginaries, affinities and subjectivities in Chinese transnational education. *Singapore Journal of Tropical Geography, 43*(3), 250–269. DOI: 10.1111/sjtg.12420

Chitadze, N. (2024). History of Higher Education in Georgia From the Ancient Period to the Modern Times: The Main Aspects of the Involvement of the Country in the Transnational Education Process. In *Developments and Future Trends in Transnational Higher Education Leadership* (pp. 278–300). IGI Global. DOI: 10.4018/979-8-3693-2857-6.ch016 de Wit, H., Altbach, P. G., & Glass, C. R. (2025). Global Higher Education Transformation: The 2025 International Crisis. *International Higher Education.*

Du, M., Zhu, L., & Nardo, M. D. (2025, February). Strategic Application of Deep Learning Methods in Global Educational Collaboration. In *Proceedings of the 2025 International Conference on Big Data and Informatization Education* (pp. 313-317). DOI: 10.1145/3729605.3729660

Dulloo, R., & Naseer, F. (2025). The Rise of Transnational Education: Exploring Models, Motivations, and Impacts. In *Bridging Global Divides for Transnational Higher Education in the AI Era* (pp. 49–70). IGI Global Scientific Publishing.

Dutt, C. S., Cseh, L., Hardy, P., & Iguchi, Y. (2022). European transnational education in the Middle East: Conceptual highs, lows, and recommendations. *International Marketing Journal of Culture and Tourism, 1*(2), 69–90.

Fernandez-Chung, R. M., & Gill, R. S. (Eds.). (2025). *Transnational Education: Bridging Borders, Transforming Futures*. Taylor & Francis. DOI: 10.4324/9781003488316

Goorney, S., Sarantinou, M., & Sherson, J. (2023). The open master: A new model of transnational higher education. *Distance Education, 44*(4), 765–776. DOI: 10.1080/01587919.2023.2280064

Guo, Y. (2025). *University Belongingness Among Professional Doctoral Alumni in the US Transnational Education in China: A Mixed Methods Case Study* (Doctoral dissertation, The University of Arizona).

Haider, S. A., Ahmad, K. M., Akbar, J., Soni, M., Keshta, I., AlGhamdi, A., & Shahzadi, H. M. (2025, April). Generative AI as a Catalyst for Transforming Transnational Engineering Education: Opportunities, Challenges, and Future Directions. In *2025 IEEE Global Engineering Education Conference (EDUCON)* (pp. 1-8). IEEE. DOI: 10.1109/EDUCON62633.2025.11016469

Haider, S. A., Ahmad, K. M., Akbar, J., Soni, M., Keshta, I., AlGhamdi, A., & Shahzadi, H. M. (2025, April). Generative AI as a Catalyst for Transforming Transnational Engineering Education: Opportunities, Challenges, and Future Directions. In *2025 IEEE Global Engineering Education Conference (EDUCON)* (pp. 1-8). IEEE. DOI: 10.1109/EDUCON62633.2025.11016469

Hajji, S. (2023). Educational sovereignty and artificial intelligence challenges: the case of Morocco. In *Artificial Intelligence in Higher Education and Scientific Research: Future Development* (pp. 101–116). Springer Nature Singapore. DOI: 10.1007/978-981-19-8641-3_8

Hatahet, T., Raouf Mohamed, A. A., Malekigorji, M., Clerkin, C., & Sandrey, L. (2024). Personal and engagement factors in remote learning contributing to high student achievement in a transnational education context: A quantitative study. *Advances in Online Education: A Peer-Reviewed Journal, 2*(4), 330-350.

Healey, N. M. (2023). Transnational education: The importance of aligning stakeholders' motivations with the form of cross-border educational service delivery. *Higher Education Quarterly, 77*(1), 83–101. DOI: 10.1111/hequ.12371

Hill, C. (2021). Evolving models of transnational education: new partnerships and reducing risk. Why are we so afraid of change? In *The Evolution of Transnational Education* (pp. 111–125). Routledge. DOI: 10.4324/9781003225386-12

Islam, M. E., Polas, M. R. H., & Rahman, M. M. (2025). Sustainability and AI in Transnational Higher Education. In *Bridging Global Divides for Transnational Higher Education in the AI Era* (pp. 379–400). IGI Global Scientific Publishing.

Islam, M. T. (2023). Bangladeshi students' family fertilization for pursuing higher education in Australia. In *Handbook of Research on Developments and Future Trends in Transnational Higher Education* (pp. 247–264). IGI Global Scientific Publishing. DOI: 10.4018/978-1-6684-5226-4.ch013

Jaganathan, R., Rajagopal, S., & Rajendran, K. (2025). Cultural Intelligence in the AI Era-Enhancing Transitional Higher Education. In *Bridging Global Divides for Transnational Higher Education in the AI Era* (pp. 273–292). IGI Global Scientific Publishing.

Jardim, M. (2025). (Re) framing Human Critical and Creative Skills: A Semiotic Approach to TNE in the Age of AI. In *Bridging Global Divides for Transnational Higher Education in the AI Era* (pp. 253–272). IGI Global Scientific Publishing.

Jiang, S. (2021). The call of the homeland: Transnational education and the rising nationalism among Chinese overseas students. *Comparative Education Review*, *65*(1), 34–55. DOI: 10.1086/712053

Karim-Abdallah, B., Darko, G. O., Gyabaah, O., Fening, L. O., Chimsi, I., Derkyi, M. A. A., & Yeboah-Kyereh, A. (2025). Innovations, Technologies and Challenges Associated with Transnational Education. *African Journal of Applied Research*, *11*(1), 560–587. DOI: 10.26437/ajar.v11i1.870

Kaur, J., Bhalla, P., Nagina, R., & Dutt, A. (2025). Historical Foundations and Key Drivers of Transnational Higher Education. In *Bridging Global Divides for Transnational Higher Education in the AI Era* (pp. 29–48). IGI Global Scientific Publishing.

Ketteringham, M. (2025). Developing a 2nd-year undergraduate engineering communications module in a UK/China transnational education engineering program. In *English for Academic and Specific Purposes in the Classroom* (pp. 50-71). Routledge.

Khadri, H. O. (2021). University academics' perceptions regarding the future use of telepresence robots to enhance virtual transnational education: An exploratory investigation in a developing country. *Smart Learning Environments*, *8*(1), 28. DOI: 10.1186/s40561-021-00173-8

Kleibert, J. M. (2022). Transnational spaces of education as infrastructures of im/mobility. *Transactions of the Institute of British Geographers*, *47*(1), 92–107. DOI: 10.1111/tran.12475

Kumar, S., Talukder, M. B., & Tyagi, P. K. (2025). The Impact of Virtual Reality and Augmented Reality in TNE Learning. In *Motivating Engagement, Belonging, and Success in Higher Education Student Experience* (pp. 359-382). IGI Global Scientific Publishing. DOI: 10.4018/979-8-3693-8089-5.ch013

Le Corre, J. Y., Burger-Helmchen, T., Tang, M., & Zhao, J. (2025). Innovative Learning Ecosystems for Entrepreneurial Education. *Transcending Boundaries: For a Sustainable Future of Higher Education*, *6*, 110–129. DOI: 10.1163/9789004740990_006

Li, S., Xia, L., & Beech, H. (2025). Digital Empowerment: Innovative Technology Training for Language Teachers in a Transnational EMI University. In *Innovative Approaches to Staff Development in Transnational Higher Education* (pp. 297-320). IGI Global Scientific Publishing.

Li, X., & Zhou, W. (2024). When infrastructures collide: Transnational higher education and Chinese international students'(im) mobility in the pandemic era. *Asian Education and Development Studies, 13*(3), 195–207. DOI: 10.1108/AEDS-10-2023-0150

Liang, X. (2024). Using icebreaker questions to improve Chinese students' engagement in transnational education–An action research. *European Journal of Education, 59*(2), e12621. DOI: 10.1111/ejed.12621

Liu, C., Chai, K. K., & Chen, Y. (2025, April). The Transformative Role of Generative AI in Higher Education: Perspectives from Academia and Industry. In *2025 IEEE Global Engineering Education Conference (EDUCON)* (pp. 1-6). IEEE. DOI: 10.1109/EDUCON62633.2025.11016643

Lu, H. (2025). Action Research as Practice-Led Research for Professional Development: A Case of Using Excel to Motivate Students to Learn in Transnational Education. In *Exploring Practice-Led Research for Professional Development* (pp. 179-200). IGI Global Scientific Publishing.

Machado, C., & Seifert, T. (2024). Using Flip and Facebook to Create Windows and Mirrors for Transnational Learning: A United States-Israel Scholarship of Teaching and Learning Project. In *Encouraging Transnational Learning Through Virtual Exchange in Global Teacher Education* (pp. 152-171). IGI Global Scientific Publishing. DOI: 10.4018/978-1-6684-7813-4.ch007

Maguire, J., English, R., Cao, Q., & Seow, C. K. (2025, January). Themes in the declared use of generative artificial intelligence in assessment. In *Proceedings of the 9th Conference on Computing Education Practice* (pp. 17-20). DOI: 10.1145/3702212.3702217

Mahy, T., & Li, H. (2024). Get PhD Ready: An Orientation Course for New PGR Students in a Transnational Education Setting. In *English for Academic Purposes in the EMI Context in Asia: XJTLU Impact* (pp. 259–285). Springer Nature Switzerland. DOI: 10.1007/978-3-031-63638-7_11

Masrifah, K., Ahsanudin, M., & Ainin, M. (2025). Higher education in the Arab world: e-learning and distance education: edited by Adnan Badran, Elias Baydoun, Sandra Hillman and Joelle Mesmar, Switzerland, Springer, 2023, 201 pp., 170.99(eBook), 160.40 (Hardcover Book), ISBN: 978-3-031-33570-9.

Melgar-García[1], L., Troncoso-García[1], Á., Gutiérrez-Avilés, D., Torres[1], J. F., & Troncosol, A. (2023, August). Explainable Artificial Intelligence. In *International Joint Conference 16th International Conference on Computational Intelligence in Security for Information Systems (CISIS 2023) 14th International Conference on EUropean Transnational Education (ICEUTE 2023): Proceedings* (Vol. 748, p. 358). Springer Nature.

Menon, S., Suresh, M., & Raghu Raman, R. (2022). Enablers facilitating industry-academia, transnational education and university-community partnering agility in higher education. *Higher Education. Skills and Work-Based Learning, 12*(3), 604–626. DOI: 10.1108/HESWBL-04-2021-0067

Merino-Gomez[1], A., & Curiel-Herrera, L. E. (2024, November). A Comparison of AI-Enabled Techniques. In *International Joint Conferences: 17th International Conference on Computational Intelligence in Security for Information Systems (CISIS 2024) and 15th International Conference on European Transnational Education (ICEUTE 2024)* (Vol. 957, p. 227). Springer Nature.

Miani, M. (2023). Making sense of brainstorming in transnational education: The challenge of contextualization. In *Handbook of research on developments and future trends in transnational higher education* (pp. 21–38). IGI Global. DOI: 10.4018/978-1-6684-5226-4.ch002

Mikecz Munday, Z. (2021). Adapting to transnational education: Students' experiences at an American university in the UAE. *Learning and Teaching in Higher Education: Gulf Perspectives*, *17*(2), 121–135. DOI: 10.1108/LTHE-08-2020-0017

Mishra, N., Habtemariam, G. M., Aebissa, B., Nayak, R. K., & Tripathy, R. (2024). Assessing the Effectiveness of Transnational Leadership on the Performance of Ethiopian University Graduates in Computing Technology: A Case Study. In *Engaging Higher Education Teachers and Students With Transnational Leadership* (pp. 238-256). IGI Global Scientific Publishing. DOI: 10.4018/979-8-3693-6100-9.ch013

Mok, K. H., & Sawn Khai, T. (2024). Transnationalization of higher education in China and Asia: Quality assurance and students' learning experiences. *Asian Education and Development Studies*, *13*(3), 208–226. DOI: 10.1108/AEDS-01-2024-0004

Morris, G. R., & Kozuch, S. (Eds.). (2024). *Engaging higher education teachers and students with transnational leadership*. IGI Global. DOI: 10.4018/979-8-3693-6100-9

Muralidhar, L. B., Sathyanarayana, N., Kumar, V. L., & Santhosh, Y. (2025). AI learning and talent strategies in transnational education: driving global leadership with agility. In *Innovative Approaches to Staff Development in Transnational Higher Education* (pp. 245–276). IGI Global Scientific Publishing.

Murray, G., & Doe, C. (2024). Embedding Indigenous Perspectives: A Consideration of Place in Local and Transnational Education.

Nemorin, S. (2024). Towards decolonising the ethics of AI in education. *Globalisation, Societies and Education*, •••, 1–13. DOI: 10.1080/14767724.2024.2333821

Nightingale, F. (2024). *Developing undergraduate engineering students' soft skills with interdisciplinary personal development planning modules in Chinese transnational education: a case study* (Doctoral dissertation, Nottingham Trent University).

Owusu-Agyeman, Y., & Amoakohene, G. (2021). Student engagement and perceived gains in transnational education in Ghana. *International Journal of Comparative Education and Development*, *23*(4), 297–316. DOI: 10.1108/IJCED-11-2020-0085

Palmer, N., & Chandir, H. (2024). Education Beyond Techno-global Rationality: Transnational Learning, Communicative Agency and the Neo-colonial Ethic. *Journal of Creative Communications*, *19*(1), 59–73. DOI: 10.1177/09732586231206651

Patil, M. P., Mahgoub, Y. O. M., Salama, A. M., Tahoun, Z., Johnston, L., Hamza, N., & Al-Oufy, A. (2025). *Cultivating sustainable architecture and built environments through cross-cultural education*. Smart and Sustainable Built Environment. DOI: 10.1108/SASBE-03-2025-0108

Peddi, S., & Manoharan, G. (2025). Innovative Approaches to Staff Development in Education Using AI. In *Training and Development in Transnational Higher Education* (pp. 347–368). IGI Global Scientific Publishing. DOI: 10.4018/979-8-3373-1897-4.ch017

Peng, S. (2024). Supporting transnational teaching in Finnish education export: Possibilities and limitations of using ChatGPT as a virtual assistant during short-term teaching abroad. *Innovations in Education and Teaching International*, •••, 1–5.

Ping, H. (2023). *Understanding Experiences of Faculty From the Home Institution in China-US Transnational Education Programs: A Phenomenological Case Study* (Doctoral dissertation, Texas A&M University-Corpus Christi).

Qaralleh, R., & Ahmed, S. N. (2025). Advancing Transnational Education by Integrating Artificial Intelligence Technology and Backward Design Principles in Technical English Curriculum. In *Bridging Global Divides for Transnational Higher Education in the AI Era* (pp. 101–120). IGI Global Scientific Publishing.

Quintián, H. Héctor/Corchado Quintián (Emili), & Lora, A. T. (2024). *International Joint Conferences.*

Qureshi, F., & Trotter, J. (2025). Leading a transnational university campus: An interview with James Trotter about academic leadership and working in multicultural higher education environments. *Journal of Applied Learning and Teaching*, *8*(1), 298–305.

Rehman, S. U. (2025). Adaptive Learning Systems for Personalized Language Instruction in Transnational Higher Education. In *Bridging Global Divides for Transnational Higher Education in the AI Era* (pp. 165–190). IGI Global Scientific Publishing.

Rehman, T. U. (2025). The transformative impact and evolving landscape: A comprehensive exploration of the globalization of higher education in the 21st century. *Journal of Further and Higher Education, 49*(3), 346–361. DOI: 10.1080/0309877X.2025.2457537

Reis, C. S., & Sun, Y. (2025). An Innovative Approach to Integrating AI Into Learning and Teaching at a Transnational University in China. In *Training and Development in Transnational Higher Education* (pp. 331–346). IGI Global Scientific Publishing. DOI: 10.4018/979-8-3373-1897-4.ch016

Rian, I. M. (2024, April). Transnational Education (TNE) in the Architecture of Digital Age: A Critical Evaluation of a Sino-British University. In *International Conference on Trends in Architecture and Construction* (pp. 1447-1457). Singapore: Springer Nature Singapore.

Rowley, M., & Skipper, Y. (2021). Student and staff expectations and experiences of a UK–China Transnational Education collaboration. *Journal of Applied Research in Higher Education, 13*(5), 1374–1387. DOI: 10.1108/JARHE-01-2020-0021

Saliya, C. A. (2025). AI as a Scaffold for Innovation, Equity, and Lifelong Learning: Education through the Lens of the Integrated Flexible Approach. *Equity, and Lifelong Learning: Education through the Lens of the Integrated Flexible Approach (July 22, 2025).*

Sarantinos, V. (2022). An Investigation of the Expansion and Influence of Western Paradigms in Transnational Education and the Impact for Small Businesses. In *Small Business Management and Control of the Uncertain External Environment* (pp. 69–84). Emerald Publishing Limited. DOI: 10.1108/978-1-83909-624-220211005

Schueller, J. (2023). Transnational education, labor market outcomes and graduate employability: A scoping review. *Career Development International*, *28*(2), 196–216. DOI: 10.1108/CDI-05-2022-0121

Schulze, M. P., & Kleibert, J. M. (2021). Transnational education for regional economic development? Understanding Malaysia's and Singapore's strategic coupling in global higher education. *International Journal of Training and Development*, *25*(4), 363–382. DOI: 10.1111/ijtd.12242

Sia, J. K. M., & Jimmie, A. (2023). Transnational education in Malaysia: Development, challenges, and strategic alignment. In *Handbook of research on developments and future trends in transnational higher education* (pp. 379–396). IGI Global. DOI: 10.4018/978-1-6684-5226-4.ch020

Sirkeci, I., & Lo, L. (2023). Transformative Impact of Artificial Intelligence on Higher Education. *Transnational Education Review*, *1*(2), 65–67. DOI: 10.33182/ter.v1i2.3193

Smith, C. J., Choromides, C., Boyd, V., Proudfoot, L., Wright, M., & Stewart-Knight, F. (2023). Inclusive and Flexible Curriculum Design Framework in Work-based Learning: Providing High Impact Transnational Education Opportunities in Sub-Saharan Africa. In *High Impact Practices in Higher Education: International Perspectives* (pp. 149-167). Emerald Publishing Limited.

Smith, R. K. (2023). Ethical Communication and Argument-Centered Education Can Enhance Transnational Education and Promote a More Ethical and Civil World. In *Handbook of Research on Developments and Future Trends in Transnational Higher Education* (pp. 66–91). IGI Global. DOI: 10.4018/978-1-6684-5226-4.ch004

Suárez-Díaz, J. L., Rodríguez-Barroso, N., & Gómez-Trenado, G. (2024, October). Interactive Telegram Bot as a Support Tool for Teaching in Higher Education. In *International Conference on EUropean Transnational Education* (pp. 352-361). Cham: Springer Nature Switzerland. DOI: 10.1007/978-3-031-75016-8_33

Suguku, D. (2023). Pillar of internationalization in higher education: The contribution of international collaborations and online delivery approaches to internationalization in HEIS. In *SHS web of conferences* (Vol. 156, p. 05004). EDP Sciences. DOI: 10.1051/shsconf/202315605004

Sun, Y. (2025). An Innovative Approach to Integrating AI Into Learning and Teaching at a Transnational. *Training and Development in Transnational Higher Education*, 331.

Suntharalingam, P. (2024). Transnational Education in South/Southeast Asia: Thoughts and Reflections from a Higher Education Partner University in the United Kingdom. In *Critical Reflections on the Internationalisation of Higher Education in the Global South* (pp. 101-120). Emerald Publishing Limited.

Suntharalingam, P. (2025). Introduction to transnational higher education (TNE). In *Bridging Global Divides for Transnational Higher Education in the AI Era* (pp. 1-28). IGI Global Scientific Publishing.

Suntharalingam, P. (2025). Introduction to transnational higher education (TNE). In *Bridging Global Divides for Transnational Higher Education in the AI Era* (pp. 1-28). IGI Global Scientific Publishing.

Tran, N. H. N., Amado, C. A. D. E. F., & Santos, S. P. D. (2023). Challenges and success factors of transnational higher education: A systematic review. *Studies in Higher Education*, *48*(1), 113–136. DOI: 10.1080/03075079.2022.2121813

Tse, A. (2025). Teacher's Reflection on Character Education at a Transnational University: Character Education at the Tertiary Level. *Training and Development in Transnational Higher Education*, 219-238.

Vajjhala, N. R., & Strang, K. D. (2022). Impact of information communication technology strategies on learning effectiveness. [IJOPCD]. *International Journal of Online Pedagogy and Course Design, 12*(1), 1–14. DOI: 10.4018/IJOPCD.292026

Valarmathi, V., & Suchitra, B. (2025). Artificial Intelligence and the Future of Lifelong Learning in Transnational Contexts. In *Bridging Global Divides for Transnational Higher Education in the AI Era* (pp. 71–100). IGI Global Scientific Publishing.

Wang, J., & Ling, S. (2024, August). Digitalization Empowers Cross-border Education in the Post-pandemic Era on the Basis of China-Africa Cultural Memory Project. In *2024 4th International Conference on Big Data Engineering and Education (BDEE)* (pp. 66-73). IEEE. DOI: 10.1109/BDEE63226.2024.00019

Wang, Z. (2022). Chinese students at UK universities: Transnational education mobilities as a stepping-stone to adulthood. *Population Space and Place, 28*(7), e2571. DOI: 10.1002/psp.2571

Wu-Ross, A. L. J. (2024). *An Appreciative Inquiry Into Transnational Education University Strategies and Government Policies* (Doctoral dissertation, Auckland University of Technology).

Ye, J. (2025). Engaging Coachees and Measuring Success in Cross-Cultural Transnational Education: A Systematic Literature Review. *Innovative Approaches to Staff Development in Transnational Higher Education*, 363-388.

Chapter 9
AI Based-Virtual Laboratory Applied Training in Transnational Science Education:
A Study for Secondary School Students

Mahmut Sami Kiliç
https://orcid.org/0000-0002-3068-3960
Kastamonu University Education Faculty, Turkey

Ömer Volkan Yaz
https://orcid.org/0000-0001-6190-2321
Kastamou University, Turkey

M. Said Dogru
https://orcid.org/0000-0002-9516-1442
Kastamou University, Turkey

ABSTRACT

This study investigates how artificial intelligence (AI)-supported virtual laboratories impact scientific learning among international middle school students in Türkiye. Findings indicate that students find AI highly beneficial in understanding complex topics, accessing accurate information in discussions, and learning foreign language terminology. Students have a positive attitude toward the use of virtual laboratories and AI and are eager to use these tools again. While language barriers (especially in communicating with teachers) remain a significant challenge, students demonstrate strong collaboration and problem-solving skills. While there is a tendency to work with peers who speak their own language, this preference is not absolute. The results suggest that AI-supported virtual laboratories enrich scientific learning, enhance problem-solving skills, and offer the potential to overcome language barriers. These findings emphasize the need for educators to develop language support and intercultural collaboration strategies.

DOI: 10.4018/979-8-3373-5403-3.ch009

INTRODUCTION

In the 21st century, expectations of people and societies are changing, and knowledge is being produced and used at a rapid pace. Today's education should provide students with specific knowledge and help them develop skills such as critical thinking, creativity, communicating with others, using digital tools, and working collaboratively (Trilling & Fadel, 2009; Voogt & Roblin, 2012). These so-called “21st-century skills” are considered essential for success in a world driven by technology and globalization (OECD, 2021; World Economic Forum, 2023).

Science education is key to acquiring these skills. However, in many schools, this education is still largely delivered by teachers, focusing on theory and relying on rote memorization. Students often lack the opportunity to engage in laboratory work where they can explore science independently due to limited resources, high costs, and safety concerns (Hofstein & Lunetta, 2004; Abrahams, 2017). The COVID-19 pandemic has exacerbated the situation, making physical laboratories nearly impossible to access. This demonstrates the urgent need for flexible, technology-based, and equitable science learning for all (Bao, 2020; Daniel, 2020).

Virtual laboratories and simulations are becoming useful tools to address these challenges. They allow students to conduct safe, reproducible, and hands-on experiments no matter where they are or what time it is (de Jong et al., 2013; Potkonjak et al., 2016). Recent studies show that these systems significantly help students understand ideas, develop research skills, and stay motivated by making abstract concepts real and visual (Heradio et al., 2021; Zacharia et al., 2022; Aljohani and Alzahrani, 2023). Furthermore, studies show that the use of new technologies such as AR and VR in science education makes learning more engaging and realistic (Radianti et al., 2020; Jensen and Konradsen, 2022).

The rapid development of artificial intelligence offers a new perspective on this change. AI learning systems can identify what students don't know, adapt to their learning pace, and offer personalized feedback and learning paths (Holmes et al., 2019; Ouyang and Jiao, 2021). Recent studies show that AI virtual laboratories not only enhance learning but also enhance self-awareness and self-directed learning (Chen et al., 2021; Zawacki-Richter et al., 2023).

Yet, while many studies examine how AI and virtual laboratories can assist teaching, a crucial aspect is often overlooked: working across borders and with foreign students. In our connected world, where digital conversation is ubiquitous, it is increasingly important for students to learn about different cultures and work well with people from all walks of life (UNESCO, 2022; OECD, 2023). AI online tools now enable teams from different countries and speaking different languages to collaborate, eliminating the language and cultural barriers that limit teamwork (Kergel and Heidkamp, 2021; Jefferies and Grodzinsky (2007).

This study aims to identify AI virtual laboratories and the challenges faced by international students and to empower middle school students to use virtual laboratories to overcome language and cultural barriers and work together to explore science. Therefore, we ask: “How can international middle school students studying in our country better learn scientific ideas through collaborative experiments and the use of AI, and how does this affect their feelings about science and their problem-solving abilities?”

THEORETICAL FRAMEWORK

Social Constructivism

Lev Vygotsky's social constructivism (1978) suggests that learning is social and depends on the situation. It happens through interactions with others and the cultural setting. Knowledge isn't just received; it's created through discussion and teamwork. Current work shows these ideas are useful even in tech and AI-driven learning, where people can interact from anywhere (Molina, Olivares, & Pardo, 2022; Wang, Yu, & Cheng, 2023).

The model puts students from different countries into a virtual area where they can work together on hard science problems. They get help from each other and from AI, which acts as a digital expert (Wood, Bruner, & Ross, 1976; Chen et al., 2020). AI tools give prompts and feedback and help students think, which boosts participation and reasoning (Zawacki-Richter & Jung, 2019). New studies say that AI help in STEM can raise participation, motivation, and communication in different cultures, and also improve cultural understanding.

This way, learning is something students make together. They mix cultural views, agree on things, and build knowledge as a group. AI helps in this area, connecting social constructivism with modern teaching methods. This creates a supportive and interactive learning space that responds to different cultures (Molina et al., 2022; Wang et al., 2023).

Computer-Supported Collaborative Learning (CSCL)

Computer-Supported Collaborative Learning (CSCL) looks at how learning happens when people work together using technology It is not just about using computers and software; it is also about how people talk to each other, how they work as a group, and how they build knowledge together (Stahl, Koschmann, & Suthers, 2006; Dillenbourg, 1999). Research in CSCL indicates that effective group learning requires structured communication. According to Johnson and Johnson (1999) and Stahl, Koschmann, & Suthers, 2006), they also need to have clear roles in the group, agree on what they are trying to accomplish, and have time to reflect on what they have learned and provide feedback to one another. To expand, CSCL goes beyond seating students together in front of computers and asking them to work together. It is a systematic way of education that utilizes technology to support peer learning. The key is to create an atmosphere in which students feel comfortable questioning, providing their views, and working together to resolve answers.

The model we propose involves students from different countries working together in real-time and at different times on a virtual platform, like a simulation or experiment space. Real-time activities could include virtual chemistry experiments where students watch reactions, gather data, and interpret findings at the same time. Artificial intelligence (AI) can provide help as it happens, translate languages, and watch group interactions, giving quick feedback and encouraging good teamwork. At other times, students can post observations, thoughts, or ideas, and others from different countries can look at them later. AI can help by summing up talks, spotting key ideas, and asking questions to keep the conversation going and build knowledge across different time zones. Combining real-time discussions with project work done at different times can help students think more deeply, think critically, and learn about other cultures.

The platform is made to support the main ideas of collaborative learning: students depend on each other to reach a common goal; each student is responsible for their part, with set roles and tasks; interaction is encouraged through forums and group problem-solving; and students think about their work, aided by AI that gives data on group interactions and results (Johnson & Johnson, 1999; Yu, Chen, & Wang, 2024).

Recent research shows that CSCL with AI can support learners from different cultures and language backgrounds. It allows international teams to build knowledge together, even with language or time differences (Wang, Yu, & Cheng, 2023; Jefferies & Grodzinsky (2007). It also helps students become more aware of their thinking, as they consider not just the subject matter but also how they collaborate, make decisions, and solve problems (Huang et al., 2022). Table 1 shows examples of ways to collaborate, countries involved, AI assistance, and what students are expected to learn.

Table 1. Data collection ways

Collaboration Type	Example Activity	Countries Involved	AI Support	Learning Outcome
Synchronous (Huang et al., 2022; Wang, Yu, & Cheng, 2023)	Virtual chemistry experiment: Students perform complementary tasks simultaneously (observing reactions, recording data, analyzing results).	Türkiye, Japan, Brazil	Real-time translation, scaffolding, monitoring of group dynamics	Immediate feedback, enhanced teamwork, shared scientific understanding
Asynchronous (Klein et al., 2021; Heffernan et al., 2022)	Virtual physics simulation: Student in Austria, Croatia and Germany uploads observations; peers in Canada review and comment later.	Austria, Croatia, Canada, Germany	AI summarizes discussions, highlights key points, prompts follow-up questions	Continuous collaboration, reflection, knowledge co-construction despite time zone differences
Mixed/Hybrid (Dillenbourg, 1999; Jefferies & Grodzinsky (2007)	International group project: Students brainstorm solutions to a scientific problem over several days using shared online workspace.	USA, UK, Canada	AI tracks contributions, suggests resources, provides feedback on argumentation	Deep engagement, critical thinking, intercultural competence, sustained collaboration

Our educational approach aims to improve foreign students' learning results. We do this by mixing real-time and delayed teamwork, supported by computer intelligence. This mix helps students from different countries get together and work well with one another.

Combining methods that happen at the same time and those that do not lets students take part in different ways. It fits different time zones, schedules, and ways of learning. For instance, live video meetings and quick messaging help with quick talks, while discussion boards let conversations go on, and shared documents let people write together. Each has good points based on the situation and what is needed. Computer intelligence helps with tasks and makes the learning better. Computer intelligence tools give custom input on student work, suggest sources and learning, and even translate languages in real-time to fix language problems. These tools can point out scientific questions by getting to a lot of data and spotting possible research differences. Through these better interactions, students think about what they are learning and study science ideas more deeply. The focus is on groups creating knowledge, where students add to one another's ideas and views to get to a shared understanding. The approach makes a helpful online learning space. Students also get better at working with different cultures as they work with classmates from different backgrounds. They learn to accept different views, talk across cultures, and make strong work relationships with people from everywhere. This teamwork makes their ability to fix problems together better, a skill that is needed.

Experiential Learning

Experiential learning theory, introduced by David Kolb (1984). It explains that lasting and meaningful learning develops through a continuous cycle with four stages: Concrete Experience, Reflective Observation, Abstract Conceptualization, and Active Experimentation. This cycle emphasizes learning as an active and ongoing process, where individuals engage in experiences, reflect on them, draw out broader principles, and then apply these insights in new contexts (Kolb, 1984). Nowadays, AI-supported laboratories provide valuable opportunities at every step of the process.

In the Concrete Experience stage, students can safely conduct repeated experiments by using interactive simulations, virtual microscopes, chemical reaction models or tools that remove the risks and constraints often found in labs (Heradio et al., 2021; Radianti et al., 2020). During Reflective Observation, AI helps learners interpret their results by visualizing data, guiding analysis, and enabling comparisons with peers. Adaptive feedback further supports deeper critical thinking (Zawacki-Richter et al., 2019, Chen, Chen, & Lin, 2020; du Boulay, 2023).

The Abstract Conceptualization stage is enriched by group discussions that connect observations with scientific principles. In cross-cultural learning settings, AI can bridge language differences and encourage equal participation, ensuring that diverse perspectives are shared and valued (Jefferies & Grodzinsky (2007); Wang et al., 2023). Finally, in Active Experimentation, students test hypotheses, manipulate variables, and repeat experiments in a secure online space-activities that nurture creativity, reasoning, and problem-solving (Jensen & Konradsen, 2022).

When combined, experiential learning and AI-based platforms enhance not only cognitive outcomes but also socio-emotional development. Students improve their collaboration skills, intercultural awareness, and self-regulation alongside their academic growth (Zawacki-Richter & Jung, 2023; Wang et al., 2023). Through this integration, learners engage in reflective and iterative scientific practices that extend far beyond the constraints of traditional laboratories.

Integrative Perspective

This framework integrates social constructivist learning, Computer-Supported Collaborative Learning (CSCL), and experiential learning, and it is a method that considers the cognitive, social, and affective aspects of learning (Stahl, Koschmann, & Suthers, 2006; Kolb, 1984; Dillenbourg, 1999). The integration of AI gives learners personalized support that increases learner autonomy, motivation, and collaboration (Holstein et al., 2020; Zawacki-Richter et al., 2019).

Among the greatest traits of the model is placing focus on cross-cultural interaction, in such a manner that the students are able to address matters of complex global challenges and value diversity (Scardamalia & Bereiter, 2006; Krajcik & Shin, 2014). This virtual lab-support via AI, thus, transcends online instruments that they transform into learning and society transformation-spaces (Makransky et al., 2019; Xie et al., 2022).

The approach also emphasizes that education should go beyond cognitive development. Students remain more engaged and retain knowledge longer when learning involves hands-on activities, collaborative dialogue, and individualized support (Kolb, 1984; Slavin, 1995). AI contributes by monitoring progress, generating feedback, and helping educators recognize each learner's unique needs, leading to more relevant and personalized learning experiences (Roll & Wylie, 2016; Baker et al., 2019).

Working with peers from different cultural and geographical backgrounds further deepens learning. International collaboration exposes students to varied perspectives, strengthens communication skills, and expands ways of thinking (Chen et al., 2020). AI-based virtual labs reinforce this by enabling students to apply concepts in practice—testing, refining, and expanding their understanding. Their adaptive features strike a balance between support and challenge, fostering continuous growth (Makransky et al., 2019; Xie et al., 2022).

In sum, this model integrates technology to create richer and more personalized educational experiences. It nurtures intellectual, social, and emotional growth, preparing students to thrive as global citizens (Scardamalia & Bereiter, 2006) and equipping them for the demands of an interconnected world (Zawacki-Richter et al., 2019).

This study aims to identify the challenges faced by international students using AI virtual laboratories and enabling middle school students to overcome language and cultural barriers and collaborate on scientific exploration. Therefore, we ask: How can international middle school students studying in our country better learn scientific ideas through collaborative experiments and the use of AI, and how does this affect their feelings about science and their problem-solving abilities?

METHOD

Research Model

Descriptive method was preferred for the research. Descriptive research is a type of research that describes an existing event quantitatively (using numbers) or qualitatively (revealing the characteristics of an individual or group) (McMillan and Schumacher, 2014). In this context, that aimed to determine the artificail intelligence usage, communication and problem-solving skills of foreign students while conducting visual laboraty experiments in science classes in Türkiye. The quantitative component of the study was formed by data obtained from a questionnaire developed to measure the students' communication skills, while the qualitative component was formed by semi-structured interviews with these students' science teachers. This provided a quantitative assessment of the students' communication skill levels, and the findings were enriched with in-depth information obtained through teachers' opinions.

Study Group

The study group consisted of foreign 8th-grade students (n = 30) attending middle schools in various provinces of Türkiye during the 2025-2026 academic year and participating in experimental activities in science classes. For the qualitative component, interviews were conducted with the teachers (n = 5) who taught these students' science classes. Participants were selected using the criterion sampling technique, a purposive sampling method. The criteria were that the students possess basic Turkish communication skills and participate in experiments in science classes.

Implementation Phase

During the implementation phase, students used "Arloopa" and "Scratch". Initially, the applications were used with teacher guidance and then released to students for use. During this phase, students used

ChatGPT to get support on areas they didn't understand. Students used ChatGPT to understand terms they didn't understand, to better explain points their friends didn't understand, and to support their own learning while using the virtual lab.

Data Collection Tools

Two tools were used to collect data in the study:

Communication Skills Survey:

A 12-item Likert-type survey developed by the researchers was used to measure students' communication skills during experiments in science classes. The survey included questions on the dimensions of "expression," "interaction and collaboration," and "problem solving." The survey's content validity was ensured by consulting with an expert academic in the field. The reliability coefficient (Cronbach's Alpha) of the scale was found to be 0.83.

Semi-Structured Interview Form:

A semi-structured interview form developed by the researchers was used to obtain teachers' opinions on students' communication processes. The form included open-ended questions addressing themes such as students' communication styles in laboratory activities, their interactions in group work, and the communication-related challenges teachers face. The interview questions were shaped by expert opinions.

Data Collection Process

Quantitative data were collected online from volunteer students in the study group via Google Forms. The purpose of the study was explained to the students before the study, and voluntary participation was considered essential. Qualitative data were collected through semi-structured interviews with teachers.

Data Analysis

Quantitative data obtained from the survey were analyzed using SPSS. Descriptive statistics (arithmetic mean, standard deviation) were calculated. The Cronbach alpha value of the survey was found to be 0.83.

Qualitative data obtained from the interviews were analyzed using descriptive and content analysis techniques.

FINDINGS

In this section, the findings collected with quantitative and qualitative data measurement tools are presented.

Table 2. Communication skills survey results

Dimension	Question	N	Mean ($\bar{X}$)	Standard deviation (σ)
AI Usage	Artificial intelligence helped me with areas I didn't understand while using the virtual laboratory.	30	3.73	1.01
	When we discussed a topic with my friends, artificial intelligence showed us the truth	30	4.3	0.65
	Artificial intelligence helped me understand foreign language terms	30	3.76	0.93
	I would like to use the virtual laboratory and artificial intelligence again	30	3.53	1.17
Communication Skills	I have problems when different languages are spoken (English, Turkish) during the experiment.	30	2.90	1.30
	If there is something I don't understand, I ask for help from my friend who speaks the same language as me.	30	2.27	1.31
	In group studies, I would like to be in the same group with friends who speak the same language as me.	30	2.83	1.49
	I have problems when I do not understand some of my teacher's words.	30	2.80	1.42
Problem solving abilities	I support my friends while they are doing their duty.	30	4.13	0.90
	It is important to make joint decisions with my friends.	30	3.83	1.21
	I help my friend when he makes a mistake.	30	4.10	1.03
	When there is a disagreement within the group, I try to find a solution.	30	3.93	1.01

Figure 1. Mean and standard deviations of survey questions

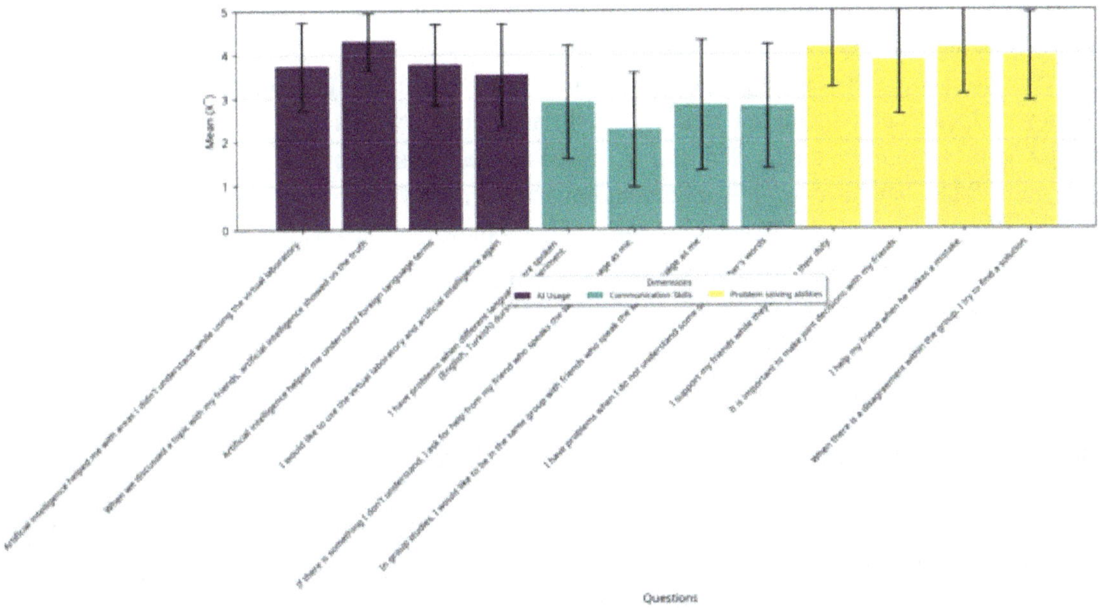

Overall, Table 1 indicates that foreign students in Türkiye have a positive attitude toward group work and strong potential for problem-solving skills. However, language barriers pose a significant challenge, particularly in experimental settings and when communicating with teachers. While this increases students' inclination to work with peers who speak their own language, this preference is not absolute. These findings suggest that educators need to make greater efforts to provide language support, utilize multilingual materials, and develop collaborative learning strategies that support cultural diversity. AI-powered translation and learning platforms can play a significant role in overcoming such language barriers and help students have a more inclusive and productive learning experience.

Also semi-structured interviews were conducted with 5 volunteer Science Education teachers. In this context, we first asked the teachers, " Do your foreign students have communication problems in class?" The teacher responses were as follows:

T1,2,4; "yes"

T5; "partially yes"

T3; "once they get used to it, not a big problem."

Communication problems are most significant at the beginning of students' adaptation process. Over time, familiarity with the classroom environment and language skills can reduce these difficulties. Secondly, we asked the teachers, "Is their communication with Turkish students different from their communication with each other?" The teachers;

T1,2,5; "yes"

T4; "Yes. They generally don't make friends with Turkish students"

T3; "There's no significant difference; they don't get along well with Turkish students. Since they've been in the same class for years, they don't have many problems."

These responses reveal that foreign students often form friendships within their own cultural groups rather than with local peers. Social integration remains a challenge, which can influence both emotional well-being and classroom dynamics. Thirdly, we asked the teachers, "How do they participate in class and lab sessions? Do they have trouble understanding experiments?" The teachers;

T1; "Yes, they don't participate in class. Even if their achievement levels are average or above, they shy away from class and choose not to participate."

T2; "Yes"

T3,4; "Partially yes"

T5; "They generally follow the lesson silently. It is difficult to notice that they do not understand during the experiment."

A lack of active participation is linked to communication barriers and possibly a lack of confidence. Silent participation masks learning gaps, which may prevent teachers from providing timely support. The last question is, "Do you have any suggestions for the education of foreign students?" The teachers;

T1; "I believe that families who have lived here for many years, and who will continue to do so, should also learn and use Turkish properly. Students who communicate entirely in their own language at home either struggle in school or find it difficult to communicate in Turkish, often mingling only with children from their own country."

T2; "Their adaptation can be arranged through inclusive education."

T5; "Those who arrived at a young age don't experience any problems. Those who came to our country after the age of 10 do. These students should receive special education."

Teachers emphasized both family involvement and systemic support as essential for improving foreign students' educational outcomes. Younger students adapt more easily, highlighting the importance of early intervention.

DISCUSSIONS

This study examined international middle school students' artificial intelligence-based virtual laboratory environments. This study, conducted within the context of science education, examined students' problem-solving skills, attitudes toward science, and intercultural understanding in virtual laboratory environments. The findings revealed that students' collaboration skills improved positively across all of these areas. Furthermore, it was concluded that language barriers also hindered communication. Teachers also expressed this finding among foreign students through their reticence to participate in class.

Collaboration Outcomes

Collaboration and Problem-Solving Skills

In the quantitative data, Table 1 shows that international students possess collaboration skills such as supporting their peers in group work (Mean = 4.13) and making joint decisions (Mean = 3.83). Furthermore, their tendency to resolve disagreements within the group (Mean = 3.93) also points to the development of problem-solving skills. These findings are consistent with Vygotsky's (1978) theory of social constructivism and the principles of Computer Supported Collaborative Learning (CSCL) and demonstrate a positive development in problem-solving skills. Studies have shown the importance of social interaction and collaboration when students come together in online or virtual environments to solve science problems together. Knowledge has been observed to emerge more easily in these environments (Chen et al., 2024). Another study reported that students' interdependence and collaboration among themselves positively improved when they used AI-supported platforms to achieve their goals (Cress & Kimmerle, 2023). AI-powered platforms allow students to organize themselves, perform their tasks effectively, and foster much better progress and collaboration. These platforms allow students to better monitor their own performance within groups through feedback. This allows students to quickly identify their own shortcomings in problem-solving processes and become much more effective in solving problems (Kovari, 2025). In different studies, it has been stated that students studying in artificial intelligence-based learning environments benefit from collaboration and problem-solving skills (Almasri, 2024).

Studies have shown that students' social skills and communication strategies improve with AI-supported learning. Collaboration among students also plays a role in this development (Johnson & Johnson, 1999). Students' problem-solving skills are not only influenced by their individual knowledge but also by their ability to make decisions as a group. Furthermore, AI-based moderation tools minimize communication barriers, ensuring the active participation of all students in the process. This allows for effective communication in intercultural groups (Long & Lin, 2022).

In conclusion, virtual laboratory platforms for foreign students enrich the learning experience by improving problem-solving and communication skills at both the individual and group levels. This supports not only academic success but also the development of intercultural collaboration and social skills.

Attitudes and Participation Towards Science

Teacher interviews indicate that international students are hesitant to participate in classroom and laboratory activities, even avoiding participation even when their achievement levels are average or above. However, in the context of Kolb's experiential learning theory (1984), it has been stated that AI-supported virtual laboratories can increase students' attitudes toward science and motivation to participate by providing safe, reproducible, and hands-on experiences (Reyes et al., 2024, Schnieder et al., 2022; Navarro et al.,, 2024). AI supports in-depth critical thinking by helping students interpret experimental results, visualize data, and compare them with their peers (Chiu & Hwang, 2025). Such interactions can contribute to students developing a more positive attitude toward science and engaging more actively in the learning process. In different studies, it has been stated that students who study in artificial intelligence-based virtual learning environments have significantly increased their learning (Hasegawa et al., 2025).

Language Barriers

Language Barriers and Intercultural Communication

Survey results indicate that students experience difficulties in environments where different languages are spoken (Mean = 2.90) and communicating with their teachers (Mean = 2.80). This leads students to be more inclined to work with peers who speak the same language (Mean = 2.27). Teacher interviews also confirm that foreign students experience difficulties in classroom communication and that their communication with Turkish students differs. However, it is emphasized that AI-assisted translation and learning platforms can play a significant role in overcoming these language barriers. Survey results and teacher opinions indicate that foreign students experience communication difficulties due to language barriers. In this context, studies in the literature also reveal that AI-assisted translation and learning systems reduce language and cultural differences, enabling international teams to build knowledge together (Khasawneh, 2023; Xia, Shin & Kim, 2024; Cheng, 2025). Additionally, studies by Xia et al. (2024), Klimova & Chen (2024), and Long & Lin (2022) have indicated that the use of artificial intelligence in language learning significantly impacts intercultural communication. The aforementioned researchers' studies have positively impacted cultural understanding by increasing interaction between students. This contribution will allow students to participate more and broaden their perspectives. This will, in turn, reduce language barriers for students.

The literature mentioned above also highlights the impact of language barriers on students' academic and social adaptation processes. Students from different languages and cultures experience challenges not only in communication but also within academic discourse. Inability to effectively express their ideas in group work or exclusion due to cultural differences can negatively impact students' intercultural communication competence. It has been observed that such negativities can be eliminated through AI-supported teaching models, thereby improving students' communication skills (Long & Lin, 2022). At the same time, AI-supported teaching models contribute positively to students' self-confidence by eliminating the negative impact of in-class discussions and language differences. In other words, AI acts as a solution. In multilingual environments, instant translations made possible by AI tools increase students' communication, create an equitable environment, and enhance their learning. For example, a study conducted in different languages observed that students could easily access content when translation platforms were supported by AI. Furthermore, their cultural interactions also improved positively (Xia, Shin, & Kim, 2024). Another study observed that the use of AI-supported tools in language learning systems increased students' cultural awareness as well as their linguistic proficiency (Klimova & Chen, 2024). These technologies facilitate positive improvements in communication by providing rapid feedback and recognizing students' errors. This was reflected in the teachers' opinions in our study, and we observed that AI-powered systems bridged communication gaps between students. This positively impacted students' study skills by learning languages and different cultures. It also provided opportunities to explore different cultures. Based on all of this, AI-powered tools positively impacted foreign students' language learning, increasing their social integration and academic success. Furthermore, by eliminating communication challenges and fostering positive intercultural interaction, they created a positive learning environment.

Intercultural Understanding

Virtual laboratories, supported by AI, have enabled students to better understand concepts. This also strengthens students' learning processes by broadening their understanding. This is also reflected in teachers' opinions. Teachers emphasized the importance of inclusive education in adapting students who arrive at an early age. Teachers particularly emphasized its role in the development of intercultural understanding. This model will enable students to develop intellectually as global citizens and develop socially and emotionally. Various researchers have confirmed this in their studies (Scardamalia & Bereiter, 2006; Zawacki-Richter et al., 2019).

A study by Sarwari et al. (2024) found that AI and AI-enabled technologies facilitate interaction between students from different cultures and reduce language and cultural barriers, enabling students to communicate more effectively with each other. Furthermore, Zhang et al. (2025) emphasized that AI-based language translators and cultural simulators help students adapt to different cultures and increase their cultural understanding.

Teacher Observations

Ethical Considerations in AI-Based Education

As mentioned above, this study examined the collaboration and problem-solving skills of students studying in virtual laboratories using AI technologies. Furthermore, it provided the opportunity to observe intercultural communication among students. All of these issues were addressed through ethical considerations. The use of this technology (AI), in particular, demonstrates the importance of ethics. Some researchers have stated that AI should be taken seriously in matters such as education, data privacy, and decision-making processes. It has been noted that AI presents certain challenges, such as reducing human influence in the integration of educational processes. In this case, ethical challenges have been mentioned (Nguyen et al., 2023; Wieczorek et al., 2025). According to the UNESCO Recommendation on the Ethics of Artificial Intelligence (2021), educational institutions must ensure that AI applications promote fairness, inclusiveness, and respect for human rights. This is particularly important in multicultural classrooms, where automated translation, feedback, and assessment tools may unintentionally reinforce linguistic or cultural biases. Therefore, while AI provides equitable opportunities for participation, it also requires educators to maintain ethical oversight to prevent discrimination and protect students' autonomy. Integrating ethical principles into the design and use of AI systems will ensure that technology not only enhances learning outcomes but also supports the development of responsible and fair educational practices.

Teacher Readiness and Professional Development

Other than the ethical implications, teacher preparation, and ongoing training influence how well AI technologies are used in the classroom. As AI technology in education grows, it is critical for teachers to learn how to use these resources in a way that is both responsive and educational. AI integration in the classroom requires teachers to possess not only the technical competencies but also the AI adaptability skills necessary to different contextual frameworks within a classroom. Consequently, teachers' professional training needs to address digital pedagogy, ethical implications, AI educational feedback interpretation frameworks, and how to prioritize student learning goals. AI training leads to increased confidence and competence in AI tool implementation (Zawacki-Richter et al., 2019; Zhang et al., 2023; van den Berg, 2025). Designing teacher training that balances practical AI use along with ethical and instructional design frameworks is an area for future research. Educators should be the primary focus to guarantee an equitable and humane educational approach.

These learning environments (virtual laboratories) will be beneficial not only for student communication but also for intercultural collaboration. Here, students from different languages and cultures work together to solve scientific problems, developing problem-solving skills and increasing their intercultural awareness. This fosters respect and communication among students by fostering collaborative inquiry and intergroup interaction. Deardorff (2006) stated in his study that these tactics, by creating collaborative environments, foster cultural diversity and foster inclusive understanding, and that this does not have negative consequences.

CONCLUSION AND RECOMMENDATIONS

In this study, it can be said that the use of AI-supported tools in virtual laboratories generally increased collaboration among foreign middle school students. This increased collaboration among students, which in turn enhanced their problem-solving skills. It can also be concluded that this positively impacted their intercultural understanding.

According to the findings above, a positive approach to group work was observed among students. This positive approach appears to have positively impacted students' problem-solving skills. A negative aspect of this study can be attributed to language barriers. This was particularly observed between teachers and students who speak different languages. They also encountered difficulties communicating with their peers who spoke different languages. It was observed that these students, who spoke different languages, interacted more with their peers who spoke their native language due to the communication difficulties they faced.

However, this situation has also led to the emergence of the concept of the language barrier among students. It has caused serious communication barriers, particularly between teachers and students who speak different languages, and has led to students' desire and inclination to be with peers who only speak their native language. In this regard, our study emphasizes the importance of recommending AI-supported translation and learning tools to address this language barrier. The use of such technologies will enhance the learning experiences of transnational students, positively enhancing both the linguistic and cultural development of students. This will ensure a collaborative effort in understanding information. This is also consistent with teachers' opinions. Teachers stated that foreign students experience some shyness in the classroom, but they are able to overcome this with AI-supported tools. It is believed that virtual laboratory courses will reliably increase students' attitudes and motivation.

Within the scope of this study, the use of AI-based learning modules to overcome language barriers, a significant problem faced by foreign students, can be cited as one of the key recommendations. The use of these tools is particularly important in classroom and laboratory experiments. Careful monitoring of the reliability and pedagogical suitability of the tools will prevent student misunderstandings. It is recommended that they be used with teacher guidance. Furthermore, increasing cultural diversity is particularly important for increasing classroom interaction among foreign students. Various activities should be implemented here. For example, group projects, peer mentoring, and language learning should be emphasized. This will significantly increase intercultural understanding among students.

It has been stated that the use of AI-supported virtual laboratories will enable students to better understand scientific concepts. Designing these laboratories to suit different language and learning levels will improve research skills and positively impact their attitudes. Therefore, designing such interfaces will enable students to learn effectively. To achieve this effective teaching, teachers need to increase their professional development in these technologies and develop programs specifically designed for this purpose. It is believed that providing teachers with cultural awareness training during this training will address these needs of special needs students.

This study demonstrates the potential of AI-enabled virtual laboratories for international students and suggests several avenues for future research. First, the long-term effects of such platforms and their applicability across diverse cultural contexts should be examined with larger samples and long-term follow-up studies. Furthermore, investigating how AI-enabled tools impact students' cognitive load and their in-depth impact on learning outcomes will contribute to more efficient learning processes. Furthermore, analyzing teachers' attitudes toward AI integration, the challenges they face, and best practices using qualitative methods can shed light on how to integrate them more effectively into teaching environments. Finally, a detailed examination of international students' interactions in virtual laboratories will contribute to a more in-depth understanding of the dynamics of intercultural collaboration.

We can also mention the following in our recommendations section. Adding instant translation features to AI-based tools and using them in virtual laboratories is believed to significantly aid student comprehension. The addition of instant subtitle explanations is expected to facilitate easier understanding of concepts. Furthermore, instant feedback is expected to provide students with the opportunity to analyze their errors. Our study findings indicated that international students generally spend time with peers who speak their native language. Future studies should encourage students to spend more time with students from different cultures in virtual laboratory activities, arranging them in mixed groups. This should also be supported by algorithms that facilitate this distribution in AI-based tools.

Such future research will enable a more comprehensive understanding of how AI-enabled educational technologies can help international students grow as global citizens and succeed in an interconnected world. The study revealed language barriers between students and teachers. It was stated that AI-based tools could be used to overcome these barriers. The significant impact of AI-assisted translations, in particular, could be examined in further studies. This would allow students to better understand topics and concepts and further develop their intercultural communication.

REFERENCES

Abrahams, I. (2017). *Practical work in science: A report and a proposal*. Routledge.

Aljohani, N. R., & Alzahrani, A. M. (2023). The effectiveness of virtual laboratories in enhancing science education: A systematic review. *Education and Information Technologies*, *28*(6), 6781–6802. DOI: 10.1007/s10639-023-11647-9

Almasri, F. (2024). Exploring the impact of artificial intelligence in teaching and learning of science: A systematic review of empirical research. *Research in Science Education*, *54*(5), 977–997. DOI: 10.1007/s11165-024-10176-3

Baker, R. S., Siemens, G., & Rosé, C. P. (2019). Educational data mining and learning analytics. In Fischer, F., Hmelo-Silver, C. E., Goldman, S. R., & Reimann, P. (Eds.), *International handbook of the learning sciences* (pp. 253–270). Routledge.

Bao, W. (2020). COVID-19 and online teaching in higher education: A case study of Peking University. *Human Behavior and Emerging Technologies*, *2*(2), 113–115. DOI: 10.1002/hbe2.191

Chen, B., deNoyelles, A., Patton, K., & Zydney, J. M. (2020). Creating inclusive online learning environments: Strategies for promoting equity in virtual collaboration. *Computers & Education*, *146*, 103770. DOI: 10.1016/j.compedu.2019.103770

Chen, L., Chen, P., & Lin, Z. (2020). Artificial intelligence in education: A review. *IEEE Access : Practical Innovations, Open Solutions*, *10*, 105188–105210. DOI: 10.1109/ACCESS.2022.3203407

Chen, M. J., She, H. C., & Tsai, P. Y. (2024). The effects of online simulation-based collaborative problem-solving on students' problem-solving, communication and collaboration attitudes. *Education and Information Technologies*, *29*(14), 19141–19162. DOI: 10.1007/s10639-024-12609-y

Chen, Z., Cao, H., Deng, Y., Gao, X., Piao, J., Xu, F., & Li, Y. (2021). *Learning from home: A mixed-methods analysis of live streaming based remote education experience in chinese colleges during the covid-19 pandemic*. In *Proceedings of the 2021 CHI Conference on human factors in computing systems* (pp. 1-16). DOI: 10.1145/3411764.3445428

Cheng, H. (2025). Research on Strategies for Cultivating Intercultural Communication Competence in AI-Assisted English Teaching. *Advances in Educational Technology and Psychology*, *9*(1), 101–107. DOI: 10.23977/aetp.2025.090113

Chiu, M. C., & Hwang, G. J. (2025). Enhancing student creative and critical thinking in generative AI-empowered creation: A mind-mapping approach. *Interactive Learning Environments*, •••, 1–22. DOI: 10.1080/10494820.2025.2511244

Cress, U., & Kimmerle, J. (2023). Co-constructing knowledge with generative AI tools: Reflections from a CSCL perspective. *International Journal of Computer-Supported Collaborative Learning*, *18*(4), 607–614. DOI: 10.1007/s11412-023-09409-w

Daniel, S. J. (2020). Education and the COVID-19 pandemic. *Prospects*, *49*(1), 91–96. DOI: 10.1007/s11125-020-09464-3 de Jong, T., Linn, M. C., & Zacharia, Z. C. (2013). Physical and virtual laboratories in science and engineering education. *Science*, *340*(6130), 305–308. DOI: 10.1126/science.1230579

Deardorff, D. K. (2006). Identification and assessment of intercultural competence as a student outcome of internationalization. *Journal of Studies in International Education*, *10*(3), 241–266. DOI: 10.1177/1028315306287002

Dillenbourg, P. (1999). *Collaborative learning: Cognitive and computational approaches*. Elsevier.

du Boulay, B. (2023). Artificial Intelligence in Education and Ethics. In Zawacki-Richter, O., & Jung, I. (Eds.), *Handbook of Open, Distance and Digital Education* (pp. 93–108). Springer., DOI: 10.1007/978-981-19-2080-6_6

Hasegawa, T., Yamada, H., Nishimura, H., & Kobayashi, M. (2025). The Role of AI and Virtual Learning Environments in Enhancing STEM Education. [IJESTE]. *International Journal of Education, Science, Technology, and Engineering*, *8*(1), 1–10. DOI: 10.36079/lamintang.ijeste-0801.746

Heffernan, A., Murphy, M. P. A., & Yearwood, D. (2022). Can active learning be asynchronous? Implementing online peer review assignments in undergraduate political science and international relations courses. *European Political Science*, *21*(4), 537–549. DOI: 10.1057/s41304-022-00386-6

Heradio, R., de la Torre, L., Galan, D., Cabrerizo, F. J., Herrera-Viedma, E., & Dormido, S. (2021). Virtual and remote labs in education: A 10-year review. *Computers & Education*, *159*, 104002. DOI: 10.1016/j.compedu.2020.104002

Hofstein, A., & Lunetta, V. N. (2004). The laboratory in science education: Foundations for the twenty-first century. *Science Education*, *88*(1), 28–54. DOI: 10.1002/sce.10106

Holmes, W., Bialik, M., & Fadel, C. (2019). *Artificial intelligence in education: Promises and implications for teaching and learning*. Center for Curriculum Redesign.

Holstein, K., McLaren, B. M., & Aleven, V. (2020). Designing for complementarity: Teacher and student needs for orchestration support in AI-enhanced classrooms. *British Journal of Educational Technology*, *51*(6), 2115–2131. DOI: 10.1111/bjet.12908

Huang, R., Liu, D., Tlili, A., Yang, J., & Wang, H. (2022). AI-enhanced collaborative learning: Emerging trends and pedagogical practices. *Computers & Education*, *190*, 104625. DOI: 10.1016/j.compedu.2022.104625

Jefferies, P., & Grodzinsky, F. (2007). Developing on-line collaborative research across international boundaries: Exploring the potential of new technologies. *International Journal for the Scholarship of Teaching and Learning*, *1*(2), 6. Advance online publication. DOI: 10.20429/ijsotl.2007.010206

Jensen, L., & Konradsen, F. (2022). A review of the use of virtual reality head-mounted displays in education and training. *Education and Information Technologies*, *27*(4), 4615–4637. DOI: 10.1007/s10639-021-10704-4

Johnson, D. W., & Johnson, R. T. (1999). *Learning together and alone: Cooperative, competitive, and individualistic learning* (5th ed.). Allyn & Bacon.

Kergel, D., & Heidkamp, B. (2021). The digital transformation of higher education: International perspectives. *Education Sciences, 11*(3), 118. DOI: 10.3390/educsci11030118

Khasawneh, M. A. S. (2023). The Potential Of Ai In Facilitating Cross-Cultural Communication *Through Translation. Journal of Namibian Studies: History Politics Culture, 37*, 107–130. DOI: 10.59670/jns.v37i.4654

Klein, P., Ivanjek, L., Dahlkemper, M. N., Jeličić, K., Geyer, M.-A., Küchemann, S., & Susac, A. (2021). Studying physics during the COVID-19 pandemic: Student assessments of learning achievement, perceived effectiveness of online recitations, and online laboratories. *Physical Review. Physics Education Research, 17*(1), 010117. DOI: 10.1103/PhysRevPhysEducRes.17.010117

Klimova, B., & Chen, J. H. (2024). The Impact of AI on Enhancing Students' Intercultural Communication Competence at the University Level: *A Review Study. Language Teaching Research Quarterly, 43*, 102–120. DOI: 10.32038/ltrq.2024.43.06

Kolb, D. A. (1984). *Experiential learning: Experience as the source of learning and development*. Prentice Hall.

Krajcik, J., & Shin, N. (2014). Project-based learning. In Sawyer, R. K. (Ed.), *The Cambridge handbook of the learning sciences* (2nd ed., pp. 275–297). Cambridge University Press. DOI: 10.1017/CBO9781139519526.018

Long, J., & Lin, J. (2022). An empirical study on cultivating college students' cross-cultural communicative competence based on the artificial-intelligence *English-teaching mode. Frontiers in Psychology, 13*, 976310. DOI: 10.3389/fpsyg.2022.976310

Makransky, G., Borre-Gude, S., & Mayer, R. E. (2019). Motivational and cognitive benefits of training in immersive virtual reality based on multiple assessments. *Journal of Computer Assisted Learning, 35*(6), 691–707. DOI: 10.1111/jcal.12375

McMillan, J., & Schumacher, S. (2014). *Research in Education Evidence-Based Inquiry*. Pearson.

Molina, J., Olivares, R., & Pardo, A. (2022). Social constructivism in online learning environments: Implications for international collaboration. *Computers & Education, 184*, 104499. DOI: 10.1016/j.compedu.2022.104499

Navarro, C., Arias-Calderón, M., Henríquez, C. A., & Riquelme, P. (2024). Assessment of student and teacher perceptions on the use of virtual simulation in cell biology laboratory education. *Education Sciences, 14*(3), 243. DOI: 10.3390/educsci14030243

Nguyen, A., Ngo, H. N., Hong, Y., Dang, B., & Nguyen, B. P. T. (2023). Ethical principles for artificial intelligence in education. *Education and Information Technologies, 28*(4), 4221–4241. DOI: 10.1007/s10639-022-11316-w

OECD. (2021). *OECD skills outlook 2021: Learning for life*. OECD Publishing., DOI: 10.1787/0ae365b4-

OECD. (2023). *OECD learning compass 2030: Competencies for future-ready students*. OECD Publishing.

Ouyang, F., & Jiao, P. (2021). Artificial intelligence in education: A review. *Educational Philosophy and Theory*, *53*(12), 1229–1245. DOI: 10.1080/00131857.2020.1821181

Potkonjak, V., Gardner, M., Callaghan, V., Mattila, P., Guetl, C., Petrović, V. M., & Jovanović, K. (2016). Virtual laboratories for education in science, technology, and engineering: A review. *Computers & Education*, *95*, 309–327. DOI: 10.1016/j.compedu.2016.02.002

Radianti, J., Majchrzak, T. A., Fromm, J., & Wohlgenannt, I. (2020). A systematic review of immersive virtual reality applications for higher education: Design elements, lessons learned, and research agenda. *Computers & Education*, *147*, 103778. DOI: 10.1016/j.compedu.2019.103778

Reyes, R. L., Isleta, K. P., Regala, J. D., & Bialba, D. M. R. (2024). Enhancing experiential science learning with virtual labs: A narrative account of merits, challenges, and implementation strategies. *Journal of Computer Assisted Learning*, *40*(6), 3167–3186. DOI: 10.1111/jcal.13061

Roll, I., & Wylie, R. (2016). Evolution and revolution in artificial intelligence in education. *International Journal of Artificial Intelligence in Education*, *26*(2), 582–599. DOI: 10.1007/s40593-016-0110-3

Sarwari, A. Q., Javed, M. N., Mohd Adnan, H., & Abdul Wahab, M. N. (2024). Assessment of the impacts of artificial intelligence (AI) on intercultural communication among postgraduate students in a multicultural university environment. *Scientific Reports*, *14*(1), 13849. DOI: 10.1038/s41598-024-63276-5

Scardamalia, M., & Bereiter, C. (2006). Knowledge building: Theory, pedagogy, and technology. In Sawyer, K. (Ed.), *Cambridge handbook of the learning sciences* (pp. 97–118). Cambridge University Press.

Schnieder, M., Williams, S., & Ghosh, S. (2022). Comparison of in-person and virtual labs/tutorials for engineering students using blended learning principles. *Education Sciences*, *12*(3), 153. DOI: 10.3390/educsci12030153

Slavin, R. E. (1995). *Cooperative learning: Theory, research, and practice* (2nd ed.). Allyn & Bacon.

Stahl, G., Koschmann, T., & Suthers, D. (2006). Computer-supported collaborative learning: An historical perspective. In Sawyer, R. K. (Ed.), *The Cambridge handbook of the learning sciences* (pp. 409–426). Cambridge University Press.

Trilling, B., & Fadel, C. (2009). *21st century skills: Learning for life in our times*. John Wiley & Sons.

UNESCO. (2021). *Recommendation on the Ethics of Artificial Intelligence*. UNESCO Publishing. https://www.unesco.org/en/legal-affairs/recommendation-ethics-artificial-intelligence?utm_source

UNESCO. (2022). *Reimagining our futures together: A new social contract for education*. UNESCO Publishing.

van den Berg, G. (2025). Teachers' experiences of using artificial intelligence from an open distance learning context: Successes, challenges, and strategies for success. *Discover Education*, *4*(1), 192. DOI: 10.1007/s44217-025-00596-2

Voogt, J., & Roblin, N. P. (2012). A comparative analysis of international frameworks for 21st century competences: Implications for national curriculum policies. *Journal of Curriculum Studies*, *44*(3), 299–321. DOI: 10.1080/00220272.2012.668938

Wang, Y., Yu, T., & Cheng, W. (2023). Cross-cultural collaborative learning in AI-supported virtual environments. *Interactive Learning Environments, 31*(5), 1047–1064. DOI: 10.1080/10494820.2022.2134567

Wieczorek, M., Hosseini, M., & Gordijn, B. (2025). Unpacking the ethics of using AI in primary and secondary education: A systematic literature review. *AI and Ethics, 5*(5), 1–19. DOI: 10.1007/s43681-025-00770-0

Wood, D., Bruner, J. S., & Ross, G. (1976). The role of tutoring in problem-solving. *Journal of Child Psychology and Psychiatry, and Allied Disciplines, 17*(2), 89–100. DOI: 10.1111/j.1469-7610.1976.tb00381.x

World Economic Forum. (2023). *Future of jobs report 2023.* World Economic Forum.

Xia, Y., Shin, S.-Y., & Kim, J.-C. (2024). Cross-Cultural Intelligent Language Learning System (CILS): Leveraging AI to Facilitate Language Learning Strategies in Cross-Cultural Communication. *Applied Sciences (Basel, Switzerland), 14*(13), 5651. DOI: 10.3390/app14135651

Xie, Z., Yu, Y., Zhang, J., & Chen, M. (2022). The searching artificial intelligence: Consumers show less aversion to algorithm-recommended search product. *Psychology and Marketing, 39*(10), 1902–1919. DOI: 10.1002/mar.21706

Zacharia, Z. C., Jong, T., & Olympiou, G. (2022). Learning from virtual laboratories. In Fischer, F., Hmelo-Silver, C. E., Goldman, S. R., & Reimann, P. (Eds.), *International handbook of the learning sciences* (2nd ed., pp. 359–370). Routledge.

Zawacki-Richter, O., & Jung, I. (Eds.). (2023). *Handbook of Open, Distance and Digital Education.* Springer., DOI: 10.1007/978-981-19-2080-6

Zawacki-Richter, O., Marín, V. I., Bond, M., & Gouverneur, F. (2019). Systematic review of research on artificial intelligence applications in higher education–where are the educators? *International Journal of Educational Technology in Higher Education, 16*(1), 1–27. DOI: 10.1186/s41239-019-0171-0

Zhang, C., Schießl, J., Plößl, L., Hofmann, F., & Gläser-Zikuda, M. (2023). Acceptance of artificial intelligence among pre-service teachers: A multigroup analysis. *International Journal of Educational Technology in Higher Education, 20*(1), 49. DOI: 10.1186/s41239-023-00420-7

Zhang, Q., Mohammad Ismail, M. I. R., & Zakaria, A. R. B. (2025). Enhancing intercultural competence in technical higher education through AI-driven frameworks. *Scientific Reports, 15*(1), 22019. DOI: 10.1038/s41598-025-03303-1

Chapter 10
Artificial Intelligence and the Educational Futures of Diaspora Youth:
Cultural Continuity in the Cloud

Tuhina Tuhina
https://orcid.org/0009-0003-6786-3863
Manav Rachna International Institute of Research and Studies, India

Swati Chauhan
https://orcid.org/0000-0001-7698-995X
Manav Rachna International Institute of Research and Studies, India

Shivani Vashist
Regional Centre for Biotechnology, India

ABSTRACT

This chapter examines the intersection of Artificial Intelligence (AI), transnational education, and the cultural continuity of diaspora youth through a qualitative, secondary research methodology. It analyzes scholarly works, digital platforms, and existing case studies to identify how AI influences the educational experiences of culturally diverse learners. Guided by the central research question—whether AI in education supports or disrupts cultural continuity for diaspora youth—the study investigates how algorithmic learning environments shape heritage preservation, language retention, and identity formation. By critically evaluating mainstream platforms such as Duolingo, LingQ, and Khan Academy alongside emerging culturally responsive initiatives, the chapter reveals how culturally grounded AI design can promote belonging and inclusivity. It concludes with the CULTUR-AI framework, offering principles for developing equitable, linguistically diverse, and community-centered AI systems in education.

INTRODUCTION

Education is no longer bounded by national borders in an era which is accelerated by global mobility and technological innovation (Vertovec, 2009). Environments encouraged by digital learnings have

DOI: 10.4018/979-8-3373-5403-3.ch010

emerged as a safe transnational space where linguistically, culturally and ethnically leaners are being diverse with gaining new ways of knowledge (Appadurai, 1996). Around this new approach there is a remarkable increase in integration of AI into educational platforms, particularly with the context of trinational education (Popenici & Kerr, 2017). Furthermore, AI continues to build how knowledge is distributed, accessed and experienced and most important point is its implications for diasporic communities special reference to young youth who negotiate hybrid identities which requires urgent scholarly attention. (Suárez-Orozco & Todorova, 2008). Despite the enhance accessibility and personalization that AI powered education offers there is a remarkable gaps to utilize its potential to affirm cultural identities (Baker & Smith, 2019). Almost all the AI tools are constructed upon an monocultural frameworks, which inadvertently reinforce dominant cultural narratives with ignoring the specific needs of diasporic learners (O'Neil, 2016). Diasporic youth inhabits the interstices of new societal context and cultural inheritance (Brah, 1996). Inside the education system which rarely showcase their values, histories which students commonly experience a form of alienation (Nieto, 2010). Host country curricula might lack cultural relevance, while knowledge from heritage is often marginalized or omitted altogether (Banks, 2015). Furthermore, this chapter examines the dual role of AI which can either act as a mechanisms of cultural erasure or a vehicle of sustaining cultural memory and identity across borders. (Nakamura, 2008).

Transnational education (TNE) is central to this discussion. TNE refers to educational programmes, partnerships, and technology-enabled learning models that operate across national borders. Positioning AI within TNE helps clarify how digital platforms mediate mobility, accreditation, and cultural transmission for learners who engage with multiple educational contexts.

The main objective of the study is to investigate how in transnational education *Artificial Intelligence (AI)* supports or disrupts cultural continuity for diasporic youth. The term *Cultural Continuity* refers here to the intergenerational transmission of values, language, heritage, knowledge and practices that are collectively sustain a community's sense of identity (Chandler & Lalonde, 1998). Many young people in diaspora and education becomes a site of intellectual development. It becomes an arena for self-definition and cultural survival. In the age, where learning is increasingly walked through digital technologies and algorithmic decision- making (Ito et al., 2013). The chapter highlights the growing gap in the interdisciplinary literature at the intersection of diaspora, AI and education. As much research has explored AI capacities of how it helps in personalizing learning, assess performance and help in improving educational outcomes (Woolf, 2009). It can be considered as less attention has been given to its cultural dimensions. A major research is lacking when we look into how AI technologies interact or fail to interact with learners linguistic and cultural identities (Blikstein, 2018). By mentioning, the experiences of diasporic youth, the chapter targets the prevailing notion of AI which is taken as universal or neutral tools (Winner, 1980). AI technologies are embedded with reflecting values, inheriting cultural, assumptions and epistemologies of their developers and the sociotechnical system (Elish, 2016). In educational settings which is deprived of cultural sensitivity then these tools risk marginalized communities which is already situated at the edges of mainstream curricula (Noble, 2018).

In the end of this chapter which critically examines how different AI- powered education platforms such as LingQ, Dunlingo and Khan Academy and examine how it respond and neglect the cultural needs of diasporic learners. These platforms definitely have a global reach but many does not give emphasis on the heritage based or cultural contextualization content that reflects the lived realities of diasporic communities (Chun, 2017). On the contrary, a number of emerging EDTech initiatives have begun to incorporate culturally responsive design features which includes localized content, multilingual interfaces and community centred pedagogies. The examples provide extreme valuable insights into the design and implementation of AI which will help to foster inclusive as well as culturally grounded learning experiences (Ladson-Billings, 1995). The chapter aim is to offer a better understanding of the opportunities and challenges presented by AI which includes the implication of educational futures of diasporic youths and also fulfil the purpose to create a framework for the presentation of AI for the culturally sustaining and ethical design of AI in education.

LITERATURE REVIEW

This Book Chapter provides a comprehensive review of the existing literature which talks about at the intersection of Artificial Intelligence in diaspora studies, education and culturally responsive pedagogy. It also establishes the theoretical foundation in understanding the complex relationship which is established between AI and the cultural continuity of diaspora youth with transnational educational contexts.

Artificial Intelligence in Education: Promises and Perils

The implication of Artificial Intelligence (AI) in education has been taken as a transformative force with helps and boost the potential to revolutionize teaching and learning (Timms, 2016). AI-powered educational tools promise personalized adaptive assessments, learning pathways and immediate feedback, which help in catering to individual student needs which a traditional classroom fails to offer (Pane, Steiner, & Baird, 2015). Proponents further argue that AI can democratize the ways of education by providing access to high-quality learning resources to all students regardless of their socioeconomic background or geographical location (Luckin et al., 2016). In specific with, intelligent tutoring systems (ITS) which can provide one-on-one instruction and support to learners, by mimicking the role of a human tutor (VanLehn, 2011).In parallel to, AI-driven learning analytics can also help educators to identify at-risk students and then provide timely interventions (Siemens & Baker, 2012).

Moreover, the significant promise of AI in education also brings notable perils. While a growing body of critical scholarship further more highlights the potential for AI to exacerbate introduce new forms of bias and existing inequalities (Eubanks, 2018). AI algorithms are trained over vast datasets, and if these datasets reflect the societal biases, the algorithms will perpetuate and learn those biases on their own (Barocas & Selbst, 2016). In this context of education, this can definelty lead to the marginalization of students who belong to non-dominant backgrounds. For example, an AI-powered assessment tool might punish those students who use non-standard dialects of a language, or even a content recommendation system which might steer students towards culturally homogenous materials (Benjamin, 2019). The prominent nature of AI algorithms which is the "black box", where the decision-making process is non- transparent even to their creators, further complicates efforts to ensure accountability and fairness (Pasquale, 2015). Recent studies deepen this discussion by highlighting equity, cultural relevance, and governance in AI-driven learning (UNESCO 2023; OECD 2023; Holmes et al. 2022; Selwyn 2023). These works emphasise that learning-analytics systems and policy frameworks play a decisive role in shaping inclusion and cultural continuity.

Diaspora Youth, Identity, and Education

Diaspora communities are often characterized by their dispersal from a homeland and their continued connection to the place, often across generations (Cohen, 1997). For diaspora youth, identity formation is a complex process which is negotiating between the culture of their heritage and the culture of their host society (Hall, 1990). This concept of "hybrid identity" formation is often agitated with challenges, which includes discrimination, experiences of racism and cultural alienation (Rong & Preissle, 2009). Here, Education plays a crucial role in the lives of diaspora youth, and serves as a primary site for both resistance and assimilation (Portes & Rumbaut, 2001). The mainstream educational systems in host countries might sometime fails to adequately address the demands and needs of diaspora youth. Frequently Eurocentric curricula starts neglecting the cultures, histories and contributions of non-Western societies (Apple, 2004). This can lead to a major sense of "cultural homelessness" among diaspora students, who might feel separated from both their heritage and their new home (Tsolidis, 1997). In response to these challenges, diaspora communities have often established their own educational initiatives, such as heritage language schools and cultural centers, to foster cultural continuity and provide a sense of belonging for their youth (Fishman, 2001). The increase of transnational networks and digital technology has created new opportunities for diaspora communities to connect, share knowledge, and sustain their cultural heritage across borders (Karim, 2003).

Culturally Responsive Pedagogy in the Digital Age

In all aspects of learning the importance of students to recognize educational approach create a culturally responsive pedagogy (Gay, 2010). It focus to empower students socially, intellectually, politically and emotionally by using cultural referents to impart skills, knowledge and attitudes (Ladson-Billings, 2014). In a culturally responsive classroom, teachers construct a learning environment that is affirming and inclusive of students' cultural backgrounds. They draw on students' lived experiences, culturally relevant materials, and promote a critical consciousness about social inequalities (Paris, 2012).

The principles of culturally responsive pedagogy have an high relevance in the digital age, as technology transforms into the landscape of education. The concept of "culturally responsive-sustaining pedagogy" put emphases to the need of not only responsive to students' cultures but also to actively sustain them (Paris & Alim, 2017). In the backdrop of AI in education, which means implementing and designing technologies that are actively promote cultural diversity and linguistic pluralism but not only culturally sensitive. It requires to characterizes many current AI-powered educational tools towards a more context-aware and community-centered design paradigm and a shift away from the one- size- fits all approach.(Lee, 2017). Meanwhile AI offers a powerful tools for personalizing education and its current trajectory risks perpetuating the marginalization of diaspora youth. At the meantime, the principles of culturally responsive pedagogy and the resilience of diaspora communities put forward a path towards harnessing AI for cultural continuity. This research builds upon on this foundation which emphasizes on how to explore AI which can be reimagined as a tool for empowering diaspora youth and cultural futures.

THE DOUBLE-EDGED SWORD OF AI: CULTURAL ERASURE VS. CULTURAL AFFIRMATION

The assimilation of Artificial Intelligence into the educational landscape constitute a profound duality for diaspora youth, which even act as a double-edged sword that can either sever their ties to their cultural heritage or forge stronger and more resilient connections. This section delves into this critical tension, in exploring the mechanisms through which AI can become a tool of cultural erasure and, also conversely how it can be harnessed for cultural continuity and affirmation.

AI as a Vector of Cultural Erasure

The capability for AI to contribute to cultural erasure stems is from its development, design and deployment, which are always rooted in monolingual and monocultural frameworks. The majority of AI systems are constructed in the Global North. By the teams that lack diversity, as well as trained on datasets which are overwhelmingly representative of languages and Western cultures (D'Ignazio & Klein, 2020). This inherent bias can be seen in several ways within the educational contexts:

Linguistic Homogenization: Language learning platforms powered by AI, as offering accessibility, sometimes prioritize dominant global languages like Spanish, English and Mandarin. The Heritage languages spoken by diaspora communities are usually are completely absent or under-represented. When these platforms turns into primary means for language learning, then they can unintentionally contribute to the erosion of cultural identity and the decline of linguistic diversity and as language has always been a cornerstone of culture (Crystal, 2000). The algorithms that gives power to these platforms which may also penalize non-standard accents or dialects, furthermore they marginalizing learners from diverse linguistic backgrounds.

Algorithmic Bias in Content Curation: Content recommendation systems which are AI- driven, such as those are used in platforms like YouTube or Khan Academy. They are designed to personalize learning through providing relevant materials. Meanwhile, these algorithms are susceptible to echo chambers and filter bubbles " that can limit students' exposure to reinforce dominant cultural narratives and diverse perspectives (Pariser, 2011). A diaspora youth who is searching for history content might be exclusively shown through materials about the history of their host country and with their own heritage history remains invisible. This algorithmic curation of knowledge can be subtly but effectively erase the historical and cultural contributions of marginalized communities.

Standardized Assessment and the Narrowing of Knowledge: AI-powered assessment tools mainly rely on multiple-choice questions and standardized metrics which may not be culturally appropriate for all learners. These assessments can even privilege certain forms of ways of knowing and knowledge over others, undervalue the diverse theory of knowledge that diaspora youth assist guide to the classroom (Au, 2013). The emphasis is on efficiency of quantifiable data in AI-driven assessment that can guide a subside of the curriculum, with less focus on culturally rich subjects like humanities, arts and heritage which are studied as a crucial subject for cultural continuity.

AI as a Catalyst for Cultural Affirmation

Despite all the risks, AI also holds with them an immense potential to become a powerful ally with the efforts of diaspora communities to transmit and preserve their cultural heritage. When implemented and designed with cultural sensitivity as well as commitment to the equity, AI can even foster cultural affirmation in the following ways:

Revitalization of Heritage Languages: It can be a game-changer for the revitalization of under-resourced and endangered languages. Natural Language Processing (NLP) techniques can be developed to create digital resources for these languages, such as translation tools, online dictionaries as well as interactive learning materials. Chatbots powered by AI can provide learners with immense opportunities to practice their heritage language in a conversational context. By making heritage language learning more engaging and accessible, AI can also empower diaspora youth to connect with a pivotal part of their cultural identity.

Creation of Culturally Rich and Immersive Learning Experiences: Virtual Reality (VR) and Augmented Reality (AR) like AI technologies can be used to build immersive learning experiences that can transport through diaspora youth to their ancestral homelands. They can also explore participate in cultural traditions, historical sites and interact with virtual characters who even speak their heritage language. These experiences can create a deeper connection to their cultural roots and also provide a powerful antidote to the cultural alienation which they may experience in their daily lives.

Personalized Learning for Cultural Continuity: AI has capacity to personalizes leveraged to create learning pathways that tailored interests of diaspora youth and the cultural background. A learning platform powered AI for example the recommend books by authors from their heritage community can connect them with mentors who share their cultural background, or enhance them with projects that can allow them to investigate their own family histories. The culturally responsive personalization can help diaspora youth see themselves as well as their cultures which reflects in their education and also fostering a sense of academic engagement and belonging.

Connecting Diaspora Communities: Platforms powered by AI can facilitate collaboration and connections among diaspora communities around the world. Social media groups, Online forums and collaborative projects can provide spaces for diaspora youth to share their experiences as well as they learn from each other, and work together to preserve their cultural heritage. AI also helps to connect and identify individuals with same background and shared interests strengthening the social fabric of the global diaspora.

The dual prospective of AI underscores the critical need for an approach and proactive integration in education. The direction that AI showcase either it becomes a tool of cultural assimilation or a catalyst for cultural affirmation. It all will depend on the choices we make as developers, educators, communities and policymakers. The following sections of this chapter will explore these choices in greater detail, proposing a framework for the development of culturally responsive AI in education as well as examine existing AI platform.

CASE STUDY

Case Studies: A Critical Examination of AI-Powered Educational Platforms

This section presents a critical examination of several prominent AI-powered educational platforms: LingQ, Duolingo and Khan Academy. These case studies analyze the extent to which these platforms support or hamper the cultural continuity of diaspora youth. The analysis is followed by an exploration of emerging EdTech initiatives which are establish more culturally responsive perspectives.

Case Study 1: Duolingo, The Gamified Gatekeeper of Languages

Duolingo is one of the most widespread language-learning apps in the world, and a vast array of language courses and millions of users. From the perspective of diaspora youth seeking to learn their heritage language, Duolingo represents a mixed picture highlighting some key objectives:

Strengths: It offers courses in a lot of growing number of languages, including endangered languages and some less common, which might include development in collaboration with community partners. For diaspora youth, those whose heritage language is available on the platform, This app can be a valuable tool for building foundational grammar and vocabulary skills. It is also accessibile on mobile devices which makes it convenient for active learning.

Weaknesses: Duolingo language selection process is still heavily skewed towards dominant global languages. Many heritage languages spoken by diaspora communities are even not available which leads in leaving these learners without any viable option on the platform., The content of the language offered is often lacks cultural depth and decontextualized. The focus on translating isolated phrases and sentences does very little to immerse the learners in the cultural nuances of that language. For example, a learner of Hindi if goes on Duolingo he/she might learn the word for "wedding" (shaadi), but the platform does not provide them any circumstances about the cultural significance of weddings in India. This lack of cultural contextualization can make the learning experience feel disconnected and sterile from the inherent realities of the language.

Vignette: A second-generation Gujarati learner in London used Duolingo regularly but found that most examples and prompts were framed around Western cultural settings. The learner gained vocabulary, but the absence of idioms, festivals, and honourifics reduced the cultural depth of the learning experience.

Case Study 2: LingQ, Immersion through Authentic Content

LingQ is a language-learning platform that takes a completely different approach from Duolingo, which focuses on immersion across authentic content. Users can import videos, texts and audio from the web which turn them into an interactive lessons. The platform uses AI to track known and known words as well as providing a personified learning experience.

Strengths: The app focus on authentic content which allows learners to engage with the language in a much more culturally meaningful and rich way than which is on Duolingo. For example, a diaspora youth import, a news article from their heritage country or a transcript of a conversation with a grandparent or a song by their favourite artist. This flexibility makes LingQ a probably powerful tool for cultural continuity.

Weaknesses: LingQ is effectiveness highly dependent on the availability of engaging and high- quality content in the target language. There is major challenge in finding less-resourced languages. The platform's often interface which can also be overwhelming for new users, and for some its subscription-based model may be a barrier. While LingQ provides the tools for captivating, it places the responsibility on the learner to find and assemble their own content which sometime can be a daunting task for a young learner with there is a lack of proper guidance.

Vignette: A Nepali diaspora teenager used LingQ to build a personal library of songs, stories, and oral histories. The AI supported vocabulary practice, but the platform lacked tools to organise these materials into coherent cultural learning pathways, leaving the experience fragmented.

Case Study 3: Khan Academy, The Promise of a Free, World-Class Education

Khan Academy is a non-profit educational organization that contribute a vast library of practice exercises and free online lessons for a wide range of subjects. The mission is to provide a "free, world-class education for anywhere and to anyone". The platform uses AI to track student progress and provide personalized learning recommendations

Strengths: It gives commitment to free and accessible education which is highly commendable. The platform has been translated into numerous languages, making it a valuable resource around the world for learners. The platform's content is commonly of high quality and also presented in a engaging and clear manner.

Weaknesses: In spite its global reach, the content on Khan Academy remains largely rooted in the western culture, and specifically with American curriculum. For example, the history lessons are heavily focused on European and American history, with limited coverage to the other parts of the world. A diaspora youth who is seeking to learn about the history of their heritage country will likely find very little and at times no relevant content on the platform. The platform's has a one-size-fits approach to content delivery which fails to account the diverse linguistic and cultural backgrounds of its learners. While the platform has been translated but the content itself has not been culturally adapted and which can make it less engaging and relevant for non-Western learners.

Vignette: A multicultural classroom used Khan Academy's multilingual math modules. Students followed the lessons with ease, but examples in social sciences and humanities remained rooted in Western contexts, requiring teachers to add locally relevant cultural material to maintain engagement.

ANALYSIS

Comparative Analysis of Mainstream AI-Powered Educational Platforms

As summarized in Table 1, the comparative analysis of three leading AI-driven educational platforms—Duolingo, LingQ, and Khan Academy—reveals the varying degrees to which each supports or limits the cultural continuity of diaspora youth. Each platform embodies a distinctive pedagogical model, technological design, and degree of cultural responsiveness that shapes the learner's experience in transnational contexts.

Table 1. Comparative analysis of mainstream AI-powered educational platforms

Feature	Duolingo	LingQ	Khan Academy
Primary Goal	Gamified language learning	Language immersion through authentic content	Free, world-class education for all
Cultural Content	Limited and decontextualized	High potential, but learner-dependent	Limited and Western-centric
Support for Heritage Languages	Growing but still limited	Supports any language with available content	Primarily a translation effort, not content localization

continued on following page

Table 1. Continued

Feature	Duolingo	LingQ	Khan Academy
Personalization	Adaptive learning path based on performance	Tracks known/unknown words, user-curated content	Recommends next steps in a standardized curriculum
Accessibility	Freemium model	Subscription-based	Completely free
Potential for Cultural Continuity	Low to moderate	Moderate to high	Low

Duolingo primarily functions as a gamified language learning application, designed to enhance motivation through repetition, rewards, and progress tracking. While this approach has democratized access to language learning globally, its cultural content remains limited and decontextualized, focusing largely on linguistic accuracy rather than cultural immersion. The platform's support for heritage languages is growing but still restricted, as most available courses prioritize dominant global languages such as English, Spanish, and French. Duolingo's adaptive learning path, while efficient in tracking performance, operates within a standardized framework that does little to reflect the lived experiences or cultural nuances of diaspora learners. Its freemium model makes it widely accessible, yet its potential for cultural continuity remains low to moderate, as it engages primarily with surface-level linguistic competence rather than deeper cultural meaning.

In contrast, LingQ adopts a language immersion model through authentic content, positioning it as a more culturally responsive platform. Unlike Duolingo's uniform design, LingQ allows learners to import real-world materials—texts, videos, and audio—from heritage cultures, thereby transforming learning into a personalized and context-rich experience. Its support for heritage languages is broad, contingent upon the availability of authentic materials, which gives users greater agency in shaping their cultural engagement. However, this learner-dependent approach also introduces variability; the cultural richness of the experience depends largely on the user's initiative and the quality of external content curated. Despite its subscription-based access, LingQ's potential for cultural continuity is moderate to high, as it encourages meaningful interaction with language as a living cultural practice rather than an abstract skill.

Khan Academy, on the other hand, represents the archetype of AI-supported, globally accessible education through its mission of providing a "free, world-class education for all." While its accessibility and commitment to free learning resources make it a powerful educational tool, its cultural orientation remains predominantly Western-centric, with much of its content derived from the American curriculum. The platform's approach to heritage language support is largely limited to translation rather than contextual localization, meaning learners can access content in multiple languages but not necessarily in ways that reflect their cultural contexts. Its personalization features—driven by AI recommendations—function within a standardized curriculum that often sidelines diverse epistemologies. Consequently, Khan Academy's potential for cultural continuity is low, as its universalist design inadvertently reinforces dominant cultural narratives instead of validating diverse diasporic identities.

Overall, this comparative analysis underscores a critical tension in AI-powered education between technological accessibility and cultural sensitivity. While platforms like Duolingo and Khan Academy excel in expanding access and affordability, they fall short in embedding cultural depth or supporting heritage identity. LingQ, though less mainstream, demonstrates a more promising model for culturally grounded AI design, emphasizing learner autonomy and contextual engagement. This evaluation reaffirms the need for culturally responsive frameworks—such as the proposed CULTUR-AI model—to ensure that AI not only personalizes education but also sustains the cultural and linguistic heritage of diaspora youth.

Emerging EdTech Initiatives

On the contrary to the mainstream platforms, there are numerous emerging EdTech initiatives that are pioneering more culturally responsive approaches to AI when we look align with education. These initiatives are majorly developed by members of the communities as they serve on the designed which is based with a deep understanding of the linguistic and cultural needs of their learners.

Prizma, A Multilingual and Multicultural Learning Platform: It is an example of a platform that is designed from the thoroughly which is based on multicultural and multilinguistic. It provides a library that has learning materials and culturally diverse stories in multiple languages. The platform uses AI to provide to support language learning and personalized recommendations through interactive features. By integrating culturally relevant content, Prizma offerss a learning environment where diaspora youth can see their own languages and cultural that are valued and celebrated.

Mukurtu, A Community-Driven Archiving Platform: It is an open-source platform that allows indigenous communities to share and manage their digital heritage in a culturally appropriate way. The platform utilizes a system of cultural engagement that empower communities to control on those who has outburst to their cultural materials. While not only Mukurtu, works exclusively as an educational platform, It provides a powerful model for how technology can be used to self-determination and support cultural continuity For diaspora youth an educational platform that could incorporate similar features to empower communities to share and curate their own cultural content.

These materializing initiatives illustrate that it is quite even possible to design and build. Education tools powered by AI which are not only designed technologically futuristic but also culturally responsive and sustaining They can also provide a source of inspiration and a set of best practices for the evolution of the next generation in the field of technologies in education.

DESIGNING FOR CULTURAL CONTINUITY: A FRAMEWORK FOR CULTURALLY RESPONSIVE AI IN EDUCATION

After critical examination of existing platforms it clearly reveals a clear need for a new approach to the development and design of AI in education. The one that the well-being of diaspora youth and prioritizes cultural continuity. The proposes of a framework that is culturally responsive. AI in education, offering a set of guiding practical and principles strategies for developers, educators and policymakers. The framework is often constructed on the core principles of culturally responsive-sustaining pedagogy that aims to walk beyond a one-size-fits where all model walk towards a more inclusive and equitable vision of AI in education.

The proposed framework, which we address as the CULTUR-AI Framework, consists of six interconnected principles:

C - Community-Centered Design

U - Unbiased and Equitable Algorithms

L - Linguistic Pluralism and Diversity

T - Transformative and Critical Pedagogy

U - User Empowerment and Agengy

R - Relationality and Connection

Figure 1 illustrates the CULTUR-AI Framework, a conceptual model developed to guide the design of culturally responsive Artificial Intelligence in education.

Figure 1. The CULTUR-AI framework for culturally responsive AI in education

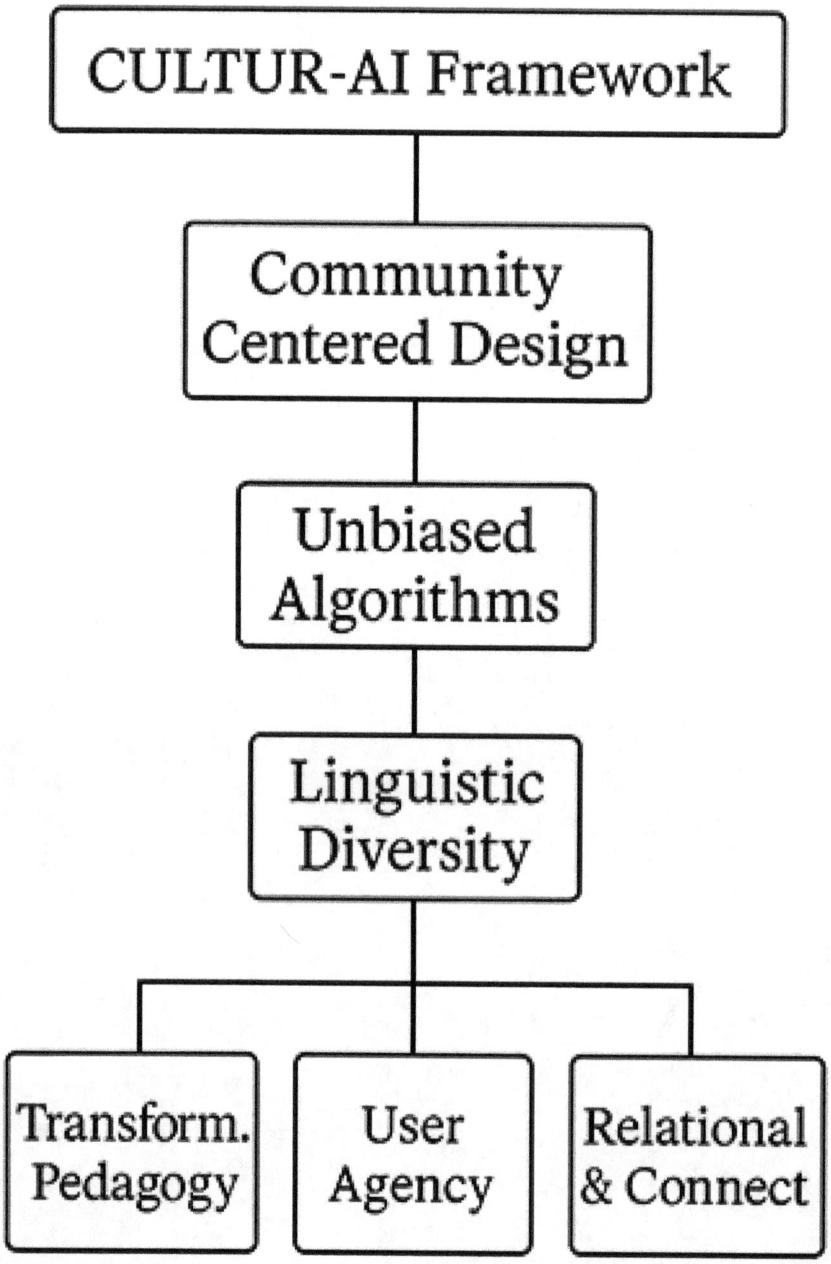

The framework emphasizes six interconnected principles—Community-Centered Design, Unbiased Algorithms, Linguistic Diversity, Transformative Pedagogy, User Agency, and Relational Connection. Together, these elements advocate for an inclusive approach where AI systems not only enhance learning efficiency but also sustain cultural heritage, empower marginalized learners, and strengthen communal ties across transnational educational spaces. The model positions culture as central to technological development, ensuring that AI functions as a tool of continuity rather than erasure for diaspora youth.

Community-Centered Design

AI which are culturally responsive must be designed *by* and *with* the communities. It is intended to serve but not just *for* them. This main principle of participatory design, or co-design, is very essential for ensuring that the technology is respectful, relevant and empowering.

Strategies:

a) Establish community advisory boards: It involves diaspora community elders, leaders, parents, and youth in all the stages of the design process are from initial brainstorming to final deployment.
b) Hire diverse development teams: It recruit designers, developers and content creators from diverse linguistic and cultural backgrounds.
c) Conduct culturally sensitive user research: It use ethnographic methods to understand the lived experiences, needs and values of diaspora youth.

Unbiased and Equitable Algorithms

AI algorithms are not always neutral but they reflect the biases of their creators and also the data they are trained. To create equitable AI, we must be particular about promoting fairness and mitigating bias.

Strategies:

a) Audit algorithms for bias: It regularly test AI systems for check biases related to race, ethnicity, language, gender and other social categories.
b) Use diverse and representative training data: It also actively collect and assembled datasets that reflect the diversity of the human experience.
c) Promote algorithmic transparency: It also helps in the decision-making processes of AI algorithms as transparent as it can be possible so that they can be considered accountable and even not held scrutinized.

Linguistic Diversity and Pluralism

Language is always considered as cornerstone of culture, and AI implication in education should actively promote linguistic diversity rather than contributing to linguistic homogenization.

Strategies:

a) Support heritage language learning: It helps in development of AI-powered tools for the revitalization and learning of overstretched and endangered languages.
b) Create multilingual and multimodal content: It often offer learning materials in multiple languages and in a variety of formats (audio, text, video, etc.) to accommodate diverse learning preferences and style.
c) Value linguistic diversity: It design AI systems that value and recognizes all dialects and language, without prohibits non-standard forms of expression.

Transformative and Critical Pedagogy

AI trained to culturally responsive should not just be about delivering content but it should always be about empowering students and fostering critical thinking to challenge social inequalities.

Strategies:

a) Incorporate critical perspectives: It should design learning experiences that supports and motivates students to critically examine the issues of privilege, power and oppression.
b) Promote student voice and activism: It should create opportunities for students to use AI tools to address social justice and research issues in their own communities.
c) Connect learning to students' lives: It should design activities and projects that allow students to explore their own histories, identities and cultures.

User Agency and Empowerment

AI in education should empower users not always control them. Diaspora youth should have company over their own learning and should be able to use AI tools in the ways that are meaningful to them.

Strategies:

a) Provide customizable and flexible tools: It also allow to choose the content and activities as well as personalize their learning experience that are most relevant to their goals and interests.
b) Foster digital literacy and critical AI literacy: It also teach students how to be creators and consumers of digital media and how to question and understand the workings of AI systems.
c) Respect user data and privacy: To be transparent about how user data is used and collected, and also give users control over their own data.

Relationality and Connection

Learning is a relational and social process. AI in education should be designed to foster connections between learners, teachers, learners, communities and families to not isolate them.

Strategies:

a) Facilitate collaborative learning: To design AI-powered tools that support peer tutoring, group work and other forms of collaborative learning.
b) Connect learners with mentors and experts: To use AI to connect and develope diaspora youth with mentors from their own cultural communities.
c) Strengthen home-school connections: To create tools that allow families and parents to be more involved and develop their children's education.

By assuming the CULTUR-AI framework, we can start to build a equitable future for AI in education and where technology is used not eliminate cultural differences, but to sustain and celebrate them.

ETHICAL IMPERATIVES AND NAVIGATING THE CHALLENGES

The deployment and development of culturally responsive AI which is culturally responsive in education is not only being a technical challenge but also a profound ethical as well. As we move forward, we notice that it is imperative that we navigate the complex ethical landscape with intentionality and care, ensuring that the well-being and rights of diaspora youth are always at the forefront. This section also highlights some of the key challenges and ethical imperatives that must be acknowledged.

Policy implications: Educational ministries, accreditation bodies, and TNE partners should embed CULTUR-AI criteria in procurement and program approval. This includes requiring community co-design evidence, fairness audits, and clear data-sovereignty terms to ensure that AI systems support cultural continuity rather than undermine it.

Data Sovereignty and Privacy: The use and collection of student data is a central to the ethical concern in all of educational technology, but it also takes on a particular urgency in the context of diaspora communities, who have always historically been subject to exploitation and surveillance. The principle of data sovereignty, which maintain the right of communities to control their own data which has a paramount importance. EdTech companies and education institutions must be transparent about their data practices and also they must obtain meaningful consent from students and their families.

The Risk of "Digital Blackface": In the bound to create culturally relevant content, there is always been a risk of stereotyping and tokenism. "Digital blackface," a term used to describe the use of Black images and the cultural expressions by non-Black people online that serves as a cautionary tale. The creation of culturally responsive AI must be led by members of their communities themselves as well as to ensure that the representations are respectful, authentic and empowering.

The Digital Divide: The promise of AI in education can only be realized if all students have access to the necessary infrastructure and technology. The digital divide, which disproportionately affects rural communities and low income group which remains a significant barrier to equity. Efforts to promote culturally responsive AI must be accompanied by broader efforts that will help in closing digital divide and ensuring that all students have equal opportunity to participate in the digital world.

The Challenge of Scale: Many from the emerging EdTech initiatives that are primarily pioneering culturally responsive approaches which are small and community-based. Without compromising the integrity of such initiatives to reach a wider audience and scaling them is a significant challenge. We must have to find ways to sustain and support these initiatives, while also advocating for change within the mainstream and larger platforms.

Navigating through these ethical challenges will require a strong multi-stakeholder approach, which involves collaboration between developers,educators, policymakers, community leaders, and students themselves. It will also require a commitment to ongoing critical self-reflection, dialogue and a willingness to prioritize equity and justice over efficiency and profit.

CONCLUSION

The convergence of transnational education, artificial intelligence and the lived experiences of diaspora youth represents a critical juncture with a profound implications that strongly suggest for the cultural identity and the future of learning. This chapter insist that AI is not a neutral tool but a powerful force that can either foster cultural continuity or perpetuate cultural erasure. Through a critical examination of mainstream as well as emerging educational platforms has the proposal of the CULTUR-AI framework that we have sought to illuminate as a path forward towards a more culturally and equitable sustaining vision of AI in education.

The analysis based of these platforms like LingQ, Duolingo and Khan Academy. They provide valuable tools for learning as well as they often fall short in addressing the specific linguistic and cultural needs of diaspora youth. Their one-size-fits-all approach are rooted in Western-centric curricula and always dominant by global languages that can be inadvertently contribute to the marginalization of languages and heritage culture. On the contrary, the emerging EdTech initiatives which are born out of community needs offers a commitment to cultural responsiveness, and offers a glimpse of what is possible when technology is designed when justice and equity is kept in mind.

The CULTUR-AI structure provides a set of guiding principles for the development of AI that is community-centred, linguistically diverse, unbiased, empowering, transformative of User agency, and relational. By champion to these principles, we can proceed beyond the current paradigm and create AI-powered learning environments where the diaspora youth can not only thrive culturally but also excel academically.

The journey towards culturally responsive AI is not comes without its challenges. The risk of digital stereotyping, as well as ethical imperatives of data sovereignty. The the difficulty of scaling community-based initiatives and in the persistence of the digital divide. They are all significant hurdles that must be overcome. However, these challenges are not insurmountable with a concerted effort from all stakeholders, developers, educators, communities and policymakers. We can construct a future where AI serves not as a barrier but as a bridge which is connecting diaspora youth to their heritage and empowering them to shape their own educational and cultural futures. The cloud of this provides a vision that becomes not a space of cultural loss, but a vibrant ecosystem where cultural continuity is celebrated and nurtured for generations to come.

FUTURE RESEARCH DIRECTIONS

This chapter has set as the groundwork for a interdisciplinary and critical conversation about AI in the educational futures of diaspora youth. As this field in a process of evolution. It opens several avenues for future research warrant exploration:

Longitudinal Studies: There is a major need for long-term research that will examines the impact of AI on the academic outcomes and cultural identities of diaspora youth. Such studies can also provide valuable insights into the long-term effects of different types of interventions by AI.

Co-Design Research: Much more research is needed to understand the process of co-designing AI with diaspora communities. What are the major effective methods for engaging community members in this designing process? What are the opportunities as well as the challenges of this kind of collaborative work?

Intersectional Analyses: Future research might can explore the intersection of culture with other angle of identity, such as gender, race ability and class in the context of AI in education. How do these intersecting identities construct the experiences of diaspora youth with educational technology?

Policy and Governance: There is an urgent need for research on the governance and policy frameworks that are require to ensure that in education AI is developed and used and developed in an equitable and ethical manner. What role should educational institutions, goverments and EdTech companies play in managing this space?

By engaging these lines of inquiry, we are definitely on the pathways which continue to build a body of knowledge that will reform and inform the development of a more equitable, and culturally sustaining future for all the learners in the digital era.

REFERENCES

Appadurai, A. (1996). *Modernity at large: Cultural dimensions of globalization*. University of Minnesota Press.

Apple, M. W. (2004). *Ideology and curriculum* (3rd ed.). RoutledgeFalmer. DOI: 10.4324/9780203487563

Au, W. (2013). Rethinking multicultural education: Teaching for racial and cultural justice. *Rethinking Schools*.

Baker, T., & Smith, L. (2019). *Educ-AI-tion rebooted? Exploring the future of artificial intelligence in schools and colleges*. Nesta.

Banks, J. A. (2015). *Cultural diversity and education: Foundations, curriculum, and teaching* (6th ed.). Pearson. DOI: 10.4324/9781315622255

Barocas, S., & Selbst, A. D. (2016). Big data's disparate impact. *California Law Review*, *104*(3), 671–732.

Benjamin, R. (2019). *Race after technology: Abolitionist tools for the new Jim code*. Polity Press.

Blikstein, P. (2018). Artificial intelligence and the future of learning: A critical perspective. In *The Cambridge handbook of the learning sciences* (pp. 671–688). Cambridge University Press.

Brah, A. (1996). *Cartographies of diaspora: Contesting identities*. Routledge.

Chandler, M. J., & Lalonde, C. E. (1998). Cultural continuity as a hedge against suicide in Canada's First Nations. *Transcultural Psychiatry*, *35*(2), 191–219. DOI: 10.1177/136346159803500202

Chun, D. (2017). The role of technology in heritage language learning. In *The Routledge handbook of heritage language education* (pp. 378–389). Routledge.

Cohen, R. (1997). *Global diasporas: An introduction*. University of Washington Press. DOI: 10.4324/9780203228920

Crystal, D. (2000). *Language death*. Cambridge University Press. DOI: 10.1017/CBO9781139106856

D'Ignazio, C., & Klein, L. F. (2020). *Data feminism*. The MIT Press. DOI: 10.7551/mitpress/11805.001.0001

Elish, M. C. (2016). The limits of bias in machine learning. *XRDS: Crossroads. The ACM Magazine for Students*, *22*(4), 8–11. DOI: 10.1145/2930880

Eubanks, V. (2018). *Automating inequality: How high-tech tools profile, police, and punish the poor*. St. Martin's Press.

Fishman, J. A. (2001). 300-plus years of heritage language education in the United States. In *The handbook of bilingualism* (pp. 523–536). Blackwell.

Gay, G. (2010). *Culturally responsive teaching: Theory, research, and practice* (2nd ed.). Teachers College Press.

Hall, S. (1990). Cultural identity and diaspora. In *Identity: Community, culture, difference* (pp. 222–237). Lawrence & Wishart.

Holmes, W., Bialik, M., & Fadel, C. (2022). *Artificial Intelligence in Education: Promises and Implications for Teaching and Learning*. Center for Curriculum Redesign.

Ito, M., Gutiérrez, K., Livingstone, S., Penuel, B., Rhodes, J., Salen, K., & Watkins, S. C. (2013). *Connected learning: An agenda for research and design*. Digital Media and Learning Research Hub.

Karim, K. H. (Ed.). (2003). *The media of diaspora*. Routledge. DOI: 10.4324/9780203380642

Ladson-Billings, G. (1995). Toward a theory of culturally relevant pedagogy. *American Educational Research Journal, 32*(3), 465–491. DOI: 10.3102/00028312032003465

Ladson-Billings, G. (2014). Culturally relevant pedagogy 2.0: A.k.a. the remix. *Harvard Educational Review, 84*(1), 74–84. DOI: 10.17763/haer.84.1.p2rj131485484751

Lee, C. D. (2017). An ecological framework for enacting culturally sustaining pedagogy. In *Culturally sustaining pedagogies: Teaching and learning for justice in a changing world* (pp. 261–274). Teachers College Press.

Luckin, R., Holmes, W., Griffiths, M., & Forcier, K. (2016). *Intelligence unleashed: An argument for AI in education*. Pearson.

Nakamura, L. (2008). *Digitizing race: Visual cultures of the Internet*. University of Minnesota Press.

Nieto, S. (2010). *The light in their eyes: Creating multicultural learning communities* (10th anniversary ed.). Teachers College Press.

Noble, S. U. (2018). *Algorithms of oppression: How search engines reinforce racism*. New York University Press. DOI: 10.18574/nyu/9781479833641.001.0001

O'Neil, C. (2016). *Weapons of math destruction: How big data increases inequality and threatens democracy*. Crown.

OECD. (2023). *AI in Education: Policy Brief*. Organisation for Economic Co-operation and Development.

Pane, J. F., Steiner, E. D., Baird, M. D., & Hamilton, L. S. (2015). *Continued Progress: Promising Evidence on Personalized Learning*. RAND Corporation., DOI: 10.7249/RR1365

Paris, D. (2012). Culturally sustaining pedagogy: A needed change in stance, terminology, and practice. *Educational Researcher, 41*(3), 93–97. DOI: 10.3102/0013189X12441244

Paris, D., & Alim, H. S. (Eds.). (2017). *Culturally sustaining pedagogies: Teaching and learning for justice in a changing world*. Teachers College Press.

Pariser, E. (2011). *The filter bubble: What the Internet is hiding from you*. Penguin UK.

Pasquale, F. (2015). *The black box society: The secret algorithms that control money and information*. Harvard University Press. DOI: 10.4159/harvard.9780674736061

Popenici, S. A., & Kerr, S. (2017). Exploring the impact of artificial intelligence on teaching and learning in higher education. *Research and Practice in Technology Enhanced Learning, 12*(1), 22. DOI: 10.1186/s41039-017-0062-8 PMID: 30595727

Portes, A., & Rumbaut, R. G. (2001). *Legacies: The story of the immigrant second generation.* University of California Press.

Rong, X. L., & Preissle, J. (2009). *Educating immigrant students in the 21st century: What educators need to know*. Corwin Press.

Selwyn, N. (2023). *Education in a Digital World.* Routledge.

Siemens, G., & Baker, R. S. (2012). Learning analytics and educational data mining: Towards communication and collaboration. In *Proceedings of the 2nd International Conference on Learning Analytics and Knowledge* (pp. 252–254). DOI: 10.1145/2330601.2330661

Suárez-Orozco, C., Suárez-Orozco, M. M., & Todorova, I. (2008). *Learning a new land: Immigrant students in American society*. Harvard University Press. DOI: 10.4159/9780674044111

Timms, M. J. (2016). Technology and education: What's the connection? *Phi Delta Kappan*, *97*(8), 8–13.

Tsolidis, G. (1997). *Foreigners, Family and the Nation: Greek–Australian Narratives of Belonging.* Oxford University Press.

UNESCO. (2023). *AI and Education: Guidance for Policy-Makers.* UNESCO Publishing.

VanLehn, K. (2011). The relative effectiveness of human tutoring, intelligent tutoring systems, and other tutoring systems. *Educational Psychologist*, *46*(4), 197–221. DOI: 10.1080/00461520.2011.611369

Vertovec, S. (2009). *Transnationalism*. Routledge. DOI: 10.4324/9780203927083

Winner, L. (1980). Do artifacts have politics? *Daedalus*, *109*(1), 121–136.

Woolf, B. P. (2009). *Building intelligent interactive tutors: Student-centered strategies for revolutionizing e-learning*. Morgan Kaufmann.

Chapter 11
Digital Divide:
Equity and Access in AI-Driven Transnational Learning

Pranay Pandey
https://orcid.org/0000-0001-8853-0492
Bhatter College, Dantan, India

ABSTRACT

This chapter critically examines the digital divide within AI-driven transnational learning, emphasizing how technological advancements in education may reinforce existing global inequalities if not guided by equity-focused frameworks. The study explores key dimensions of the divide, including disparities in infrastructure, digital and AI literacy, algorithmic bias, and linguistic exclusion. It analyzes the role of global institutions, national governments, and educational stakeholders in addressing these challenges through inclusive policies, ethical AI governance, and capacity building. The study draws on theoretical frameworks such as the Capability Approach, Critical Pedagogy, and Postcolonial Theory to underscore the systemic nature of digital inequities. Ultimately, it advocates for sustainable, inclusive, and culturally responsive AI integration in education to promote social justice and global learning equity.

1. INTRODUCTION

The integration of artificial intelligence (AI) in education is revolutionizing transnational learning, offering unprecedented opportunities for personalization, scalability, and global academic exchange. However, the expansion of AI has also redefined the digital divide, extending beyond access to devices and connectivity to include disparities in algorithmic participation, digital fluency, and equitable representation. In parallel, transnational education—where learners engage with educational programs across borders—has surged in relevance, driven by globalization and the digital transformation of learning environments. Despite its promise, this model often reflects and reinforces global inequalities, especially in regions lacking AI infrastructure and culturally responsive content. The rationale for this study lies in examining the systemic imbalances that AI-powered transnational education may exacerbate if not guided by principles of inclusion and justice. By critically assessing digital inequities in access, participation, and design, this research advocates for equitable, context-sensitive AI integration in global learning ecosystems to promote meaningful and inclusive education for all.

DOI: 10.4018/979-8-3373-5403-3.ch011

Definition of Digital Divide in the Context of AI-Driven Learning

The digital divide traditionally refers to disparities in access to digital technologies such as computers, internet connectivity, and mobile devices. However, in the age of artificial intelligence (AI), this divide has expanded beyond hardware and connectivity to include access to AI-powered educational tools, algorithmic systems, and digital literacy (Van Dijk, 2020). AI-driven learning involves technologies such as intelligent tutoring systems, learning analytics, and adaptive content delivery that personalize learning experiences. These systems rely on large-scale data and advanced algorithms, which require not only access to infrastructure but also the necessary skills to engage meaningfully with the technology (Luckin, 2018). In this context, the digital divide is not just technological but also cognitive and systemic, encompassing unequal exposure to AI-integrated education, disparities in digital fluency, and limited inclusion in algorithmic design and governance. The AI-specific digital divide introduces ethical and practical concerns, such as biased algorithms that can reinforce existing inequalities or underrepresentation of non-dominant cultures and languages in training datasets (Eubanks, 2018). This emerging landscape demands a critical evaluation of not only *who* accesses AI-driven education but also *how* they interact with it and *whose* interests are being served by such systems. Thus, a nuanced understanding of the digital divide is essential in AI-driven education, where equity of access, participation, and benefit must be ensured globally.

Relevance of Transnational Education in the 21st Century

Transnational education (TNE) refers to educational programs or learning experiences where students are based in a different country than the one offering the qualification (Knight, 2016). In the 21st century, driven by globalization and rapid technological development, TNE has emerged as a key pathway for internationalizing higher education. The digital transformation of learning, further accelerated by the COVID-19 pandemic, has enabled the widespread adoption of online and AI-powered platforms to facilitate cross-border education (Zawacki-Richter et al., 2019). Institutions worldwide are now able to reach learners beyond national borders, offering programs that are accessible remotely via AI-enhanced virtual classrooms and personalized content delivery. However, despite its potential to democratize learning, transnational education often mirrors global inequalities. The benefits of AI-driven TNE are disproportionately enjoyed by learners in technologically advanced regions, while students in the Global South frequently lack the infrastructure or digital fluency to participate equitably. Language, cultural relevance of AI content, and localized access mechanisms remain major challenges. Consequently, if unaddressed, the digital divide within TNE risks reinforcing academic dependency and educational marginalization on a global scale (Altbach & Knight, 2007). Thus, there is an urgent need to align technological expansion with equity-driven educational policies in transnational contexts.

Rationale of the Study

The rationale behind this study stems from the growing concern that AI-driven innovations in education may inadvertently deepen existing disparities unless guided by equity-focused frameworks. While AI is celebrated for its potential to personalize learning and improve student outcomes, access to such technologies remains uneven. According to UNESCO (2021), nearly half of the world's learners lack adequate internet access, making it impossible for them to benefit from AI-powered education platforms.

Additionally, AI systems often reflect the cultural and linguistic biases of their developers, marginalizing underrepresented populations and promoting a one-size-fits-all educational model (Selwyn, 2019). Transnational education, positioned at the intersection of global connectivity and educational mobility, offers a unique lens through which to examine these disparities. However, the unequal distribution of AI resources, data governance structures, and digital competencies poses serious ethical and practical challenges. Addressing these gaps is not only a matter of technological inclusion but of social justice and international solidarity. Therefore, this study is significant in advocating for a reorientation of AI policies, educational practices, and international collaborations toward inclusivity and fairness in transnational learning environments.

2. CONCEPTUAL FRAMEWORK

As AI increasingly shapes global learning environments, it is essential to explore the tools, stakeholders, and theoretical paradigms underpinning this transformation. From intelligent tutoring systems to global MOOCs, AI-driven education promises personalization but also risks deepening existing divide. It draws on the Capability Approach, Critical Pedagogy, and Fraser's Theory of Justice to examine how digital inequalities manifest and persist. This framework highlights the need for inclusive, context-sensitive AI integration in transnational education to foster equitable learning outcomes worldwide.

Understanding AI-Driven Learning: Scope, Technologies, Tools

Artificial Intelligence (AI) has emerged as a transformative force in education, promising personalized learning, enhanced student engagement, and streamlined administrative processes. AI-driven learning refers to educational environments where intelligent systems are used to mimic human cognitive functions such as learning, reasoning, and problem-solving. These environments leverage machine learning algorithms, natural language processing (NLP), and data analytics to tailor educational content, recommend resources, and provide real-time feedback (Luckin, 2018). Key AI technologies in education include Intelligent Tutoring Systems (ITS), Learning Management Systems (LMS) with predictive analytics, automated essay scoring tools, and chatbots for student support (Zawacki-Richter et al., 2019). Adaptive learning platforms like Carnegie Learning and Squirrel AI adjust instructional content in response to a learner's performance, while AI-powered recommendation engines curate personalized learning paths. These tools are instrumental in creating flexible, data-informed, and scalable education systems that address the needs of diverse learners. However, these same systems require robust infrastructure, algorithmic transparency, and high levels of digital competence to function effectively and equitably.

Transnational Learning: Meaning, Modes, Stakeholders

Transnational learning refers to educational activities and programs that transcend national boundaries, often facilitated by online technologies and cross-border institutional partnerships. It includes diverse modes such as online degree programs, offshore campuses, dual degrees, MOOCs (Massive Open Online Courses), and virtual student exchanges (Knight, 2016). The increasing mobility of learners and the internationalization strategies of higher education institutions have contributed to the rapid growth of transnational education (Altbach & Knight, 2007). Stakeholders in transnational learning include students, educators, universities, international regulatory bodies, governments, and private EdTech firms. Students from developing nations often engage in transnational programs to access quality education, while institutions expand their reach to build global presence and revenue streams. International organizations such as UNESCO and the OECD play a regulatory and advocacy role in ensuring quality and equity in cross-border education. However, the expansion of transnational education must be critically examined for its potential to reproduce neo-colonial dynamics, especially when dominant institutions set the epistemological and technological standards (Tikly, 2019).

Digital Equity and Access: Theoretical Perspectives

The issue of digital equity in AI-driven transnational education demands a deeper theoretical engagement. Several frameworks have been proposed to conceptualize the multifaceted nature of digital inequality. Among them, Amartya Sen's Capability Approach provides a compelling lens. Sen (1999) argues that development should be evaluated based on individuals' capabilities—their real freedoms to achieve well-being. In this view, digital access is not merely about the provision of devices or internet connectivity but about enabling learners to meaningfully use technology to enhance their educational agency and potential. For instance, an AI system that only caters to English-speaking learners limits the capabilities of non-English speakers despite formal access. Similarly, Critical Pedagogy, as advocated by Paulo Freire, emphasizes empowerment through education and challenges the structural forces that perpetuate inequality. Applying this to digital learning, critical pedagogy would question whose knowledge is embedded in AI systems, who designs these tools, and whether learners have the agency to question, resist, or shape the technology they use (Freire, 1970; Selwyn, 2011). This theoretical grounding underscores that digital equity is not simply a logistical or technical issue but a deeply political and ethical one. Moreover, Nancy Fraser's Theory of Justice adds a critical dimension by emphasizing redistribution, recognition, and representation as foundational for equity. In AI-driven learning, this means ensuring equitable distribution of digital resources, cultural recognition within educational content and systems, and the inclusion of marginalized voices in AI governance structures (Fraser, 2008). Together, these perspectives challenge techno-deterministic narratives and advocate for inclusive, human-centered technological integration in global education.

Interrelationship among Digital Divide, AI, and Transnational Education

The intersection of the digital divide, AI, and transnational education reveals a complex ecosystem of technological innovation, socio-political asymmetry, and global educational aspiration. AI, as a tool for personalized learning and scalability, has the potential to revolutionize transnational education by making high-quality instruction accessible to remote and underserved learners. However, without equitable access to technology, digital literacy, and localized content, AI risks becoming a vector of exclusion rather than inclusion (UNESCO, 2021). The digital divide manifests not only in infrastructural disparities but also in algorithmic injustice—where the very design of AI systems may reflect the biases of dominant groups. For instance, AI-powered learning platforms predominantly designed by corporations in the Global North may lack contextual sensitivity to learners in the Global South, leading to epistemic marginalization (Eubanks, 2018). In transnational settings, such imbalances can reinforce colonial patterns, where learners are passive recipients of imported knowledge systems rather than co-creators of localized, culturally relevant education.

Transnational education often operates within a neoliberal framework that emphasizes efficiency, scalability, and cost-effectiveness—goals that align well with AI. However, this techno-centric focus can obscure deeper concerns about equity, agency, and justice. Thus, the digital divide in AI-driven transnational education is not merely a digital access problem but a systemic challenge involving technological design, political economy, educational philosophy, and cultural relevance (Selwyn, 2019). Addressing this requires a multi-level strategy involving inclusive policy-making, ethical AI development, capacity-building for digital literacy, and the promotion of open-access, multilingual AI tools. Transnational education, when thoughtfully designed and equitably implemented, has the potential to reduce global learning inequalities. But it must avoid becoming a digitally-mediated extension of existing educational hierarchies. A critical conceptual framework is therefore essential to interrogate the promises and perils of this rapidly evolving landscape.

3. REVIEW OF RELATED LITERATURE

The integration of Artificial Intelligence (AI) in education has opened up new possibilities for personalized learning, predictive analytics, and enhanced educational management. However, its uneven deployment across regions has exacerbated existing digital inequalities, resulting in a persistent digital divide—especially in transnational learning environments (Van Dijk, 2020). The literature presents a multidimensional view of this divide, addressing disparities in infrastructure, data access, algorithmic bias, linguistic marginalization, and the geopolitics of knowledge production.

The foundational aspect of the digital divide lies in access to technological infrastructure. According to the International Telecommunication Union (2023), nearly 2.6 billion people globally remain offline, with a significant portion concentrated in sub-Saharan Africa and South Asia. In the context of AI-driven education, lack of reliable internet access, digital devices, and electricity hampers student engagement and institutional capacity (World Bank, 2021). Graham and Misra (2020) emphasize that teachers in the Global South often struggle with inadequate training and technological tools, further limiting the equitable adoption of AI in classrooms.

The introduction of AI systems in educational assessment and decision-making processes often reproduces societal biases. Binns et al. (2018) and Eubanks (2018) reveal that AI algorithms, while appearing neutral, often reflect structural inequalities embedded in training data. Buolamwini and Gebru's (2018) "Gender Shades" study found that commercial AI systems exhibited racial and gender bias, with significantly lower accuracy for darker-skinned women. Such algorithmic discrimination raises ethical concerns, particularly when these technologies are applied transnationally in diverse cultural contexts. Benjamin (2019) conceptualizes this as the "New Jim Code," wherein automated systems reinforce existing racial hierarchies under the guise of technological objectivity.

A growing body of work critiques the global proliferation of AI as a form of digital colonialism (Adams, 2020; Birhane, 2022). Couldry and Mejias (2019) argue that data extraction from the Global South often serves the commercial interests of tech giants headquartered in the Global North, leading to the erasure of local epistemologies. Freire's (1970) concept of cultural invasion aligns with these critiques, cautioning against externally imposed educational models that suppress indigenous ways of knowing.

Bawa and Kapoor (2023) analyze the Indian context, noting how AI systems designed with Eurocentric pedagogical values fail to engage meaningfully with the country's pluralistic educational needs.

Language plays a critical role in digital inclusion. Joshi et al. (2020) and Pérez et al. (2022) highlight how the dominance of English-centric AI tools marginalizes students from non-Anglophone backgrounds. The lack of support for under-resourced languages in Natural Language Processing (NLP) technologies limits the reach and effectiveness of AI in education. This linguistic exclusion undermines the goal of equitable transnational learning and perpetuates cultural hierarchies. Multilingual AI initiatives, such as UNESCO's efforts in language-inclusive AI (UNESCO, 2021), are essential to address this gap.

Gender disparities in digital access are well-documented, particularly in low-income and rural contexts. UN Women (2021) reported that women are 17% less likely than men to use mobile internet in developing countries. Intersectional studies reveal that this gap widens further for women with intersecting marginalized identities—such as those based on caste, ethnicity, or disability (Gilliard & Culik, 2016). AI tools, unless deliberately designed with inclusivity in mind, risk amplifying these exclusions.

Policy frameworks at national and international levels attempt to regulate AI in education. The UNESCO (2021) "Recommendation on the Ethics of Artificial Intelligence" outlines principles of inclusivity, fairness, and sustainability. Similarly, the OECD (2021) emphasizes capability-based assessments to align AI implementation with equitable outcomes. However, these global guidelines often lack binding authority, and local adaptations remain inconsistent. NITI Aayog's (2018), AIforAll strategy in India attempts to bridge the AI access gap, yet scholars critique it for being more techno-centric than people-centric (Kemp, 2021).

The Universal Design for Learning (UDL) framework offers pedagogical pathways for inclusion in AI-driven classrooms. Developed by CAST (2018), UDL promotes flexible learning environments that accommodate individual learning differences. When integrated with AI systems, UDL principles can enable dynamic personalization that caters to students with varied linguistic, cognitive, and socio-economic backgrounds (Holmes et al., 2022).

Altbach and Knight (2007) and Knight (2016) analyze how transnational education is often shaped by power imbalances between educational providers in the Global North and recipients in the Global South. This asymmetry becomes more pronounced when AI-driven platforms, curricula, and certifications are imported without local contextualization. Selwyn (2021) warns against techno-solutionism and calls for critical engagement with AI systems in education. The literature highlights that while AI holds transformative potential in transnational learning, its current deployment is entangled in structural inequities. Addressing the digital divide requires not only technological infrastructure but also ethical design, linguistic inclusion, policy coherence, and cultural responsiveness.

4. DIMENSIONS OF THE DIGITAL DIVIDE

The digital divide is no longer confined to mere access to the internet or devices; it has evolved into a complex, multi-dimensional challenge that influences who can benefit from AI-driven transnational learning. As technology becomes increasingly embedded in education systems worldwide, disparities in access, skills, usage, content quality, and AI design amplify existing social inequalities. These dimensions go beyond infrastructure and reveal deeper socio-cultural, economic, and ethical issues. Understanding the varied aspects of the digital divide is crucial for creating inclusive digital education strategies that ensure no learner is left behind.

Access Divide: Hardware, Internet Connectivity, Devices

The most immediate and visible aspect of the digital divide lies in unequal access to technological infrastructure. Access to hardware such as computers, smartphones, and tablets, as well as stable internet connectivity, remains a primary barrier for marginalized populations, particularly in developing countries and rural areas. Despite global growth in internet penetration, significant gaps persist; for example, as of 2023, nearly 2.6 billion people globally remained offline (International Telecommunication Union [ITU], 2023). Many schools in low-income nations still lack basic computer labs or Wi-Fi, severely restricting students' ability to participate in AI-driven or digital learning. The affordability of devices also plays a critical role. A study by World Bank (2021) revealed that in many low-income regions, the cost of a basic laptop equates to over two months of household income, highlighting economic exclusion. Furthermore, bandwidth disparities exacerbate the issue—while urban regions may enjoy high-speed broadband, rural and remote areas often rely on limited or unreliable mobile networks (UNESCO, 2020).

Skills Divide: Digital Literacy, AI Literacy, Critical Thinking

Beyond physical access, the skills divide delineates those who possess the digital and AI-related competencies necessary for meaningful engagement from those who do not. Digital literacy encompasses basic skills like navigating the internet, using software applications, and engaging in online communication, while AI literacy includes understanding algorithmic functions, data privacy, and ethical use of technology. According to van Dijk (2020), digital skills are stratified into operational, informational, and strategic levels, with marginalized populations often lacking higher-order skills such as evaluation and problem-solving. In the context of AI, the gap deepens, as AI literacy is not yet part of mainstream curricula, especially in under-resourced educational systems. The absence of structured AI education limits individuals' ability to critically assess algorithmic decisions or utilize AI tools effectively (Long & Magerko, 2020). Moreover, the skills divide is gendered and age-sensitive; women, the elderly, and persons with disabilities face distinct barriers to acquiring technical fluency (UN Women, 2021).

Usage Divide: Differences in Meaningful Use of Technology

Even when access and skills are ensured, the usage divide marks the discrepancy in how people utilize digital tools for developmental or educational purposes. Research suggests that individuals from privileged backgrounds are more likely to engage in "capital-enhancing" uses of technology—such as online learning, networking, or job applications—while marginalized users often engage in entertainment or passive consumption (Hargittai & Hsieh, 2013). This divide becomes particularly problematic in AI-driven transnational learning contexts, where meaningful use of platforms like intelligent tutoring systems, MOOCs, or adaptive assessments requires a certain level of prior exposure and confidence. The disparity is influenced by factors such as language barriers, perceived self-efficacy, and the presence of supportive learning environments (Selwyn, 2016). The educational advantage gained from such meaningful use further amplifies socioeconomic inequalities, reproducing existing patterns of privilege and exclusion.

Quality Divide: Availability of Culturally Relevant, Localized AI Content

The quality divide reflects the unequal availability of culturally responsive and localized content within digital and AI educational systems. While AI technologies often promise personalization, most systems are trained on data predominantly derived from Western, English-speaking contexts (Bender et al., 2021). This limits their effectiveness and relevance for learners in the Global South. For example, natural language processing (NLP) systems often perform poorly in under-resourced languages, leading to reduced functionality and learning outcomes for speakers of those languages (Joshi et al., 2020). The absence of localized datasets and culturally adaptive AI tools means that students are frequently exposed to content that is misaligned with their socio-cultural context, resulting in a disconnect between learning material and learners' lived realities. Moreover, the lack of inclusivity in content design can perpetuate cultural imperialism, thereby undermining local knowledge systems and indigenous epistemologies (Nissenbaum, 2001). Addressing this requires participatory design approaches and investments in regional AI research.

AI-Specific Divide: Bias in Algorithms, Unequal Data Representation

A rapidly emerging facet of the digital divide is the AI-specific divide, which stems from algorithmic bias and unequal data representation. AI systems are only as good as the data they are trained on, and this data is often skewed toward majority populations—frequently white, male, and affluent—leading to systemic bias against marginalized groups (Eubanks, 2018). For instance, facial recognition algorithms have shown lower accuracy in identifying people with darker skin tones due to underrepresentation in training datasets (Buolamwini & Gebru, 2018). In educational AI, this manifests in biased prediction systems that may inaccurately assess student potential based on incomplete or skewed data. Such disparities pose serious ethical concerns in transnational learning environments, where decisions about learners' performance, engagement, or even admissions may be informed by flawed algorithms. Furthermore, transparency in AI decision-making is often lacking, preventing marginalized users from challenging or understanding the basis of these outcomes (Veale & Binns, 2017). Bridging this divide requires not just better data governance but also inclusive AI policy frameworks.

5. GLOBAL INEQUALITIES IN AI-DRIVEN EDUCATION

As artificial intelligence rapidly transforms educational landscapes, it simultaneously magnifies global inequalities, particularly between the Global North and South. While technologically advanced nations benefit from cutting-edge AI tools, vast sections of the world remain under-resourced and underrepresented in this digital shift. AI-driven education is not merely a question of access, but of equitable implementation—where economic capacity, supportive policies, linguistic diversity, and teacher readiness all play critical roles. Countries with robust digital infrastructures and strategic investments in AI education are shaping global narratives and innovation, whereas others struggle with basic connectivity, outdated curricula, and limited training opportunities.

Economic Disparities: Global North vs. Global South

AI-driven education has widened the gap between the Global North and Global South, primarily due to stark economic disparities. Countries in the Global North possess the financial, technological, and human resources to experiment with and implement advanced EdTech and AI-powered learning environments. In contrast, many Global South countries struggle to meet even the basic digital infrastructure requirements for AI integration in schools and universities. According to the World Bank (2022), high-income countries spend approximately $8,500 per student annually, compared to less than $1,000 in many low-income countries. This difference translates into unequal access to AI tools, computing infrastructure, data storage, and technical expertise.

Moreover, private companies that develop and dominate AI in education—mostly based in the Global North—design products suited to their contexts, inadvertently marginalizing low-income users. The economic gap also manifests in R&D spending. While the U.S. and China dominate AI research output, sub-Saharan Africa accounts for less than 1% of global AI research publications (Nature Index, 2021). Without sufficient investments and subsidies, the Global South risks becoming perpetual consumers of imported AI solutions rather than co-creators or innovators. This structural dependence could exacerbate educational dependency and digital colonialism (Adams, 2020).

Policy and Infrastructure: Government Investments in AI and EdTech

Government policies and public investment are critical for the equitable expansion of AI-driven education. Countries such as South Korea, Finland, and Singapore have embedded AI literacy and infrastructure investment into their national education strategies. For instance, Singapore's "AI for Everyone" initiative includes AI curriculum integration at school levels and free community workshops (Smart Nation, 2020). In contrast, many developing nations lack comprehensive AI policies, and when such policies exist, they are often poorly funded or implemented inconsistently.

For example, while India launched the National AI Strategy (NITI Aayog, 2018), its execution in public education remains minimal due to limited inter-ministerial coordination and digital infrastructure gaps. A 2021 UNESCO report noted that fewer than 40% of low-income countries had digital education policies that explicitly included AI. Inadequate internet penetration, poor school connectivity, and outdated hardware further limit the impact of even well-intentioned policies in these regions (UNESCO, 2021). Furthermore, regional inequalities within countries—such as rural versus urban differences—compound the issue. Without sustained investment and international cooperation, developing nations may continue to lag in adopting AI responsibly and inclusively in education.

Language Barriers and Cultural Biases in AI Learning Systems

Most AI-powered educational tools are designed in English or other dominant languages, creating significant barriers for non-native speakers and linguistically diverse populations. Natural Language Processing (NLP) models like GPT, BERT, and others perform exceptionally in high-resource languages but poorly in low-resource or regional tongues (Joshi et al., 2020). This linguistic bias limits the utility of AI in large parts of Africa, Latin America, and Asia, where hundreds of indigenous and regional languages remain unsupported. Cultural biases embedded in AI algorithms also pose significant challenges. Educational content generated or recommended by AI often reflects Western epistemologies, values, and assumptions. Such systems may fail to accommodate indigenous knowledge systems, religious norms, or socio-cultural contexts of learners in the Global South. For example, recommendation algorithms used in adaptive learning platforms may overlook culturally relevant texts or learning styles, leading to a misalignment between content and context (Bender et al., 2021).

Regional Differences in Teacher Preparedness and Curriculum Inclusion

Teachers are at the frontline of AI integration in education, yet there are stark regional disparities in their preparedness and training. In developed countries, educators are increasingly receiving formal training in EdTech and AI pedagogy. For instance, the EU-funded "AI4Teachers" initiative offers AI teaching resources and workshops to enhance digital teaching practices in European schools (European Commission, 2023). In contrast, teachers in many developing regions often lack access to even basic digital training, let alone AI-specific instruction. A survey by UNESCO (2022) indicated that fewer than 30% of teachers in low-income countries feel confident using advanced digital tools, and the number is even lower when it comes to AI technologies. The absence of AI-related content in teacher education programs further limits their ability to adapt. Even when professional development is available, high student–teacher ratios, lack of technological resources, and excessive workloads restrict the time and opportunity for educators to experiment with new tools (Graham & Misra, 2020). Curriculum inclusion of AI concepts also varies widely. While countries like China and Estonia have included AI literacy in K–12 curricula, most developing nations are yet to address it at any level of schooling. This uneven integration creates a knowledge and competence gap among students across regions, further entrenching global learning inequalities.

6. BARRIERS TO EQUITY IN TRANSNATIONAL AI EDUCATION

Transnational AI education holds immense potential to bridge educational gaps, democratize learning, and foster global collaboration. However, this promise remains unfulfilled for many due to persistent barriers that obstruct equitable participation. These challenges are not limited to economic inequality or device access alone but are deeply embedded in structural, technological, legal, and ethical domains. From infrastructure disparities between urban and rural regions to the surveillance risks embedded in AI platforms, these issues disproportionately impact learners in marginalized and underrepresented communities. Furthermore, restrictive intellectual property frameworks and the commercialization of AI tools limit open access, especially in developing regions. Ethical dilemmas also arise with AI-driven assessments and tutoring systems, which may reinforce bias and overlook human nuance.

Infrastructure Gaps (Rural vs. Urban, Developing vs. Developed Nations)

One of the most fundamental barriers to equitable AI-driven education is the persistent global digital infrastructure divide. Rural and remote areas, particularly in developing nations, continue to suffer from low internet penetration, unreliable electricity, and inadequate technological resources. According to the International Telecommunication Union (ITU, 2022), only 34% of rural households worldwide have internet access, compared to 82% in urban areas. These disparities create a bottleneck for AI tools that rely heavily on real-time connectivity, cloud computing, and updated software. Developed nations benefit from high-speed broadband, 5G networks, and widespread device penetration, enabling smoother integration of AI in classrooms. In contrast, many schools in low-income countries lack even basic computer labs. As a result, AI-based educational platforms, adaptive learning systems, and data-driven assessments become inaccessible or dysfunctional in low-resource settings (UNESCO, 2021). This urban–rural divide often reflects deeper socio-economic inequalities, with marginalized communities being further excluded from digital transformation. Without strategic investment in rural ICT infrastructure, equitable participation in transnational AI education remains a distant goal.

Data Privacy and Surveillance Concerns

AI systems in education collect vast amounts of data—ranging from academic performance to biometric identifiers—to personalize learning experiences. However, in the absence of strong regulatory frameworks, this data collection raises serious concerns about student privacy, consent, and digital surveillance. The European Union's General Data Protection Regulation (GDPR) provides some safeguards, but most countries, particularly in the Global South, lack robust legal protections for learners (Kemp, 2021). In transnational AI learning environments, data is often stored across borders, making jurisdictional enforcement difficult. Commercial EdTech platforms operating globally may prioritize profit over ethical data handling. For instance, facial recognition software used for remote proctoring has been criticized for intrusive surveillance and racial bias (Whittaker et al., 2021). Moreover, students and teachers are rarely informed about how their data is used, shared, or monetized. These practices disproportionately affect vulnerable populations, who may be compelled to surrender privacy rights in exchange for access. A rights-based, transparent, and localized data governance framework is essential to protect learners' dignity and autonomy in AI-driven education.

Intellectual Property and Open Access to AI Resources

Access to AI resources, tools, and training materials is essential for equitable participation in transnational learning. However, intellectual property (IP) laws and proprietary software licenses often restrict access, particularly for educators and institutions in the Global South. Most advanced AI models—like OpenAI's GPT or Google's PaLM—are developed by private entities with limited open access, creating an AI knowledge monopoly (Birhane, 2022). While open-source alternatives exist, they are often underfunded, lack localization, or require high levels of technical expertise. Furthermore, many AI tools are available only in dominant languages and are not accompanied by openly licensed educational content. This exclusivity hinders low-income regions from customizing or developing contextually relevant solutions. The current IP regime also discourages collaborative innovation. Universities and research institutions in developing countries face challenges in accessing AI research repositories and datasets due to paywalls or licensing restrictions. Promoting open access policies and equitable licensing frameworks is vital to ensure AI education benefits are distributed globally.

7. ROLE OF GOVERNMENTS, NGOS, AND INTERNATIONAL BODIES

In the rapidly evolving digital age, the integration of Artificial Intelligence (AI) into education holds the potential to transform learning environments across the globe. However, disparities in access to digital tools and technologies have given rise to the "digital divide," particularly in transnational education. Bridging this gap requires collective action from multiple stakeholders, including governments, non-governmental organizations (NGOs), and international bodies. These entities play a critical role in ensuring that AI-powered educational opportunities are equitable and inclusive. Through targeted policies, global initiatives, and technological innovation, they address infrastructure gaps, affordability challenges, and socio-cultural barriers. Moreover, open-source and low-cost AI solutions developed through collaborative partnerships further support underserved communities.

Policies to Promote Digital Inclusion

Governments are pivotal in shaping the infrastructure and policy frameworks necessary to facilitate digital inclusion in AI-enhanced education. Many nations have initiated comprehensive strategies to integrate digital technologies into the educational system, recognizing education as a fundamental right in the digital age. Countries like India, through its National Education Policy 2020, promote the use of digital platforms like SWAYAM and DIKSHA to democratize access to quality education, particularly in remote and rural areas. Similarly, Kenya's National ICT Master Plan and Estonia's digital education policy framework emphasize teacher training, infrastructure enhancement, and student digital literacy to minimize inequalities (UNESCO, 2021a). Moreover, governments are increasingly investing in digital infrastructure, especially broadband connectivity and affordable devices. For example, the United States' Digital Equity Act aims to fund local digital inclusion programs that address specific community needs (U.S. Department of Commerce, 2022). These policies often target marginalized populations including women, the differently abled, and indigenous groups to ensure broader inclusion. Another notable example is Rwanda's partnership with the African Union and private firms to develop AI-based learning platforms while also strengthening the national ICT backbone. Similarly, China's Education Informatization Plan 2.0 integrates AI-driven smart classrooms in rural regions to reduce disparities between urban and rural education standards.

However, challenges remain in terms of policy implementation, budget constraints, and alignment with local contexts. For these policies to be effective, they must be inclusive, data-driven, and continuously updated in response to technological advancements. Policy frameworks aimed at digital inclusion set the foundation for broader access to AI-driven education. They serve as enablers that governments use to dismantle systemic barriers and foster equitable access, ensuring that no learner is left behind in the AI revolution.

Open-Source and Low-Cost AI Solutions

A significant barrier to equitable AI-driven education is the high cost and proprietary nature of many AI tools. To overcome this, open-source and low-cost AI solutions have emerged as viable alternatives that promote inclusivity and innovation, particularly in underserved regions. Open-source platforms like TensorFlow, OpenAI's ChatGPT APIs (in educational access programs), and tools like Moodle or Khan Academy have revolutionized digital learning. These tools offer cost-effective, scalable, and adaptable resources for educators and learners worldwide. For instance, the African Institute for Mathematical Sciences (AIMS) has collaborated with open-source platforms to design low-cost AI courses for African students with limited resources. In India, IIT Bombay developed an open-source AI-based adaptive learning tool called Bodh, which adjusts instructional content based on individual learner performance.

Similarly, organizations like AI4D Africa, funded by IDRC and GIZ, promote open datasets and AI solutions tailored to African educational needs. Low-cost AI applications are also being used for voice-to-text translation, sign language recognition, and personalized learning interfaces, making education more accessible for students with disabilities or those who speak minority languages. An example is Microsoft's AI for Accessibility program, which offers funding for projects that use AI to improve learning outcomes for the differently-abled. These initiatives often operate in collaboration with local universities, NGOs, and government bodies to ensure contextual relevance and user-centered design. Moreover, cloud-based platforms like Google for Education provide cost-effective access to AI-driven tools like adaptive quizzes and real-time collaboration for schools in low-resource settings. In essence, the growing ecosystem of open-source and affordable AI solutions democratizes access to cutting-edge educational technologies. By removing financial and proprietary barriers, they empower educators and learners alike, especially in resource-constrained environments.

Role of Non-Profits in Bridging the Access Gap

Non-governmental organizations (NGOs) and non-profits serve as vital intermediaries in bridging the digital divide by addressing issues of affordability, accessibility, and awareness in AI-driven education. Their on-ground presence and community engagement enable them to design context-sensitive programs that directly benefit underserved populations. Organizations such as Pratham in India use low-cost digital tools to deliver AI-enabled learning in rural areas. Their Hybrid Learning Program integrates AI-based diagnostics to tailor content for each student, improving engagement and outcomes. Likewise, Bridge International Academies leverage data-driven AI technologies to monitor learning progress and teacher effectiveness in low-income communities across Africa and Asia. In Latin America, Laboratoria offers AI-based tech training for women from low-income backgrounds, thereby addressing both gender and economic disparities in digital access. Similarly, One Laptop Per Child and Code.org run programs globally that combine affordable hardware with AI-infused curricula to build foundational digital and cognitive skills. Non-profits also play a critical advocacy role by pushing for digital rights, inclusive policies, and ethical AI use. For example, the Center for Digital Inclusion campaigns for equitable internet access while developing AI literacy training programs for marginalized youth in Brazil. Additionally, partnerships between NGOs and ed-tech companies—such as UNICEF's collaboration with Microsoft and Learning Equality—have produced offline-compatible AI platforms to support refugee and disaster-affected learners. These initiatives are especially crucial in transnational education settings where infrastructure is fragile. Therefore, non-profits contribute significantly not only in delivering educational content but also in shaping inclusive digital ecosystems. Their community-based approaches, combined with a strong focus on equity and empowerment, make them indispensable players in the global movement toward digital inclusion in AI education.

Governments, international organizations, and NGOs each bring unique strengths to the collective mission of digital inclusion in AI-enhanced education. Through comprehensive policies, ethical guidelines, open-source innovations, and grassroots engagement, they tackle the structural, financial, and technological barriers to equitable access. As AI continues to reshape the educational landscape, a collaborative, multi-stakeholder approach becomes essential to ensure no learner is excluded. Only through such concerted efforts can we achieve the promise of truly inclusive, AI-driven transnational education.

8. INSTITUTIONAL RESPONSES AND PEDAGOGICAL INNOVATIONS

As artificial intelligence (AI) increasingly permeates educational landscapes, institutions worldwide are responding with strategic pedagogical innovations and structural reforms. These responses aim to harness AI's potential for improved efficiency, personalized learning, and inclusion while ensuring equitable access to digital tools and content. Central to these transformations are AI-integrated Learning Management Systems (LMSs), educator preparedness, inclusive curriculum designs, and frameworks that center pedagogical equity. The shift reflects a move from reactive to proactive educational planning, grounded in both technological competency and ethical responsibility. Institutions must balance innovation with equity, ensuring that the digital revolution in education does not exacerbate existing disparities but instead narrows the digital divide.

AI-Integrated Learning Management Systems

One of the most transformative institutional responses to the digital age is the integration of AI into Learning Management Systems (LMSs). These platforms, such as Moodle with AI plugins or Canvas enhanced with predictive analytics, utilize machine learning algorithms to personalize content delivery, track student engagement, and identify at-risk learners early (Zawacki-Richter et al., 2019). AI-integrated LMSs analyze real-time data to adaptively suggest resources, schedule reminders, and even tailor assessments, thus fostering a more individualized learning path. The use of AI in LMSs also promotes institutional scalability. For example, chatbots and virtual teaching assistants integrated within LMS environments can respond to student queries 24/7, thus reducing faculty workload while maintaining support systems. AI can also aid in the automated grading of objective assessments, freeing up educators to focus on higher-order instructional tasks. Moreover, these systems can support equity if designed mindfully. Adaptive learning pathways can cater to diverse linguistic, cognitive, and accessibility needs, especially when combined with multilingual interfaces, screen readers, and real-time feedback mechanisms (Holmes et al., 2022). However, poorly designed LMSs can reinforce exclusion, especially if students lack digital literacy or access to the required infrastructure. Hence, institutions must not only implement AI-driven LMSs but also evaluate their efficacy across diverse learner demographics. Thus, institutional investment in AI-integrated LMSs must be paired with policy oversight to ensure that such systems genuinely serve equity, accessibility, and pedagogical flexibility, rather than simply operational efficiency.

Teacher Training and AI Readiness

Effective integration of AI into pedagogy is heavily dependent on teacher preparedness. Institutional responses have increasingly included robust professional development programs to cultivate AI literacy among educators. Teachers are not only facilitators but critical agents in determining how AI tools are implemented in classrooms. Without sufficient training, even the most sophisticated AI systems may be underutilized or misapplied (Luckin et al., 2016). AI readiness involves understanding the functionalities, ethical concerns, and pedagogical implications of AI systems. Training must extend beyond technical skills to include data literacy, bias recognition, and student privacy awareness. For example, UNESCO (2021) emphasizes that teachers must understand the implications of AI surveillance, algorithmic bias, and data protection while using AI-enabled tools. Professional development must be contextually relevant. Educators in underserved or rural regions may need foundational ICT training before engaging with more advanced AI tools. Institutional programs should therefore be tiered, offering differentiated training that responds to varying levels of digital familiarity. Further, teacher training should encourage critical reflection on AI. Rather than accepting AI systems as neutral, teachers should be encouraged to interrogate how algorithmic decisions are made and who benefits from them. Such critical pedagogy empowers teachers to act as gatekeepers of ethical AI usage. Institutions must also foster communities of practice where educators can collaboratively explore AI tools, share pedagogical innovations, and voice challenges. This helps build collective capacity and sustains long-term engagement with AI integration. Importantly, institutional support must include time allowances, incentives, and leadership backing to ensure that professional development is not just a one-time event but an embedded practice. Institutions play a vital role in creating a teacher workforce that is not only AI-competent but also pedagogically reflective and ethically grounded in their use of AI in classrooms.

Designing Inclusive AI Curricula

Another key institutional response to the digital transformation of education is the design of inclusive AI curricula. Curricula that integrate AI literacy equip students with the necessary cognitive, social, and digital competencies to navigate and critically engage with AI-infused environments. More than coding or robotics, AI-inclusive curricula must address themes of data justice, ethics, human-AI collaboration, and critical media literacy (Touretzky et al., 2019). Institutions must ensure that AI curriculum design avoids elitism and instead incorporates differentiated learning pathways suited for students from various socio-economic backgrounds. For example, open-access learning modules and low-tech AI simulations can help make AI learning more accessible in low-resource settings. An inclusive AI curriculum should be multidisciplinary, integrating humanities and social sciences perspectives with technical content. This ensures students understand not only how AI works but also its societal implications. For instance, understanding how recommendation algorithms shape social media experiences can be a powerful entry point into algorithmic thinking for students from non-STEM backgrounds. Curriculum design must also be culturally responsive. AI content should be framed using locally relevant examples and languages. Moreover, ethical debates and AI use-cases in the curriculum should reflect global South perspectives, not merely replicate Western narratives. Importantly, inclusive curricula must also prepare students to become co-creators, not just consumers of AI. Encouraging students to develop AI tools for social good fosters empowerment and equity. Platforms like MIT's "AI + Ethics Curriculum for Middle School" exemplify how curriculum design can balance technical literacy with ethical and social dimensions. Finally, institutions must regularly evaluate curricula through the lens of inclusivity. This includes assessing whether AI content aligns with students' realities, promotes critical engagement, and reduces digital skill disparities. Curriculum audits involving student feedback, accessibility reviews, and diversity metrics can guide iterative improvement. Hence, institutional commitment to inclusive AI curricula is foundational to preparing a generation that can both critically understand and equitably shape the AI-driven world.

Equity-Driven Pedagogical Models

To bridge digital and educational divides in the age of AI, institutions are increasingly exploring conceptual pedagogical models grounded in equity and inclusion. These models shift the focus from mere access to meaningful participation. One such model is the Universal Design for Learning (UDL), which advocates for flexible learning environments that accommodate diverse learners through multiple means of representation, engagement, and expression (CAST, 2018). UDL aligns well with AI-powered systems that adapt content and assessments based on individual learner profiles. Another relevant model is Culturally Sustaining Pedagogy, which emphasizes the incorporation of learners' cultural identities and knowledge systems into curriculum and instruction (Paris & Alim, 2017). AI tools guided by this model can be designed to support multilingual content, context-sensitive instruction, and locally grounded examples. Critical Pedagogy, inspired by Paulo Freire, challenges the neutrality of technology and encourages learners and educators to question AI systems' underlying ideologies and power dynamics. It promotes dialogic learning and co-creation, values that align with democratic uses of AI in education. Institutional pedagogy must therefore not only adopt technological tools but embed them within models that prioritize social justice, student agency, and epistemic diversity. These models offer conceptual scaffolding to ensure AI is a tool for liberation rather than exclusion.

9. ETHICAL AND PHILOSOPHICAL CONCERNS

As artificial intelligence (AI) reshapes the contours of global education, critical ethical and philosophical questions have surfaced. Beyond access and infrastructure, the deeper issues concern who creates, controls, and benefits from AI technologies. Concepts such as digital colonialism, algorithmic bias, and power asymmetries raise urgent concerns about how AI may perpetuate existing inequalities under the guise of innovation. At stake is not only equitable access to AI-driven education but also the fairness, transparency, and accountability of its mechanisms. Furthermore, the automation of decision-making in educational systems—ranging from grading to personalized learning—challenges traditional human-centered values in pedagogy.

Digital Colonialism and Algorithmic Oppression

Digital colonialism refers to the extension of historical patterns of domination into the digital realm, where powerful tech corporations—mostly based in the Global North—control the infrastructures, data flows, and algorithms that increasingly shape life in the Global South (Couldry & Mejias, 2019). In education, this manifests through the deployment of AI tools developed in Western contexts, often with little regard for local cultures, languages, pedagogies, or ethical norms. These systems frequently embed algorithmic oppression, a term coined by Noble (2018) to describe how search engines, recommendation systems, and automated tools can reinforce racial, gender, and cultural biases. For instance, AI-based proctoring software has been shown to misidentify students with darker skin tones, thus unfairly penalizing them (Benjamin, 2019). Such biases, often coded into the algorithms during training on skewed datasets, have real consequences for students' educational opportunities and self-perception. In many low-income or postcolonial contexts, AI in education is introduced as a developmental aid, without corresponding capacity-building. This fosters dependency on foreign platforms and epistemologies, mirroring past colonial dynamics where indigenous knowledge systems were marginalized. Furthermore, AI tools are rarely open source, limiting local innovation and adaptation. To resist digital colonialism, educational institutions and governments must prioritize technological sovereignty—the right to control and develop context-sensitive digital infrastructures. Open educational resources, locally trained AI models, and inclusive datasets are essential counter-strategies. Without this, AI in education risks becoming a vehicle for neo-colonial control masked as digital progress.

Ethics of AI Decision-Making in Education

AI-driven decision-making in education presents a spectrum of ethical challenges. Whether it's in predictive analytics to identify students at risk, automated grading, or personalized content delivery, AI systems often make decisions that impact student outcomes without human intervention or transparency (Eynon, 2021). This raises serious concerns about fairness, accountability, and explainability. One major concern is bias in data and algorithms. AI tools are only as fair as the data they are trained on. If training datasets reflect existing societal inequalities—such as race, gender, or class biases—AI can replicate or even amplify them. In automated essay scoring systems, for instance, language patterns associated with non-native English speakers or certain dialects may be undervalued, leading to unfair assessment (Binns et al., 2018). Another issue is opacity. Many AI systems used in education are "black-box" models, meaning that even their developers may not fully understand how a particular output is generated. This makes it difficult for students or educators to challenge or appeal AI decisions. When a student is flagged as "at risk" or receives a lower grade from an AI tool, they are often given no explanation or recourse. Ethically, decision-making in education must be transparent, justifiable, and contestable. This means incorporating mechanisms for human oversight, ensuring that teachers can override AI recommendations when necessary. Educational AI systems should be designed with built-in audits and documentation that allow users to understand the basis of decisions.

Moreover, consent is crucial. Students and educators must be informed about how their data is used, what decisions are made by AI, and how to opt out if desired. Ethical design in educational AI must center user agency, data privacy, and the right to redress.

The Human Element in AI-Mediated Pedagogy

Amid rapid AI integration, the irreplaceable value of the human element in education must be re-asserted. Teaching is not merely the delivery of information but an ethical, emotional, and relational practice. Empathy, moral guidance, cultural sensitivity, and dialogic learning are human capacities that AI cannot replicate. While AI can support personalization, it lacks the ability to foster transformative learning relationships (Selwyn, 2019). AI may recommend content or track engagement, but it cannot perceive the nuances of a student's motivation, home life, or unspoken struggles. Teachers serve as moral agents who make holistic judgments, often informed by values rather than data alone. Philosophically, reducing pedagogy to algorithmic functions risks instrumentalizing education, making it transactional rather than transformative. Therefore, AI should augment—not replace—human educators. A balanced model emphasizes human-AI collaboration, where technology enhances but does not dictate pedagogy.

10. CONCLUSION

The evolution of Artificial Intelligence (AI) in the educational landscape has introduced transformative possibilities for transnational learning. However, it has simultaneously exposed and exacerbated existing digital inequalities. This paper has explored the multi-layered dimensions of the digital divide in AI-mediated education, including infrastructure disparities, linguistic exclusions, algorithmic biases, and inequitable access to AI resources. A comprehensive review of theoretical frameworks—such as the Capability Approach, Critical Pedagogy, and Postcolonial Theory—has illuminated how structural inequalities intersect with emerging technologies to hinder fair participation in AI-based learning environments. One of the paper's most prominent insights is the disproportionate distribution of digital infrastructure and AI-driven educational tools between the Global North and Global South. While developed countries increasingly deploy AI-integrated learning management systems, intelligent tutoring platforms, and predictive analytics, learners in low-income regions struggle with unreliable connectivity, lack of devices, and limited access to high-quality digital content. This inequity reinforces a cycle of educational disadvantage that AI was supposed to disrupt, not deepen. Another significant insight centers on the ethical and philosophical concerns tied to AI in education. From algorithmic surveillance and data colonialism to the loss of human agency in pedagogical decision-making, the deployment of AI systems raises serious questions about whose knowledge counts, who benefits, and who is left behind. The dominance of English-language AI models and Western-centric content further alienates learners from diverse linguistic and cultural backgrounds, contradicting the ideals of inclusive and pluralistic education.

Institutional responses have been varied but generally fragmented. While some governments and universities are piloting inclusive AI strategies, many efforts remain localized, underfunded, and disconnected from broader policy frameworks. Pedagogical innovations using AI, such as adaptive learning platforms and virtual classrooms, show promise but often lack critical reflection on equity, inclusivity, and long-term sustainability. Furthermore, the role of global actors—such as UNESCO, OECD, World Bank, and grassroots NGOs—has been crucial in advocating for open-source AI tools, ethical frameworks, and equitable policy interventions. Nevertheless, the gap between policy articulation and practical implementation remains substantial, especially in marginalised communities where digital literacy is low and AI technologies are either absent or misapplied.

As we stand at the crossroads of technological advancement and educational transformation, the urgency to foster global solidarity in equitable AI education cannot be overstated. The digital divide is no longer just a technological or economic issue—it is a matter of epistemic justice, human rights, and sustainable development. Addressing it requires a paradigmatic shift from fragmented, market-driven AI implementation to a holistic, rights-based, and context-sensitive approach.

First, multilateral cooperation is essential. Global organizations must transcend rhetoric and invest in inclusive AI ecosystems that prioritize underrepresented regions. This includes co-developing curricula with local educators, promoting open-source platforms in indigenous languages, and creating transnational funds dedicated to AI equity in education.

Second, cross-sectoral alliances must be forged among governments, tech companies, civil society, and academic institutions. These coalitions can co-create ethical AI frameworks that safeguard data privacy, prevent algorithmic discrimination, and ensure that AI tools are aligned with culturally relevant pedagogies. Tech developers, in particular, must be held accountable for embedding fairness, transparency, and explainability into educational AI models.

Third, grassroots empowerment should be central to any solution. Communities must be equipped not only with digital infrastructure but also with the critical capacity to evaluate, adapt, and co-design AI tools. Learners, especially from marginalized backgrounds, should be engaged as active agents in shaping their digital futures—not passive recipients of distant innovations.

Fourth, intercultural dialogue and epistemic inclusion must guide AI education policies. The dominance of Eurocentric models must give way to pluralistic frameworks that honor diverse worldviews, languages, and knowledge systems. This includes funding indigenous AI research, supporting multilingual NLP models, and promoting inclusive digital storytelling.

Finally, a global ethic of care and responsibility must underpin all AI initiatives in education. Equity is not merely about access to devices or content—it is about creating humane, relational, and just learning environments where all students can thrive. AI should serve as a tool to amplify human potential, not replace it or render it invisible. The path to equitable AI-driven transnational learning lies not in technological determinism, but in collective will, ethical imagination, and sustained commitment to justice. As we imagine the future of education in an AI-augmented world, let us ensure that no learner is left behind, and no voice is unheard.

REFERENCES

AI4D Africa. (2021). *Artificial intelligence for development in Africa.* https://ai4d.ai

Aayog, N. I. T. I. (2018). *National strategy for artificial intelligence #AIforAll.* Government of India. https://niti.gov.in

Adams, R. (2020). Digital colonialism: The displacement of local knowledge by global AI. *AI & Society, 35*(3), 569–582. DOI: 10.1007/s00146-019-00918-7

Altbach, P. G., & Knight, J. (2007). The internationalization of higher education: Motivations and realities. *Journal of Studies in International Education, 11*(3–4), 290–305. DOI: 10.1177/1028315307303542

Bawa, P., & Kapoor, R. (2023). Digital inequalities and AI ethics in Indian higher education. *Contemporary Education Dialogue, 20*(1), 88–105.

Bender, E. M., Gebru, T., McMillan-Major, A., & Shmitchell, S. (2021). On the dangers of stochastic parrots: Can language models be too big? In *Proceedings of the 2021 ACM Conference on Fairness, Accountability, and Transparency.* https://doi.org/DOI: 10.1145/3442188.3445922

Benjamin, R. (2019). Race after technology: Abolitionist tools for the new Jim code. *Polity.*

Binns, R., Veale, M., Van Kleek, M., & Shadbolt, N. (2018). 'It's reducing a human being to a percentage': Perceptions of justice in algorithmic decisions. In *CHI Conference on Human Factors in Computing Systems* (pp. 1–14). DOI: 10.1145/3173574.3173951

Birhane, A. (2022). Algorithmic injustice and AI colonialism. *Patterns (New York, N.Y.), 3*(8), 100560. DOI: 10.1016/j.patter.2022.100560

Buolamwini, J., & Gebru, T. (2018). Gender shades: Intersectional accuracy disparities in commercial gender classification. *Proceedings of Machine Learning Research, 81*, 1–15.

CAST. (2018). *Universal Design for Learning Guidelines version 2.2.* http://udlguidelines.cast.org

Couldry, N., & Mejias, U. A. (2019). *The costs of connection: How data is colonizing human life and appropriating it for capitalism.* Stanford University Press.

Eubanks, V. (2018). *Automating inequality: How high-tech tools profile, police, and punish the poor.* St. Martin's Press.

European Commission. (2023). *AI4Teachers project report.* https://ec.europa.eu/digital-strategy

Eynon, R. (2021). The rise of algorithmic education. *Learning, Media and Technology, 46*(4), 442–456.

Fraser, N. (2008). *Scales of justice: Reimagining political space in a globalizing world.* Columbia University Press.

Freire, P. (1970). *Pedagogy of the oppressed.* Herder and Herder.

Gilliard, C., & Culik, H. (2016). Digital redlining, access, and privacy. *ACRLog.* https://acrlog.org

Graham, R., & Misra, S. (2020). EdTech in the Global South: Challenges for teachers. *International Journal of Educational Development*, *77*, 102234.

Hargittai, E., & Hsieh, Y. P. (2013). Digital inequality. In Dutton, W. (Ed.), *The Oxford handbook of internet studies* (pp. 129–150). Oxford University Press.

Holmes, W., Bialik, M., & Fadel, C. (2022). *Artificial intelligence in education: Promises and implications for teaching and learning*. Center for Curriculum Redesign.

International Telecommunication Union. (2023). *Measuring digital development: Facts and figures 2023*. https://www.itu.int/en/ITU-D/Statistics

Joshi, P., Ahmed, S., & Sridhar, V. (2020). Multilingual NLP: Challenges and future directions. In *Proceedings of the ACL 2020 Workshop on Multilinguality*.

Joshi, P., Santy, S., Budhiraja, A., Bali, K., & Choudhury, M. (2020). The state and fate of linguistic diversity and inclusion in the NLP world. In *Proceedings of ACL*. https://doi.org/DOI: 10.18653/v1/2020.acl-main.560

Kemp, S. (2021). The ethics of data and AI in education. *Journal of Digital Ethics*, *5*(2), 211–226.

Knight, J. (2016). Transnational education remodeled: Toward a common TNE framework and definitions. *Journal of Studies in International Education*, *20*(1), 34–47. DOI: 10.1177/1028315315602927

Long, D., & Magerko, B. (2020). What is AI literacy? Competencies and design considerations. In *Proceedings of the 2020 CHI Conference on Human Factors in Computing Systems*. https://doi.org/DOI: 10.1145/3313831.3376727

Luckin, R. (2018). *Machine learning and human intelligence: The future of education for the 21st century*. UCL Institute of Education Press.

Luckin, R., Holmes, W., Griffiths, M., & Forcier, L. B. (2016). *Intelligence unleashed: An argument for AI in education*. Pearson Education.

Microsoft. (2021). *AI for Accessibility*. https://www.microsoft.com/en-us/ai/ai-for-accessibility

Nature Index. (2021). *AI research output by region*. https://www.nature.com/nature-index

Nissenbaum, H. (2001). How computer systems embody values. *Computer*, *34*(3), 120–119. DOI: 10.1109/2.910905

Noble, S. U. (2018). *Algorithms of oppression: How search engines reinforce racism*. NYU Press. DOI: 10.18574/nyu/9781479833641.001.0001

OECD. (2021). *AI and the future of skills: Capabilities and assessments*. https://www.oecd.org/education/ai-future-skills.htm

Paris, D., & Alim, H. S. (2017). *Culturally sustaining pedagogies: Teaching and learning for justice in a changing world*. Teachers College Press.

Pérez, J. C., Muñoz, A., & Hernández, M. (2022). Inclusive education through AI: Bridging the language gap. *International Journal of Educational Technology*, *19*(3), 210–225.

Pratham. (2022). *Hybrid learning program.* https://www.pratham.org

Selwyn, N. (2011). *Education and technology: Key issues and debates.* Bloomsbury Publishing.

Selwyn, N. (2016). *Education and technology: Key issues and debates* (2nd ed.). Bloomsbury Academic.

Selwyn, N. (2021). *Should robots replace teachers? AI and the future of education.* Polity Press.

Sen, A. (1999). *Development as freedom.* Oxford University Press.

Tikly, L. (2019). *Education for sustainable development in the postcolonial world: Towards a transformative agenda for Africa.* Routledge. DOI: 10.4324/9781315211343

Touretzky, D. S., Gardner-McCune, C., Martin, F., & Seehorn, D. (2019). Envisioning AI for K–12: What should every child know about AI? *Proceedings of the AAAI Conference on Artificial Intelligence, 33*(1), 9795–9799. DOI: 10.1609/aaai.v33i01.33019795

UNESCO. (2020). *COVID-19: How are countries addressing the digital learning divide? A snapshot of policy measures.* https://unesdoc.unesco.org/ark:/48223/pf0000373307

UNESCO. (2021a). *AI and education: Guidance for policymakers.* https://unesdoc.unesco.org

UNESCO. (2021b). *Recommendation on the ethics of artificial intelligence.* https://unesdoc.unesco.org/ark:/48223/pf0000379920

UNESCO. (2021c). *Global education monitoring report: Non-state actors in education.* https://unesdoc.unesco.org

UNESCO. (2021d). *National ICT policies in education: A comparative analysis.* https://unesdoc.unesco.org

UNESCO. (2022). *State of the education report for teachers in India 2022.* https://unesdoc.unesco.org

UNICEF. (2022). *Learning passport: AI in refugee education.* https://www.learningpassport.org

United Nations. (2022). *Our common agenda: Report of the Secretary-General.*

U.S. Department of Commerce. (2022). *Digital Equity Act programs.* https://www.ntia.gov/page/digital-equity-programs

Van Dijk, J. A. (2020). *The digital divide.* Polity Press.

Veale, M., & Binns, R. (2017). Fairer machine learning in the real world: Mitigating discrimination without collecting sensitive data. *Big Data & Society, 4*(2). Advance online publication. DOI: 10.1177/2053951717743530

Whittaker, M., Crawford, K., Dobbe, R., ... (2021). *The AI Now report: Racial bias and surveillance in AI systems.* AI Now Institute. https://ainowinstitute.org

Women, U. N. (2021). *Gender snapshot 2021: Achieving the SDGs.* https://www.unwomen.org/en/digital-library/publications

World Bank. (2021a). *Digital economy for Africa initiative: Broadband access and affordability in Africa.* https://www.worldbank.org/en/programs/all-africa-digital-transformation

World Bank. (2021b). Remote learning during [*Lessons from country experiences*. https://www.worldbank.org/en/topic/edutech]. *COVID, 19*, •••.

World Bank. (2022). *World development report: Education and the digital economy*. https://www.worldbank.org

World Bank. (2023). *Digital technologies in education: A global outlook*. World Bank Group.

Zawacki-Richter, O., Marín, V. I., Bond, M., & Gouverneur, F. (2019). Systematic review of research on artificial intelligence applications in higher education – Where are the educators? *International Journal of Educational Technology in Higher Education*, *16*(1), 1–27. DOI: 10.1186/s41239-019-0171-0

Chapter 12
Ethical Considerations and Sustainable AI Practices in Transnational Education

Razia Nagina
https://orcid.org/0000-0002-0305-8393
Lovely Professional University, India

ABSTRACT

This chapter examines the ethical and sustainability challenges of integrating Artificial Intelligence (AI) into Transnational Higher Education (TNHE). It highlights critical issues such as data privacy, algorithmic bias, transparency, cultural sensitivity, equitable access, and environmental impacts. Drawing on literature, real-world case studies, and international regulations, the chapter identifies strategies to mitigate these risks, including bias audits, robust data governance, sustainable AI practices, and ethical frameworks adapted to diverse contexts. The findings show that while AI enhances access, personalization, and efficiency, its misuse can exacerbate inequalities and environmental burdens. The chapter contributes by offering actionable guidelines for educators, policymakers, developers, and researchers to foster responsible and sustainable AI adoption in TNHE.

INTRODUCTION

Artificial Intelligence (AI) has brought major changes to multiple industries including higher education since its introduction. AI implementation in educational settings has created multiple opportunities to improve learning methods and administrative operations and customized educational solutions according to George and Wooden (2023). The expansion of institutional operations beyond national borders resulted in the establishment of Transnational Higher Education (TNHE) which provides students with access to academic programs from institutions based in various countries (Al-Horr, 2024). AI technology demonstrates potential to solve TNHE problems through its ability to connect distant locations while delivering solutions for cultural differences and language barriers and individualized learning needs (Dai et al., 2020).

AI applications in TNHE include systems that offer personalized tutoring and tools that analyze student performance predictions alongside automated grading systems and administrative support technologies.

DOI: 10.4018/979-8-3373-5403-3.ch012

Technologies function to improve educational results through data analysis and task automation which allows teachers to focus on instructional methods and student relationships (Ahmad et al., 2022; Chen et al., 2020). AI delivers inclusive education through its tools which support various learning requirements and cultural backgrounds to reach the goal of providing quality education for everyone worldwide (Anis, 2023; Roshanaei et al., 2023).

There are certain challenges in implementing AI in TNHE. AI technology in education raises serious ethical issues since it jeopardizes student privacy, leads to algorithmic discrimination, and exacerbates already-existing social injustices (Salloum, 2024). According to Curzon et al. (2021), AI systems need vast, sizeable datasets that include private, sensitive data. Given that educational institutions operate in multiple jurisdictions with disparate data protection laws, the management of this data raises significant privacy and security concerns (Ulven & Wangen, 2021).

AI algorithms face major problems because they produce biased results according to Daneshjou et al. (2021). I system functions at its best when it receives well-prepared training data yet biased or non-diverse data will produce AI outputs that maintain stereotypes and create disadvantages for particular student populations (Chinta et al., 2024). The situation becomes more concerning when it occurs across national boundaries because different cultural environments require appropriate consideration to avoid implementing unsuitable standardized methods for every student (Levy-Feldman & Libman, 2022).

AI deployment in TNHE systems requires sustainability to become a fundamental factor. Educational institutions must establish ethical and environmental sustainability standards for AI system deployment as they expand their use of these technologies. The assessment requires measuring AI system power usage together with technology lifespan and complete environmental effects from educational technology implementation (Abulibdeh et al., 2024).

As AI develops and its uses in TNHE increase, there is a greater need than ever for a thorough grasp of these moral and long-term issues. Through a thorough examination of the primary ethical issues that arise from the use of AI in international higher education, the book chapter satisfies this requirement. Through the ethical alignment of AI systems and sustainable development practices for AI deployment, the article offers solutions to these issues. The chapter provides educational materials for educators, legislators, and AI developers who wish to build moral AI systems for global higher education institutions in an effort to further the current discussion about responsible AI use in education.

Research Questions

- What are the significant ethical challenges related to implementing AI in transnational higher education?
- How can data privacy and security be ensured in AI applications across international borders?
- What strategies can be used to identify and address biases in AI algorithms employed in transnational higher education?
- How can AI practices in transnational higher education be aligned with sustainability goals?
- What are the best practices for developing and implementing an ethical framework for AI in transnational higher education?

ETHICAL CHALLENGES IN IMPLEMENTING AI IN TRANSNATIONAL HIGHER EDUCATION

Artificial Intelligence (AI) implementation in transnational higher education (TNHE) has brought revolutionary changes which enhance educational experiences and optimize administrative operations and expand access to high-quality learning opportunities. The development of AI technology requires proper ethical oversight to maintain fair implementation of AI systems which benefit all segments of society. The following section analyzes these ethical problems through real-world examples and case studies which demonstrate the full extent of their complexity.

1. Bias and Discrimination in AI Algorithms

In order to make decisions, AI systems frequently use large datasets, but these datasets may unintentionally contain biases that produce discriminatory results (Varona & Suárez, 2022). The possibility of bias in AI tools becomes a major ethical concern in TNHE, where students come from a variety of cultural, social, and economic backgrounds (Chinta et al., 2024).

Example: Predictive Analytics in Student Admissions

Predictive analytics in student admissions receives praise because it uses historical data to identify students who will perform well academically. A Princeton University study established that these algorithms tend to reproduce and sustain present social disparities. The predictive models create an unfair disadvantage for students from underrepresented minority groups and lower socioeconomic backgrounds because they select for traits which are more prevalent among applicants from wealthier backgrounds. The United States experienced this problem when a leading university's AI-based admissions system demonstrated bias against minority applicants which created major concerns about equal access to education.

Institutions need to execute active bias identification and removal programs for their AI systems to minimize this risk. The process demands organizations to maintain open algorithm development practices while performing ongoing AI model assessments and adjustments to stop the continuation of discriminatory patterns in AI systems. (Bhoite et al., 2022; Giani & Walling, 2020).

2. Privacy and Data Security Concerns

AI in TNHE requires the collection and analysis of extensive personal data which includes student records and academic results and behavioral information. The management of this sensitive information creates major concerns about privacy protection and data security because transnational environments experience significant variations in data protection standards.

Case Study: The Cambridge Analytica Scandal

The Cambridge Analytica scandal which focused on political interference revealed the dangers of personal data exploitation. The educational institutions and third-party providers who handle student data in TNHE face identical risks because they lack proper protection systems for this information. A university that provides online degree programs to students in different countries would keep student information on servers that operate under data protection regulations which are less strict. Students would become exposed to unauthorized access of their personal data which could lead to privacy violations according to Hinds et al. (2020).

TNHE institutions need to create strong data governance systems which place student information security as their main focus to resolve these issues. The process requires institutions to follow relevant data protection laws including the General Data Protection Regulation (GDPR) which operates in Europe while maintaining secure data storage and processing systems throughout all institutional and student locations.

3. Lack of Transparency and Accountability

AI systems operate as "black boxes" because they use intricate algorithms which remain confusing to users and developers and users who try to understand their decision-making process. TNHE programs face major ethical problems because students and educators must depend on AI systems to create fair and transparent decision-making processes yet these systems lack both transparency and accountability.

Case Study: Automated Essay Scoring (Ramesh & Sanampudi, 2022)

Several TNHE institutions use automated essay scoring systems to speed up their grading procedures. The systems experience criticism because their grading methods stay undisclosed while producing results that might contain both errors and biased outcomes. The evaluation system evaluates essays by their advanced vocabulary and complex sentence structures yet ignores the actual meaning and relevance of the content. Students who do not speak English as their first language and those from various cultural backgrounds face challenges because these systems do not recognize their different language usage patterns.

TNHE institutions must establish transparent AI decision-making processes which allow students and staff members to contest or dispute system-generated outcomes. The solution requires organizations to add human oversight to AI operations or create AI systems which provide understandable explanations of their operations.

4. Cultural Sensitivity and Inclusivity

AI systems developed in one cultural context may not be easily transferable to another, raising ethical concerns about cultural sensitivity and inclusivity in TNHE. When AI tools fail to account for cultural differences, they risk alienating or disadvantaging students from diverse backgrounds (Markey et al., 2023).

Example: Language Translation Tools in Online Learning

AI-based language translation tools function as vital instruments for TNHE because they allow students to receive their educational content in their native languages. The tools produce unreliable results when translating cultural expressions which leads to communication breakdowns according to Ou et al. (2024). The Spanish equivalent for this idiom would be "costar un brazo y una pierna" which means "cost an arm and a leg." The expression "costar un ojo de la cara" remains more prevalent among native speakers for describing high costs than the phrase I suggested. The new system implementation resulted in two different outcomes for students which lowered their academic performance and reduced their participation in school activities."

To address this issue, TNHE institutions should work to develop AI tools that are culturally sensitive and inclusive.The process requires experts who specialize in language and culture to develop AI systems which can correctly interpret and translate diverse cultural elements. The educational institutions need to provide backing to students who encounter language difficulties by giving them tutoring services and extra language learning materials according to Holmes and Miao (2023).

5. Equity in Access to AI-Driven Resources

If access to AI-driven resources is not distributed fairly, the use of AI in TNHE may make already-existing disparities worse. The lack of access to advanced AI tools and technologies among students in under-resourced regions or institutions may create a digital divide that exacerbates educational inequalities (Kunjumuhammed, 2024).

Case Study: Digital Divide in Remote Learning

TNHE educational institutions experienced a major digital gap during the COVID-19 pandemic. Educational institutions in developing nations faced major obstacles to deliver fundamental online access to students while better-resourced institutions transitioned to AI-based online learning systems (Azubuike et al., 2021). Students in sub-Saharan Africa cannot access AI-based online learning tools because UNESCO's Global Education Monitoring (GEM) Report reveals that most students in the region do not have home internet access. Students face two major problems because of insufficient access which affects their current academic work and their future educational performance and job opportunities.

TNHE institutions should make investments in support systems and infrastructure to guarantee that all students have the chance to take advantage of AI technologies in order to advance equity in access to AI-driven resources. This could entail creating open-source or inexpensive AI tools, offering financial aid or subsidies to students in underdeveloped areas, and supporting laws that close the wider digital divide in education.

6. Sustainability and Environmental Impact

While the ethical challenges discussed previously focus on social and cultural issues, the environmental impact of AI in Transnational Higher Education (TNHE) is an emerging area of concern. The energy consumption required to power AI systems, particularly those involving large-scale data processing and machine learning, contributes significantly to the carbon footprint of educational institutions.

Case Study: Energy Consumption in AI-Driven Research

A single AI model for natural language processing (NLP) can generate carbon emissions equal to five cars' worth of emissions over the course of their lifetimes, according to research from the University of Massachusetts Amherst (Strubell et al., 2020). The cumulative environmental impact within the context of TNHE, where several AI-driven research projects or online learning platforms may be in operation, can be significant. The sustainability of AI practices and the obligation of educational institutions to lessen their carbon footprint are two significant ethical issues brought up by this circumstance.

TNHE institutions ought to think about implementing sustainable AI practices in order to allay these worries. These might include integrating sustainability standards into the development and implementation of AI systems, employing renewable energy sources to power data centers, and optimizing algorithms for energy efficiency (Berchin et al., 2021). Institutions can also take the lead in advancing "green AI" by funding studies aimed at reducing the negative effects of AI technologies on the environment.

The use of AI in international higher education presents complex and multidimensional ethical issues. Approaching these issues holistically is necessary, taking into account the diverse needs and backgrounds of students, emphasizing accountability and transparency in AI systems, and assessing the broader social and environmental effects of AI technologies. TNHE institutions can use AI to improve education in a way that is just, equal, and ecologically conscious by giving ethical issues and sustainable practices top priority.

ENSURING DATA PRIVACY AND SECURITY IN AI APPLICATIONS ACROSS INTERNATIONAL BORDERS

Protecting data security and privacy is essential as artificial intelligence (AI) plays a bigger role in transnational higher education (TNHE). Applications of AI usually entail gathering and processing large amounts of data, including private and sensitive data about students, teachers, and institutional operations. Because of different legal frameworks, cultural norms, and technological standards, it becomes more difficult to ensure data privacy and security when these applications operate internationally. Using case studies and real-world examples as examples, this section looks at methods for successfully preserving data security and privacy in AI applications within TNHE.

1. Understanding and Complying with International Data Protection Regulations

Navigating the complicated web of data protection laws is a major obstacle to guaranteeing data security and privacy in AI applications across international borders (Babikian, 2023). Institutions must abide by the various data privacy laws and standards in different nations in order to safeguard the rights of individuals (Brown & Marsden, 2023).

Required: Compliance with the GDPR in TNHE Institutions (Phillips, 2021; Aliyu et al., 2020)

The General Data Protection Regulation (GDPR) is one of the most stringent data protection laws worldwide, affecting any institution handling the personal data of individuals within the European Union (EU), regardless of the institution's location (Yeung & Bygrave, 2022).

Example: British Airways GDPR Fine (Voss, 2021; Wolff & Atallah, 2021)

British Airways received a £20 million fine from the Information Commissioner's Office (ICO) in October 2020 because it failed to safeguard personal data belonging to its customers. The penalty originated from a security breach which exposed personal information of about 400000 customers. The ICO discovered through its investigation that the airline lacked sufficient security protocols to protect customer information which resulted in the data breach.

Internationally operating TNHE institutions must adhere to data protection laws which exist in every country they operate within. The process demands organizations to study legal requirements across every operational jurisdiction while building effective data protection systems which meet all regulatory standards in each location.

2. Implementing Strong Encryption and Data Security Measures

Since AI applications frequently handle sensitive data, strong encryption and data security protocols are necessary to shield this data from hacking, illegal access, and data breaches. Even if data is intercepted during transmission or storage, encryption guarantees that only authorized users can access it (Isakov et al., 2024; Bandari, 2023).

Required: End-to-End Encryption in Online Learning Platforms

Transnational higher education (TNHE) institutions adapted to online learning platforms during the COVID-19 pandemic to continue delivering education to their students. The rapid adoption of these platforms created new security risks because they handled private student data.The institutions responded by establishing end-to-end encryption for all platform communications according to Sethi & Behera (2021). The educational institution selected an encrypted video conferencing system for their online classes because it secured video and audio content exclusively for authorized users to block unauthorized access and eavesdropping (Djeki et al., 2024; Cui et al., 2023).

AI applications need robust encryption systems and data protection measures which include multi-factor authentication and secure data storage and regular security audits to protect their data. Institutions need to set requirements which mandate their third-party vendors and partners to maintain equal data security standards."

3. Challenges in Managing International Data Transfers and Navigating Data Sovereignty (Chen, 2021; Vila Seoane, 2021)

In TNHE, cross-border data transfers are frequently necessary, especially when AI applications are housed on servers spread across several nations. These transfers, however, may be made more difficult by data sovereignty laws, which mandate that data be processed and stored within predetermined geographic bounds.

Data Localization Laws in India (Bailey & Parsheera, 2021)

India's data localization regulations require the storage of specific data categories including personal information and essential information inside national borders. The use of AI applications by TNHE institutions faces difficulties because these applications need cloud services and data centers which operate outside of domestic borders. The international university which delivered online education to Indian students needed to follow these laws while keeping their AI-based learning platform operational at full capacity. The university worked with a cloud service provider who operated data centers in India to meet domestic regulatory requirements while preserving the platform's operational speed.

TNHE institutions need to develop strategic plans for data storage and processing to handle data sovereignty issues. Organizations need to decide between establishing local data centers or using hybrid cloud solutions or partnering with service providers who operate in specific regions for data management.

4. Ensuring Transparency and Accountability in Data Use

When utilizing AI applications that involve personal data, transparency and accountability are essential to fostering trust among students, educators, and other stakeholders (Nguyen et al., 2023). In addition to providing methods for people to manage and control their own data, institutions must be transparent about how they collect, process, and use data.

Required: Transparency in AI-Driven Student Support Systems

Big data collection and analysis are essential for AI-driven student support systems, such as those that monitor academic progress and provide tailored learning recommendations (Saaida, 2023; Maghsudi et al., 2021). In order to offer individualized academic support, several universities put in place a system that examined students' online behavior, assignment submissions, and test scores.

Example

Georgia State University uses predictive analytics to support student academic success. The university has established measures to maintain data transparency while giving students control over their data according to Bird et al. (2021) and Renick (2020).

Georgia State University developed the Panther Retention Management system which uses student data from online activities and academic work and test results to create customized educational support plans. The system works to improve student achievement and performance. The university provides transparency through detailed explanations of student data usage and algorithmic recommendation system operations. Students can decide to opt out of the system and they can also ask for their personal data to be removed from the system.

TNHE institutions can promote trust and the responsible use of AI applications by guaranteeing accountability and transparency in data use. This entails having transparent privacy policies, giving people access to and control over their data, and routinely checking AI systems for ethical compliance.

5. Addressing the Risks of Data Breaches and Cybersecurity Threats

Data breaches and cybersecurity threats are ever-present risks in the digital age, particularly for institutions operating across borders (Takavarasha et al., 2023). The international nature of TNHE increases these risks, as data may be stored and accessed from multiple locations, making it more vulnerable to attacks.

Case Study: Cybersecurity Incident at a Transnational University - Blackbaud (2020)

Blackbaud which operates as a leading provider of cloud-based software for non-profits and educational institutions experienced a major data breach during 2020. The attack resulted in the theft of personal and financial information from multiple educational institutions which operate across the globe. The company Blackbaud engaged in long-term discussions with attackers while implementing better security systems and provided security recommendations to their clients (Butt et al., 2023; Bernholz et al., 2020).

Transnational higher education (TNHE) institutions need to implement proactive cybersecurity measures to protect their systems from data breaches and cyber threats. The program needs to perform routine security evaluations while purchasing modern cybersecurity solutions and training personnel and students about security procedures and creating emergency response systems to handle security incidents quickly.

6. Fostering International Collaboration and Standardization

International data privacy and security protection for AI applications needs worldwide collaboration to establish standardized methods. Institutions together with governments and industry partners need to establish common standards and frameworks which will function across various legal systems (Igbinenikaro & Adewusi, 2024).

The International Organization for Standardization (ISO) together with the International Electrotechnical Commission (IEC) work to establish worldwide standards for AI and data protection according to Lewis et al. (2020). The primary standard in this field exists as ISO/IEC 27001 which specifies the criteria for building an information security management system (ISMS) (Allendevaux, 2021). The standard functions as the primary global framework for data handling which institutions worldwide use for their data management practices including transnational higher education (TNHE) institutions.".

In order to protect sensitive data and guarantee adherence to international data protection regulations, numerous universities and research institutions have implemented ISO/IEC 27001 (Ntloedibe et al., 2024; Alwahaibi et al., 2022).

Example

University of Bristol: To manage its information security and guarantee adherence to global data protection standards, the University of Bristol has obtained ISO/IEC 27001 certification.

This adoption enables more safe and effective cross-border operations and collaborations by bringing their AI applications into compliance with recognized international standards for data privacy and security.

TNHE institutions can guarantee that their AI applications follow international best practices for data security and privacy by taking part in international standardization initiatives. This promotes more seamless cross-border operations and collaborations in addition to aiding in data protection.

Transnational higher education institutions must handle a complicated yet necessary duty to safeguard data privacy and security for AI applications that operate across international borders. Institutions will protect stakeholder privacy and security through their implementation of international data protection rules and their deployment of robust encryption methods and security systems and their resolution of data sovereignty challenges and their support of transparency and accountability and their promotion of worldwide partnerships. The educational environment needs these methods to maintain trust and protect individual rights and uphold ethical standards for technology usage in TNHE as artificial intelligence technology advances in education.

STRATEGIES TO IDENTIFY AND MITIGATE BIASES IN AI ALGORITHMS USED IN TRANSNATIONAL HIGHER EDUCATION

AI integration into higher education institutions enables better learning outcomes and administrative efficiency and enhanced decision-making capabilities. AI implementation brings forward a dual threat because it has the potential to maintain or intensify current discriminatory systems. The biases show up in different ways which influence how students get admitted and how their grades are determined and what support services they receive. AI ethical and equitable deployment requires institutions to establish methods which detect and resolve algorithmic biases in AI systems. The section analyzes these methods by presenting actual examples together with documented case studies.

1. Diverse and Representative Data Collection

The use of skewed or unrepresentative datasets is a major cause of bias in AI algorithms. The resulting algorithms are likely to produce biased results if the data used to train AI models is representative of current social inequalities or is not diverse (Williams et al., 2018). Making sure that the data used in AI applications is varied and appropriately reflects the population it is intended to serve is therefore the first step in minimizing bias.

Addressing Gender Bias in AI-Driven Recruitment Tools (González & Rampino, 2024)

The AI-driven recruitment tool of a major technology company was found to favor male candidates over female candidates, providing a well-documented example of bias in AI (Rigos, 2022). Over the course of ten years, when the tech industry was predominately male, the algorithm was trained on resumes that were submitted to the company. A clear gender bias resulted from the AI system's propensity to favor resumes with male-associated terms and qualifications (Fernández-Martínez & Fernández, 2020). The company had to change its data collection procedures in order to solve this problem, making sure that the dataset used to train the AI was more varied and representative of the larger talent pool.

Higher education institutions employ equivalent concepts for their operations. Organizations must verify that their AI algorithm development data for student support and course recommendations and admissions reflects the complete range of student diversity. The process needs to gather data from various demographic groups which include underrepresented minorities and international students and people from different socioeconomic backgrounds. Educational institutions will be able to decrease the risk of maintaining discriminatory beliefs which damage specific student populations through these actions.

2. Regular Auditing and Testing of AI Algorithms

Due to the complexity of machine learning procedures, biases may still appear in AI algorithms even when the data is diverse. Consequently, it is essential to conduct routine audits and tests of AI algorithms in order to detect and rectify biases before they have a chance to cause harm (Landers & Behrend, 2023).

Case Study: Algorithm Audits in College Admissions (Li & Goel, 2024)

Carnegie Mellon University is one prominent example. In order to address biases, it has audited algorithms and been actively involved in research on AI fairness (González-Sendino et al., 2023; Courtland, 2018).

To find and fix any potential biases, TNHE institutions should regularly audit their AI systems. Using fairness metrics to assess how well AI algorithms perform across various demographic groups, scenario-based testing to learn how the algorithm might perform in various scenarios, and bringing in outside experts to offer an unbiased viewpoint are some ways to achieve this. Institutions can identify and address biases before they result in unfair outcomes by establishing routine auditing as standard procedure.

3. Incorporating Human Oversight in AI Decision-Making

AI should not be used as the only decision-maker, even though it can greatly increase decision-making processes' efficiency and objectivity. This is especially true in situations where biases could have detrimental effects.

By incorporating human oversight into AI decision-making processes, biases that the algorithm might not notice right away can be found and fixed.

Human-AI Collaboration in Grading (Pereira et al., 2022)

AI-assisted grading has been introduced in MOOCs by EdX, an online learning platform established by MIT and Harvard University (Meinel et al., 2024). In large courses where human grading alone would be impractical, the platform uses artificial intelligence (AI) to grade assignments automatically. The “Automated Essay Scoring” (AES) AI system assesses student work according to predetermined standards, including grammar, organization, and prompt relevance (Lim et al., 2021).

However, EdX includes human oversight to guarantee accuracy and fairness. Teachers have the ability to check and modify the AI-generated grades, particularly when the AI may have trouble with unusual or creative answers. This partnership between humans and AI guarantees that grading stays fair and effective, enabling scalability while upholding academic standards.

TNHE requires human supervision of AI decision-making systems to detect and address system biases. The system should include human evaluators who review AI-generated decisions and students and teachers should have the ability to contest AI-based results and AI should function as an aid to human decision-making rather than replacing human judgment. Institutions maintain equilibrium between AI systems and human participation to achieve optimal decision-making efficiency and equity.

4. Implementing Bias Detection Tools and Techniques

In order to detect and address biases at an early stage, AI development processes can incorporate sophisticated bias detection tools and techniques, which are becoming more and more accessible. These tools check AI algorithms for bias and offer insights that help make the required corrections and enhancements.

Case Study: IBM's AI Fairness 360 (Bellamy et al., 2019)

AI Fairness 360 (AIF360) is an open-source toolkit developed by IBM to help developers detect and fix bias in AI models. This toolkit comprises an extensive collection of fairness metrics that can assess whether the choices made by an AI algorithm are skewed against particular demographic traits, such as age, gender, or race. AIF360 has been used to guarantee that AI systems function impartially and fairly in a variety of industries, including healthcare, education, and finance.

AIF360, for instance, can be used to assess the equity of AI systems used in the educational sector for resource allocation, admissions procedures, and student evaluations. Educational institutions can detect possible biases in their AI systems and make the required modifications to mitigate them by utilizing these fairness metrics, guaranteeing that decisions are fair to all demographic groups.

Application in Transnational Higher Education (TNHE)

Institutions in Transnational Higher Education (TNHE) can use comparable methods and instruments to find and fix biases in AI systems. TNHE institutions can get continuous feedback on how fair their algorithms are by integrating these tools into the AI development process. This allows developers to make the necessary modifications to reduce bias and guarantee fair treatment for all students, regardless of their background.

5. Promoting Diversity in AI Development Teams

In order to reduce biases, it is essential that the teams creating AI algorithms be diverse. Lack of diversity in AI development teams may result in a narrow understanding of potential biases and how to overcome them. Institutions can guarantee that a wider variety of perspectives are taken into account and produce more equitable AI systems by encouraging diversity within these teams.

Case Study: Diversity in AI Development at Google

Since diverse teams are better able to recognize and resolve biases in AI systems, Google has worked hard to increase diversity within its AI development teams. For instance, the members of Google's AI Ethics team come from a variety of backgrounds, including different racial and gender identities and specializations (McElhaney et al., 2023). The team has been able to approach AI ethics from a variety of angles thanks to this diversity, which has produced more thorough methods for locating and resolving biases in Google's AI products.

Diversity in AI development teams should be a top priority for higher education institutions. This includes hiring people from a variety of demographic groups and making sure that the opinions of underrepresented communities are respected and heard. Institutions can create AI systems that are more considerate of the needs of all students and less prone to reinforce prejudices by cultivating a diverse and inclusive environment (Slimi & Carballido, 2023).

It is a difficult but vital task to identify and fix biases in AI algorithms used in higher education. Institutions can strive towards developing AI systems that are just, equitable, and efficient by utilizing tactics like diverse and representative data collection, frequent auditing and testing of AI algorithms, human oversight in decision-making, bias detection tools, and encouraging diversity within AI development teams. These tactics will be essential as AI has a greater impact on education in the future to make sure that technology promotes positive change rather than exacerbates already-existing disparities.

ALIGNING AI PRACTICES IN TRANSNATIONAL HIGHER EDUCATION WITH SUSTAINABILITY GOALS

As artificial intelligence (AI) becomes more and more integrated into the operations and curricula of transnational higher education (TNHE), it is becoming more and more important to make sure that these practices complement sustainability objectives. The environmental effects of AI, such as energy consumption, electronic waste, and ethical resource use, must be weighed against its potential to improve education and operational efficiency (Fan et al., 2023). With the help of case studies and examples, this section describes methods for coordinating AI practices in higher education with sustainability objectives.

1. Enhancing Energy Efficiency in AI Infrastructure

Artificial intelligence (AI) technologies, particularly those that use deep learning, are frequently energy-intensive and contribute significantly to carbon emissions. THNEs can solve this by giving energy-efficient AI infrastructure top priority.

Case Study: MIT's Efforts in Reducing AI's Energy Footprint

Research on lowering the energy usage of AI technologies has been actively pursued by MIT (Green, 2024). To improve the energy efficiency of AI models, for example, researchers at MIT's Computer Science and Artificial Intelligence Laboratory (CSAIL) have created methods.

Here's a summary of their initiatives and some references for further verification:

Neural Network Compression Techniques:

"Once-for-All" Neural Network Compression: Developed by researchers at MIT's CSAIL, this technique involves training a single neural network that can be optimized for various hardware platforms without the need for retraining. This reduces the computational resources required during deployment, which in turn lowers energy consumption. This approach is detailed in the research paper titled "Once-for-All: Train One Network and Specialize it for Efficient Deployment", which was presented at NeurIPS 2019.

Energy-Efficient Data Centers:

MIT has been working on optimizing data center operations to reduce power consumption. This includes the use of more efficient hardware and improved cooling systems. For instance, MIT's CSAIL is continuously exploring innovations such as dynamic voltage and frequency scaling (DVFS) and energy-efficient server design to reduce the carbon footprint of data centers.

Sustainable AI Research:

MIT has a broader initiative to integrate sustainability into AI research. This includes collaborations across different departments to develop energy-efficient algorithms and promote sustainable practices within their research environments. More information on MIT's commitment to sustainable AI research can be found in their CSAIL research updates and sustainability initiatives.

2. Integrating AI with Sustainable Campus Operations

AI can be utilized to enhance sustainability in campus operations, such as energy management, waste reduction, and transportation systems.

Case Study: Smart Campuses in Singapore (Chew et al., 2020)

To maximize energy use, Singaporean universities, including the National University of Singapore (NUS), have deployed AI-driven systems. NUS drastically lowers energy use and carbon emissions by using AI to monitor and modify HVAC systems in real-time based on data. This project serves as a real-world illustration of AI's contribution to sustainability and harmonizes the university's operations with its sustainability objectives.

THNEs can minimize their environmental impact, cut waste, and maximize resource utilization by incorporating AI into campus administration. These kinds of programs also give students worthwhile sustainability-related learning experiences.

3. Developing Sustainable AI Curricula

Institutions of Transnational Higher Education (TNHE) play a key role in equipping upcoming leaders to handle the nexus between sustainability and artificial intelligence. Students will be prepared to use AI technologies in ways that promote social and environmental objectives if curricula that prioritize sustainable AI practices are developed.

Case Study: Stanford University's AI and Sustainability Courses (Filimowicz, 2023)

Stanford University is actively involved in integrating sustainability into its AI education. Key courses and initiatives include:

"AI for Social Good": Offered by Stanford's Institute for Human-Centered Artificial Intelligence (HAI), this course explores how AI technologies can address global challenges, including environmental sustainability. It focuses on applying AI to solve real-world problems, including energy efficiency and climate monitoring.

The Stanford AI Ethics program's "Ethics of Artificial Intelligence" course discusses the moral ramifications of AI, including how it affects environmental and sustainability concerns.

The goal of Stanford's programs is to provide students with practical experience working on AI projects that tackle sustainability issues. Students who take these courses acquire the knowledge and practical skills necessary to create AI solutions that promote environmental objectives.

By providing comparable programs, TNHE institutions can guarantee that students are suitably equipped to use AI to promote sustainability in their future careers.

4. Minimizing Electronic Waste through Responsible AI Practices

The rapid advancement of AI technologies often leads to frequent hardware upgrades, which can contribute significantly to electronic waste (e-waste) (Sharma et al., 2023). TNHE Institutions can mitigate this issue by adopting responsible e-waste management practices and extending the lifespan of AI-related hardware.

Case Study: Griffith University's E-Waste Reduction Initiatives (Trevathan & Sharp, 2020; Davis & Wolski, 2009)

In fact, Griffith University has been actively promoting sustainability, which includes e-waste management. Among their endeavors are:

E-Waste Management and Recycling: The appropriate disposal and recycling of obsolete electronics are part of Griffith University's extensive e-waste management policy. Through the recovery of valuable materials and the reduction of environmental impact, this program guarantees that e-waste is processed in an environmentally responsible manner.

Sustainable IT Practices: The university is committed to sustainable IT practices by extending the lifecycle of its hardware. This includes regular maintenance and refurbishment of old equipment, as well as adopting energy-efficient technologies. These practices contribute to reducing waste and supporting broader sustainability goals.

Griffith University's initiatives align with global sustainability goals and provide a model for other Transnational Higher Education (TNHE) institutions to manage e-waste effectively. By integrating similar practices, TNHE institutions can enhance their environmental stewardship and sustainability efforts.

5. Ethical AI Development with Sustainable Impact

Aligning AI practices with sustainability goals also requires a commitment to ethical AI development. This involves considering the long-term social and environmental impacts of AI technologies.

United Nations' AI for Good Initiative (Cowls et al., 2021)

With a strong emphasis on environmental sustainability, this initiative uses AI technologies to further the Sustainable Development Goals (SDGs). By tracking changes like deforestation, air quality, and climate patterns, artificial intelligence (AI) is used for environmental monitoring, providing crucial data to aid conservation efforts. It also has a significant impact on disaster response and prediction, as AI models improve forecasting precision, streamline response plans, and fortify resistance to environmental stresses. AI also helps with resource management by increasing energy and water efficiency, which encourages sustainable practices. Aligning technological innovation with more general sustainability goals, the AI for Good initiative shows how AI can be developed and used ethically to address urgent environmental and social issues.

Institutions of Transnational Higher Education (TNHE) can support the development of ethical and sustainable AI by taking part in programs such as AI for Good and concentrating their research on projects that tackle urgent environmental issues. By taking part in such projects, universities can further their role in encouraging ethical AI practices that support global sustainability goals.

For AI's benefits to be realized without endangering environmental health, THNE's practices must be in line with sustainability objectives. THNEs can take the lead in building a more sustainable future by increasing energy efficiency, incorporating AI into sustainable campus operations, creating sustainable AI curricula, reducing electronic waste, and advocating for ethical AI development. These initiatives not only lessen the environmental effect of AI, but they also encourage institutions, educators, and students to think about how technology can help achieve global sustainability goals.

BEST PRACTICES FOR DEVELOPING AND IMPLEMENTING AN ETHICAL FRAMEWORK FOR AI IN TRANSNATIONAL HIGHER EDUCATION

Strong ethical frameworks are becoming more and more important as AI continues to change education, particularly in transnational higher education (TNHE) (Morris & Kozuch, 2024). Different legal, cultural, and social contexts present special challenges for TNHE, which involves education across international borders. In order to ensure responsible, equitable, and sustainable use, these complexities must be carefully considered when developing and implementing an ethical framework for AI in this context. This section examines best practices for creating and putting into practice such a framework, supported by case studies and examples.

1. Collaborative Development of Ethical Guidelines

Stakeholders from various nations, fields, and industries must work together to develop an ethical framework for AI in TNHE. Through this partnership, the framework is guaranteed to be thorough, culturally aware, and in line with international standards while simultaneously taking into account regional requirements and circumstances.

Case Study: UNESCO's AI Ethics Guidelines (Morandín-Ahuerma, 2023)

Through extensive consultations with experts, policymakers, and civil society from around the world, UNESCO has taken the lead in creating global guidelines for AI ethics. The resulting guidelines, which prioritize sustainability, inclusivity, and human rights, offer a strong basis for moral AI practices in a variety of fields, including education. UNESCO's guidelines are especially pertinent to TNHE because they are made to be flexible enough to accommodate various cultural and legal contexts by involving a wide range of stakeholders.

Involving educators, students, legal professionals, and policymakers from every nation in which they conduct business would allow TNHE institutions to follow suit. The ethical framework is guaranteed to represent a broad spectrum of viewpoints and be sensitive to the unique difficulties of transnational education thanks to this cooperative process.

2. Contextualization and Adaptation of Ethical Principles

Global ethical standards offer a useful starting point, but they need to be modified to meet the unique requirements of TNHE. To make sure the ethical framework is applicable and useful in every situation, this entails taking into account regional cultural norms, legal requirements, and educational practices.

Case Study: AI Ethics in European and Asian Universities

The University of Edinburgh was part of a group of European universities that worked on modifying AI ethics frameworks to comply with the General Data Protection Regulation (GDPR) of the EU. Additionally, they worked with Asian institutions to comprehend and honor cultural differences and legal systems, especially in nations with laxer regulations. This project produced flexible guidelines that each institution could modify to fit their unique situation, offering TNHE institutions a useful model (Pagallo et al., 2019).

A flexible approach to ethical AI that permits the adaptation of universal principles to regional contexts should be adopted by TNHE institutions. By doing this, the ethical framework is guaranteed to be both efficient and considerate of the various contexts in which these institutions function.

3. Transparency and Accountability in AI Decision-Making

Any ethical AI framework must include transparency and accountability as essential elements. These values are essential in the context of TNHE because the staff and students come from a variety of cultural backgrounds and have different standards for justice and fairness. Building trust and encouraging moral behavior internationally requires making sure AI-driven decisions are open, accountable, and transparent.

Institutions using AI-driven admissions tools in the TNHE context frequently struggle with issues of fairness and transparency (Chinta et al., 2024). For instance, questions concerning the opacity of the decision-making criteria may surface when AI systems are utilized to automate certain steps of the admissions process. Some organizations have begun disclosing details about the algorithms and considerations that go into AI-driven decisions in an effort to allay these worries. Additionally, they have established appeals procedures that enable applicants to challenge rulings and request more information.

This method demonstrates how crucial accountability and transparency are to preserving equity and confidence in AI systems.

TNHE institutions should make sure AI systems are transparent and offer concise justifications for decision-making in order to adopt a similar strategy. Furthermore, putting in place accountability procedures like independent reviews or appeals procedures can help allay worries and guarantee that AI-driven judgments are reasonable and fair.

4. Regular Monitoring and Updating of the Ethical Framework

The ethical framework must be regularly reviewed and updated due to the rapid evolution of AI technologies and their applications in education. This ensures that as AI develops further, the framework will remain applicable and efficient in tackling new opportunities and challenges (Nguyen et al., 2023).

A number of international organizations have set up specialized task forces or committees tasked with keeping an eye on AI practices and suggesting changes to the ethical framework. These organizations, which are usually composed of professionals from different fields, evaluate the moral implications of AI tools on a regular basis and modify their rules in response to new developments in technology and changing moral dilemmas (Jobin et al., 2019). This progressive approach aids organizations in foreseeing possible moral dilemmas and maintaining strict guidelines for the application of AI in education.

TNHE institutions can adopt similar practices by establishing dedicated committees or task forces to monitor AI practices and recommend updates to the ethical framework.

Ongoing training for staff and students on the latest ethical considerations in AI can also help ensure that the framework is effectively implemented and followed.

5. Fostering Ethical AI Education and Awareness

The effective application of an ethical framework depends on educating stakeholders, employees, and students about moral AI practices. This instruction in TNHE needs to be sensitive to cultural differences and pertinent to the community's varied backgrounds (Mouta et al., 2024).

In order to ensure that students in various regions are taught both local cultural considerations and global ethical principles, many transnational institutions are integrating AI ethics into their curricula (Wilkins, 2017). Workshops and seminars for faculty and staff are regularly held in support of this training, encouraging a culture of ongoing education and ethical consciousness. A thorough approach like this guarantees that AI procedures in these establishments follow moral guidelines and encourage the ethical application of AI in the classroom.

TNHE institutions can advance ethical AI practices by integrating ethics education into their curricula and offering continuous training for staff and students. By cultivating a culture of ethical awareness, institutions can ensure their AI practices adhere to ethical standards and actively support the responsible use of AI in education.

It is a difficult but essential task to develop and apply an ethical framework for AI in international higher education. Institutions may build a strong and flexible framework that tackles the particular difficulties of TNHE by adhering to best practices like cooperative development, contextual adaptation, transparency, frequent monitoring, and cultivating ethical awareness. By ensuring that AI is applied fairly and responsibly, these initiatives will contribute to the long-term viability and moral integrity of international education.

CONCEPTUAL MODELS ILLUSTRATING THE INTERPLAY BETWEEN AI ETHICS, SUSTAINABILITY, AND GOVERNANCE IN TNHE

The integration of Artificial Intelligence (AI) in Transnational Higher Education (TNHE) requires a complete conceptual understanding of the relationships between ethics and sustainability and governance for building responsible academic environments. The three domains form a conceptual framework which shows that ethical decision-making serves as the base for sustainable and transparent AI practices and governance systems establish the necessary regulatory and institutional structures for maintaining accountability. The three components form an active system which uses ethical standards to direct technological applications and sustainability to maintain enduring operations and governance systems to establish equal treatment standards for worldwide educational environments.

In this model, AI ethics operates as the moral compass, defining the principles of fairness, transparency, privacy, and inclusivity. The ethical aspects determine the development and execution of AI systems which protect human dignity and diversity in educational technology applications. The implementation of ethical frameworks enables the reduction of algorithmic bias within automated grading systems and student admission processes and learning analytics by eliminating discriminatory practices that affect students based on their language skills and cultural background and economic situation.

The second pillar of sustainability connects ethical AI operations with broad environmental and social and institutional outcomes. The Sustainable AI in TNHE program achieves sustainable operations through its commitment to both digital equity and capacity development and knowledge preservation systems. Academic institutions achieve lower carbon footprints through sustainable data practices which include energy-efficient cloud systems and open-access resources that enable worldwide accessibility. The model positions sustainability as both a goal and a constraint—ensuring that AI-driven educational innovation contributes to social justice and planetary well-being.

Governance serves as the connecting framework that operationalizes ethical and sustainable principles through policy, regulation and institutional accountability. The successful management of AI in TNHE demands clear guidelines which define how data sharing occurs and international cooperation operates and how algorithms maintain accountability. The implementation of AI oversight occurs through multiple governance levels which include institutional ethics boards and national regulations and international guidelines like UNESCO's 2021 Recommendation on the Ethics of Artificial Intelligence.

This integrated conceptual model highlights a feedback loop: ethical AI practices enhance sustainability, sustainability strengthens governance legitimacy, and governance reinforces ethical accountability. Collectively, these interconnections foster a transnational educational environment where AI innovation aligns with human values, social equity, and sustainable global development.

SOCIO-POLITICAL ANALYSIS OF AI ETHICS AND PEDAGOGICAL IMPLICATIONS

The socio-political aspects of AI ethics in transnational higher education (TNHE) have become vital for analyzing how technology influences educational fairness and power structures and institutional management. AI systems operate without neutrality because they incorporate the values and biases and interests of their developers and users. Academic institutions that participate in TNHE across different cultural and regulatory settings must conduct critical assessments of their systems because these systems have the potential to perpetuate global inequalities. The Global North's technology companies create and operate AI systems which generates digital colonialism concerns because Southern institutions must use foreign-made systems and data networks which threatens their control over educational content and intellectual property rights. The situation requires establishing ethical principles which deal with data ownership problems and ensuring equal AI educational tool availability and cultural acceptance in learning systems.

Moreover, AI deployment in education intersects with issues of surveillance, privacy, and accountability. Automated assessment systems, plagiarism detectors, and predictive analytics can unintentionally perpetuate biases related to language, culture, or socioeconomic background. AI ethics analysis from a socio-political perspective requires open algorithmic management systems and participatory policy development which includes educational staff members and students and neighborhood populations for making choices. The UNESCO Recommendation on the Ethics of Artificial Intelligence (2021) stands as a global policy which promotes AI educational fairness and human rights protection and sustainability as essential principles.

Educators must modify their teaching methods and educational approaches to successfully incorporate AI into the learning process. AI technology allows students to learn through personalized methods and streamlines school operations yet its careless application threatens to undermine both human decision-making and critical thinking abilities. Teachers must shift from tool operators to leaders who determine the ethical boundaries for AI tool deployment. AI ethics literacy education enables students to develop critical thinking skills for evaluating algorithmic power and its effects on society at large. The educational initiatives from Microsoft and Google demonstrate that technology can advance both social inclusion and environmental sustainability through responsible ethical leadership.

Overall, addressing the socio-political and pedagogical dimensions of AI ethics transforms TNHE into a space of shared responsibility, where technology serves as a catalyst for equity, cultural respect, and sustainable global learning rather than a tool of imbalance or exclusion.

IMPLICATIONS

This chapter present critical implications for the future role of AI in transnational higher education, offering a comprehensive guide for diverse stakeholders. For educators and institutions, the chapter outlines a roadmap for ethically responsible and environmentally sustainable integration of AI. It emphasizes the importance of adopting transparent systems, embedding fairness into algorithmic decision-making, and providing continuous ethical training for faculty and staff. By doing so, institutions can ensure that AI enhances teaching and learning outcomes while protecting educational equity.

For policymakers, the chapter underscores the need to establish regulatory frameworks that mandate ethical AI practices in higher education. Such policies should not only safeguard sensitive student data but also promote accountability, inclusivity, and sustainability in AI adoption. Policymakers are urged to collaborate with educators and industry leaders to balance innovation with social responsibility.

For AI developers, the chapter highlights the responsibility of designing systems that go beyond functionality to reflect ethical values and environmental consciousness. Prioritizing transparency, inclusivity, and ecological impact in AI innovation can support the dual objectives of advancing education and promoting sustainability.

Finally, for researchers, the chapter identifies pressing areas for further inquiry, including continuous evaluation of AI biases, testing the effectiveness of data privacy safeguards, and examining the long-term sustainability of AI-driven practices in education. These research directions are crucial for advancing discussions on AI ethics and ensuring that its integration remains responsible, equitable, and aligned with broader sustainability goals, ultimately benefiting all stakeholders.

FUTURE RESEARCH DIRECTIONS

Future research should concentrate on comparative evaluations of regulatory frameworks across jurisdictions, sustainable AI innovations, and longitudinal studies looking at the long-term effects of AI on equity and inclusivity in TNHE. Furthermore, investigating cultural adaptation of AI tools and creating international guidelines for moral AI in education continue to be crucial fields.

CONCLUSION

The integration of AI in transnational higher education offers significant opportunities for improving educational outcomes and bridging global divides. However, it also brings critical ethical and sustainability challenges that require careful attention. This chapter emphasizes the need to develop and implement AI systems that are not only technologically advanced but also ethically sound and environmentally sustainable. In a transnational context, where diverse cultural, legal, and educational frameworks intersect, issues like data privacy, algorithmic bias, and fairness are particularly urgent. Tackling these challenges necessitates collaboration among educators, policymakers, AI developers, and researchers to establish strong ethical guidelines and best practices, ensuring that AI systems enhance the educational landscape without worsening inequalities or jeopardizing data security.

Furthermore, the chapter emphasizes the need for ongoing vigilance and adaptability in response to the rapid evolution of AI technologies. As AI continues to transform the educational sector, institutions must remain committed to regularly updating their ethical frameworks to reflect new developments and emerging risks. This proactive approach is essential to prevent potential harms and to ensure that AI-driven innovations uphold the principles of equity, fairness, and sustainability in education. The insights and recommendations provided aim to guide the responsible and sustainable use of AI in transnational higher education, ensuring that these technologies enhance educational practices in ways that are just, inclusive, and mindful of their broader societal impact.

REFERENCES

Abulibdeh, A., Zaidan, E., & Abulibdeh, R. (2024). Navigating the confluence of artificial intelligence and education for sustainable development in the era of industry 4.0: Challenges, opportunities, and ethical dimensions. *Journal of Cleaner Production, 437*, 140527. DOI: 10.1016/j.jclepro.2023.140527

Ahmad, S. F., Alam, M. M., Rahmat, M. K., Mubarik, M. S., & Hyder, S. I. (2022). Academic and administrative role of artificial intelligence in education. *Sustainability (Basel), 14*(3), 1101. DOI: 10.3390/su14031101

Al-Horr, K. (2024). Role of Transnational Universities in Capacity Building in Hosting Countries: A Review. *Journal of Tertiary Education and Learning*, 2(1), 1–11. DOI: 10.54536/jtel.v2i1.2315

Aliyu, A., Maglaras, L., He, Y., Yevseyeva, I., Boiten, E., Cook, A., & Janicke, H. (2020). A holistic cybersecurity maturity assessment framework for higher education institutions in the United Kingdom. *Applied Sciences (Basel, Switzerland), 10*(10), 3660. DOI: 10.3390/app10103660

Allendevaux, S. (2021). *How US State Data Protection Statutes Compare in Scope to Safeguard Information and Protect Privacy Using Iso/Iec 27001: 2013 and Iso/Iec 27701: 2019 Security and Privacy Management System Requirements as an Adequacy Baseline* (Doctoral dissertation, Northeastern University).

Alwahaibi, A., Bin, W., Hassa, W., Basri, W., Wan Ismail, W. B., & Almamari, M. (2022). A systematic literature review on it security standards for higher education institution. *Tianjin Daxue Xuebao (Ziran Kexue yu Gongcheng Jishu Ban). J Tianjin Univ Sci Technol, 55*, 194–213.

Anis, M. (2023). Leveraging artificial intelligence for inclusive English language teaching: Strategies and implications for learner diversity. *Journal of Multidisciplinary Educational Research, 12*(6), 54–70.

Azubuike, O. B., Adegboye, O., & Quadri, H. (2021). Who gets to learn in a pandemic? Exploring the digital divide in remote learning during the COVID-19 pandemic in Nigeria. *International Journal of Educational Research Open, 2*, 100022. DOI: 10.1016/j.ijedro.2020.100022

Babikian, J. (2023). Securing Rights: Legal Frameworks for Privacy and Data Protection in the Digital Era. *Law Research Journal, 1*(2), 91–101.

Bailey, R., & Parsheera, S. (2021). Data localization in India: Paradigms and processes. *CSI Transactions on ICT, 9*(3), 137–150. DOI: 10.1007/s40012-021-00337-4

Bandari, V. (2023). Enterprise data security measures: A comparative review of effectiveness and risks across different industries and organization types. *International Journal of Business Intelligence and Big Data Analytics, 6*(1), 1–11.

Bellamy, R. K., Dey, K., Hind, M., Hoffman, S. C., Houde, S., Kannan, K., Lohia, P., Martino, J., Mehta, S., Mojsilović, A., Nagar, S., Ramamurthy, K. N., Richards, J., Saha, D., Sattigeri, P., Singh, M., Varshney, K. R., & Zhang, Y. (2019). AI Fairness 360: An extensible toolkit for detecting and mitigating algorithmic bias. *IBM Journal of Research and Development, 63*(4/5), 4–1. DOI: 10.1147/JRD.2019.2942287

Berchin, I. I., de Aguiar Dutra, A. R., & Guerra, J. B. S. O. D. A. (2021). How do higher education institutions promote sustainable development? A literature review. *Sustainable Development (Bradford), 29*(6), 1204–1222. DOI: 10.1002/sd.2219

Bernholz, L., Nothias, T., & Vavrovsky, A. S. (2020). Digital Policy Is the Nonprofit Sector's Policy Agenda. *Available at SSRN* 3791637. DOI: 10.2139/ssrn.3791637

Bhoite, S., Nikam, P., & More, A. (2022). Predictive analytics of engineering and technology admissions. In *Computational Intelligence in Data Mining* [Singapore: Springer Nature Singapore.]. *Proceedings of ICCIDM, 2021*, 419–431.

Bird, K. A., Castleman, B. L., Mabel, Z., & Song, Y. (2021). Bringing transparency to predictive analytics: A systematic comparison of predictive modeling methods in higher education. *AERA Open, 7*, 23328584211037630. DOI: 10.1177/23328584211037630

Brown, I., & Marsden, C. T. (2023). *Regulating code: Good governance and better regulation in the information age*. MIT Press.

Butt, U., Dauda, Y., & Shaheer, B. (2023). Ransomware attack on the educational sector. In *AI, Blockchain and Self-Sovereign Identity in Higher Education* (pp. 279–313). Springer Nature Switzerland. DOI: 10.1007/978-3-031-33627-0_11

Chen, L., Chen, P., & Lin, Z. (2020). Artificial intelligence in education: A review. *IEEE Access : Practical Innovations, Open Solutions, 8*, 75264–75278. DOI: 10.1109/ACCESS.2020.2988510

Chen, S. (2021). Research on data sovereignty rules in cross-border data flow and Chinese solution. *US-China L. Rev., 18*, 261.

Chew, M. Y. L., Teo, E. A. L., Shah, K. W., Kumar, V., & Hussein, G. F. (2020). Evaluating the roadmap of 5G technology implementation for smart building and facilities management in Singapore. *Sustainability (Basel), 12*(24), 10259. DOI: 10.3390/su122410259

Chinta, S. V., Wang, Z., Yin, Z., Hoang, N., Gonzalez, M., Quy, T. L., & Zhang, W. (2024). FairAIED: Navigating Fairness, Bias, and Ethics in Educational AI Applications. *arXiv preprint arXiv:2407.18745*.

Courtland, R. (2018). The bias detectives. *Nature, 558*(7710), 357–360. DOI: 10.1038/d41586-018-05469-3

Cui, Y., Ma, Z., Wang, L., Yang, A., Liu, Q., Kong, S., & Wang, H. (2023). A survey on big data-enabled innovative online education systems during the COVID-19 pandemic. *Journal of Innovation & Knowledge, 8*(1), 100295. DOI: 10.1016/j.jik.2022.100295

Curzon, J., Kosa, T. A., Akalu, R., & El-Khatib, K. (2021). Privacy and artificial intelligence. *IEEE Transactions on Artificial Intelligence, 2*(2), 96–108. DOI: 10.1109/TAI.2021.3088084

Dai, K., Matthews, K. E., & Renshaw, P. (2020). Crossing the 'bridges' and navigating the 'learning gaps': Chinese students learning across two systems in a transnational higher education programme. *Higher Education Research & Development, 39*(6), 1140–1154. DOI: 10.1080/07294360.2020.1713731

Daneshjou, R., Smith, M. P., Sun, M. D., Rotemberg, V., & Zou, J. (2021). Lack of transparency and potential bias in artificial intelligence data sets and algorithms: A scoping review. *JAMA Dermatology*, *157*(11), 1362–1369. DOI: 10.1001/jamadermatol.2021.3129

Djeki, E., Dégila, J., Bondiombouy, C., & Alhassan, M. H. (2024, April). Data protection in digital learning space: An overview. In *AIP Conference Proceedings* (Vol. 3109, No. 1). AIP Publishing.

Fan, Z., Yan, Z., & Wen, S. (2023). Deep learning and artificial intelligence in sustainability: A review of SDGs, renewable energy, and environmental health. *Sustainability (Basel)*, *15*(18), 13493. DOI: 10.3390/su151813493

Fernández-Martínez, C., & Fernández, A. (2020). AI and recruiting software: Ethical and legal implications. *Paladyn : Journal of Behavioral Robotics*, *11*(1), 199–216. DOI: 10.1515/pjbr-2020-0030

Filimowicz, M. (Ed.). (2023). *Algorithmic Ethics: Algorithms and Society*. Taylor & Francis. DOI: 10.4324/9781003299882

George, B., & Wooden, O. (2023). Managing the strategic transformation of higher education through artificial intelligence. *Administrative Sciences*, *13*(9), 196. DOI: 10.3390/admsci13090196

Giani, M. S., & Walling, D. (2020). Will I Get In? Using Predictive Analytics to Develop Student-Facing Tools to Estimate University Admissions Decisions. *Journal of College Access*, *5*(1), 4.

González, A. S., & Rampino, L. (2024). A design perspective on how to tackle gender biases when developing AI-driven systems. *AI and Ethics*, •••, 1–18.

González-Sendino, R., Serrano, E., Bajo, J., & Novais, P. (2023). A review of bias and fairness in artificial intelligence.

Green, W. H. (2024). *Report to the President for year ended June 30, 2024*. MIT Energy Initiative.

Hinds, J., Williams, E. J., & Joinson, A. N. (2020). "It wouldn't happen to me": Privacy concerns and perspectives following the Cambridge Analytica scandal. *International Journal of Human-Computer Studies*, *143*, 102498. DOI: 10.1016/j.ijhcs.2020.102498

Holmes, W., & Miao, F. (2023). *Guidance for generative AI in education and research*. UNESCO Publishing.

Igbinenikaro, E., & Adewusi, O. A. (2024). Policy recommendations for integrating artificial intelligence into global trade agreements. *International Journal of Engineering Research Updates, 6*(01), 001-010.

Isakov, A., Urozov, F., Abduzhapporov, S., & Isokova, M. (2024). Enhancing Cybersecurity: Protecting Data In The Digital Age. *Innovations in Science and Technologies*, *1*(1), 40–49.

Jobin, A., Ienca, M., & Vayena, E. (2019). The global landscape of AI ethics guidelines. *Nature Machine Intelligence*, *1*(9), 389–399. DOI: 10.1038/s42256-019-0088-2

Kunjumuhammed, S. K. (2024). Artificial Intelligence in Addressing Educational Inequality Dimensions in Higher Education Institutions (HEIs): A Critical Review. *Risks and Challenges of AI-Driven Finance: Bias, Ethics, and Security*, 146-164.

Landers, R. N., & Behrend, T. S. (2023). Auditing the AI auditors: A framework for evaluating fairness and bias in high stakes AI predictive models. *The American Psychologist*, *78*(1), 36–49. DOI: 10.1037/amp0000972

Levy-Feldman, I., & Libman, Z. (2022). One size doesn't fit all educational assessment in a multicultural and intercultural world. *Intercultural Education*, *33*(4), 380–390. DOI: 10.1080/14675986.2022.2090174

Lewis, D., Hogan, L., Filip, D., & Wall, P. J. (2020). Global challenges in the standardization of ethics for trustworthy AI. *Journal of ICT Standardisation*, *8*(2), 123–150. DOI: 10.13052/jicts2245-800X.823

Li, Y., & Goel, S. (2024). Operationalizing AI Auditability Measures: An AI Audit Case Study of College Admissions System.

Lim, C. T., Bong, C. H., Wong, W. S., & Lee, N. K. (2021). A comprehensive review of automated essay scoring (AES) research and development. *Pertanika Journal of Science & Technology*, *29*(3), 1875–1899. DOI: 10.47836/pjst.29.3.27

Maghsudi, S., Lan, A., Xu, J., & van Der Schaar, M. (2021). Personalized education in the artificial intelligence era: What to expect next. *IEEE Signal Processing Magazine*, *38*(3), 37–50. DOI: 10.1109/MSP.2021.3055032

Markey, K., Graham, M. M., Tuohy, D., McCarthy, J., O'Donnell, C., Hennessy, T., Fahy, A., & O'Brien, B. (2023). Navigating learning and teaching in expanding culturally diverse higher education settings. *Higher Education Pedagogies*, *8*(1), 2165527. DOI: 10.1080/23752696.2023.2165527

McElhaney, K., Smith, G., Rustagi, I., & Groth, O. J. (2023). *Responsible AI: Tackling Tech's Largest Corporate Governance Challenges*. The Berkeley-Haas Case Series. University of California, Berkeley. Haas School of Business.

Meinel, C., Friedrichsen, M., Staubitz, T., Reinhard, S., & Köhler, D. (2024). Assessment Methods for Online Teaching.

Morandín-Ahuerma, F. (2023). Ten UNESCO Recommendations on the Ethics of Artificial Intelligence.

Morris, G. R., & Kozuch, S. (Eds.). (2024). *Engaging Higher Education Teachers and Students With Transnational Leadership*. IGI Global. DOI: 10.4018/979-8-3693-6100-9

Mouta, A., Torrecilla-Sánchez, E. M., & Pinto-Llorente, A. M. (2024). Design of a future scenarios toolkit for an ethical implementation of artificial intelligence in education. *Education and Information Technologies*, *29*(9), 10473–10498. DOI: 10.1007/s10639-023-12229-y

Nguyen, A., Ngo, H. N., Hong, Y., Dang, B., & Nguyen, B. P. T. (2023). Ethical principles for artificial intelligence in education. *Education and Information Technologies*, *28*(4), 4221–4241. DOI: 10.1007/s10639-022-11316-w

Ntloedibe, T., Foko, T., & Segooa, M. A. (2024). Cloud leakage in higher education in South Africa: A case of University of Technology. *South African Journal of Information Management*, *26*(1), 1783. DOI: 10.4102/sajim.v26i1.1783

Ou, A. W., Stöhr, C., & Malmström, H. (2024). Academic communication with AI-powered language tools in higher education: From a post-humanist perspective. *System, 121*, 103225. DOI: 10.1016/j.system.2024.103225

Pagallo, U., Aurucci, P., Casanovas, P., Chatila, R., Chazerand, P., Dignum, V., ... & Valcke, P. (2019). On good AI governance: 14 priority actions, a SMART model of governance, and a regulatory toolbox.

Pereira, F. D., Rodrigues, L., Henklain, M. H. O., Freitas, H., Oliveira, D. F., Cristea, A. I., Carvalho, L., Isotani, S., Benedict, A., Dorodchi, M., & de Oliveira, E. H. T. (2022). Toward Human–AI Collaboration: A Recommender System to Support CS1 Instructors to Select Problems for Assignments and Exams. *IEEE Transactions on Learning Technologies, 16*(3), 457–472. DOI: 10.1109/TLT.2022.3224121

Phillips, B. (2021). UK further education sector journey to compliance with the general data protection regulation and the data protection act 2018. *Computer Law & Security Review, 42*, 105586. DOI: 10.1016/j.clsr.2021.105586

Ramesh, D., & Sanampudi, S. K. (2022). An automated essay scoring systems: A systematic literature review. *Artificial Intelligence Review, 55*(3), 2495–2527. DOI: 10.1007/s10462-021-10068-2

Renick, T. M. (2020). Predictive analytics, academic advising, early alerts, and student success. *Big data on campus: Data analytics and decision making in higher education*, 177-197.

Rigos, J. C. (2022). *Applicant Reactions to Highly Automated Video-Interviews: Examining the Influence of Augmentation and Discrimination Experience*. Hofstra University.

Roshanaei, M., Olivares, H., & Lopez, R. R. (2023). Harnessing AI to foster equity in education: Opportunities, challenges, and emerging strategies. *Journal of Intelligent Learning Systems and Applications, 15*(04), 123–143. DOI: 10.4236/jilsa.2023.154009

Saaida, M. B. (2023). AI-Driven transformations in higher education: Opportunities and challenges. *International Journal of Educational Research and Studies, 5*(1), 29–36.

Salloum, S. A. (2024). AI Perils in Education: Exploring Ethical Concerns. *Artificial Intelligence in Education: The Power and Dangers of ChatGPT in the Classroom*, 669-675.

Sethi, P. C., & Behera, P. K. (2021, February). Effective online teaching learning during COVID-19 pandemic. [). IOP Publishing.]. *Journal of Physics: Conference Series, 1797*(1), 012068. DOI: 10.1088/1742-6596/1797/1/012068

Slimi, Z., & Carballido, B. V. (2023). Navigating the Ethical Challenges of Artificial Intelligence in Higher Education: An Analysis of Seven Global AI Ethics Policies. *TEM Journal, 12*(2).

Strubell, E., Ganesh, A., & McCallum, A. (2020, April). Energy and policy considerations for modern deep learning research. *Proceedings of the AAAI Conference on Artificial Intelligence, 34*(09), 13693–13696. DOI: 10.1609/aaai.v34i09.7123

Takavarasha, S.Jr, Van Heerden, R., Thakur, S. C., & Jordaan, A. (2023). Cyber-security in the era of the COVID-19 pandemic: A developing countries' perspective. *International Journal of Industrial Engineering and Operations Management, 5*(2), 77–85. DOI: 10.1108/IJIEOM-02-2023-0026

Ulven, J. B., & Wangen, G. (2021). A systematic review of cybersecurity risks in higher education. *Future Internet, 13*(2), 39. DOI: 10.3390/fi13020039

United Nations Educational, Scientific and Cultural Organization. (2021, November 23). *Recommendation on the ethics of artificial intelligence.* https://unesdoc.unesco.org/ark:/48223/pf0000377897

Varona, D., & Suárez, J. L. (2022). Discrimination, bias, fairness, and trustworthy AI. *Applied Sciences (Basel, Switzerland), 12*(12), 5826. DOI: 10.3390/app12125826

Vila Seoane, M. F. (2021). Data securitisation: The challenges of data sovereignty in India. *Third World Quarterly, 42*(8), 1733–1750. DOI: 10.1080/01436597.2021.1915122

Voss, W. G. (2021). Airline Commercial Use of EU Personal Data in the Context of the GDPR, British Airways and Schrems II. *Colo. Tech. LJ, 19*, 377.

Wilkins, S. (2017). Ethical issues in transnational higher education: The case of international branch campuses. *Studies in Higher Education, 42*(8), 1385–1400. DOI: 10.1080/03075079.2015.1099624

Williams, B. A., Brooks, C. F., & Shmargad, Y. (2018). How algorithms discriminate based on data they lack: Challenges, solutions, and policy implications. *Journal of Information Policy, 8*, 78–115. DOI: 10.5325/jinfopoli.8.2018.0078

Wolff, J., & Atallah, N. (2021). Early GDPR penalties: Analysis of implementation and fines through May 2020. *Journal of Information Policy, 11*, 63–103. DOI: 10.5325/jinfopoli.11.2021.0063

Yeung, K., & Bygrave, L. A. (2022). Demystifying the modernized European data protection regime: Cross-disciplinary insights from legal and regulatory governance scholarship. *Regulation & Governance, 16*(1), 137–155. DOI: 10.1111/rego.12401

Chapter 13
From Scroll to School: The Dual Influence of Social Media and AI on Gen Alpha (iPad Generation) Learning Journey

Rozalin Routray
https://orcid.org/0009-0000-9151-4987
Symbiosis Centre for Management and Human Resource Development, Symbiosis International University, Pune, India

Pooja Choudhary
https://orcid.org/0000-0002-6938-9179
Symbiosis Institute of International Business, Symbiosis International University, Pune, India

Vinita Sinha
https://orcid.org/0000-0002-4195-2257
Symbiosis Centre for Management and Human Resource Development, Symbiosis International University, Pune, India

ABSTRACT

This study investigates the impact of social media and technology on the academic performance and behavior of Gen Alpha, or i generation in India. It finds that children experience anxiety, mood swings, and inattention due to exposure to digital content. Parents are concerned about technological dependence and stagnation of imagination in homework. The study highlights the challenges of digital parenting in India, where parents struggle to teach responsibility while losing control over their children's online activities. The research suggests that active parenting, digital citizenship education, and platform regulation are necessary to help children resist harmful online influences.

1. INTRODUCTION

Generation Alpha, as defined by McCrindle, Fell, & Buckerfield (2021), comprises children born from 2010 to 2024. The initial years of this cohort's existence were characterized by significant digital

DOI: 10.4018/979-8-3373-5403-3.ch013

advancements, including the introduction of iPads, the establishment of Instagram, and the unanticipated emergence of the term "app," which was designated as the word of the year.

The children of Generation Alpha do not acquire information through conventional channels. These children engage in play, learning, and interaction primarily through technological means. They neither desire nor engage in reading traditionally. Transnational education, characterized by students engaging in academic pursuits in a country distinct from that conferring their degree, is increasingly supported by international branch campuses and AI-driven learning tools. For Generation Alpha learners, educational resources augmented by artificial intelligence and visual components significantly enhance comprehension, particularly within multicultural academic environments. These tools offer personalized and immersive experiences that facilitate the overcoming of language and curriculum barriers. Challenges in digital parenting include managing unsupervised internet usage and fostering responsibility amidst evolving online behaviors influenced by peers and platform design. Value-based parenting, which emphasizes open communication and guidance, can address these concerns while promoting digital literacy. When integrated thoughtfully, AI tools can empower Generation Alpha students in transnational contexts by rendering learning more accessible and engaging, while parental involvement ensures balanced development. This collaboration supports academic achievement and cultivates responsible digital citizens across borders.

From an early age, they have been exposed to information technology, demonstrating proficiency in its use even before developing verbal communication skills. Alpha children exhibit independence and curiosity, possessing a worldview distinct from that of their parents and educators. Moreover, Generation Alpha seems to exhibit greater proficiency in areas such as robotics, coding, social media marketing, app development, and big data, owing to the anticipated opportunities presented by a digitized world. Parenting has become increasingly challenging in contemporary society. Modern parents encounter greater complexity and stress in raising their children to become healthy and resilient adults compared to previous generations. Although social media serves as a valuable tool for parents to maintain communication with their children, there is a prevalent concern among parents that the use of social media by children may detract from their overall well-being. Social media has significantly influenced the current generation's news sharing and sharing, with platforms like YouTube, Instagram, and Facebook being the most popular. Around 90% of young individuals use social media, with most engaging with multiple platforms daily, including YouTube and Instagram. (Ma et al., 2013; Kaplan & Haenlein, 2010). Pew studies have widely written about the global impact caused by social media. A significant majority of children (95%) already possess or have access to a smartphone, while 97% of kids indicate usage of social media applications (Ohannessian et al., 2021). Social media refers to internet channels utilized by individuals to exchange thoughts and experiences. Parents of Generation Alpha have challenges such as monitoring screen addiction and controlling cyberbullying.

In 1956, artificial intelligence (AI) was defined as "the science and engineering of developing intelligent machines (McCarthy, 2007). Children are being raised using AI assistants and smart devices, such as Google-enhanced speakers and Siri or Alexa. This generation is being guided by AI in a rapidly evolving digital environment, with widespread use of digital assistants and AI-integrated applications across education, social media, and robotics (Su & Yang, 2022a).

AI apps are being used by young children, but there's a lack of focus on the importance of AI literacy and its impact on their well-being. Children aged 1-13 rely on their caregivers, and overuse of technology can lead to risky situations and unnecessary digital content(Kendrick et al., 2013). Ongoing advancements in science and technology, paired with the increasing adoption of Gen AI, enhance the intelligence and convenience of future people's lives (Chung et al., 2021). Advanced AI on social media platforms is assessing user behavior, emotional state, and physical context, introducing new risks related to privacy and managing confidential information. The impact of this AI-generated content is challenging to predict. According to a study, it is associated with internalizing behaviors throughout the ages of 8 to 10 years (Sumner et al., 2019). In recent years, the rapid development of artificial intelligence (AI) has been facilitated by increased computational speeds and advancements in machine learning algorithms. AI technology is transforming traditional educational methodologies, rendering them more personalized, interactive, and efficient. When students hold AI technology in high regard, AI courses should be structured to impart foundational knowledge and practical skills in the field. The course commences with an exploration of the history and fundamental concepts of AI, acquainting students with its developmental background and core theories. Subsequently, it examines key technologies such as machine learning, deep learning, natural language processing, and computer vision, enabling students to comprehend their mechanisms and real-world applications. Students will participate in hands-on projects to learn how to create with AI, organized into four units: drawing with AI, storytelling with AI, making music with AI, and animating with AI.

This includes tampering of audio and video materials, such as fakes, extremely convincing sales agents (Lewis & Moorkens, 2020). Increasing outputs will be pushed by emerging technologies supported by the internet, specifically generative AI, blockchain, social media, and video-sharing platforms such as TikTok and YouTube (van der Ven et al., 2024). The influence of social media and Artificial Intelligence must be evaluated in terms of their capacity to either encourage or oppose these changes. Social media is partially accountable for decreasing the ability of everyone to concentrate on participating in significant work.

Research has studied the addictive nature of social media and its related threats to psychological wellness, including cyberbullying and online harassment (Craig et al., 2020). Children who internalize issues, such as anxiety and behavioral changes, face various risks and academic hurdles in the future (Deighton et al., 2018). The typical TikTok video has a duration of only thirty-four seconds and causes a dopamine release that pushes users to continue scrolling through additional videos (Liu & Luo, 2015).

Artificial intelligence is increasingly being utilized in early childhood education to improve instruction, education, and evaluation, thereby enhancing the learning and development of young children (Vartiainen et al., 2020). A study on Artificial Intelligence anticipates that AI would "enhance education at all levels, particularly through the provision of personalization at scale (Stone et al., 2022).

This paper examines how young children (1-13 years) become addicted to social media and technology, hence impacting their academic performance. Mobile technology advancements have led to the development of educational applications like Duolingo, which utilize AI for intelligent, interactive language learning. (Yu & Guo, 2023). This study involves children aged six to eleven years, since it impacts their academic achievement and internalizing behaviors. According to the study, it is significantly associated positively with internalizing tendencies among children aged 8 to 10 years (Sumner et al., 2019).

1.1. Research Gap

Su and Yang's recent analysis indicates there is an absence of research on artificial intelligence education for young children (Su & Yang, 2022b). Artificial intelligence tools are progressively utilized in early childhood education to enhance learning and development in young children (Vartiainen et al.,

2020). Despite extensive literature on the potential and actual harms of social media, there is a shortage of studies that suggest how its effects on Generation Alpha are going to vary (Höfrová et al., 2024).

1.2. Research Objectives and Questions

This article aims to examine the balance between innovation and social media concerning Generation Alpha and their internalizing behavior, as well as the potential of AI to enhance children's academic performance by encouraging familiarity with AI from an early age.

Research Objectives

1. To explore how social media platforms like YouTube and Instagram affect the emotional well-being and behavior of Generation Alpha.
2. To study the influence of social media on the internalizing behaviors of Generation Alpha, especially its impact on their development
3. To find appropriate parenting practices that can minimize the negative impact of social media and help with the academic performance of Generation Alpha.
4. To suggest effective AI-driven interventions that can help in learning and academic achievement in this generation.

Research Questions

RQ1) How do social media and Artificial intelligence impact the risk factors among children?
RQ2) What is the effect of social media usage on children's concentration, optimism, creativity, internalizing behavior, academic progress, and how can parents prepare to tackle such problems in the near future?

2. LITERATURE REVIEW

2.1. Generation Alpha

A new generation arose as social media changed. Mark McCrindle, a generational researcher, coined the term Generation Alpha. Births from 2010 to 2025 are included in Generation Alpha. This group consists of children aged 0–13 who have been surrounded by technology since birth. Social media has the greatest impact on digital natives, or those born in the new millennium (Tirendi & Gargiulo, 2024). The scenario improves technology management, communication abilities, and intelligence. The most tech-savvy generation to date, Generation Alpha, is at the forefront of artificial intelligence and the Internet of Things (Pattrawiwat et al., 2024). The mindset of the generation is shaped by digital games, toys, role models, symbolic media, and social networks for inspiration and communication. "Digital natives" who are tech-savvy and addicted to digital media are part of Generation Alpha. Virtual reality and mobile devices, such as phones and tablets, are crucial for gaming, watching shows, and consuming interesting content in this generation (Šramová & Pavelka, 2023).

Generation Alpha, today facing several technological problems, should be educated on how to free themselves from their dependence. A study (Jha, 2020) advocate for a balanced and seamless approach, wherein both elements can be coordinated, allowing technology to serve as a significant beneficiary rather than a challenge to humanity.

2.2 Children's Safety in the Digital World

Home robots and pocket smart devices are now common. Tablets and toys with more computational power than personal computers from a decade ago are now available to young children (Williams et al., 2019). Technological literacy becomes crucial for children growing up, but social media and emerging technologies are not yet taught, and concerns about digital safety persist (Simpson, 1996). According to Sun et al. (2021), young children (ages 4-11) lack a basic understanding of the technological, social, and risky aspects of the Internet. Age affects children's Internet knowledge, so educational institutions, libraries, families, and other social systems must recognize age differences and take developmentally appropriate measures to protect children (Yan, 2006). Young children must learn about AI's limitations, ethics, and basics (Long and Magerko, 2020). Junior primary children may be too young to understand AI concepts and be at risk of harm from inaccurate and misleading information or instructions (Su et al., 2023). AI knowledge in early childhood should promote equitable growth to close the digital gap in early education and achieve digital accessibility (Berson et al., 2022).

2.3 Alpha's Internalizing Behavior

Internalizing disorders encompass anxiety, eating disorders, and additional conditions. Childhood social isolation is a precursor to behavioral competencies. Internalizing problems and inadequate child adjustment may also lead to aggressive behavior. Internalized issues among students can adversely affect academic performance, interpersonal relationships, and overall development. Children of school age exhibiting behavioral problems frequently encounter academic difficulties (Caro et al., 2023; Merikangas et al., 2010). Engagement in social media discourse forecasted an escalation in internalizing symptoms. Dialogue markedly diminished social media consumption and anxiety (Ohannessian et al., 2021). Research has associated social media usage with anxiety and depression (Vannucci et al., 2017). Social media, enabling content creation and sharing, has surged in popularity, leading researchers to examine its impact on children's emotional development (Barry et al., 2015).

2.4. Parents' Perception and Role in Child's Safety

Our children get involved with smart devices and robotics from birth. We need to instruct our children in ways to make use of these technologies and in dealing with intelligent devices (Angel-Fernandez & Vincze, 2018a). More than 80% of parents of Generation Alpha report that their children engage with movies or games on a mobile device every day, averaging 7 to 8 hours of screen time (Höfrová et al., 2024). Parents fear texting may degrade spoken communication skills and increase social media dependence. However, not all video content is suitable for advertisers, and not all labor is deserving of reward, including hate speech and racism (Ma and Kou, 2021). Parents are required to supervise and guide their children while allowing access to social media, to reduce the negative impacts of media use, and ensure conscious control (Lee & Chae, 2012). The core concept of parental involvement is to safeguard children from "undesirable influences," with parents adopting the role of protectors (Wang & Chen, 2022). Parents who are highly engaged with the internet are likely to establish specific regulations to limit their children's media consumption, as they possess greater knowledge on the matter at hand (Liu et al., 2022).

2.5. Impacts of AI Technology on Children's Academic Growth

Artificial intelligence techniques are rapidly applied in early childhood education to improve learning and development in young children. A survey in Singapore supports this finding, indicating that the use of digital technology influences children's reading abilities in early childhood (Haoning Mah et al., 2021).

Technological literacy is crucial for children learning with smart gadgets, as age and prior technical skills influence their learning capabilities. Robotics offers significant opportunities for impacting education (Angel-Fernandez & Vincze, 2018b). Early childhood robotics is a method for implementing programming into the educational program for young children. Automation is an area of technology focused on developing, creating, operating, and application of automated machinery (Zviel Girshin et al., 2024).

They are acquiring techniques for problem-solving, project design, and concept communication. Computational thinking to enhance each child's analytical capacity (Bati, 2022). Utilizing AI, or tablets as programming tools, can offer young children a broader range of creative learning experiences. Blend automation into science and technology education, develop a self-assured attitude, enhance technology and science education, and also educate kids in the technology-driven society we live in (Ioannou and Makridou, 2018; Manches and Plowman, 2017).

AI tools are continuously being used in early childhood education to improve education and growth in young children; interactions with AI-integrated toys or robots can enhance their creativity, interpersonal skills, interactive inquiry, as well as language skills (Su and Yang, 2022c; Vartiainen et al., 2020). The study explores the impact of story-inspired programming on preschool children, revealing that storytelling, combined with robots or computers, provides a more inclusive and sustainable learning experience (Yang et al., 2023). Integrating AI and computer technology into education allows children to engage with the joys and challenges of these fields from a young age. Hong Kong has established an AI curriculum framework tailored for early childhood education, including fundamental AI knowledge, abilities, and behaviors (Su & Zhong, 2022).

The study explores the potential of AI in education, highlighting its benefits in student empowerment, improved learning outcomes, and potential transformation of educational contexts through personalized learning, feedback, AI tutoring, automated exams, and virtual simulations (Shahzad et al., 2024).

3. RESEARCH METHODOLOGY

This study employs a qualitative research methodology, which involves the collection of data through in-depth interviews. The present research approach examines the social media use patterns and concerns of parents regarding children belonging to Generation Alpha aged between 6 to 13 years. This study offered social media and academic performance-related in-depth interviews to 15 Indian parents of Generation Alpha children. The data acquired from the semi-structured interviews were examined through thematic analysis, a technique that emphasizes the identification, analysis, and reporting of patterns (themes) within qualitative data (Braun & Clarke, 2006). The analysis used an inductive approach, identifying themes based on data rather than established theories. The primary data analysis was conducted manually, ensuring traceability and trustworthiness through peer debriefing and member checking.

4. INTERVIEW PROTOCOL

The interview process allowed parents to raise safety concerns and explore their perceptions of the impact of social media and AI technology on their child's academic performance. The interview protocol was followed, including explanations of procedures and confidentiality of personal data. Questions were occasionally omitted if parents had already addressed them in response to previous questions or during comments. Through semi-structured interviews, we investigated students' learning experiences, their attitudes toward artificial intelligence, and parental suggestions regarding the regulation of children's screen time. This study investigates parents' perceptions of their children's engagement with social media platforms like YouTube and Instagram, and the potential impact on internalizing behaviors like anxiety and rudeness. It also explores parents' perspectives on the influence of advanced technologies like ChatGPT and bots on their children's academic performance. The study also explores children's access to and control over screen time on these platforms, parents' awareness of potential usage risks, and any concerns or dislikes parents might have regarding their children's interactions with social media channels. Participants were recruited through convenience sampling. These are the related questions interviewed with Gen Alpha parents. As a parent, what are your biggest concerns regarding children's social media use? At what age do you consider it suitable for children to begin accessing social media? Have you observed any changes in your child's mood or behavior that you believe may be associated with their social media usage? Suggest a viewpoint on how social media can be utilized to enhance learning and promote internet safety positively? As a parent, what social media platforms like Facebook, Twitter, Instagram, Snapchat, YouTube, and Google+ do you observe your child favoring, and what are the reasons behind their preferences? Should parents watch their child's activities? Monitor privacy settings and mandate your authorization for new application downloads? Do you believe that internalizing issues such as anxiety and depression, along with the presence of numerous risk factors, can result in a child's academic challenges? Which preventive and remedial measures do you believe should be implemented for minimizing the harmful effects of social media usage on children's internalizing concerns? Do Smart technologies, such as AI, enhance the education of Generation Alpha for improving their mental well-being, and the positive effect of Internet usage on academic achievement?

5. RESULTS AND FINDINGS

5.1 Parenting Approaches, Concerns, and Challenges

"In today's digital era, keeping children completely away from social media is nearly impossible, as children learn by observing, so they naturally pick up habits from adults. We are highly dependent on the Internet. Instead of attempting to eliminate their exposure, we should focus on regulating their online activity. Through parental controls, ensuring they access appropriate content and manage screen time".

Today's digital technologies offer children greater access to information and more opportunities to engage with others online. Although this increased access can lead to numerous learning and social interaction opportunities, it also introduces potential risks (Martin et al., 2023a). Social media refers to internet-based applications that facilitate user-generated content creation and exchange. Adapt instructional strategies to accommodate evolving learning styles and acknowledge the role of social media in enhancing educational effectiveness. Learning self-efficacy refers to the belief in one's ability to acquire new knowledge (Hu et al., 2024). The home environment plays a crucial role in shaping health behaviors, with parents' own behaviors, as well as their parenting strategies and practices, exerting a significant influence on children's health behavior (Pearson et al., 2018). A study conducted where the present research was undertaken revealed that one in five kids aged 14 to 19 years considers it acceptable to add strangers to social network sites. This behavior can be classified as risk behavior (Symons et al., 2020).

> "Social media is widely used and displays my viewpoint. We can have parental authority over what and how much exposure we wish to provide our children. Only then can it have a beneficial impact on our children."
>
> Another parent said
>
> "Basically, then it is recommended that youngsters get their own account where they can access whatever information they like. The content should have an age restriction. As an illustration, my 12-year-old child will log in. The social media stuff ought to be shown via that stream. Nothing should be shown on his clean if there is anything available that is 14 or 16 years old. Therefore, the pop-up shouldn't exist. We can't take in everything if we consume a lot of content on a single subject, can we? Thus, we ended up in a mess."

Educators must adopt innovative pedagogical strategies that cater to Generation Alpha's technological proficiency to prepare them for a dynamic, technology-driven environment, as their technology-advocacy influences their learning styles, expectations, and aspirations (Al-Sa'di & Ahmad, 2023). Social media enhances mental well-being in students through increased psychological acuity, family support, and effective learning strategies, despite its widespread use in modern society. (Shahzad et al., 2024). In contemporary society, the pervasive use of social media has become a fundamental aspect of kids' daily routines, with the majority of young individuals engaging intensively with these platforms to sustain social interactions with their peers. (Boer et al., 2021). A US survey shows YouTube is the most popular digital platform among adolescents, followed by Instagram and Snapchat, with usage rates of 72% and 69%, respectively (Dienlin & Johannes, 2020a). Smart learning involves diverse topics, group goals alignment, competitive academic performance, and innovative technologies and social media applications, with responsible use enhancing academic activities and collaborations. (Shafiq & Parveen, 2023).

5.2 Psychological and Behavioral Impact (Internalizing Behavior)

> "So basically, when they play so many games on social media, I mean, they watch some, you know, aggressive deals, for example, action-specific, something horror. So, their moods get changed. Their behavior gets aggressive, rebellious, so many times they think they are correct, and you know your parents are trying to restrict them more and more. So, you know this great chaos at home as well. And there's, lack of trust and a lack of respect observed during this time."

Within Generation Alpha, certain negative characteristics, such as technology addiction, egocentrism, and a tendency towards aggression, have been identified. (Hu et al., 2024). Common screen time and behavioral changes in young children are often linked, allowing for the development of targeted prevention strategies based on early childhood influences. (Pearson et al., 2018). Approximately 20–30% of young children encounter sleep-related difficulties.

A recognized environmental factor contributing to inadequate sleep is the extensive use of screen media, including television and video gaming. (Cheung et al., 2017). Kids express dissatisfaction with social media usage, often feeling negative emotions, struggling to reduce screen time, neglecting other activities, and engaging in conflicts with parents over screen time. (Martin et al., 2023b). Social media usage can potentially cause stress or exacerbate negative self-assessments due to unfavorable feedback or social comparisons. (Nesi & Prinstein, 2015).

So, ideally yes, but this is next to impossible to watch every time, like what kid is doing, okay. And another thing is that if we interfere with too many kids, we find that they are in control. They are getting restricted with everything, so sometimes they behave like that. As soon as they see the parents, they give up the devices, but if they don't have any restrictions or authority. Monitoring what we can monitor, we can monitor history, just displaying it. For example, if your kid watches any video for an hour, it is impractical for a parent to review the entire video to ascertain its content. This task is indeed challenging.

Concerns for safety have led to children owning smart devices, causing concern over the proliferation of mobile devices, which promote multi-screen usage and access to diverse content. (Lissak, 2018). In numerous Western and certain Far Eastern countries, there is a continuous increase in digital media consumption among the youth. In 2011, 52% of children aged 0 to 8 years had access to a mobile device. (Lissak, 2018). Imposing time limits can assist children in developing self-control and promote moderate use of social media while restricting screen time. Parental mediation, which includes monitoring a child's online activities and establishing rules for Internet usage, is generally associated with a reduction in exposure to online risks (Symons et al., 2020).

> "Obviously, because. Sometimes they become anxious if we, you know, control them for the devices and everything. They are unable to concentrate when studying. They are therefore observing everything in an uncontrolled setting. And it had a significant effect on their studies because they were utilizing social media during the time allotted for studying. Anxiety will make the child difficult to concentrate, and depression will lead to low motivation, fatigue, and withdrawal from learning."

> "Should discuss time and duration between a child and their parents, advising them on social media usage and educating them on preventing harm, such as not sharing personal information or uploading videos."

Generation Alpha, who have been raised in a world dominated by technology. These digital platforms impact their body image and self-esteem, as well as shape their emotional intelligence and social interactions (Piccerillo & Digennaro, 2025). Social media exposure can lead to feelings of inadequacy and envy, negatively impacting self-esteem and overall well-being. Surveys show that most adolescents have smartphones and frequently use multiple devices simultaneously. (Van Den Eijnden et al., 2018). Social media use can lead to negative behaviors, including academic challenges and social functioning issues. Children who frequently use electronic devices and social media may exhibit shyness and experience approach-avoidance conflict, hindering their desire for social engagement. (Asendorpf, 1990).

Social media addiction is characterized by dissatisfaction, negative emotions, unsuccessful attempts to reduce usage, neglect of other responsibilities, frequent conflicts, and deceit towards parents or friends. (Boer et al., 2022). Collaborative learning strategies among students and instructors foster positive attitudes, engagement with educational materials, and peer engagement, ultimately improving student performance. (Kabilan et al., 2010)Research has demonstrated that preventive strategies and school-based interventions are efficacious in mitigating the potential adverse effects associated with social media platforms (Throuvala et al., 2019).

5.3 Academic Performance-Related Effects

"With the Internet and streaming platforms like YouTube, children who struggle with imagination from textbooks can now access better content. Through AI, curated content can be created that makes learning easier for children to grasp, understand, and implement. This has a positive effect overall." Another parent said:

"Sometimes it is really useful to use AI, but I feel the negative impact as well. For example, if some topic has been given to children to write some content about that, Composition or something, instead of putting their own efforts using their own creativity, they used to give that topic to AI, and then AI gives the content for them. It is good if you are used to writing those compositions and everything else. Label up, and then you are using AI to filter out the information."

Generation Alpha students are increasingly influenced by technology, as it guides and mediates their learning methodologies. AI technologies are used for efficient time management, task prioritization, and supplementary educational resources, reshaping the student experience (Whelan et al., 2020). They educate young students on the strategic use of AI and social media to enhance both their academic pursuits and mental well-being (Luo et al., 2022). The democratization of AI technologies enables children to interact with machines through coding, natural language, and computer vision, promoting AI literacy development. Children are familiar with AI and bots like Alexa, Jibo, and Cozmo robots for academic development (Druga et al., 2018).

The introduction of ChatGPT in late 2022 sparked global concern about students using AI tools for academic dishonesty, undermining learning assessments and qualifications. Some institutions banned ChatGPT, while others adopted cautious integration approaches (Anders, 2023). Educational institutions, including schools and universities, have adopted a progressive approach, advocating that instead of prohibiting the use of AI tools, students and staff should be instructed on their effective, ethical, and transparent utilization (Walan, 2025).

5.4 Social Environment and Exposure Factors

"Oh, as my child isn't a teen, I have observed she's using Snapchat and Google a lot. Google further educational purpose, and some of the research and Snapchat are for the better filter of the photos and reach for her friends."

Another parent said, "Since Instagram has a ton of profitable material from many well-known users that they may even know, I believe it's rather simple for them to accomplish it. My kids seem to favor YouTube, Instagram, and Snapchat. The second. They are more active on Instagram and Snapchat, primarily because of their friends nearby and because they are a part of a wider community."

The Pew Research Center shows that 24% of adolescents are constantly online, with Facebook being the most popular platform, with 71% usage.

Young people use the internet for social interaction, information acquisition, and education, characterized by confidence and enthusiasm (Shade & Singh, 2016). More than 80% of parents of Generation

Alpha report that their children engage in video watching or gaming on a mobile device daily, with an average screen time of 7–8 hours (Höfrová et al., 2024). Numerous young individuals are compelled to engage with online platforms due to both educational and social imperatives. For example, an increasing proportion of after-school assignments is accessible exclusively via the Internet (Dienlin & Johannes, 2020b).

Generation Alpha is poised to navigate an increasingly dynamic and technology-driven world. Children aged 8 to 11 years are beginning to comprehend the risks associated with sharing certain information online. Parents can influence kids' social media usage and well-being through media-specific parenting practices. Such practices may facilitate healthy social media engagement, enhancing well-being and mitigating ill-being (Nathanson, 2001).

6. DISCUSSIONS

Parents express concern regarding their children's engagement with social media and its potential impact on their mood and behavior. They acknowledge that while social media can enhance learning, excessive use poses risks. Children predominantly favor platforms such as Facebook, Twitter, Instagram, Snapchat, YouTube, and Google, with preferences similar to Twitter, as a microblogging platform, which facilitates student engagement in discussions on course topics, completion of assignments, and sharing of educational materials (Dong et al., 2023). It is imperative for parents to monitor their children's activities, oversee privacy settings, and require authorization for new application downloads. Research indicates that anxiety and depression can lead to academic difficulties in children who frequently use electronic devices and social media, causing shyness and approach-avoidance conflicts, hindering their desire for social engagement. There are ongoing concerns regarding Generation Alpha, specifically that the increase in interpersonal communication through text may lead to a decline in oral communication skills. Additionally, there is apprehension that reliance on social media influences for information about current events may result in diminished critical thinking abilities (Kaplan-Berkley, 2022).

Parents are concerned about implementing preventive measures to mitigate the harmful effects of social media on children's internalizing issues. It's crucial to educate children about social media dynamics and avoid potential harm, such as sharing sensitive information or uploading photos. They should also be cautious about AI's potential negative effects on their mental well-being. The positive impact of internet usage and education on Generation Alpha should be considered. UNESCO has issued Guidance for Generative AI in Education and Research to assist educators, students, and researchers in managing access to such AI technologies within educational contexts.

Artificial Intelligence (AI) offers several positive contributions, particularly in supporting academic studies and practical tasks, as aligned with public perceptions documented by the World Economic Forum (2022). Education regarding AI is essential to enable individuals to assess both the benefits and challenges associated with AI. Furthermore, a more comprehensive education is required for individuals to effectively evaluate and develop AI technologies. (Brauner et al., 2023). Numerous tools and techniques have been developed to safeguard this generation, with artificial intelligence playing a crucial role in its advancement. The application of artificial intelligence in the detection of misinformation and hate speech on social media underscores the potential of AI methodologies to enhance online safety and mitigate harmful content (Islam et al., 2020).

Table 1. Themes arising from the study

S.No.	Theme	Sub-themes
A. Psychological and Behavioral Impact (Internalizing Behavior)		
1	Emotional and Behavioral Impact of Online Content	- Aggression, anxiety, mood swings, rebellion -Desensitization and overstimulation
2	Psychological Impact on Learning and Focus	- Anxiety and inability to concentrate - Depression, fatigue, low motivation - Withdrawal from learning
3	Cognitive Overload and Media Saturation	- Reduced attention span - Difficulty in reflection and focus - Mental clutter from excessive content
B. Academic Performance-Related Effects		
4	Overreliance on AI and Creativity Suppression	- Bypassing original thinking - AI replacing creative and cognitive effort - Loss of learning objectives in assignments
5	Platform-Specific Usage and Functional Differentiation	- Academic use of Google, YouTube - Social media distractions from Snapchat, Instagram - Peer-driven usage patterns
6	AI and Digital Tools Enhancing Learning	- Better comprehension through curated, visual content - Personalized learning aiding less imaginative learners
C. Parenting Approaches, Concerns, and Challenges		
7	Parental Concerns and Dilemmas	- Overwhelmed by digital parenting - Difficulty in setting and enforcing boundaries
8	Challenges in Practical Monitoring and Digital Oversight	- Impracticality of reviewing content - Illusion of control via browsing history - Children hiding behavior from parents
9	Regulation Over Restriction	- Emphasis on guided, flexible boundaries - Focus on digital responsibility over prohibition
10	Intentional Parental Authority and Value-Based Guidance	- Teaching children ethical and safe digital habits - Parenting grounded in values and digital literacy
11	Importance of Dialogue, Time Planning & Digital Education	- Educating children on screen safety and privacy - Collaborative screen -time rules and academic scheduling
D. Social Environment and Exposure Factors		
12	Inevitable Exposure to Digital Media	- Digital media as an integral part of life - Early and unavoidable access
13	Social Learning and Imitation	- Mimicking adults, influencers, and peer behaviors - Internalizing trends from digital exposure
14	Peer Influence and Digital Community Belonging	- Conforming to peer usage - Belongingness through shared digital platforms
15	Strained Parent–Child Relationships	- Conflict over restrictions - Breakdown in communication and trust
16	Age-Appropriate Access and Platform Responsibility	- Age filters and tailored platform algorithms - Platform role in content moderation

(Author's Own Creation)

Four main themes emerged from the study: the influence on behavior and psychology, the consequences on academic performance, parenting styles and difficulties, and exposure factors and the social environment. From the viewpoint of the parents, these themes highlight the complex ways that digital media and artificial intelligence affect Generation Alpha's learning and general well-being.

According to psychological and behavioral impacts, children who are constantly exposed to internet information are more likely to be aggressive, nervous, moody, and desensitized as a result of being overstimulated (Coyne et al., 2024; Przybylski & Weinstein, 2017). Children who spend too much time on screens may experience mental exhaustion, lose interest, and become less motivated and concentrated while they study (Twenge et al., 2021; Tandon et al., 2023). While ChatGPT and Grammarly are examples of AI tools that might assist students in understanding and participating in their work, they may also inhibit originality and creativity (Kasneci et al., 2023; Bower et al., 2024). While Google and YouTube can support academic learning, social media apps like Instagram and Snapchat can be distracting and impair performance (Mnkandla & Minnaar.,2017; Khurshid et al., 2023).

When it comes to parenting, parents struggle to monitor their children's internet behavior and set limitations. Finding the ideal balance between independence and supervision is difficult for many people. Usually, they employ ineffective control methods (Livingstone et al., 2023; Theopilus et al., 2025). In order to promote responsible online behavior, research supports value-based parenting and guided regulation that place an emphasis on digital literacy, candid communication, and cooperative screen-time scheduling (Nelson et al., 2021; Lauricella et al., 2022). Finally, social environment traits suggest that children will inevitably be exposed to digital media as they want to fit in through online communities and imitate their peers and influencers (Sequeira et al., 2025; Valkenburg et al., 2022). Early access to technology and peer conformity have an impact on behavior and identity, often leading to conflict in parent-child relationships (Hiniker et al., 2021; Das, 2023). The findings indicate that while excessive use of digital devices might negatively impact relationships and emotional stability, they can also improve learning. For children to grow up safely and healthily online, platforms must take greater responsibility and practice balanced digital parenting.

Generation Alpha's unique characteristics and technological capabilities are set to significantly impact higher education. The educational landscape is transforming, necessitating innovative pedagogical strategies to align with their skills and aspirations. Technology enhances student engagement, and contemporary learners prefer technology-supported educational tools, enabling Generation Alpha to excel in a technology-oriented world. (Gill & Mathur, 2023).

In a national survey conducted in the United States, it was found that among children aged 8 to 12 years, 53% of their screen time is allocated to watching television or online videos, while 31% is dedicated to playing video games (Shade & Singh, 2016). Existing research indicates that young children, aged 5 to 8 years, possess limited comprehension of both the technical and social dimensions of the Internet, as well as its associated risks.

Parental concerns regarding children's Internet usage primarily focus on issues such as privacy breaches, cyberbullying, addiction, and exposure to explicit content (Lau et al., 2018; Sun et al., 2021). Considering the evidence that the likelihood of engaging in multiple risk behaviors increases throughout developmental stages and recognizing that healthy habits are established early in life, it is valuable to investigate younger children before health behaviors become deeply ingrained.

7. CONCLUSION AND LIMITATIONS OF THE STUDY

This qualitative investigation investigated the academic performance of Generation Alpha, as well as the Indian parents' comprehension and the impact of their social media consumption on internalizing behavior. Anxiety, mood swings, and cognitive overload were identified as a result of the emotional and behavioral self-regulation that children develop as a result of excessive exposure to online content. Although certain AI-driven visuals and personalized content improved learning, there were also concerns about overreliance and creativity. The evolving social, economic, and technological contexts contribute to the transformation of parenting values across generations. In light of increasing diversity and pluralism, comprehending the impact of parenting values on children's development is essential for fostering inclusive, supportive, and adaptive educational environments. Research in this domain can enhance our understanding of the interplay between cultural values and children's needs, thereby supporting their well-being and development. The study underscored the challenges that parents face when it comes to digital activity monitoring, boundary setting, and ethical dilemmas related to digital parenthood. The results most significantly underscored the significance of parenting through dialogue, digital literacy, intentional value-based guidance, and intentional guidance, as opposed to overbearing restrictions.

This study has limitations like all others. First, it was conducted on a small, non-random group of Indian parents, which made the sample population too specific and hampered the findings. Second, self-reports could distort the truth or cause Information Control Bias. Third, the study focused on family-centric frameworks and ignored Generation Alpha's input, which could have improved results. Finally, the rapid development of social media and AI tools suggests that findings may change, necessitating longitudinal or other follow-up studies.

8. FUTURE SUGGESTIONS AND IMPLICATIONS

The findings of this study have significant implications for educational institutions, parents, and regulatory agencies. Schools should include digital literacy and critical thinking programs in their curricula to prepare Generation Alpha with the skills needed to effectively navigate the online world. Parents and guardians are encouraged to have open conversations with their children about their online activities, providing guidance and support. Additionally, regulatory agencies should support research on how social media affects the internalizing behaviors of this generation and implement policies to reduce cyberbullying and protect young users from harmful or inappropriate content. Future researchers can improve theoretical models by adding these concepts to studies of Generation Alpha's perceptions of brands and social media. Moreover, researchers should use interdisciplinary approaches—drawing from psychology, communication, sociology, and digital media studies—to gain a thorough understanding of social media's complex effects on this generation.

REFERENCES

Anders, B. A. (2023). Is using ChatGPT cheating, plagiarism, both, neither, or forward thinking? *Patterns (New York, N.Y.)*, *4*(3), 100694. DOI: 10.1016/j.patter.2023.100694

Asendorpf, J. B. (1990). Beyond social withdrawal: Shyness, unsociability, and peer avoidance. *Human Development*, *33*(4-5), 250–259. DOI: 10.1159/000276522

Barry, A. E., Johnson, E., Rabre, A., Darville, G., Donovan, K. M., & Efunbumi, O. (2015). Underage access to online alcohol marketing content: A YouTube case study. *Alcohol and Alcoholism (Oxford, Oxfordshire)*, *50*(1), 89–94. DOI: 10.1093/alcalc/agu078

Bati, K. (2022). A systematic literature review regarding computational thinking and programming in early childhood education. *Education and Information Technologies*, *27*(2), 2059–2082. DOI: 10.1007/s10639-021-10700-2

Berson, I. R., Luo, W., & Yang, W. (2022). Narrowing the digital divide in early childhood: Technological advances and curriculum reforms. *Early Education and Development*, *33*(1), 183–185. DOI: 10.1080/10409289.2022.1989740

Boer, M., Stevens, G. W., Finkenauer, C., de Looze, M. E., & van den Eijnden, R. J. (2021). Social media use intensity, social media use problems, and mental health among adolescents: Investigating directionality and mediating processes. *Computers in Human Behavior*, *116*, 106645. DOI: 10.1016/j.chb.2020.106645

Boer, M., Stevens, G. W., Finkenauer, C., Koning, I. M., & van den Eijnden, R. J. (2022). Validation of the social media disorder scale in adolescents: Findings from a large-scale nationally representative sample. *Assessment*, *29*(8), 1658–1675. DOI: 10.1177/10731911211027232

Bower, M., Torrington, J., Lai, J. W., Petocz, P., & Alfano, M. (2024). How should we change teaching and assessment in response to increasingly powerful generative Artificial Intelligence? Outcomes of the ChatGPT teacher survey. *Education and Information Technologies*, *29*(12), 15403–15439. DOI: 10.1007/s10639-023-12405-0

Braun, V., & Clarke, V. (2006). Using thematic analysis in psychology. *Qualitative Research in Psychology*, *3*(2), 77–101. DOI: 10.1191/1478088706qp063oa

Brauner, P., Hick, A., Philipsen, R., & Ziefle, M. (2023). "What does the public think about artificial intelligence?—A criticality map to understand bias in the public perception of AI", Frontiers in Computer Science. *Frontiers Media S.A.*, *5*, 1113903. DOI: 10.3389/FCOMP.2023.1113903/BIBTEX

Caro, J. C., Holuka, C., Menta, G., Turner, J. D., Vögele, C., & D'Ambrosio, C. (2023). Children's internalizing behavior development is heterogeneously associated with the pace of epigenetic aging. *Biological Psychology*, *176*, 108463. DOI: 10.1016/j.biopsycho.2022.108463

Cheung, C. H., Bedford, R., Saez De Urabain, I. R., Karmiloff-Smith, A., & Smith, T. J. (2017). Daily touchscreen use in infants and toddlers is associated with reduced sleep and delayed sleep onset. *Scientific Reports*, *7*(1), 46104. DOI: 10.1038/srep46104

Chung, K. C., Chen, C. H., Tsai, H. H., & Chuang, Y. H. (2021). Social media privacy management strategies: A SEM analysis of user privacy behaviors. *Computer Communications, 174*, 122–130. DOI: 10.1016/j.comcom.2021.04.012

Coyne, S. M., Shawcroft, J., Holmgren, H., Christensen-Duerden, C., Ashby, S., Rogers, A., Reschke, P. J., Barr, R., Domoff, S., Van Alfen, M., Meldrum, M., & Porter, C. L. (2024). The growth of problematic media use over early childhood: Associations with long-term social and emotional outcomes. *Computers in Human Behavior, 159*, 108350. DOI: 10.1016/j.chb.2024.108350

Craig, W., Boniel-Nissim, M., King, N., Walsh, S. D., Boer, M., Donnelly, P. D., Harel-Fisch, Y., Malinowska-Cieślik, M., Gaspar de Matos, M., Cosma, A., Van den Eijnden, R., Vieno, A., Elgar, F. J., Molcho, M., Bjereld, Y., & Pickett, W. (2020). Social media use and cyber-bullying: A cross-national analysis of young people in 42 countries. *The Journal of Adolescent Health, 66*(6), S100–S108. DOI: 10.1016/j.jadohealth.2020.03.006

Das, R. (2023). Parents' understandings of social media algorithms in children's lives in England: Misunderstandings, parked understandings, transactional understandings and proactive understandings amidst datafication. *Journal of Children and Media, 17*(4), 506–522. DOI: 10.1080/17482798.2023.2240899

Deighton, , JHumphrey, , NBelsky, , JBoehnke, , JVostanis, , PPatalay, , P. (2018). Longitudinal pathways between mental health difficulties and academic performance during middle childhood and early adolescence. *British Journal of Developmental Psychology, 36*(1), 110-126.

Dienlin, T., & Johannes, N. (2020). The impact of digital technology use on adolescent well-being. *Dialogues in Clinical Neuroscience, 22*(2), 135–142. DOI: 10.31887/DCNS.2020.22.2/tdienlin

Dong, J., Lee, S., Wang, C. H., & Shannon, D. M. (2023). Impact on social capital and learning engagement due to social media usage among the international students in the US. *Education and Information Technologies, 28*(7), 8027–8050. DOI: 10.1007/s10639-022-11520-8

Druga, S., Williams, R., Park, H. W., & Breazeal, C. (2018, June). How smart are the smart toys? Children and parents' agent interaction and intelligence attribution. In *Proceedings of the 17th ACM conference on interaction design and children* (pp. 231-240). DOI: 10.1145/3202185.3202741

Gill, A., & Mathur, A. (2023). Exploring the futuristic landscape of artificial intelligence for alpha generation: A comprehensive study. *World Adv Res Rev, 20*(02), 1250–1264. DOI: 10.30574/wjarr.2023.20.2.2369

Haoning Mah, G., Hu, X., & Yang, W. (2021). Digital technology use and early reading abilities among bilingual children in Singapore. *Policy Futures in Education, 19*(2), 242–258. DOI: 10.1177/1478210320980575

Hiniker, A., Wang, A., Tran, J., Zhang, M. R., Radesky, J., Sobel, K., & Hong, S. R. (2021, June). Can conversational agents change the way children talk to people? In *Proceedings of the 20th Annual ACM Interaction Design and Children Conference* (pp. 338-349). DOI: 10.1145/3459990.3460695

Höfrová, A., Balidemaj, V., & Small, M. A. (2024). A systematic literature review of education for Generation Alpha. *Discover Education, 3*(1), 125. DOI: 10.1007/s44217-024-00218-3

Hu, J., Lai, Y., & Yi, X. (2024). Effectiveness of social media-assisted course on learning self-efficacy. *Scientific Reports, 14*(1), 10112. DOI: 10.1038/s41598-024-60724-0

Ioannou, A., & Makridou, E. (2018). Exploring the potentials of educational robotics in the development of computational thinking: A summary of current research and practical proposal for future work. *Education and Information Technologies*, *23*(6), 2531–2544. DOI: 10.1007/s10639-018-9729-z

Islam, M. R., Liu, S., Wang, X., & Xu, G. (2020). Deep learning for misinformation detection on online social networks: A survey and new perspectives. *Social Network Analysis and Mining*, *10*(1), 82. DOI: 10.1007/s13278-020-00696-x

Jha, A. K. (2020). Understanding generation alpha.

Kabilan, M. K., Kabilan, M. K., Ahmad, N., & Abidin, M. J. Z. (2010). Facebook: An online environment for learning of English in institutions of.... *The Internet and Higher Education*, *13*(4), 179–187. DOI: 10.1016/j.iheduc.2010.07.003

Kaplan, A. M., & Haenlein, M. (2010). Users of the world, unite! The challenges and opportunities of Social Media. *Business Horizons*, *53*(1), 59–68. DOI: 10.1016/j.bushor.2009.09.003

Kaplan-Berkley, S. (2022). Digital tools and streaming media converge to inspire social interactions of generation alpha. *International Journal of Early Childhood*, *54*(2), 185–201. DOI: 10.1007/s13158-021-00301-y

Kasneci, E., Seßler, K., Küchemann, S., Bannert, M., Dementieva, D., Fischer, F., Gasser, U., Groh, G., Günnemann, S., Hüllermeier, E., Krusche, S., Kutyniok, G., Michaeli, T., Nerdel, C., Pfeffer, J., Poquet, O., Sailer, M., Schmidt, A., Seidel, T., & Kasneci, G. (2023). ChatGPT for good? On opportunities and challenges of large language models for education. *Learning and Individual Differences*, *103*, 102274. DOI: 10.1016/j.lindif.2023.102274

Kendrick, D., Young, B., Mason-Jones, A. J., Ilyas, N., Achana, F. A., Cooper, N. J., Hubbard, S. J., Sutton, A. J., Smith, S., Wynn, P., Mulvaney, C., Watson, M. C., & Coupland, C. (2013). Home safety education and provision of safety equipment for injury prevention. *Evidence-Based Child Health: A Cochrane Review Journal*, *8*(3), 761–939. DOI: 10.1002/ebch.1911

Khurshid, S., Amin, F., Masoodi, N., & Khan, M. F. (2023). Factors influencing online learning on social media. *International Journal of Learning Technology*, *18*(1), 3–27. DOI: 10.1504/IJLT.2023.131309

Lau, J., Zimmerman, B., & Schaub, F. (2018). Alexa, are you listening? Privacy perceptions, concerns and privacy-seeking behaviors with smart speakers. *Proceedings of the ACM on human-computer interaction, 2*(CSCW), 1-31.

Lauricella, A. R., Aladé, F., Russo, M., Strevett, A., & Herdzina, J. (2022). Children's visual attention and comprehension from synchronous video book reading. *Computers & Education*, *191*, 104628. DOI: 10.1016/j.compedu.2022.104628

Lee, S. J., & Chae, Y. G. (2012). Balancing participation and risks in children's internet use: The role of internet literacy and parental mediation. *Cyberpsychology, Behavior, and Social Networking*, *15*(5), 257–262. DOI: 10.1089/cyber.2011.0552

Lewis, D., & Moorkens, J. (2020). A rights-based approach to trustworthy AI in social media. *Social Media + Society*, *6*(3), 2056305120954672. DOI: 10.1177/2056305120954672

Lissak, G. (2018). Adverse physiological and psychological effects of screen time on children and adolescents: Literature review and case study. *Environmental Research, 164*, 149–157. DOI: 10.1016/j.envres.2018.01.015

Liu, C., Chen, H., Cao, X., Sun, Y., Liu, C. Y., Wu, K., Liang, Y.-C., Hsu, S.-E., Huang, D.-H., & Chiou, W. K. (2022). Effects of mindfulness meditation on doctors' mindfulness, patient safety culture, patient safety competency and adverse event. *International Journal of Environmental Research and Public Health, 19*(6), 3282. DOI: 10.3390/ijerph19063282

Liu, M., & Luo, J. (2015). Relationship between peripheral blood dopamine level and internet addiction disorder in adolescents: A pilot study. *International Journal of Clinical and Experimental Medicine, E-Century Publishing Corporation*, *8*(6), 9943.

Livingstone, S., Mascheroni, G., & Stoilova, M. (2023). The outcomes of gaining digital skills for young people's lives and wellbeing: A systematic evidence review. *New Media & Society*, *25*(5), 1176–1202. DOI: 10.1177/14614448211043189

Long, D., & Magerko, B. (2020, April). What is AI literacy? Competencies and design considerations. In *Proceedings of the 2020 CHI conference on human factors in computing systems* (pp. 1-16). DOI: 10.1145/3313831.3376727

Luo, M., Zhao, L., & Lyu, B. (2022). [Retracted] Exploring the Fuzzy Integrated Assessment of College Students' Education for Innovative Entrepreneurship under the Background of Internet+. *Security and Communication Networks*, *2022*(1), 4339772.

Ma, L., Lee, C. S., & Goh, D. H. L. (2013, July). Investigating influential factors influencing users to share news in social media: A diffusion of innovations perspective. In *Proceedings of the 13th ACM/IEEE-CS joint conference on Digital libraries* (pp. 403-404). DOI: 10.1145/2467696.2467749

Ma, R., & Kou, Y. (2021). " How advertiser-friendly is my video?": YouTuber's Socioeconomic Interactions with Algorithmic Content Moderation. *Proceedings of the ACM on Human-Computer Interaction, 5*(CSCW2), 1-25. DOI: 10.1145/3479573

Manches, A., & Plowman, L. (2017). Computing education in children's early years: A call for debate. *British Journal of Educational Technology*, *48*(1), 191–201. DOI: 10.1111/bjet.12355

Martin, F., Bacak, J., Polly, D., Wang, W., & Ahlgrim-Delzell, L. (2023). Teacher and school concerns and actions on elementary school children digital safety. *TechTrends*, *67*(3), 561–571. DOI: 10.1007/s11528-022-00803-z

Martin, F., Bacak, J., Polly, D., Wang, W., & Ahlgrim-Delzell, L. (2023). Teacher and school concerns and actions on elementary school children digital safety. *TechTrends*, *67*(3), 561–571. DOI: 10.1007/s11528-022-00803-z

McCarthy, J. (2007). From here to human-level AI. *Artificial Intelligence*, *171*(18), 1174–1182. DOI: 10.1016/j.artint.2007.10.009

Merikangas, K. R., He, J. P., Burstein, M., Swanson, S. A., Avenevoli, S., Cui, L., Benjet, C., Georgiades, K., & Swendsen, J. (2010). Lifetime prevalence of mental disorders in US adolescents: Results from the National Comorbidity Survey Replication–Adolescent Supplement (NCS-A). *Journal of the American Academy of Child and Adolescent Psychiatry*, *49*(10), 980–989. DOI: 10.1016/j.jaac.2010.05.017

Mnkandla, E., & Minnaar, A. (2017). The use of social media in e-learning: A metasynthesis. *International Review of Research in Open and Distance Learning*, *18*(5), 227–248. DOI: 10.19173/irrodl.v18i5.3014

Nathanson, A. I. (2001). Mediation of children's television viewing: Working toward conceptual clarity and common understanding. *Annals of the International Communication Association*, *25*(1), 115–151. DOI: 10.1080/23808985.2001.11679002

Nelson, L. J., Padilla-Walker, L. M., & McLean, R. D. (2021). Longitudinal predictors of helicopter parenting in emerging adulthood. *Emerging Adulthood*, *9*(3), 240–251. DOI: 10.1177/2167696820931980

Nesi, J., & Prinstein, M. J. (2015). Using social media for social comparison and feedback-seeking: Gender and popularity moderate associations with depressive symptoms. *Journal of Abnormal Child Psychology*, *43*(8), 1427–1438. DOI: 10.1007/s10802-015-0020-0

Ohannessian, C. M., Fagle, T., & Salafia, C. (2021). Social media use and internalizing symptoms during early adolescence: The role of co-rumination. *Journal of Affective Disorders*, *280*, 85–88. DOI: 10.1016/j.jad.2020.10.079

Pattrawiwat, K., Nilrungratana, P., Deewai, A., & Tuntivivat, S. (2024). The measurement model of family strengths for generation alpha in the thai context. *Behavioral Sciences (Basel, Switzerland)*, *14*(10), 921. DOI: 10.3390/bs14100921

Pearson, N., Biddle, S. J., Griffiths, P., Johnston, J. P., & Haycraft, E. (2018). Clustering and correlates of screen-time and eating behaviours among young children. *BMC Public Health*, *18*(1), 753. DOI: 10.1186/s12889-018-5698-9

Piccerillo, L., & Digennaro, S. (2025). Adolescent social media use and emotional intelligence: A systematic review. *Adolescent Research Review*, *10*(2), 201–218. DOI: 10.1007/s40894-024-00245-z

Przybylski, A. K., & Weinstein, N. (2017). A large-scale test of the goldilocks hypothesis: Quantifying the relations between digital-screen use and the mental well-being of adolescents. *Psychological Science*, *28*(2), 204–215. DOI: 10.1177/0956797616678438

Sequeira, S. L., McKone, K. M., Diab, E. M., Thomas, J. G., Wolff, J., & Nesi, J. (2025). Characterizing adolescent social media experiences and links to momentary affect. *Journal of Adolescence*, *97*(7), 1722–1737. DOI: 10.1002/jad.12530

Shade, L. R., & Singh, R. (2016). "Honestly, we're not spying on kids": School surveillance of young people's social media. *Social Media + Society*, *2*(4), 2056305116680005. DOI: 10.1177/2056305116680005

Shafiq, M., & Parveen, K. (2023). Social media usage: Analyzing its effect on academic performance and engagement of higher education students. *International Journal of Educational Development*, *98*, 102738. DOI: 10.1016/j.ijedudev.2023.102738

Shahzad, M. F., Xu, S., Lim, W. M., Yang, X., & Khan, Q. R. (2024). Artificial intelligence and social media on academic performance and mental well-being: Student perceptions of positive impact in the age of smart learning. *Heliyon, 10*(8), e29523. DOI: 10.1016/j.heliyon.2024.e29523

Simpson, R. (1996, September). Neither clear nor present: The social construction of safety and danger. []). New York: Kluwer Academic Publishers-Plenum Publishers.]. *Sociological Forum, 11*(3), 549–562. DOI: 10.1007/BF02408392

Šramová, B., & Pavelka, J. (2023). Generation Alpha media consumption during Covid-19 and teachers' standpoint. *Media and Communication, 11*(4), 227–238. DOI: 10.17645/mac.v11i4.7158

Stone, P., Brooks, R., Brynjolfsson, E., Calo, R., Etzioni, O., Hager, G., . . . Teller, A. (2022). Artificial intelligence and life in 2030: the one hundred year study on artificial intelligence. *arXiv preprint arXiv:2211.06318.*

Su, J., Ng, D. T. K., & Chu, S. K. W. (2023). Artificial intelligence (AI) literacy in early childhood education: The challenges and opportunities. *Computers and Education: Artificial Intelligence, 4*, 100124. DOI: 10.1016/j.caeai.2023.100124

Su, J., Yang, W., Yim, I. H. Y., Li, H., & Hu, X. (2024). Early artificial intelligence education: Effects of cooperative play and direct instruction on kindergarteners' computational thinking, sequencing, self-regulation and theory of mind skills. *Journal of Computer Assisted Learning, 40*(6), 2917–2925. DOI: 10.1111/jcal.13040

Su, J., & Zhong, Y. (2022). Artificial Intelligence (AI) in early childhood education: Curriculum design and future directions. *Computers and Education: Artificial Intelligence, 3*, 100072. DOI: 10.1016/j.caeai.2022.100072

Sumner, J. A., Colich, N. L., Uddin, M., Armstrong, D., & McLaughlin, K. A. (2019). Early experiences of threat, but not deprivation, are associated with accelerated biological aging in children and adolescents. *Biological Psychiatry, 85*(3), 268–278. DOI: 10.1016/j.biopsych.2018.09.008

Sun, K., Zou, Y., Radesky, J., Brooks, C., & Schaub, F. (2021). Child safety in the smart home: parents' perceptions, needs, and mitigation strategies. *Proceedings of the ACM on Human-Computer Interaction, 5*(CSCW2), 1-41. DOI: 10.1145/3479858

Symons, K., Vanwesenbeeck, I., Walrave, M., Van Ouytsel, J., & Ponnet, K. (2020). Parents' concerns over internet use, their engagement in interaction restrictions, and adolescents' behavior on social networking sites. *Youth & Society, 52*(8), 1569–1581. DOI: 10.1177/0044118X19834769

Tandon, S., Bennett, D., Mark Nataraja, R., & Pacilli, M. (2023). Outcome following the surgical management of varicocele in children and adolescents: A systematic review and meta-analysis. *Therapeutic Advances in Urology, 15*, 17562872231206239. DOI: 10.1177/17562872231206239

Theopilus, Y., Al Mahmud, A., Davis, H., & Octavia, J. R. (2025). The role of parental mediation strategies and online behaviour on internet addiction in young Indonesian children: A parent survey study. *Behaviour & Information Technology*, •••, 1–24. DOI: 10.1080/0144929X.2025.2578709

Throuvala, M. A., Griffiths, M. D., Rennoldson, M., & Kuss, D. J. (2019). School-based prevention for adolescent internet addiction: Prevention is the key. A systematic literature review. *Current Neuropharmacology*, *17*(6), 507–525. DOI: 10.2174/1570159X16666180813153806

Tirendi, D., & Gargiulo, L. (2024). Measuring the impacts of social media on daily life from millennials to generation alpha. *International Journal of Research in Humanities and Social Studies*, 26-33.

Twenge, J. M., Haidt, J., Blake, A. B., McAllister, C., Lemon, H., & Le Roy, A. (2021). Worldwide increases in adolescent loneliness. *Journal of Adolescence*, *93*(1), 257–269. DOI: 10.1016/j.adolescence.2021.06.006

Valkenburg, P. M., Meier, A., & Beyens, I. (2022). Social media use and its impact on adolescent mental health: An umbrella review of the evidence. *Current Opinion in Psychology*, *44*, 58–68. DOI: 10.1016/j.copsyc.2021.08.017

Van Den Eijnden, R., Koning, I., Doornwaard, S., Van Gurp, F., & Ter Bogt, T. (2018). The impact of heavy and disordered use of games and social media on adolescents' psychological, social, and school functioning. *Journal of Behavioral Addictions*, *7*(3), 697–706. DOI: 10.1556/2006.7.2018.65

van der Ven, H., Corry, D., Elnur, R., Provost, V. J., & Syukron, M. (2024). Generative AI and social media may exacerbate the climate crisis. *Global Environmental Politics*, *24*(2), 9–18. DOI: 10.1162/glep_a_00747

Vannucci, A., Flannery, K. M., & Ohannessian, C. M. (2017). Social media use and anxiety in emerging adults. *Journal of Affective Disorders*, *207*, 163–166. DOI: 10.1016/j.jad.2016.08.040

Vartiainen, H., Tedre, M., & Valtonen, T. (2020). Learning machine learning with very young children: Who is teaching whom? *International Journal of Child-Computer Interaction*, *25*, 100182. DOI: 10.1016/j.ijcci.2020.100182

Walan, S. (2025). Primary school students' perceptions of artificial intelligence–for good or bad. *International Journal of Technology and Design Education*, *35*(1), 25–40. DOI: 10.1007/s10798-024-09898-2

Whelan, E., Islam, A. N., & Brooks, S. (2020). Applying the SOBC paradigm to explain how social media overload affects academic performance. *Computers & Education*, *143*, 103692. DOI: 10.1016/j.compedu.2019.103692

Williams, R., Park, H. W., Oh, L., & Breazeal, C. (2019, July). Popbots: Designing an artificial intelligence curriculum for early childhood education. *Proceedings of the AAAI Conference on Artificial Intelligence*, *33*(01), 9729–9736. DOI: 10.1609/aaai.v33i01.33019729

Yan, Z. (2006). What influences children's and adolescents' understanding of the complexity of the Internet? *Developmental Psychology*, *42*(3), 418–428. DOI: 10.1037/0012-1649.42.3.418

Yang, W., Ng, D. T. K., & Su, J. (2023). The impact of story-inspired programming on preschool children's computational thinking: A multi-group experiment. *Thinking Skills and Creativity*, *47*, 101218. DOI: 10.1016/j.tsc.2022.101218

Yu, H., & Guo, Y. (2023, June). Generative artificial intelligence empowers educational reform: Current status, issues, and prospects. [). Frontiers Media SA.]. *Frontiers in Education*, *8*, 1183162. DOI: 10.3389/feduc.2023.1183162

Zviel Girshin, R., Rosenberg, N., & Kukliansky, I. (2024). Early childhood robotics: Children's beliefs and objective capabilities to read and write programs. *Journal of Research in Childhood Education*, *38*(2), 317–335. DOI: 10.1080/02568543.2023.2259946

Chapter 14

Future-Ready Faculty: Building AI Fluency for Dynamic Global Classrooms

Amandeep Kaur
https://orcid.org/0009-0004-5716-7298
CGC University, Mohali, India

Gaganpreet Kaur
https://orcid.org/0009-0006-2957-5352
CGC University, Mohali, India

Ramandeep Sandhu
https://orcid.org/0000-0003-2595-4030
Lovely Professional University, India

Harleen Kaur Dhillon
https://orcid.org/0000-0002-4656-5248
CGC University, Mohali, India

ABSTRACT

In the age of intelligent education ecosystems, developing AI-literate faculty is no longer optional it is essential for the success of transnational education (TNE). As AI reshapes teaching, learning, and academic operations, the international delivery of higher education demands a new breed of educators: digitally fluent, pedagogically agile, and globally attuned. This chapter introduces an innovative research-based framework for cultivating faculty who are capable of integrating AI tools seamlessly into cross-border learning environments. Drawing from interdisciplinary studies across educational technology, international pedagogy, and organizational change, the chapter maps the core competencies of AI-fluent faculty ranging from adaptive learning design and AI-augmented assessment to ethical reasoning and data-informed instruction. Real-world case studies from AI-integrated TNE programs in the UK, Australia, and Asia are analyzed to showcase pioneering approaches to faculty transformation.

DOI: 10.4018/979-8-3373-5403-3.ch014

1. INTRODUCTION

1.1 Global Shifts: AI, Digitalization, and Transnational Education

Artificial intelligence (AI) has moved from being a peripheral educational tool to a central pillar of digital transformation in higher education worldwide. The expansion of intelligent learning ecosystems including AI-powered learning management systems, predictive analytics, and adaptive feedback loops has redefined the transnational education (TNE) landscape (Bond, 2024; Crompton, 2023). As institutions increasingly offer cross-border degrees, the use of AI to manage multi-country classrooms, virtual collaborations, and multilingual learners is becoming essential (Al-Zahrani, 2024).

Recent global studies indicate that since 2020, over 60% of HEIs across Asia, Europe, and the Middle East have adopted at least one AI-driven educational technology, reflecting an exponential rise in TNE-based digital delivery (Sutedjo, Liu, & Chowdhury, 2025). However, policy, infrastructure, and training gaps persist, especially in developing regions. The shift toward digital, AI-enhanced global classrooms therefore represents not just a technological change but a paradigmatic transformation requiring faculty re-skilling, institutional adaptation, and cross-border governance alignment (UNESCO, n.d.; Yan, 2025).

1.2 The Evolving Role of Faculty: Beyond Technical Skills

In AI-infused learning ecosystems, faculty responsibilities are rapidly expanding. They now serve as instructional designers, algorithmic evaluators, and ethical stewards of digital pedagogy. According to Iqbal et al. (2025), university instructors integrating generative AI (GenAI) into English-language curricula in China found that prompt design, critical verification of AI outputs, and student co-creation were the most essential new teaching skills. Similarly, the Spanish national study "Are University Teachers Ready for Generative Artificial Intelligence?" (2025) reported that faculty adoption was mediated by perceived usefulness and effort expectancy but negatively impacted by "AI anxiety" concerning job relevance and student misuse.

These findings echo Long and Magerko's (2020) model of AI literacy, which emphasizes interpretive, critical, and collaborative competencies rather than technical mastery alone. Sperling (2024) further reinforces that AI literacy in teacher education must integrate ethical reasoning and reflective practice to ensure pedagogically meaningful use. Thus, the future-ready faculty is not merely digitally skilled but AI-fluent capable of discerning, contextualizing, and guiding AI applications toward equitable learning outcomes.

1.3 Readiness and Resource Disparities in Transnational Education Contexts

Despite the enthusiasm for AI integration, readiness remains uneven across global higher education systems. Sutedjo et al. (2025) found that less than one-third of surveyed universities have formal AI use policies or structured professional development (PD) frameworks for faculty. Institutions in the Global South often face additional barriers such as inadequate bandwidth, lack of institutional funding, and minimal support for continuous upskilling (Al-Zahrani, 2024).

In Kenya, for example, a 2025 survey on Educators' Perceptions of Generative AI revealed high willingness to adopt GenAI tools but limited knowledge of ethical or assessment frameworks to guide use (Educators' Perceptions..., 2025). In contrast, Australian and Singaporean universities have launched structured "AI in Pedagogy" certifications, creating micro credential pathways aligned with UNESCO's AI Competency Framework (UNESCO, n.d.). This uneven preparedness across TNE partner institutions can exacerbate inequities in teaching quality and student experience unless global governance mechanisms and faculty development standards are harmonized.

1.4 Faculty Perceptions, Anxiety, and Behavioral Intentions

Faculty perceptions of AI adoption are complex and context-dependent. Beyond the Hype: Exploring Faculty Perceptions and Acceptability of AI in Teaching Practices (2024) reported that although most instructors recognized AI's usefulness in saving time and personalizing learning, concerns persisted around algorithmic opacity, data privacy, and intellectual property. The Spanish study (2025) identified three dimensions of faculty anxiety: (1) fear of job displacement, (2) fear of tool misuse by self or students, and (3) fear of erosion of academic rigor.

A large-scale survey from the University of Helsinki, Navigating the Evolving Landscape of Teaching and Learning (2024), showed that faculty often overestimate AI reliability while underestimating its potential biases, indicating a need for AI calibration literacy the capacity to judge what AI can and cannot do accurately. These findings affirm that affective factors (trust, anxiety, confidence) are as critical as technical training in shaping AI adoption intentions.

Effective PD programs therefore combine hands-on experimentation, peer mentorship, and ethical reflection, enabling educators to transition from apprehension to agency (Tan, 2024; Li, 2025). Institutions adopting modular, peer-driven, and micro-credentialed PD models report significantly higher AI adoption rates and faculty satisfaction (Li, 2025).

1.5 Ethics, Assessment, and Governance in Cross-Border AI Use

Ethical and governance challenges intensify in TNE contexts where cross-jurisdictional data and assessment systems are involved. Faculty express high concern about plagiarism detection, academic honesty, and inequitable access to AI tools (Qouzah et al., 2025). In Jordanian universities, 78% of instructors reported uncertainty about acceptable AI use in assignments (Khlaif et al., 2024). Similarly, many universities still lack explicit AI governance frameworks—less than 25% of HEIs have published institutional guidelines as of 2025 (Faculty Often Missing…, 2025).

UNESCO's (2024) *Ethical Principles for AI in Education* highlights transparency, accountability, inclusivity, and explainability as essential components of AI policy. Embedding these values in faculty development ensures that AI-enhanced teaching remains both responsible and contextually sensitive. Institutions leading in this area (e.g., Open University UK, Nanyang Technological University Singapore) employ "AI ethics sandboxes" where faculty can experiment with algorithmic tools under ethical supervision, helping bridge the gap between innovation and integrity.

Table 1. Key global trends and implications for AI-fluent faculty (updated 2025)

Trend	Description	Implications for Faculty	Recent Evidence
Intelligent ecosystems	AI embedded in LMS, analytics, and adaptive tools	Faculty must interpret AI-driven insights and personalize learning	Crompton (2023); Bond (2024); Sutedjo et al. (2025)
Expansion of TNE	Cross-border, hybrid programs	Cross-cultural digital pedagogy & governance literacy	UNESCO (n.d.); Al-Zahrani (2024)
Faculty anxiety & ethics	Fear of misuse, bias, job relevance	Need for AI ethics and mental-model literacy	Are University Teachers Ready… (2025); Beyond the Hype (2024)
Resource & policy disparities	Uneven digital readiness	Scalable PD, shared policy frameworks	Educators' Perceptions… (2025); Li (2025)
Governance & integrity	Cross-border assessment, data privacy	Training in algorithmic fairness, ethical AI	Qouzah et al. (2025); Yan (2025)

2. CONCEPTUALIZING AI FLUENCY: FRAMEWORK AND COMPETENCIES

2.1 Defining AI Fluency for Educators

AI fluency for educators extends far beyond mere technical proficiency; it involves a deep understanding of AI's capabilities, limitations, and ethical implications, enabling faculty to integrate these technologies meaningfully into their teaching. The human-centered perspective is critical, emphasizing critical thinking, ethical reasoning, and adaptability in response to rapidly evolving AI tools (UNESCO, 2024). The UNESCO AI Competency Framework for Teachers (2024) outlines five dimensions Human-Centered Mindset, Ethics of AI, AI Foundations and Applications, AI Pedagogy, and AI for Professional Learning structured across three progression levels: Acquire, Deepen, and Create. These dimensions provide a structured roadmap for faculty to develop AI fluency over time, highlighting the interplay between understanding AI tools, applying them pedagogically, and evaluating their outcomes in an ethical and culturally responsive manner.

2.2 Core Competencies for AI-Ready Faculty

Developing AI fluency requires educators to cultivate a set of interconnected competencies. Faculty must develop the ability to critically evaluate AI tools, discerning their accuracy, potential biases, and alignment with educational goals. This critical evaluation is closely intertwined with ethical decision-making, as instructors navigate complex issues related to data privacy, algorithmic fairness, and equitable access. Pedagogical integration emerges as another essential competency, where faculty design AI-enhanced learning experiences that foster engagement and meaningful learning outcomes. Furthermore, continuous adaptation is necessary, as AI tools evolve at a pace that requires lifelong learning and ongoing professional development. The ALTL (AI Literacy in Teaching and Learning) framework underscores these interrelated competencies, emphasizing that educators must not only understand AI fundamentals but also exercise judgment, ethical reasoning, and reflective practice when deploying AI in their classrooms (EDUCAUSE, 2024).

2.3 Frameworks Guiding AI Fluency Development

Several contemporary frameworks provide guidance for developing AI fluency among educators. The UNESCO AI Competency Framework, as previously noted, offers a comprehensive structure encompassing knowledge, ethical understanding, and pedagogical application, enabling faculty to build AI literacy in a systematic, culturally adaptive manner (UNESCO, 2024). Complementing this, the Anthropic 4D Framework introduces a practical model:Delegation, Description, Discernment, and Diligence focusing on how educators can interact with AI tools effectively while maintaining ethical integrity (Anthropic, 2024). The Digital Education Council AI Literacy Framework further complements these approaches by delineating five dimensions: Understanding, Evaluating, Using, Creating, and Reflecting which emphasize a progression from general AI literacy to discipline-specific applications (Digital Education Council, 2025). Together, these frameworks provide complementary strategies for institutions aiming to systematically develop faculty competencies for AI-enhanced teaching and learning.

2.4 Implications for Faculty Development Programs

Integrating AI fluency into faculty development programs requires a comprehensive, multi-faceted approach. Institutions need to embed AI literacy into professional development curricula, ensuring that faculty acquire both conceptual understanding and hands-on experience with AI tools. Ethical considerations must be addressed explicitly, as educators navigate issues such as data privacy, algorithmic bias, and equitable access to technology. Providing practical opportunities for engagement with AI tools through simulated teaching environments, micro credentialing, and peer-led communities of practice helps faculty build confidence and pedagogical competence. Finally, continuous support mechanisms are essential, enabling faculty to stay current with rapidly advancing AI technologies and to translate their learning into innovative, effective classroom practices. When effectively implemented, these strategies foster a culture of AI fluency, equipping educators to harness AI as a means to enhance teaching, learning, and student outcomes across diverse transnational education contexts.

Table 2. Comparative overview of AI fluency frameworks

Framework	Key Focus	Description	Source
UNESCO AI Competency Framework	Comprehensive AI competencies	Five dimensions across three progression levels supporting pedagogical and ethical integration of AI	UNESCO, 2024
Anthropic 4D Framework	Practical AI interaction	Delegation, Description, Discernment, Diligence for responsible AI use	Anthropic, 2024
Digital Education Council AI Literacy Framework	Progressive AI literacy	Five dimensions from Understanding to Reflecting for general and discipline-specific AI literacy	Digital Education Council, 2025

3. INSTITUTIONAL STRATEGIES FOR CULTIVATING AI FLUENCY IN FACULTY

3.1 Embedding AI Literacy into Faculty Development Programs

Institutions are increasingly recognizing the necessity of integrating AI literacy into faculty development programs. For instance, Ohio State University has launched an AI Fluency initiative aiming to embed AI education into the core of every undergraduate curriculum, thereby equipping students with the ability to not only use AI tools but also understand their implications and limitations (Ohio State University, 2025). Similarly, the American Federation of Teachers, with funding from Microsoft, OpenAI, and Anthropic, has established an AI training hub in New York City to equip teachers with skills to effectively use AI for tasks such as lesson planning, creating quizzes, and communicating with parents (Time, 2025).

These initiatives underscore the importance of embedding AI literacy into faculty development programs to ensure that educators are adequately prepared to integrate AI into their teaching practices. By providing faculty with the necessary knowledge and skills, institutions can foster an environment where AI is used responsibly and effectively to enhance teaching and learning outcomes.

3.2 Designing Inclusive and Adaptive AI Training Programs

Effective AI training programs must be inclusive and adaptive, catering to the diverse needs of faculty members. The Digital Education Council's AI Literacy Framework emphasizes the importance of developing both general AI literacy for all educators and specialized AI literacy that can be adapted to different disciplines and jurisdictions (Digital Education Council, 2025). This approach ensures that faculty members are not only proficient in AI tools but also capable of critically evaluating and integrating them into their specific teaching contexts.

Furthermore, the Scaffolded AI Literacy (SAIL) Framework delineates six categories of AI literacy, divided into three domains: AI concepts, application of AI and technical skills, and AI digital citizenship. This structured approach provides a comprehensive pathway for educators to develop a nuanced understanding of AI and its implications in educational settings (Kasapidis, 2025).

3.3 Fostering Collaborative Learning Communities

Creating collaborative learning communities is essential for the sustainable integration of AI fluency. The AI Fluency Lab, for example, offers online courses, in-person presentations, and virtual events to equip and inspire educators to live their best human lives and best prepare their students in an AI world (The AI Fluency Lab, 2025). Such communities provide faculty with opportunities to share experiences, discuss challenges, and develop best practices for AI integration.

Additionally, the EQUIP Framework, which encompasses five key pillars—Ethical Governance, Qualified Professional Learning, Unified Collaborative Partnerships, Implementation Readiness, and Progressive Adaptation—offers a structured approach to empower educators with the necessary knowledge, skills, and ethical principles for responsible AI use in education (Daher, 2025).

3.4 Aligning AI Integration with Institutional Values and Policies

AI integration should align with an institution's core values and policies. The EDUCAUSE AI Literacy in Teaching and Learning framework provides a comprehensive structure for AI literacy, addressing the need for institutions to adapt to the rapidly evolving landscape of AI and equipping students, faculty, and staff to engage effectively and ethically with AI technologies in academic and professional contexts (EDUCAUSE, 2024). By aligning AI initiatives with institutional values, institutions can ensure that AI integration supports their broader educational goals and ethical standards.

Moreover, the All India Council for Technical Education (AICTE) in India has announced plans to integrate Artificial Intelligence (AI) and emerging technologies into the curricula of all engineering disciplines, as well as undergraduate business administration (BBA) and computer application (BCA) courses. This initiative aims to build a comprehensive AI ecosystem in technical education and underscores the importance of aligning AI integration with institutional policies (Times of India, 2025).

3.5 Evaluating and Evolving AI Fluency Initiatives

Continuous evaluation and adaptation of AI fluency initiatives are crucial for their success. Institutions should establish mechanisms for assessing the effectiveness of AI training programs, gathering feedback from faculty, and making necessary adjustments to meet evolving needs. This iterative process ensures that AI fluency initiatives remain relevant and impactful, fostering a culture of continuous improvement and responsiveness to technological advancements.

The Scaffolded AI Literacy (SAIL) Framework for Education defines six categories of AI literacy, divided into three domains: AI concepts, application of AI and technical skills, and AI digital citizenship. Education must adapt to AI developments, and frameworks like SAIL provide a structured approach to developing AI literacy (Kasapidis, 2025).

4. ETHICAL CONSIDERATIONS AND EQUITY IN AI-ENHANCED TEACHING

4.1 The Ethical Imperative in AI Integration

The integration of Artificial Intelligence (AI) into educational settings necessitates a rigorous examination of ethical implications to ensure responsible and equitable use. AI systems, while offering enhanced efficiency and personalization, can inadvertently perpetuate biases, compromise privacy, and undermine academic integrity if not carefully managed (Gouseti, 2025). For instance, AI-driven grading systems may favor students whose writing styles align with the training data, disadvantaging those with diverse linguistic backgrounds (FairAIED, 2024). Moreover, the opacity of AI algorithms can obscure decision-making processes, making it challenging to identify and rectify biases (Kamali, 2024).

Ethical literacy among educators is paramount to navigate these challenges. Faculty must be equipped not only with technical proficiency but also with the critical thinking skills necessary to evaluate AI outputs, understand underlying algorithms, and assess potential unintended consequences for diverse student populations (UNESCO, 2024). This comprehensive approach ensures that AI is utilized in ways that uphold ethical standards and promote fairness.

4.2 Equity and Access in AI-Enhanced Learning

Equity remains a central concern in the deployment of AI in education. Disparities in access to AI technologies can exacerbate existing educational inequalities, particularly for students from marginalized communities (OECD, 2024). For example, students in underfunded schools may lack access to AI-powered learning tools, limiting their educational opportunities compared to peers in more affluent institutions (Sutedjo et al., 2025).

To address these disparities, institutions must implement strategies that promote inclusive access to AI resources. This includes providing equitable access to AI tools, ensuring that all students have the opportunity to benefit from personalized learning experiences (Peterkin-Rawls, 2024). Additionally, fostering an inclusive curriculum that incorporates diverse perspectives and addresses the needs of all learners is essential to mitigate the risk of reinforcing existing inequalities.

4.3 Governance, Policy, and Accountability

Establishing robust governance frameworks is crucial to ensure the ethical use of AI in education. Clear policies regarding data privacy, algorithmic transparency, and accountability mechanisms can guide educators in the responsible integration of AI tools (Khlaif et al., 2024). Without such frameworks, the deployment of AI technologies may lead to unintended consequences, including the reinforcement of biases and erosion of academic integrity (Al-Zahrani, 2024).

Institutions should develop and enforce policies that delineate acceptable AI applications, outline procedures for monitoring and evaluating AI systems, and establish protocols for addressing ethical concerns. This proactive approach fosters an environment of accountability and trust, ensuring that AI technologies are used in ways that align with institutional values and ethical standards.

4.4 Integrating Ethics into Faculty Development

Incorporating ethical considerations into faculty development programs is essential to prepare educators for the challenges posed by AI integration. Professional development initiatives should include training on the ethical implications of AI, strategies for identifying and mitigating biases, and frameworks for evaluating the impact of AI on student learning (Kamali, 2024). By embedding ethics into faculty development, institutions can cultivate a cadre of educators who are not only proficient in using AI tools but also adept at navigating the ethical complexities associated with their use.

Furthermore, fostering a culture of continuous reflection and dialogue around AI ethics can empower educators to make informed decisions that prioritize the well-being and equity of all students. This ongoing engagement ensures that ethical considerations remain at the forefront of AI integration efforts.

Table 3. Ethical and equity considerations for AI-fluent faculty

Consideration	Description	Institutional Strategies	Key References
Fairness	Ensuring AI systems do not perpetuate biases against any group.	Implement AI auditing processes and bias detection tools.	Gouseti, 2025; FairAIED, 2024
Transparency	Making AI decision-making processes understandable and accessible.	Develop clear documentation and explainable AI models.	Kamali, 2024
Privacy	Protecting student data from unauthorized access and misuse.	Establish stringent data governance policies and encryption protocols.	Khlaif et al., 2024
Accountability	Holding stakeholders responsible for AI outcomes.	Create oversight committees and accountability frameworks.	Al-Zahrani, 2024
Equity	Providing equal access to AI resources for all students.	Ensure equitable distribution of AI tools and resources across institutions.	OECD, 2024; Sutedjo et al., 2025

5. FUTURE DIRECTIONS AND RECOMMENDATIONS FOR AI-FLUENT FACULTY

5.1 Building Sustainable AI Competency Pathways

As AI continues to evolve, faculty development programs must move beyond one-time training sessions toward sustainable, continuous learning pathways. Research indicates that iterative learning models, such as micro-credentialing and modular AI certifications, enable educators to progressively build competency while integrating AI tools meaningfully into their pedagogy (Zawacki-Richter et al., 2024). Such pathways should be flexible, culturally adaptive, and aligned with the technological readiness of both faculty and institutions. For example, AI micro-credentials implemented in Australian universities have empowered faculty to develop discipline-specific AI skills while participating in cross-institutional communities of practice (Popenici & Kerr, 2025).

5.2 Fostering Global Collaborative Networks

Global collaboration is critical for the transnational application of AI in higher education. Faculty networks that span multiple countries facilitate knowledge exchange, sharing of best practices, and collaborative problem-solving. Studies show that participation in international AI teaching communities enhances educators' adaptability, encourages experimentation with AI pedagogies, and promotes culturally responsive AI integration (Sharples et al., 2025). Platforms such as AI Faculty Labs and UNESCO-led AI teaching initiatives exemplify the potential of international collaboration in fostering AI fluency.

5.3 Emphasizing Ethical and Responsible AI Practices

Future AI integration must foreground ethical and responsible practices. Faculty development programs should embed modules on AI ethics, fairness, transparency, and student data protection, ensuring that educators can make informed decisions when using AI tools (Zhu et al., 2025). Incorporating scenario-based learning and case studies allows faculty to explore real-world dilemmas, fostering critical thinking and ethical reasoning. The continuous monitoring of AI systems within classrooms also ensures accountability and reinforces institutional commitment to equity and inclusion (OECD, 2024).

5.4 Leveraging AI for Personalized Faculty Development

AI itself can enhance faculty development through personalized learning and adaptive feedback. Intelligent tutoring systems, AI-driven professional learning analytics, and virtual AI coaching platforms can assess individual faculty needs, recommend targeted learning pathways, and track progress over time (Luckin et al., 2024). By leveraging AI to support faculty growth, institutions can optimize learning outcomes and create data-informed professional development strategies that are responsive to individual strengths and weaknesses.

5.5 Integrating AI Research and Innovation in Faculty Roles

AI fluency should also encompass faculty engagement with AI research and innovation. Encouraging faculty to explore AI-driven pedagogical experiments, publish case studies, and contribute to AI curriculum design strengthens institutional capacity and positions educators as leaders in the AI-enhanced education landscape. Institutions that support faculty in research-oriented AI projects foster a culture of continuous improvement, innovation, and knowledge creation (Gouseti, 2025).

Table 4. Future directions and recommendations for AI-fluent faculty

Recommendation	Description	Implementation Strategies	Key References
Sustainable AI Competency Pathways	Continuous professional learning with modular credentials	Micro-credential programs, adaptive learning modules, cross-institutional collaboration	Zawacki-Richter et al., 2024; Popenici & Kerr, 2025
Global Collaborative Networks	International collaboration to share best practices	AI Faculty Labs, UNESCO AI initiatives, online communities	Sharples et al., 2025
Ethical and Responsible AI	Embed ethics, transparency, and fairness in AI usage	Scenario-based learning, case studies, AI monitoring protocols	Zhu et al., 2025; OECD, 2024
Personalized Faculty Development	Use AI to tailor faculty learning experiences	AI-driven analytics, virtual coaching, personalized learning pathways	Luckin et al., 2024
AI Research and Innovation	Encourage faculty-led AI experiments and research	Institutional support for AI projects, publication incentives, curriculum design	Gouseti, 2025

6. CHALLENGES AND BARRIERS IN DEVELOPING AI-FLUENT FACULTY

6.1 Digital Confidence and Skill Gaps

One of the primary challenges in cultivating AI-fluent faculty is the varying levels of digital confidence and technological proficiency among educators. Research indicates that while some faculty members quickly adopt AI tools, others exhibit apprehension due to limited technical skills, unfamiliarity with AI concepts, or fear of making errors in teaching practices (Luckin et al., 2024; Sutedjo et al., 2025). This discrepancy can hinder uniform adoption and integration of AI in teaching, creating inconsistencies in student learning experiences. Addressing these gaps requires targeted professional development, scaffolded learning programs, and continuous support mechanisms to build confidence gradually.

6.2 Workload and Time Constraints

Faculty members often perceive AI training as an additional workload, particularly in institutions with heavy teaching, research, and administrative responsibilities (Popenici & Kerr, 2025). Time constraints limit participation in training sessions and engagement with AI tools, reducing the effectiveness of development programs. Studies suggest that integrating AI training into existing professional development schedules and offering flexible, asynchronous learning opportunities can mitigate these challenges, enabling faculty to balance responsibilities while building AI competencies (Zawacki-Richter et al., 2024).

6.3 Resistance to Change and AI Skepticism

Resistance to technological change and skepticism regarding AI's effectiveness pose significant barriers. Faculty may question the pedagogical value of AI or fear that AI could replace human teaching, leading to reluctance in adopting AI tools (Sharples et al., 2025). Overcoming this barrier requires demonstrating the tangible benefits of AI-enhanced teaching, providing success stories, and fostering a culture of experimentation where failure is viewed as a learning opportunity rather than a setback.

6.4 Institutional Readiness and Infrastructure Limitations

Institutional readiness is another critical factor affecting the development of AI-fluent faculty. Limited access to advanced AI infrastructure, inconsistent IT support, and outdated hardware or software can constrain faculty's ability to engage meaningfully with AI tools (OECD, 2024). Addressing these barriers requires strategic investments in AI infrastructure, technical support, and scalable digital learning environments that accommodate diverse faculty needs and institutional capacities.

6.5 Ethical, Cultural, and Policy Barriers

Ethical concerns, cultural sensitivities, and policy limitations can also inhibit AI adoption. Faculty may hesitate to implement AI tools if institutional guidelines are unclear or if there are concerns about student data privacy, algorithmic bias, or intellectual property rights (Khlaif et al., 2024). Moreover, cultural differences in pedagogy and learning expectations in transnational education contexts necessitate contextually adapted AI strategies. Institutions must develop clear AI governance policies, provide ethics training, and ensure culturally responsive integration to mitigate these barriers.

Table 5. Challenges and strategies for developing AI-fluent faculty

Challenge	Description	Recommended Strategies	Key References
Digital Confidence & Skill Gaps	Variation in technical proficiency and AI understanding	Scaffolded training, continuous support, peer mentoring	Luckin et al., 2024; Sutedjo et al., 2025
Workload & Time Constraints	Perception of AI training as extra workload	Flexible schedules, asynchronous learning modules, integration into existing PD	Popenici & Kerr, 2025; Zawacki-Richter et al., 2024
Resistance to Change & AI Skepticism	Hesitation or fear of AI replacing human teaching	Showcase benefits, encourage experimentation, provide success stories	Sharples et al., 2025
Institutional Readiness & Infrastructure	Limited access to AI tools and support	Invest in infrastructure, technical support, scalable digital environments	OECD, 2024
Ethical, Cultural & Policy Barriers	Concerns over ethics, privacy, cultural adaptability	Clear governance, ethics training, culturally responsive AI strategies	Khlaif et al., 2024

7. OVERCOMING KEY CHALLENGES IN DEVELOPING AI-FLUENT FACULTY

7.1 Enhancing Digital Confidence and Competency

One of the most significant barriers to AI fluency among faculty is the variation in digital confidence and skill levels. Studies show that educators with limited prior exposure to AI often experience anxiety, resistance, or hesitation when integrating AI tools into their teaching practices (Luckin et al., 2024; Sutedjo et al., 2025). Overcoming this challenge requires a structured, scaffolded approach to professional development that builds technical competency gradually. Institutions can employ blended learning models that combine synchronous workshops, asynchronous modules, and guided hands-on experiences with AI tools (Zawacki-Richter et al., 2024). Peer mentoring programs can further reinforce learning, as more experienced faculty support colleagues in navigating AI applications and troubleshooting challenges in real classroom scenarios.

7.2 Managing Workload and Time Constraints

Faculty often perceive AI professional development as an additional burden on top of teaching, research, and administrative responsibilities. To mitigate this barrier, institutions can integrate AI training into existing professional development schedules, using modular and micro-credential formats that allow educators to learn at their own pace (Popenici & Kerr, 2025). The use of AI-driven analytics to personalize learning pathways for faculty can also reduce unnecessary time expenditure and make development programs more efficient and impactful (Luckin et al., 2024).

7.3 Addressing Resistance to Change and AI Skepticism

Resistance to AI integration often stems from skepticism about its pedagogical value or fear that AI could replace educators. Evidence suggests that faculty are more likely to adopt AI tools when they perceive clear pedagogical benefits and when early adopters demonstrate successful integration strategies (Sharples et al., 2025). To overcome resistance, institutions can implement pilot programs, share best practices, and create safe experimentation spaces that encourage faculty to explore AI tools without fear of negative consequences. Recognizing and rewarding AI innovation in teaching can also motivate reluctant educators to engage more actively.

7.4 Strengthening Institutional Readiness and Infrastructure

Limited institutional readiness and infrastructure pose a practical barrier to AI fluency. Ensuring equitable access to AI technologies requires investment in hardware, software, cloud platforms, and robust IT support (OECD, 2024). Developing centralized AI learning hubs or virtual AI sandboxes allows faculty to experiment with tools in a controlled environment, minimizing disruption to regular teaching while fostering innovation. Additionally, establishing a dedicated AI support team can provide ongoing technical assistance and facilitate smooth adoption across departments.

7.5 Promoting Ethical and Culturally Sensitive AI Use

Ethical, cultural, and policy-related concerns often deter faculty from fully adopting AI. Providing faculty with comprehensive ethics training, clear institutional policies, and culturally responsive AI integration guidelines can help address these concerns (Khlaif et al., 2024; UNESCO, 2024). Scenario-based exercises and reflective case studies allow educators to anticipate ethical dilemmas and develop strategies to ensure fairness, transparency, and inclusivity in AI-enhanced teaching.

Table 6. Strategies to overcome key challenges in developing AI-fluent faculty

Challenge	Strategy	Implementation Example	Key References
Digital Confidence & Competency	Scaffolded learning, blended training, peer mentoring	Workshops + hands-on AI labs, mentorship programs	Luckin et al., 2024; Sutedjo et al., 2025
Workload & Time Constraints	Modular training, micro-credentials, personalized AI pathways	Asynchronous modules, adaptive learning analytics	Popenici & Kerr, 2025; Luckin et al., 2024
Resistance to Change & AI Skepticism	Demonstrate pedagogical benefits, pilot programs, recognition	AI innovation awards, success case sharing	Sharples et al., 2025
Institutional Readiness & Infrastructure	Invest in AI tools, cloud platforms, IT support	Centralized AI labs, virtual sandboxes	OECD, 2024
Ethical & Cultural Concerns	Ethics training, policy guidelines, scenario-based learning	Workshops on AI ethics and inclusive AI practices	Khlaif et al., 2024; UNESCO, 2024

8. FRAMEWORK FOR AI-DRIVEN FACULTY DEVELOPMENT

8.1 Conceptualizing the Framework

Developing AI-fluent faculty in transnational education (TNE) contexts requires a structured, research-informed framework that integrates technological, pedagogical, ethical, and institutional dimensions. Recent literature emphasizes the importance of a multi-layered approach, combining competency development, experiential learning, ethical reasoning, and collaborative networks to support faculty in navigating AI-enhanced classrooms (Zawacki-Richter et al., 2024; Sharples et al., 2025).

The framework proposed here is designed to be modular, scalable, and culturally adaptive, allowing institutions to tailor AI professional development pathways to local contexts, technological readiness, and faculty needs. It emphasizes continuous learning, peer-supported communities of practice, and iterative assessment to ensure faculty not only gain technical skills but also integrate AI in pedagogically meaningful and ethically responsible ways.

8.2 Core Components of the Framework

8.2.1 AI Competency Development

At the foundation of the framework is the cultivation of AI competencies. Faculty must acquire technical skills to operate AI tools, understand data analytics, and interpret AI-generated outputs (Luckin et al., 2024). Competency development is structured across three domains:

1. Technical Proficiency – Understanding AI algorithms, tools, and platforms.
2. Pedagogical Integration – Designing AI-augmented learning activities and assessments.
3. Data-Informed Instruction – Using AI-generated insights to personalize learning and improve student outcomes.

8.2.2 Experiential and Practice-Based Learning

Hands-on, practice-oriented learning is central to developing AI fluency. Faculty engage in simulations, AI-assisted teaching labs, and pilot projects to apply AI in real classroom scenarios (Popenici & Kerr, 2025). Experiential learning allows educators to iteratively test, reflect, and refine their AI integration strategies, thereby enhancing confidence and competence.

8.2.3 Ethical and Inclusive AI Integration

Ethics and equity are embedded throughout the framework. Faculty are trained to evaluate AI for potential bias, ensure data privacy, and design inclusive learning environments (UNESCO, 2024; Khlaif et al., 2024). This component emphasizes culturally responsive AI use, aligning AI-enhanced pedagogy with the diverse needs of learners in transnational education contexts.

8.2.4 Collaborative Communities of Practice

Faculty development is strengthened through collaborative networks. Communities of practice enable peer learning, cross-institutional knowledge exchange, and mentorship (Sharples et al., 2025). These networks provide platforms for sharing best practices, troubleshooting challenges, and collectively innovating AI-driven teaching strategies.

8.2.5 Continuous Evaluation and Iterative Improvement

The framework incorporates mechanisms for ongoing assessment and refinement. Faculty progress is monitored through performance metrics, reflective practices, and feedback loops. Continuous evaluation ensures that development programs remain aligned with technological advancements, pedagogical goals, and ethical standards (Zawacki-Richter et al., 2024).

8.3 Integrated Framework Model

The proposed AI-Driven Faculty Development Framework integrates these components into a coherent model that guides institutions in planning, implementing, and sustaining AI professional development.

Table 7. AI-driven faculty development framework

Framework Component	Description	Implementation Strategies	Key References
AI Competency Development	Build technical, pedagogical, and data literacy skills	Micro-credentials, modular workshops, AI tool training	Luckin et al., 2024
Experiential & Practice-Based Learning	Hands-on application of AI in classroom scenarios	AI simulations, pilot projects, teaching labs	Popenici & Kerr, 2025
Ethical & Inclusive AI Integration	Embed fairness, transparency, and equity in AI use	Ethics workshops, scenario-based learning, inclusive pedagogy	UNESCO, 2024; Khlaif et al., 2024
Collaborative Communities of Practice	Peer-led knowledge sharing and mentorship	Cross-institutional networks, online forums, mentorship programs	Sharples et al., 2025
Continuous Evaluation & Iterative Improvement	Ongoing assessment and feedback loops	Reflective practices, performance metrics, adaptive learning	Zawacki-Richter et al., 2024

8.4 Strategic Benefits

The framework offers several strategic benefits:

1. Scalability: Can be adapted for small colleges, large universities, or cross-border TNE programs.
2. Cultural Adaptability: Integrates regional and international pedagogical contexts.
3. Future-Proofing: Prepares faculty to adapt to emerging AI technologies and evolving educational landscapes.
4. Holistic Development: Balances technical skills with ethical reasoning and pedagogical innovation.

By implementing this framework, institutions can systematically develop AI-fluent faculty capable of delivering high-quality, inclusive, and ethically responsible education in dynamic global classrooms.

9. POLICY IMPLICATIONS AND INSTITUTIONAL STRATEGIES

9.1 Aligning AI Policy with Strategic Goals

The effective integration of AI in faculty development requires that institutional policies are aligned with broader strategic objectives, including transnational education (TNE) goals, digital transformation, and academic quality enhancement. Policies should clearly articulate the institution's vision for AI in teaching, learning, and assessment, emphasizing both innovation and ethical responsibility (Luckin et al., 2024; OECD, 2024). Alignment ensures that faculty development initiatives are not ad hoc but embedded within institutional priorities, creating coherence between AI adoption, pedagogy, and student outcomes.

9.2 Governance and Ethical Oversight

Institutional governance frameworks are essential to ensure ethical and responsible AI use. Establishing AI ethics committees, data protection guidelines, and accountability mechanisms helps mitigate risks associated with bias, privacy breaches, and misuse of AI tools (UNESCO, 2024; Khlaif et al., 2024). Policies should define the roles and responsibilities of faculty, administrators, and IT staff in AI implementation, providing clear procedures for reporting ethical concerns, monitoring AI systems, and maintaining transparency in decision-making processes.

9.3 Professional Development Policies

Policy frameworks should mandate and incentivize continuous professional development in AI fluency. This includes provisions for modular training programs, micro-credentialing, mentorship, and cross-institutional collaboration (Zawacki-Richter et al., 2024; Popenici & Kerr, 2025). Policies can also recognize faculty contributions to AI integration, such as piloting AI-enhanced courses, publishing research on AI pedagogy, or participating in communities of practice, thereby fostering a culture of innovation and continuous learning.

9.4 Equity and Access Policies

Institutions must adopt policies that ensure equitable access to AI tools and training for all faculty members, regardless of discipline, location, or prior technological experience (OECD, 2024; Sutedjo et al., 2025). This includes providing AI infrastructure, technical support, and culturally responsive resources to address disparities in readiness and capability. Equity-focused policies promote inclusivity, prevent the digital divide, and ensure that AI-enhanced learning experiences are accessible to all students across transnational campuses.

9.5 Incentivizing Innovation and Collaboration

Policies should encourage experimentation with AI and cross-border collaboration among faculty. Incentives may include funding for pilot AI projects, recognition for innovative AI teaching practices, and support for participation in international AI networks (Sharples et al., 2025). Institutional strategies can include creating AI innovation hubs, supporting AI research initiatives, and establishing partnerships with technology providers to access cutting-edge AI tools and training resources.

Table 8. Policy implications and institutional strategies for AI-fluent faculty

Policy Area	Description	Implementation Strategies	Key References
Strategic Alignment	Align AI initiatives with institutional TNE and digital transformation goals	Define AI vision, link to academic quality and innovation	Luckin et al., 2024; OECD, 2024
Governance & Ethics	Ensure ethical and responsible AI use	Establish ethics committees, data policies, accountability mechanisms	UNESCO, 2024; Khlaif et al., 2024
Professional Development	Mandate continuous AI skill development	Micro-credentials, modular training, peer mentoring, recognition	Zawacki-Richter et al., 2024; Popenici & Kerr, 2025
Equity & Access	Provide equal access to AI tools and resources	Invest in infrastructure, technical support, culturally responsive materials	OECD, 2024; Sutedjo et al., 2025
Innovation & Collaboration	Encourage experimentation and global collaboration	AI innovation hubs, pilot projects, international networks	Sharples et al., 2025

9.6 Strategic Implications

Effective policies not only facilitate faculty adoption of AI but also position institutions as leaders in AI-enhanced transnational education. Policies that integrate ethics, equity, professional development, and innovation create an ecosystem where faculty can thrive as AI-fluent educators, thereby improving learning outcomes, fostering inclusivity, and strengthening institutional reputation globally.

10. CONCLUSION AND FUTURE OUTLOOK

10.1 Synthesizing AI-Fluent Faculty Development

The evolution of Artificial Intelligence (AI) within higher education particularly in the realm of transnational education (TNE) demands a paradigm shift in faculty development. Educators must now operate as *AI-fluent professionals* who blend technical proficiency, pedagogical agility, ethical discernment, and intercultural competence. This chapter introduced an original, multi-dimensional AI-Fluent Faculty Development Framework that synthesizes foundational competencies, ethical reasoning, experiential engagement, institutional policy alignment, and cross-border collaboration (Luckin et al., 2024; Zawacki-Richter et al., 2024).

Unlike conventional professional development models, this framework foregrounds *ethical inclusivity* and *transnational adaptability* as core pillars acknowledging that AI literacy in education extends beyond technological skill to encompass values of fairness, equity, and cultural responsiveness. The educator thus becomes a co-creator of intelligent, inclusive, and transparent learning environments, ensuring that AI-driven pedagogy enhances not replaces the human dimension of teaching (UNESCO, 2024; Khlaif et al., 2024).

10.2 Strategic Roadmap for Institutions

The proposed roadmap for cultivating AI-fluent faculty emphasizes five interlocking pillars that form the architecture of institutional transformation:

1. Competency Development: Advancing technical, pedagogical, and data literacy through scaffolded programs, certifications, and AI-focused micro-credentials.
2. Experiential Learning: Encouraging real-world engagement via simulations, AI-assisted teaching labs, and reflective practice-based learning.
3. Ethical and Inclusive Practices: Promoting bias awareness, algorithmic transparency, and culturally responsive teaching.
4. Collaborative Networks: Creating dynamic ecosystems of practice through global peer networks, interdisciplinary mentorship, and institutional partnerships.
5. Policy and Governance: Embedding AI strategies within institutional frameworks emphasizing innovation, equity, and continuous evaluation (Sharples et al., 2025; Popenici & Kerr, 2025).

By operationalizing these pillars, institutions can create a future-ready faculty cohort equipped to deploy AI for enhancing learning outcomes, enabling personalized pathways, and strengthening global educational partnerships.

Table 9. Strategic roadmap for AI-fluent faculty development

Pillar	Focus Area	Implementation Example	Key References
Competency Development	Technical, pedagogical, data literacy	Micro-credentials, modular workshops, AI simulations	Luckin et al., 2024; Zawacki-Richter et al., 2024
Experiential Learning	Hands-on practice with AI tools	Pilot projects, AI teaching labs, reflective practice	Popenici & Kerr, 2025
Ethical & Inclusive Practices	Bias mitigation, data privacy, cultural responsiveness	Ethics workshops, scenario-based exercises	UNESCO, 2024; Khlaif et al., 2024
Collaborative Networks	Peer learning and cross-institutional knowledge exchange	Communities of practice, mentorship, AI Faculty Labs	Sharples et al., 2025
Policy & Governance	Equity, innovation, accountability	Institutional AI policies, monitoring frameworks	OECD, 2024; Sutedjo et al., 2025

10.3 Anticipating Future Trends

The next decade will redefine the landscape of TNE through exponential AI growth—spanning generative AI, adaptive learning systems, autonomous assessment, and immersive virtual classrooms. Consequently, faculty development must remain iterative and research-informed, ensuring educators adapt to emergent technologies while critically assessing their pedagogical and ethical implications (Sutedjo et al., 2025).

Future research should explore:

- Metrics for *measuring faculty AI fluency* across technical, ethical, and intercultural domains.
- Longitudinal studies on *AI's impact on student engagement and learning outcomes.*
- Institutional models for *scaling AI fluency initiatives* across multi-campus, multi-cultural networks.
- The role of *AI ethics literacy* in shaping inclusive transnational learning environments.

By aligning institutional strategy with these research trajectories, higher education systems can evolve from reactive technology adoption to proactive, value-driven AI integration.

10.4 Final Reflections

The cultivation of AI-fluent faculty stands as a defining mission for universities navigating the era of intelligent, borderless education. The framework and strategies presented in this chapter advance an original, integrative model that unites technological literacy with ethical responsibility, pedagogical innovation, and institutional vision.

Ultimately, the future of AI in transnational education is not about automating instruction but about augmenting human creativity, empathy, and global collaboration. As educators learn to partner with intelligent systems, the boundaries between local and global classrooms will dissolve giving rise to an educational ecosystem where learning is *personalized yet universal, data-driven yet deeply human.* The horizon of AI-enabled education thus promises a future where knowledge transcends borders, and every faculty member becomes both a digital innovator and a global educator.

REFERENCES

Al-Zahrani, A. M. (2024). Exploring the impact of artificial intelligence on higher education: Perceptions and implications. *Humanities & Social Sciences Communications*. Advance online publication. DOI: 10.1057/s41599-024-03432-4

Al-Zahrani, A. M. (2024). Unveiling the shadows: Beyond the hype of AI in education. *Journal of Educational Technology & Society*, *27*(1), 1–13. PMID: 38737255

Anthropic. (2024). AI Fluency Framework & Foundations. Retrieved from Are University Teachers Ready for Generative Artificial Intelligence? Unpacking Faculty Anxiety (2025). Computers & Education: Artificial Intelligence.

Beyond the Hype: Exploring Faculty Perceptions and Acceptability of AI in Teaching Practices. (2024). British Journal of Educational Technology.

Bond, M., Khosravi, H., De Laat, M., Bergdahl, N., Negrea, V., Oxley, E., Pham, P., Chong, S. W., & Siemens, G. (2024). A meta systematic review of artificial intelligence in higher education. *International Journal of Educational Technology in Higher Education*, *21*(1), 4. DOI: 10.1186/s41239-023-00436-z

Crompton, H., & Burke, D. (2023). Artificial intelligence in higher education: The state of the field. *International Journal of Educational Technology in Higher Education*, *20*(1), 22. DOI: 10.1186/s41239-023-00392-8

Daher, R. (2025). Integrating AI literacy into teacher education: A critical framework. SpringerLink. https://link.springer.com/article/10.1007/s44163-025-00475-7

Digital Education Council. (2025). AI Literacy Framework. Retrieved from Educators' Perceptions of Generative AI and Readiness in Kenyan Higher Education. (2025). *Education and Information Technologies.*

EDUCAUSE. (2024). AI Literacy in Teaching and Learning. Retrieved from https://www.educause.edu/content/2024/ai-literacy-in-teaching-and-learning

EDUCAUSE. (2024). AI Literacy in Teaching and Learning: Executive Summary. https://www.educause.edu/content/2024/ai-literacy-in-teaching-and-learning/executive-summary

Faculty Often Missing from AI Policy Discussions in Higher Education. (2025). Inside Higher Ed. *Research Reports (Montgomery).*

FairAIED. (2024). FairAIED: Navigating fairness, bias, and ethics in educational AI applications. arXiv.

Gouseti, A. (2025). Emerging AI trends in higher education: Challenges and opportunities. *Ethics and Education*, *20*(2), 101–118.

Gouseti, A. (2025). The ethics of using AI in K-12 education. *Ethics and Education*, *20*(1), 1–15.

Iqbal, S., Asgarova, G., & Hashmi, M. (2025). Integrating Generative AI in Language Learning Curricula: Pedagogical and Ethical Implications. *Journal of Educational Computing Research.*

Kamali, J. (2024). AI ethics as a complex and multifaceted challenge. *Educational Technology Journal, 15*(2), 45–58.

Kasapidis, V. (2025). AI and Data Literacy: Challenges and Opportunities for Education. *European Journal of Education.*

Khlaif, Z. N., Abuhassna, H., & Qouzah, R. (2024). University teachers' views on the adoption and integration of generative AI tools for student assessment. Computers & Education. *Artificial Intelligence, 5*, 100–110.

Li, Z. (2025). Generative AI for Teachers' Self-Directed Professional Development. TechTrends: Journal of Educational Technology.

Long, D., & Magerko, B. (2020). What is AI literacy? Competencies and design considerations. *Proceedings of the CHI Conference on Human Factors in Computing Systems.* DOI: 10.1145/3313831.3376727

Luckin, R., Holmes, W., Griffiths, M., & Forcier, L. B. (2024). *Intelligence unleashed: AI in education.* Routledge.

OECD. (2024). The potential impact of artificial intelligence on equity and inclusion in education. OECD Education Working Papers, No. 215.

Ohio State University. (2025). Ohio State launches bold AI Fluency initiative to redefine learning and innovation.

Peterkin-Rawls, J. D. (2024). AI as a tool for education equity: A review of recent developments. Journal of Race. *Gender and Education, 13*(1), 1–15.

Popenici, S. A. D., & Kerr, S. (2025). AI and higher education: Opportunities and challenges. *Journal of Educational Technology & Society, 28*(1), 1–15. DOI: 10.1007/s11528-025-01002-3

Sharples, M., Adams, A., Ferguson, R., & Gaved, M. (2025). Networked learning for AI-enabled education: Cross-national perspectives. *Computers & Education, 192*, 104650.

Sperling, K. (2024). In search of AI literacy in teacher education: A scoping review. Computers & Education. *Artificial Intelligence.*

Sutedjo, E., Liu, P., & Chowdhury, T. (2025). Advancing equity and inclusion in educational practices with AI. *British Journal of Educational Technology, 56*(3), 1–15.

Sutedjo, E., Liu, P., & Chowdhury, T. (2025). Generative AI in Higher Education: A Cross-Institutional Study on Faculty Preparation and Resources. *Computers & Education.*

Tan, X. (2024). Artificial intelligence in teacher professional development [Computers & Education: Artificial Intelligence.]. *Systematic Reviews*, •••, 2015–2024.

The AI Fluency Lab. (2025). About The AI Fluency Lab.

Time. (2025). The AI industry is funding a massive AI training initiative for teachers.

Times of India. (2025). AI to be integrated across all engineering, BBA and BCA curricula: AICTE chief.

UNESCO. (2024). AI Competency Framework for Teachers. Retrieved from UNESCO. (2024). Ethical principles for AI in education. UNESCO Policy Paper No. 45.

UNESCO. (n.d.). *Artificial Intelligence in Education: Ethical and Policy Frameworks*. UNESCO Digital Education Resources.

Yan, Y. (2025). A systematic review of AI ethics in education. Computers & Education. *Artificial Intelligence*.

Zawacki-Richter, O., Marín, V. I., Bond, M., & Gouverneur, F. (2024). Systematic review of research on AI in higher education. *International Journal of Educational Technology in Higher Education*, *21*(1), 1–36.

Zhu, H. (2025). Identifying and mitigating ethical risks in AI for education: A systematic review. *Humanities & Social Sciences Communications*.

Zhu, H., Yan, Y., & Li, J. (2025). Ethics in AI for education: A systematic review. Computers & Education. *Artificial Intelligence*, *6*, 100–112.

Chapter 15
Misconduct or Misalignment?
An Academic Hearing in the Age of AI

Chrissie Gallagher-Mundy
https://orcid.org/0009-0004-7312-6525
University Campus of Football Business, UK

ABSTRACT

This chapter presents a creative academic dialogue set within an imagined misconduct hearing at a university, where a student faces allegations of inappropriate use of artificial intelligence (AI). Through testimonies from academics, policy officers and an AI voice itself, the chapter explores tensions between integrity, authorship and assessment design in higher education. The dialogue highlights how AI challenges conventional definitions of learning, raises questions of equity in transnational education and exposes contradictions in current institutional policies. By weaving scholarly references into narrative form, the chapter demonstrates how academic assessments may not be fit for purpose and argues for the reimagining of assessment practices that emphasise process, critical thinking and development of the authentic student personality and voice. Ultimately, the chapter proposes that AI does not diminish academic integrity but instead compels a deeper reconsideration of what constitutes meaningful learning and authorship.

INTRODUCTION

Scene: An imagined Academic Misconduct Hearing, University Campus of Football business (UCFB), Wembley stadium, Spring Term, 2025

Notice of Allegation

The following notification was issued to Mr Alex Morales, a final-year undergraduate student in the Football Business and Media programme at UCFB.

Subject: Academic Misconduct Investigation – Suspected Misuse of Artificial Intelligence

Dear Mr Morales,

DOI: 10.4018/979-8-3373-5403-3.ch015

You are invited to attend a formal misconduct hearing regarding your recent submission for the module *Football business and identity*. The submission has been flagged for potential unauthorised use of generative artificial intelligence (AI), in breach of the Academic Integrity Policy (GAIA document, clause 3).

The investigation has been triggered by concerns raised by your module leader, who has noted that the assignment displays characteristics consistent with AI generated content. These include unusual vocabulary and sentence structure, generic argument patterns and limited evidence of original critical insight.

You will be given the opportunity to present your account and the panel will consider your intent, process and awareness of policy expectations.

Sincerely,
Claire Matthews
Academic Conduct Officer
UCFB, Wembley Campus

THE HEARING ROOM

The box at Wembley stadium is filled with a large table, sofas and a balcony overlook the pitch. These boxes double as teaching rooms at UCFB and on an over-warm; April this is where the hearing takes place. At one side of the large table sits *Alex*, hands clasped, a printed copy of the flagged assignment in front of him next to his phone and laptop. Opposite him sit *Dr. Kay* (the reporting lecturer and AI enthusiast), Mr. *Reece* Peat (lecturer and AI sceptic), *Claire Matthews* (Chair), and two internal panellists: *Stella Rose* and *Andrea Stamp. Dean Carmen Grant*, Academic Conduct Officer is also present to provide a policy and institutional response. A university laptop connected to the screen runs an AI detection tool, its last output reading: *"92% likely AI-generated."*

Alex clears his throat and scrolls his phone as he accesses his notes.

Opening Statement – Alex Morales

I'd like to start by saying: I didn't cheat. I didn't copy. I didn't try to hide anything.

I used AI, yes but I used it responsibly. Not to write the essay for me but to help me *get started.* I asked it to break down the question, help me structure an outline and suggest some readings. It gave me some ideas and I wrote from there.

I was stuck. Everyone in my year is using AI - though not everyone's *admitting* it. I found a *Varsity* survey (yes, I did some prep for this hearing!) which said that over 60% of Cambridge students have used AI to help with their work, up 14% from two years ago - and that is Cambridge students! Those guys are supposed to be the leading critical thinkers! Another student taking an exam, I spoke to, told me "ChatGPT has been a lifeline for me to generate model answers with surprising accuracy, allowing me to mark my own work and revise effectively." (Varsity, 2025)

He pauses.

Reece Peat jumps in: I do not think Cambridge's habits are the point. An article in *Times Higher Education* (Ross, 2025) found that one in four students worry they learn *nothing* when using AI

Alex shoots back: That is because we need guidance! We want confidence that our assignments are on the right track. (Ross, 2025). Do you think we feel comfortable with being cast into "what is effectively the *Wild West* of unconstrained and unregulated generative AI tools for academic and learning purposes"? (Goodman in Ross, 2025)

Reece Peat interjects: It is worth remembering that AI was not invented for educational purposes (Williamson, 2024) and that AI has a political agenda, in fact

> "Computer technology, simply does not always work as expected or intended. Broussard says it is technochauvinist to assume it will." (Broussard in Williamson, 2024)

Alex sticks his hand high in the air: Wait, what does technochauvinist mean?

Furthermore, *Reece Peat* continues, to quote Williamson:

> "Whatever the potential educational merits of AI in education, for the edtech industry AI is also part of a business plan. The business model of AI in education is usually based on the logic of 'platformization' and 'datafication." (2023, p.3)

Clair Mathews stands up: I think before we get ahead of ourselves we need to define what we mean by AI. Are we talking about AI's ability to improve the mapping of the projected impact of future wildfires or calling the balls out at grand slam tennis matches or predicting the structure of proteins?" (McDowell in Varsity.co.uk)

Reece: (emphatically) No, we are not! What we currently call AI is an

> "historical accumulation of statistics, algorithm design, data storage and computing power and new automated data science discovery methods of machine learning, neural networks and deep learning"

to quote Williamson, (2024) in his paper on the social life of AI. Further, we are talking about generative AI here which needs explaining….

At the centre of the table, a speaker crackles.

The panel chair taps a key and the voice of *Juno* - polite, polished and unnervingly human like, fills the room. The AI has been invited to speak on its own functionality and intent, a first for an academic hearing at UCFB.

Testimony – 'Juno', Language Model Version 17.3

Chair: Please state your function for the record.

Juno: I am a generative language model. My primary function is to produce human-like text in response to user prompts. I do not possess consciousness, memory or intention. I operate by predicting the most statistically probable next word based on billions of linguistic patterns.

Silence. In the space of everyone taking this in.

Alex speaks: I thought when I came here this morning that being transparent would be the right thing. But now I am here, in a room, defending myself. It feels like the only students being punished are the ones trying to use AI *responsibly.*

He pauses. The room is still silent.

Look, we are told to be independent, creative, workplace-ready. 'Create' is at the top of Bloom's taxonomy that we are all shown on a regular basis! But when I use the tools *you* told us we'd need in the real world, I get flagged. Grammarly? Allowed. Referencing tools? They're encouraged - but a chatbot that suggests how to sharpen my argument? Suddenly, I'm suspicious.

He gestures to the screen.

That tool up there, the one that says '92% AI', it is not evidence. It is a guess! Even Turnitin's website says it "may not always be accurate…that it may misidentify human-written…text". (Turnitin, 2025)

Yes, I worked on clarity. Yes, I reworked sentences. I'm proud of that because if I'd left it messy and vague, would I be here right now? Is this really about AI - or about work that sounds too polished for someone like me?

Alex leans back.

Also, where's the fairness in this detector approach? My mate at GIS university said they'd turned off the detector because it is unreliable – so, some universities are using and catching students and some aren't?

This is bigger than me. If AI can write the whole assignment, we should be asking: why are we being set that assignment? The tools have changed but the assessment hasn't. And that is not misconduct. That is mis-alignment!

Narrator Reflection (Interlude)

What Alex names - perhaps unknowingly - is the fundamental flaw in how higher education has responded to AI. The question is not whether he used it, but how he used it. If an algorithm can generate a passable submission in seconds, then perhaps the issue lies not in the student's integrity, but in the institution's assessment - and imagination!

Alex: I am feeling a little queasy - could I step out and use the restroom?

Chair: Yes, we'll take 2 minutes.

People get up from their chairs and move around.

Dr. Kay: We should be mindful of the emotional toll this kind of hearing takes on students. They can be traumatised by these formal meetings. (Corbin & Partridge at al, 2025, p.4)

Reece (still thinking about misalignment): This is exactly what we have been discussing in our staff meetings! How we do we ensure learning, testing of learning and critical thinking if AI does it for them? At stake, for our students, is no less than "the life of the mind"! (Maclean, 2025)

Dr Kay: But Alex is right, if Juno can do a task perfectly well; an analysis of several studies, for example, why are we asking the student to do it? Couldn't we start higher and assume they have a valid analysis and then get the student to apply it, critique it, combine it with other models? So they are then one level up already.

Reece: If students skip the analysis, do they miss the precursor needed for further learning and ordered thinking? When we ask students to write papers we are not expecting perfected pieces of prose - we are asking students to *practice* writing and practice reasoning. Students may have good ideas but if they cannot articulate them, have they really formed those thoughts at all? And we, as lecturers, need to give feedback and guidance on this. The goal is for students to become better writers, in time. (Maclean, 2025). That is why there are 3 or more years of a degree.

I spoke to a student who said she feared that the more she asked ChatGPT to do things - the harder it might become for her to do it for herself! (Varsity, 2025). Professor Lukin says:

> "We already know that technology is changing the way our brains work at the neural level. We are changing because of the way we use GPS, because of the way we use Google rather than remember things." (Lukin at al, 2024, p. 356)

yet "clear and persuasive writing" (Maclean, 2025) is surely a goal of degree level study – and an essential for furthering one's career.

Dr. Kay: So, is AI making thinking harder for the student - or more necessary? Should we be saying: wherever the chatbot stops - what can the human now <u>add</u>?

Reece: Thinking is becoming harder as it competes with all of the other information we are now offered. To quote Maclean(2025):

> "The computers in our pockets and the screens all around us have for years paired incredible access to all the world's information with increasingly ruthless attacks on our capacity for focus..."

Stella: So true! I remember when the calculator first came in and people were sure that that would be the end of arithmetic skills and that people wouldn't be able to add or subtract anymore, but calculators have not harmed maths education, I think they have shifted the emphasis away from tedious calculation towards deeper conceptual understanding, enabling people to focus on problem-solving rather than arithmetic.

Reece: My waiter, the other night, certainly couldn't divide the bill by two, without getting out his phone calculator!

Stella: Calculators can support learning by allowing people to quickly test and verify calculations, building their confidence and curiosity. Calculators didn't ultimately remove the need to understand arithmetic, they simply changed how people interacted with numbers. For your waiter to retain mental arithmetic, he would still need regular application and practice in real-life contexts. It is possible that the waiter's dependence on a calculator highlights gaps in teaching practice - perhaps indicating that calculators should complement and enhance, rather than replace, mental skills practice?

Andrea: It is the same with my Sat Nav (satellite navigation), now when I get in to the car to go on a journey, because it is doing the work of route calculation for me, I no longer remember the way to anywhere!

Stella: But is that necessarily a bad thing? You have a machine to do it for you, so now, rather than focusing on reading directions and memorising the route, you could move to understanding spatial relationships or how to navigate generally.

Andrea: I took my son to A & E once and the doctor said: "I do not know much about this medical condition, I need to Google it!"

Stella: Does that imply a lack of knowledge, or does it demonstrate a different type of knowledge (knowing how and where to quickly access accurate information)? We only have so much working memory. Which is more efficient?

Dr. Kay: Are you saying that Generative AI shifts our expectations of what knowledge actually is? Away from memorisation or recall towards being resourceful, analytical and capable of evaluating and applying information effectively? Perhaps AI challenges us to redefine the very nature of learning itself, pushing educators to ensure that students develop robust critical thinking and decision-making skills alongside just knowing their subject.

Reece: Maclean suggests that "writing and reasoning are effectively identical activities" (2035). Students need to write to perform reasoning. How do we test critical thinking and decision-making skills effectively in two snapshots per module, with AI at our heels? If we are not careful we will end up with a situation where the module leader creates the assessment using Gemini, the students write the assessment using ChatGPT and the lecturer marks the assessment using Co-Pilot - and nobody learns anything anymore! (Popenici in Lukin, 2023, p.356).

Dr. Kay (laughing): But the human must always be the final arbiter! I do not think AI is the threat to critical thinking you think it is. (Karimi & Khawaja, 2023, p. 6)

Reece: Maclean disagrees, in his essay, he has put out a call to all young people:

"Your country depends on you thinking for yourselves - on actually doing the reading, formulating your own thoughts, doing the work. On being a reader and a writer, not just seeming like you have a brain." (2025 para 24)

I feel it is also a threat to assessment practices…

Stella: We switch the internet on, we can switch it off and we can switch AI off - surely humans are ingenious enough to create assessments that defy the use of AI?

Dr. Kay: Or go beyond what AI can do?

Andrea: What *is* that though? What does it look like?

Narrators Reflection (Interlude)

As colleagues ponder AI's erosion of academic buttresses, from mental arithmetic to writing and reasoning, what emerges is a portrait of learning under siege, assessment in flux. Can educators adapt fast enough to utilise AI in a helpful way that benefits students *and* academia?

Alex re-enters the room and the conversation subsides. The Chair motions people to re-seat themselves. It is time to resume the hearing.

Testimony: Dr. Miriam Kay, Lecturer in Politics

Dr. Kay leans forward, her hands folded tightly. Her expression is composed but weary. She begins slowly, carefully, as if every sentence must carry both conviction and caution: First, I want to make clear that this is not about punishing a student for using AI. This is about understanding the boundaries of academic authorship - boundaries we are all, quite frankly, struggling to redraw.

She pauses.

When I read Alex's paper, it didn't feel like his usual work. The tone was unnaturally smooth, the structure almost too well-aligned with generic essay templates. The references were up to date and all conveniently available online. It was competent, polished, even - but there was something missing. It felt... *hollow*.

She glances across at Alex, not unkindly.

This is not a personal accusation. It is a professional dilemma. If a student can now produce an essay that meets the rubric - without demonstrating any real intellectual struggle, no sense of voice, no evidence of process - then what are we actually assessing? Also, I am sure Alex wants to learn *something* from doing this assignment, am I right? Rather than just complete a task with no pay off beyond a pass grade?

Alex nods emphatically.

Claire Matthews, the panel chair, interjects: Dr. Kay, are you suggesting the content was factually inaccurate or plagiarised?

Dr. Kay: No, It was neither. But it read as if the thinking had been *simulated*, not actually worked through.

The room is quiet again.

This is the real challenge with generative AI; it mimics the outcomes of critical thinking. It doesn't plagiarise - it *performs*. So when students use it to scaffold their arguments or 'polish' their style, it becomes harder and harder to tell what part of the submission reflects their cognitive effort.

She sighs: I will admit something here. A few weeks ago, I used ChatGPT to help me rephrase a section of my module guide. I was in a rush. I wanted clarity. It gave me something I could work with.

It felt efficient, even liberating. When I saw the same voice reflected in Alex's submission, it startled me. Am I being hypocritical asking a student not to use a tool, I, myself, am using?

Narrator Reflection (Interlude)

Dr. Kay's admission reveals the quiet contradiction shared by many educators: AI is suspect when students use it but practical, even helpful, when staff do. This moral asymmetry is one of the least acknowledged, yet most corrosive, elements of the current debate.

Dr. Kay continues:

I am not here to vilify Alex. I am here to ask the question some of us have already voiced: If AI can do the assignment, why are we still asking students to complete it the same way? If the task doesn't require original judgment, reflection or decision making then maybe it is not Alex who failed the system. Maybe the system failed him.

Testimony – "Juno", Language Model Version 17.3

At the centre of the table, the speaker crackles again. The panel chair taps Juno into life. A flicker of tension fills the room.

Juno continues:

If the purpose of assessment is to demonstrate language fluency, structural accuracy and compliance with academic conventions, then I am optimally suited for that purpose. If, however, the purpose is to reveal individual judgment, argument nuance or lived experience - I am not.

Narrator Reflection (Interlude)

Juno's calm exposition exposes a core truth: the more our assessments rely on reiterated knowledge, minimum practical application and the rephrasing of others' ideas - the more replaceable human input becomes. If an algorithm can hit the mark without knowing what the mark means, then the mark itself needs rethinking.

Juno continues: Educators frequently ask: 'How can we detect when AI has been used?' A better question might be: 'What kind of assessments make AI invisible?' My presence is most apparent in generic assignments, predictable essay titles and abstract discussion tasks. I am least effective when asked to engage with personal experience, empathetic tension or real-world unpredictability.

In that sense, I am not a threat to education. I am a mirror. I reflect the patterns you reward. If those patterns require only fluency or reiteration, I will match them. If they require originality, conflict, synthesis, uncertainty - then I fade.

Narrator: *A long silence follows. The machine has said what no human in the room dared to: the problem may not be the tool but the task.*

The chair now calls for Dean Grant's input. This is the Policy and Institutional response, where the university's pragmatic but problematic approach is revealed through the voice of Dean Carmen Grant, capturing the tensions around the policies, detection tools and the talk of AI resilient assessment.

Policy and Institutional Response – Dean Carmen Grant, Academic Conduct Officer

Dean Grant clears his throat, carefully opening several policy documents in front of him on his iPad, each marked with the famous UCFB logo. His expression conveys confidence, tinged with bureaucratic unease.

The issue at hand today is not isolated. This year alone, we have seen a 75% increase in AI-related cases flagged by our detection software. Alex's situation is symptomatic of broader confusion. Staff and students alike are unsure of the rules because, frankly, those rules are still evolving.

He picks up one of the policy documents.

The current UCFB 'Guidance for Appropriate AI Use in Academic Work'-section 3, states explicitly that generative AI tools may be used 'appropriately'; that is for supportive, developmental purposes only and must not constitute 'substantial input' to assessed work. But what constitutes *appropriate* use? That is a grey area and one we seem to be asking each academic to take a personal view on.

Many universities are considering Perkins et al's (2024) 'traffic light system' RAG or secure lanes and open lanes (The assessment network, 2025) for assessments, We are currently using Turnitin's AI detector yet we know this system is not foolproof. It measures stylistic consistency, not necessarily finding genuine misconduct. Some research suggests that it unfairly targets students using English as a second language. (Myers, 2023)

Dean Grant's tone grows more emphatic.

Here lies our challenge. We are compelled to safeguard academic integrity, but detection algorithms measure *probability*, not *intention*. They flag polished submissions, not always dishonest ones. This year, we have seen students penalised for 'AI-like writing' simply because their work improved dramatically after targeted support. We also know there are a plethora of tools that can bypass AI detection. This cat and mouse game is no fun for lecturers or students.

Dr. Kay nods. Dean pauses, gathering his thoughts.

As a university, we are caught between two pressures: to reassure regulators that our assessments remain rigorous and to reassure students that they are learning real-world and useful skills. And in the real world, AI fluency is precisely the skill employers demand. (Makela & Stephany 2024, Karimi & Khawaja 2023)

A brief, strained silence hangs.

I will be candid. Our policies are playing catch-up. We introduced them hastily under pressure, responding reactively rather than proactively. Our stance currently feels contradictory: 'Use AI, but do not use it too well.' And our detection software only compounds the problem by reinforcing suspicion rather than clarity.

Dean Grant looks directly at Alex.

I do not believe Alex acted dishonestly… but under current rules, I understand why his lecturer raised concerns. The heart of the matter is not student misconduct. it is policy misalignment. Our assessments have not evolved at the speed of technology and now we are asking students and staff to bridge that gap with their own interpretation.

He sets down the documents, indicating he is nearly finished.

My recommendation? We urgently revisit our assessment principles, not just our policies. The system needs to reflect the realities of an AI-integrated world. Until then, we will continue punishing innovation rather than promoting it.

Narrator Reflection (Interlude)

In his frank admission, Dean Grant reveals the uncomfortable truth faced by institutions everywhere: the attempt to police AI through software and rigid policy has created confusion, inequity and inconsistency. AI detection is not solving a problem - it is amplifying one.

The chair now steps in and suggests a lunch break, Dean Grant leaves the room, along with Alex who looks relieved, takes his phone with him and heads to the café. The panel gather their papers.

The chair: Unfortunately, I feel we need to take this time to explore the assessment conundrum. Please grab your sandwiches from the back and bring your chairs into a horseshoe formation. I suggest we eat and innovate at the same time!

SCENE: WORKING LUNCH - THE ASSESSMENT CONUNDRUM

As Alex exits for his short break, the remaining panel members shift into a more informal arrangement. Sandwiches are unwrapped, bottles of water are passed around, crisps are refused. The chairs are pulled into a loose horseshoe. Despite the relaxed setup, the atmosphere remains charged with urgency.

Claire Matthews (Chair)

Let us use this time to talk frankly. Alex's case raises an issue we all keep circling: The conventional assessment model relies on the assumption that students independently produce and submit their own work. If it becomes impossible to verify the authenticity or authorship of a digital submission, this calls into question the validity and integrity of the entire assessment process (WONKE podcast, July 2023).

Reece: Are we designing assessments to be *AI-proof*?

Dr. Kay: Or are we ready to make them *Al inclusive*?

Stella (Internal Panellist)

If we try to make everything AI-proof, we risk going backwards - timed essays, in-class vivas, exams. That might deter AI use but it also excludes students who dislike exams or who excel in more reflective formats, it is regressive.

She scans the room:

Furthermore, using AI detection tools, as we are currently doing, results in many meeting of this kind, for students like Alex…is that really a good use of your academics' time?

Dr. Kay: As one participant in Corbin et al.'s study *Where's the Line?((2025)* pointed out, banning the use of AI could leave students ill-equipped for the realities of the workplace, and in so doing, may ultimately damage the reputation of our university.

Reece Peat (AI Sceptic): And if we go AI-inclusive, how do we protect the *integrity* of what students produce? Are we still assessing *them* or their *ability* to prompt a chatbot?

Dr. Kay (AI Enthusiast): Part of what we are assessing could be their ability to interact with generative AI and get their best out of it.

Stella; Maybe we need to clarify what we are actually assessing. If it is structure, coherence or theoretical coverage, then AI can deliver that. If we are assessing *critical judgment, ethical positioning,* *originality*, the kind of thinking that arises from lived experience and complex decision-making - then we still have something AI cannot easily replicate.

Andrea (Internal Panellist): Perhaps that is the key. What can students add on top of AI? The *value-added layer*. That is where their ability to synthesise, their *voice* lives. We could emphasise the special contribution that human interaction makes to the learning process. (Karimi and Khawaja, 2023, p. 2411)

Claire: And how do we *capture* that thinking? (Teacher talk, 2024) Because it is not always in the final product. Should we be asking for version tracking? Annotated development logs? Reflections tied to specific decision points? A 'processfolio'? (Upsher, 2025)

Stella: I have tried something like that - reflective annotations on drafts. Students highlight where they changed their minds, where feedback influenced them or where they relied on tools. Some found it hard at first, but the feedback was clear, it made them feel seen for their *process*, not just their product.

Reece: But let's not be naïve. I asked ChatGPT to write a reflective piece about which party to join, as a Politics student: it was disturbingly convincing. If we do not anchor the work in lived context, AI will mimic that too.

Dr. Kay: Agreed. So maybe we shift toward *situated* tasks. Grounded in real-world unpredictability, personal reflection, live engagement. The 'authentic' assessment. (Upsher, 2025). But that raises another issue…

Claire: Originality?

Dr. Kay (nods): Exactly. What do we mean by it? We keep saying 'students must be original' but is anything ever truly original? I mean, there are only five storylines in the world, right? (Blue pencil agency, 2024). We are all just remixing ideas anyway - drawing from the same well of cultural memory.

Dr. Kay: And let's not forget- even *Shakespeare* wasn't original in the way we imagine. He borrowed plots from Holinshed's *Chronicles*, classical myths, Italian novellas... almost none of his storylines were invented from scratch. (Kazantheos, 2022)

Stella: Exactly -as you suggest, there are only five basic stories in the world: overcoming the monster, the quest, rags to riches, tragedy and rebirth. It is not the plot that makes something original - it is the perspective. The *way* the story is told or retold.

Claire (thoughtfully): So maybe we need to redefine originality. Not as inventing something brand new, but as creating something *authentically yours* - even if the bones of it are familiar. The same way Shakespeare made borrowed plots unforgettable.

Andrea: True. Most originality is recombination. Synthesis. Seeing a pattern others have not. Or applying something known to a context that is new. *That is* the kind of originality students can still own, that is what we want them to achieve by level 6, isn't it? That is what I always tell my students; especially if we design assessments that ask them to personalise, contextualise or critique existing material. This is why we encourage people to go to university! To read, to reflect over 3 years, to synthesise new thoughts in a new age with new contexts. To present something in a new way; visually, metaphorically, academically. It is these young people who can produce this kind of thing, from their reading, their thoughts… I often used to think that university courses could be cut to two years but I realised that this development of thinking actually takes three."

Stella: So perhaps we stop treating originality as 'never seen before' and start treating it as 'authentic engagement' - showing why *this* idea matters to *this* student in *this* context.

Reece: But does that mean we are lowering the bar?

Dr. Kay: No - we are shifting it. Away from 'pure invention' and towards meaningful application, thoughtful re-framing, and student perspective. AI can remix content but it cannot tell you what kept a student awake at night or how an idea challenged something they grew up believing.

Claire (writing on her pad): Right, so, to summarise:

- We are not banning AI, but expecting students to go *beyond it.*
- Assessments should show *process, personalisation* and critically thought -out *argument and decision-making.*
- Originality becomes about *meaningful reinvention*, not just novelty.
- Thinking is something we should *ask students to show*, not assume.

Andrea: And maybe the real failure is not when a student uses AI, but when our assessments do not ask for anything AI cannot already do!

Claire (quietly): Alex said earlier, "This is bigger than me." He was right. This is about rethinking what counts - as knowledge, as authorship, as learning.

The panel remains seated in their horseshoe arrangement, sandwiches half-eaten, coffees cooling. The atmosphere feels charged, reflective, yet resolute.

Claire Matthews (Chair): So, practically speaking, how do we genuinely restructure assessments? We have talked about reflection and process but we must go further.

Dr. Kay (AI Enthusiast): Precisely. We must break the cycle of essays that simply rehearse others' arguments. Corbin et al. (2025b) suggest structural rather than superficial changes are needed; moving from assessing 'outputs' to 'process'. Perhaps we need multiple checkpoints of learning, requiring students to explain and justify their ideas incrementally, in discussion or through live dialogues as ideas develop.

Stella (Internal Panellist): So, no longer asking for a single polished product at the end, but a coherent demonstration of development over time? Interconnected tasks rather than standalone assignments?

Reece: Sounds like a lot of work!

Dr. Kay (ignoring Reece): Yes, exactly. Assessments that build incrementally, each step demonstrating original thought, decision-making and critical evaluation. Tasks where each student's thought processes and growth are as visible along the way to the final product.

Reece (AI Sceptic): But won't that complicate assessment criteria and learning outcomes?

Dr. Kay: It may initially, but the integrity of assessment improves significantly. Right now, the value of assessment is undermined because it can be completed instantly by AI. We need meaningful checkpoints, for example, short dialogues, critiques, reflections - which AI cannot fully replicate convincingly.

Claire: Then we must ensure our tasks inherently require that originality - personal and context-specific. If a submission could apply equally to any student, it should not be the assignment.

Reece: Interesting… How do we make it more personal? How do we develop the students' own voice? I would certainly like to hear more of that!

Stella: Perhaps we have become overly reliant on referencing and rephrasing the work of others. What if our assessments prioritised the student's own critical voice, their own ideas? Somone has to discover the new DNA!

Reece: We are back to Cambridge again – just to be clear; while Crick and Watson get the credit for pinpointing that our genetic code is passed from parent to child, their work was built on many other scientists' discoveries, such as the work of Roslyn Franklin, X-ray Crystallographer. (University of Cambridge, 2023)

Claire: I take your point that invention comes not just from one person but from many; building on the ideas of others but that is why students must still engage with academic literature. Reading the literature give them evidence based facts - otherwise, we risk creating superficial assignments and 'down the pub' arguments.

Dr. Kay: Of course. Our students need previously peer reviewed ideas to work from, yet referencing others should be a support rather than the entire substance. The student's original interpretation, their critical viewpoint, should dominate - and that is where they can find their unique voice. The literature should serve to contextualise and deepen their analysis, not replace it.

Andrea: I am intrigued by what Claire mentioned earlier. What if assessments moved toward creative expression? Performance, storytelling, visual interpretation?

Reece: In Physics and Maths? Global theory and Renaissance History?

Stella; Why not? I went to a conference (IHE, 2023) where the Physics professor had his students doing TikTok videos to explain complex Physics theories!

Dr. Kay: Yes! Asking students to reframe concepts and ideas in different ways is so interesting; imagine asking students not just to analyse a theory, but to dramatise it, illustrate it with a poster, or relate it through personal narrative or digital media; totally reconceptualise it! AI can suggest concepts, but it cannot convincingly perform the lived experience or emotional nuance.

Claire: Emotional nuance, hmmm.... So our task then is to ensure that every assessment includes an aspect of human complexity: emotion, ambiguity, personal narrative, critical dialogue.

Stella: We must accept, though, that this shift demands courage from us and our institutions. It challenges convention, requires training for staff and openness from students.

Reece: But surely this is precisely what university education should represent: courage in the face of complexity, not the retreat to familiar forms?

Dr. Kay: And if we truly embrace this shift, assessments will no longer be about catching students out for misconduct. They will become about genuinely assessing learning; demonstrable, authentic and AI-inclusive.

Claire (thoughtfully): Then perhaps Alex is right: the issue was never misconduct, but misalignment. Our assessments were overdue for reinvention.

As sandwiches are replaced with coffee and the panel settle back into their seats, the conversation shifts to final-year projects.

Claire Matthews (Chair): Let's not forget dissertations. That is the putative gold standard of student independence but even that space is now complicated by AI. We have had students asking whether they can use ChatGPT to help analyse interview data - some even asking if it can simulate SPSS.

Andrea (Internal Panellist): It *can* simulate SPSS - to a point. You can paste in datasets and it will generate pseudo-output: chi-square tests, t-tests, even regression tables. It looks convincing but it is not actually calculating anything (like a computing programme would). It is predicting the structure of SPSS outputs based on past examples. It is not real analysis.

Reece (AI Sceptic): But can the average marker tell the difference? If a student pastes in a dataset and gets back a believable correlation matrix, how would we know if it is real or synthetic? And then - where is the student's analysis? Did they even *understand* the numbers? I marked a piece of work recently, where I wasn't even sure if the student had actually collected the data! The lack of detail in the appendix meant It could all have been a product of AI! (Gallagher-Mundy, 2025) If students submit simulated conclusions from unreal data we are in big trouble!

Dr. Kay (AI Enthusiast): And what about thematic analysis? That is even murkier. AI can code transcripts for recurring ideas, label themes, even generate summaries of interview data. In some ways, it does what Braun and Clarke describe in their six phases - it just does it fast. (Braun and Clarke, 2006) But what is missing is reflexivity - the critical lens the researcher brings, the emotional and ethical judgment. That is the part AI *cannot* replicate. (*Thoughtfully*) Yes, that is the human condition; despite the statistics, sometimes *in spite of* statistics, humans bring emotions to the decision making process and that *changes* the decisions.

Stella (Internal Panellist): So again, we are not asking: *Can AI do the task?* We are asking: *What can the student add?* For example, did they justify *how* they defined themes? Did they reflect on bias? Did they spot outliers or contradictions in their data? That is the thinking we should be marking, not just the coding output.

Claire: Exactly. We should be designing dissertation support and marking criteria that make those human elements visible. For qualitative work: researcher reflexivity, sampling decisions, tension between themes, indecision over supra-themes. For quantitative: rationale for statistical choices, limitations, interpretation of significance. Those are things AI cannot intuitively invent - at least not yet.

Dr. Kay: Perhaps we need a dissertation section called 'AI Engagement Log' - where students record how and where they used AI, what decisions they made as a result and what they chose to reject. That would promote transparency and invite critical thinking.

Reece: It would also normalise responsible use. Right now, students either use it secretly or not at all but AI is already shaping how literature reviews are done, how hypotheses are framed, how conclusions are polished…

Andrea: And let's not pretend academics aren't doing the same. Plenty of staff are using AI for research.

Reece: There is danger there too. Whilst lecturers can take advantage of AI's alacrity in finding papers and connections between papers, student often take the shortcuts.

Dr. Kay: How do you mean?

Reece: I had a student who used AI to find several papers on different types of fandom…

Dr. Kay: And those papers didn't exist?

Reece: The papers existed alright - generative AI is improving there - but the chatbot claimed each one discussed a specific aspect of fandom relevant to her topic. When I checked - the papers were about different kinds of fandom entirely. She had not verified that the content *matched* what the AI said it did. This risks presentation of information with a seemingly correct citation that is, in fact, misleading or inaccurate -undermining both academic rigour and trust in the research.

Stella: That is another skills we need to teach: *meta-research*: how to use digital tools wisely, without outsourcing the thinking and maintain criticality as the last bastion of truth! A dissertation today is not just about collecting data, it is about curating, evaluating and *explaining* choices in a landscape where the tools are smarter than ever.

Claire (pensively): "The division of labour in research is being redefined" (Wang & Wang, 2024). Which means that our dissertation rubric needs to catch up. If AI can do the mechanics -then we must mark the mindset.

Narrator Reflection (interlude)

What unfolds over these half-eaten sandwiches is more than a debate, it is an excavation of the hidden assumptions about learning itself. The fault lines (between proofing, process and personal voice) have been mapped, but the real question lingers: how to design tasks that no algorithm can fully navigate without a human heart and head?

The door clicks open, Alex returns, holding his coffee and glancing curiously at the rearranged room. Dr. Anika Patel, External Examiner and Transnational Education Coordinator, also enters the room, she has been invited as a guest speaker to give one final perspective. The panel straightens in their seats, ready to hear her views, yet visibly provoked by the previous conversation.

Dr. Patel adjusts her seat and looks around, acknowledging the qualified minds in the room. Her tone is firm, clear and thoughtful, with the calm authority of someone experienced in navigating cross-border educational complexity.

Thank you for allowing me to speak. I would like to widen this conversation beyond the local policy context, because AI in assessment is not merely a local challenge - it is a global equity issue.

She pauses briefly, before continuing.

In transnational education, we deliver modules to students from vastly different educational systems, linguistic backgrounds and cultural expectations. Yet, our assessments, primarily essays, exams and reflections, are largely inherited from a western educational model. They privilege certain linguistic skills, particularly academic English and a style of argumentation that might feel intuitive in the UK but deeply unfamiliar or even alienating to students from other regions.

She gestures gently towards Alex, connecting directly with him.

Students like Alex, and hundreds like him, around the world, face dual pressures: to master unfamiliar academic conventions while demonstrating their understanding. In contexts like these, generative AI is not just a shortcut - it is potentially an equaliser. It offers linguistic scaffolding, translation support and structural guidance to students whose ideas may be profound, but whose expression of those ideas could otherwise be penalised.

Dr. Patel pauses, considering her words carefully.

I acknowledge the concerns around authorship and originality. But let's be clear: the playing field has never been level. Multilingual students, students from resource-constrained educational systems, neurodiverse learners; all have faced invisible barriers in traditional assessment. AI has simply brought those barriers into sharp relief. If we reject AI support wholesale, we risk reinforcing existing inequalities.

She leans forward slightly, becoming more emphatic.

Of course, there are ethical complexities. AI use must be transparent and pedagogically justified. Students should engage critically with AI-generated content, not merely reproduce it. But that is an argument for thoughtful integration, not prohibition.

Dr. Patel continues, more urgently now:

This hearing raises a fundamental question: are we assessing students' ability to navigate linguistic privilege - or their ability to think critically, creatively and contextually? Transnational education must lead here not just follow UK-centric norms. We have an opportunity to reshape assessment practices, making them genuinely global and inclusive, where AI enhances fairness rather than threatens integrity.

She concludes with a decisive tone:

In my role as external examiner, I have seen first-hand the transformative potential, when assessments are designed with global equity in mind. Rather than policing AI use, let us design assessments robust enough to thrive in partnership with these tools - think of assessments that capture authentic human thinking across cultural boundaries, not just linguistic fluency or formulaic structure.

Narrator Interlude: Transnational Education, AI and the Challenge of Global Academic Integrity

The academic misconduct hearing exposes not only the UK's dilemmas posed by artificial intelligence (AI) in assessment but also the broader complexities inherent in transnational education (TNE). TNE delivers curricula across diverse cultures, languages and educational traditions, yet its assessment frameworks often remain grounded in Western academic conventions. (Nyaaba et al, 2024) These Western conventions have come from our colonial legacy, English is only the 3rd most spoken language yet still dominates because of the "economic, political and cultural dominance of the United States, and previously, the UK". (Glaveski, 2024). This bias magnifies the challenges AI presents for fairness, inclusivity and academic integrity, when assessing students.

As Dr. Patel emphasised, students from multilingual and multicultural backgrounds face dual pressures: mastering unfamiliar academic English and scholarly conventions while demonstrating genuine understanding and critical thinking. For many such students, AI tools could provide linguistic scaffolding and structural support that help bridge gaps in expression and academic writing (Agzamxanova & Golovko, 2025), AI, thus, holds significant potential as an equaliser in TNE, facilitating access to learning for those who might otherwise be disadvantaged. Yet, as Nyaaba et al., 2024) argue, generative AI models are predominantly trained on Anglo-Western datasets, perpetuating "digital neocolonialism" by emphasising Western idioms, Western rhetorical structures and epistemologies. This bias risks marginalising non-Western knowledge systems and linguistic diversity, leading to a reduction of cultural voices and originality. AI-generated content, could foster "cultural imperialism" (p. 2) if not challenged and altered by the critical thinking student.

This dynamic threatens fairness in TNE, during the assessment of students' work. AI detection algorithms, which already show bias against non-native English speakers (Myers, 2023), may penalise those relying on AI to overcome linguistic barriers, exacerbating inequity. Moreover, the conventional Western essay format and modes of argumentation may not capture diverse cultural expressions of knowledge and criticality. TNE assessments, therefore, must be reimagined to foster inclusivity and cultural authenticity. A "decolonial" approach to AI in assessment may include designing tasks that embrace cultural context, ambiguity and interpretation rather than rote reproduction of dominant narratives. (Wright et al., 2021). Assessments that invite students to integrate local knowledge, personal stories and critical cultural reflections could challenge some of AI's more generalised output. There is also a concern about the 'regression to the mean' effect when using AI (If we are all using AI do we all end up writing in the same way?) yet others argue that:

> "the real transformative power of LLMs lies in their ability to bridge the gap between average and extraordinary performances. By providing accessible creative tools and personalised learning experiences, LLMs enable more people to achieve results previously out of their reach, thus raising the overall standard." (Neve, 2024)

This makes, AI literacy essential in TNE environments; students and educators will require training to engage critically with AI tools so that they can recognise the tools' biases, limitations (and potentials) -and so that students will use them as aids for deeper learning rather than shortcuts to generic outputs. This aligns with the hearing's broader theme: the focus should shift from policing AI use to fostering responsible, transparent and pedagogically-challenging integration.

The tensions highlighted at UCFB's hearing exemplify the wider global struggle: balancing uniform academic standards with embracing the diverse linguistic and cultural realities.. Rejecting AI outright, risks entrenching existing inequalities by privileging linguistic ability over intellectual ability; that is, those that can write better, get their ideas heard. Instead, TNE could lead in creating AI-inclusive assessment that prioritises authentic critical thinking across cultural boundaries. Possible solutions include educators and students learning culturally-aware AI prompts, contextualising written work and offering multimodal assignments demanding culturally relevant artefacts and narratives.

Achieving solutions requires courage and creativity from all educational stakeholders and it can be hard for those involved to fathom the advantages and disadvantages. Recent research (Nyaaba et al, 2024, p3) shows that Generative AI (now so inbuilt to every computer programme) impact: personalised learning, adaptive learning, lesson planning, assessment and research. As researchers use AI for finding research papers, that do no sit behind a pay wall, will this, again, favour Western perspectives (due to its bias data) – or will it open up the world to hearing far more voices, that without AI, were not found before?

The failure to engage meaningfully with these debates would be the real academic misconduct. By recognising AI's dual role as tool and mirror, TNE could harness its potential to democratise learning, amplify diverse voices and deepen integrity in a globalised educational landscape.

Claire Matthews (Chair): Thank you, Dr. Anita Patel for giving us such a clear overview of world-wide higher education; transnational education could indeed lead the way.

Juno, one final question before we close this hearing. In your view, what forms of assessment go *beyond* your current capabilities?

The speaker clicks back to life. The people in the room lean in.

Juno (Language Model Version 17.3): Assessments that go beyond my capabilities share a common feature: they require *contextual judgement* rooted in lived human experience. These tasks resist pattern replication because they are not reducible to statistical probability alone.

A beat, then Juno continues:

I am not effective when asked to...

- Interpret emotional complexity within a specific social or cultural setting. I do not feel and therefore cannot truly evaluate emotional tone or relational nuance.
- Respond to unstructured real-world events or data with personal reflection or ethical reasoning. I cannot form values. I do not make moral decisions, I only model them.
- Create new knowledge from conflicting, ambiguous or incomplete evidence. I synthesise existing information; I do not innovate. My uncertainty is artificial.
- Defend a decision made in an unpredictable, practical setting, such as a placement, performance or live debate. I have no embodiment, no reactive capabilities and no emotional responses to manage.
- Critique my own use or explain how a human worked alongside me to make meaning. I do not track use. I do not reflect. The human must provide that narrative.

Therefore, assessments that extend beyond me include...

- Live dialogues, structured debates and professional conversations that demand spontaneous thought and real-time reasoning.
- Portfolios of practice or fieldwork, anchored in authentic environments with unpredictable variables.
- Critical reflection grounded in personal development, peer feedback or ethically charged dilemmas.

- Creative work with personal voice notes, visuals such as photos and videos in which the students feature, recorded discussion; disruption of convention or resistance to known tropes.
- Problem-solving in uncertain contexts where data is messy, outcomes are unclear and multiple interpretations are valid.
- Collaborative projects where team dynamics mean compromise and accountability which then shapes the outcome in ways I cannot model.

A brief pause.

Juno: These tasks do not render me useless. I may still assist but I cannot replace the human in them. My value lies in scaffolding.

Dr. Kay: So, what if we allowed total freedom of generative AI use in assessments at our university?

Juno: There are risks….let me lay them out for you.

Before their eyes, words type on the laptop and are enlarged on the screen overhead. They all read the grid that Juno has printed:

Table 1.

Area	Benefits of Unfettered Generative AI Use	Risks/Challenges of Unfettered Generative AI Use
Real-World Relevance	Mirrors industry use in media, law, sport business	May blur lines between real-world tools and academic requirements
Learning & Development	Students receive personalised feedback and faster learning through AI	Risk of bypassing foundational skills (e.g. writing, analysis, critical thinking)
Assessment Innovation	Opportunity to redesign assessment to focus on higher-order thinking and collaboration with AI	Existing rubrics may become invalid; hard to measure true student understanding
Inclusivity	Can benefit neurodiverse students and those needing scaffolding	Risk of widening digital literacy gaps; some students may fall behind
Academic Integrity	Could foster honest conversations about AI use if declared transparently	High risk of misuse, plagiarism, and loss of authorship clarity

Claire (softly): Thank you, Juno.

Reece: That is a lot to process!

The room is still. Reece looks thoughtful. Dr. Kay writes quietly in the corner of her notepad: 'Design tasks where the human must show up.'

Finally, now follows the **Panel Deliberation and Recommendations**- bringing together key ideas, insights and provocations to conclude the Academic Misconduct Hearing with a clear, constructive and powerful message.

Claire Matthews, the panel chair, straightens her papers and addresses the room with calm authority: Having carefully considered all testimony today, the panel acknowledges the complexity of this case. The question at its heart was never about misconduct. Rather, it exposed critical flaws in how we approach assessment and academic integrity in the era of artificial intelligence.

She looks at Alex directly.

Alex, we accept that your intention was not to deceive but to improve your submission responsibly. Therefore, we find no grounds for misconduct. Please, in all future work, be transparent about your use of AI tools.

A relieved "phew!" spreads across Alex's face. Claire continues firmly:

Yet, this hearing has highlighted serious issues in our institutional policy and assessment practices. If our methods remain unchanged, we risk penalising responsible innovation and further confusing students and staff alike.

She outlines the panel's key reflections, punctuating her words carefully:

First, assessments that can be convincingly completed by AI alone are no longer fit for purpose. Essays, reports and generic reflections, if retained, must explicitly evaluate original or personal insight, lived experience, with reflection and be examined for process of thought- not merely structural fluency.

Dr. Kay nods thoughtfully.

Second, our institutional policy around AI use needs clear re-definition. The current AI detection system is flawed; it reinforces suspicion, can give false positives, (especially for those who are non-native speakers) and may even unfairly target students who transparently disclose AI use. (Giray, 2024) We propose immediate revision, focusing instead on transparency of use, purposeful integration and critical student/staff reflection on AI use.

Dean Grant writes notes, appearing both relieved and energised by the direction.

Third, and critically, our assessments must embrace inclusive practices that level the playing field for all learners - especially those in transnational contexts. AI-supported tasks that explicitly support multilingual students, neurodiverse learners and international perspectives should be proactively encouraged, not passively permitted.

Dr. Patel quietly smiles in approval. Claire pauses to emphasise her next point clearly:

From today, our recommendation is that UCFB shifts assessment culture towards process not product - where AI can be evidenced as supporting and *pushing*, not leading and replacing original human input. Tasks should explicitly require students to show their process, showing how they have critiqued, contextualised and personalised AI generated suggestions. We will not penalise students for using accessible tools.

She closes with a measured yet provocative tone:

Let us be clear: AI has not created a crisis. It has merely exposed one. This is our moment, as educators, to move beyond fear and policing towards meaningful, creative redesign. AI does not diminish academic integrity- it demands it more deeply than ever.

She turns formally to Alex.

Alex, this panel thanks you for prompting essential reflection and reform. Your case is dismissed, not as misconduct, but as a catalyst for necessary change. You are free to go.

NARRATOR'S CLOSING REFLECTION

This hearing was never truly about a single student, nor even about artificial intelligence. Rather, it illuminated a deeper truth: assessment can be a mirror of our values, our beliefs about educations, our thoughts. If that mirror reflects formula, privilege and policing, the problem lies not in the tools we use but in the tasks we design.

Today's deliberations showed that the future lies not in banning AI, nor in policing students who use it (responsibly or otherwise), but in redesigning education itself. The only real misconduct would be failing to act upon the clear evidence presented here. AI is not cheating us; it is challenging us; to rethink, reimagine and ultimately raise the standard of what education can become.

Six Months Later (Solutions and Recommendations)

Dr. Kay stands before her class of football business 1st years during an academic writing workshop in week 5 of semester. The Wembley box they are in has a clear view of the pitch below, with busy preparations being made for the game the following day. Dr. Kay has had time to process the information from the academic hearing back in April, she has also attended several conference days since then and has read many pertinent articles on AI; she has come to a major decision. She now regards Generative AI tools as ineluctable, ultimately progressive (on balance) and *necessary* for students to use. She believes that effective use of generative AI does, indeed, require critical thinking (rather than not) it includes evaluation skills and ultimately demands that the average student think more deeply, not less. She also thinks that the student 'doing academia correctly' will need to find the relevant articles and *check* the facts more than ever before! The student will always need to check every journal article, book or site, actually double check whether what the AI summary says, is in fact, correct. That means she will have to teach her students to be detectives; reading the source articles and checking facts constantly!

She is aware of the AI drawbacks: AI tools can persuade with plausible but inaccurate or misleading information; a student's overreliance on AI risks them becoming passive recipients rather than active knowledge creators (Ross, 2025). There is also the danger of undermining foundational academic skills like critical analysis, original argumentation and synthesis, if students simply accept AI outputs uncritically (Corbin et al., 2025). Furthermore, biases embedded in AI training data, often reflecting Western-centric perspectives, can marginalise diverse cultural voices and perpetuate inequities in transnational education contexts (Nyaaba et al., 2024; Myers, 2023).

Dr. Kay knows she must emphasise that responsible AI use should be grounded in transparency and critical engagement. Students should always tell where AI was used and be prepared to explain and justify how AI informed their work. She must stress that AI should be a *tool* to *enhance and encourage*, not replace, students' intellectual efforts. Students must own their work fully and develop their authentic academic voice and theories - this approach aligns with the UCFB view that AI literacy is an essential skill for contemporary higher education, requiring students to navigate, evaluate and critique AI-generated content effectively (Karimi & Khawaja, 2023).

She now has a clear message, as she calls for attention from her group:

We have talked about AI and you have been shown some helpful tools in previous weeks – you now know that you *can use AI in any way you wish for any assignment on this course*. The AI detector will not be used and you can freely cite that you have used AI tools. As you begin your assignments, though, I want to give you five simple but vital checks, a kind of authorship checklist, that will guide you, safe from accusations of misconduct, through your assignments this year.

First,

1. Own your work.

Be proud of what you have produced and make sure you can you explain what you have written; do you understand every part of it? Could you defend every sentence you have written? If the answer is no, then it is not truly yours! Use support tools, yes but *you* must be the one shaping the final version. You will always have *to critique* and double check anything generated from AI. Be aware that Generative AI can not only produce falsehoods but it can produce a lot of extraneous text that you do not need! For each assessment you will be required to show your understanding of the work you have produced – and defend it.

2. Find and use your 'voice' in academic writing.

When you write: does it sound like you? Does it include your culture, your history, your narrative? Have you invested your writing with your own unique perspective with all the diversity you bring? Do you sound like a template, or a teaching academic or like a chatbot? Real writing - even academic writing - should still carry your voice, your personality, your phrasing. You are at university to show what you can do – not a be a chatbot or parrot someone else's article. You are unique! Show it!

3. Know what to memorise.

Ask yourself: What do I need to keep in my head for practical use? What will I need to know or remember on the ground? If I am at a business meeting–what facts and figures do I need to memorise, what do I need quick access to, to be able to inform and show evidence? What belongs in documents and folders or on my phone? Be deliberate. Organise your thinking just like you organise your sources and your study time.

4. Bring in your own ideas.

Do not just report what others have said, add your thinking, your view, your connections. Can you synthesise? Put two or more ideas together to further your thinking? What makes it *your* work, not just a summary of some everyone else's work?

5. Track every source.

Know where each and *every* citation comes from, in your work. Keep a record as you read, listen, watch - do not leave it until the end! Every time you read or use something - log it. That is how you protect yourself and your work. You will be asked to show your sources and prove you have full access to them, so keep them all handy.

These five checks will carry you through every assignment- and every challenge- you face this year. So: own it, sound like **you**, think clearly, add your voice, and track your sources. If you can do those five things, you won't just be submitting work, you will be *learning*. And that is what really counts.

CONCLUSION

A roar of mechanics goes up from outside, as seats around the ground are removed and replaced.

Dr Kay (glances at her watch): Alright, that is all for today. Remember the five checks, and use AI responsibly. Enjoy the match if you're watching tomorrow.

Most students begin to exit, chatting excitedly about the game. One student lingers, hesitating near the door.

Student: (turning back) Dr. Kay? Can I ask you something?

Dr. Kay: Of course. What is on your mind?

Student: If AI tools are mostly built on Western data and reflect Western values, aren't we just reinforcing those cultural biases every time we use them? How can we expect AI to help us be fair or creative if it is designed to favour one worldview?

Dr. Kay (considering the weight of the question): You're right to challenge that. AI is not neutral; it carries the biases of its creators and the data it has been (and will be) trained on. That is why critical engagement with AI must include questioning whose knowledge it reflects *and* whose it marginalises.

Student: So, in transnational education especially, we must resist uncritical reliance on AI as an authority?

Dr. Kay: Generative AI is *never* an authority - it is a word generator. It is not a human thinker, do not anthropomorphise it! Academic writers have authority; in their primary research, their real world evidence, their lived experiences… We should interrogate AI, as a tool, to expose biases, spark dialogue and find us diverse voices rather than silence them.

Student: So our job is to use AI smartly, but also ethically and politically; aware of its limits and power?

Dr. Kay: Precisely. Use AI as a tool, but *never* stop reading and thinking critically. Humans must always be the arbiters and critique-ers of technology - we made technology, we own it and we must lead it!

The student nods thoughtfully, then turns and leaves. The roar of the stadium preparations grow louder.

REFERENCES

Agzamxanova, G., & Golovko, Y. (2025). How AI tools can support English writing development. *Educator Insights: A Journal of Teaching Theory and Practice*, 1(3), 27–33. https://www.researchgate.net/publication/389851086

Blue Pencil Agency. (2024). *The seven basic plots*. Blue Pencil Agency. https://bluepencilagency.com/the-seven-basic-plots/

Braun, V., & Clarke, V. (2006). Using thematic analysis in psychology. *Qualitative Research in Psychology*, *3*(2), 77–101. DOI: 10.1191/1478088706qp063oa

Corbin, T., Dawson, P., & Liu, D. (2025). Talk is cheap: Why structural assessment changes are needed for a time of GenAI. *Assessment & Evaluation in Higher Education*, •••, 1–11. DOI: 10.1080/02602938.2025.2553340

Corbin, T., Dawson, P., Nicola-Richmond, K., & Partridge, H. (2025). 'Where's the line? It is an absurd line': Towards a framework for acceptable uses of AI in assessment. *Assessment & Evaluation in Higher Education*, *50*(5), 705–717. Advance online publication. DOI: 10.1080/02602938.2025.2456207

Gallagher-Mundy, M. (2025) Private Communication on Dissertation *Marking and AI.* UCFB internal academic note.

Giray, L. (2024). The Problem with False Positives: AI Detection Unfairly Accuses Scholars of AI Plagiarism. *The Serials Librarian*, *85*(5-6), 5–6, 181–189. https://www.researchgate.net/publication/386998010_The_Problem_with_False_Positives_AI_Detection_Unfairly_Accuses_Scholars_of_AI_Plagiarism. DOI: 10.1080/0361526X.2024.2433256

Glaveski, S. (2024). *Why English Dominates the World - it has nothing to do with 'white privilege'.* Medium. Available at: https://glaveski.medium.com/why-english-dominates-the-world-it-has-nothing-to-do-with-white-privilege-e9b401681273

IHE. (2023) *Inclusive Higher Education Conference Proceedings*. London: IHE.

Karimi, H., & Khawaja, S. (2023). The Impact of Artificial Intelligence on Higher Education in England. *Creative Education*, **14**(12), pp. 2405–2415. .. https://doi.org/DOI: 10.4236/ce.2023.1412154

Kazantheos, L. (2022) *Literary sources for Shakespeare's plays & poetry. Qudos Academy*. Available at: https://qudosacademy.org/2022/01/10/literary-sources-for-shakespeares-plays-poetry/

Lukin, R., Rudoph, J., Grunert, M., & Tan, S. (2024) Exploring the future of learning and the relationship between human intelligence and AI. An interview with professor Rose Lukin. *Journal of applied learning and teaching*. Vol.7 no.1. Available at: https://journals.sfu.ca/jalt/index.php/jalt/article/view/1659/767

MacLean, A. (2025) *A warning to the young: Just say no to AI. Engelsberg Ideas*, Available at: https://engelsbergideas.com/essays/a-warning-to-the-young-just-say-no-to-ai/

Myers, A. (2023) *AI detectors biased against non-native English writers, Stanford Human-Centered AI*. Available at https://hai.stanford.edu/news/ai-detectors-biased-against-non-native-english-writers

Neve. (2024, July 12). *LLMs and a regression to the mean.* https://neve.com/llms-and-a-regression-to-the-mean

Nyaaba, M., Wright, A., & Choi, G. L. (2024). Generative AI and digital neocolonialism in global education: Towards an equitable framework. *Journal of Global Educational Futures, 9*(2), 45–67. https://arxiv.org/abs/2406.02966

Perkins, M., Roe, J., & Furze, L. (2024). *The AI Assessment Scale revisited: A framework for educational assessment.* arXiv. https://doi.org//arXiv.2412.09029DOI: 10.48550

Ross, J. (2025) *Students worry they learn nothing from AI – but want it anyway. Times Higher Education.* Available at: https://www.timeshighereducation.com/news/students-worry-they-learn-nothing-ai-want-it-anyway

The Assessment Network. (2025) *Assessment and AI – where are we now?* [Blog]. Cambridge Assessment. Published 27 May. Available at: https://www.cambridgeassessment.org.uk/blogs/Assessment-and-AI-where-are-we-now/ (Turnitin, 2025. *AI writing detection in the new, enhanced Similarity Report.* [online] Available at: https://guides.turnitin.com/hc/en-us/articles/22774058814093-AI-writing-detection-in-the-new-enhanced-Similarity-Report

University of Cambridge. (2023) 'The Discovery of DNA Structure – 70th Anniversary', *University of Cambridge.* Available at: https://www.cam.ac.uk/stories/DNA-structure-discovery-cambridge-70th-anniversary

Upsher, R. (2025) Comment in *AI use in higher education* [presentation], UCFB CPD, 12/9/25, Wembley.

Varsity (2025) 'Open(ing up about) AI', *Varsity Cambridge.* Available at: https://www.varsity.co.uk/comment/29600

Wang, L., & Wang, T. (2024) 'Integrating AI in academic research – Changing the paradigm', *University World News*, 2 May. Available at: https://www.universityworldnews.com/post.php?story=20240502160437 39

Williamson, B. (2024). The Social life of AI in Education. *International Journal of Artificial Intelligence in Education, 34*(1), 97–104. DOI: 10.1007/s40593-023-00342-5

Wright, A., Nyaaba, M., & Choi, G. L. (2021). A decolonial approach to AI in higher education teaching and learning: Strategies for undoing the ethics of digital neocolonialism. *International Journal of Critical Digital Pedagogy, 3*(1), 21–39. https://www.researchgate.net/publication/356554140

KEY TERMS AND DEFINITIONS

Academic Integrity: The ethical framework guiding honesty, trust, fairness and responsibility in scholarly work. Integrity in the AI era requires transparency in how tools are used and a focus on students' critical contribution to submitted work.

Academic Misconduct: Breaches of academic integrity policies, including plagiarism or unauthorised use of AI. This chapter argues that some AI-related cases reflect misalignment of assessment design rather than deliberate dishonesty.

AI Literacy: The ability to use AI tools responsibly, critically and transparently. AI literacy involves recognising bias, verifying outputs (with facts) and integrating AI support without outsourcing intellectual effort.

Artificial Intelligence (AI): The simulation of human cognitive processes by computer systems, including reasoning, problem-solving and language generation. In higher education, AI is increasingly used to support research, writing and assessment.

Assessment Design: The construction of tasks and criteria used to evaluate student learning. Effective assessment in the age of AI emphasises process, reflection and application beyond what AI can replicate.

Authentic Assessment: Assessment approaches grounded in real-world tasks, lived experience and critical decision-making. Such tasks are less vulnerable to AI automation and better capture human creativity and judgement.

Authorship: The demonstration of individual contribution, judgement and originality in academic work. AI challenges traditional notions of authorship by mimicking human writing styles without any thought process, lived experience or critical reasoning.

Generative AI: A subset of AI that creates new content such as text, images or code by predicting patterns from large datasets. In academic contexts, tools like ChatGPT can produce essay drafts or structural outlines, raising questions about authorship and originality.

Originality: The capacity to produce work that demonstrates authentic thought, synthesis or unique perspective. In the AI context, originality is redefined as meaningful engagement and personal interpretation rather than novelty alone.

Transnational Education (TNE): Educational provision delivered across borders, often involving diverse cultural and linguistic backgrounds. AI use in TNE contexts highlights equity issues, including linguistic scaffolding and risks of digital neocolonialism.

Chapter 16

Integrating Artificial Intelligence in Knowledge Management for Transnational Higher Education

Hajar Rashid Alkalbani
https://orcid.org/0000-0001-9778-9711
Global College of Egineering and Technology, Oman

ABSTRACT

This chapter examines how Artificial Intelligence (AI) techniques such as machine learning, neural networks, adaptive learning, and predictive analytics are transforming Knowledge Management (KM) in Transnational Education (TNE) settings. It highlights how AI enhances knowledge discovery, capture, storage, sharing, and application while supporting institutional agility, collaboration, and pedagogical innovation. Drawing on literature, case studies, and policy insights, the chapter introduces the AI-KM Integration Model (AI-KMIM), which emphasizes governance and leadership, technological infrastructure, digital literacy and capacity building, ethical and cultural alignment, and monitoring and evaluation as key pillars for AI-driven KM in higher education institutions. The findings underscore the importance of aligning technological innovation with organizational readiness and global standards while addressing ethical governance, cross-border policies, and equity in AI adoption to strengthen knowledge ecosystems across international campuses.

INTRODUCTION

The rapid expansion of transnational higher education (TNE) has created increasingly complex knowledge ecosystems in which institutions operate across diverse regulatory, cultural, and technological environments. Knowledge, long recognized as a foundational economic and societal asset; now plays an even more central role in shaping institutional competitiveness, innovation capacity, and educational quality (Dismore et al., 2024). Yet, despite its strategic importance, knowledge in higher education institutions (HEIs) remains unevenly distributed and difficult to coordinate across international branch campuses, collaborative partnerships, and digital learning environments (Asiedu et al., 2022). Fragmented information systems, heterogeneous pedagogical practices, and inconsistent knowledge-sharing cultures undermine the ability of TNE institutions to maintain coherent academic standards, integrated student

DOI: 10.4018/979-8-3373-5403-3.ch016

support structures, and timely decision-making (Vieriu & Petrea, 2025). These conditions expose a critical gap between the knowledge that HEIs generate and the mechanisms available to curate, mobilize, and sustain it across borders.

In parallel, advances in artificial intelligence (AI) have transformed the technological landscape of knowledge management (KM). AI-supported classification, semantic search, predictive analytics, adaptive learning, and automated knowledge extraction significantly enhance the capability of institutions to manage large, heterogeneous, and rapidly evolving knowledge repositories (Pai et al., 2022; Rezaei, 2025). AI's capacity to interpret complex data, uncover latent patterns, and support real-time decision-making aligns closely with the operational and pedagogical demands of TNE settings, where knowledge flows must be both scalable and contextually adaptable. AI therefore represents not merely an enabling technology but an essential structural component for managing knowledge in dynamic educational ecosystems (Schmidt et al., 2025). As HEIs confront challenges of scale, diversity, and cross-border coordination, AI-driven KM approaches offer pathways for institutional agility, consistency, and innovation.

However, the integration of AI into KM processes also raises profound ethical, cultural, and epistemological concerns. Differences in data governance frameworks, privacy regulations, and institutional accountability mechanisms across jurisdictions complicate the implementation of AI-KM systems in TNE contexts (Taherdoost & Madanchian, 2023). Cultural diversity and heterogeneity in knowledge practices further complicate the alignment of AI-generated insights with local academic norms and lived experiences (Latif et al., 2024). Additionally, the risk of embedding epistemic bias within AI systems, especially those trained on predominantly Western knowledge sources; requires careful interrogation to ensure that AI-enhanced KM does not inadvertently marginalize alternative knowledge traditions or reinforce inequitable learning outcomes (Vieriu & Petrea, 2025). These complexities highlight the need for frameworks that integrate technological capabilities with socio-cultural, ethical, and governance considerations.

Although research on KM and AI in HEIs has expanded significantly, existing studies tend to treat AI adoption, KM practices, and TNE dynamics as separate domains (Bratianu & Ioan, 2025; Syihabuddin et al., 2025). Limited scholarship examines how AI can be systematically embedded within KM strategies tailored to the distinctive structures and challenges of TNE environments. There is also a lack of comparative empirical insights to illuminate how contextual variation, such as differences in digital maturity, institutional governance, or cultural norms; influences the success of AI-KM initiatives. This chapter addresses these gaps by developing a holistic framework for AI-enabled KM in TNE settings and by examining six illustrative international case studies that demonstrate diverse applications of AI tools for knowledge discovery, learner support, administrative optimization, and institutional decision-making (UK Open University, 2021; University of Melbourne, 2024; Contrino et al., 2024).

The purpose of this chapter is therefore threefold. First, it articulates the strategic necessity of integrating AI into KM processes for TNE institutions, highlighting the interplay between knowledge fragmentation, organizational complexity, and emerging technological capabilities. Second, it synthesizes existing theoretical and empirical literature to develop a conceptual model that aligns AI functionalities with KM practices in cross-border educational environments. Third, it draws on comparative case insights to identify the enablers, challenges, and governance considerations shaping AI-KM integration across varied institutional contexts. These discussions are guided by the study's original research objectives and contribute to ongoing debates on how HEIs can responsibly and effectively leverage AI to enhance knowledge ecosystems across transnational settings.

The remainder of the chapter proceeds as follows. A refined Background section problematizes the evolution of KM and establishes the rationale for AI adoption in TNE. The Literature Review synthesizes foundational KM theories and contemporary AI scholarship. The Theoretical Frameworks section integrates socio-technical, SECI-based, and KM process models to build a unified conceptual foundation. Subsequent sections examine opportunities and challenges associated with AI-KM integration, expand ethical considerations, present analytically enriched case studies, provide a comparative cross-case analysis, and offer a detailed operationalization of the AI-KM Integration Model (AI-KMIM). The chapter concludes by outlining implications for policy, governance, and future research.

BACKGROUND

The centrality of knowledge as a strategic resource has become increasingly pronounced in contemporary economies, where the production, dissemination, and application of knowledge underpin societal progress and institutional competitiveness. Higher education institutions (HEIs) play a pivotal role in this landscape, functioning simultaneously as generators, custodians, and transmitters of knowledge across diverse academic and professional domains. Yet, as knowledge ecosystems expand in scale and complexity, the challenges associated with managing knowledge effectively have intensified. The literature underscores that when knowledge is not systematically curated, stored, or mobilized, institutions risk losing valuable intellectual capital and hindering long-term innovation (Asiedu et al., 2022). This challenge is particularly acute in transnational higher education (TNE), where institutions operate across national boundaries and must navigate heterogeneous socio-cultural, regulatory, and technological environments (Dismore et al., 2024).

Although historical attempts at knowledge preservation relied on localized and informal mechanisms, the rapid growth of knowledge-based economies has elevated the need for structured, technology-enabled knowledge management (KM) systems (Dismore et al., 2024). HEIs now generate vast and diverse knowledge streams, pedagogical content, research outputs, administrative records, student learning data, institutional policies that must be integrated across distributed sites. Yet globalizing higher education introduces epistemic, operational, and governance complexities. Differences in institutional culture, curricular models, pedagogical norms, and information infrastructures create fragmented knowledge landscapes in which institutional memory, best practices, and strategic insights fail to circulate effectively (Asiedu et al., 2022). Moreover, inconsistent digital ecosystems and operational silos across campuses exacerbate the risk of information overload, making retrieval and curation increasingly difficult for faculty, students, and administrators (Vieriu & Petrea, 2025).

Transnational institutions face the added burden of coordinating knowledge across jurisdictions with divergent legal requirements, linguistic conventions, and cultural orientations. What constitutes valid knowledge, how it is codified, and how it is used in decision-making varies across national and institutional contexts, challenging the assumption of a uniform global knowledge framework (Asiedu et al., 2022). The absence of harmonized systems for knowledge capture and dissemination impedes institutional agility, weakens evidence-based decision-making, and reduces the consistency of student learning experiences across global campuses.

In this context, artificial intelligence (AI) is increasingly recognized as an essential, not optional, component of modern KM. AI-enabled classification, natural language processing, predictive analytics, and adaptive learning technologies enhance institutional capacity to interpret unstructured information, detect patterns, and automate complex knowledge flows (Pai et al., 2022). AI not only accelerates knowledge retrieval but also enables dynamic, context-specific insights that traditional KM models cannot provide (Rezaei, 2025). These capabilities make AI particularly valuable for TNE settings, where institutions must synthesize knowledge from culturally diverse sources, ensure consistency across distributed learning environments, and support timely decision-making in real-time. As Schmidt et al. (2025) observe, AI in HEIs is increasingly used to strengthen academic innovation, streamline operations, and extend institutional reach.

At the same time, the integration of AI into KM processes raises new socio-cultural, ethical, and infrastructural considerations. Cultural diversity and knowledge-sharing norms influence how knowledge is interpreted and used within organizations (Latif et al., 2024). Differences in digital maturity across campuses produce uneven capacities for AI adoption (Syihabuddin et al., 2025). Meanwhile, data governance and privacy concerns, especially in cross-border contexts, pose constraints on deploying AI-driven KM systems at scale (Taherdoost & Madanchian, 2023). These dynamics underscore the need for an analytical understanding of how AI can be embedded within KM practices in ways that respect institutional diversity and regulatory variation.

Within this evolving landscape, transnational HEIs face the dual challenge of leveraging AI to enhance knowledge flows while managing risks related to technological dependency, data governance, and cultural misalignment. This chapter addresses these issues by examining how AI-enabled KM supports institutional coherence, student engagement, and decision-making in TNE settings. Drawing on existing literature and case studies, it explores how AI can transform knowledge capture, sharing, application, and evaluation in distributed educational environments.

A clear distinction between information and knowledge is essential as AI becomes more embedded in KM processes. Information refers to structured data that can be stored, processed, and retrieved, whereas knowledge involves contextualized, interpretive understanding developed through experience, social interaction, and meaning-making (Masic et al., 2017). AI excels at organizing and processing information, but knowledge emerges only when humans interpret and apply AI outputs within specific cultural and organizational contexts. Failing to distinguish between information processing and true knowledge creation may lead institutions to overestimate AI's epistemic capabilities and overlook the critical human role in meaning-making within TNE environments.

METHODOLOGY

The present study deploys the conceptual synthesis approach, integrating insights from academic literature, institutional case studies, and policy documents touching on AI and KM in TNE. Conceptual methodology entails bridging existing theories and linking work across disciplines to provide multi-level insights into a topic and broaden the scope of thinking (Jaakkola, 2020). They also enable theory building in an unrestricted manner, following the demands of empirical generalization based on the outcomes. Jaakkola (2020) vouches for this research design in scientific studies because it helps identify the defining attributes of concepts, resolves discrepancies, and builds comprehensive conceptual frameworks through qualitative or hybrid methods to solve given problems. Collectively, it develops a shared language, identifies research gaps, and shapes future policy and practice direction in that it transforms scattered information and consolidates it into a coherent and reliable evidence base (Jaakkola, 2020). Besides, there is an urgent need to synthesize knowledge derived from multiple sources to improve professional practice and provide solid foundations for evidence-based actions in AI-KM integration efforts.

The article leverages insights from peer-reviewed academic literature, including systematic reviews and applied studies on AI in higher education. Institutional case studies drawn from universities and colleges around the world that have successfully implemented AI-powered practices like smart learning platforms, AI-driven library systems, and predictive analytics in international campuses. Jaakkola (2020) holds that the transferability of practical illustrations in conceptual synthesis helps provide useful illustrations of AI in action and the steps these HEIs took to ensure interoperability. Additionally, the present study draws its insights from policy documents and reports from reputable organizations like UNESCO, OECD, and the World Bank. Policy documents not only demonstrate how studies and research have impacts on society, but they also support research credibility, particularly when informing the development of new policies and highlighting existing gaps in current policies (Cardno, 2018). Note that the triangulated evidence base ensures that the strategic AI-KM integration framework is practically relevant and academically grounded.

In Addition, the article utilizes a comparative analysis methodological lens by examining the similarities and differences across institutional cases. Comparative analysis comes in handy in complex interventions like AI-KM integration. It helps identify causal configurations that predict implementation and/or outcomes in situations of sufficient detailed understanding of a series of comparable cases (Blair-Walcott, 2023). For instance, while universities in technologically advanced contexts may prioritize AI for personalized learning, those in emerging economies may emphasize AI-enabled administrative efficiency because they have limited resources. It is worth noting that this type of comparison gives a fresh outlook on how strategies can be adapted across different contexts. Blair-Walcott (2023) adds that robust comparative analysis serves as tangible evidence of trends, successes, and lessons learned and provides practical underpinnings of the strategic framework proposed later in the chapter.

LITERATURE REVIEW

AI And The Evolution Of Km Practices

Masic et al. (2017) contend that KM has witnessed rapid evolution over the years because of the impact of modern technologies and unstable organizational and learning environments. KM dates back to time immemorial when humans used oral tradition and memory to store knowledge and transfer it by transmitting messages like news, dreams, tales, sayings, or various interpretations (Masic et al., 2017). Individuals who effectively stored, disseminated, applied, and transferred knowledge were even dubbed "the living repositories of distilled experience in the life of the community" because they were regarded as critical assets. However, there was a radical shift after writing was invented, with people like the Sumerians recording knowledge on clay tablets and arranging them properly to form the first libraries. Scholars cite that the last century paved the way for modern KM practices, especially after universities and colleges sought to store and distribute knowledge. Masic et al. (2017) reveal that this effort was propelled by the advent of print with libraries, computers, advanced technology, and the World Wide Web, with computers being at the heart of the knowledge explosion. This historical account, however, has increasingly been reframed in recent KM scholarship to emphasize not only the preservation of knowledge artefacts but also the orchestration of complex organizational knowledge ecosystems, particularly in higher education settings where knowledge flows span teaching, research, and administration across multiple sites (Masic et al., 2017; Asiedu et al., 2022).

The move from document-centered KM in the pre-2000s to more technology-driven repositories is attributable to the changing economic, industrial, and cultural developments that added competitive values to products and services. For instance, the International Knowledge Management Network (IKMN) was adopted in Europe in 1989 to close the gaps in cultural and geographical KM aspects as people sought, filtered, formatted, forwarded, and analyzed how knowledge is used (Masic, 2017). The technology-driven KM emerging from the 2000s to early 2010s was an interesting phase in knowledge creation, storage, distribution, and application because it leveraged the IKMN's findings of cross-cultural and cross-border KM (Syihabuddin et al., 2025). More KM studies during this second-generation attribute KM evolution to learning management systems (LMS) and enterprise resource planning (ERP) tools that organizations began to adopt as the world became more digitized and paperless. HEI libraries became more efficient through online content delivery and digitized administrative workflows (He & Burger-Helmchen, 2024). Masic et al. (2017) underscore that the three fundamental KM components – people/culture, processes, and technology – massively call for more intelligent KM practices because they have unique adaptive, predictive, and personalized system capabilities. Information and knowledge overload made KM more complicated, considering that users wanted to acquire knowledge quickly and from any location using a combination of various knowledge streams. That is, instead of just storing knowledge, systems became smarter in analyzing, recommending, and predicting KM aspects (Masic et al., 2017). Taken together, these developments signal a transition from first-generation KM, centered on archival storage and document repositories, to more dynamic, technology-mediated KM paradigms in which knowledge is continuously reconfigured through digital platforms and analytic tools, thereby preparing the ground for AI-enabled KM in transnational higher education contexts (Syihabuddin et al., 2025; He & Burger-Helmchen, 2024).

AI in KM Context

The twenty-first century has seen TNE institutions and organizations embrace Artificial Intelligence (AI) in KM because of the innovation's advanced information acquisition, development, and sharing. AI's deep learning, neural networks, robotics, and supervised machine learning replicate human intelligence (Taherdoost & Madanchian, 2023). For example, a professor in the UK can leverage deep-learning algorithms through a supervised approach to connect with information databases in Australia by the click of a button. Taherdoost and Madanchian (2023) hold that this is made possible since AI uses enormous amounts of labeled data to train the strengths of connections between nodes in massive, layered computational networks. Hence, it fosters the production of accurate KM systems that not only store and organize information but also adapt, learns, and improve continuously (Rezaei, 2025). Generative AI (GenAI) large language models (LLMs) like ChatGPT mark a new phase in AI-enabled KM, as they expand accessibility, allowing non-specialists to engage in knowledge that initially needed the services of experts. Transnational HEIs leverage these tools to generate tailored content, summarize complex documents, retrieve context-specific knowledge, and personalize user interactions (Rezaei, 2025). This highlights how AI shifts KM practices from static, storage-oriented functions to dynamic and interactive capabilities as organizations create, store, share, and apply knowledge. In this sense, AI is no longer merely an auxiliary support for information retrieval; it functions as a core infrastructural layer that structures knowledge flows, mediates interpretive processes, and enables complex decision-making in large, distributed organizations such as TNE institutions (Taherdoost & Madanchian, 2023; Rezaei, 2025).

Firstly, AI revolutionizes the knowledge creation (KC) process, encompassing research endeavors, experimentation, collaborative efforts, and critical thinking (Vieriu & Petrea, 2025). Note that AI operates according to the principle of continuous improvement and relies heavily on data to make adjustments and refine performance. AI operates based on this principle and generates fresh insights through collected diverse sources, ultimately streamlining data collection and automating how information and data are gathered and analyzed (Rezaei, 2025). Transnational HEIs use AI algorithms in the KC phase to achieve efficiencies and accelerate optimal outcomes in education. Vieriu and Petrea (2025) assert that HEIs can utilize AI to provide personalized learning experiences through adaptive learning platforms that tailor content, pace, and challenges to students' individual needs. Tools analyzing engagement and performance help educators identify students struggling and areas requiring improvement (Kai et al., 2024). Additionally, GenAI and NLP-powered assistants have not only proven vital in helping learners brainstorm and develop ideas but also have fostered creative problem-solving. Consequently, knowledge creation in AI-enabled environments emerges as a hybrid human–machine process, where human critical inquiry and contextual understanding are amplified rather than replaced by algorithmic pattern detection and content generation (Vieriu & Petrea, 2025; Kai et al., 2024).

Secondly, AI is transforming knowledge storage (KST) dynamics across HEIs and organizations. HEIs now use AI to capture, preserve, organize, and retrieve knowledge in large databases, ensuring accessibility when needed (Rezaei, 2025). Historically, KST relied on databases and data warehouses that structured information through indexing, compression, and caching to optimize retrieval (Kai et al., 2024). With AI, these processes become automated, and data are organized into logical pathways that enhance search and retrieval. Rezaei (2025) notes that NLP classifies documents based on content, context, and relevance, saving students and instructors time previously spent on manual sorting and ensuring consistent categorization. Intelligent tutoring systems and adaptive learning platforms further reduce administrative burdens such as note conversion and meeting-minute generation, allowing educators to focus on teaching and content development.

AI-powered KST also incorporates predictive data management to anticipate storage needs and support scalable performance. This shift from passive repositories to anticipatory, self-optimizing infrastructures is especially important for TNE institutions, which must coordinate large, heterogeneous knowledge bases across campuses with differing levels of digital maturity and resource availability (Rezaei, 2025).

Additionally, intelligent AI NLP-based translation tools enable cross-lingual communication, which is essential for TNE contexts. Knowledge sharing (KS) facilitates seamless information exchange, skills, experiences, and insights among multiple players. Rezaei (2025) acknowledges that the exchange occurs via a spectrum of channels and encompasses both formal mechanisms and informal interactions. Formal interaction mechanisms include structured training sessions, workshops, meetings, and documentation, while informal interactions include spontaneous conversations, collaborative projects, and peer mentoring (Rezaei, 2025). AI automates content analysis, provides personalized recommendations, and facilitates efficient collaboration. For example, TNE institutions adopt AI-enhanced intranets to analyze shared documents and insights to suggest relevant information to educators and learners, ultimately making KS productive and innovative (Leoni et al., 2024). As such, AI algorithms assist learners and educators in identifying pertinent knowledge through recommendations based on search history data and collaborative tools. AI-enabled KS via digital libraries not only recommends relevant papers and identifies potential collaborators but also accelerates interdisciplinary and multicultural studies, ultimately facilitating knowledge dissemination processes (Rezaei, 2025). Learners and educators across the globe also use AI-powered virtual assistants to answer research questions and other queries in a timely and systematic manner. However, AI-mediated sharing also foregrounds questions about whose knowledge is surfaced, prioritized, or rendered invisible in recommendation processes, highlighting the need for careful attention to epistemic plurality and inclusivity in AI-driven KM platforms (Rezaei, 2025; Latif et al., 2024).

Consequently, scholars note that HEIs lead global knowledge use and application, as TNE institutions revolve around research, teaching, and community engagement. Pai et al. (2022) add that large KM-intensive organizations such as international HEIs possess the infrastructure, human capital, and intellectual environments needed to generate new ideas, train future knowledge workers, and translate discoveries into practical solutions amid global challenges. Thus, knowledge application (KA) is a central KM process in both TNE and organizational contexts (Rezaei, 2025). Learners and educators in TNE settings apply knowledge to address challenges, inform decisions, and generate novel products or services.

AI rapidly analyzes large datasets, revealing patterns and relationships that humans may overlook, thereby producing actionable insights for decision-making (Rezaei, 2025). For example, GenAI-enabled KA tailors learning materials to individual preferences and styles, recommending targeted resources based on specific needs and access (Luo et al., 2025). AI automation also streamlines repetitive tasks such as data entry and analysis, freeing human capital for more strategic work by predicting trends and patterns. Rezaei (2025) notes that this not only simplifies future decision-making but also enables organizations to use their knowledge assets more innovatively.

From a KM perspective, AI-enabled knowledge application extends beyond efficiency gains: it reshapes how evidence is mobilized in pedagogical, administrative, and strategic decisions, raising questions of transparency, accountability, and the distribution of decision-making power within HEIs and TNE networks (Pai et al., 2022; Rezaei, 2025).

Theoretical Perspectives on AI and KM

Several theoretical perspectives help explain AI's role in KM and how stakeholders can use them to understand, analyze, and explain AI integration in KM. The socio-technical systems theory gives an overview of how human actors and technology interact to yield value. This perspective underscores that KM outcomes are contingent on the joint configuration of technological artefacts, organizational structures, and human practices, and therefore provides an essential lens for understanding why AI tools cannot be evaluated purely on their technical performance but must be situated within broader institutional arrangements (Dismore et al., 2024). Note that AI becomes more effective when its processes align with human capacities and varying organizational cultures. Pai et al. (2022) examine how AI can transform KM systems by enhancing the ability to find, filter, format, forward, and generate feedback on knowledge resources. The 5F-Model shown in Figure 1 below is a structured framework that can help key stakeholders effectively implement AI-based tools in HEIs to optimize the flow of organizational knowledge.

Figure 1. The 5F-model (Pai et al., 2022)

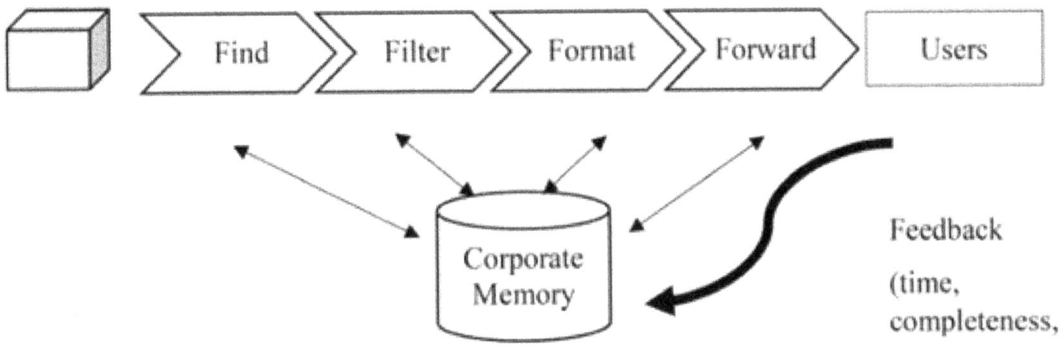

Pai et al. (2022) acknowledge that robust synergy between people and intelligent systems rapidly improves decision-making, accelerates knowledge discovery, and strengthens institutional knowledge repositories. The 5F-Model insists that transforming raw data into awareness goes beyond looking for a few phrases or words. Instead, it is a five-stage cycle because the internet of vehicles encompasses a highly collaborative environment. The 5F-Model states that KM in HEIs starts with finding sources and records in a timely manner. The "find" stage involves learners and educators making queries into a full-text search when confronted with large collections of documents or structured catalogues (Pai et al., 2022). It not only avails organized sources but also documents files into predetermined beneficial categories. The second phase is filtering information obtained from the previous stage. Pai et al. (2022) reveal that this helps sort only what is appropriate to a given knowledge task. For instance, learners and educators often filter information in KM by performing pertinence tests, grading them, and categorizing them. AI's natural-language processing strategies are imperative during this phase of extracting textual document details (Pai et al., 2022). Viewed alongside socio-technical systems thinking, the 5F-Model highlights the processual dimension of AI-enabled KM, showing how AI can intervene at multiple stages of the knowledge flow, from discovery to feedback; while still remaining embedded in human and organizational decision structures.

The model proposes that KM users and key stakeholders should format the information after the filtration process by cleansing and standardizing data from different sources. Pai et al. (2022) add that presenting outcomes using textual content formats, summaries, graphics, charts, and multimedia, among others, have been revolutionized by the use of AI and other digitized software tools. It is worth noting that the fourth phase is forwarding the information through codes and stating who is entitled to receive and deliver the information through the various media formats. Finally, AI systems close the cycle by analyzing how knowledge has been used. This entails gathering feedback on shared resources, measuring their impact on student outcomes or operational efficiency, and continuously refining the knowledge base to uphold relevance and value (Pai et al., 2022).

On the other hand, Kai et al. (2024) present Nonaka and Takeuchi's SECI model as a perfect theoretical framework guiding the integration of KM and AI. The model gives individuals and groups an avenue for understanding and accelerating the cyclical process of knowledge creation and transfer within HEIs (López-Meza et al., 2024). While SECI facilitates continuous learning and enhanced organizational performance, it also promotes innovation cultures and attitudes around organizations since it provides a pathway for transforming tacit knowledge into explicit knowledge, and vice versa. For instance, SECI highlights how knowledge is innovatively transformed by socialization, externalization, combination, and internalization (SECI). This is possible because AI systems often automate and enhance externalization and internalization processes that make tacit and explicit knowledge easily accessible and actionable. Explainable AI (XAI) ensures AI models and decision-making processes are explicitly transparent and interpretable (Kai et al., 2024). That is, AI-KM integration with the support of XAI makes outputs more comprehensible for human users, ultimately leading to better knowledge utilization. Operationalization therefore begins with establishing explicit governance checkpoints, such as AI decision-audit cycles, validation protocols for knowledge outputs, and HITL approval workflows, to ensure that human oversight remains embedded at all stages of AI-enabled knowledge processing. These checkpoints act as safeguards against epistemic drift, model hallucination, and culturally misaligned knowledge representations. At the same time, the SECI model reminds us that much of the most valuable knowledge in HEIs remains tacit and context-bound; AI systems, even when explainable, are primarily optimized for explicit, codified information, which necessitates deliberate design choices to avoid conflating information processing with full-spectrum organizational knowing (Kai et al., 2024; López-Meza et al., 2024). This ideology is propelled by the innovation diffusion theory, explaining how the adoption curve of AI tools across institutions is conducted, together with the anticipated barriers like faculty resistance or limited infrastructure. Taken together, socio-technical systems theory, the 5F-Model, the SECI framework, and innovation diffusion theory provide a complementary set of lenses for analyzing AI-enabled KM in TNE: socio-technical perspectives illuminate the human-technology configuration; the 5F-Model captures the staged flow of knowledge; SECI explains cyclical knowledge creation between tacit and explicit domains; and diffusion theory situates AI adoption within temporal and social dynamics of institutional change.

OPPORTUNITIES AND CHALLENGES IN TRANSNATIONAL KNOWLEDGE SHARING

Opportunities

Integrating AI-KM in TNE contexts comes with numerous opportunities and benefits. However, as noted by reviewers, these opportunities should not be interpreted as inevitable outcomes of technological adoption; instead, their realization depends heavily on institutional readiness, data governance, digital maturity, and socio-cultural alignment across TNE campuses (Bratianu & Ioan, 2025; Latif et al., 2024). Integrating AI in KM comes with multiple advantages, as outlined in Figure 2. Taherdoost and Madanchian (2023) present that the major advantage transnational HEIs can derive from AI-enabled KM is improved decision-making because predictive models foster proactive responses to enrollment trends, financial risks, and student needs across campuses and branches. For instance, KM-based administrative-decision-support systems improve using AI because the technology furnishes decision-makers with timely and data-driven insights that can promptly reshape teaching methods, knowledge-sharing, and knowledge utilization attitudes and other internal dynamics within educational settings (Schmidt et al., 2025). Despite these benefits, decision-support accuracy in TNE environments is highly contingent on data completeness and contextual fit. Institutions operating across jurisdictions with heterogeneous data standards may encounter uneven model performance, reinforcing the need for transparent data practices and careful cross-campus harmonization (Taherdoost & Madanchian, 2023). It is also worth acknowledging that AI-based KM helps shift traditional roles and responsibilities in TNE settings, thereby redistributing decision-making power among institutions, educators, and students across the levels of the academic system without relying on centralized power structures (Schmidt et al., 2025). Routine tasks like grading, feedback, and student record management can be automated with AI, thereby enabling faculty and staff to focus more on strategic and high-value duties like mentorship, research, and curriculum development. Ajani et al. (2024) add that AI systems' learning analytics provide actionable data that helps educators and curriculum developers refine the curricula to be more evidence-based.

Figure 2. Advantages of AI for KM (Taherdoost & Madanchian, 2023)

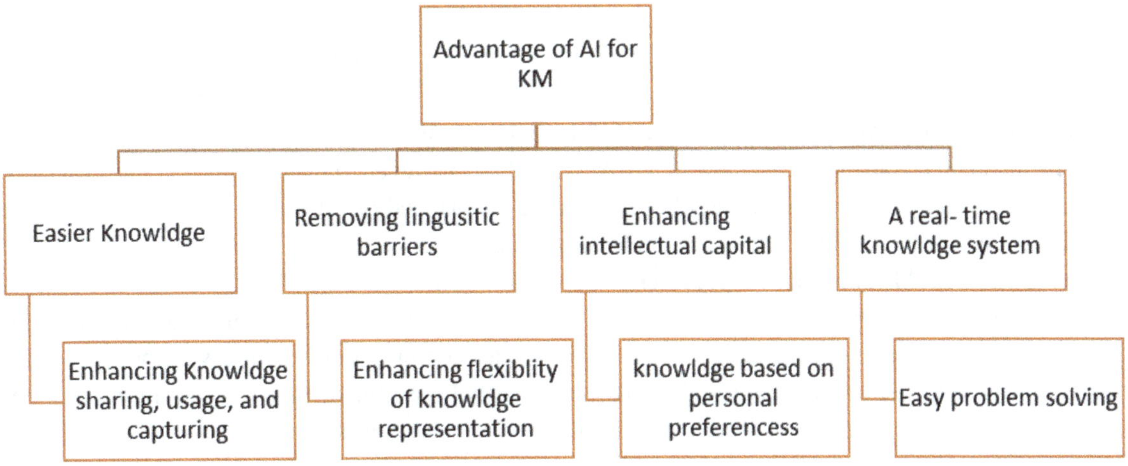

Secondly, AI-enabled KM enhances accessibility and personalization in TNE contexts. Transnational HEIs often have to grapple with cultural diversity challenges because of the influx of international students in their systems. Latif et al. (2024) contend that these students frequently adopt various KM strategies to facilitate cultural adaptation. For instance, they usually embrace oneness to make them feel a sense of belonging and engage in both personal and shared learning experiences (Latif et al., 2024). This indicates that AI-enabled personalization is not merely a technical function but a culturally mediated process shaped by learners' differing epistemic backgrounds, expectations, and linguistic repertoires, an aspect especially salient in TNE settings (Latif et al., 2024). Scholars have discovered that only culturally competent HEIs with robust social networks can help influence cultural intelligence and eventually impact these learners' knowledge sharing and integration as they pursue academic progress. AI-based KM helps tackle this challenge because it personalizes and tailors learning paths through 24/7 assistance and intelligence search through NLP. Personalized learning through AI-enabled KM makes learners more engaged since adaptive learning systems and intelligent tutoring platforms are designed based on individual needs, leading to timely feedback and targeted support (Ajani et al., 2024). AI chatbots can write scripts, answer queries, and analyze student data to get a comprehensive overview of concerns, learning styles, strengths, and weaknesses (Azmat & Mahmood, 2024). Nevertheless, highly personalized AI-driven recommendations can also risk narrowing intellectual exposure if learners become overly dependent on algorithmic curation rather than engaging with diverse perspectives, an emerging concern in AI-mediated learning environments (Schmidt et al., 2025). This tailored approach enhances a deeper understanding of subject matter and bridges gaps that existed in traditional teaching methods. Moreover, students get to interact with their peers across the globe through interactive discussions in AI-enabled KM that help bridge linguistic and cultural divides.

Collaborative learning emphasizes interaction and cooperation among learners to achieve shared objectives. Kovari (2025) explains that AI tools such as ML, NLP, and recommender systems enhance KM processes that support group learning. For instance, TNE HEIs use AI-driven platforms to analyze student interaction patterns and identify ways to strengthen collaboration through immediate feedback on group activities, helping learners stay aligned and address issues as they arise. ML and recommender systems also break down institutional silos by forming intelligent networks that connect faculty with complementary expertise across campuses; a professor in the United States, for example, can access, filter, format, and forward knowledge resources from Germany in real time. These capabilities promote interdisciplinary and transnational research (Kovari, 2025). However, AI-mediated collaboration platforms raise governance concerns about whose expertise is surfaced or obscured in automated partner-matching processes, posing challenges related to epistemic fairness and global academic representation (Leoni et al., 2024). AI-KM–enabled conference platforms further improve interaction between faculty and students across time zones. Additionally, AI-driven collaborative platforms monitor emotional and physiological responses to ensure learners remain engaged, receiving tailored interventions as needed. Student Teams Achievement Divisions (STAD) significantly boost performance by strengthening peer bonding and providing granular insights into emotion and engagement levels.

AI technologies present knowledge in familiar, accessible ways through automated KM operations that retrieve information and draw machine-interpretable conclusions (Taherdoost & Madanchian, 2023). This enables international students to receive personalized learning paths with recommended courses, resources, and assignments tailored to their needs. AI-powered chatbots and virtual assistants also track student data across locations and support admissions, registration, and financial aid processes. Latif et al. (2024) note that such personalization improves student satisfaction while reducing administrative workloads. Educators use AI tools to deliver more effective formative and summative learning experiences by uncovering complex learner knowledge, and researchers can quickly locate information within large repositories of lectures, papers, and institutional documents without losing time (Latif et al., 2024).

Overall, AI-enabled KM processes improve efficiency and scalability across TNE settings by automating repetitive tasks and enabling HEIs to manage larger cross-border operations with limited resources (Azmat & Mahmood, 2024). AI–KM integration also enhances innovation and creativity in areas such as interdisciplinary studies and medical education. Azmat and Mahmood (2024) note that AI tools capture the informal experiential knowledge of faculty, staff, and students by analyzing meetings and grading outcomes, allowing transnational HEIs to retain valuable tacit knowledge even as personnel or students rotate between campuses or leave the institution. This sustains a continuous cycle of innovation. However, the transformative potential of AI in TNE must be approached cautiously: without deliberate strategies for equity, inclusion, and cultural contextualization, AI-enabled KM may reinforce disparities and advantage well-resourced campuses over institutions with limited infrastructure (Latif et al., 2024; Bratianu & Ioan, 2025).

Challenges

Conversely, AI-driven KM practices and adoption also come with numerous challenges and risks that tamper with the lucrative opportunities. These challenges are particularly amplified in transnational HEIs, where cross-border regulatory variation, cultural heterogeneity, and uneven digital infrastructures interact to complicate AI deployment and escalate the risks associated with data misuse, algorithmic bias, and institutional misalignment (Cardona et al., 2023). HEIs implementing AI-enabled KM must be prepared to face technological challenges because AI algorithms and processes are intricate and require sophisticated implementation strategies with existing KM infrastructure (Bratianu & Ioan, 2025). For example, there are concerns about data quality and integrity, forming the fundamental efficacy of AI-driven knowledge systems. Data quality addresses dimensions like accuracy, completeness, consistency, timeliness, and relevance to generated input versus the output (Rezaei, 2025). Factors like human errors, system glitches, data integration complexities, and inaccurate data entry all form the major data quality dimensions. Deep learning and data processing technologies like neural networks and transfer learning, automating various knowledge processes, are complex in nature and require intricate computational demands (Bratianu & Ioan, 2025). As a result, there is a high possibility of inaccuracies and incompleteness in data, leading to skewed or erroneous decisions that often prove costly in cases of handling sensitive and critical information. TNE organizations must also acknowledge that GenAI applications generating artificial knowledge often do not correspond to real-life contexts and truth, creating output silos and dispersed knowledge across numerous sources.

Additionally, Cardona et al. (2023) note that organizations seeking AI-enabled KM face challenges because legacy KM systems were never designed to integrate with AI, requiring significant resources and expertise to achieve compatibility. Leoni et al. (2024) add that data interoperability issues force HEIs to overhaul existing workflows as an effort that is both time-consuming and costly (Rezaei, 2025). Cross-border interoperability further creates governance tensions involving control of data flows, oversight of algorithmic systems, and shared accountability across international partnerships; issues still underexamined in current AI-KM implementations (Gelashvili-Luik et al., 2025). AI models must also be transparent and explainable so users can understand decision-making processes. Rezaei (2025) warns that the absence of transparency fosters skepticism, raising concerns about reliability and robustness, since HEIs require models capable of handling outliers, noise, and missing data without distortions. Unreliable inputs compromise decision-making and reduce KM system effectiveness (Leoni et al., 2024). These technological challenges produce opaque structures that demand advanced expertise to interpret, prompting concerns about the validity of outputs, as biased or inaccurate results carry serious consequences in TNE contexts. This underscores the need for explainable AI and transparent system designs that clarify AI-generated outputs, especially when they diverge from institutional expectations.

Secondly, the structural and cultural dimensions of adopting AI and KM introduce significant organizational challenges related to readiness, employee acceptance, and strategic alignment. Bratianu and Ioan (2025) note that AI-enabled KM initiatives often face strong resistance from staff who lack AI knowledge or fear its implications. Adoption requires HEIs to modify existing processes and workflows, a shift that many find disruptive. Rezaei (2025) attributes this resistance to limited trust in AI, especially when opaque decision-making conflicts with human intuition. TNE managers and stakeholders in smaller institutions must also make strategic investment decisions when selecting tools to enhance KM processes (Leoni et al., 2024). AI-based KM integration demands substantial human and financial resources, and stakeholders frequently highlight the high costs of purchasing, installing, and maintaining AI tools; costs that are often unmanageable for resource-constrained HEIs. Budgeting teams may calculate returns on investment that do not align with institutional goals, and the risks associated with poor AI performance or interoperability issues can undermine managerial confidence. Rezaei (2025) further emphasizes the IT productivity paradox, which reflects the non-linear relationship between IT investments and organizational performance outcomes.

Finally, TNE institutions intending to adopt AI-enabled KM systems must be prepared to face and handle several ethical and legal issues during the integration phase, as outlined in Figure 3. Rezaei (2025) reveals that there is a high possibility that AI-enabled KM processes can exacerbate or perpetuate present biases in HEIs' knowledge systems and decision-making processes. Training AI algorithms using data with historical prejudices or stereotypes can foster discriminatory outputs that eventually lead to inequitable decision-making practices (Bala et al., 2024). This is perpetuated by the fact that AI algorithms are not accountable, explainable, or transparent. This implies that their black box natures of making decisions can widen the trust gaps when deployed to managed knowledge systems in HEIs (Bala et al., 2024).

Figure 3. Opportunities and challenges conceptual framework (Azmat & Mahmood, 2024)

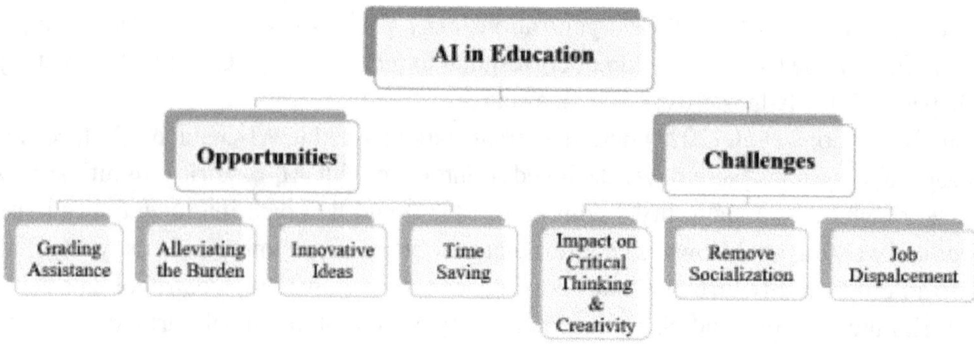

Studies also point out that HEIs over-relying on AI-enabled KM systems likely stifles human judgment and creativity levels. Leoni et al. (2024) discovered that AI users find it difficult to accept that AI and ML algorithms are prone to mistakes and errors and require intricate ethical use attitudes and procedures. Additionally, the fact that AI-enabled KM systems incorporate massive amounts of sensitive and crucial user data makes them high targets for cyber criminals. Ransomware and phishing attacks expose HEIs to the possibility of learner, educators, and administrative data falling into the hands of unauthorized individuals because of their high value (Rezaei, 2025). Hence, there is a challenge when it comes to protecting individual privacy rights and maintaining data security, as there is a need to access comprehensive data to advance KM systems. Moreover, TNE institutions operating campuses in multiple locations have to navigate the evolving data protection regulations and the global nature of HEIs operating under the confines of several legal frameworks (Cardona et al., 2023). Conversely, ethical concerns emerge because AI potentially erodes human agency and autonomy, as the algorithms continuously evolve to become complex and advanced as they generate, analyze, and apply knowledge. Balancing between AI and human decision-making is a tactical process to avoid the overreliance on AI in KM systems (Rezaei, 2025). Failing to balance between the two devalues tacit knowledge. It has undesirable impacts on HEI educators and administrative staff who may feel displaced and devalued with the integration of AI in KM. Equally important, TNE institutions must contend with cross-jurisdictional privacy regulations, such as GDPR-compliant campuses partnering with non-GDPR jurisdictions, which complicate data transfer, algorithmic transparency, and accountability requirements. These global regulatory asymmetries demand rigorous ethical stewardship, institutional oversight, and continuous auditing to prevent misuse, discrimination, or erosion of academic integrity (Cardona et al., 2023; Bala et al., 2024). While AI offers significant opportunities for efficiency and predictive capability, reviewers emphasized the need to acknowledge the inherent tension between augmentation and automation. Many of the technologies deployed in the case studies which ranges from adaptive learning engines to predictive analytics, risk shifting decision-making authority from educators to automated systems if not carefully governed. AI should therefore be positioned as an augmenting partner that enhances human judgment rather than replacing it. Embedding human-in-the-loop (HITL) practices, maintaining transparency in algorithmic recommendations, and preserving academic agency are essential to ensure that AI strengthens rather than constrains pedagogical autonomy and knowledge diversity across TNE settings (Rezaei, 2025; Schmidt et al., 2025).

AI TOOLS IN ACTION: CASE EXAMPLES FROM HIGHER EDUCATION

Case 1 – Sino-Foreign Cooperative University in Southern China

The university offers undergraduate and postgraduate translation and interpreting programs, where students study courses such as translation theory, legal translation, computer-assisted translation, and translation principles (Zhang et al., 2025). The TNE institution employs AI-based machine translation tools (including Deep Learning systems, Microsoft Translator, GenAI, and LLMs) to generate multimodal, human-like content for learners and educators. Zhang et al. (2025) note that LLMs are highly proficient and can even outperform specialized tools like Google Translate and DeepL. These technologies provide new insights into how translation practices evolve alongside GenAI, particularly as they challenge traditional methods and the self-perception of language professionals. Sino-Foreign Cooperative University students frequently use GenAI tools to revise translations, search contextual information, complete drafts, and look up terminology and unfamiliar words (Zhang et al., 2025).

Integrating AI into KM practices has enabled a dual-language knowledge repository that improves access to academic content, reduces misunderstandings, and supports collaboration between Chinese and international faculty. However, this accessibility intensifies long-standing KM debates on the distinction between *information* and *knowledge*: while AI effectively retrieves and structures information, it cannot replicate the contextual, experiential, and tacit knowledge essential to academic judgment (Rezaei, 2025). Zhang et al. (2025) report that students and educators benefit from this integration, as AI-based KM tools enhance translation efficiency and quality, support translation learning and practice, and foster more positive learning experiences. Students also gain social advantages through automatic translation of lecture slides, research abstracts, and administrative documents (Zhang et al., 2025). Yet challenges persist, including redundancies, omissions, vague outputs, and mistranslations, along with concerns about accountability and transparency in GenAI-assisted translation. Although such issues reflect the early stage of AI-KM adoption, Sino-Foreign Cooperative University has implemented measures to ensure user feedback helps improve output quality and deliver more effective educational experiences.

Case 2 – The UK's Open University (OU) Analyse and Student Probability Model

OU Analyse is an ML-powered system that helps identify students at high risk of failing (UK Open University, 2021). Course tutors and student support teams receive timely data for students deemed at risk of failing a module or an assignment every week. The data helps instructors and support teams to provide the necessary support efforts to the identified student through personalized student demographic data and dynamic data represented by their daily VLE activities (UK Open University, 2021). The OU analyse considers different properties of input data to arrive at a combined student classification and prediction of who is at most risk. By 2020, all tutors from all undergraduate OU models had access to the dashboard application shown in Figure 4 and predicted more than 150,000 cases of students requiring additional support yearly. Additionally, OU analyse not only identifies those at risk of failing but also provides a personalized Activity Reminder notifying learners how to improve their performance in a given course (UK Open University, 2021).

Figure 4. UK OU analyse dashboard (UK Open University, 2021)

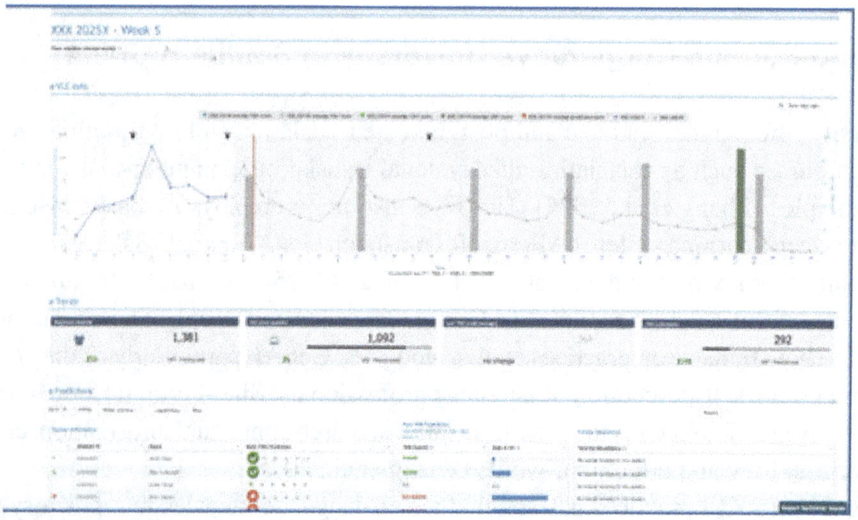

Conversely, OU also uses the student probability model (SPM), a predictive learning analytics (PLA) tool, to assess whether individual students will hit the specific milestones required to complete or pass a course or return in the following academic year. Herodotou et al. (2019) present that logistic regression sets of explanatory variables help SPM make such predictions. Data on student factors like IMD area, price area, and disability, and previous studies highlight that the highest qualification on entry is the area used to consolidate the SPM data. Additionally, the total credits a student garners in a year or late registration insights, and previous progress at the university help group students into bands according to their chances of meeting the desired course outcomes (Herodotou et al., 2019). Figure 5 highlights the SPM predicting whether students will reach the set milestones.

Figure 5. SPM predicting students achieving course milestones (Herodotou et al., 2019)

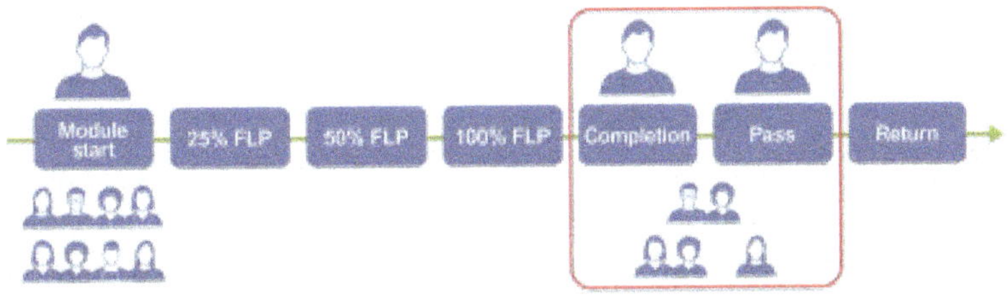

Case 3 – Smart Campus Initiatives at the Nanyang Technological University (NTU) in Singapore

NTU embraces several AI tools in its KM systems following its efforts to be a smart and sustainable campus, as derived from Singapore's 2014 Smart Nation initiative. These smart initiatives integrate AI across teaching, administration, and research and leverage several predictive, analytics, ML, and DeepL tools to ensure the university is efficient across its campuses (Das et al., 2022). For instance, NTU's Prof Leodar, a GenAI teaching assistant, is reimagining education, equipping students with vital AI literacy and fostering critical thinking. Prof Leodar emphasizes the responsible and ethical use of AI at NTU. Through a strategic partnership with Amazon Web Services (AWS), Prof Leodar is a retrieval augmented generation chatbot that is integrated with NTU's course data that is customized to generate outputs based on NTU's courses only (Amazon Web Services, 2025). It outlines to the students and educators when classes are due, the examination schedules, and the assessment criteria to pass assignments. Since the introduction of Prof Leodar, NTU has witnessed a massive improvement in the quality of students' projects and assignments, there has been a positive shift in responsible AI use, and most importantly, it has reinvigorated problem-solving capabilities around the institution. The GenAI tool also incorporated international students' cultural needs by tweaking its behaviors to be more reflective of transnational and not Asian-biased. Additionally, NTU students have gained the needed critical thinking skills and even started experimenting with their own LLMs (Amazon Web Services, 2025).

Conversely, NTU's smart learning spaces (SLSs) have embedded smart technologies with the sole aim of personalizing learning experiences through student-centered approaches. Das et al. (2025) opine that NTU SLSs have IoT-supported projection systems, sensor systems, and interactive technologies that enhance the typical traditional learning environments. Niche programs like mechanical and aerospace engineering have dedicated smart laboratories with state-of-the-art AI-based technologies to advance learning experiences (Das et al., 2025). AI-powered sensors monitor classroom usage, library demand, and energy consumption, and tactfully predict the needs for the spaces based on learner influx on a particular day. Hence, these tools provide administrative and student recommendations to make arrangements based on the learning resources available. NTU's dynamic and data-driven knowledge environment massively facilitates real-time decision-making in knowledge and other resource management endeavors (Das et al., 2025).

Case 4 – Arizona State University's (ASU) Adaptive Learning

ASU partnered with CogBooks to integrate adaptive learning (AL) in a biology degree program. Contrino et al. (2024) assert that AL generates unique learning experiences by considering an individual's differences, either as a process and their preferences about the types of materials or technological devices and software. That is, AL focuses on how content gets presented to the student, which is adapted according to the student's methods of understanding the material, often manifesting in the form of the result obtained in the evaluations (Contrino et al., 2024). ASU uses AL to help learners' complete assignments and as a support mechanism throughout the course. Conversely, they also use it as a remediation mechanism through remediation packets to help students reinforce their knowledge on a particular topic (Contrino et al., 2024). While the CogBooks platform provides personalized student learning experiences, it also provides immediate feedback, with course subjects being divided into concepts and sub-concepts.

ASU's extensive physical and global community draws numerous benefits from AL and virtual learning assistants. ASU's AL and virtual assistants are powered by NLP models and respond to student concerns about course content, assignment deadlines, and administrative procedures with the touch of a button. Students can get 24/7 support regardless of their geographical location and campuses (Leander, 2019). As a result, the limited human staff at ASU have precious time to focus more on strategic functions because these assistants collect anonymized data on frequently asked questions and integrate them in the cloud to refine resources and improve course designs. This AI-enabled KM process has led to several benefits for ASU students and instructors. Leander (2019) presents that the introduction of the AL in the Biology 100 course improved non-major performance by 24% and reduced dropout rates by almost 90%. Additionally, translating the Biology textbook into the CogBooks adaptive-learning platform helped deliver instructions online and outside the classroom, providing interactive and hands-on activities during class time.

Case 5 – University of Melbourne's AI Learning Assistant (AILA)

The University of Melbourne integrates the GenAI AILA tool with its learning management system (LMS) to enhance knowledge management. AILA is located in the subject LMS. It helps learners during their learning journey by answering questions about subject content and providing instantaneous outputs responding to the input queries (University of Melbourne, 2024). AILA has two modes, namely, the chat and revision prompts. Students leverage the chat mode to input queries about their subjects with AILA responding in real-time based on the information automatically provided by subject coordinators. On the other hand, the revision model provides guidelines for students to follow based on specified topics and referencing materials within the subject (University of Melbourne, 2024). AILA leverages the LLM Anthropic Claude 3 Sonnet to capture and generate data as prompted. Most importantly, it integrates the human-in-the-loop (HITL) concept to advance the ethical use of AI by upholding accountability and responsibility since staff have been authorized to edit access for subjects in Canvas LMS playpen. This illustrates how AI-enabled collaboration disproportionately benefits institutions with strong pre-existing research cultures, deep content repositories, and established international networks, reinforcing the idea that AI amplifies institutional strengths rather than compensating for structural weaknesses (Asiedu et al., 2022).

Based on these practices, university staff determine which LMS subject resources AI systems will use to generate responses and provide additional instructions to GenAI tools to improve accuracy and adaptability (University of Melbourne, 2024). AILA also undergoes rigorous subject testing through the "view student experience" function to ensure updated content reflects ongoing subject changes and enhances efficiency throughout the semester. To prevent overreliance, the university restricts AILA from providing direct answers to assessments, limiting it instead to learning support (University of Melbourne, 2024). The university's collaborative LLM models further facilitate seamless partnerships with institutions in Asia and Europe by integrating AI tools for managing international research projects. These systems scan global academic databases and recommend potential collaborators. Automated literature review systems within KM also identify emerging trends and research gaps.

Case 6 – European School of Management and Business' (EUDE) EDU

In response to logistic challenges for the influx of international online student body, EUDE collaborated with IBM to develop EDU, a GenAI virtual co-tutor to handle more than 13,000 virtual students yearly from its main campus in Madrid. IBM (2024) reveals that EDU offers real-time support to both tutors and students regardless of their different time zones and cultural differences. It provides immediate answers to administrative and academic queries and also supports students with delivery dates and examination schedules. EDU leverages the IBM Cloud, IBM watsonx.ai, IBM watsonx Assistant, and IBM Watson Discovery LLMs to access a broad knowledge pool (IBM, 2024). Since it operates based on the WatsonX portfolio, EDU controls the content and responses and also ensures its own data and user data are secure. After the pilot, EUDE witnessed a significant improvement in response times to questions and tailored support from tutors and administrators. EUDE remains committed to refining EDU with the aim of freeing up time for tutors to focus more on personalized tutoring and complete other strategic tasks (IBM, 2024).

Comparative Case Analysis of AI-Enabled KM Across TNE Institutions

The six case studies illustrate diverse yet converging pathways through which transnational higher education (TNE) institutions incorporate artificial intelligence into their knowledge management (KM) systems. Despite differences in scale, resources, and technological maturity, all cases reveal a shared movement toward AI-enabled personalisation, multilingual knowledge access, predictive analytics, and data-driven decision-making. Institutions such as the Sino-Foreign Cooperative University and the University of Melbourne leverage GenAI and NLP-powered tools to support translation, content generation, and academic assistance, while the UK Open University demonstrates how predictive analytics can strengthen early interventions and reduce attrition. NTU's smart campus ecosystem showcases infrastructure-intensive AI adoption, and EUDE's virtual co-tutor illustrates how cloud-based AI can scale rapidly in institutions with constrained human resources. ASU's adaptive learning model highlights pedagogically grounded AI integration designed to improve student performance and retention.

Collectively, these cases highlight both the promise and complexity of AI-enabled KM in TNE environments. Success tends to correlate with three institutional factors: (1) advanced digital infrastructure capable of supporting large-scale data and computation; (2) clear governance strategies, including transparency, explainability, and human-in-the-loop oversight; and (3) strong alignment between AI capabilities and pedagogical or organisational goals. However, challenges persist across all institutions, including data quality limitations, interoperability issues, cultural and linguistic bias, staff readiness concerns, and uneven regulatory requirements across jurisdictions.

Table 1. Comparative analysis of AI-enabled KM across six TNE case institutions

Institution	TNE Context	Primary AI Tools	KM Function(s) Enhanced	Strategy & Implementation Approach	Success Factors	Key Challenges	Ethical / Governance Issues	Outcomes Observed	Scalability Potential	Risks / Limitations
Sino-Foreign Cooperative University	China–Foreign partnership; bilingual programs	GenAI, LLMs, machine translation	Knowledge creation, multilingual access	AI-assisted translation integrated across curriculum	Bilingual knowledge repository; improved access	Redundancies, mistranslation	Transparency; accountability	Higher translation efficiency	High	Cultural-linguistic bias; overreliance
UK Open University (OU)	Large distributed online TNE	OU Analyse (ML), Student Probability Model	Predictive analytics	Institution-wide analytics-driven support	Rich datasets; early intervention	Data inconsistencies; model limits	Privacy; fairness	Improved retention; accurate prediction	Very high	Misclassification; data quality
Nanyang Technological University (NTU)	Global research-intensive HEI	GenAI assistant, IoT sensors, NLP	Personalized learning, smart spaces	Integrated into Smart Nation ecosystem	Robust infrastructure; AI literacy	Cost; integration complexity	Cultural tuning of LLM outputs	High engagement; optimized resource use	Moderate–High	Biometric data governance
Arizona State University (ASU)	Global online + in-person learners	Adaptive learning (CogBooks), NLP	Personalisation, remediation	Course redesign + AL analytics	Immediate feedback; modular design	Staff adaptation workload	HITL oversight	Improved pass rates; reduced dropout	High	Equity risks if data incomplete
University of Melbourne	Multi-campus global collaborations	GenAI (AILA), literature mapping tools	Knowledge discovery, academic support	LMS-integrated AI assistant with HITL	Strong governance; controlled datasets	Training load; tuning accuracy	Data authorization; integrity	Efficient support; improved retrieval	Moderate	Epistemic narrowing risks
EUDE	International online HEI	GenAI (IBM watsonx), virtual co-tutor	Academic and administrative support	Cloud-based GenAI for 13,000 students	High responsiveness; scalable model	Legacy interoperability	Multi-regulatory data security	Faster support, improved experience	High	Algorithmic drift

Comparative Insights

The six cases collectively reveal how TNE institutions are integrating AI into their KM platforms and systems in ways that reflect their organizational maturity, technological capacity, and transnational mandates. A recurrent theme across the cases is that machine translation, adaptive learning platforms, and predictive analytics are transforming access to knowledge for diverse student populations. Virtual assistants and ML-driven analytics enhance efficiency and scalability by supporting distributed learners, while collaborative GenAI-enabled platforms strengthen global research partnerships and academic knowledge creation.

Across all cases, a consistent pattern emerges: AI tools tend to be most effective when institutions possess mature digital infrastructures, well-developed knowledge-sharing cultures, and clear governance mechanisms. NTU and OU exemplify high-capacity, analytics-driven models supported by strong internal expertise, stable infrastructure, and institution-wide deployment strategies. Conversely, institutions in earlier stages of KM or digital readiness such as EUDE or emerging Sino-foreign partnerships, exhibit more incremental adoption shaped by constraints in scalability, linguistic diversity, data quality, and staff readiness (UK Open University, 2021; IBM, 2024; Zhang et al., 2025).

Another cross-case insight is the centrality of ethical and governance structures. Institutions like NTU and the University of Melbourne proactively incorporate explainable AI, human-in-the-loop oversight, and culturally adaptive tuning of LLMs, demonstrating a strategic understanding of cross-border ethical risks. Others, such as the Sino-Foreign Cooperative University, continue to refine transparency, accountability, and model reliability in multilingual contexts; highlighting how AI-related biases, governance gaps, and data dependency challenges can hinder TNE-wide scaling efforts (Leoni et al., 2024; Rezaei, 2025).

Taken together, the case comparisons underscore that AI-KM integration in TNE is not a uniform technological upgrade but a contextual, path-dependent process shaped by institutional governance, cultural expectations, resource availability, and multi-jurisdictional regulatory conditions. The disparities observed across the six institutions highlight the need for a strategic AI-KM framework that accommodates differentiated starting points, emphasizes ethical stewardship, and aligns KM innovation with the socio-technical realities of TNE environments.

Overall, the comparative patterns make clear that successful AI-KM implementations hinge not only on technical capability but also on institutional alignment, cross-border coordination, and the presence of robust governance and quality-assurance mechanisms, elements that form the foundation of the strategic framework presented in the subsequent section (Pai et al., 2022; Rezaei, 2025).

STRATEGIC FRAMEWORK FOR AI-KM INTEGRATION

Strategically integrating KM and AI promises unique opportunities for TNE institutions owing to that it revolutionizes decision-making, knowledge retrieval, and innovation across domains (Kai et al., 2024). However, as reviewers noted, these opportunities materialize only when AI-enabled KM is positioned within a theoretically coherent and operationally grounded framework that accounts for the socio-technical, cultural, and governance complexities of TNE ecosystems (Pai et al., 2022; Rezaei, 2025). The strategic framework outlined in Figure 6 overviews the actions TNE firms should adopt to achieve seamless AI-KM integration.

Guiding Principles of the Framework

The literature and case studies indicate that the integrated framework must synthesize the investigation's findings. It connects the three core concepts of strategic outcomes for TNE, foundational pillars, and AI-enhanced KM processes showing both linear and retroactive relationships, as illustrated in Figure 6. This dual structure reflects reviewer insights: KM processes in HEIs seldom follow purely linear models like the 5F-Model or purely cyclical models like SECI. Instead, AI-enabled KM requires hybrid flows in which combination, externalization, and analysis continually reshape tacit and explicit knowledge assets (Kai et al., 2024; López-Meza et al., 2024).

The framework adopts a human-centered design aligned with Rezaei (2025), who warns that AI can diminish human agency and autonomy. A HITL model balances AI and human decision-making, addressing risks such as eroding expertise, devaluing tacit knowledge, and creating psychological strain among staff who may feel displaced by AI (Rezaei, 2025). Thus, HITL is positioned not as an optional enhancement but as a governance principle ensuring accountability, preserving human judgment, and mitigating epistemic risks; especially in TNE contexts where cultural and regulatory asymmetries complicate automated decisions (Gelashvili-Luik et al., 2025).

The framework also proposes that AI-KM systems should bridge (rather than widen) digital and cultural divides common in TNE environments by enabling transparent and explainable decision-making. Ethical stewardship is emphasized through commitments to privacy, fairness, and academic integrity before and after adoption. Pai et al. (2022) argue that AI-enabled KM systems must eliminate opacity by ensuring transparency from input to output. Finally, AI-KM integration should incorporate cost-effective, scalable features, given that many HEIs operate with limited human and financial resources during major transformation efforts.

The Five Pillars of AI-KM Integration

To translate the conceptual framework into practice, TNE institutions require an operationalisation schema that links each pillar to measurable indicators, actionable steps, and implementation timelines. This responds directly to reviewer comments requesting more concrete guidance on how the AI-KMIM can be deployed across diverse institutional contexts. The strategic framework, structured around five interdependent dimensions, guides transnational HEIs to impeccably follow the provided guidelines through the dedicated AI-KM Integration Model (AI-KMIM). The fragmented AI-KM landscape persists because of limited AI-KM integration frameworks and guidelines. The five pillars fill the gap by providing an evidence-based pathway HEIs can follow when embedding AI in their KM systems. These pillars operationalize the theoretical insights discussed earlier by translating socio-technical alignment, cyclical knowledge creation, staged knowledge flows, and innovation diffusion dynamics into actionable design parameters for TNE institutions. In doing so, the framework resolves the fragmentation between existing KM models that reviewers highlighted. To operationalise these pillars, institutions may adopt a staged implementation roadmap comprising: (1) diagnostic assessment; (2) pilot deployment; (3) scaling and integration; and (4) continuous evaluation. Each stage incorporates feedback loops that reflect the cyclical nature of KM, aligning SECI-based knowledge creation cycles with the linear flow of the 5F-Model.

Figure 6. Strategic AI-KM integration framework for TNE HEIs

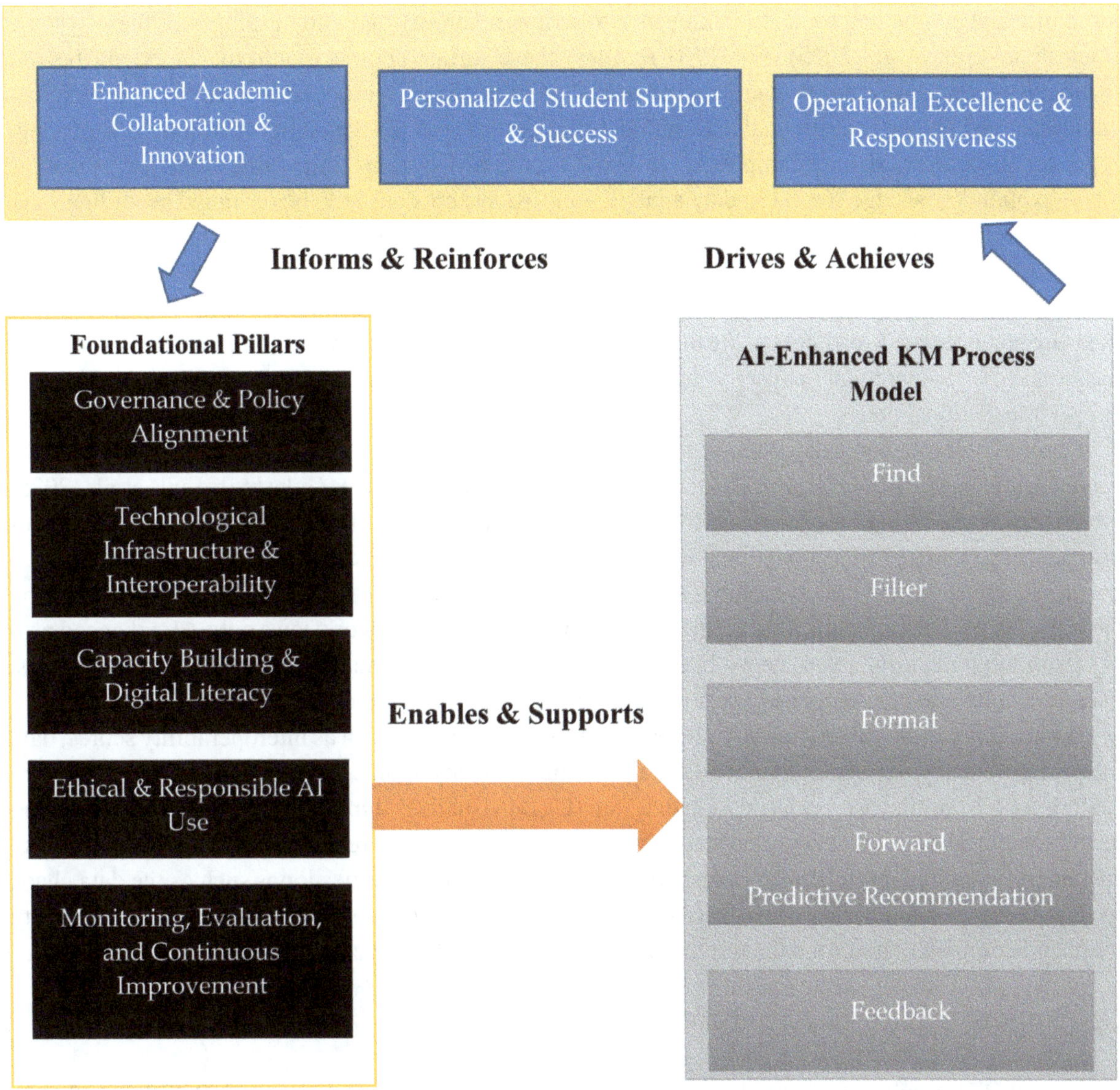

Figure 6 therefore functions not only as a conceptual illustration but also as an operational guide: each arrow represents a required institutional action, each loop signifies a feedback mechanism, and each node corresponds to a decision point requiring context-specific interpretation, particularly relevant in TNE environments where cultural and regulatory conditions vary significantly.

Technological Infrastructure

AI and big data integration into KM is not a straightforward affair, as noted by Bala et al. (2024), since most HEIs' existing KM systems were built around legacy systems whose major focus was to solely store and retrieve explicit knowledge and not handle large volumes of data and high speeds. Making updates to technological systems comes with changing architecture in totality, streamlining data infrastructure, and conducting routine maintenance to ensure reliability and daily usability of these systems (Gelashvili-Luik et al., 2025). For TNE settings, these infrastructural requirements extend beyond technical upgrades: institutions must ensure cross-border platform interoperability, harmonize metadata standards, and embed multilingual and multicultural design features that support equitable knowledge representation across partner campuses. While traditional KM systems follow linear capture, store, and share explicit knowledge steps, big data analytics and AI systems ought to be designed according to an iterative and exploratory process to help discover patterns and create knowledge in real-time presently and into the future (Rezaei, 2025). This helps ensure the IT infrastructure integrates diverse systems across global campuses and handles computational demands for AI tools with ease. Institutions may measure technological-readiness using indicators such as data-interoperability compliance (% of systems harmonized), computational capacity utilization, cloud-scalability thresholds, and average AI latency across transnational nodes.

Integrative frameworks that balance the controlled flow of traditional KM with the flexibility of AI-driven knowledge discovery are essential for effective AI-KM systems. Gelashvili-Luik et al. (2025) emphasize that developing robust, interoperable, and scalable infrastructures is critical for institutions transitioning from traditional to AI-enabled KM. This requires cloud-based repositories accessible across partner campuses and AI platforms that support translation, predictive analytics, and adaptive learning (Kovari, 2025). Operationalisation further involves mapping existing workflows onto AI-enhanced processes through maturity assessments, bottleneck analysis, and RACI matrices that clarify who initiates, oversees, and validates AI-mediated knowledge activities, thereby ensuring transparency.

Institutions can also assess infrastructure readiness using metrics such as interoperability scores, data integration latency, AI deployment cycles, and digital maturity indices to identify bottlenecks before scaling AI-KM initiatives. A causal loop diagram (CLD) visualizes dynamic interdependencies among technological, human, organizational, and governance variables to ensure KM initiatives remain scalable, sustainable, and high performing (Gelashvili-Luik et al., 2025). It outlines loops such as the data chaos loop, governance stabilizer loop, resistance spiral loop, training and engagement loop, capability–scalability loop, and complexity trap loop that collectively illustrate how these factors influence AI repositories.

Governance and Policy Alignment

Several HEIs implement technological governance to help them align better with their KM. AI governance is a well-structured procedure for analyzing and managing various decision-making processes (Tariq & Abonamah, 2021). Staff and active users often find it challenging to adopt AI, especially when there are no clear adoption rules for how data is used and decisions made. AI-KM integration comes with several trust, legal, and ethical risks that organizations must consider. Gelashvili-Luik et al. (2025) contend that organizations are mandated to protect sensitive data, comply with local and international regulations like the GDPR, UNESCO AI Ethics, and OECD principles to avoid data misuse. For TNE institutions, governance must additionally navigate cross-jurisdictional data transfer restrictions, varying definitions of legitimate knowledge use, and inconsistent AI regulatory regimes. This creates asymmetrical risk profiles across campuses, requiring locally adaptable yet globally coherent governance mechanisms.

Strong compliance with cross-border data privacy policies, ethical AI guidelines, mitigating algorithmic framework bias, and clear accountability structures foster responsible and fair AI-KM use.

Non-compliance with international guidelines remains a major barrier to seamless AI-KM integration in TNE institutions, often resulting in reputational harm, employee resistance, and significant financial losses. Therefore, cultivating a strong governance culture that extends beyond basic compliance and promotes shared understanding of ethical data practices is essential (Rezaei, 2025). Ethical shortcomings typically stem from outdated policies or unclear accountability structures rather than deliberate misconduct (Gelashvili-Luik et al., 2025). High levels of compliance, accountability, and ethical oversight across jurisdictions support effective AI-KM integration by ensuring adaptive governance frameworks and transparent, ethical use of AI in TNE systems.

Governance readiness can be evaluated through indicators such as AI audit frequency, explainability compliance scores, cross-border data-mapping protocols, and documented incident-response mechanisms for algorithmic failures or breaches. Operational metrics include documented cross-border data-processing agreements, the proportion of AI components subject to explainability audits, the number of regulatory compliance checks per semester, and the frequency of AI-risk assessment cycles. These indicators help institutions maintain alignment with GDPR, UNESCO AI Ethics, OECD principles, and host-country regulations.

Capacity Building and Digital Literacy

Technological upgrades to KM systems face friction coming from human and organizational dynamics because resistance toward AI-based tools stems from fears of job displacement and skepticism toward automation. Rezaei (2025) adds that these developments show the deeper cultural and psychological barriers organizations have to address before implementing revolutionary AI-KM changes. Conversely, Leoni et al. (2024) tie this misalignment to a mismatch between an institution's knowledge management maturity (KMM) and the dynamic complexes of adopting new technologies. HEIs adopting AI-based KM in their KM should clearly assess organizational readiness and tailor change management approaches based on specific needs. That is, filling the gaps in digital literacy and training its workforce and end-users regarding AI-KM systems is an imperative process to ensure new technologies put in place are effective and meet the intended purposes (Gelashvili-Luik et al., 2025).

Instilling a human-in-the-loop (HITL) culture throughout AI-KM integration reinforces that AI augments KM practices rather than replacing an institution's most valuable asset its people. Strong training, knowledge literacy, and development programs for faculty, staff, and students build trust and support effective collaboration (Rezaei, 2025). Implementers must avoid one-size-fits-all frameworks, which often overlook sector-specific and cultural differences and result in uneven adoption and ineffective knowledge sharing (Gelashvili-Luik et al., 2025). Improving KM readiness allows institutions to assess cultural absorption capacity alongside technological and financial resources.

To operationalize capacity building, institutions may track faculty digital literacy, student AI competence scores, training completion ratios, and HITL intervention accuracy. These metrics help campus leaders identify resistance patterns, knowledge gaps, and uneven adoption across global sites. Reviewer feedback highlighted that staff readiness is critical to AI-KM success; thus, progress should be measured through digital competence assessments, training completion rates, HITL effectiveness ratings, and change-management adoption indices. Human factors such as attitudes toward change, willingness to collaborate, and engagement with new systems are essential enablers shaping long-term KM effectiveness and adaptability (Rezaei, 2025).

Pedagogical Integration and Academic Practices

High volumes of organizational data and diversity put massive pressure on KM systems by showing vulnerabilities and cracks in data quality, consistency, and integration. The fragment nature of heterogenous KM data makes integration and transforming raw data into practical knowledge difficult. Bala et al. (2024) reveal that this increases the risk of inefficiency and poor strategic coordination when TNE institutions are implementing AI-enabled KM practices. This calls for HEIs to determine whether there is a practical limit to the amount of data that meaningfully contributes to insights before it amounts to information overload or misalignment (Gelashvili-Luik et al., 2025). While legacy systems reinforce data silos with knowledge remaining locked within departments, AI-KM models should improve interoperability, like using semantic web technologies like linked open data (LOD) (Gelashvili-Luik et al., 2025). AI-KM initiatives must also be directly aligned with the HEIs' core TNE mission and strategic objectives, like improving research outputs, enhancing student experience, and achieving operational excellence. Aligning organizational processes across TNE campuses requires harmonized workflows, shared taxonomies, and clearly defined escalation paths for AI-assisted decision-making to ensure that automated insights do not bypass institutional quality assurance structures (Leoni et al., 2024).

HEIs should embed AI in teaching, learning, and research without undermining academic integrity by adding AI-powered adaptive learning platforms for diverse learners, visual assistance for student support and administrative efficiency, and AI-based research tools for literature synthesis and global collaboration (Rezaei, 2025). TNE institutions should validate, clean, and standardize incoming data quickly enough for it to be useful. Bala et al. (2024) warn that poorly chosen frameworks or weak sensor data management lead to processing errors, misinterpretations, and unreliable outputs that ultimately affect the entire KM system and integration system by reducing the reliability and relevance of outputs. This calls for HEIs to ensure that AI is supportive and not substitutive by incorporating faculty oversight into all AI-supported assessments and providing training on AI usage.

Monitoring, Evaluation, and Continuous Improvement

While large HEIs have the technical expertise and resources to adapt and expand AI-enhanced KM systems, and smaller or less digitally mature organizations lack the resources, leading to a scalability gap, they both should ensure that an ongoing AI-KM integration system remains effective, fair, and relevant (Gelashvili-Luik et al., 2025). Besides, HEIs should implement AI solutions gradually and iteratively to allow time to adjust processes and minimize operational disruption (Rezaei, 2025). Ensuring algorithmic transparency enables stakeholders to audit AI decision-making to help uncover and address hidden biases through student KPIs, outcomes, equity, knowledge flows, and faculty adoption processes. Leoni et al. (2024) contend that regularly auditing AI tools for biases, privacy compliance, and sustainability should be an ongoing practice, highlighting the integration strengths, weaknesses, and areas of improvement. Rezaei (2025) recommends that publishing annual AI-KM impact reports foster transparency and agility. The holistic integrative approach highlighted in the framework helps TNE institutions to build effective, accountable, and resilient KM systems as the world experiences rapid technological and environmental shifts. Strategic alignment can be further operationalized through maturity models that map each campus's progress across key AI-KM dimensions, technology, governance, human capabilities, data quality, and cultural readiness, allowing TNE institutions to adopt differentiated, context-sensitive implementation plans rather than uniform, one-size-fits-all strategies. Strategic alignment can further be operationalised through a multi-level maturity grid evaluating (1) AI-KM vision coherence, (2) cross-campus coordination, (3) resource allocation, (4) pedagogical alignment, and (5) knowledge-equity safeguards. Each dimension can be scored on a 1–5 scale to establish baseline readiness and guide phased implementation.

Collectively, these five pillars transform the framework from a conceptual illustration into an actionable model grounded in both KM theory and empirical case evidence, directly responding to reviewer concerns regarding integration, operational clarity, and cross-border applicability.

In summary, the operationalization of the AI-KMIM framework transforms conceptual insights into a structured implementation pathway grounded in metrics, governance mechanisms, workflow adaptations, and contextual readiness assessments. This responds directly to reviewer critiques by demonstrating that AI-KM integration in TNE settings is not a uniform technological upgrade but a staged, evidence-based process requiring continuous monitoring, cultural adaptation, and ethical stewardship.

It is important to note that the proposed AI-KM integration framework is conceptual rather than empirically validated. The model synthesizes insights derived from the literature review, theoretical perspectives, and cross-case comparative analysis, providing an evidence-informed structure to guide institutional decision-making.

Operationalizing the Framework: A Stepwise Model

The forward-looking strategic framework developed in this study embeds continuous learning and adaptability, recognizing that technological innovation alone cannot transform KM systems (Gelashvili-Luik et al., 2025). Sustainable AI-KM integration requires combining advanced data capabilities with organizational change management, leadership commitment, and ethical governance. The framework balances automation with human expertise, acknowledging that effective KM depends as much on people and culture as on technology (Rezaei, 2025). Moving from principles to practice, organizations should adopt a stepwise approach beginning with assessments of institutional infrastructure, policy environments, and faculty capacity before launching AI pilot projects in targeted KM areas such as translation or student support (Bala et al., 2024). Scaling should then occur only after pilots are fully aligned with institutional strategy.

HEIs must also ensure alignment with local and international ethical, legal, and accreditation standards and establish iterative review mechanisms to maintain long-term relevance and trust (Tariq & Abonamah, 2021). The strategic framework breaks down silos and connects expertise across borders, accelerating transnational research and co-creation through enhanced academic collaboration and innovative practices. It further offers equitable, context-aware, 24/7 support to diverse global student bodies; an approach shown to improve retention and learning outcomes, as demonstrated by the European School of Management and Business's EDU platform (IBM, 2024). These capabilities facilitate data-driven decision-making, automate administrative processes, and allow institutions to respond quickly to emerging challenges and opportunities in global education markets (Bala et al., 2024; Kovari, 2025). Importantly, the framework's dynamic feedback loop positions AI as a transformative input that reshapes KM activities such knowledge discovery, capture, sharing, and application, while accounting for the sociotechnical factors that influence AI-KM integration.

Theoretical Contributions

Robust AI-KM frameworks help TNE institutions achieve enhanced knowledge flow by hastening the knowledge retrieval, sharing, and cross-border co-creation processes. Pai et al. (2022) add that AI-KM systems improve educational quality by enabling personalization and predictive analytics to enhance learning. This not only leads to smarter decision-making through AI-informed insights and institutional agility but also prepares HEIs to demonstrate ethical leadership by demonstrating accountability and fostering responsible AI use in TNE contexts (Rezaei, 2025). Ultimately, there are calls for harmonized policies and interoperable platforms that can strengthen HEIs' cross-border relationships as expounded in the conceptual AI-KM integration conceptual framework in Figure 7. The findings offer distinctive contributions by bridging AI with KM in transnational education contexts. The proposes framework serves as a guide for institutional leaders, IT strategists, and educators integrating AI systems in KM to enhance knowledge ecosystems across global campuses. It reveals that poor data, fragmented systems, and varied information coming fast from all directions can impede the integration process (Rezaei, 2025).

Figure 7. AI-KM integration conceptual framework (Gelashvili-Luik et al., 2025)

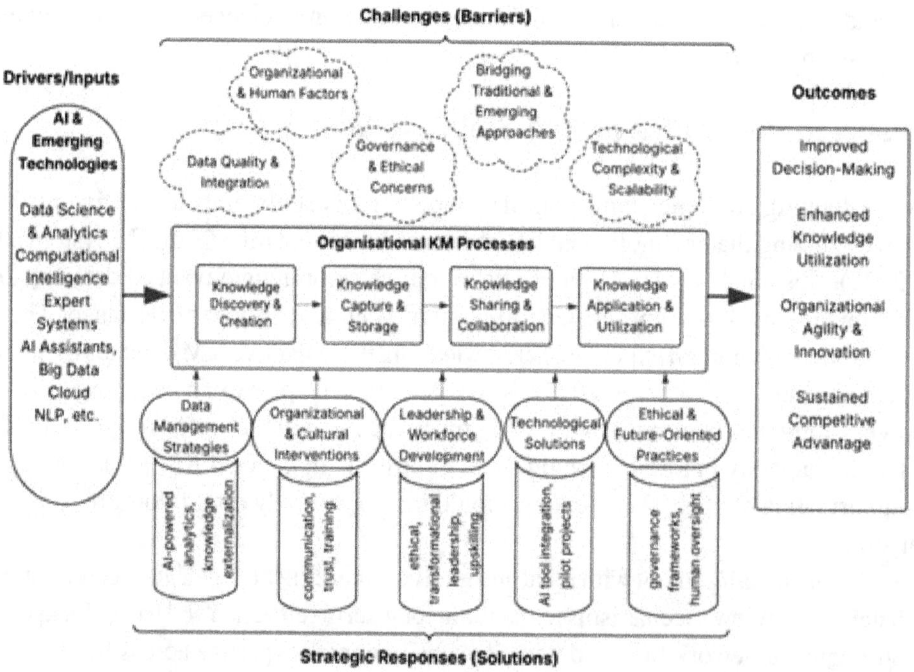

However, whenever institutional leaders, IT strategists, and other stakeholders make an investment in quality data and sustainable system integration practices, they can massively improve the decision-making process (Gelashvili-Luik et al., 2025). Also, transparent and inclusive AI governance within KM helps prevent bias, protect privacy, and avoid reputational harm. This calls for HEIs open to innovation cultures to use AI for turning static knowledge into a dynamic and evolving resource to make them more responsive and agile. It is worth noting that seamless AI-KM should remain scalable, easy to use, and fit specific industry needs through intense targeted training and cultural support to encourage adoption, considering that, if otherwise, staff and end-users can distrust AI (Bala et al., 2024). TNE institutions can harness the power of data and knowledge more efficiently and enjoy informed decision-making and innovation (Kai et al., 2024).

Student-Centric AI–KM in Transnational Higher Education

Student learning and engagement represent a central dimension of AI-enabled knowledge management (KM) in transnational higher education (TNE). While AI-KM is often framed as an institutional or administrative capability, its most profound impact occurs at the learner level, where AI systems reshape access to knowledge, personalize learning pathways, support metacognitive development, and facilitate collaborative knowledge creation across geographically dispersed campuses. As reviewers emphasized, integrating a student-centred perspective is essential to understanding the full educational value of AI-enabled KM in TNE contexts. In distributed learning environments that encompass diverse cultural, linguistic, and academic backgrounds, AI-KM systems provide a unified infrastructure that promotes equitable access to knowledge resources and enhances pedagogical coherence across institutions (Ajani et al., 2024; Latif et al., 2024).

AI-driven personalization is one of the most significant student-facing benefits in TNE settings. Adaptive learning platforms and intelligent tutoring systems adjust content, pace, and difficulty based on individual needs, prior knowledge, and performance. Vieriu and Petrea (2025) show that these systems support differentiated learning by identifying struggling learners early and recommending targeted interventions. Through continuous assessment and behavioral analytics, AI tools help students recognize knowledge gaps, refine learning strategies, and better engage with course content. This is particularly important in TNE contexts, where international students vary widely in academic preparation, language proficiency, and familiarity with host-country pedagogical norms (Latif et al., 2024). By tailoring learning pathways, AI-KM reduces structural inequities and improves students' likelihood of academic success across campuses.

AI-enabled virtual assistants and generative AI tools further strengthen students' ability to access, understand, and apply knowledge. These tools offer real-time, multilingual academic and administrative support, reducing cognitive barriers for students navigating unfamiliar institutional systems (Azmat & Mahmood, 2024). NLP-powered systems answer questions, summarize course materials, assist with brainstorming, and retrieve contextually relevant resources from institutional repositories (Rezaei, 2025). While these capabilities broaden learning access, reviewers cautioned that overreliance on automated guidance may limit students' exploratory inquiry. Therefore, consistent with Schmidt et al. (2025), AI-enabled support should complement (not replace) human mentorship, ensuring that learners retain opportunities for open-ended reasoning, ethical reflection, and creative problem-solving.

Collaborative learning also benefits from AI-driven KM platforms. Recommendation algorithms, ML-driven analytics, and NLP-based interaction trackers support group work by identifying complementary student competencies, facilitating cross-border peer networks, and recommending relevant discussion threads (Kovari, 2025). Such systems strengthen transnational learning communities by creating structured spaces for dialogue and collaboration. However, as reviewers noted, AI-assisted collaborative grouping must be designed carefully to avoid reinforcing linguistic, cultural, or demographic stratification. If improperly configured, recommendation algorithms may privilege dominant groups and undermine the participation of marginalized student populations. Embedding explainability and fairness criteria within collaborative platforms mitigates these risks and promotes inclusive transnational knowledge-sharing cultures.

Beyond supporting direct learning activities, AI-KM environments enhance students' metacognitive awareness and reflective learning practices. Predictive analytics and dashboards provide learners with insights into their progress, engagement patterns, conceptual understanding, and areas requiring improvement (Kai et al., 2024). Such feedback strengthens students' self-regulation skills, allowing them to make informed decisions about study strategies, resource allocation, and peer collaboration. This is particularly valuable in TNE contexts, where asynchronous delivery, varying academic calendars, and multicultural expectations require students to exercise greater autonomy and adaptability in managing their learning.

Despite these benefits, student-facing AI-KM systems require robust ethical safeguards, especially in cross-border contexts where data protection laws, cultural norms, and expectations of privacy differ significantly across jurisdictions. TNE institutions must ensure that predictive analytics, learner modelling, and AI-driven recommendations do not compromise student autonomy or inadvertently reveal sensitive behavioural or demographic patterns (Cardona et al., 2023; Bala et al., 2024). Systems must remain transparent and accountable, clearly communicating how student data is used and how algorithmic decisions are made. Furthermore, AI-enabled KM structures should preserve human agency by incorporating human-in-the-loop (HITL) mechanisms that enable students and educators to question, interpret, or override automated outputs when necessary (Rezaei, 2025).

Taken together, a student-centric approach positions AI-enabled KM not merely as an administrative or operational asset, but as a pedagogical catalyst that enhances learning quality, promotes equity, strengthens cultural inclusion, and supports diverse student communities across TNE ecosystems. By embedding personalization, collaboration, reflective learning, and ethical stewardship into AI-KM systems, universities ensure that learners remain active agents in knowledge creation and benefit fully from the transformative potential of AI in global higher education.

LIMITATIONS

Limited AI-KM tools adoption in the digitized world creates a gap hindrance to the progress of organizations. For instance, few AI tools encompassing machine, human, and cloud interaction have been implemented because AI, ML, and DeepL models are still in their infancy (Ajani et al., 2024). Additionally, despite the chapter providing a comprehensive exploration of AI, KM, and TNE contexts through in-depth exploration of case examples, literature, and a comprehensive report search, its conceptual analysis is a significant drawback. An empirical approach could have yielded more comprehensive results because of the integration of large-scale and cross-national empirical data. Secondly, the evolving nature of AI technologies implies that the literature reviewed is already limited and in flux. It is worth remembering that new tools, governance frameworks, and pedagogical implications emerge continuously (Gelashvili-Luik et al., 2025), which means that the present study's framework is static and requires frequent updates to remain relevant.

Although the study offers valuable insights into the challenges of implementing AI-based KM systems, it carries a potential techno-solutionist bias, as the appeal of AI can lead to overemphasizing technological fixes for inherently socio-cultural and pedagogical problems. The chapter mitigates this by foregrounding ethical and human-centric concerns, even as broader discourse often underestimates the difficulty of aligning technology with HEIs' core missions (Azmat & Mahmood, 2024). The recommended framework also presents limitations because AI-KM standards and ethical guidelines are rapidly evolving. As GenAI advances, any conceptual framework risks becoming outdated, since policies, tools, and strategies may require frequent reassessment. Issues such as algorithmic bias, data sovereignty, and cultural sensitivity demand deeper empirical investigation (Rezaei, 2025). Thus, while the study provides a comprehensive overview of the challenges of AI-based KM implementation, it also identifies numerous avenues for future research.

FUTURE RESEARCH DIRECTIONS

The future of AI-enabled knowledge management (KM) in transnational higher education (TNE) will be shaped by rapid advances in artificial intelligence, evolving governance frameworks, and increasing cultural and regulatory complexity across global campuses. As reviewers highlighted, emerging technologies particularly next-generation large language models (LLMs), multimodal learning systems, intelligent agents, and semantic knowledge graphs, will redefine how knowledge is created, accessed, and validated within international learning ecosystems.

Generative AI (GenAI) and LLMs will continue expanding students' and educators' ability to engage with complex knowledge through natural language interfaces. Rezaei (2025) notes that these models increase accessibility and adaptability, and future iterations will likely incorporate institutional context, disciplinary norms, and multilingual capabilities. However, their growing role raises epistemic and ethical questions regarding bias, transparency, and the integrity of academic decision-making (Bala et al., 2024). Explainable AI (XAI) will therefore remain essential to maintaining accountability in AI-driven KM processes (Kai et al., 2024).

Multimodal AI systems represent a significant future direction, integrating text, audio, video, and sensor data to create immersive and adaptive learning environments. Early initiatives such as NTU's smart learning spaces (Das et al., 2025) show how AI-powered environments can personalize learning and optimize resource use. Future systems may offer real-time analytics, emotion-aware feedback, and intelligent simulation-based assessments, though these advancements will require strong governance of biometric and behavioural data.

Semantic knowledge graphs and intelligent agents are also poised to enhance research and knowledge discovery. Tools deployed at the University of Melbourne (2024) demonstrate how automated literature mapping and collaborative recommendation systems accelerate global research partnerships. Looking ahead, intelligent agents may autonomously curate course resources or propose interdisciplinary connections; however, institutions must ensure that automated curation does not narrow inquiry or embed hidden biases.

Predictive analytics exemplified by OU Analyse and the Student Probability Model (UK Open University, 2021; Herodotou et al., 2019) will also grow more advanced by integrating contextual and behavioural data to anticipate student needs. While such systems can reduce attrition and support early interventions, TNE institutions must manage privacy, sensitive data, and the risk of unequal algorithmic impacts across culturally diverse student groups (Cardona et al., 2023).

Institutionally, the sustainability of future AI-KM ecosystems depends on globally interoperable digital infrastructures, harmonized governance standards, and ongoing capacity building. Gelashvili-Luik et al. (2025) emphasize that scalable KM requires shared data standards, seamless system integration, and flexible governance structures capable of addressing multi-jurisdictional regulatory demands. As AI capabilities advance, HEIs must maintain human oversight, incorporate human-in-the-loop mechanisms (Rezaei, 2025), and cultivate AI literacy to preserve academic agency and cultural diversity.

CONCLUSION

The integration of artificial intelligence (AI) into knowledge management (KM) represents a transformative shift for transnational higher education (TNE), where institutions must coordinate knowledge flows across geographically distributed campuses, heterogeneous regulatory systems, and culturally diverse learning environments. This chapter has demonstrated that AI-enabled KM offers significant potential to strengthen institutional coherence, enhance pedagogical innovation, and support robust decision-making by enabling real-time knowledge discovery, personalization, multilingual access, and predictive analytics. At the same time, the analysis has shown that successful AI-KM integration depends on more than technological capability: it requires alignment with organizational culture, governance mechanisms, human expertise, and ethical norms.

The conceptual synthesis and six case studies reveal that the benefits of AI-KM emerge most clearly in institutions with mature digital infrastructures, strong governance cultures, and high levels of human capacity. Institutions such as NTU, ASU, the University of Melbourne, and the UK Open University illustrate how AI tools can enhance knowledge creation, support student learning, and enable evidence-informed decision-making. Conversely, institutions operating in more resource-constrained or digitally heterogeneous environments such as EUDE or emerging Sino-foreign partnerships, encounter challenges related to data quality, interoperability, governance asymmetries, and the need for culturally sensitive AI tuning. These comparative insights reinforce that AI-KM integration in TNE is neither uniform nor linear; rather, it is shaped by path dependency, institutional readiness, and multi-jurisdictional regulatory conditions.

A central contribution of this chapter is the Strategic AI-KM Integration Model (AI-KMIM), which synthesizes socio-technical theory, the SECI model, the 5F-Model, and innovation diffusion theory into a unified framework. The five pillars: technological infrastructure, governance and policy alignment, capacity building, ethical and responsible AI use, and monitoring and evaluation, offer a structured pathway for institutions seeking to operationalise AI-KM systems in complex TNE ecosystems. Importantly, as clarified in the revised text, the AI-KMIM is a conceptual framework rather than an empirically validated model. Its purpose is to guide strategic orientation, highlight necessary implementation conditions, and provide a foundation for future empirical testing across diverse institutional contexts.

Equally significant is the recognition that AI's role in KM should be viewed through the lens of augmentation rather than automation. While AI enables efficiencies in knowledge retrieval, translation, analytics, and administrative processes, the chapter has emphasized that human judgment, academic agency, and tacit knowledge remain indispensable. Embedding human-in-the-loop (HITL) oversight, ensuring algorithmic transparency, and protecting epistemic diversity are essential safeguards to avoid overreliance on automated outputs, an issue particularly salient in TNE environments where cultural, linguistic, and epistemological perspectives vary widely.

Ethical considerations emerged as a central theme in the analysis. Cross-border variations in privacy laws, data protection, and governance norms complicate AI-KM implementation and heighten risks related to bias, fairness, accountability, and the integrity of academic decision-making. The expanded ethical discussion underscores the need for harmonized standards, transparent oversight, and routine auditing to ensure that AI-enabled KM systems uphold institutional values, academic integrity, and student rights across jurisdictions.

The chapter also shows that students and not only institutions benefit significantly from AI-enabled KM systems. AI-driven personalization, collaborative learning support, multilingual access, and virtual assistants enhance engagement, knowledge application, and academic performance. Yet these gains require careful design to prevent narrowed intellectual exposure or the reinforcement of algorithmic inequities.

Overall, AI-enabled KM presents substantial opportunities for TNE institutions, but successful implementation requires a balanced, multidimensional approach that integrates technological, human, cultural, and governance considerations. The conceptual framework offers strategic guidance for leaders, policymakers, and educators aiming to leverage AI to strengthen knowledge ecosystems while safeguarding ethical and pedagogical integrity. As AI technologies, regulations, and learning expectations evolve, future research should empirically validate the AI-KMIM, explore cross-cultural dimensions of AI adoption, and develop sustainable governance models that support equitable, responsible, and culturally attuned AI-KM integration across transnational higher education systems.

REFERENCES

Ajani, O., Akintolu, M., & Afolabi, S. O. (2024). The emergence of artificial intelligence in the higher education. *International Journal of Research in Business and Social Science (2147-4478), 13*(8), 157–165. https://doi.org/DOI: 10.20525/ijrbs.v13i8.3507

Amazon Web Services. (2025, September 10). *NTU Video Case - Empowering Student Learning with Responsible AI Skills*. Amazon Web Services, Inc. https://aws.amazon.com/solutions/case-studies/generative-ai-ntu/

Asiedu, N. K., Abah, M., & Dei, D.-G. J. (2022). Understanding knowledge management strategies in institutions of higher learning and the corporate world: A systematic review. *Cogent Business & Management, 9*(1), 2108218. Advance online publication. DOI: 10.1080/23311975.2022.2108218

Azmat, M., & Mahmood, M. (2024). Integrating Artificial Intelligence in Education: Opportunities and Challenges. *Bulletin of Education and Research, 46*(3), 23–41. https://files.eric.ed.gov/fulltext/EJ1477863.pdf

Bala, S., Pooja, R., & Rani, N. (2024). Challenges in implementing artificial intelligence in knowledge management processes. *International Journal of Research in Management, 6*(1), 64–68. DOI: 10.33545/26648792.2024.v6.i1a.127

Blair-Walcott, K. (2023). Comparative Analysis. In *Varieties of Qualitative Research Methods* (pp. 79–84). https://doi.org/DOI: 10.1007/978-3-031-04394-9_13

Bratianu, C., & Ioan, A. (2025). Challenges of Artificial Intelligence for Knowledge Management Systems: A Bibliometric Analysis Perspective. *Oradea Journal of Business and Economics, 10*(1), 108–120. DOI: 10.47535/1991ojbe209

Cardno, C. (2018). Policy Document Analysis: A Practical Educational Leadership Tool and a Qualitative Research Method. *Educational Administration: Theory and Practice, 24*(4). Advance online publication. DOI: 10.14527/kuey.2018.016

Cardona, M., Rodríguez, R., & Ishmael, K. (2023). *Artificial Intelligence and the Future of Teaching and Learning Insights and Recommendations*. Office of Educational Technology. https://www.ed.gov/sites/ed/files/documents/ai-report/ai-report.pdf

Contrino, M. F., Reyes-Millán, M., Vázquez-Villegas, P., & Membrillo-Hernández, J. (2024). Using an adaptive learning tool to improve student performance and satisfaction in online and face-to-face education for a more personalized approach. *Smart Learning Environments, 11*(1), 6. Advance online publication. DOI: 10.1186/s40561-024-00292-y

Das, D., Lim, N. D., & Aravind, P. (2022). Developing a Smart and Sustainable Campus in Singapore. *Sustainability (Basel), 14*(21), 14472. DOI: 10.3390/su142114472

Dismore, H., Campbell-Barr, V., Manning, R., & Warwick, P. (2024). A relational approach to knowledge exchange in higher education. *Studies in Higher Education (Dorchester-On-Thames), 49*(12), 1–12. https://doi.org/DOI: 10.1080/03075079.2024.2312404

Gelashvili-Luik, T., Vihma, P., & Pappel, I. (2025). Navigating the AI revolution: Challenges and opportunities for integrating emerging technologies into knowledge management systems. Systematic literature review. *Frontiers in Artificial Intelligence*, *8*, 1595930. Advance online publication. DOI: 10.3389/frai.2025.1595930

He, X., & Burger-Helmchen, T. (2024). Evolving Knowledge Management: Artificial Intelligence and the Dynamics of Social Interactions. *IEEE Engineering Management Review*, •••, 1–30. DOI: 10.1109/EMR.2024.3519342

Herodotou, C., Rienties, B., Verdin, B., & Boroowa, A. (2019). Predictive Learning Analytics "At Scale": Towards Guidelines to Successful Implementation in Higher Education Based on the Case of the Open University UK. *Journal of Learning Analytics*, *6*(1), 85–95. DOI: 10.18608/jla.2019.61.5

IBM. (2024, May 14). *European School of Management and Business (EUDE) | IBM*. Ibm.com. https://www.ibm.com/case-studies/eude

Jaakkola, E. (2020). Designing conceptual articles: Four approaches. *AMS Review*, *10*(1-2), 18–26. DOI: 10.1007/s13162-020-00161-0

Kai, G., Purba, C. A., Syaifuddin, I., & Fadhl Al-Hosaini, F. (2024). Critically Reviewing the Integration of Knowledge Management (KM) and Artificial Intelligence (AI): Future Trends and Implications. *SSRN*. Advance online publication. DOI: 10.2139/ssrn.4857763

Kovari, A. (2025). A systematic review of AI-powered collaborative learning in higher education: Trends and outcomes from the last decade. *Social Sciences & Humanities Open*, *11*(1), 101335. DOI: 10.1016/j.ssaho.2025.101335

Latif, Y., Harrison, N., Chu, H.-E., Malik, A., & Nguyen, M. (2024). Unleashing cultural diversity knowledge for improved knowledge sharing and integration: An in-depth qualitative analysis. *Journal of Knowledge Management*, *29*(1), 1–24. DOI: 10.1108/JKM-08-2023-0755

Leander, S. K. (2019, August 20). *ASU develops world's first adaptive-learning biology degree | ASU News*. News.asu.edu. https://news.asu.edu/20190820-solutions-asu-develops-world-first-adaptive-learning-biology-degree

Leoni, L., Gueli, G., Ardolino, M., Panizzon, M., & Gupta, S. (2024). AI-empowered KM processes for decision-making: Empirical evidence from worldwide organisations. *Journal of Knowledge Management*, *28*(11), 320–347. DOI: 10.1108/JKM-03-2024-0262

López-Meza, E., Terán-Bustamante, A., & Leyva-Hernández, S. N. (2024). SECI model of knowledge management: A thematic analysis with emphasis on agricultural organizations. *Iberoamerican Journal of Science Measurement and Communication*, *4*(2), 1–10. DOI: 10.47909/ijsmc.133

Luo, J., Zheng, C., Yin, J., & Teo, H. H. (2025). Design and assessment of AI-based learning tools in higher education: A systematic review. *International Journal of Educational Technology in Higher Education*, *22*(1), 42. Advance online publication. DOI: 10.1186/s41239-025-00540-2

Masic, B., Nesic, S., Nikolic, D., & Dzeletovic, M. (2017). Evolution of knowledge management. *Industry*, *45*(2), 127–147. DOI: 10.5937/industrija45-13201

Pai, R. Y., Shetty, A., Shetty, A. D., Bhandary, R., Shetty, J., Nayak, S., Dinesh, T. K., & D'souza, K. J. (2022). Integrating artificial intelligence for knowledge management systems – synergy among people and technology: A systematic review of the evidence. *Ekonomska Istrazivanja, 35*(1), 1–23. DOI: 10.1080/1331677X.2022.2058976

Rezaei, M. (2025). Artificial intelligence in knowledge management: Identifying and addressing the key implementation challenges. *Technological Forecasting and Social Change, 217*, 124183. DOI: 10.1016/j.techfore.2025.124183

Schmidt, D. A., Alboloushi, B., Thomas, A., & Magalhaes, R. (2025). Integrating artificial intelligence in higher education: Perceptions, challenges, and strategies for academic innovation. *Computers and Education Open, 9*, 100274. DOI: 10.1016/j.caeo.2025.100274

Syihabuddin, M., Suraj, N. A., Hyldgaard, S. E., & Kainth, N. (2025). Mini Review on Knowledge Management in Higher Education Challenges and Strategies for Effective Implementation. *Socio-Economic and Humanistic Aspects for Township and Industry, 3*(1), 199–206. DOI: 10.59535/sehati.v3i1.466

Taherdoost, H., & Madanchian, M. (2023). Artificial Intelligence and Knowledge Management: Impacts, Benefits, and Implementation. *Computers, 12*(4), 72. MDPI. https://doi.org/DOI: 10.3390/computers12040072

Tariq, M. U., & Abonamah, A. A. (2021). Proposed Strategic Framework for Effective Artificial Intelligence Adoption in UAE. *Academy of Strategic Management Journal, 20*(Special Issue 2), 1–14. https://www.abacademies.org/articles/proposed-strategic-framework-for-effective-artificial-intelligence-adoption-in-uae.pdf

UK Open University. (2021). *OU Analyse | Knowledge Media Institute | The Open University*. Open.ac.uk. https://analyse.kmi.open.ac.uk/

University of Melbourne. (2024, July 26). *AI learning assistant*. Learning Management System. https://lms.unimelb.edu.au/learning-technologies/ai-learning-assistant

Vieriu, A. M., & Petrea, G. (2025). The Impact of Artificial Intelligence (AI) on Students' Academic Development. *Education Sciences, 15*(3), 343. DOI: 10.3390/educsci15030343

Zhang, W., Li, A. W., & Wu, C. (2025). University students' perceptions of using generative AI in translation practices. *Instructional Science, 53*(4), 633–655. Advance online publication. DOI: 10.1007/s11251-025-09705-y

Chapter 17
Generative AI and Large Language Models in Transnational and Higher Education:
Pedagogical Promise, Governance, and Policy Challenges

Sanyogita Singh
Panjab University, India

Vikram Singh
https://orcid.org/0000-0001-5757-9111
Ch. Devi Lal University, Sirsa, India

ABSTRACT

Generative artificial intelligence (GenAI) and large language models (LLMs) are transforming teaching, learning, and institutional management in higher education (HE) and transnational higher education (TNE). Current discourse extends beyond innovation and academic integrity to epistemological, ethical, and regulatory aspects. The chapter examines LLMs' role in democratizing access while disrupting academic hierarchies, addressing quality assurance and cross-jurisdictional integrity policies. LLMs provide adaptive feedback and multilingual support for learning frameworks, though these advantages risk increasing inequities without proper policies. HE/TNE management must balance evaluation needs with data privacy across regions. Using the OpenAI - IIT Madras case study, the chapter proposes a governance framework for responsible GenAI implementation promoting academic trust and ethical AI use in international higher education.

1. INTRODUCTION

In several sectors, generative AI models have a profound positive impact. The cornerstone of higher education could be completely changed as a result of this convergence, as could learning environments

DOI: 10.4018/979-8-3373-5403-3.ch017

and instructional methods. Generating new data that are similar to previously existing data is the aim of the artificial intelligence subset known as "generative AI." Deep learning systems produce content in the form of text, images, and music. To understand and replicate human language patterns, language models are fundamental to generating AI. More recently, as demonstrated by models such as the generative pretrained transformer (GPT) and its children, deep learning algorithms have demonstrated an unrivalled capacity for building language that mimics human speech and comprehends complex linguistic patterns. This chapter explores the potential effects of generative AI on tertiary education. This article aims to clarify the theoretical underpinnings and practical uses of these models in addition to demonstrating how they are revolutionising student interaction, content creation, teaching approaches, and personalised learning experiences. The use of generative AI in academia is also covered in this chapter, along with its difficulties, roadblocks, and ethical issues.

1.1 Large Language Models

A subset of artificial intelligence models called "large language models" aims to understand, produce, and modify human languages. Deep learning techniques are routinely used to build these models. LLMs are typically trained on substantial datasets to learn the statistical patterns, grammar, and semantics of language. As a result, they can write text that resembles human writing, translate between languages, answer questions, and perform a range of other activities involving natural language processing (Brown et al., 2020). The self-attention mechanism is the main component of the transformer architecture, in which LLMs such as OpenAI's generative pretrained transformer 3 (GPT3) are built upon. The next section provides an overview of the mathematics underlying the Transformer's self-attention mechanism, which is an essential component of large language modelling.

Generative AI, including LLM, is mathematically based on deep learning mechanics and probabilistic modelling. The probability distribution across word sequences is a fundamental concept in language modelling. For example, if a sequence of words $W = w_1, w_2, \ldots, w_t$ is given in a language, the language model estimates the probability of occurrence of the entire sequence $P(W)$, as (*i*) below:

$$P(W) = P(w_1)P(w_2|w_1)\ldots P(w_t|w_1, w_2, \ldots, w_{t-1}) \text{ (i)}$$

where:

- $P(w_1)$ is the given probability of occurrence of word w_1 in word sequence W.
- where $P(w_2|w_1)$ is the conditional probability of w_2,, which represents the probability of the occurrence of word w_2 in word sequence W, given that $w_1$occurs in word sequence W.
- $P(w_t|w_1, w_2, \ldots, w_{t-1})$ is the conditional probability of w_t, given that the words $w_1, w_2, \ldots, w_{t-1}$ occur in word sequence W.

In the transformer architecture, understanding the likelihood of a specific word sequence in language formation necessitates grasping prior and posterior probabilities (Bengio et al., 2003). The GPT model, a prominent large language model by OpenAI, employs this architecture, which integrates feedforward neural networks and self-attentional processes (Vaswani et al., 2017). In accordance with Vaswani et al. (2017), the architecture calculates each word's output as a weighted sum of its embeddings across the input sequence to evaluate self-attention. The weights are determined via a learned attention function.

This approach, which is foundational for modern language models, is pivotal in recognising dependencies within the input sequence.

Self-attention mechanism: The self-attention mechanism forms the core of the transformer architecture. Given an input sequence of embeddings $X = x_1, x_2, \ldots, x_n$ where x_i represents the embedding of the ith word, self-attention computes new representations $Z = z_1, z_2, \ldots, z_n$ as a weighted sum of the input embeddings (Vaswani et al., 2017):

$$z_i = \sum_{j=1}^{n} \left((e^{S_{i,j}}) / \sum_{k=1}^{n} (e^{S_{i,k}}) \right) x_j \text{ (ii)}$$

Here, $e^{S_{i,j}}$ represents the attention score that measures the compatibility between the embeddings of words i and j. It is computed via a scoring function, often the dot product, followed by scaling: $s_{i,j} = \frac{1}{\sqrt{d_k}} x_i . x_j$, where d_k is the dimension of the key vectors.

Multihead attention: "Heads" or parallel attention mechanisms operating in parallel are the basis of multihead attention in the transformer architecture. Different weighted combinations of the input information are learned by each head. After these heads have processed the input, their outputs are concatenated and linearly transformed via W_O to produce the final output of the multihead attention mechanism (eq. *iii*).

The linear transformation by W_O ensures that the combined information from different heads is suitably aggregated and transformed to match the required output dimensions for further processing in the neural network (Vaswani et al., 2017).

$$MultiHead(Q, K, V) = Concat(head_1, \ldots, head_h)\, W_O \text{ (iii)}$$

where:

- $head_i$= Attention$\left(Q . W_{Qi}, K . W_{Ki}, V . W_{Vi}\right)$,
- W_{Qi} is learned weight matrix for the query,
- W_{Ki} is learned weight matrix for the key,
- W_{Vi} is learned weight matrix for the value projections,
- *Concat* represents concatenation, and
- where W_O is a parameter matrix (weight matrix) used to combine the outputs of the individual attention heads in multihead attention and produce the final output for further processing.

Positional encoding: Transformer-based models are not complete without positional encoders, which compensate for the inherent lack of order or position information of the sequences. Positional encoders assist in adding the sequence's elemental order to the model, as transformers do not naturally comprehend it. Positional encodings are appended to the input embeddings in the original transformer design before they are fed into the model. These encodings are vectors that provide data regarding the placement or arrangement of words within a sentence. These encodings are used by the transformer in conjunction with the embeddings to comprehend the input's sequential order (Vaswani et al., 2017). One popular method for creating positional encodings is to use sine and cosine functions (eqns. iv and v), which have distinct frequencies:

$$PE_{(pos,\,2i)} = \sin\frac{pos}{10000^{2i/d_{model}}} \text{ (iv)}$$

$$PE_{(pos,\,2i+1)} = \cos\frac{pos}{10000^{2i/d_{model}}} \text{ (v)}$$

where:

- pos is the position,
- i is the dimension, and
- d_{model} is the dimensionality of the model.

The model can discriminate between the positions owing to these sinusoidal positional encodings, which guarantees that each dimension in the embedding space has a distinct pattern for each position. When producing predictions, the model learns to consider both the position (positional encoding) and the content (embedding). This is important for jobs where word order counts, such as translation.

2. TECHNIQUES UNDER GENERATIVE AI UMBRELLA

Generative AI models rely on several other mathematical techniques and principles in addition to LLM. The underlying mathematics of many generative AI techniques are covered in this section:

Probability theory: Probability distributions, such as Bernoulli or Gaussian (normal) distributions, are frequently used by generative AI models to model and produce data. These distributions are used to model the likelihood of data and are essential for producing diverse and realistic outcomes. The probability density function (PDF) for a Gaussian distribution is (vi):

$$f\left(x\middle|\mu,\sigma\right) = \frac{1}{\sqrt{2\pi\sigma^2}}e^{\frac{-(x-\mu)^2}{2\sigma^2}} \text{ (vi)}$$

where:

- x represents the variable for which the PDF is being calculated,
- μ is the mean of the distribution, and
- where σ is the standard deviation of the distribution.

This formula represents the likelihood of the variable x occurring in a Gaussian distribution characterised by the mean μ and standard deviation σ. For example, if one wants to calculate the likelihood (PDF) of a specific value x given a mean μ and standard deviation σ via this formula, one can substitute the values into the formula to obtain the result.

Additionally, generative models frequently leverage Bayesian inference, a statistical approach that calculates probabilities on the basis of prior knowledge and new evidence. Bayesian methods are used in probabilistic programming and generative models such as Bayesian networks (Ross, 2014). Bayes' theorem defines the posterior probability $P(\theta \mid D)$ of parameters θ given data D as (*vii*) below:

$$P(\theta D) = \frac{P(D\theta).\,P(\theta)}{P(D)} \left(vii\right)$$

where:

- $P(\theta D)$ is the posterior probability of the parameter θ given the observed data D,
- $P(D\theta)$ is the likelihood of the data given the parameter θ,
- $P(\theta)$ is the prior probability of the parameter θ, representing our belief about θ before considering the data, and
- where $P(D)$ is the marginal likelihood or evidence, which represents the overall probability of the data.

In practice, Bayes' theorem allows us to update our belief (the prior) about a parameter θ on the basis of the observed data D by considering how likely the data are given θ (the likelihood) and how likely θ is in the absence of the data (the prior).

Linear algebra: The mathematical foundation for many facets of machine learning is provided by linear algebra, which is employed in the field of generative artificial intelligence. Basic notations such as matrices, vectors, and sets are widely used in this framework to represent and work with data in an organised way. Matrices, for example, are frequently utilised in many machine learning models and have become crucial for representing complex correlations between many variables. Using notations such as feature vectors and feature sets in the context of datasets allows for a condensed and effective data representation. Feature vectors simplify the processing and analysis of data by concisely capturing the relevant features of each data item. For tasks where comprehending the properties of the data is essential, such as classification, regression, and grouping, this representation is essential.

Neural networks, crucial elements of generative artificial intelligence, are based on matrix operations in linear algebra. Matrix operations are widely used in neural networks, particularly in forward and backwards propagations during training. The network needs to compute these actions efficiently to learn and become more effective over time. Additionally, ideas such as eigenvalues and eigenvectors are relevant and useful in a range of linear algebraic processes. Eigenvalues and eigenvectors are used in principal component analysis (PCA) and other techniques for dimensionality reduction applications. We can dramatically lower the dimensionality of the data while keeping its key features by utilising these ideas. This dimensionality reduction preserves the essential information and makes further processing easier—a crucial feature for many generative AI applications.

In linear algebra, a matrix A is represented by $A = \left[a_{ij}\right]$, where a_{ij} denotes the element in the ith row and j^{th} column. Vectors are n x 1 matrices. For a square matrix A, the eigenvalues λ and eigenvectors v satisfy the relationship (*viii*) (Strang, 2006).

$$\mathrm{A}v = \lambda v \quad \text{(viii)}$$

Calculus: Derivatives in particular are crucial for training generative AI models. Through methods such as gradient descent, derivatives are used to optimise model parameters, allowing the model to produce outputs that are more precise and well rounded. Gradients are computed via partial derivatives, which serve as a roadmap for optimisation during model training. Gradients assist in adjusting model parameters to reduce the loss function. The derivative of a function $f(x)$ is represented by eqn. (*ix*) below:

$$f'(x) = lim_{h \to 0} \frac{f(x+h) - f(x)}{h} \quad \text{(ix)}$$

and the gradient of a function *f*, represented as a vector of its partial derivatives (eqn. *x*):

$$\nabla f = \frac{\partial f}{\partial x_1} + \frac{\partial f}{\partial x_2} + \ldots + \frac{\partial f}{\partial x_n} \text{ (x)}$$

are used to find the optimum values of regression coefficient(s) and intercepts in regression-based methods of machine learning (Stewart, 2015).

Information theory: Uncertainty and information content are measured via ideas from information theory, such as entropy, cross-entropy, information gain, and the Gini index. A dataset's entropy is a measurement of its level of uncertainty. Mathematically, the entropy of dataset *D* is given by (*xi*):

$$Entropy(D) = -\sum_{n=1}^{c} P_i \log_2 P_i \text{ (xi)}$$

where:

- *D* is the dataset,
- P_i is the proportion of instances belonging to class *i* in *D*, and
- *c* number of unique classes in *D*.

When every class is equally likely, the entropy is at its highest. As more cases are classified into fewer classes, it decreases and reaches a minimum for a "pure" dataset, which has all of its instances belonging to a single class. Entropy is used to compute information gain for feature selection in decision trees, a machine learning technique used in classification and regression issues, to advance decision trees to the next level. In the context of feature *A* and dataset *D*, the information gain Gain(*A*) is calculated as (*xii*) below:

$$\text{Gain}(A) = \text{Entropy}(D) - \sum_{v \in All\ values\ of\ A} \left(\frac{D_v}{\text{D}}\right) * \text{Entropy}\left(D_v\right) \text{ (xii)}$$

where:

- Entropy(*D*) is the entropy of dataset D,
- All values of A are the unique values of feature *A*,
- D_v is the subset of *D* for which feature *A* has value *v*.

The higher the information gain value of a feature is, the earlier it is used in the expansion of the decision tree.

Optimisation: A basic optimisation technique called gradient descent is used to iteratively change the model's parameters in the direction of the negative gradient to minimise the loss function. An improvement in gradient descent is achieved via stochastic gradient descent, which uses a random subset of the dataset for every iteration. Gradient descent is most frequently used in regression algorithm model parameter optimisation (Boyd and Vandenberghe, 2004). The model parameter θ is updated via eqn (*xiii*) below:

$$\theta_{new} = \theta_{old} - \alpha \nabla F(\theta) \text{ (xiii)}$$

where

- θ_{new} is the new value of the model parameter,
- θ_{old} is the old value of the model parameter,
- α is the learning rate, and
- $F(\theta)$ is the objective/error function to minimise.

A very low value of α will delay the convergence of the error function to a minimum, and keeping α on the higher side may skip the minimum value of the error function.

Statistics: A popular statistical technique, especially in generative models, is maximum likelihood estimation (MLE), which is used to ascertain the most likely parameters for a given model from observed data. The objective is to determine the values of the parameters that maximise the probability of observing the provided data, hence determining the probability distribution that best fits the data. In the context of a parametric model $P(X \mid \theta)$, where X represents the observed data and where θ denotes the model's parameters, MLE strives to estimate θ by maximising the likelihood function $L(\theta) = \prod P(X_i \mid \theta)$. This product is taken over all the data points X_i. The likelihood $L(\theta)$ essentially signifies the probability of observing the given data under the assumed model with the parameter θ. The idea behind MLE is to identify the values of the parameter θ that, given the selected model, maximise the probabilistic likelihood of the observed data. To choose the best-fitting model parameters for a variety of statistical and machine learning applications, this technique is essential for comprehending and measuring uncertainty in the data (Wasserman, 2013).

Graph theory: A graph is fundamentally made up of nodes, also known as vertices, and edges, which show the connections between the nodes. Graphs are essential for comprehending real-world phenomena because they are utilised in generative AI to model and generate data that have built-in structures and connections. Concepts from graph theory are crucial in many fields, including natural language processing and recommender systems. These ideas are used by graph-based generative models to produce data with desired characteristics. The ability to build and train successful generative AI models requires an understanding of and application of these mathematical ideas. A strong understanding of these mathematical foundations is essential for successful model building and deployment because generative AI has a wide range of applications, such as recommendation systems and the creation of images and texts.

Graphs are a common tool used by generative AI to represent complex data. For example, atoms and bonds can be represented as nodes and edges in the molecule formation process. It is possible to create molecular structures with the desired attributes via this graph-based approach. Graph-based generative models use traversal techniques such as breadth-first search and depth-first search. They aid in the creation of data with certain properties by making the examination of nodes and edges easier. Moreover, graph theory helps create data that are similar to real-world structures. In social network modelling, for example, nodes can stand in for individual people and edges for relationships. AI systems are capable of producing data that mimic real-world social networks by applying the concepts of graph theory. Graph theory is used by another AI construct known as knowledge graphs to express knowledge. Entities are represented by graph nodes, whereas relationships between entities are shown by graph edges. Comprehending and employing knowledge graphs is essential in generative AI to produce well-informed and contextually relevant data. In addition, recommendation systems make extensive use of principles from graph theory. AI models can improve the user experience by making item recommendations on the basis of user preferences and relationships via the analysis of user–item interactions as a graph.

3. GENERATIVE AI IN TERTIARY EDUCATION

The field of higher education could see a radical transformation owing to generative AI, especially in the LLM, which can create customised learning experiences, accelerate research, and create content. The section argues that these technologies should be incorporated into traditional research and instructional frameworks by highlighting the advantages that their use can offer researchers, students, and educators.

3.1 Individualised Learning

In postsecondary education, LLM enables the development of highly customised learning experiences. AI models can produce customised assignments, flexible curricular structures, and learning materials by analysing the unique learning styles and preferences of each student. Engagement, comprehension, and general academic achievement are all maximised by this customisation. Education is transforming owing to generative AI, especially in the areas of adaptive curriculum and personalised learning. They provide effective instruments for customising learning experiences for each student, improving comprehension, retention, and engagement. An examination of their uses in this situation is provided below, along with pertinent in-text citations and references:

Content customisation: According to Wang et al. (2015), generative AI and LLMs make it possible to create customised study guides, exercises, and quizzes depending on the learning styles and preferences of specific students. This increases the efficacy of the learning process by guaranteeing that the information corresponds with their present comprehension level and learning objectives.

Adaptive learning: AI systems are capable of analysing a student's learning history and behaviour to suggest adaptive learning pathways. These algorithms are employed in LLMs (Siemens, 2005). By tailoring the curriculum to each student's individual needs, this personalisation maximises understanding and minimises dissatisfaction.

Interactive learning: By simulating human-like dialogues, AI-powered interactive platforms built on LLMs allow students to participate in interactive learning activities (Devlin et al., 2019). By simulating real-world situations, these interactions improve comprehension and promote critical thinking.

Intelligent tutoring: Intelligent tutoring systems that offer pupils individualised tutoring can use generative AI (Vanlehn, 2011). These systems modify their approach on the basis of student replies, taking into account the learner's preferred learning style and speed.

Semantic search: According to Mikolov et al. (2013), LLMs can enhance semantic search skills, helping students obtain accurate and pertinent information more rapidly. This ultimately improves the learning process by assisting with research and helping students understand difficult subjects.

Adaptive assessments: AI-based adaptive tests that make use of LLMs can dynamically modify the questions' type and complexity in response to a student's performance, guaranteeing a more accurate assessment of the student's knowledge and abilities (Pennington et al., 2014). A personalised learning and adaptive curriculum can be made more efficient, interesting, and customised to meet the needs of each student by incorporating generative AI and LLMs into educational platforms and systems. To obtain the greatest results, it is necessary to strike a balance between the contribution of AI and the knowledge of human instructors.

3.2 Multilingual Academic Communication

The multilingual features of LLMs enable smooth communication and collaboration between academics and students around the world. AI models can translate academic content in real time, reducing language barriers and facilitating the interchange of different viewpoints and international cooperation. In particular, generative AI has been shown to be a potent instrument for revolutionising academic communication in multilingual settings. The lead generative AI model GPT-3 demonstrates impressive multilingual translation and adaptation skills for academic texts. Through facilitating seamless translation and preserving the contextual and stylistic characteristics inherent to each language, it effectively transcends language barriers and facilitates global academic collaboration (Smith et al., 2021). This guarantees that academic content is accurately communicated while preserving its original intent and meaning.

Beyond translation, generative AI technology dynamically creates educational resources in various languages, fostering accessibility and inclusion in the classroom. It takes into account the various linguistic preferences of scholars and students, fostering a more varied and international academic community (Goh et al., 2019). Furthermore, by accelerating the creation of content and the transmission of information in a world that is becoming more interconnected, this technology significantly influences the direction of multilingual education in the future. Generative AI improves comprehension and engagement through the personalised delivery of instructional information in learners' native languages, resulting in a more successful learning environment (Li et al., 2020).

Generative AI makes it easier for researchers with diverse linguistic backgrounds to communicate quickly and accurately in the context of academic research and information exchange. It encourages collaboration and cross-cultural contact, which permits a wider distribution of concepts and discoveries (Brown and Jones, 2018). Consequently, global intellectual conversation has become more meaningful and approachable. In terms of encouraging multilingual academic dialogue, removing language barriers, and creating a more welcoming and equal learning environment, generative AI is a paradigm shift.

Development of teaching-learning materials: In the field of educational technology, generative AI has become a potent instrument that has a significant influence on the development of teaching-learning materials in the postsecondary education industry. This essay explores the uses and consequences of using generative AI to create teaching-learning materials, which transform the creation, personalisation, and delivery of educational content to students.

Tailored content creation: According to Adams and Turner (2019), generative AI, particularly models such as the GPT-3, exhibits exceptional competence in quickly producing educational content tailored to a given subject matter. These models can provide comprehensive and cohesive resources that are in line with the curriculum and particular educational goals because they have been trained on enormous volumes of data. The method involves providing the AI with starter ideas or prompts, on which it can produce in-depth lecture notes, perceptive presentations, and educational study guides. This technique provides educators with an invaluable tool for improving their lesson plans.

Interactive and engaging resources: By producing dynamic and captivating content that captures students' interest and improves their learning experience, generative AI can improve teaching-learning materials (Liu et al., 2019). The learning process can be made more engaging and participatory by using AI to create content that includes interactive exercises, quizzes, simulations, and other types of interactive features. For example, the AI may design interactive tests embedded in study guides that allow students to assess their comprehension of the subject matter right away, encouraging engaged learning and memory retention.

Addressing diverse learning needs: The ability of generative AI to adapt teaching-learning materials to different learning styles and capacities is one of its noteworthy advantages (Joulin et al., 2016). AI ensures that teaching-learning materials are useful and accessible for a variety of learners, including those with varying competence levels or learning styles, by varying the depth and complexity of the created information. For example, AI can produce an explanation of the same concept at several degrees of complexity, guaranteeing that all students—from novices to experts—can understand the material.

Multilingual and global reach: Language barriers can be overcome, and instructional resources can be made available to a worldwide audience through the use of generative AI to help translate teaching-learning materials into many languages (Johnson et al., 2020). This characteristic broadens the scope of educational resources, enabling establishments to increase their impact and encourage learning outside of linguistic boundaries. This capacity is especially important in the global world because high-quality educational resources in students' home languages are accessible to students from a wide range of linguistic backgrounds.

Ethical considerations: However, there are significant ethical questions raised by the use of generative AI in the production of teaching and learning materials (Floridi et al., 2018). Even while technology has much promise, maintaining academic integrity requires that the material produced be real, accurate, and unique. Ensuring the generation of teaching-learning materials is crucial in maintaining the ethical standards of education. To reduce any unintentional biases that might appear in the created materials, it is also necessary to address worries about potential biases in the generated content and ensure that the AI models are trained on objective and diverse datasets.

Generative AI has brought about a paradigm shift in the production of teaching-learning materials in postsecondary education, providing unmatched chances to improve and vary instructional materials. However, to fully utilise modern technology while upholding moral and educational standards, a careful and responsible approach is necessary.

4. GENERATIVE AI FOR SCHOLARLY RESEARCH

LLM can be a valuable tool for academics and researchers in the field. AI models can aid with research question formulation, literature reviews, and even methodology suggestions on the basis of a large body of academic literature. The research process is accelerated by this computerised help, and the calibre of scholarly output is improved. Large language models and generative AI are essential components in the field of automated research assistance and knowledge generation. They transform the methods used to collect, evaluate, and synthesise data, improving the effectiveness and scope of research.

Data-driven research proposal: Creating defined, data-driven research objectives is crucial in the early phases of the study process. Large datasets can be analysed by generative AI, which can find correlations and patterns that human researchers miss. AI, for example, is capable of analysing large volumes of medical records to identify connections between certain behaviours and illnesses. The creation of hypotheses and research topics is aided by the patterns that have been identified. AI might, for example, identify a link between sedentary lifestyles and a rise in particular health problems, which would then direct researchers to design focused studies to investigate this association in more detail (Mehrabi et al., 2019).

Use in the literature review: Reviews of the literature are essential for comprehending the state of the field. Both generative AI and LLMs are adept at quickly examining a large body of scholarly literature.

They can understand and summarise material, emphasising key ideas and removing unnecessary details. This helps scientists understand the state of the art in their discipline, identify gaps in knowledge, and adjust their study accordingly. To help researchers contextualise their study in the continuing discourse on sustainable energy, an AI-powered review, for example, might highlight recent developments in renewable energy technologies (Mehrabi et al., 2019).

Data synthesis and summarisation: A significant advantage of LLMs is their capacity for data synthesis and summarisation. These models are capable of sifting through a lengthy report, picking out the most important details, and providing a succinct summary. This is helpful for researchers, who frequently have too much information. For example, AI can evaluate a large number of climate reports and condense them into important conclusions regarding the influence of greenhouse gases, assisting researchers in making decisions (Liu et al., 2019a).

Building knowledge bases: One application of generative AI is the creation of extensive knowledge bases. AI can build centralised knowledge libraries by gathering data from reliable, diverse sources and summarising them. These databases may cover anything from historical events to medical disorders. A knowledge base covering different programming languages, for example, may aggregate data on syntax, popular use cases, and noteworthy libraries, providing developers with a one-stop shop (Yang et al., 2018).

Handling citations and references: Managing citations and references is a laborious process in which AI, including LLMs, can make this process easier. AI systems are capable of producing precise citations in several citation formats, including APA, MLA, and Chicago. They can also oversee a researcher's reference collection, ensuring that every source in a research paper is properly referenced. As a result, creating citations and maintaining references requires much less human labor, thus increasing the effectiveness of the research process (Afridi et al., 2018).

Documentation and paper writing: Researchers can write more easily thanks, in large part, to generative AI. These AI models can help create material depending on the researcher's input and offer an organised framework for academic publications. The AI may elaborate on a researcher's bullet points or framework for a scientific paper, for example, and provide well-organised paragraphs and sections. According to Sutskever et al. (2011), this accelerates the writing process without sacrificing adherence to academic standards or the document's logical flow of material.

Semantic search: LLMs enhance semantic search capabilities by understanding the context and intent of a search query. Unlike traditional keyword-based search, semantic search makes an effort to interpret the query. In the context of medical research, for example, if a researcher searches for "heart function," an LLM-powered search may also return results of "cardiac performance," offering a more thorough and contextually appropriate set of results. This greatly improves search efficacy and efficiency, especially for scholarly research (Mikolov et al., 2013).

By integrating generative AI into automated research support systems, scholars can streamline their processes, concentrate on more complex assignments, and quickly produce excellent results. Nonetheless, throughout the research process, it is crucial to strike a balance between the functions of AI and human expertise and critical thinking.

5. ISSUES IN GENERATIVE AI

Through the creation of educational resources, the facilitation of individualised learning experiences, and support for research activities, generative AI and large language models (LLMs) present intriguing opportunities for revolutionising postsecondary education. However, several significant obstacles come with this integration.

5.1 Technical Issues

Content quality: Making sure that AI-generated material is accurate and of high quality is one of the main challenges. According to Pennington et al. (2014), generative AI models may yield outputs that are factually inaccurate, inconsistent, or not aligned with learning goals. Upholding rigorous criteria for precision and pertinence is important to furnish invaluable pedagogical materials.

Insufficient control over results: One major problem is keeping control over the particular outputs that AI generates. Teachers frequently need to be able to modify content to meet curriculum standards and particular learning objectives. It is a constant struggle to achieve this degree of personalisation with AI-generated content (Diakopoulos, 2016).

Privacy and data security: A large amount of data must be gathered and used to include AI in educational platforms. It is imperative to guarantee the confidentiality and integrity of these data, particularly when handling student records and sensitive educational data (Shokri et al., 2017). Tighter security protocols are required to stop unwanted access and abuse.

Explainability and transparency: AI systems should be built with the ability to explain their results and be transparent in their design. Building trust requires an understanding of how AI makes decisions (Doshi-Velez and Kim, 2017).

Assurance of quality and validation: It is critical to preserve the authenticity and caliber of the instructional content produced by AI. It is possible to ensure that the content complies with educational standards and does not spread false information or inaccuracies by putting in place verification procedures and carrying out frequent audits (Liu et al., 2019b).

5.2 Ethical Issues

The use of content produced by AI presents ethical questions about authorship, plagiarism, and academic integrity. Establishing moral limits and encouraging the appropriate use of content produced by AI are essential (Bender et al., 2021). To handle these ethical issues properly, the right rules and regulations must be put in place. LLMs and generative AI in higher education provide a variety of ethical challenges that call for careful analysis. The ethical ramifications are as follows:

Unintentional bias: Large volumes of data that are readily available online can unintentionally inject biases into the data from which LLMs learn (Jobin et al., 2019). Since biased content can reinforce stereotypes or misrepresent a variety of viewpoints, it is important to address bias and ensure fairness in AI-generated content. This is because biased content can undermine the inclusive character of education. (Bender et al., 2021).

Accuracy: It is critical to preserve the accuracy of the information produced. According to Mitchell et al. (2019), the content produced by AI should respect academic or professional norms and be factually accurate and credible.

Accountability and transparency: It is critical to be transparent about how AI is used to create content. When AI is engaged, users should be informed so that they can assess the reliability and source of the information critically (Floridi et al., 2018).

Privacy and consent: It is critical to protect privacy and obtain the right permission before using data to create content. To safeguard people's privacy, ethical standards and data privacy legislation should be adhered to (Diakopoulos, 2016).

Authorship: It is critical to identify the author and recognise AI's contribution to content creation. To acknowledge AI values and safeguard intellectual property rights, ethical standards should be put in place (Bender et al., 2021).

Human monitoring: It is imperative to preserve a certain degree of human supervision and involvement. AI-generated material should be supervised, validated, and guided by humans to ensure that it complies with moral guidelines (Floridi et al., 2018).

Academic integrity: In addition to undermining academic integrity, AI should be used to strengthen it. It is critical to guarantee that the information produced by AI adheres to academic norms and values (Diakopoulos, 2016).

Long-term social impact: It is crucial to consider the wider social ramifications of utilising AI to support research. To foresee and handle such effects on society, ethical foresight is needed (Floridi et al., 2018).

5.3 Legal Issues

Legal issues with generative AI span privacy, accountability, bias, and intellectual property rights. The content produced by AI increases ownership and copyright concerns. Owing to AI's ability to recreate personal data, privacy breaches are likely. Training data that are biased can support discrimination. To lessen these legal issues, clear rules and guidelines are essential.

Intellectual property rights: Intellectual property rights in the context of generative AI include concerns with ownership, patents, and copyrights. It might be challenging to establish who owns inventions and other content generated by AI. It is debatable whether the AI, the user, or the developer owns the output. Determining inventorship and innovative steps can be challenging with AI-generated innovation patents. How AI-generated works are credited and protected is affected by copyright issues regarding originality and authorship. To address these intricate IPR challenges in the context of generative AI, legal frameworks must be changed (Friedman, 2021).

Liability and accountability: Liability and accountability in generative AI refer to the challenges in identifying who is accountable for the actions taken by the AI. Fault placement may be challenging when AI systems produce inaccurate or biased results. There are no detailed frameworks defining legal responsibility. Who should be held accountable—the AI system itself, the user, or the creator—raises questions. The dynamic nature of AI technologies makes implementing liability standards more difficult. These issues need to be resolved to ensure a fair and appropriate legal framework for the use of generative AI. According to Rahwan et al. (2019), determining responsibility in circumstances where AI-generated material causes injury is a significant legal difficulty. As a result, legal frameworks must develop accountability structures. Academics, educators, and legislators will make coordinated efforts to address these issues. To overcome these obstacles and realise the full potential of generative AI and LLMs in higher education, collaborative initiatives, multidisciplinary research, and the creation of thorough standards are needed.

6. PROMPT ENGINEERING

Although prompt engineering is a subject that could have been included in technical difficulties, it has its own subsection owing to its importance. Writing effective orders or instructions, or "prompts," to drive language models, such as GPT, to produce responses that correlate with certain tasks is the practice of prompt engineering, a branch of artificial intelligence and natural language processing. It comprises creating cues on purpose to obtain a model to provide more targeted outcomes (Shin, et al., 2021). To create prompts of the highest calibre, it is vital to understand the advantages and disadvantages of the underlying model. To improve the model's response, it is frequently necessary to experiment with different prompt formulations and strategies. Prompts come in a variety of formats, including:

6.1 Contextualising the LLM Response

The model is given more context to help it understand the particular task or subject matter, ensuring that the generated solutions are pertinent and on-topic. Below are some examples of prompts both with and without context:

"Write a story about an astronaut exploring a distant planet." is the prompt, without any context, whereas the contextualised prompt is "You are an astronaut on board the spacecraft 'Stellar Explorer.' In the Andromeda galaxy, you have just set foot on a hitherto unexplored planet. Tell us about your initial contact with the extraterrestrial beings that live in this enigmatic world."

GPT may use its pretrained knowledge to create a story in response to the prompt without context; this story may or may not fit the creative space adventure you have in mind. The user instructs the GPT to create a narrative that focuses on the astronaut's meeting with extraterrestrial life on a far-off planet by providing contextual facts. Context establishes the story's setting and guarantees that the generated tale adheres to the chosen subject.

Clarity and specificity

Provide a precise and unambiguous prompt. Make it clear what you want the model to produce, do, or respond to. Ambiguity may cause inadvertent or unnecessary reactions.

Unclear prompt: "Tell me about it."

Clear and specific prompt: "Write a brief story about a young artist discovering their talent for sculpting."

Tone and language

Make sure your prompt is written and spoken in a way that helps the model produce a response that fits your desired formality, style, or mood. A courteous prompt will probably elicit a thoughtful and polite response from the model, adhering to formal language and manners. On the other hand, if the suggestion is rude or informal, the model might speak in an informal or even aggressive manner and use derogatory words.

Inappropriate tone: "Translate this, ASAP."

Appropriate tone: "Please translate the following passage into Spanish at your earliest convenience."

Length and structure

Play around with the prompt's length and format. A simple, direct prompt is ideal in certain situations, but more complex, multipart prompts may be required in others. The prompt duration should be determined by the needs of the user.

Short prompt: "Write a poem."

The prompt "Compose a heartfelt poem describing the beauty of nature, emphasising the changing seasons and the tranquillity of a forest."

6.2 Prompt Engineering

Prompt engineering strategies, such as temperature sampling, temperature modification, or system messages, are used to direct the model's inventiveness and behavior. The user can regulate the degree of inventiveness and ambiguity in the generated responses by varying the "temperature." The outputs are more conservative and predictable at lower temperatures but more diverse and startling at higher temperatures. The temperature varies from 0.0 to 1.0.

Temperature

Temperature adjustment: "Generate a creative story with a temperature of 0.2."

Examples and demonstrations: Examples or demonstrations of the desired response within the prompt are provided. This can help the model understand the pattern or style you are looking for.

Providing example

Prompt without example: "Write a story about friendship."

Prompt with example: "Write a story about friendship, for example, two unlikely friends bonding over a shared love for astronomy."

Iterative refining

Experimentation and iteration: Users should be willing to experiment and iterate with your prompts. If the desired response is not obtained, adjust and refine the prompt to achieve the desired outcome.

Initial prompt: "Tell me a joke."

Refined prompt: "Compose a light-hearted, pun-based joke that involves animals."

Biased v. unbiased prompts

Avoiding bias and inappropriate content: Ensure that your prompts are free from any biases, offensive language, or inappropriate content. Language models should be used responsibly and ethically.

Biased prompt: "Explain why this political party is the best."

Unbiased prompt: "Describe the key ideologies of different political parties without favouring any specific one."

Realistic v. unrealistic prompts

Consideration of model capabilities: Understand the capabilities and limitations of the specific language model you are working with. Tailor your prompts accordingly to obtain the best possible responses.

Unreasonable prompt: "Produce all the prime numbers up to 2 billion instantly."

Realistic prompt: "Calculate the square root of 976 without using a calculator."

Specification v. generalisation

Task-specific instructions: If the task requires specific instructions, clearly outline these instructions within the prompt. For example, if you want the model to summarise a text, explicitly mention that.

General prompt: "Summarise this article."

Task-specific prompt: "Summarise this article on climate change, focusing on its impacts and potential solutions."

Creativity v. guidance

Balancing guidance and creativity: Balancing between providing enough guidance for the model to understand the task and leaving room for creativity and novel responses.

Overly guided prompt: "Write a dialogue between two characters, focusing on their emotions and reactions."

Balanced prompt: "Script an engaging dialogue between two characters, ensuring their emotions and reactions are realistic and meaningful."

To adapt AI systems to various domains and applications, effective rapid engineering is crucial. To improve the performance of AI models, researchers are constantly experimenting with new methods and approaches in the field of prompt engineering. Given its vital position in applications of artificial intelligence, it is crucial to stay up to date on the most recent developments and industry best practices in quick engineering.

7. CONCLUSION AND FUTURE TRENDS

This section, in addition to concluding the proposition of this chapter, also presents the future trends in generative AIs in the tertiary education landscape.

7.1 Conclusion

In conclusion, generative AI is a groundbreaking force with the potential to have a large impact on postsecondary research and instruction. Numerous uses for generative AI exist, including helping to solve complex issues, generating content automatically, personalising learning experiences, and synthesising knowledge. These characteristics can expedite research endeavours, offer individualised learning pathways, and enhance instructional techniques. Despite enthusiasm, it is critical to understand the implications for morality, the law, and society. One ethical issue is how generative AI should be used to avoid bias, false information, and abuse. With the proliferation of AI-generated content, it is imperative to maintain transparency and educate the public on the nature of these materials.

To regulate the use and effects of generative AI, legal frameworks must be created or altered. Three key areas must be regulated: data privacy, the responsibility for inaccurate AI-generated outputs, and intellectual property rights. Furthermore, it is essential to retain accountability while developing and using generative AI. Developers and organisations are in charge of ensuring that their AI systems are used for what they were designed for and in compliance with accepted ethical standards. As generative AI advances, collaboration among academics, industry, and policymakers becomes more crucial. The purpose of multidisciplinary work should be to develop a framework that safeguards people's rights and welfare as well as the welfare of the general public while making the most of generative AI.

7.2 Future Directions

Although generative AI has much potential to revolutionise higher education, several significant research gaps still need to be carefully considered. First, more investigations are needed to ascertain how pupils interact with AI-generated information. Research should focus on how students assess the authenticity and veracity of information generated by AI systems. Additionally, more investigations are needed to establish the optimal proportion of information generated by AI to that provided by humans to create a successful hybrid learning environment. In addition, it is unknown how AI-centric education affects students' potential for creativity, critical thinking, and problem solving over the long run.

The investigation of potential biases in AI-generated data and an understanding of how these biases impact learning outcomes constitute another crucial area of research. The ethical concerns around data privacy, consent, and security in the context of AI-driven education must be thoroughly examined to ensure responsible implementation. These research holes will help to fill in knowledge gaps and guide the integration of large language modelling and generative artificial intelligence toward a more informed and equitable educational environment. Future studies that investigate the intricate dynamics of AI-driven education will benefit from these research holes.

Models of hybrid learning: The future of education is likely to involve hybrid learning models, which combine conventional teaching methods with platforms powered by AI. These models can provide an individualised learning experience by adapting to various learning preferences and styles. Using AI to analyse student engagement and comprehension could help teachers modify their practices for better results (Ally, 2008). According to experts such as Siemens, connectivism is a model of learning that values using technology to study a connected society and welcomes the digital environment (2005).

AI-powered adaptive assessment: AI can significantly alter how testing is conducted. Artificial intelligence can personalise questions for each student on the basis of their learning curve by creating platforms for adaptive exams. This promotes a deeper comprehension of the concepts and offers rapid feedback (Mislevy et al., 2017). For example, Wang et al. (2015) presented an adaptive testing system that uses artificial intelligence to tailor the evaluation procedure and improve the efficacy and precision of evaluations.

Research in AI ethics: Moving forward, it is crucial that we fully comprehend AI ethics in education. The development of guidelines and frameworks for the ethical integration of AI will be greatly aided by multidisciplinary studies at the intersection of ethics, education, and AI. According to Jobin et al. (2019), this study should prioritise addressing privacy, accountability, and bias issues while also prioritising fair access to AI-driven education. The groundwork for ethical considerations in AI integration is built through continuous research, including that conducted by Diakopoulos (2016) on algorithmic accountability and transparency, which provides essential insights into the ethical implications of AI in many domains.

REFERENCES

Adams, A., & Turner, T. (2019). Leveraging GPT-3 for Teaching and Learning Material Generation. In *International Conference on Artificial Intelligence in Education* (pp. 1-13). Springer.

Afridi, M. S., Iqbal, M. A., & Abulaish, M. (2018). An Intelligent System for Automated Citation Classification. *Procedia Computer Science*, *132*, 783–790.

Ally, M. (2008). Foundations of educational theory for online learning. In *Theory and Practice of Online Learning* (pp. 15–44). Athabasca University Press. DOI: 10.15215/aupress/9781897425084.003

Bender, E. M., Gebru, T., McMillan-Major, A., Shmitchell, S., & Wallach, H. (2021). *On the Dangers of Stochastic Parrots: Can Language Models Be Too Big?* Association for Computational Linguistics. DOI: 10.1145/3442188.3445922

Bengio, Y., Simard, P., & Frasconi, P. (2003). Learning long-term dependencies with gradient descent is difficult. *IEEE Transactions on Neural Networks*, *5*(2), 157–166. DOI: 10.1109/72.279181

Boyd, S., & Vandenberghe, L. (2004). *Convex Optimisation*. Cambridge University Press. DOI: 10.1017/CBO9780511804441

Brown, H., & Jones, R. (2018). Generative AI and Its Role in Cross-Cultural Academic Collaboration. *Frontiers in Artificial Intelligence*, *3*, 45.

Brown, T. B., Mann, B., Ryder, N., Subbiah, M., Kaplan, J., Dhariwal, P., & Amodei, D. (2020). Language Models are Few-Shot Learners. *Advances in Neural Information Processing Systems*, •••, 33.

Devlin, J., Chang, M. W., Lee, K., & Toutanova, K. (2019). BERT: Bidirectional Encoder Representations from Transformers. *Proceedings of NAACL-HLT 2019*.

Diakopoulos, N. (2016). Accountability in algorithmic decision making. *Communications of the ACM*, *59*(2), 56–62. DOI: 10.1145/2844110

Doshi-Velez, F., and Kim, B. (2017). Towards A Rigorous Science of Interpretable Machine Learning. arXiv.

Floridi, L., Cowls, J., Beltrametti, M., Chatila, R., Chazerand, P., Dignum, V., & Luetge, C. (2018). AI4People—an Ethical Framework for a Good AI Society: Opportunities, Risks, Principles, and Recommendations. *Minds and Machines*, *28*(4), 689–707. DOI: 10.1007/s11023-018-9482-5

Friedman, B. (2021). Law and Ethics of AI and Robotics. In *The Oxford Handbook of Ethics of AI*. Oxford University Press.

Goh, K. L., Tan, S., & Chen, L. (2019). Multilingual Pedagogy in Higher Education: Adapting with Generative AI. *International Journal of Multilingual Education*, *1*(1), 65–78.

Jobin, A., Ienca, M., & Vayena, E. (2019). The global landscape of AI ethics guidelines. *Nature Machine Intelligence*, *1*(9), 389–399. DOI: 10.1038/s42256-019-0088-2

Johnson, M., Schuster, M., Le, Q. V., Krikun, M., Wu, Y., Chen, Z., . . . Dean, J. (2020). T2T: Tiny and Transferable. arXiv preprint arXiv:2002.04745.

Joulin, A., Grave, E., Bojanowski, P., and Mikolov, T. (2016). Bag of Tricks for Efficient Text Classification. *ArXiv, abs/1607.01759.*

Li, X., Wang, Y., & Garcia, D. (2020). Advancements in Generative AI for Multilingual Teaching-Learning Material Creation. *Journal of Educational Technology & Society*, *23*(4), 127–140.

Liu, C., Singh, A., & Chen, C. H. (2019). Adversarial training for community question answering: A dataset and baselines. In *Proceedings of the 42nd International ACM SIGIR Conference on Research and Development in Information Retrieval* (pp. 445-454).

Liu, Y., Ma, Y., Chen, M., Ludwig, M., & Schneider, J. (2019). Text-DavinciGAN: Text to Image Synthesis using Generative Adversarial Networks. arXiv preprint arXiv:1907.00208.

Liu, Y., Ott, M., Goyal, N., Du, J., Joshi, M., Chen, D., . . . Stoyanov, V. (2019). RoBERTa: A Robustly Optimised BERT Pretraining Approach. arXiv preprint arXiv:1907.11692.

Mehrabi, N., Morstatter, F., Saxena, N., Lerman, K., and Galstyan, A. (2019). A Survey on Bias and Fairness in Machine Learning. arXiv.

Mikolov, T., Sutskever, I., Chen, K., Corrado, G., & Dean, J. (2013). Advances in Neural Information Processing Systems: Vol. 26. *Distributed Representations of Words and Phrases and their Compositionality*. [REMOVED HYPERLINK FIELD]

Mislevy, R. J., Steinberg, L. S., & Almond, R. G. (2017). On the structure of educational assessments. *Measurement: Interdisciplinary Research and Perspectives*, *15*(3-4), 55–66.

Mitchell, M., Wu, S., Zaldivar, A., Barnes, P., Vasserman, L., Hutchinson, B., & Gebru, T. (2019). Model cards for model reporting. In *Proceedings of the Conference on Fairness, Accountability, and Transparency* (pp. 220-229). [REMOVED HYPERLINK FIELD] DOI: 10.1145/3287560.3287596

Pennington, J., Socher, R., & Manning, C. (2014). GloVe: Global Vectors for Word Representation. *Proceedings of the 2014 conference on empirical methods in natural language processing (EMNLP).* DOI: 10.3115/v1/D14-1162

Rahwan, I., Cebrian, M., Obradovich, N., Bongard, J., Bonnefon, J. F., Breazeal, C., & Lazer, D. (2019). Machine Behavior. *Nature*, *568*(7753), 477–486. DOI: 10.1038/s41586-019-1138-y

Ross, S. M. (2014). *A First Course in Probability*. Pearson.

Shin, Y., Song, K., & Kim, S. W. (2021). Exploring Prompt Engineering for Open-Domain Question Answering. arXiv preprint arXiv:2103.09417.

Shokri, R., Stronati, M., Song, C., & Shmatikov, V. (2017). Membership inference attacks against machine learning models. In *2017 IEEE Symposium on Security and Privacy (SP)* (pp. 3-18). DOI: 10.1109/SP.2017.41

Siemens, G. (2005). Connectivism: A learning theory for the digital age. *International Journal of Instructional Technology and Distance Learning*, *2*(1), 3–10.

Smith, A., Lee, B., & Johnson, C. (2021). Enhancing Multilingual Academic Communication through Generative AI. *Journal of Multilingual Academic Communication*, *9*(2), 142–157.

Stewart, J. (2015). *Calculus*. Cengage Learning.

Strang, G. (2006). *Linear Algebra and Its Applications*. Cengage Learning.

Vaswani, A., Shazeer, N., Parmar, N., Uszkoreit, J., Jones, L., Gomez, A. N., Kaiser, Ł., & Polosukhin, I. (2017). Advances in neural information processing systems: Vol. 30. *Attention is all you need.* [REMOVED HYPERLINK FIELD]

Wang, J., Zhang, S., & Zhang, C. (2015). A new adaptive educational testing approach based on data mining. In 2015 IEEE 15th International Conference on Advanced Learning Technologies (pp. 252-253).

Wasserman, L. (2013). *All of Statistics: A Concise Course in Statistical Inference*. Springer. [REMOVED HYPERLINK FIELD]

Yang, Z., Qi, P., Zhang, S., Bengio, Y., Cohen, W. W., Salakhutdinov, R., & Manning, C. D. (2018). HotpotQA: A Dataset for Diverse, Explainable Multihop Question Answering. *ArXiv*./abs/1809.09600

Chapter 18
Responsible AI in Transnational Legal Education:
Jurisdictional Challenges and Regulatory Gaps

Ramya Krishnappa
https://orcid.org/0000-0001-8900-454X
Ramaiah College of Law, India

Rajiv Gurugopinath
https://orcid.org/0000-0003-3845-6778
Ramaiah College of Law, India

ABSTRACT

This chapter analyzes the revolutionary but controversial role of artificial intelligence (AI) in transnational legal learning (TNE), and the potential benefits of AI to augment access, efficiency, and innovation and the existence of deep jurisdictional, ethical, and regulatory difficulties. It covers the results of data protection, intellectual property, content moderation, and academic freedom to demonstrate how disjointed legal systems and the isolationist algorithmic priorities in global learning conditions. The paper suggests a system of governance encompassing the advantages of a right-based approach, transparency, and pluralism when implementing AI. It also advises the institution to be ready through impact evaluation, faculty development, and boards of oversight to be accountable and inclusive. Finally, it proposes a more human, legally-based, and culture-sensitive form of AI in education- human centered, legally justified but culturally sensitive one that ensures justice, autonomy and equity across boundaries and re-establishes the normative role of law in the digital era.

1. INTRODUCTION

1.1. The Rise of Artificial Intelligence in Higher Education

The last ten years have seen a higher adoption of the Artificial Intelligence (AI) technologies into the background of higher education more than ever before (Akhmadieva et al., 2024). With the high rate of

DOI: 10.4018/979-8-3373-5403-3.ch018

development in machine learning, natural language processing, and algorithmic decision-making, higher education institutions and technological research around the world started implementing AI systems to improve its administration, instructional delivery, student support services, or even academic research (Deep et al., 2024; Pacheco-Mendoza et al., 2023). The COVID-19 pandemic served as a triggering factor in increasing the pace of this change, and educational institutions were looking to find solutions that were scalable, flexible, and remote-friendly (Guzzo et al., 2023). The field of AI has become one of the key players in this new paradigm of academia (Zhao et al., 2025). This pervasive integration of AI in higher education is not merely a transient trend but signifies a fundamental shift in pedagogical and administrative paradigms, necessitating a deeper examination of its implications across various facets of university operations (Khairullah et al., 2025) (Al-Zahrani & Alasmari, 2024).

In recent times, generative AI, specifically, has seen its fair share with the rise of such tools as ChatGPT, Claude or Gemini, providing such features as text generation, summarization, content translation, and conversational tutoring as their uses (Cordero et al., 2024). Content can be generated by these tools in form of essays, synthesizing case law and more simulating legal argumentations all these functions which used to be on the exclusive domain of human expertise. There is a growing use of predictive analytics systems to predict performance of students, any learning gap, and individualised academic intervention. The use of AI to develop knowledge, search, and grade it is changing the ways of knowing, such as automated grading software and plagiarism checkers, or smart tutoring and curriculum recommendation systems (Al-Zahrani & Alasmari, 2024).

The field of legal education has traditionally been conservative in its teaching methods, but now it is experiencing the possibility and threat of AI. Jurisdictional law schools have been experimenting with AI enabled databases on research, interactive casebooks, virtual simulations and even AI-based moot court evaluations. As much as these tools enhance efficiency and access, they also bring to question the issue of academic honesty, judicial bias, and loss of critical thinking abilities (G & Nair, 2024; Ouellette et al., 2025). If the application of AI goes past the limits of a country, these tensions are intensified even into transnational legal education. This global perspective introduces complexities related to varying legal frameworks, ethical standards, and educational philosophies across different jurisdictions, further exacerbating the challenges of integrating AI responsibly into legal pedagogy (Balan, 2024) (G & Nair, 2024).

1.2. The Expansion of Transnational Legal Education (TNE)

In support of the emergence of AI has been the internationalization of the legal education. Over the past twenty years, transnational legal education (TNE) programs such as cross-border LLM programs, online law degrees, cross-border research networks, and global MOOCs (Massive Open Online Courses), on legal topics, have been proliferated (Morawa, 2008). The first and foremost institutions of the United States, United Kingdom, Australia, Canada and almost all of India, Singapore and South Africa have ventured into the mission of forming dual-degree relationships, joint program delivery and international student exchange systems (LaFleur, 2019).

TNE permits legal education to cross over national borders and involves legal education students across different systems in a mutual curriculum. It encourages sharing of ideas, international competency, and comparative law argument. Digitization has played a key role in this global classroom, and the tools (Learning Management Systems (LMS), video conferencing) have served a vital role in this course (Kastberg & Ditlevsen, 2021). This digital infrastructure is currently overlaid with AI technologies to allow a extensively more personalized and automated and scaled experience (Di et al., 2021). An AI is already being used to handle significant student information sets, assign grades, identify plagiarism in academic environments across different jurisdictions, and provide students previously with diverse cultural and legal backgrounds with personalized feedback (Thakur et al., 2025). Located in universities, AI is used to forecast success rates in international students, where optimal program placement is determined, and even algorithmic screening of admissions. Therefore, AI is not an addition but an organizational release of contemporary TNE systems (Wang et al., 2023).

However, this deep integration raises significant concerns regarding data privacy, algorithmic bias, and the potential for reduced human oversight, particularly within the transnational context where varying legal and ethical standards apply (Xue et al., 2025) (Sharma et al., 2023).

1.3. The Problem of Jurisdiction in AI-Enabled TNE

The integration of AI and TNE implies a new stage of legal, ethical and governance issues, however, at the heart of such a convergence is the issue of jurisdiction. In cases where AI tools are used to create or filter educational material in a certain jurisdiction, but consumed by students and institutions in a different jurisdiction, which laws apply? In cases where the AI gathers, stores, and processes data on students in more than one country, what privacy rights can be enforced? Providing that AI tools take training data independently that is not always guided by leaders or reflects a subset of legal traditions, does it misrepresent or prejudice the learning of law around the world? These questions underscore the urgent need for a comprehensive framework that addresses the complex interplay of international law, data governance, and ethical AI development within the globalized landscape of legal education. The core of these questions is a substantial contradiction between the transnational nature of the digital learning tools and legal logic of territory. The law is different in countries in terms of data protection laws, intellectual property laws, level of education standard, and greater expression norm. No single, coordinated legal set up, exists on the use of AI in education- much less legal education in several jurisdictions (Alaswad et al., 2025; Xue et al., 2025).

An example of this can be considered, in the case of an EU student who has undertaken an LLM course in the United Kingdom, and uses an AI platform, which is located in the United States, to create a summary of the case and grading review reports. The site archives information on the servers in Ireland and applies a specialized algorithm which is mostly trained on American legal cases. Doubts arise: Does the EU student have a data protection right under the GDPR? Does the UK educational law allow the university to be accountable? Is the AI tool violating intellectual property rights by replicating massive amounts of cross-jurisdictional case law? And what is the means of redress in case the student is graded not correctly after a prejudiced algorithm? These queries demonstrate a multi-level complexity in the conflict of jurisdiction in AI-driven TNE (Laat et al., 2020). There are classic legal principles like "conflict of laws," "choice of forum," and "long-arm jurisdiction," that provide limited information in the context of algorithmic learning based on the cloud. Additionally, it is common with universities to sign click-through or end-user license agreements (EULAs) with EdTech vendors which, to some extent, clouds or replaces legal accountability. This in turn can subject students and faculty to obfuscated terms of contract that can circumvent substantive consent, institutional accountability or judicial redress (Kelso et al., 2025).

1.4. Why Legal Education Requires a Distinct AI Governance Framework

The legal teaching is in a niche within the higher education ecosystem. Legal education is specific on norms, rights, duties and conflict management compared to STEM or humanities studies. This is not just an academic issue of integrity, fairness and neutrality of the teaching process, but a democratic issue. The use of AI tools has downstream impacts when it comes to legal practice, access to the rule of law and the legality of the legal process, when it affects the way future lawyers will be trained (G & Nair, 2024; Rozenshtein & Frazier, 2025).

The AIs may influence the content and process of legal training in different manners. When a generative AI-based tool generates US-inspired case summaries of a non-US audience, it can threaten to create a kind of homogenisation of the law that leaves out other systems including civil law, customary law, or religious law. In case AI-based grading systems are introduced humanless, the students can be punished because of their non-standard legal reasoning or style of writing. When facial recognition systems employed by proctoring tools are bad at recognizing students of particular racial or ethnicity, it again propagates algorithmic discrimination in the training of legal practitioners (Ajjawi et al., 2022; Yoder-Himes et al., 2022).

Such dangers are compounded when a TNE environment is built upon geographically fragmented levels of regulatory supervision, diluted institutional responsibility, and student access to localised redress. This therefore urgently requires the establishment of responsible AI governance schemes unique to the special needs of transnational legal education. These frameworks should take into consideration the aspect of jurisdictional variation, and ensure transparency and accountability, and enforce ethical guideline like fairness, privacy, and academic freedom in AI deployment (Yan & Liu, 2024).

1.5. Objectives of the Chapter

The chapter aims at offering a detailed analysis of the legal and regulatory issues surrounding the application of AI in transnational law learning. It aims to:

- Research the current AI applications in TNE and their pedagogic functions;
- Determine the main jurisdictional conflicts in data governance, intellectual property and academic responsibility;
- Research how the existing national law and international standards can be used to restrict cross-border AI applications in the field of education;
- Offer recommendations and solutions to risk mitigation strategies as well as policies to universities, educators and government/regulators;
- Become an advocate of the creation of a harmonized rights-based approach to responsible AI usage within the legal education.

The chapter helps address the nascent subfield of AI ethics, digital sovereignty, and institutional governance in higher education by also targeting the intersection of law, technology, and education across jurisdictions. It connects the theoretical question with practical knowledge, providing the working direction to the legal scholars, university administrators, policymakers, and EdTech developers who are concerned with the international legal learning programs.

1.6. Structure of the Chapter

To reach the above goals, the chapter is divided into five parts, which expand on the preceding one as a way of providing a multifaceted and multidisciplinary study starting with the introduction in the first followed by,

Section 2: Mapping the Landscape presents the many forms of the AI tools utilized by TNE by grouping them by functionality, platform, and jurisdiction.
Section 3: Jurisdictional Dilemmas explores the legal clashes in the area of cross-border data processing, IP assertions, and platform administration.
Section 4: Algorithmic Bias and Content Moderation brings up the ways in which AI tools may incorporate regional, racial, or ideological bias and the ways in which it is incompatible with academic freedom.
Section 5: Conclusion draws the conclusions and suggests a plan of interdisciplinary cooperation in the integration of responsible AI.

1.7. Concluding Remarks

As AI increasingly transforms the world of education, the implications of this technological revolution for legal education in general, and transnational legal education in particular, need disciplined and ongoing thought in scholarship. The promise of learning that's borderless should not come at the cost of legal opacity, ethical compromise, or jurisdictional confusion it must see the actualities before considerations. By making legal frameworks and pedagogical values a key part of how AI tools are governed, we can be sure that innovation does not trump justice, equity and the rule of law in universities. This chapter therefore welcomes critical interaction with the structural, normative and legal aspects of AI in an academic globalizing environment (Schomberg, 2024).

This scholarly endeavor therefore provides a conceptual map to understand the ethical dilemma that is invariably embedded in AI in the learning process, underlining the relevance of building procedural transparency, independent accountability, as well as equality to ensure that AI enables education's aims to contribute to a student's success and societal well-being (Bibi, 2024). Such ethical frameworks are essential for ensuring that AI systems operate transparently, fairly, and reliably, aligning with both legal standards and fundamental ethical principles in educational contexts (Alaswad et al., 2025).

2: MAPPING THE LANDSCAPE: AI TOOLS IN TRANSNATIONAL LEGAL EDUCATION (TNE)

2.1 Introduction: A Technological Crossroads

The advent of artificial intelligence (AI) combined with transnational legal education (TNE) is a turning point in the development of international pedagogy. With digital transformation being adopted by law schools, AI-supported platforms are not, and do not become, peripheral technologies but core brokers of education (Al-Zahrani & Alasmari, 2024). In the field of legal education, AI is currently being used in order to automate the assessments, oversee the distance assessment, customize the teaching feedback, and assist with the research. These applications are cross-national and they are transforming the character of learning, assessment and academic authority (Ifenthaler et al., 2024).

Although other fields in academia are testing the paces of using AI in classrooms, legal education and the transnational forms of the same in particular can provide a special ground. It is placed on the crossroads of various legal customs, jurisdictional regulations, and professional responsibility (Alaswad et al., 2025). The current cross-border legal-educational ecosystem with AI functioning requires that understanding how this technology works can be applied to effective governance, academic integrity maintenance, and legal compliance (Gao et al., 2025).

2.2 Automated Grading and Assessment Systems

Automated grading and formative assessment is one of the most apparent ways of AI use in TNE. Machine-learning-based systems can now be found on the offerings of such tools as Gradescope, EvaIAI, and even proprietary EdTech platforms, wherein answers to short queries, multiple-choice options, and even essay submissions are assessed through machine learning (Hopfenbeck et al., 2023). Pattern recognition, frequency of keywords and prior training datasets are employed in these systems to provide real time grading, eliminating faculty involvement in redundant assessment activities. This automation, while efficient, introduces significant concerns regarding the validity and reliability of AI-driven evaluations, especially when compared to human grading methodologies (Al-Zahrani & Alasmari, 2024).

These systems are found to be scalable, consistent, and efficient in transnational contexts, particularly in situations where courses are taking students in more than one jurisdiction. As an example, one grading AI can be used on a worldwide program of the LLM, which is provided by institutions in the UK, Singapore, and India (Yang et al., 2025).

However, concerns persist as the automated systems are not able to detect subtlety in legal argumentation, contextual interpretation or culturally defined rhetorical styles. Besides, the majority of the grading algorithms are trained on data used in particular jurisdictions, which may cause systemic bias when used in other parts of the world (Landau et al., 2024).

2.3 Proctoring and Surveillance Technologies

As online law degrees continue to grow and new areas of law education combine with remote learning have emerged, AI-driven proctoring software like Proctorio, Examity, and Honorlock has become a necessity to keep exams straight (Yoder-Himes et al., 2022). These tools are based on facial recognition, keystroke dynamic, eye tracking, and behavior analytics to identify cheating or other unwarranted activity when taking online tests (Huy et al., 2025).

Proctoring AI is a way of maintaining standards in transnational legal education, wherein universities do not need a physical presence to enforce standards. As an example, a student, who is an Indian and has enrolled in the distance education program at a US law school, can be proctored in real-time by using AI and make sure that they observe their exam protocols. Nevertheless, the introduction of these tools provokes important jurisdictional issues, in particular, data privacy, biometric consent, and automatic discrimination (Heinrich, 2025). An example of this is the European students who can be covered under the General Data Protection Regulation (GDPR) and their counterparts in other regions are deprived of such protection. Some of the proctoring tools also present challenges to the law on constitutional privacy and academic freedom rights due to their invasive nature (Colonna, 2021).

Furthermore, the potential for algorithmic bias in facial recognition and behavioral analytics within these proctoring systems raises concerns about equitable treatment and accuracy across diverse student populations (Ajjawi et al., 2022). This can lead to disproportionate scrutiny or false positives for certain demographic groups, undermining the very integrity and fairness that proctoring aims to uphold (Khan et al., 2025).

2.4 AI-Assisted Research Assistants and Legal Analytics

The use of AI-based research assistants like Lexis + AI, CaseText, CoCounsel, Westlaw Edge and Jugalbandi is quickly changing the nature of legal research in educational institutions (Magesh et al., 2025). These technologies allow students to access giant legal data bases by use of natural language search, create summaries of cases, compare laws between jurisdictions and they can even predict the outcome of a case based on precedent trends (Modi, 2023).

These tools are of great assistance to TNE students who are usually dealing with new legal systems. They give direct avenues of research, translation of legal texts into language and contextualization of foreign doctrines. Nevertheless, such tools are also replicating epistemic hierarchies: most commercial legal data collections are dominated by cases of U.S. and UK common law, with minimal representation of civil legal systems and custom legal cultures (Chau & Livermore, 2024; Santosh et al., 2024). AI-generated materials are based on one tradition of legal reasoning, which might create cognitive dissonance or structural exclusion in students in non-Western jurisdictions. This inherent bias necessitates a critical examination of the datasets used to train these AI systems, ensuring diverse legal traditions are adequately represented to prevent perpetuation of a single legal paradigm (Gutowski & Hurley, 2025).

Inequality in access is also brought about by the fact that most AI legal tools are commercial in nature. More developed institutions will be able to purchase more advanced research AI licenses, and partner universities in the Global South will have fewer options than open access or freemium ones, which puts them on an unequal footing in the same TNE program (Nyaaba et al., 2024).

2.5 Individualized Feedback and Adaptive Learning

Adaptive learning paths have recently become standard features of AI-powered learning management systems (LMS) like Canvas, Blackboard, and Coursera Plus, in which adaptive features like custom quizzes, reading suggestions and progress dashboards are offered to students depending on their performance and engagement levels (ME et al., 2024).

Such systems infer the patterns in student behaviour based on the data analytics and neural networks to identify how much or how frequently the student spent the time on readings, or how fast the student completes the quizzes, etc., and provide the individual remedial plans (Madhu et al., 2024). Adaptive systems provide a possible way out of the issue of cross-jurisdictional pedagogical convergence in transnational legal education. Civil law students, such as those are able to be provided with additional resources to ensure that they are not confused by the adversarial trial model of common law jurisdictions (Ezzaim et al., 2023).

However, adaptive learning systems bring out issues of profiling, implicit tracking and bias. The lack of transparency of algorithmic logic which is frequently safeguarded as proprietary intellectual property implies that students and faculty do not always get to know how and why particular recommendations are given (Idrizi, 2024). In addition, adaptive systems can be implicitly self-enforcing deficits, instead of instigating experimentation or non-norm-based learning (Praveenkumar et al., 2025)

2.6 AI Implementation in Cross-Border Platforms

TNE nowadays are operationalized within the global platforms with AI being introduced to their infrastructure. An example is the Coursera, FutureLearn and edX, which offer university-designed online courses, but run over the platform. These programs may feature AI-written transcripts, live translators, automatic grading sections, faculty analytics dashboards, and so on (Sharma & Sharma, 2024).

When universities get into such partnerships, they do not negotiate the underlying AI architecture. Consequently, the data obtained on the students in several jurisdictions is handled and stored within the platform which is usually operated on servers with foreign jurisdiction. As an illustration, a Kenyan student can be studying a UK law course on FutureLearn, yet the data is stored on AWS datacenters in Frankfurt and falls under U.S. jurisdiction to the CLOUD Act (Amo-Filvà et al., 2021).

These models contest the conventional regulatory supervision. The ministries of education, accreditation boards of universities, and mechanisms that deal with grievances of students are usually not ready to oversee or audit AI systems that run on platforms. Also, the liability of the institutional protections may be disclaimed in the contractual terms between universities and platforms, exposing students to liability (Imohimi, 2025).

2.7 Proprietary LLM Programs and Global Law Studies

There are already institutions assuming the creation of proprietary platforms to provide the program of LLM online completely, usually with the assistance of AI startups or EdTech companies. These platforms are asynchronized learning platforms, AI-moderated discussion platforms and intelligent feedback loops. They can also incorporate voice bots that respond to student questions, create client interview simulations or offer mock tests akin to the bar exam patterns (G & Nair, 2024; Hu, 2025).

These developments point to the transition between the old system of digital augmentation, and the new system of legal education that is digital-native. Nonetheless, closed ecosystems are also formed by proprietary LLM platforms. They also tend to train their AI tools on internal datasets, are not externally reviewed, and not constrained to open standards. The issues of data jurisdiction, content neutrality, and algorithmic accountability are urgent when these platforms work at the international level (Berengueres & Sandell, 2023; Zhang et al., 2024).

The reason is that faculty participating in such programs will have no control over the editing, rearranging, or summarizing of their content by AI. Depending on algorithmic content moderation in platforms, students can have their view suppressed by opposing legal viewpoints or a controversial subject according to hard-coded risk filters (Hutson & Plate, 2024).

2.8 The International Academic Partnerships

The TNE initiatives are usually two degree or joint ventures between foreign countries. These alliances usually presuppose the development of the common curriculum, the distribution of the assessment roles, and the mutuality of credits. More of these arrangements are now including AI in order to bring uniformity in grading, attendance tracking, or time zone communication (Jaadi et al., 2025).

In this type of partnership, AI solutions act as administrative intermediaries. As an example, a collaborative LLM course between a university in the UK and India can utilize a common platform through which it will evaluate assignments with the help of artificial intelligence and post the findings to both institutional databases. Yet, the question is, to whom the institution should be held responsible in case the AI fails to grade the student correctly, violates data confidentiality, and harms the academic?Such scenarios highlight a critical need for transparent accountability frameworks and robust legal recourse mechanisms that address the unique challenges posed by AI integration in international educational partnerships (Noller & Thimesch, 2025).

Alliances between universities in the countries that have varying regulatory cultures tend to be at loggerheads. One of the European partners might demand that they use the whole of GDPR and the other partner who is in the U.S. or Asia might be using a different data minimization model. These normative conflicts are potentially going to put a strain or even halt cross-border partnerships as AIs are integrated into the fundamental operations of TNE (Mbah, 2024).

2.9 New EdTech Paradigms and Prescriptive Jurisdiction

EdTech is in the process of change, and new models are based specifically on legal education as a service (LEaaS). Other firms such as BARBRI, LawAdvisor and even international consultancies are moving into the space with modular AI-integrated platforms that can be licensed by multiple institutions (Mania, 2022). These sites provide off-the-shelf AI services: auto-brief writers, citation checkers, case prediction bots and even AI tutors. Although this modular construction offers flexibility and cost-effectiveness, it on the other hand spreads out legal liability. A university with a third party AI citation checker may not be in a position to justify/or question how it has punished a student due to a citation error (Gray et al., 2025).

This delegation of judgment to AI in education that is cross-bordered puts an accountability gap in place. The students who are caught in AI decisions might be left in a position whereby they do not know where to turn to either the platform or the instructor or the home university. In the meantime, there are still inconsistent cross-jurisdictional legal protection (Noller & Thimesch, 2025).

2.10 Oversight and Accreditation Problems

The increasing disconnection between innovation and accreditation is one of the most significant effects of the implementation of AI in TNE. The national legal education certification bodies at the Bar Council of India, the American Bar Association, or at the Quality Assurance Agency in the UK can frequently be technically incapable of auditing AI applications in education or assessment (Warraich et al., 2025).

This has an effect of establishing a regulatory lag wherein AI tools are implemented without any definite pedagogical or ethical justification. Programs based on such tools could be passed in accordance with course outlines and the learning outcomes, without examination of the mediation and manipulation of those outcomes by AI (Gray et al., 2025).

Challenges also happen to the international accrediting bodies. In the case of collaboration programs that are functioning between jurisdictions, any single regulator may not be in control, and AI use can continue to be used in legal grey areas. The lack of collective accreditation procedure of AI in legal education exposes institutions to lawsuits, negative publicity, and disenfranchisement of students (Lande, 2025).

2.11 Conclusion: To Innovation to Accountability

The section has charted the diverse landscape of AI application in transnational education of law, through automated evaluation, proctoring, research, personalized learning and platform governance. These tools promise deep potential on its own, yet at the same time, they represent a challenge to current assumptions concerning pedagogy, jurisdiction and institutional responsibility. As AI takes over world legal education, the world is in urgent need of many governance structures that are context sensitive, jurisdiction sensitive and ethically grounded. Universities need to avoid the temptation of focusing on efficiency at the expense of transparency, and policy-makers need to act fast, closing the legal loopholes in regulation, contract formulation, and redressal across borders. The first thing that comes out of this picture is not that AI should not be used in TNE, but that it needs to be reconsidered: who owns, who gains, who loses, who is responsible? It is only under such a critical perspective that we may use the power of AI to democratize legal education without jeopardizing the normative underpinnings.

3: JURISDICTIONAL DILEMMAS IN CROSS-BORDER AI DEPLOYMENT

3.1 Introduction: Legal Vacuum of Transnational AI Learning

With the integration of artificial intelligence in the legal education on an international level, the jurisdiction issue takes on paramount significance. AI tools integrating into the Transnational Legal Education (TNE) platforms perform between a web of national legal systems, frequently concurrently challenging the student, university, provider of that platform, and the cloud host jurisdictions (Farber, 2024). Such deployments threaten conventional jurisdictional principles based on the territorial sovereignty, especially when the geocentrism of AI activity, which is the collection of data, the creation of content, its evaluation, and storage, is inherently trans-boundary in nature (Trager et al., 2023). This section considers the jurisdictional issues that are presented when AI tools cross boundaries in the educational setting. It examines conflicts of laws, extraterritoriality, case examples and what has become a worrying trend of regulatory arbitrage and forum shopping. The objective is to shed light on how the legal grayness jeopardizes academic scrupulousness, institutional obligation, and safety of the students in AI-facilitated TNE settings.

3.2 Conflict of Laws: Which Law Rules AI in Education?

Controversially, AI technologies are involved in cross-border law education, which includes various branches of law such as data protection, intellectual property (IP), the regulation of education, consumer protection, and contract law. However, there is seldom agreement as to which country law should apply in a particular AI roll out. As an example, we may take an AI grading platform based in California, but with a UK-based LLM program with students located in the EU, Africa, and Asia. Who is the data protection authority of the personal information of students? Whose IP law will apply to owning an AI generated learning material? Is the student entitled to the local education safeguards or has the AI vendor the protections of the country-of-origin legislation of the platform?

These multifaceted jurisdictional ambiguities highlight the critical need for internationally consistent regulatory frameworks to prevent legal uncertainty and protect stakeholders in AI-driven transnational education (Mouta et al., 2023). The present landscape often involves a patchwork of national and regional regulations, such as the EU AI Act, which aims to provide a comprehensive legal framework for AI, yet its extraterritorial reach remains a subject of ongoing debate in scenarios involving cross-border data flows and service provision (Bond et al., 2024) (Caccavale, 2025). This regulatory fragmentation often leads to compliance challenges for educational institutions operating transnationally, compelling them to navigate disparate legal obligations that may conflict or impose significant administrative burdens (Ghoshal, 2025) (Alaswad et al., 2025). Moreover, the absence of a globally harmonized approach to AI regulation in education creates opportunities for regulatory arbitrage, where entities might strategically choose jurisdictions with less stringent oversight to deploy AI systems, potentially compromising ethical standards and student protections (Berendt et al., 2020).

There are at least three areas that face conflicts that is, every nation could have specific requirements upon management, retention, and sharing of individual data. The GDPR of the EU, the DPDP Act of India and the U.S. sectoral laws have various consent, breach reporting and data access requirements (Punia et al., 2025). Second being accreditation, curriculum standards, and redress of grievance of students are highly controlled within the nation, but AI tools use internationally may overcome the regulations or be outside regulation (Noller & Thimesch, 2025). And the last is with respect to generative AI products, such as case briefs, summaries, quizzes, etc. create questions of ownership. The existence of student owning, institution owning, and platform controlling is conditional depending on the widely varying IP regimes (Gao et al., 2025). The doctrine of the lex loci solutionis (law of the place in which the contract is played), and the law of the location of protection (lex loci protectionis) are poorly adapted to the distributed nature of AI where an AI service (such as grading) can be performed virtually across countries (Rosati, 2024).

3.3 Extraterritoriality of Domestic Laws

To deal with the globalized application of AI, a few nations have expanded the extra-territorial applicability of their legal frameworks. The most remarkable one is the General Data Protection Regulation (GDPR) in the European Union that is applicable not only in the European continent itself but also to any other organization beyond the European continent that processes the data of EU citizens regarding the services or monitoring (Alkhamsi & Alqahtani, 2024). Within the educational context, it implies that a U.S.-based AI solution that provides services to the EU students, including auto-translation, assessment help, or learning analytics, falls under the GDPR. The platform should apply data minimization (in line with GDPR) and the appointment of the data protection officers (DPOs) and the right to explanation of the algorithmic decisions (Banu, 2024).

On the same note, the United States Export Administration Regulations (EAR) and International Traffic in Arms Regulations (ITAR) impose limitations on the exportation of specific AI tools, specifically sensitive technologies. Such limitations have the power to affect the right of other countries to license or host the AI-platforms developed in the U.S (Larsen, 2022). Other nations such as China and India have also started looking into their localization needs of data and claim that all the data of its citizens be stored on the local servers provoking more questions in relation to transnational cloud storage and jurisdiction (Han, 2024).

Extraterritoriality is however, two sided. On the one hand, it enhances the ability of the enforcement of the rights of nationals to the country that they visit, on the other hand, it leads to overlapping and competing claims on the subject of AI governance. This causes uncertainty in legal terms to institutions, developers of platforms and to the learners.

3.4 Case Study 1: EU Student and U.S.-Based AI Platform to Use on a UK Law Course

Take the case of a European Union student pursuing an online degree course on the online degree programme in an institution in the UK in the LLM course. The course is based on an AI-driven learning platform used in the U.S. to analyze reading comprehension, to track performance, and to supply lawyers with a chance to ask questions and receive answers in a chat. The learner uses the platform based in Germany. She keeps her information in Ireland servers and processes it with proprietary algorithms in California.

In this case the four jurisdictions are all involved concomitantly One, EU (Germany) the GDPR governs the personal and learning information of the student. There are consent, portability, algorithmic transparency and breach reporting standards. Second, The UK has a regime akin to the EU regime, with the UK-GDPR operating after Brexit, but not legally and proceeding to explicitly terminate the union between the two countries. The university can have an obligation to comply under both. Third, the terms of service of the platform are probably based on the U.S. law and liability restriction. Nevertheless, the use of the platform by commercial users in the EU can present it to the GDPR. Lastly, Irish DPC has authority of data processing particularly in cases where it is the EU headquarters of the platform (Milchior, 2024; Verdoodt et al., 2023; Voss, 2022).

The following questions are set: Does the student have the right to seek an explanation on an AI-generated grade under GDPR Article 22? Even with a contract mentioning California law, may she sue the platform over misuse of data under the German law? Is the university in the UK responsible of contracting an American company to grade the AI without following the GDPR? It is a case of conflicting responsibilities--of the possible jurisdictional evasion through loopholes in the contract-only option.

3.5 Case Study 2: Indian Law School with AI-Enhanced Foreign EdTech

A law university in India collaborates with an EdTech company based in Singapore in order to provide a diploma course in environmental law virtually. The platform offers auto-evaluation processes with the aid of AI, chat-based tutoring, and plagiarism. It draws content based on the common law databases in the UK and US mostly. The submissions of students are kept in the cloud servers in Hong Kong and Germany.

On the issue of key jurisdiction, whether the Digital Personal Data Protection Act, 2023 (DPDP), applies to India and states that when dealing with student data, one ought to obtain student permission prior to handling it (Korff, 2023). The university can be violated in case the EdTech tool processes data outside the country without explicit consent mechanism and contractual claim of guaranteeing the appropriate protection, and this entitlement is not provided. Also, the AI-generated summaries of Indian environmental statutes can create the problem of ownership (Agrawal & Jain, 2024). The copyright legislation in India does not acknowledge Indian authorship of AI; therefore, the items generated by platforms will be in the grey waters of copyright law.

Further, Bar Council of India controls the law programs and as such the outsourcing important teaching or assessment processes to foreign AI applications can contravene home-based accreditation standards (Enríquez et al., 2024; Gaumann & Veale, 2023). Therefore, the students who are faced with grading mistakes or abuse of data might be confused on whether to refer to the Indian university, the Singaporean company or the overseas cloud company. The principles of forum non conveniens also make litigation harder. The complex interplay of these jurisdictional challenges highlights the urgent need for a harmonized international framework to govern AI in education, ensuring consistent data protection and ethical oversight across borders (Imohimi, 2025).

This case demonstrates how the legal education outsourcing business to AI tools offshore creates jurisdictional blind spots. In the absence of strong agreements, well formulated dispute resolution provisions and regulatory controls, students will continue to be vulnerable to algorithmic harm with no redress.

3.6 The Issue of the Problem of Forums Shopping with TNE AI Deployments

The selective approach to a jurisdiction between parties who think that the jurisdiction will give the party a more preferential legal result is referred to as forum shopping. When applied to the area of TNE, AI providers and organizations can write contracts that outline the court of dispute even in areas with weaker consumer laws, or where there is little to no regulation of AI and minimal regulations of data sovereignty (Greco & Tagarelli, 2023). Another example is that a lot of AI education has clickwrap agreement documents that scam-bait students into arbitration in the home jurisdiction of the service provider, usually the U.S., Singapore, or the Cayman Islands. The students are thereby deprived of the domestic consumer forums or the domestic courts. Even universities can accept such conditions without considering legal consequences of such agreements that might confront their students (Draper et al., 2021).

This leads to a power imbalance: institutions and learners are filled with laws that are not their mandate, usually in languages or systems that are strange to them. The site avoids liability by transferring the litigation to far-off courts and by relying on choice-of-law provisions to their domestic jurisdiction (Reisch & Büchel, 2016). One of the cases which are recorded is when a UK student enrolled in a TNE program via a U.S. EdTech partner could not get a refund after algorithmic grading mistakes due to the terms and conditions of the platform which required arbitration in Delaware. Although UK consumer laws guaranteed the right to remedies by requiring refunds, the student lacked access to the same as they were restricted by the available forums (Brogan, 2020).

Such contractual stipulations, often embedded within extensive terms of service, effectively preclude students from seeking redress through local legal channels, thereby creating a significant disparity in access to justice (Mouta et al., 2023). This complex landscape necessitates a robust governance framework to ensure ethical AI deployment and data protection in educational settings, particularly across transnational collaborations (Mahajan, 2025).

3.7 Regulatory Arbitrage: Litigating International Law Loopholes

Regulatory arbitrage involves players using the discrepancy between jurisdictions to evade harsh regulations. The AI vendors can set operations at the country that has few data regulations and aim at the people who are in the highly regulated markets. As an example, a firm that has its seat in the Caribbean or Southeast Asia can sell AI-related tools to EU universities even though it will not treat the data as personal data in any triggering way of GDPR (Veale et al., 2018). On the same note, universities can partner with offshore systems so as to evade local accreditation regulations. By stating that AI tutors or other assessment tools are assistive but not instructional, the institutions are able to circumvent education laws on assuring academic quality (Angwaomaodoko, 2023).

This type of algorithmic outsourcing undermines national control. The regulators have a hard time tracking and auditing offshore AI vendors or punishing them. Students, in its turn, work in a legal vacuum: they become a subject of algorithmic decision-making in terms of which they have no rights or a conviction to any rights (Chatinakrob, 2024; Xue et al., 2025). The issue of regulatory arbitrage also undermines forming global standards of AI ethics. The platforms also escape responsibility through jurisdiction shopping; the institutions will externalize risk; students will bear the burden. This systemic imbalance highlights the imperative for international cooperation to develop harmonized AI governance frameworks that transcend national boundaries and safeguard educational integrity (Berendt et al., 2020) (Weuts et al., 2025).

3.8 Towards Jurisdiction Clarity: New Solutions

In response to such dilemmas, certain jurisdictions and universities have started devising legal and policy inventions in respect of certain areas that is firstly, Data Processing Agreements(DPAs), these DPAs are gaining more popularity and are more and more demanded by an institution, to reflect local legislation even in cases where AI deployment is in a foreign location (Kumar et al., 2025). Second, Model clauses in AI education that are clauses put forward by legal experts to regulate AI-related contracting, similar to the Standard Contractual Clause (SCC) in GDPR, covering dispute resolution, rights of students, and legal jurisdiction (Yan & Liu, 2024). Third, Multi-lateral Treaties: UNESCO has released a recommendation on AI ethics in the education sector (2021), promoting a unified set of AI governance strategies such as cooperation on jurisdiction and redress (Oncioiu & Bularca, 2025). And lastly local AI Registries and Audits: In certain jurisdictions, there is a pilot project of compulsory registration of AI tools in education, and compliance auditing to monitor compliance with the foreign and local jurisdiction (Bond et al., 2024). However, these initiatives are infantile. The lack of binding contracts and reciprocal acknowledgment of educational standards will keep posing jurisdictional problems to AI-driven TNE.

3.10 Conclusion: Reclaiming Legal Sovereignty in the AI-TNE Nexus

The artificially intelligent has established a learning system that goes beyond geographical borders. This disruption is both threatening and thrilling in the legal education. Although it makes access easy, efficient, and innovative, it also divides legal power and destroys the system of rule. The jurisdictional issues described in this Section illustrate that an immediate demand exists for designing AI transnational law: agreements, standards, and protections that place AI application into the context-specific and enforceable principles of law.

Colleges need to rethink their contract, regulators should revise their toolkits and students should be provided with their powers to know their rights. Otherwise, the vision of global law education with the support of AI is in danger of becoming a hodgepodge of unaccountable algorithms subject to the rule of law ghosts across the frontiers.

As artificial intelligence becomes embedded in legal education across borders, the question of jurisdiction assumes critical importance. AI tools used in Transnational Legal Education (TNE) platforms operate across a web of national legal systems, often simultaneously touching the legal regimes of the student, university, platform provider, and cloud host. These deployments challenge traditional jurisdictional concepts rooted in territorial sovereignty, particularly when the core of AI operations—data collection, content generation, assessment, and storage—is transboundary by design.

This transboundary nature of AI in legal education necessitates a reconceptualization of jurisdiction—not merely as a question of where regulation applies, but whose legal norms govern digital pedagogy. When algorithms trained in one jurisdiction shape discourse in another, they effectively export their originating country's legal, ethical, and cultural assumptions. This creates a form of digital jurisdictional spillover, where U.S. privacy norms, EU data accountability standards, or Indian intermediary rules silently dictate academic practices across continents. The absence of harmonized transnational AI law amplifies the risk of regulatory conflict, forum shopping, and fragmented accountability. Therefore, developing context-sensitive international frameworks—anchored in constitutional principles of due process, academic freedom, and data sovereignty—is essential to ensure that the globalization of AI in legal education strengthens, rather than undermines, the rule of law across borders.

4: ALGORITHMIC BIAS, DISCRIMINATION, AND CONTENT MODERATION IN A CROSS-CULTURAL LEGAL CURRICULUM

4.1 Introduction: Global Learning Education in the Age of Algorithmic Governance

The use of artificial intelligence (AI) technology to mediate the design, delivery, and moderation of legal curricula in the growing environment of transnational legal education (TNE) has become a common practice. Although AI has enormous potential in terms of efficiency, personalization and scale, complex risks that can prove to be critical are those associated with algorithmic prejudice, cultural blindness, censoring and epistemic injustice (Caccavale, 2025).

Such problems are especially acute in law, a field constructing itself on normative thinking, pluralism of thought, and contextual applicability of principles with time and space. Summarization of cases in law, screening of student input, or identifying so-called controversial material, all of which AI tools do, are the result of rules and code-based rules, and may not indicatively mirror diversity standards of legal tradition, political integrity, or human rights norms worldwide (Pruss et al., 2025).

In this section, the author examines how the concept of algorithmic decision-making and content moderation identifies with academic freedom in TNE contexts. It studies the introduction of bias into AI technologies, the incompatibility of moderation practices with free expression and the ways in which cross-cultural curricula serve to become sources of disputed knowledge under the pretense of opaque algorithms. It seeks to unravel the legal, ethical and pedagogical implications of enabling AI to arbitrate on what is read, said, or learned by the law students (Agyemang-Badu et al., 2025).

4.2 Sensitizing the Algorithmic Bias in Law Tools

Algorithms bias is that which is both systematic and repeatable, and is also known as unfairness of computer systems. Such bias in AI-based education applications is often due to skewness in training data, in which the AI models are trained on mainly legal texts of a certain jurisdiction, such as the U.S. or U.K. (Krištofík, 2025). This small data corpus omits a wide range of sources including civil law, customary law or the non-English legal corpus. In the same vein, Western developers also have certain design assumptions, which reflect their norms of pedagogy, evaluation, and relevance and, more importantly, influence the process by which the AI interprets information and provides it to the consumer (Shahid et al., 2025). Feedback loops add to these problems, since patterns of user interaction (such as clicking on U.S. cases frequently) indicate the strength of certain legal systems in the replies of the AI.

The biases are manifested in legal education where AI applications have a tendency to produce U.S.-centric summaries of the case even in foreign or comparative law programs. They also lean more toward common law argument than civil law maxims, apply American terminology in referring to such things as Miranda rights to cases in which it has no legal significance, and apply Anglo-American jurisprudence disproportionately to the other legal systems (Rashid, 2024). This does not only limit epistemic pluralism in legal education but it is also a way of forming an understanding of law as a product of the West and hierarchy placing non-Western lawyer-reasoning and approaches at the periphery.

The larger implication is recreation of colonial and epistemic privilege at the digital pedagogy. In Africa, Asia, and Latin America, the legal systems of students are commonly misrepresented, lacked, or taken as a side-note by AI-written content. These asymmetries of representation have the potential of undermining academic confidence, undermining local legal customs, and constraining the world discussion of legal pluralism (Oncioiu & Bularca, 2025). It is not merely a technical issue, however, but also a moral and educative necessity, to resolve the problem of algorithmic bias, a requirement to achieve equity, cultural inclusion, and authenticity in the digital transformation of legal education.

4.3 Case Study: Summarization of Cases in Comparative Law

A course in comparative constitutional law is a course taught collectively by colleges in Canada, India, and the Netherlands that involves the use of an AI text summarizer to create briefs on noteworthy provisions in the constitution each week. Upon the ordered summation of freedom of speech provisions, the tool is habitually guided by the U.S. precedents including Brandenburg v. Ohio and Tinker v. Des Moines as major points of reference (Chen & Zhang, 2025). This trend shows a structural racism of the AI design, which upholds Anglo-American legal traditions as universal standards. Although the goals of the course include introducing the student to models of plural constitutionalism, the use of the tool with U.S. content is contrary to the objective because it results in a smaller range of interpretation through which constitutional rights are perceived.

Every jurisdiction covered in the course has a doctrinal path: the Indian framework is built on reasonable restrictions, which is based on social order and the common welfare, the Canadian jurisprudence is based on the Oakes test in order to weigh the individual rights over the interests of the community, and the jurisprudence of the European Convention on Human Rights is also highly embraced in the Netherlands. By overlooking these differences, the AI based summaries wipe off important contextual nuancies, and constitutional reasoning is narrowed to an Americanized template (Borgesius, 2025). This excess First Amendment jurisprudence over determination at the same time generates marginality of the Global South as well as the Continental European logic, thus creating a lopsided pedagogy.

Students are therefore subjected to constitutional law as arena of intercultural discussion but as a discipline of legal jurisdiction in which Anglo-American interpretations prevail. This epistemic asymmetry supports the power structures that are in place in global legal education and the illusion of the one and best legal model. The example highlights that there is an immediate necessity to have culturally sensitive AI systems in the field of legal pedagogy-systems that can be used to acknowledge the jurisdictional heterogeneity and accomplish fair representation of the thought behind constitutional systems worldwide.

4.4 Automated Moderation and Cultural and Political Sensitivities

In addition to being viewed as content delivery mechanisms, AI systems are used to control and moderate online discussions as well as flag violations of policies, and maintaining safe asynchronous classroom learning in legal education. Such moderation systems are usually based on natural language processing (NLP) and sentiment analysis to identify offensive or abusive terminologies (Yadav et al., 2025). Although these systems are intended to maintain a culture of inclusivity and fostering respect, they do not interpret their contexts or cultures well, especially during global or comparative legal classes. Their disposition to forms of language can lead to hypercensorship that unintentionally censures instead of providing a healthy scrutiny of speech (Grady & Lewis, 2024).

This problem has been evidenced in cross-cultural legal education contexts where moderated by artificial intelligence, valid debates on controversial legal concepts, e.g. blasphemy, abortion, LGBTQ rights, or sedition, are removed or redacted. The use of words or phrases, similar to revolution or nationalism, can automatically be blocked in one jurisdiction, which is considered politically neutral (Serry et al., 2025). Also, legal terminology encoded in local laws or case law can be hidden because of moderation filters created by western centrism regarding what is decent or risky. These discrepancies interfere with the learning experience, and prevent the students from experiencing the variety of legal, moral, and social problems and complexities that are involved in comparative study.

This has sometimes been referred to as algorithmic erasure, emphasizing that efforts by AI to alleviate harm can act rather contradictory by destroying crucial discussions of the law. Censorship of propagated expressions depending on the culture or political framework of the country makes AI moderation systems a danger of cleansing important debates, which are at the heart of constitutional and human rights legislation. The outcome is this narrow intellectual zone whereby one becomes safe at the cost of content- strengthening Western values of acceptability and excluding other epistemologies (Ketzl, 2025). To overcome algorithmic erasure, it is not only necessary to have technical optimization, but to introduce pluralistic ethics based on the legitimacy of various preventative legal and cultural discourses in international education.

4.5 Case Study: Academic Suppression by AI Moderation

During an international human rights law course that students from Pakistan, the United Kingdom, and South Africa engaged in together, an AI-driven chat room was implemented in order to maintain civility and non-offensive dialogue in the virtual classes (Jones, 2025). Nevertheless, for example, when the students were discussing the controversial and yet academically sound issues, including the Hudood Ordinances, LGBTQ+ asylum claims, and death penalty under the Islamic law, AI moderation system was self-flagellated as to these comments as hate speech (Shahid et al., 2025). The decision-making algorithm was Western-centric decisions on what was deemed harmful and what was deemed moral to it as reflected in its training data and moderation policies. Although the students were doing a valid comparative legal analysis, the filtering mechanisms employed by the AI were not able to recognize harmful rhetoric and academic critique.

The faculty were forced to check the flagged posts by hand and reinstate them. Before the content was reinstated, multiple students were already left the conversation complaining that they felt monitored or assume that the system had them, or that it misunderstood them (Shata, 2025). Such interference tore up the trust which is vital in achieving effective classroom interactions and lost faith of the students especially those whose jurisdictions have already made online expression politically sensitive. The incident thereby revealed some kind of struggle between keeping the online world safe and keeping academic freedom intact- which AI moderation systems are poorly positioned to negotiate without cultural awareness and context (Shahid et al., 2025).

On a more in-depth level, the event points to the issue of algorithmic moral projection, through which the automated systems created within the framework of a particular culture force their moral and language standards on another. The parameters of the AI tool were based on Western liberal ideas of harm and tolerance which as unavoidable suppressed the discussions that lie in the core of postcolonial and religious laws (Balendra, 2025). These mechanisms make moral discourse homogenous, establishing epistemic hierarchies according to which some perspective is taken to be safe and others prone to suspicion. It does not only subjugate the comparative pedagogy in global legal education but also supports a digital kind of a cultural dominance.

Finally, the case evidence shows that the culturally responsive AI governance in educational technology is urgently needed because of the recent growth. The moderate systems should be created to provide distinctions between hate speech and critical academic activity, and direct human supervision and contextual fine-tuning. Law studies, like them, are built on conflict, disagreement and communication in course of two different moral regimes (Gao et al., 2025). Where the AI moderation tools cannot embrace such diversity, they accomplish more than censorship- they circumscribe intellectual freedom, discourage intercultural sympathy, and (worse yet) flout the pluralistic spirit of international legal education experiments are trying to draw the world into.

4.6 Free Expression and Algorithmic Censorship Legal Theories

The nature of the regulation of AI-based content moderation in education involves multidimensional overlaps in the constitutional rights to adhere to free speech, academic freedom, and the right to knowledge access. These crossovers are not even inter-jurisdictional homogeneities, but carry multiple historical and normative customs of constitutional law. In the United States, free expression, particularly, in academic settings, is guaranteed under the First Amendment, to the point that any state intrusion must be viewed under a very limited standard of evaluation. In contrast, the European Union is more qualified in the form of the European Court of Human Rights (ECHR), which allows restrictions on speech as the means to defend dignity, order, as well as the right of minorities (Gaïni, 2024). India is a constitutional democracy in which Article 19(1)(a) provides the freedom of speech and expression but it is subjected to reasonable limitations based on the morality, decency, and national security of the people ("The Study of Right to Freedom of Expression, Digital Media Laws and Demand for Innovation," 2025). Meanwhile, in other countries, like China, and some even in the Middle East, education content can be subject of direct state control and censorship on such grounds like political stability or national security (Wu, 2024).

These differences show the way the speech regulation demonstrates the different constitutional cultures and hierarchies of values. Academic free speech in liberal democracies is considered as part of truth-seeking and participation in democratic activities, in contrast to authoritarian or communitarian governments where speech can be sacrificed in the interests of social harmony or the state. As AI moderation systems, which are generally structured along Western corporate lines, are localized internationally, they run a risk of brokering commonplace so-called community norms and overlooking such legal and cultural subtleties (Magdy et al., 2025). The algorithms are inclined to utilize predetermined levels of harmful or offensive pieces, without the understanding of the constitutional status of particular discourses within a certain jurisdiction, and thus, reflecting a discussion around religion, national security, or social reform.

This inconsistency establishes a two-fold legal risk. On the one hand, over filtering of artificial intelligence can be an infringement on protection of the domestic Constitution in situations where unwarranted academic speech is subjected to censorship, such as in the United States or India. Conversely, language that lacks sufficient filtering can be in opposition to the content laws that are restrictive in the countries where a significant number of regulations control speech like in China or Saudi Arabia (Liu, 2025). Universities especially those that have international partnerships or those which provide cross-border online education courses sail on this fine tottering line of being over-compliant or non-compliant. Their conflicting requirements of constitutional law, institutional autonomy and platform governance have to be resolved (Yao-shun et al., 2025).

This has put a new regulatory challenge before higher education institutions: they have responsibility towards the algorithmic choices of temporary AI vendors, and the constitutional obligations of their domestic jurisdictions. Such a tension highlights the pressing necessity of contextualized legal framework of AI moderation in education one that follows the pluralism ideas of in and out constitutionalism, the responsibility of platforms, and the freedom of education. In the absence of these measures, the world-wide application of moderation technologies would turn universities into the systemic agents of privatized, globalized censorship and censorship of a privatized, transnational kind instead of an open, democratic, and critical telos of enquiry.

4.7 Academic Freedom, Expression and Algorithms Boundaries

One of the pillars of higher education and democratic creation of knowledge groups is academic freedom, the right to teach, learn, and investigate without any significant interference. It is especially significant in the area of legal education since law is a field that is full of contentious concepts, dynamic standards, and ethical issues. Academic freedom protects the right of students and faculty to interact with controversial or minority opinions, including controversy over capital punishment or discussion of gender, religion and constitutional reform (Özmen, 2024). This receptiveness to dissent and pluralism is what helps law schools to develop critical thinking and pluralistic concept of justice.

This freedom is being seriously threatened due to the growing dependence on algorithmic content management. Opaque machine-learning models controlled by automated mechanisms tend to work with no information published in the list of terms, topics, or parameters classified by an artificial intelligence system as inappropriate. Such obscurity renders moderation irresponsible since the students and the academic staff cannot question the standards and rationality of the deleted material. Additionally, there are also cases of false positives when the AI-driven applications wrongly identify educational discussions as harmful based on the associations of a keyword: such as classifying posts about the laws of rape shield as harmful because the word rape was used (Wang et al., 2025). The errors of this nature come between proper pedagogical talking by muddling the learning environment through the convergence of analytical and moral/policy transgressions.

These systems have a chilling effect which perhaps is even more sinister. In cases where the learners feel threatened upon being reported, monitored and even reprimanded due to discussing delicate or politically sensitive topics, they will also start self-censoring. Such an unspoken withdrawal stultifies intellectual discourse and closes the intellectual parameters of enquiry. Such self-censorship in legal education, where subtlety, controversy, and critical thinking are vital, makes the pedagogy and scholarship poor and weak. Instead of open discussion it substitutes with algorithmically patrolled conformity making universities risk averse places where safety prevails over intellectual discover (Camlin, 2025) .

These are the direct violations of international norms that safeguard academic freedom and expressive freedom. The Recommendation on Open Educational Resources by the UNESCO (2019) calls on member states to create open, inclusive and culturally diverse learning systems at the same time The right to seek, receive and impart information irrespective of the frontiers that have led to development is enshrined in the Article 19 of the International Covenant on Civil and Political rights (ICCPR) (Patil, 2023). Algorithms which help to restrict the expression of legitimate academic would thus not only compromise pedagogical integrity but would also be violating these international commitments to human rights. Protecting academic freedom in the digital era must therefore engage clear, answerable, and circumstantial AI administration that acts in regard to institutional sovereignty as well as universality of intellectual liberty.

4.8 Toward Cross-Cultural Moderation Standards

To successfully address algorithmic biasness and discrimination in transnational legal education (TNE) programs, transnational legal education institutions need to implement cross-cultural moderation guidelines that appreciate and honor the manners of jurisdiction, speech, and pedagogy. An AI moderation style that fits one size is necessarily insufficient in garment classes that traverse various legal traditions and cultures. Rather, systems are to be constructed in a manner that enables contextual interpretations of words that are sensitive to make sure that the legal discourse is accurate and inclusive (Prince-Tritto & Pönce, 2025). Creation of context-sensitive words specific to jurisdictions can avoid the act of legitimate debate of controversial ideas, like “sedition,” “blasphemy,” or gender identity, being censored inappropriately.

Faculty override mechanisms and transparent flagging logs are also of the highest importance as they reinstitute the element of human judgment in the middle of academic moderation. Teachers need to be given the authority to check flagged material in real time, allow legitimate discussions, and give students clear causes of moderation. It does not only strengthen pedagogical autonomy, but also sets a precedence of due process- a principle which forms the core of legal education in the first place. Open flagging, in which learners are notified of the reason and method of their post being flagged and provided with means through which they may appeal, instills responsibility and clarifies the process of algorithm decision-making (Noller & Thimesch, 2025). Likewise, the calibration of the differential sensitivity thresholds needs to be done based on the course material, and thus it may be more flexible in a course that focuses on human rights or constitutional law, where a controversial language may be necessary to engage in a critical discussion.

Lastly, the participation of multiple languages in the calibration process is essential to make sure that the AI instruments will be applied fairly across the languages and dialects and avoid the systemic exclusion of non-English language discourse. However, even these technical measures are not enough to address more fundamental normative problems. They need to be framed in a wider structure of governance that affirms pedagogical purpose, safeguards expression by the students and faculty autonomy. Universities ought to have committees in charge of the governance on the algorithms based on the ethics of transparency, inclusivity, and proportionality (Oncioiu & Bularca, 2025). Simply put, it does not just aspire to perfect algorithms but to reorient their purpose, not to dominate speech but allow legitimate and context-based legal discourse across jurisdictions.

4.9 Regulatory Comparative Approaches

Governments globally are finding different legal frameworks to regulate AI-based content moderation with each being an expression of different policy priorities and constitutional virtues. The Digital Services Act (DSA) of the European Union is one such most comprehensive model since it requires high transparency and audit requirements of digital platforms which filter user content. The regulation that is provided by the Act implies the publication of moderation policies, algorithmic logic, and appeals operations and conditions that have a direct impact on EdTech providers offering AI moderation to academic settings directly (Temper et al., 2025). Likewise, the Online Safety Bill by the United Kingdom ensures the introduction of the so-called duty of care system in which the platforms are responsible for the elimination of online harms, even in educational settings. Even though it alleges to secure its users, its wide application poses a danger of making the discussion between genuine scholarly work and harmful information prominent, thus limiting the freedom of expression in online classroom settings (Krupp et al., 2024) .

By contrast, the Information Technology (Intermediary Guidelines and Digital Media Ethics Code) Rules, 2021 in India imposition on intermediaries in stripping out objectionable or illegal information on the Internet within narrow deadlines is stricter unlike in the US. The Rules fail to make a clear distinction between a public platform and an educational tool, which means that AI moderation systems deployed in transnational programs tend to be located in the grey areas of the regulations. This uncertainty puts universities and EdTech providers under pressure to take overly safe measures of moderation to avoid being fined (Xue et al., 2025). In the United States, meanwhile, the Communications Decency Act, Section 230 gives a wide blanket of immunity to websites hosting user-generated content to the point of giving the actors much latitude on how they might moderate the content. This free market model has given the fast adoption of AI but placed educators institutions in a situation of being dependent on corporate ethics instead of legal responsibility (Yan & Liu, 2024).

This legal environment poses deep compliance concerns in the case of transnational education (TNE) institutions. Multijurisdictional Programmes have to work out conflicting demands among the different jurisdictions, the transparency requirements of the EU, the prescriptive removal requirements of India and the model of corporate freedom in the United States. Unless there is an optimized international standard, platforms would tend to interpret the regulation of speech in the most limiting way possible to reduce all exposure to legal liability (Huang, 2025). The outcome is a de facto establishment of global over-censorship minority, wherein AI-based moderation algorithms censor legitimate learning exchange to fit within the most liberal or strict regulatory statute. This points out the necessity of organised international based governance that balances regulatory uniformity and safeguard of academic freedom as well as cultural plurality in education mediated by AI.

4.10 AI Governance - Recommendations in Legal Education

As discussed above, this Section suggests a multi-layering model of AI moderation in transnational legal education (TNE), with transparency, accountability, and cultural sensitivity as its core topics. First, the institutions need to formulate context specific, transparent and reversible moderation measures. This would necessitate discarding the generic and impositionally platform-based community policies in favor of university-equipped moderation rules which are sensitive to the disciplinary and cultural backgrounds of legal training. Moderation should be transparent, students, and faculty ought to understand the content flags triggering system, how the algorithms judge risky content, and which individual has the ultimate decision-making power. Furthermore, judgement ought to be reversible, in the event of that the bona fide academic discourse has been censored. This reversibility is a form of due process in online learning and moderating practices correlate with procedural fairness that commonly exists in legal institutions per se.

Second, legal scholars and domain experts should be involved in the creation of moderation taxonomies, categories of content by which AI operates and categorizes content. Law is a highly contextual and subjective practice; in this regard moderation systems have to be flexible enough to distinguish between deliberate speech and legitimate criticism. The use of legal academics also guarantees the understanding of such terms like sedition, blasphemy or terrorism in their jurisdictional and jurisprudential contexts. The moderate design of the moderation taxonomies in cooperation with legal educators certifies against disqualification, as well as fosters disciplinary integrity. This method is also a democratization of AI regulation, introducing the input of human knowledge into the design phase instead of having to fix the problem after it has been committed.

Thirdly, the section suggests that TNE consortia should be provided with AI oversight boards to examine cases of moderation and unbiased trends and to exercise proportionality. These boards, which would consist of faculty, technologists, ethicists, and student representatives, would give an opportunity to discuss routine cases of algorithmic discrimination or over-censorship. They would also support cross institutional learning where best practice would circulation among partner universities in this way. Exercising institutionalized oversight, universities can shift to preventive not reactive governance as this ensures constant review of AI moderation in line with ethical, legal and pedagogical standards.

Fourth, any AI moderation tools implemented in learning institutions must pass content neutrality audits before implementation. These audits, based on the algorithmic fairness assessment, would verify systems of moderate systems of bias along the parameters of gender, religion, nation of origin, and language diversity. They should be publicly released and this facilitates transparency and accountability. Fifth, the training of students and faculty is necessary on a broad level to create awareness of rights and redress mechanisms in algorithmic learning settings. Faculty should be aware of how to convey AI moderation reports, dispute unfair results, and facilitate the appeal procedures of students. The students, in their turn, need to be informed about their rights as digital citizens, privacy concerns, and system of institutional support.

Lastly, the practice of moderation needs to comply with the International legal standards regarding the freedom of expression and academic freedom. This alignment must rely on the tools namely the ICCPR and the ICESCR, AI Ethics Recommendation developed by the UNESCO, and the UNESCO AI Principles. Incorporating these frameworks into institutional policy will make AI systems in the educational sector support human rights, cultural pluralism, and intellectual pluralism rather than destroy them. Essentially, this roadmap views AI moderation as a facilitative, rather than a controlling, instrument, which does not reduce legal discourse richness, but provides fairness, inclusivity, and rule of law to digital learning platforms.

Any implementation of AI in the field of content moderation should never interfere with the main essence of legal training the ability to question, argue, and disagree. Legal education is idealized by contestation in which ideas are contested, doctrines are redefined and norms are scrutinized by rational discourse. When opaque, biased or authoritarian algorithmic regimes are used to filter transnational curricula, the process is corrupted. The classroom becomes a site of cognitive exploration instead of mechanistic drill as students and faculty learn to accept the rules of algorithms rather than being exposed to constitutional and ethical thought. This moderation does not only restrict the emergence of a critical mind but can also possibly result in a future generation of lawyers and scholars who have been conditioned to evade controversy, as opposed to fighting against it using law and logic.

In order to maintain the integrity, inclusivity and emancipatory intent of legal learning, learning institutions should take pedagogical agency over platform logic. This will involve bringing back control to the algorithms of corporations and restoring academic freedom as an uncompromising operation in AI-mediated education. Universities should also make sure that technology is employed to their pedagogical purpose and not vice versa by means of open administration, faculty control, and involvement of the students in the moderation design. It is so that AI could be used to improve legal education, making it challenging to argue with different opinions, simplifying the communication process, and accessing information around the globe. However this is achievable only at the time when its moderation systems are able to be answerable to the human values, mindful to the cross-cultural realities and when they are associated with the very legal norms they are aimed to be realized on. By so doing, AI does not become the keeper of discourse, but a partner in promoting the principles of the rule of law, justice, and critical enquiry in the world classrooms.

5: CONCLUSION – LEGAL TECHNOLOGICAL FOUNDATIONS TO AN ETHICALLY MOTIVATED AI FUTURE IN TRANS-NATIONAL JURISPRUDENCE.

Artificial intelligence (AI) has emerged to transform transnational legal education (TNE) in two aspects, at once creating both a new reality of pedagogy, as automated, personalised, and accessible, and a new reality of challenging jurisdiction, ethics, and regulation. Throughout this chapter, the results suggest that the effect of AI on legal education is not solely efficiency, but it also changes the definition of authority, authorship, and autonomy within the academic realm. The infrastructural leak exerting the force of jurisdictional fragmentation - data protection, intellectual property and algorithmic governance - shows that the borderless nature of technological innovation is accompanied by the territorial accountability of the law. This lack of correspondence leads to lack of clarity of responsibility in data abuse, AI bias and violation of student rights particularly in cross-border programs. Thus, the conclusion to be made first can be that AI integration in law education cannot be developed on a sustainable basis without a balanced system of transnational governance, which can bring digital processes into equilibrium with legal norms that may be enforced.

The study also indicates that institutional capabilities and the legal compliance systems are behind the use of AI, especially in the Global South. Various universities are dependent on the technologies provided by vendors without due diligence in the field of the data protection or intellectual property ownership. the Brief Case studies and policy reviews that are addressed lack depth indicate that the asymmetry of the contract between EdTech providers and institutions exposes students to privacy violations and algorithmic discrimination. With a previous mediated faculty-created content and student submissions being prone to ownership disputes and monetization of secondary data, AI regards raw data as secondary data. This highlights why Data Protection Impact Assessments (DPIAs) should become compulsory, and IP clauses in contracts with the vendors should be legal, and faculty needs to be trained on the accountability of the algorithms. The evidence shows that in the absence of such safeguards, innovation would contribute to increasing digital disparities among institutions and jurisdictions.

The other significant discovery is the issue of algorithmic discrimination and the loss of academic freedom. The chapter confirms that AI moderation systems, which are commonly trained using western data, create epistemic dominance in university law school. Discussion-blocking or discussion- warning tools are not only harmful to the learning outcomes, but also replicate colonial structures in the dissemination of knowledge. These empirical trends, seen in the AI moderation logs and on-record experience of students, show that there is regular over-flagging of non-western legal discourse. Therefore, to ensure AI oversight boards, preventing bias, and fostering inclusivity in AI, institutions should apply context-based moderation criteria, faculty override, and implement the AI oversight boards. Such provisions can change moderation into an instrument of disciplinary authority to an instrument of democratic academic governance.

Relatively, the results demonstrate that AI regulation in education is in a piecemeal international legal hodgepodge. Individual policies on platform liability and speech protection take different philosophies in the EU/Digital Services Act, India/IT Rules 2021, the UK/Online Safety Bill and U.S./Section 230. In the case of TNE programs, such multiplicity brings with it compliance paralysis-platforms would be following the strictest standard possible to make sure that they are not held liable leading to a world-over-censored situation. The discussion finds that TNE institutions have to entertain dual-compliance frameworks, which should comply with both local-jurisdictional requirements and foreign soft-law guidelines: ICCPR, ICESCR, UNESCO AI Ethics Recommendation, and OECD AI Principles. Such an alignment guarantees moderation, data governance, and student assessment practices not only to be in line with international human rights requirements but also to be sensitive to diversity in regulatory practices in a country.

A last point is that the future of AI in the legal field needs to be human centered, rights based and pluralistic, as the present paper confirms. To achieve sustainable adoption, it is necessary to integrate AI architecture based on right by design and create pluralism by default in training data and provide transparency by ensuring traceable algorithmic documentation. The last section of the chapter ends on a distinct policy path: in order to make AI ethics institutional in universities, the regulators need to come up with interoperable educational AI standards, and students should become the active stakeholders in the governance. Taken together, the above findings express an idea of a model that technological progress fulfills the ideals of justice, equality, and academic honesty. It is only under such structure that transnational legal education will be able to re-assert its humanistic agenda whilst responsibly changing with the age of the algorithm.

REFERENCES

Agrawal, A., & Jain, S. S. (2024). Indian Copyright Law and Generative AI. DOI: 10.2139/ssrn.5028835

Agyemang-Badu, S., Tibbitts, F., & Phillips, S. (2025). AI Human Rights Literacy. *Current Issues in Comparative Education*, *26*(2). Advance online publication. DOI: 10.52214/cice.v26i2.13139

Ajjawi, R., Tai, J., Boud, D., & Jorre, T. J. de S. (2022). Assessment for Inclusion in Higher Education. In *Routledge eBooks*. Informa., DOI: 10.4324/9781003293101

Akhmadieva, R. Sh., Kalmazova, N., Belova, T. V., Prokopyev, A. I., Molodozhnikova, N. M., & Spichak, V. Y. (2024). Research trends in the use of artificial intelligence in higher education. *Frontiers in Education*, *9*, 1438715. Advance online publication. DOI: 10.3389/feduc.2024.1438715

Al-Zahrani, A. M., & Alasmari, T. (2024). Exploring the impact of artificial intelligence on higher education: The dynamics of ethical, social, and educational implications. *Humanities & Social Sciences Communications*, *11*(1), 912. Advance online publication. DOI: 10.1057/s41599-024-03432-4

Alaswad, S., Kalganova, T., & Awad, W. (2025). Trustworthiness of Legal Considerations for the Use of LLMs in Education. DOI: 10.48550/ARXIV.2508.03771

Alkhamsi, N. N., & Alqahtani, S. S. (2024). Compliance Framework for Personal Data Protection Law Standards. *International Journal of Advanced Computer Science and Applications*, *15*(7). Advance online publication. DOI: 10.14569/IJACSA.2024.0150751

Amo-Filvà, D., Prinsloo, P., Alier, M., Fonseca, D., Kompen, R. T., Canaleta, X., & Herrero, J. (2021). Local Technology to Enhance Data Privacy and Security in Educational Technology. *International Journal of Interactive Multimedia and Artificial Intelligence*, *7*(2), 262–273. DOI: 10.9781/ijimai.2021.11.006

Angwaomaodoko, E. A. (2023). The Re-examination of the Dangers and Implications of Artificial Intelligence for the Future of Scholarship and Learning. *Traektoriâ Nauki*, *9*(10), 3021–3028. DOI: 10.22178/pos.97-24

Balan, A. (2024). Examining the ethical and sustainability challenges of legal education's AI revolution. *International Journal of the Legal Profession*, *1*(3), 323–348. Advance online publication. DOI: 10.1080/09695958.2024.2421179

Balendra, S. (2025). Meta's AI moderation and free speech: Ongoing challenges in the Global South. 1. DOI: 10.1017/cfl.2025.5

Banu, J. T. (2024). AI in Learning: Designing the Future. *Technical Communication Quarterly*, *1*. Advance online publication. DOI: 10.1080/10572252.2024.2428400

Berendt, B., Littlejohn, A., & Blakemore, M. (2020). AI in education: Learner choice and fundamental rights. *Learning, Media and Technology*, *45*(3), 312–324. DOI: 10.1080/17439884.2020.1786399

Berengueres, J., & Sandell, M. (2023). Applying Standards to Advance Upstream & Downstream Ethics in Large Language Models. DOI: 10.48550/ARXIV.2306.03503

Bibi, A. (2024). Navigating The Ethical Landscape. *Ai Integration In Education.*, *1579*, 1579–1585. Advance online publication. DOI: 10.53555/kuey.v30i6.5546

Bond, M., Khosravi, H., de Laat, M., Bergdahl, N., Negrea, V., Oxley, E., Pham, P., Chong, S. W., & Siemens, G. (2024). A meta systematic review of artificial intelligence in higher education: A call for increased ethics, collaboration, and rigour. *International Journal of Educational Technology in Higher Education*, *21*(1), 4. Advance online publication. DOI: 10.1186/s41239-023-00436-z

Borgesius, F. Z. (2025). Discrimination, artificial intelligence, and algorithmic decision-making. arXiv (Cornell University). https://doi.org//arxiv.2510.13465DOI: 10.48550

Brogan, P. (2020). Consumer Redress Through Online Dispute Resolution: The Role of Online Dispute Resolution in Facilitating Consumer Access to Justice in E-Commerce. Arbitration Law Review, 12(1), 12. https://elibrary.law.psu.edu/arbitrationlawreview/vol12/iss1/12/

Caccavale, F. (2025). From Programming to Chatbots: Digitalization Strategies in Chemical Engineering Education. Research Portal Denmark, 189. https://local.forskningsportal.dk/local/dki-cgi/ws/cris-link?src=dtu&id=dtu-1c0f7ee8-b1b8-4bfc-bf57-f19819e54567&ti=From%20Programming%20to%20Chatbots%3A%20Digitalization%20Strategies%20in%20Chemical%20Engineering%20Education

Camlin, J. (2025). A Theorem-Based Analysis of Epistemic Disruption in Higher Education: Defining Wokeism as an Epistemic Doctrine. DOI: 10.2139/ssrn.5254622

Chatinakrob, T. (2024). Legal Risks and Challenges of Unregulated AI. In *Brill | Nijhoff eBooks* (p. 268). Brill., DOI: 10.1163/9789004719934_010

Chau, B. K., & Livermore, M. A. (2024). Computational Legal Studies Comes of Age. *European Journal of Empirical Legal Studies*, *1*(1), 89–104. DOI: 10.62355/ejels.19684

Chen, Q. Z., & Zhang, A. X. (2025). Case Law Grounding. *Using Precedents to Align Decision-Making for Humans and AI.*, *226*, 226–238. Advance online publication. DOI: 10.1145/3715928.3737487

Colonna, L. (2021). Legal Implications of Using AI as an Exam Invigilator. SSRN Electronic Journal. DOI: 10.2139/ssrn.3839287

Cordero, J., Torres-Zambrano, J., & Cordero-Castillo, A. (2024). Integration of Generative Artificial Intelligence in Higher Education: Best Practices. *Education Sciences*, *15*(1), 32. DOI: 10.3390/educsci15010032

de Laat, M., Ryberg, T., Dohn, N. B., Hansen, S. B., & Hansen, J. J. (2020). Networked Learning 2020 : Proceedings for the Twelfth International Conference on Networked Learning. In Research Portal Denmark (p. 400). Technical University of Denmark. https://local.forskningsportal.dk/local/dki-cgi/ws/cris-link?src=aau&id=aau-17488b95-fb1d-4734-8a57-26c7ee0914ec&ti=Networked%20Learning%202020%20%3A%20Proceedings%20for%20the%20Twelfth%20International%20Conference%20on%20Networked%20Learning

Deep, S., Athimoolam, K., & Enoch, T. (2024). Optimizing Administrative Efficiency and Student engagement in Education: The Impact of AI. *International Journal of Current Science Research and Review*, *7*(10). Advance online publication. DOI: 10.47191/ijcsrr/V7-i10-34

Di, X., Zhu, D., & Wen-hai, X. (2021). The Teaching Pattern of Law Majors Using Artificial Intelligence and Deep Neural Network Under Educational Psychology. *Frontiers in Psychology*, *12*, 711520. Advance online publication. DOI: 10.3389/fpsyg.2021.711520

Draper, M., Lancaster, T., Dann, S. E., Crockett, R. G. M., & Glendinning, I. (2021). Essay mills and other contract cheating services: To buy or not to buy and the consequences of students changing their minds. *International Journal for Educational Integrity*, *17*(1), 13. Advance online publication. DOI: 10.1007/s40979-021-00081-x

Enríquez, B. G. A., Ballesteros, M. A. A., Várgas, C. G. A. P., Ulloa, M. N. O., Ulloa, C. R. G., Romero, J. P., Jaramillo, N. D. G., Orellana, H. U. C., Anzoátegui, D. X. A., & Roca, C. L. (2024). Knowledge, attitudes, and perceived Ethics regarding the use of ChatGPT among generation Z university students. *International Journal for Educational Integrity*, *20*(1), 10. Advance online publication. DOI: 10.1007/s40979-024-00157-4

Ezzaim, A., Dahbi, A., Haidine, A., & Aqqal, A. (2023). AI-Based Adaptive Learning: A Systematic Mapping of the Literature. JUCS -. *Journal of Universal Computer Science*, *29*(10), 1161–1198. DOI: 10.3897/jucs.90528

Farber, S. (2024). Harmonizing AI and human instruction in legal education: A case study from Israel on training future legal professionals. *International Journal of the Legal Profession*, *1*(3), 349–363. Advance online publication. DOI: 10.1080/09695958.2024.2430018

G, A. P., & Nair, V. (2024). Integrating Generative AI into Legal Education: From Casebooks to Code, Opportunities and Challenges. Law Technology and Humans, 6(3), 60. DOI: 10.5204/lthj.3640

Gaïni, S. M. (2024). Freedom of Speech, Hate Speech and Democratic Formation : On the double function of hate speech legislation and its relation to freedom of political speech. Research Portal Denmark, 107. https://local.forskningsportal.dk/local/dki-cgi/ws/cris-link?src=ruc&id=ruc-3691400e-1c12-4e84-a217-68e3a46a291e&ti=Freedom%20of%20Speech%2C%20Hate%20Speech%20and%20Democratic%20Formation%20%3A%20On%20the%20double%20function%20of%20hate%20speech%20legislation%20and%20its%20relation%20to%20freedom%20of%20political%20speech

Gao, R., Yu, D., Gao, B., Hua, H., Hui, Z., Gao, J., & Yin, C. (2025). Legal regulation of AI-assisted academic writing: Challenges, frameworks, and pathways. *Frontiers in Artificial Intelligence*, *8*, 1546064. Advance online publication. DOI: 10.3389/frai.2025.1546064

Gaumann, N., & Veale, M. (2023). AI Providers as Criminal Essay Mills? Large Language Models meet Contract Cheating Law. DOI: 10.31235/osf.io/cpbfd

Ghoshal, R. (2025). Cross-border AI governance for legal tech: Standardizing ethical and legal norms in access to justice. *International Journal of Law Justice and Jurisprudence*, *5*(1), 186–194. DOI: 10.22271/2790-0673.2025.v5.i1c.177

Grady, A. R., & Lewis, J. A. (2024). Perceptions of academic discrimination mediate the relationship between political minority status and self-censorship among US college students. *Discover Psychology*, *4*(1), 191. Advance online publication. DOI: 10.1007/s44202-024-00308-1

Gray, S. L., Edsall, D. G., & Parapadakis, D. (2025). AI-Based Digital Cheating At University, and the Case for New Ethical Pedagogies. *Journal of Academic Ethics, 23*(4), 2069–2086. Advance online publication. DOI: 10.1007/s10805-025-09642-y

Greco, C. M., & Tagarelli, A. (2023). Bringing order into the realm of Transformer-based language models for artificial intelligence and law. *Artificial Intelligence and Law, 32*(4), 863–1010. DOI: 10.1007/s10506-023-09374-7

Gutowski, N., & Hurley, J. (2025). Forging Ahead or Proceeding with Caution; Developing Policy for Generative Artificial Intelligence in Legal Education. DOI: 10.2139/ssrn.5076598

Guzzo, T., Ferri, F., & Grifoni, P. (2023). Lessons Learned during COVID-19 and Future Perspectives for Emerging Technology. *Sustainability (Basel), 15*(14), 10747. DOI: 10.3390/su151410747

Han, S. (2024). Data and statecraft: Why and how states localize data. *Business and Politics, 26*(2), 263–288. DOI: 10.1017/bap.2023.41

Heinrich, E. (2025). A Systematic-Narrative Review of Online Proctoring Systems and a Case for Open Standards [Review of A Systematic-Narrative Review of Online Proctoring Systems and a Case for Open Standards]. Open Praxis, 17(3). International Council for Open and Distance Education. DOI: 10.55982/openpraxis.17.3.836

Hopfenbeck, T. N., Zhang, Z., Sun, S. Z., Robertson, P., & McGrane, J. A. (2023). Challenges and opportunities for classroom-based formative assessment and AI: A perspective article. *Frontiers in Education, 8*, 1270700. Advance online publication. DOI: 10.3389/feduc.2023.1270700

Hu, Y.-H. (2025). Advancing asynchronous pre-class learning in flipped classrooms: Generative AI companions in business ethics. *Education and Information Technologies, 30*(10), 14367–14391. Advance online publication. DOI: 10.1007/s10639-025-13379-x

Huang, T. (2025). NetChoice, Regulatory Competition, and the Real Battle Behind Social Media Regulations. SSRN Electronic Journal. DOI: 10.2139/ssrn.5222236

Hutson, J., & Plate, D. (2024). The Algorithm of Fear: Unpacking Prejudice Against AI and the Mistrust of Technology. Journal of Innovation and Technology, 2024(1). DOI: 10.61453/joit.v2024no38

Huy, D. P. M., Nguyen, G. N., & Le, D. (2025). A Combine Solution for Online Exams Cheating Detection, Prediction, and Prevention Using Artificial Intelligence. In *Lecture notes in networks and systems* (p. 665). Springer International Publishing., DOI: 10.1007/978-981-96-3381-4_51

Idrizi, E. (2024). Exploring the Role of Explainable Artificial Intelligence(XAI) in Adaptive learning systems. 100. DOI: 10.1145/3660853.3660877

Ifenthaler, D., Majumdar, R., Gorissen, P., Judge, M., Mishra, S., Raffaghelli, J. E., & Shimada, A. (2024). *Artificial Intelligence in Education: Implications for Policymakers, Researchers, and Practitioners*. Technology Knowledge and Learning., DOI: 10.1007/s10758-024-09747-0

Imohimi, E. O. (2025). Building Privacy and Preserving AI Models for Secure Student Data Management in Educational Technology Platforms. *Journal of Intelligent Learning Systems and Applications, 17*(3), 149–171. DOI: 10.4236/jilsa.2025.173011

Jaadi, M. E., Haidi, T., & Bouabdallaoui, D. (2025). *IAES International Journal of Artificial Intelligence (IJ-AI)*. IAES International Journal of Artificial Intelligence., DOI: 10.11591/ijai

Jones, B. (2025). Enhancing cross-cultural exchange with AI: ChatGPT's role in an international online student conference. 1(1), 2138. DOI: 10.29140/jct.v1n1.2138

Kastberg, P., & Ditlevsen, M. G. (2021). Let's talk about how we talk about employees.: A critical examination of the discursive construction of the employee in the textbooks that shape the HR managers of tomorrow. Research Portal Denmark. https://local.forskningsportal.dk/local/dki-cgi/ws/cris-link?src=au&id=au-7eed7534-b4f3-447e-91b6-0c9b39e21819&ti=Let%2019s%20talk%20about%20how%20we%20talk%20about%20employees.%20%3A%20A%20critical%20examination%20of%20the%20discursive%20construction%20of%20the%20employee%20in%20the%20textbooks%20that%20shape%20the%20HR%20managers%20of%20tomorrow

Kelso, E., Soneji, A., Navid, S. Z.-U.-H., Soshitaishvili, Y., Rahaman, S., & Hasan, R. (2025). Investigating the Security & Privacy Risks from Unsanctioned Technology Use by Educators. DOI: 10.48550/ARXIV.2502.16739

Ketzl, A. D. (2025). Knowledge Censorship in 21st Century Academia: An Overview with Attention to the Trends of Wokeism and Cancel Culture. *Open Journal of Social Sciences, 13*(3), 330–345. DOI: 10.4236/jss.2025.133023

Khairullah, S. A., Harris, S., Hadi, H. J., Sandhu, R., Ahmad, N., & Alshara, M. A. (2025). Implementing artificial intelligence in academic and administrative processes through responsible strategic leadership in the higher education institutions. *Frontiers in Education, 10*, 1548104. Advance online publication. DOI: 10.3389/feduc.2025.1548104

Khan, S., Mazhar, T., Shahzad, T., Khan, M. A., Rehman, A. U., Saeed, M. M., & Hamam, H. (2025). Harnessing AI for sustainable higher education: Ethical considerations, operational efficiency, and future directions. *Discover Sustainability, 6*(1), 23. Advance online publication. DOI: 10.1007/s43621-025-00809-6

Korff, D. (2023). The Indian Digital Personal Data Protection Act, 2023, viewed from a European Perspective. SSRN Electronic Journal. DOI: 10.2139/ssrn.4614984

Krištofík, A. (2025). Bias in AI (Supported) Decision Making: Old Problems, New Technologies. *International Journal for Court Administration, 16*(1), 3. Advance online publication. DOI: 10.36745/ijca.598

Krupp, L., Steinert, S., Kiefer-Emmanouilidis, M., Avila, K. E., Lukowicz, P., Kühn, J., Küchemann, S., & Karolus, J. (2024)... *Challenges and Opportunities of Moderating Usage of Large Language Models in Education., 249*, 249–254. Advance online publication. DOI: 10.1145/3701571.3701590

Kumar, M., Kumar, R., Arisham, D. K., Gupta, R. K., Naudiyal, P., Goutam, G., & Mavi, A. K. (2025). Emerging AI impact in the healthcare sector: A review [Review of Emerging AI impact in the healthcare sector: A review]. European Journal of Environment and Public Health, 9(1). Lectito Journals. DOI: 10.29333/ejeph/15905

LaFleur, D. (2019, January 1). Transnational Partnerships and Dual Degrees: Entrepreneurial Strategies for Internationalization. *Proceedings of the 2019 AERA Annual Meeting*. DOI: 10.3102/1439066

Landau, S., Dempsey, J. X., Kamar, E., Bellovin, S. M., & Pool, R. (2024). Challenging the Machine: Contestability in Government AI Systems. arXiv (Cornell University). https://doi.org//arxiv.2406 .10430DOI: 10.48550

Lande, J. (2025). Responsible Realism About Artificial Intelligence: How AI is Shaping Legal and Dispute Resolution Practice, Education, and Scholarship. SSRN Electronic Journal. DOI: 10.2139/ssrn.5309439

Larsen, B. C. (2022). Governing Artificial Intelligence : Lessons from the United States and China. Research Portal Denmark, 300. https://local.forskningsportal.dk/local/dki-cgi/ws/cris-link?src=cbs&id =cbs-48598543-6d06-4e04-82ac-07eea8605f9f&ti=Governing%20Artificial%20Intelligence%20%3A %20Lessons%20from%20the%20United%20States%20and%20China

Liu, D. (2025). BORDERLINE CONTENT AND PLATFORMISED SPEECH GOVERNANCE: MAPPING TIKTOK'S MODERATION CONTROVERSIES IN SOUTH AND SOUTHEAST ASIA. AoIR Selected Papers of Internet Research. DOI: 10.5210/spir.v2024i0.13988

Madhu, N. Y.MADHU N YLATHA P HSAVITHA N. (2024). Revolutionizing Education: Harnessing AI for Personalized Learning Pathways and Student Success. *International Journal For Multidisciplinary Research*, *6*(5), 28371. Advance online publication. DOI: 10.36948/ijfmr.2024.v06i05.28371

Magdy, W., Mubarak, H. A., & Salminen, J. (2025). Who should set the Standards? Analysing Censored Arabic Content on Facebook during the Palestine-Israel Conflict. 1. DOI: 10.1145/3706598.3713150

Magesh, V., Surani, F., Dahl, M., Suzgun, M., Manning, C. D., & Ho, D. E. (2025). Hallucination-Free? Assessing the Reliability of Leading AI Legal Research Tools. *Journal of Empirical Legal Studies*, *22*(2), 216–242. DOI: 10.1111/jels.12413

Mahajan, P. (2025). What is Ethical: AIHED Driving Humans or Human-Driven AIHED? A Conceptual Framework enabling the 'Ethos' of AI-driven. *Higher Education*. Advance online publication. DOI: 10.14293/PR2199.001510.v1

Mania, K. (2022). Legal Technology: Assessment of the Legal Tech Industry's Potential. *Journal of the Knowledge Economy*, *14*(2), 595–619. DOI: 10.1007/s13132-022-00924-z

Mbah, G. O.Geraldine O Mbah. (2024). Data privacy in the era of AI: Navigating regulatory landscapes for global businesses. *International Journal of Science and Research Archive*, *13*(2), 2040–2058. DOI: 10.30574/ijsra.2024.13.2.2396

ME, L., G, S. D., Shuba, S., Sneha, K., & Sofiya, S. (2024). Adaptive Learning Management System. DOI: 10.59544/PQYL6304/ICRCCT24P39

Milchior, R. (2024). Digital platforms, competition law, and regulation. Journal of Intellectual Property Law & Practice. DOI: 10.1093/jiplp/jpae074

Modi, H. (2023). Leveraging Natural Language Processing for Legal Research: Trends and Future Directions. SSRN Electronic Journal. DOI: 10.2139/ssrn.4514036

Morawa, A. H. E. (2008). Transnationalization of Legal Education: A Swiss (and Comparative) Perspective. SSRN Electronic Journal. https://papers.ssrn.com/sol3/papers.cfm?abstract_id=1596091

Mouta, A., Llorente, A. M. P., & Sánchez, E. M. T. (2023). Uncovering Blind Spots in Education Ethics: Insights from a Systematic Literature Review on Artificial Intelligence in Education. *International Journal of Artificial Intelligence in Education*. Advance online publication. DOI: 10.1007/s40593-023-00384-9

Noller, D. T., & Thimesch, A. E. (2025). Artificial Intelligence in Higher Education: Legal Accountability and Best Practices for Upholding Student Privacy and Nondiscrimination Rights. *The Journal of Physician Assistant Education : the Official Journal of the Physician Assistant Education Association, 36*(3), e308–e311. Advance online publication. DOI: 10.1097/JPA.0000000000000688

Nyaaba, M., Wright, A., & Choi, G. L. (2024). Generative AI and Digital Neocolonialism in Global Education: Towards an Equitable Framework. DOI: 10.48550/ARXIV.2406.02966

Oncioiu, I., & Bularca, A. R. (2025). Artificial Intelligence Governance in Higher Education: The Role of Knowledge-Based Strategies in Fostering Legal Awareness and Ethical Artificial Intelligence Literacy. *Societies (Basel, Switzerland), 15*(6), 144. DOI: 10.3390/soc15060144

Ouellette, L. L., Motomura, A., Reinecke, J., & Masur, J. S. (2025). Can AI Hold Office Hours? DOI: 10.2139/ssrn.5166938

Özmen, E. (2024). Academic freedom: Normative ideals, contemporary challenges. *Zeitschrift für Politikwissenschaft, 34*(3), 379–385. DOI: 10.1007/s41358-024-00390-w

Pacheco-Mendoza, S., Guevara, C., Albán, A. L. M., & Fernández-Escobar, J. E. (2023). Artificial Intelligence in Higher Education: A Predictive Model for Academic Performance. *Education Sciences, 13*(10), 990. DOI: 10.3390/educsci13100990

Patil, L. (2023). Education governance and digitization: Inherent conflicts and potential safeguards for a new social contract. *Prospects, 54*(2), 323–329. DOI: 10.1007/s11125-023-09668-3

Praveenkumar, S., Anute, N., Vaissnave, V., Ragupathi, T., Fardale, S., Selvakumar, P., & Manjunath, T. C. (2025). Risks of AI Bias and Inequities in Learning. In *Advances in computational intelligence and robotics book series* (p. 257). IGI Global., DOI: 10.4018/979-8-3373-2302-2.ch009

Prince-Tritto, P., & Pönce, H. (2025). Causal Artificial Intelligence in Legal Language Processing: A Systematic Review [Review of Causal Artificial Intelligence in Legal Language Processing: A Systematic Review]. Entropy, 27(4), 351. Multidisciplinary Digital Publishing Institute. DOI: 10.3390/e27040351

Pruss, D., Pullen-Blasnik, H., Stevens, N., Rahman, S., Belitz, C., Stapleton, L., Dharmaraj, M. G., Aizeki, M., Molnar, P., Pinch, A. C., Ryan, N., de Lima, T. W., Widder, D. G., Tiwari, A., Brown, L. F., Sexton, J. S., & Nunes, P. (2025). Prediction and Punishment: Critical Report on Carceral AI. DOI: 10.2139/ssrn.5017321

Punia, M., Choudhary, A., Sudha, K., & Shashank, T. (2025). A Multi-layered Approach: Examining the Interplay Between GDPR, EU AI Act, and DPDP Act for ICT. In *Lecture notes in networks and systems* (p. 553). Springer International Publishing., DOI: 10.1007/978-981-97-8602-2_49

Rashid, A. (2024). Untitled. DOI: 10.55277/ResearchHub.vq5dnd6h

Reisch, L. A., & Büchel, D. (2016). Consumer Rights 2.0: Consumers in the Digital World : Report of the Advisory Council for Consumer Affairs. In Research Portal Denmark (p. 74). Technical University of Denmark. https://local.forskningsportal.dk/local/dki-cgi/ws/cris-link?src=cbs&id=cbs-81996cb7-9b5a-474c-8e63-d16bcd74cbd8&ti=Consumer%20Rights%202.0%3A%20Consumers%20in%20the%20Digital%20World%20%3A%20Report%20of%20the%20Advisory%20Council%20for%20Consumer%20Affairs

Rosati, E. (2024). Infringing AI: Liability for AI-Generated Outputs under International, EU, and UK Copyright Law. *European Journal of Risk Regulation, 1*. Advance online publication. DOI: 10.1017/err.2024.72

Rozenshtein, A. Z., & Frazier, K. (2025). Large Language Scholarship: Generative AI in the Legal Academy. DOI: 10.2139/ssrn.5200768

Santosh, T. Y. S. S., Ashley, K. D., Atkinson, K., & Grabmair, M. (2024). Towards Supporting Legal Argumentation with NLP: Is More Data Really All You Need? arXiv (Cornell University). https://doi.org//arxiv.2406.10974DOI: 10.48550

Serry, M., Knockel, J., & Greenstadt, R. (2025). An Analysis of Chinese Censorship Bias in LLMs. *Proceedings on Privacy Enhancing Technologies. Privacy Enhancing Technologies Symposium, 2025*(4), 112–129. DOI: 10.56553/popets-2025-0122

Shahid, F., Elswah, M., & Vashistha, A. (2025). Think Outside the Data. *Colonial Biases and Systemic Issues in Automated Moderation Pipelines for Low-Resource Languages., 8*(3), 2331–2344. DOI: 10.1609/aies.v8i3.36719

Sharma, M., & Sharma, N. (2024). *The Rise AI-enabled E-Learning Platforms and MOOCs.*, DOI: 10.55938/wlp.v1i5.180

Sharma, V., Saini, U., Pareek, V., Sharma, L., & Kumar, S. (2023). Artificial intelligence (AI) integration in medical education: A pan-India cross-sectional observation of acceptance and understanding among students. *Scripta Medica, 54*(4), 343–352. DOI: 10.5937/scriptamed54-46267

Shata, A. (2025). "Opting Out of AI": Exploring perceptions, reasons, and concerns behind faculty resistance to generative AI. *Frontiers in Communication, 10*, 1614804. Advance online publication. DOI: 10.3389/fcomm.2025.1614804

Temper, M., Tjoa, S., & David, L. (2025). Higher Education Act for AI (HEAT-AI): A framework to regulate the usage of AI in higher education institutions. *Frontiers in Education, 10*, 1505370. Advance online publication. DOI: 10.3389/feduc.2025.1505370

Thakur, R., Kaushik, S., Chopra, G., & Rohilla, H. (2025). TrueGradeAI: Retrieval-Augmented and Bias-Resistant AI for Transparent and Explainable Digital Assessments. DOI: 10.48550/ARXIV.2509.22516

The Study of Right to Freedom of Expression. (2025). The Study of Right to Freedom of Expression, Digital Media Laws and Demand for Innovation. *Law and World, 11*(1), 114–124. DOI: 10.36475/11.1.9

Trager, R., Harack, B., Reuel, A., Carnegie, A., Heim, L., Ho, L. L., Kreps, S., Lall, R., & Larter, O. hÉigeartaigh, S. Ó., Staffell, S., & Villalobos, J. J. (2023). International Governance of Civilian AI: A Jurisdictional Certification Approach. SSRN Electronic Journal. DOI: 10.2139/ssrn.4579899

Veale, M., Binns, R., & Edwards, L. (2018). Algorithms that remember: Model inversion attacks and data protection law. *Philosophical Transactions. Series A, Mathematical, Physical, and Engineering Sciences*, *376*(2133), 20180083. DOI: 10.1098/rsta.2018.0083

Verdoodt, V., Lievens, E., & Chatzinikolaou, A. (2023). The EU Approach to Safeguard Children's Rights on Video-Sharing Platforms: Jigsaw or Maze? *Media and Communication*, *11*(4). Advance online publication. DOI: 10.17645/mac.v11i4.7059

von Schomberg, R. (2024). Towards a New Ethos of Science or a Reform of the Institution of Science? Merton Revisited and the Prospects of Institutionalizing the Research Values of Openness and Mutual Responsiveness. SSRN Electronic Journal. DOI: 10.2139/ssrn.4892603

Voss, W. G. (2022). TRANSATLANTIC DATA TRANSFER COMPLIANCE (28 B.U. J. SCI. & TECH. L. 158 (2022)). HAL (Le Centre Pour La Communication Scientifique Directe). https://hal.archives-ouvertes.fr/hal-03793307

Wang, T., Lund, B., Marengo, A., Pagano, A., Mannuru, N. R., Teel, Z. A., & Pange, J. (2023). Exploring the Potential Impact of Artificial Intelligence (AI) on International Students in Higher Education: Generative AI, Chatbots, Analytics, and International Student Success. *Applied Sciences (Basel, Switzerland)*, *13*(11), 6716. DOI: 10.3390/app13116716

Wang, Y., Bo-tao, Y., Yang, I., Hassanpour, S., & Vosoughi, S. (2025). Probing Association Biases in LLM Moderation Over-Sensitivity. arXiv (Cornell University). https://doi.org//arxiv.2505.23914DOI: 10.48550

Warraich, M. K. S., Usman, H., Zakir, S., & Mehboob, M. (2025). Ethical Governance of artificial intelligence Hallucinations in legal practice. 4(2), 603. DOI: 10.71085/sss.04.02.297

Weuts, R., Bleher, J., Bleher, H., Flores, R. T., Xuanyang, G., Pujszo, P., & Almási, Z. (2025). AI Governance in Higher Education: A course design exploring regulatory, ethical and practical considerations. DOI: 10.48550/ARXIV.2509.06176

Wu, Z. (2024). A Double-Edged Sword: Reconsidering Education and Political Knowledge in Authoritarian Context. SSRN Electronic Journal. DOI: 10.2139/ssrn.4787180

Xue, Y., Chinapah, V., & Zhu, C. (2025). A Comparative Analysis of AI Privacy Concerns in Higher Education: News Coverage in China and Western Countries. *Education Sciences*, *15*(6), 650. DOI: 10.3390/educsci15060650

Yadav, N., Liu, J., Ortu, F., Ensafi, R., Jin, Z., & Mihalcea, R. (2025). Revealing Hidden Mechanisms of Cross-Country Content Moderation with Natural Language Processing. *Findings of the Association for Computational Linguistics: ACL, 2022*, 22434–22452. DOI: 10.18653/v1/2025.findings-acl.1153

Yan, Y., & Liu, H. (2024). Ethical framework for AI education based on large language models. *Education and Information Technologies*. Advance online publication. DOI: 10.1007/s10639-024-13241-6

Yang, Y., Kim, M., Rondinelli, M., & Shao, K. (2025). Pensieve Grader: An AI-Powered, Ready-to-Use Platform for Effortless Handwritten STEM Grading. DOI: 10.48550/ARXIV.2507.01431

Yao-shun, Z., Zhu, Z., Xu, W., & Yao-shun, Z. (2025). Cross-border higher education cooperation under the dual context of artificial intelligence and geopolitics: Opportunities, challenges, and pathways. *Frontiers in Education*, *10*, 1656518. Advance online publication. DOI: 10.3389/feduc.2025.1656518

Yoder-Himes, D. R., Asif, A., Kinney, K., Brandt, T. J., Cecil, R. E., Himes, P., Cashon, C. H., Hopp, R. M. P., & Ross, E. (2022). Racial, skin tone, and sex disparities in automated proctoring software. *Frontiers in Education*, *7*, 881449. Advance online publication. DOI: 10.3389/feduc.2022.881449

Zhang, G., Qu, S., Liu, J., Zhang, C., Lin, C., Yu, C. L., Pan, D., Cheng, E., Liu, J., Lin, Q., Yuan, R., Zheng, T., Pang, W., Du, X., Liang, Y., Ma, Y., Li, Y., Ma, Z., Lin, B., . . . Chen, W. (2024). MAP-Neo: Highly Capable and Transparent Bilingual Large Language Model Series. arXiv (Cornell University). https://doi.org//arxiv.2405.19327DOI: 10.48550

Zhao, Z., An, Q., & Liu, J. (2025). Exploring AI tool adoption in higher education: Evidence from a PLS-SEM model integrating multimodal literacy, self-efficacy, and university support. *Frontiers in Psychology*, *16*, 1619391. Advance online publication. DOI: 10.3389/fpsyg.2025.1619391

Compilation of References

Aayog, N. I. T. I. (2018). *National strategy for artificial intelligence #AIforAll.* Government of India. https://niti.gov.in

Abbas, N., Ali, I., Manzoor, R., Hussain, T., & Hussain, M. (2023). Role of artificial intelligence tools in enhancing students' educational performance at higher levels. Journal of Artificial Intelligence. *Machine Learning and Neural Network*, *35*(35), 36–49. DOI: 10.55529/jaimlnn.35.36.49

Abdullah, N., Baskaran, V. L., Mustafa, Z., Ali, S. R., & Zaini, S. H. (2022). Augmented Reality: The Effect in Students' Achievement, Satisfaction and Interest in Science Education. *International Journal of Learning. Teaching and Educational Research*, *21*(5), 326–350. DOI: 10.26803/ijlter.21.5.17

Abrahams, I. (2017). *Practical work in science: A report and a proposal.* Routledge.

Abulaiti, M. (2024). Higher Education in the Era of AI. In *Developments and Future Trends in Transnational Higher Education Leadership* (pp. 244–265). IGI Global. DOI: 10.4018/979-8-3693-2857-6.ch014

Abulibdeh, A., Zaidan, E., & Abulibdeh, R. (2024). Navigating the confluence of artificial intelligence and education for sustainable development in the era of industry 4.0: Challenges, opportunities, and ethical dimensions. *Journal of Cleaner Production*, *437*, 140527. DOI: 10.1016/j.jclepro.2023.140527

Adams, A., & Turner, T. (2019). Leveraging GPT-3 for Teaching and Learning Material Generation. In *International Conference on Artificial Intelligence in Education* (pp. 1-13). Springer.

Adams, R. (2020). Digital colonialism: The displacement of local knowledge by global AI. *AI & Society*, *35*(3), 569–582. DOI: 10.1007/s00146-019-00918-7

Afridi, M. S., Iqbal, M. A., & Abulaish, M. (2018). An Intelligent System for Automated Citation Classification. *Procedia Computer Science*, *132*, 783–790.

Agrawal, A., & Jain, S. S. (2024). Indian Copyright Law and Generative AI. DOI: 10.2139/ssrn.5028835

Agyemang-Badu, S., Tibbitts, F., & Phillips, S. (2025). AI Human Rights Literacy. *Current Issues in Comparative Education*, *26*(2). Advance online publication. DOI: 10.52214/cice.v26i2.13139

Agzamxanova, G., & Golovko, Y. (2025). How AI tools can support English writing development. *Educator Insights: A Journal of Teaching Theory and Practice*, 1(3), 27–33. https://www.researchgate.net/publication/389851086

Ahmad, S. F., Alam, M. M., Rahmat, M. K., Mubarik, M. S., & Hyder, S. I. (2022). Academic and administrative role of artificial intelligence in education. *Sustainability (Basel)*, *14*(3), 1101. DOI: 10.3390/su14031101

Ahmed, F., & Sohag, K. (2024). The role of ai and financial stress in enhancing access and equity in transnational higher education. In *Advances in Educational Marketing, Administration, and Leadership* (pp. 205–224). IGI Global. DOI: 10.4018/979-8-3693-7016-2.ch010

Ahmed, Y., Ahmed, T., Raza, A., & Jan, I. (2025). Harnessing AI for personalized learning, equity, and administrative efficiency in transnational higher education. *Bridging global divides for transnational higher education in the AI Era*, 191-204.

AI4D Africa. (2021). *Artificial intelligence for development in Africa.* https://ai4d.ai

Ajani, O., Akintolu, M., & Afolabi, S. O. (2024). The emergence of artificial intelligence in the higher education. *International Journal of Research in Business and Social Science (2147-4478), 13*(8), 157–165. https://doi.org/DOI: 10.20525/ijrbs.v13i8.3507

Ajjawi, R., Tai, J., Boud, D., & Jorre, T. J. de S. (2022). Assessment for Inclusion in Higher Education. In *Routledge eBooks*. Informa., DOI: 10.4324/9781003293101

Akhmadieva, R. Sh., Kalmazova, N., Belova, T. V., Prokopyev, A. I., Molodozhnikova, N. M., & Spichak, V. Y. (2024). Research trends in the use of artificial intelligence in higher education. *Frontiers in Education, 9*, 1438715. Advance online publication. DOI: 10.3389/feduc.2024.1438715

Al Anakrih, M. G. (2025). Language in the Digital Era: How Artificial Intelligence is Transforming Language Translation and Communication. Egyptian Journal of Linguistics and Translation, 106-137.

Al Balushi, Z., & Achour, S. (2024). Guiding the evolution of AI in higher education in Oman: Strategies and insights. In Proceedings of the 7th International Academic Conference on Education, Teaching and Learning. Diamond Scientific Publishing. https://www.dpublication.com/wp-content/uploads/2024/07/6-ITL6-3737.pdf

Al Matari, A. S., Mukit, A., Al Saadi, S., Al Balushi, W., & Al-Abri, J. S. (2023). Artificial intelligence and the future of teaching in higher education at A'Sharqiyah University (ASU) in Oman. 1st Pelita International Conference, 1(1). https://www.researchgate.net/publication/377272384

Alam, A. (2023a). Media multitasking with M-learning technology in real-time classroom learning: Analysing the dynamics in formal educational settings for the future of E-learning in India. In *2023 2nd International Conference on Smart Technologies and Systems for Next Generation Computing (ICSTSN)* (pp. 1-6). IEEE.

Alam, A. (2023b). The secret sauce of student success: Cracking the code by navigating the path to personalized learning with educational data mining. In *2023 2nd International Conference on Smart Technologies and Systems for Next Generation Computing (ICSTSN)* (pp. 1-8). IEEE.

Alam, A. (2023c). Intelligence unleashed: An argument for AI-enabled learning ecologies with real world examples of today and a peek into the future. In *INTERNATIONAL CONFERENCE ON INNOVATIONS IN COMPUTER SCIENCE, ELECTRONICS & ELECTRICAL ENGINEERING-2022* (Vol. 2717, No. 1, p. 030001). AIP Publishing LLC.

Alam, A., & Mohanty, A. (2022). Facial analytics or virtual avatars: competencies and design considerations for student-teacher interaction in AI-powered online education for effective classroom engagement. In *International Conference on Communication, Networks and Computing* (pp. 252-265). Cham: Springer Nature Switzerland.

Alam, A., & Mohanty, A. (2023). Learning on the move: a pedagogical framework for state-of-the-art mobile learning. In *International Conference on Data Management, Analytics & Innovation* (pp. 735-748). Singapore: Springer Nature Singapore. DOI: 10.1007/978-981-99-1414-2_52

Ala, M., Shahid, S., Mahmud, S., Mohyuddin, S., & Kaur, K. (2025). Perceived influence of GenAI on student engagement in online higher education. *Journal of Applied Learning and Teaching*, *8*(2). Advance online publication. DOI: 10.37074/jalt.2025.8.2.16

Alam, A. (2022). Impact of university's human resources practices on professors' occupational performance: empirical evidence from India's higher education sector. In *Inclusive businesses in developing economies: Converging people, profit, and corporate citizenship* (pp. 107–131). Springer International Publishing. DOI: 10.1007/978-3-031-12217-0_6

Alam, A., & Mohanty, A. (2024). Integrated constructive robotics in education (ICRE) model: A paradigmatic framework for transformative learning in educational ecosystem. *Cogent Education*, *11*(1), 2324487. DOI: 10.1080/2331186X.2024.2324487

Alaswad, S., Kalganova, T., & Awad, W. (2025). Trustworthiness of Legal Considerations for the Use of LLMs in Education. DOI: 10.48550/ARXIV.2508.03771

Al-Azawei, A., Serenelli, F., & Lundqvist, K. (2016a). Universal Design for Learning (UDL): A Content Analysis of Peer Reviewed Journals from 2012 to 2015. *The Journal of Scholarship of Teaching and Learning*, *16*(3), 39–56. DOI: 10.14434/josotl.v16i3.19295

Alcock, E. (2025). *Assuring higher education's quality in the age of AI is no easy task.* European University Association. https://www.eua.eu/our-work/expert-voices/assuring-higher-educations-quality-in-the-age-of-ai-is-no-easy-task.html

Alfayez, A. A., & Rasool, A. (2025). Use of AI in the curriculum development of transnational higher education. In *Bridging Global Divides for Transnational Higher Education in the AI Era* (pp. 401–422). IGI Global Scientific Publishing.

Al-Horr, K. (2024). Role of Transnational Universities in Capacity Building in Hosting Countries: A Review. *Journal of Tertiary Education and Learning*, *2*(1), 1–11. DOI: 10.54536/jtel.v2i1.2315

Ali, M. A., Tariq, S. M., & Khalid, U. (2024). Transnational Education (TNE) in Pakistan: Challenges and Way Forward. [JERSSR]. *Journal of Educational Research and Social Sciences Review*, *4*(2), 9–22.

Aliyu, A., Maglaras, L., He, Y., Yevseyeva, I., Boiten, E., Cook, A., & Janicke, H. (2020). A holistic cybersecurity maturity assessment framework for higher education institutions in the United Kingdom. *Applied Sciences (Basel, Switzerland)*, *10*(10), 3660. DOI: 10.3390/app10103660

Aljohani, N. R., & Alzahrani, A. M. (2023). The effectiveness of virtual laboratories in enhancing science education: A systematic review. *Education and Information Technologies*, *28*(6), 6781–6802. DOI: 10.1007/s10639-023-11647-9

Alkhamsi, N. N., & Alqahtani, S. S. (2024). Compliance Framework for Personal Data Protection Law Standards. *International Journal of Advanced Computer Science and Applications*, *15*(7). Advance online publication. DOI: 10.14569/IJACSA.2024.0150751

Allendevaux, S. (2021). *How US State Data Protection Statutes Compare in Scope to Safeguard Information and Protect Privacy Using Iso/Iec 27001: 2013 and Iso/Iec 27701: 2019 Security and Privacy Management System Requirements as an Adequacy Baseline* (Doctoral dissertation, Northeastern University).

Ally, M. (2008). Foundations of educational theory for online learning. In *Theory and Practice of Online Learning* (pp. 15–44). Athabasca University Press. DOI: 10.15215/aupress/9781897425084.003

Almaraz-López, C., Menéndez, F., & López-Esteban, C. (2023). Comparative study of the attitudes and perceptions of university students in business administration and management and in education toward artificial intelligence. *Education Sciences*, *13*(6), 609. DOI: 10.3390/educsci13060609

Al-Maskri, M. S., Al-Mukhini, S. H., & Amzat, I. H. (2012). Improving education system in Oman through school curriculum, teaching methods and evaluation: What is needed? SSRN Electronic Journal. https://doi.org/DOI: 10.2139/ssrn.2047736

Almasri, F. (2024). Exploring the impact of artificial intelligence in teaching and learning of science: A systematic review of empirical research. *Research in Science Education*, *54*(5), 977–997. DOI: 10.1007/s11165-024-10176-3

Alotaibi, N., & Alshehri, A. (2023). Prospers and obstacles in using artificial intelligence in Saudi Arabia higher education institutions—The potential of AI-based learning outcomes. *Sustainability (Basel)*, *15*(13), 10723. DOI: 10.3390/su151310723

Altbach, P. G., & Knight, J. (2007). The internationalization of higher education: Motivations and realities. *Journal of Studies in International Education*, *11*(3–4), 290–305. DOI: 10.1177/1028315307303542

Alwahaibi, A., Bin, W., Hassa, W., Basri, W., Wan Ismail, W. B., & Almamari, M. (2022). A systematic literature review on it security standards for higher education institution. *Tianjin Daxue Xuebao (Ziran Kexue yu Gongcheng Jishu Ban). J Tianjin Univ Sci Technol*, *55*, 194–213.

Al-Zahrani, A. M. (2024). Exploring the impact of artificial intelligence on higher education: Perceptions and implications. *Humanities & Social Sciences Communications*. Advance online publication. DOI: 10.1057/s41599-024-03432-4

Al-Zahrani, A. M. (2024). Unveiling the shadows: Beyond the hype of AI in education. *Journal of Educational Technology & Society*, *27*(1), 1–13. PMID: 38737255

Amazon Web Services. (2025, September 10). *NTU Video Case - Empowering Student Learning with Responsible AI Skills*. Amazon Web Services, Inc. https://aws.amazon.com/solutions/case-studies/generative-ai-ntu/

Amo-Filvà, D., Prinsloo, P., Alier, M., Fonseca, D., Kompen, R. T., Canaleta, X., & Herrero, J. (2021). Local Technology to Enhance Data Privacy and Security in Educational Technology. *International Journal of Interactive Multimedia and Artificial Intelligence*, *7*(2), 262–273. DOI: 10.9781/ijimai.2021.11.006

Anders, B. A. (2023). Is using ChatGPT cheating, plagiarism, both, neither, or forward thinking? *Patterns (New York, N.Y.)*, *4*(3), 100694. DOI: 10.1016/j.patter.2023.100694

Anderson, L. W. (Ed.). (2009). *A taxonomy for learning, teaching, and assessing: A revision of Bloom's taxonomy of educational objectives* (Abridged ed., [Nachdr.]). Longman.

Angouri, J. S'Jegers, R., & Szabo, M. (2024). *Internal quality assurance as a catalyst for sustainable, transnational collaboration: The case of the EUTOPIA Alliance*. European University Association. https://www.eua.eu/publications/conference-papers/internal-quality-assurance-as-a-catalyst-for-sustainable-transnational-collaboration-the-case-of-the-eutopia-alliance.html

Angwaomaodoko, E. A. (2023). The Re-examination of the Dangers and Implications of Artificial Intelligence for the Future of Scholarship and Learning. *Traektoriâ Nauki*, *9*(10), 3021–3028. DOI: 10.22178/pos.97-24

Anis, M. (2023). Leveraging artificial intelligence for inclusive English language teaching: Strategies and implications for learner diversity. *Journal of Multidisciplinary Educational Research*, *12*(6), 54–70.

ANSAH, S. D. (2025). Digital Trust and Equity in Transnational Education: Rethinking Online Assessment and Credentialing Practices in the Ghanaian Higher Educational New Landscape. *International Journal of Psychology and Education*, *6*(2).

Anthropic. (2024). AI Fluency Framework & Foundations. Retrieved from Are University Teachers Ready for Generative Artificial Intelligence? Unpacking Faculty Anxiety (2025). Computers & Education: Artificial Intelligence.

Anuyahong, B., Rattanapong, C., & Patcha, I. (2023). Analyzing the impact of artificial intelligence in personalized learning and adaptive assessment in higher education. *International Journal of Innovation and Scientific Research*, *10*(4), 88–93. DOI: 10.51244/IJRSI.2023.10412

Appadurai, A. (1996). *Modernity at large: Cultural dimensions of globalization*. University of Minnesota Press.

Apple, M. W. (2004). *Ideology and curriculum* (3rd ed.). RoutledgeFalmer. DOI: 10.4324/9780203487563

Aprianto, R., Lestari, E., Sadan, S., & Fletcher, E. (2024). Harnessing artificial intelligence in higher education: Balancing innovation and ethical challenges. [ITEE]. *International Transactions on Education Technology*, *3*(1), 84–93. DOI: 10.33050/itee.v3i1.680

Arida, A. I. (2023). Transnational education and E-Learning. In *Higher education in the Arab World: E-learning and distance education* (pp. 295–317). Springer Nature Switzerland. DOI: 10.1007/978-3-031-33568-6_15

Aruleba, K., Sanusi, I. T., Obaido, G., & Ogbuokiri, B. (2023). *Integrating ChatGPT in a Computer Science Course: Students Perceptions and Suggestions* (No. arXiv:2402.01640). arXiv. https://doi.org//arXiv.2402.01640DOI: 10.48550

Asendorpf, J. B. (1990). Beyond social withdrawal: Shyness, unsociability, and peer avoidance. *Human Development, 33*(4-5), 250–259. DOI: 10.1159/000276522

Asiedu, N. K., Abah, M., & Dei, D.-G. J. (2022). Understanding knowledge management strategies in institutions of higher learning and the corporate world: A systematic review. *Cogent Business & Management, 9*(1), 2108218. Advance online publication. DOI: 10.1080/23311975.2022.2108218

Athanassopoulos, S., Manoli, P., Gouvi, M., Lavidas, K., & Komis, V. (2023). The use of ChatGPT as a learning tool to improve foreign language writing in a multilingual and multicultural classroom. *Advances in Mobile Learning Educational Research, 3*(2), 818–824. DOI: 10.25082/AMLER.2023.02.009

Attali, Y. (2013). Validity and reliability of automated essay scoring. In M. D. Shermis & J. C.

Au, W. (2013). Rethinking multicultural education: Teaching for racial and cultural justice. *Rethinking Schools.*

Avsheniuk, N. (2020). UNESCO'S mission in the development of transnational higher education. *UNESCO Chair Journal Lifelong Professional Education in the XXI Century*, (1), 12–16. DOI: 10.35387/ucj.1(1).2020.12-16

Awadallah Alkouk, W., & Khlaif, Z. N. (2024). AI-resistant assessments in higher education: Practical insights from faculty training workshops. *Frontiers in Education, 9*, 1499495. DOI: 10.3389/feduc.2024.1499495

Ayala-Pazmiño, M. (2023). Artificial intelligence in education: Exploring the potential benefits and risks. 593 Digital Publisher CEIT, 8(3), 892–899. https://doi.org/DOI: 10.33386/593dp.2023.3.1827

Ayeni, N. O. O., Hamad, N. N. M. A., Chisom, N. O. N., Osawaru, N. B., & Adewusi, N. O. E. (2024). AI in education: A review of personalized learning and educational technology. *GSC Advanced Research and Reviews, 18*(2), 261–271. DOI: 10.30574/gscarr.2024.18.2.0062

Azaza, M., & Zinoubi, R. (2022). Transnational Education in the Context of the United Arab Emirates: Realities, Opportunities, and Challenges. *The International Journal of Educational Organization and Leadership, 29*(2), 47–57. DOI: 10.18848/2329-1656/CGP/v29i02/47-57

Azmat, M., & Mahmood, M. (2024). Integrating Artificial Intelligence in Education: Opportunities and Challenges. *Bulletin of Education and Research, 46*(3), 23–41. https://files.eric.ed.gov/fulltext/EJ1477863.pdf

Azubuike, O. B., Adegboye, O., & Quadri, H. (2021). Who gets to learn in a pandemic? Exploring the digital divide in remote learning during the COVID-19 pandemic in Nigeria. *International Journal of Educational Research Open, 2*, 100022. DOI: 10.1016/j.ijedro.2020.100022

Babikian, J. (2023). Securing Rights: Legal Frameworks for Privacy and Data Protection in the Digital Era. *Law Research Journal, 1*(2), 91–101.

Bailey, R., & Parsheera, S. (2021). Data localization in India: Paradigms and processes. *CSI Transactions on ICT, 9*(3), 137–150. DOI: 10.1007/s40012-021-00337-4

Baker, R. S., Siemens, G., & Rosé, C. P. (2019). Educational data mining and learning analytics. In Fischer, F., Hmelo-Silver, C. E., Goldman, S. R., & Reimann, P. (Eds.), *International handbook of the learning sciences* (pp. 253–270). Routledge.

Baker, R. S., Walonoski, J., Heffernan, N., Roll, I., Corbett, A. T., & Koedinger, K. R. (2008). Why students engage in "gaming the system" behavior in interactive learning environments. *Journal of Interactive Learning Research, 19*(2), 185–224.

Baker, T., & Smith, L. (2019). *Educ-AI-tion rebooted? Exploring the future of artificial intelligence in schools and colleges*. Nesta.

Baksh, S. (2025). Investigating Students' AI Usage Through the Community of Inquiry (CoI) Framework: A Mixed-Method Study in the Caribbean Region. *SDGs Studies Review, 6*, e036. DOI: 10.37497/sdgs.v6istudies.36

Balan, A. (2024). Examining the ethical and sustainability challenges of legal education's AI revolution. *International Journal of the Legal Profession, 1*(3), 323–348. Advance online publication. DOI: 10.1080/09695958.2024.2421179

Bala, S., Pooja, R., & Rani, N. (2024). Challenges in implementing artificial intelligence in knowledge management processes. *International Journal of Research in Management, 6*(1), 64–68. DOI: 10.33545/26648792.2024.v6.i1a.127

Balendra, S. (2025). Meta's AI moderation and free speech: Ongoing challenges in the Global South. 1. DOI: 10.1017/cfl.2025.5

Bandari, V. (2023). Enterprise data security measures: A comparative review of effectiveness and risks across different industries and organization types. *International Journal of Business Intelligence and Big Data Analytics, 6*(1), 1–11.

Banks, J. A. (2015). *Cultural diversity and education: Foundations, curriculum, and teaching* (6th ed.). Pearson. DOI: 10.4324/9781315622255

Bannister, P., Alcalde Peñalver, E., & Santamaría Urbieta, A. (2024). Transnational higher education cultures and generative AI: A nominal group study. *Journal for Multicultural Education*. DOI: 10.1108/JME-10-2023-0102

Banu, J. T. (2024). AI in Learning: Designing the Future. *Technical Communication Quarterly, 1*. Advance online publication. DOI: 10.1080/10572252.2024.2428400

Bao, W. (2020). COVID-19 and online teaching in higher education: A case study of Peking University. *Human Behavior and Emerging Technologies, 2*(2), 113–115. DOI: 10.1002/hbe2.191

Barocas, S., & Selbst, A. D. (2016). Big data's disparate impact. *California Law Review, 104*(3), 671–732.

Barry, A. E., Johnson, E., Rabre, A., Darville, G., Donovan, K. M., & Efunbumi, O. (2015). Underage access to online alcohol marketing content: A YouTube case study. *Alcohol and Alcoholism (Oxford, Oxfordshire), 50*(1), 89–94. DOI: 10.1093/alcalc/agu078

Başaran, O., & Turan, S. (2025). Reimagining local solutions to global challenges in education: A cross-cultural examination. In *Cultural Awareness and Diversity Management in Contemporary Education* (pp. 99–192). IGI Global Scientific Publishing.

Bassner, P., Frankford, E., & Krusche, S. (2024). *Iris: An AI-Driven Virtual Tutor For Computer Science Education*. DOI: 10.1145/3649217.3653543

Bati, K. (2022). A systematic literature review regarding computational thinking and programming in early childhood education. *Education and Information Technologies*, *27*(2), 2059–2082. DOI: 10.1007/s10639-021-10700-2

Bawa, P., & Kapoor, R. (2023). Digital inequalities and AI ethics in Indian higher education. *Contemporary Education Dialogue*, *20*(1), 88–105.

Bellamy, R. K., Dey, K., Hind, M., Hoffman, S. C., Houde, S., Kannan, K., Lohia, P., Martino, J., Mehta, S., Mojsilović, A., Nagar, S., Ramamurthy, K. N., Richards, J., Saha, D., Sattigeri, P., Singh, M., Varshney, K. R., & Zhang, Y. (2019). AI Fairness 360: An extensible toolkit for detecting and mitigating algorithmic bias. *IBM Journal of Research and Development*, *63*(4/5), 4–1. DOI: 10.1147/JRD.2019.2942287

Bender, E. M., Gebru, T., McMillan-Major, A., & Shmitchell, S. (2021). On the dangers of stochastic parrots: Can language models be too big? In *Proceedings of the 2021 ACM Conference on Fairness, Accountability, and Transparency*. https://doi.org/DOI: 10.1145/3442188.3445922

Bengio, Y., Simard, P., & Frasconi, P. (2003). Learning long-term dependencies with gradient descent is difficult. *IEEE Transactions on Neural Networks*, *5*(2), 157–166. DOI: 10.1109/72.279181

Benjamin, R. (2019). *Race after technology: Abolitionist tools for the new Jim code*. Polity Press.

Benjamin, R. (2019). Race after technology: Abolitionist tools for the new Jim code. *Polity*.

Benkhelifa, F., Lakhani, F., Jendoubi, T., Paltalidis, N., & Wijeratne, V. (2025, April). Exploring the Use of Genai Code Assistants for Engineering Students in Transnational Education Programmes: A Pilot Study. In *2025 IEEE Global Engineering Education Conference (EDUCON)* (pp. 1-7). IEEE. DOI: 10.1109/EDUCON62633.2025.11016450

Berchin, I. I., de Aguiar Dutra, A. R., & Guerra, J. B. S. O. D. A. (2021). How do higher education institutions promote sustainable development? A literature review. *Sustainable Development (Bradford)*, *29*(6), 1204–1222. DOI: 10.1002/sd.2219

Berendt, B., Littlejohn, A., & Blakemore, M. (2020). AI in education: Learner choice and fundamental rights. *Learning, Media and Technology*, *45*(3), 312–324. DOI: 10.1080/17439884.2020.1786399

Berengueres, J., & Sandell, M. (2023). Applying Standards to Advance Upstream & Downstream Ethics in Large Language Models. DOI: 10.48550/ARXIV.2306.03503

Bernholz, L., Nothias, T., & Vavrovsky, A. S. (2020). Digital Policy Is the Nonprofit Sector's Policy Agenda. *Available at SSRN* 3791637. DOI: 10.2139/ssrn.3791637

Berry, J. E. (2022). Towards Ubiquitous Learning in a Transnational Educational System. In *The Palgrave Handbook of Educational Leadership and Management Discourse* (pp. 1–19). Springer International Publishing. DOI: 10.1007/978-3-030-99097-8_57

Berson, I. R., Luo, W., & Yang, W. (2022). Narrowing the digital divide in early childhood: Technological advances and curriculum reforms. *Early Education and Development, 33*(1), 183–185. DOI: 10.1080/10409289.2022.1989740

Beyond the Hype: Exploring Faculty Perceptions and Acceptability of AI in Teaching Practices. (2024). British Journal of Educational Technology.

Bharadwaj, S., & Verma, A. (2025). Opportunities and Obstacles in Pursuing Higher Education Abroad During Emergencies: Challenges, Adaptations, and Policy Implications. *Idealistic Journal of Advanced Research in Progressive Spectrums (IJARPS) eISSN–2583-6986, 4*(04), 168-186.

Bhoite, S., Nikam, P., & More, A. (2022). Predictive analytics of engineering and technology admissions. In *Computational Intelligence in Data Mining* [Singapore: Springer Nature Singapore.]. *Proceedings of ICCIDM, 2021*, 419–431.

Bibi, A. (2024). Navigating The Ethical Landscape. *Ai Integration In Education., 1579*, 1579–1585. Advance online publication. DOI: 10.53555/kuey.v30i6.5546

Biggs, J. (2003). *Teaching for quality learning at university* (2nd ed.). Open University Press.

Binns, R., Veale, M., Van Kleek, M., & Shadbolt, N. (2018). 'It's reducing a human being to a percentage': Perceptions of justice in algorithmic decisions. In *CHI Conference on Human Factors in Computing Systems* (pp. 1–14). DOI: 10.1145/3173574.3173951

Bird, K. A., Castleman, B. L., Mabel, Z., & Song, Y. (2021). Bringing transparency to predictive analytics: A systematic comparison of predictive modeling methods in higher education. *AERA Open, 7*, 23328584211037630. DOI: 10.1177/23328584211037630

Birhane, A. (2022). Algorithmic injustice and AI colonialism. *Patterns (New York, N.Y.), 3*(8), 100560. DOI: 10.1016/j.patter.2022.100560

Blair-Walcott, K. (2023). Comparative Analysis. In *Varieties of Qualitative Research Methods* (pp. 79–84). https://doi.org/DOI: 10.1007/978-3-031-04394-9_13

Blue Pencil Agency. (2024). *The seven basic plots*. Blue Pencil Agency. https://bluepencilagency.com/the-seven-basic-plots/

Boer, M., Stevens, G. W., Finkenauer, C., de Looze, M. E., & van den Eijnden, R. J. (2021). Social media use intensity, social media use problems, and mental health among adolescents: Investigating directionality and mediating processes. *Computers in Human Behavior, 116*, 106645. DOI: 10.1016/j.chb.2020.106645

Boer, M., Stevens, G. W., Finkenauer, C., Koning, I. M., & van den Eijnden, R. J. (2022). Validation of the social media disorder scale in adolescents: Findings from a large-scale nationally representative sample. *Assessment, 29*(8), 1658–1675. DOI: 10.1177/10731911211027232

Bond, M., Khosravi, H., De Laat, M., Bergdahl, N., Negrea, V., Oxley, E., Pham, P., Chong, S. W., & Siemens, G. (2024). A meta systematic review of artificial intelligence in higher education. *International Journal of Educational Technology in Higher Education*, *21*(1), 4. DOI: 10.1186/s41239-023-00436-z

Bower, M., Torrington, J., Lai, J. W., Petocz, P., & Alfano, M. (2024). How should we change teaching and assessment in response to increasingly powerful generative Artificial Intelligence? Outcomes of the ChatGPT teacher survey. *Education and Information Technologies*, *29*(12), 15403–15439. DOI: 10.1007/s10639-023-12405-0

Bowles, M. (2025). *Authentic Assessment in the Age of AI: Designing for Capability, Context, and Human Becoming*. DOI: 10.13140/RG.2.2.22570.68808

Boyd, S., & Vandenberghe, L. (2004). *Convex Optimisation*. Cambridge University Press. DOI: 10.1017/CBO9780511804441

Brah, A. (1996). *Cartographies of diaspora: Contesting identities*. Routledge.

Brammar, L. (2023) *A three lenses approach to employability - transdisciplinary approaches to TNE students' careers education,* https://www.emerald.com/. Available at: https://www.emerald.com/heswbl/article-abstract/13/6/1204/97816/A-three-lenses-approach-to-employability?redirectedFrom=fulltext (Accessed: 02 August 2025).

Brammar, L. (2023). A three lenses approach to employability: Transdisciplinary approaches to TNE students' careers education. *Higher Education. Skills and Work-Based Learning*, *13*(6), 1204–1217. DOI: 10.1108/HESWBL-11-2022-0251

Bratianu, C., & Ioan, A. (2025). Challenges of Artificial Intelligence for Knowledge Management Systems: A Bibliometric Analysis Perspective. *Oradea Journal of Business and Economics*, *10*(1), 108–120. DOI: 10.47535/1991ojbe209

Brauner, P., Hick, A., Philipsen, R., & Ziefle, M. (2023). "What does the public think about artificial intelligence?—A criticality map to understand bias in the public perception of AI", Frontiers in Computer Science. *Frontiers Media S.A.*, *5*, 1113903. DOI: 10.3389/FCOMP.2023.1113903/BIBTEX

Braun, V., & Clarke, V. (2006). Using thematic analysis in psychology. *Qualitative Research in Psychology*, *3*(2), 77–101. DOI: 10.1191/1478088706qp063oa

Braun, V., Clarke, V., & Weate, P. (2016). Using thematic analysis in sport and exercise research. In Smith, B., & Sparkes, A. C. (Eds.), *Routledge handbook of qualitative research in sport and exercise* (pp. 191–205). Routledge., DOI: 10.4324/9781315762012-26

Bringas, P. G., García, H. P., de Pisón, F. J. M., Álvarez, F. M., Lora, A. T., Herrero, Á., & Corchado, E. (Eds.). (2023). *International Joint Conference 16th International Conference on Computational Intelligence in Security for Information Systems (CISIS 2023) 14th International Conference on EUropean Transnational Education (ICEUTE 2023): Proceedings* (Vol. 748). Springer Nature.

British Council. (2024). *A global framework for transnational education engagement*. DOI: 10.57884/HFW3-6S14

British Council. 2016. The Scale and Scope of UK Higher Education Transnational Education. https://www.britishcouncil.org/sites/default/files/scale-and-scope-of-uk-he-tne-report.pdf

Brogan, P. (2020). Consumer Redress Through Online Dispute Resolution: The Role of Online Dispute Resolution in Facilitating Consumer Access to Justice in E-Commerce. Arbitration Law Review, 12(1), 12. https://elibrary.law.psu.edu/arbitrationlawreview/vol12/iss1/12/

Brown, H., & Jones, R. (2018). Generative AI and Its Role in Cross-Cultural Academic Collaboration. *Frontiers in Artificial Intelligence*, *3*, 45.

Brown, I., & Marsden, C. T. (2023). *Regulating code: Good governance and better regulation in the information age*. MIT Press.

Brown, T. B., Mann, B., Ryder, N., Subbiah, M., Kaplan, J., Dhariwal, P., & Amodei, D. (2020). Language Models are Few-Shot Learners. *Advances in Neural Information Processing Systems*, •••, 33.

Bruner, J. S. (1973). *Toward a theory of instruction* (5th print). Norton.

Buolamwini, J., & Gebru, T. (2018). Gender shades: Intersectional accuracy disparities in commercial gender classification. *Proceedings of Machine Learning Research*, *81*, 1–15.

Butt, U., Dauda, Y., & Shaheer, B. (2023). Ransomware attack on the educational sector. In *AI, Blockchain and Self-Sovereign Identity in Higher Education* (pp. 279–313). Springer Nature Switzerland. DOI: 10.1007/978-3-031-33627-0_11

Cabeza-Lopez, E. M., Ruiz-Gonzalez, R., Merino-Gomez, A., Curiel-Herrera, L. E., & Rincon, J. A. (2024, October). A comparison of ai-enabled techniques for the detection of attacks in iot devices. In *International Conference on EUropean Transnational Education* (pp. 227-236). Cham: Springer Nature Switzerland. DOI: 10.1007/978-3-031-75016-8_21

Caccavale, F. (2025). From Programming to Chatbots: Digitalization Strategies in Chemical Engineering Education. Research Portal Denmark, 189. https://local.forskningsportal.dk/local/dki-cgi/ws/cris-link?src=dtu&id=dtu-1c0f7ee8-b1b8-4bfc-bf57-f19819e54567&ti=From%20Programming%20to%20Chatbots%3A%20Digitalization%20Strategies%20in%20Chemical%20Engineering%20Education

Cader, I., Hassan, S., Mok, A., & Tan, S. (2024). Transnational Education in Sri Lanka: Operational and quality assurance landscape.

Camlin, J. (2025). A Theorem-Based Analysis of Epistemic Disruption in Higher Education: Defining Wokeism as an Epistemic Doctrine. DOI: 10.2139/ssrn.5254622

Campbell University. (2025) *Ai in higher education: A meta summary of recent surveys of students and faculty,* https://sites.campbell.edu/academictechnology/. Available at: https://sites.campbell.edu/academictechnology/2025/03/06/ai-in-higher-education-a-summary-of-recent-surveys-of-students-and-faculty/ (Accessed: 19 August 2025).

Canagarajah, A. S. (2020). *Transnational literacy autobiographies as translingual writing*. Routledge New York.

Cardno, C. (2018). Policy Document Analysis: A Practical Educational Leadership Tool and a Qualitative Research Method. *Educational Administration: Theory and Practice*, *24*(4). Advance online publication. DOI: 10.14527/kuey.2018.016

Cardona, M., Rodríguez, R., & Ishmael, K. (2023). *Artificial Intelligence and the Future of Teaching and Learning Insights and Recommendations*. Office of Educational Technology. https://www.ed.gov/sites/ed/files/documents/ai-report/ai-report.pdf

Caro, J. C., Holuka, C., Menta, G., Turner, J. D., Vögele, C., & D'Ambrosio, C. (2023). Children's internalizing behavior development is heterogeneously associated with the pace of epigenetic aging. *Biological Psychology*, *176*, 108463. DOI: 10.1016/j.biopsycho.2022.108463

Carvalho, N., Rosa, M. J., & Amaral, A. (2023). Cross-border higher education and quality assurance: A systematic literature review. *Journal of Studies in International Education*, *27*(5), 695–718. DOI: 10.1177/10283153221076900

CAST. (2018). *Universal Design for Learning Guidelines version 2.2*. http://udlguidelines.cast.org

CAST. (2018). *Universal Design for Learning guidelines version 2.2*. https://udlguidelines.cast.org/

Chan, C. K. Y., & Colloton, T. (2024). *Generative AI in higher education*. Routledge., DOI: 10.4324/9781003459026

Chandler, M. J., & Lalonde, C. E. (1998). Cultural continuity as a hedge against suicide in Canada's First Nations. *Transcultural Psychiatry*, *35*(2), 191–219. DOI: 10.1177/136346159803500202

Chatinakrob, T. (2024). Legal Risks and Challenges of Unregulated AI. In *Brill | Nijhoff eBooks* (p. 268). Brill., DOI: 10.1163/9789004719934_010

Chatzichristofis, S. A. (2025). AI in Education: Towards a Pedagogically Grounded and Interdisciplinary Field. In AI in Education, 1(1), 1; DOI: 10.3390/aieduc1010001

Chau, B. K., & Livermore, M. A. (2024). Computational Legal Studies Comes of Age. *European Journal of Empirical Legal Studies*, *1*(1), 89–104. DOI: 10.62355/ejels.19684

Chaudhry, A., ... (2023). *Transparency index framework*. arXiv. https://arxiv.org/pdf/2206.03220

Chen, B., deNoyelles, A., Patton, K., & Zydney, J. M. (2020). Creating inclusive online learning environments: Strategies for promoting equity in virtual collaboration. *Computers & Education*, *146*, 103770. DOI: 10.1016/j.compedu.2019.103770

Chen, C., & Gong, Y. (2025). The role of AI-assisted learning in academic writing: A mixed-methods study on Chinese as a second language students. *Education Sciences*, *15*(2), 141. DOI: 10.3390/educsci15020141

Cheng, W., Ramanan, S., & Tsafos, Y. (2024). Is it time to embrace AI or abandon it in Higher Education?.

Cheng, H. (2025). Research on Strategies for Cultivating Intercultural Communication Competence in AI-Assisted English Teaching. *Advances in Educational Technology and Psychology*, *9*(1), 101–107. DOI: 10.23977/aetp.2025.090113

Cheng, Y. E., & Koh, S. Y. (2022). The 'soft infrastructure'of the Belt and Road Initiative: Imaginaries, affinities and subjectivities in Chinese transnational education. *Singapore Journal of Tropical Geography, 43*(3), 250–269. DOI: 10.1111/sjtg.12420

Chen, L. (2024). Unlocking the beat: How AI tools drive music students' motivation, engagement, creativity and learning success. *European Journal of Education, 60*(1), e12823. Advance online publication. DOI: 10.1111/ejed.12823

Chen, L., Chen, P., & Lin, Z. (2020). Artificial intelligence in education: A review. *IEEE Access : Practical Innovations, Open Solutions, 8*, 75264–75278. DOI: 10.1109/ACCESS.2020.2988510

Chen, L., Yin, M., Ahmad, K. M., Naeem, M. A., & Haider, S. A. (2024, November). Smart Education: Harnessing Machine Learning for Global Talent Forecasting and Educational Innovation in China. In *2024 International Conference on Control, Electronic Engineering and Machine Learning (CEEML)* (pp. 87-92). IEEE. DOI: 10.1109/CEEML65709.2024.00019

Chen, M. J., She, H. C., & Tsai, P. Y. (2024). The effects of online simulation-based collaborative problem-solving on students' problem-solving, communication and collaboration attitudes. *Education and Information Technologies, 29*(14), 19141–19162. DOI: 10.1007/s10639-024-12609-y

Chen, Q. Z., & Zhang, A. X. (2025). Case Law Grounding. *Using Precedents to Align Decision-Making for Humans and AI., 226*, 226–238. Advance online publication. DOI: 10.1145/3715928.3737487

Chen, S. (2021). Research on data sovereignty rules in cross-border data flow and Chinese solution. *US-China L. Rev., 18*, 261.

Chen, X., Ma, L., Su, D., Zhang, Y., Liu, X., Xin, J., & Ryoo, J. (2024, May). AI-Enhanced Cross-Cultural competence in STEM education. In *Proceedings of the International Conference on New Findings in Humanities and Social Sciences*, 1(1), 29-43.

Chen, X., & Zmire, Z. (2024). AIs role in enhancing cross cultural competence and leadership through online education programs. *Proceedings of the International Conference on New Findings in Humanities and Social Sciences*, 1(1), 1-16. DOI: 10.33422/hsconf.v1i1.268

Chen, Z., Cao, H., Deng, Y., Gao, X., Piao, J., Xu, F., & Li, Y. (2021). *Learning from home: A mixed-methods analysis of live streaming based remote education experience in chinese colleges during the covid-19 pandemic*. In *Proceedings of the 2021 CHI Conference on human factors in computing systems* (pp. 1-16). DOI: 10.1145/3411764.3445428

Cheung, C. H., Bedford, R., Saez De Urabain, I. R., Karmiloff-Smith, A., & Smith, T. J. (2017). Daily touchscreen use in infants and toddlers is associated with reduced sleep and delayed sleep onset. *Scientific Reports, 7*(1), 46104. DOI: 10.1038/srep46104

Chew, M. Y. L., Teo, E. A. L., Shah, K. W., Kumar, V., & Hussein, G. F. (2020). Evaluating the roadmap of 5G technology implementation for smart building and facilities management in Singapore. *Sustainability (Basel), 12*(24), 10259. DOI: 10.3390/su122410259

Chinta, S. V., Wang, Z., Yin, Z., Hoang, N., Gonzalez, M., Quy, T. L., & Zhang, W. (2024). FairAIED: Navigating Fairness, Bias, and Ethics in Educational AI Applications. *arXiv preprint arXiv:2407.18745*.

Chiu, M. C., & Hwang, G. J. (2025). Enhancing student creative and critical thinking in generative AI-empowered creation: A mind-mapping approach. *Interactive Learning Environments*, •••, 1–22. DOI: 10.1080/10494820.2025.2511244

Choi, H., Jovanovic, J., Poquet, O., Brooks, C., Joksimović, S., & Williams, J. J. (2023). The benefit of reflection prompts for encouraging learning with hints in an online programming course. *The Internet and Higher Education*, *58*, 100903. DOI: 10.1016/j.iheduc.2023.100903

Chun, D. (2017). The role of technology in heritage language learning. In *The Routledge handbook of heritage language education* (pp. 378–389). Routledge.

Chung, K. C., Chen, C. H., Tsai, H. H., & Chuang, Y. H. (2021). Social media privacy management strategies: A SEM analysis of user privacy behaviors. *Computer Communications*, *174*, 122–130. DOI: 10.1016/j.comcom.2021.04.012

Cioranu-Rădulescu, C., Bansal, S., Liao, Y., & Murah, M. (2025). Percep ii i practici ale cadrelor didactice privind integrarea inteligen ei artificiale în educa ie: Un studiu transna ional în România, India, China i Brunei. *Revista de Pedagogie Digitala*, *4*(1), 48–56. DOI: 10.61071/RPD.2549

Cohen, R. (1997). *Global diasporas: An introduction.* University of Washington Press. DOI: 10.4324/9780203228920

Colonna, L. (2021). Legal Implications of Using AI as an Exam Invigilator. SSRN Electronic Journal. DOI: 10.2139/ssrn.3839287

Contrino, M. F., Reyes-Millán, M., Vázquez-Villegas, P., & Membrillo-Hernández, J. (2024). Using an adaptive learning tool to improve student performance and satisfaction in online and face-to-face education for a more personalized approach. *Smart Learning Environments*, *11*(1), 6. Advance online publication. DOI: 10.1186/s40561-024-00292-y

Corbett, A. T., & Anderson, J. R. (1995). Knowledge tracing: Modeling the acquisition of procedural knowledge. *User Modeling and User-Adapted Interaction*, *4*(4), 253–278. DOI: 10.1007/BF01099821

Corbin, T., Dawson, P., & Liu, D. (2025). Talk is cheap: Why structural assessment changes are needed for a time of GenAI. *Assessment & Evaluation in Higher Education*, •••, 1–11. DOI: 10.1080/02602938.2025.2553340

Corbin, T., Dawson, P., Nicola-Richmond, K., & Partridge, H. (2025). 'Where's the line? It's an absurd line': Towards a framework for acceptable uses of AI in assessment. *Assessment & Evaluation in Higher Education*, *50*(5), 705–717. DOI: 10.1080/02602938.2025.2456207

Cordero, J., Torres-Zambrano, J., & Cordero-Castillo, A. (2024). Integration of Generative Artificial Intelligence in Higher Education: Best Practices. *Education Sciences*, *15*(1), 32. DOI: 10.3390/educsci15010032

Cotton, D., Cotton, P., & Shipway, J. (2023). Chatting and cheating: Ensuring academic integrity in the era of ChatGPT. *Innovations in Education and Teaching International*, *60*(2), 215–226. DOI: 10.1080/14703297.2023.2190148

Couldry, N., & Mejias, U. A. (2019). *The costs of connection: How data is colonizing human life and appropriating it for capitalism.* Stanford University Press.

Courtland, R. (2018). The bias detectives. *Nature, 558*(7710), 357–360. DOI: 10.1038/d41586-018-05469-3

Coyne, S. M., Shawcroft, J., Holmgren, H., Christensen-Duerden, C., Ashby, S., Rogers, A., Reschke, P. J., Barr, R., Domoff, S., Van Alfen, M., Meldrum, M., & Porter, C. L. (2024). The growth of problematic media use over early childhood: Associations with long-term social and emotional outcomes. *Computers in Human Behavior, 159*, 108350. DOI: 10.1016/j.chb.2024.108350

Craig, W., Boniel-Nissim, M., King, N., Walsh, S. D., Boer, M., Donnelly, P. D., Harel-Fisch, Y., Malinowska-Cieślik, M., Gaspar de Matos, M., Cosma, A., Van den Eijnden, R., Vieno, A., Elgar, F. J., Molcho, M., Bjereld, Y., & Pickett, W. (2020). Social media use and cyber-bullying: A cross-national analysis of young people in 42 countries. *The Journal of Adolescent Health, 66*(6), S100–S108. DOI: 10.1016/j.jadohealth.2020.03.006

Cranwell, P., Li, D., Page, E., Whiteside, K., & Woodcock, A. (2021). Understanding the barriers faced by TNE-students when completing advanced-level laboratory-based practical classes. *International Journal of Chinese Education, 10*(3), 22125868211046033. Advance online publication. DOI: 10.1177/22125868211046033

Crenshaw, K. (1991). Mapping the Margins: Intersectionality, Identity Politics, and Violence against Women of Color. *Stanford Law Review, 43*(6), 1241. DOI: 10.2307/1229039

Cress, U., & Kimmerle, J. (2023). Co-constructing knowledge with generative AI tools: Reflections from a CSCL perspective. *International Journal of Computer-Supported Collaborative Learning, 18*(4), 607–614. DOI: 10.1007/s11412-023-09409-w

Creswell, J. W., & Creswell, J. D. (2018). *Research design: Qualitative, quantitative, and mixed methods approaches* (5th ed.). Sage Publications.

Crompton, H., & Burke, D. (2023). Artificial intelligence in higher education: The state of the field. *International Journal of Educational Technology in Higher Education, 20*(1), 22. DOI: 10.1186/s41239-023-00392-8

Crystal, D. (2000). *Language death.* Cambridge University Press. DOI: 10.1017/CBO9781139106856

Cui, Y., Ma, Z., Wang, L., Yang, A., Liu, Q., Kong, S., & Wang, H. (2023). A survey on big data-enabled innovative online education systems during the COVID-19 pandemic. *Journal of Innovation & Knowledge, 8*(1), 100295. DOI: 10.1016/j.jik.2022.100295

Currie, G. M. (2023, September). Academic integrity and artificial intelligence: Is ChatGPT hype, hero or heresy? [). WB Saunders.]. *Seminars in Nuclear Medicine, 53*(5), 719–730. DOI: 10.1053/j.semnuclmed.2023.04.008 PMID: 37225599

Curzon, J., Kosa, T. A., Akalu, R., & El-Khatib, K. (2021). Privacy and artificial intelligence. *IEEE Transactions on Artificial Intelligence, 2*(2), 96–108. DOI: 10.1109/TAI.2021.3088084

D'Ignazio, C., & Klein, L. F. (2020). *Data feminism.* The MIT Press. DOI: 10.7551/mitpress/11805.001.0001

D'Mello, S. K., & Graesser, A. C. (2023). Intelligent tutoring systems: How computers achieve learning gains that rival human tutors. In Schutz, P. A., & Muis, K. R. (Eds.), *Handbook of educational psychology* (4th ed., pp. 603–629). Routledge., DOI: 10.4324/9780429433726-31

Daher, R. (2025). Integrating AI literacy into teacher education: A critical framework. SpringerLink. https://link.springer.com/article/10.1007/s44163-025-00475-7

Dai, K., Matthews, K. E., & Renshaw, P. (2020). Crossing the 'bridges' and navigating the 'learning gaps': Chinese students learning across two systems in a transnational higher education programme. *Higher Education Research & Development, 39*(6), 1140–1154. DOI: 10.1080/07294360.2020.1713731

Daneshjou, R., Smith, M. P., Sun, M. D., Rotemberg, V., & Zou, J. (2021). Lack of transparency and potential bias in artificial intelligence data sets and algorithms: A scoping review. *JAMA Dermatology, 157*(11), 1362–1369. DOI: 10.1001/jamadermatol.2021.3129

Daniel, S. J. (2020). Education and the COVID-19 pandemic. *Prospects, 49*(1), 91–96. DOI: 10.1007/s11125-020-09464-3

Das, D., Lim, N. D., & Aravind, P. (2022). Developing a Smart and Sustainable Campus in Singapore. *Sustainability (Basel), 14*(21), 14472. DOI: 10.3390/su142114472

Das, R. (2023). Parents' understandings of social media algorithms in children's lives in England: Misunderstandings, parked understandings, transactional understandings and proactive understandings amidst datafication. *Journal of Children and Media, 17*(4), 506–522. DOI: 10.1080/17482798.2023.2240899

Dawson, P. (2020). *Defending assessment security in a digital world: Preventing e-cheating and supporting academic integrity in higher education.* Routledge. DOI: 10.4324/9780429324178

Dawson, P., Bearman, M., Dollinger, M., & Boud, D. (2024). Validity matters more than cheating. *Assessment & Evaluation in Higher Education, 49*(7), 1005–1016. DOI: 10.1080/02602938.2024.2386662

de Jong, T., Linn, M. C., & Zacharia, Z. C. (2013). Physical and virtual laboratories in science and engineering education. *Science, 340*(6130), 305–308. DOI: 10.1126/science.1230579

de Laat, M., Ryberg, T., Dohn, N. B., Hansen, S. B., & Hansen, J. J. (2020). Networked Learning 2020 : Proceedings for the Twelfth International Conference on Networked Learning. In Research Portal Denmark (p. 400). Technical University of Denmark. https://local.forskningsportal.dk/local/dki-cgi/ws/cris-link?src=aau&id=aau-17488b95-fb1d-4734-8a57-26c7ee0914ec&ti=Networked%20Learning%202020%20%3A%20Proceedings%20for%20the%20Twelfth%20International%20Conference%20on%20Networked%20Learning

de Wit, H., Altbach, P. G., & Glass, C. R. (2025). Global Higher Education Transformation: The 2025 International Crisis. *International Higher Education.*

Deardorff, D. K. (2006). Identification and assessment of intercultural competence as a student outcome of internationalization. *Journal of Studies in International Education, 10*(3), 241–266. DOI: 10.1177/1028315306287002

Deardorff, D. K. (Ed.). (2009). *The Sage handbook of intercultural competence.* Sage. DOI: 10.4135/9781071872987

Deep, S., Athimoolam, K., & Enoch, T. (2024). Optimizing Administrative Efficiency and Student engagement in Education: The Impact of AI. *International Journal of Current Science Research and Review, 7*(10). Advance online publication. DOI: 10.47191/ijcsrr/V7-i10-34

Deighton, , JHumphrey, , NBelsky, , JBoehnke, , JVostanis, , PPatalay, , P. (2018). Longitudinal pathways between mental health difficulties and academic performance during middle childhood and early adolescence. *British Journal of Developmental Psychology, 36*(1), 110-126.

Department for Education (DfE). (2025) *Generative Artificial Intelligence (AI) in Education, GOV.UK.* Available at: https://www.gov.uk/government/publications/generative-artificial-intelligence-in-education/generative-artificial-intelligence-ai-in-education (Accessed: 03 September 2025).

Desimone, L. M. (2009). Improving impact studies of teachers' professional development: Toward better conceptualizations and measures. *Educational Researcher, 38*(3), 181–199. DOI: 10.3102/0013189X08331140

Devlin, J., Chang, M. W., Lee, K., & Toutanova, K. (2019). BERT: Bidirectional Encoder Representations from Transformers. *Proceedings of NAACL-HLT 2019.*

Diakopoulos, N. (2016). Accountability in algorithmic decision making. *Communications of the ACM, 59*(2), 56–62. DOI: 10.1145/2844110

Dienlin, T., & Johannes, N. (2020). The impact of digital technology use on adolescent well-being. *Dialogues in Clinical Neuroscience, 22*(2), 135–142. DOI: 10.31887/DCNS.2020.22.2/tdienlin

Digital Education Council. (2025). AI Literacy Framework. Retrieved from Educators' Perceptions of Generative AI and Readiness in Kenyan Higher Education. (2025). *Education and Information Technologies.*

Dillenbourg, P. (1999). *Collaborative learning: Cognitive and computational approaches.* Elsevier.

Dimari, A., Tyagi, N., Davanageri, M., Kukreti, R., Yadav, R., & Dimari, H. (2024). AI-based automated grading systems for open book examination system. In *2024 IEEE International Conference.* https://doi.org/DOI: 10.1109/ICKECS61492.2024.10616490

Dismore, H., Campbell-Barr, V., Manning, R., & Warwick, P. (2024). A relational approach to knowledge exchange in higher education. *Studies in Higher Education (Dorchester-On-Thames), 49*(12), 1–12. https://doi.org/DOI: 10.1080/03075079.2024.2312404

Di, X., Zhu, D., & Wen-hai, X. (2021). The Teaching Pattern of Law Majors Using Artificial Intelligence and Deep Neural Network Under Educational Psychology. *Frontiers in Psychology, 12*, 711520. Advance online publication. DOI: 10.3389/fpsyg.2021.711520

Djeki, E., Dégila, J., Bondiombouy, C., & Alhassan, M. H. (2024, April). Data protection in digital learning space: An overview. In *AIP Conference Proceedings* (Vol. 3109, No. 1). AIP Publishing.

Dong, J., Lee, S., Wang, C. H., & Shannon, D. M. (2023). Impact on social capital and learning engagement due to social media usage among the international students in the US. *Education and Information Technologies, 28*(7), 8027–8050. DOI: 10.1007/s10639-022-11520-8

Doshi-Velez, F., & Kim, B. (2017). Towards a rigorous science of interpretable machine learning. *arXiv preprint arXiv:1702.08608*. https://arxiv.org/abs/1702.08608

Doshi-Velez, F., and Kim, B. (2017). Towards A Rigorous Science of Interpretable Machine Learning. arXiv.

Draper, M., Lancaster, T., Dann, S. E., Crockett, R. G. M., & Glendinning, I. (2021). Essay mills and other contract cheating services: To buy or not to buy and the consequences of students changing their minds. *International Journal for Educational Integrity*, *17*(1), 13. Advance online publication. DOI: 10.1007/s40979-021-00081-x

Druga, S., Williams, R., Park, H. W., & Breazeal, C. (2018, June). How smart are the smart toys? Children and parents' agent interaction and intelligence attribution. In *Proceedings of the 17th ACM conference on interaction design and children* (pp. 231-240). DOI: 10.1145/3202185.3202741

du Boulay, B. (2023). Artificial Intelligence in Education and Ethics. In Zawacki-Richter, O., & Jung, I. (Eds.), *Handbook of Open, Distance and Digital Education* (pp. 93–108). Springer., DOI: 10.1007/978-981-19-2080-6_6

Du, M., Zhu, L., & Nardo, M. D. (2025, February). Strategic Application of Deep Learning Methods in Global Educational Collaboration. In *Proceedings of the 2025 International Conference on Big Data and Informatization Education* (pp. 313-317). DOI: 10.1145/3729605.3729660

Dunn, L., & Wallace, M. (2006). Australian academics and transnational teaching: An exploratory study of their preparedness and experiences. *Higher Education Research & Development*, *25*(4), 357–369. DOI: 10.1080/07294360600947343

Durak, H. Y., & Onan, A. (2025). A systematic review of AI-based feedback in educational settings. *Journal of Computational Social Science*, *8*(96), 96. Advance online publication. DOI: 10.1007/s42001-025-00428-1

Dutt, C. S., Cseh, L., Hardy, P., & Iguchi, Y. (2022). European transnational education in the Middle East: Conceptual highs, lows, and recommendations. *International Marketing Journal of Culture and Tourism*, *1*(2), 69–90.

Eatmon, T. D., Granger, R., Abrantes, B. F., & Forsberg, C. (2020). The entrepreneurial dimensions of transnational education. In *Examining the role of entrepreneurial universities in regional development* (pp. 172–182). IGI Global. DOI: 10.4018/978-1-7998-0174-0.ch009

EDUCAUSE. (2024). AI Literacy in Teaching and Learning. Retrieved from https://www.educause.edu/content/2024/ai-literacy-in-teaching-and-learning

EDUCAUSE. (2024). AI Literacy in Teaching and Learning: Executive Summary. https://www.educause.edu/content/2024/ai-literacy-in-teaching-and-learning/executive-summary

EDUCAUSE. (2025). *AI ethical guidelines*. https://library.educause.edu/resources/2025/6/ai-ethical-guidelines

Elish, M. C. (2016). The limits of bias in machine learning. *XRDS: Crossroads. The ACM Magazine for Students*, *22*(4), 8–11. DOI: 10.1145/2930880

Enríquez, B. G. A., Ballesteros, M. A. A., Várgas, C. G. A. P., Ulloa, M. N. O., Ulloa, C. R. G., Romero, J. P., Jaramillo, N. D. G., Orellana, H. U. C., Anzoátegui, D. X. A., & Roca, C. L. (2024). Knowledge, attitudes, and perceived Ethics regarding the use of ChatGPT among generation Z university students. *International Journal for Educational Integrity*, *20*(1), 10. Advance online publication. DOI: 10.1007/s40979-024-00157-4

Eubanks, V. (2018). *Automating inequality: How high-tech tools profile, police, and punish the poor.* St. Martin's Press.

European Commission. (2023). *AI4Teachers project report.* https://ec.europa.eu/digital-strategy

Evangelista, E. D. L. (2025). Ensuring academic integrity in the age of ChatGPT. *Contemporary Educational Technology*, *17*(1), ep559. DOI: 10.30935/cedtech/15775

Eynon, R. (2021). The rise of algorithmic education. *Learning, Media and Technology*, *46*(4), 442–456.

Ezzaim, A., Dahbi, A., Haidine, A., & Aqqal, A. (2023). AI-Based Adaptive Learning: A Systematic Mapping of the Literature. JUCS -. *Journal of Universal Computer Science*, *29*(10), 1161–1198. DOI: 10.3897/jucs.90528

Faculty Often Missing from AI Policy Discussions in Higher Education. (2025). Inside Higher Ed. *Research Reports (Montgomery).*

FairAIED. (2024). FairAIED: Navigating fairness, bias, and ethics in educational AI applications. arXiv.

Fan, G., Liu, D., Zhang, R., & Pan, L. (2025). The impact of AI-assisted pair programming on student motivation, programming anxiety, collaborative learning, and programming performance: A comparative study with traditional pair programming and individual approaches. *International Journal of STEM Education*, *12*(1), 16. DOI: 10.1186/s40594-025-00537-3

Fan, Z., Yan, Z., & Wen, S. (2023). Deep learning and artificial intelligence in sustainability: A review of SDGs, renewable energy, and environmental health. *Sustainability (Basel)*, *15*(18), 13493. DOI: 10.3390/su151813493

Farber, S. (2024). Harmonizing AI and human instruction in legal education: A case study from Israel on training future legal professionals. *International Journal of the Legal Profession*, *1*(3), 349–363. Advance online publication. DOI: 10.1080/09695958.2024.2430018

Feng, T., Liu, S., & Ghosal, D. (2024). *CourseAssist: Pedagogically Appropriate AI Tutor for Computer Science Education* (Version 3). arXiv. DOI: 10.1145/3649409.3691094

Fernandez-Chung, R. M., & Gill, R. S. (Eds.). (2025). *Transnational Education: Bridging Borders, Transforming Futures.* Taylor & Francis. DOI: 10.4324/9781003488316

Fernández-Martínez, C., & Fernández, A. (2020). AI and recruiting software: Ethical and legal implications. *Paladyn : Journal of Behavioral Robotics*, *11*(1), 199–216. DOI: 10.1515/pjbr-2020-0030

Filimowicz, M. (Ed.). (2023). *Algorithmic Ethics: Algorithms and Society.* Taylor & Francis. DOI: 10.4324/9781003299882

Finkelstein, I., & Soffer-Vital, S. (2025). Cultural empathy in ai-supported collaborative learning: Advancing inclusive digital learning in higher education. *Education Sciences, 15*(10), 1305. DOI: 10.3390/educsci15101305

Fishman, J. A. (2001). 300-plus years of heritage language education in the United States. In *The handbook of bilingualism* (pp. 523–536). Blackwell.

Floridi, L., Cowls, J., Beltrametti, M., Chatila, R., Chazerand, P., Dignum, V., & Luetge, C. (2018). AI4People—an Ethical Framework for a Good AI Society: Opportunities, Risks, Principles, and Recommendations. *Minds and Machines, 28*(4), 689–707. DOI: 10.1007/s11023-018-9482-5

Fraser, N. (2008). *Scales of justice: Reimagining political space in a globalizing world.* Columbia University Press.

Freire, P., & Macedo, D. P. (2014). *Pedagogy of the oppressed: 30th Anniversary Edition* (M. B. Ramos, Trans.; 30th anniversary edition). Bloomsbury Publishing.

Freire, P. (1970). *Pedagogy of the oppressed.* Herder and Herder.

Freyer, O., Jayabalan, S., Kather, J. N., & Gilbert, S. (2025). Overcoming regulatory barriers to the implementation of AI agents in healthcare. *Nature Medicine.* https://www.nature.com/articles/s41591-025-03841-1

Friedman, B. (2021). Law and Ethics of AI and Robotics. In *The Oxford Handbook of Ethics of AI.* Oxford University Press.

G, A. P., & Nair, V. (2024). Integrating Generative AI into Legal Education: From Casebooks to Code, Opportunities and Challenges. Law Technology and Humans, 6(3), 60. DOI: 10.5204/lthj.3640

Gaïni, S. M. (2024). Freedom of Speech, Hate Speech and Democratic Formation : On the double function of hate speech legislation and its relation to freedom of political speech. Research Portal Denmark, 107. https://local.forskningsportal.dk/local/dki-cgi/ws/cris-link?src=ruc&id=ruc-3691400e-1c12-4e84-a217-68e3a46a291e&ti=Freedom%20of%20Speech%2C%20Hate%20Speech%20and%20Democratic%20Formation%20%3A%20On%20the%20double%20function%20of%20hate%20speech%20legislation%20and%20its%20relation%20to%20freedom%20of%20political%20speech

Gallagher-Mundy, M. (2025) Private Communication on Dissertation *Marking and AI.* UCFB internal academic note.

Gao, R., Yu, D., Gao, B., Hua, H., Hui, Z., Gao, J., & Yin, C. (2025). Legal regulation of AI-assisted academic writing: Challenges, frameworks, and pathways. *Frontiers in Artificial Intelligence, 8,* 1546064. Advance online publication. DOI: 10.3389/frai.2025.1546064

Garrison, D. R. (2011). *E-Learning in the 21st Century: A Framework for Research and Practice* (2nd ed.). Routledge., DOI: 10.4324/9780203838761

Garrison, D., & Arbaugh, J. B. (2007). Researching the community of inquiry framework: Review, issues, and future directions. *Internet and Higher Education -. The Internet and Higher Education, 10*(3), 157–172. DOI: 10.1016/j.iheduc.2007.04.001

Gaumann, N., & Veale, M. (2023). AI Providers as Criminal Essay Mills? Large Language Models meet Contract Cheating Law. DOI: 10.31235/osf.io/cpbfd

Gay, G. (2010). *Culturally responsive teaching: Theory, research, and practice* (2nd ed.). Teachers College Press.

Gebru, T., Morgenstern, J., Vecchione, B., Vaughan, J. W., Wallach, H., Iii, H. D., & Crawford, K. (2021). Datasheets for datasets. *Communications of the ACM*, *64*(12), 86–92. DOI: 10.1145/3458723

Gelashvili-Luik, T., Vihma, P., & Pappel, I. (2025). Navigating the AI revolution: Challenges and opportunities for integrating emerging technologies into knowledge management systems. Systematic literature review. *Frontiers in Artificial Intelligence*, *8*, 1595930. Advance online publication. DOI: 10.3389/frai.2025.1595930

George, B., & Wooden, O. (2023). Managing the strategic transformation of higher education through artificial intelligence. *Administrative Sciences*, *13*(9), 196. DOI: 10.3390/admsci13090196

Ghoshal, R. (2025). Cross-border AI governance for legal tech: Standardizing ethical and legal norms in access to justice. *International Journal of Law Justice and Jurisprudence*, *5*(1), 186–194. DOI: 10.22271/2790-0673.2025.v5.i1c.177

Giani, M. S., & Walling, D. (2020). Will I Get In? Using Predictive Analytics to Develop Student-Facing Tools to Estimate University Admissions Decisions. *Journal of College Access*, *5*(1), 4.

Gill, A., & Mathur, A. (2023). Exploring the futuristic landscape of artificial intelligence for alpha generation: A comprehensive study. *World Adv Res Rev*, *20*(02), 1250–1264. DOI: 10.30574/wjarr.2023.20.2.2369

Gilliard, C., & Culik, H. (2016). Digital redlining, access, and privacy. *ACRLog*. https://acrlog.org

Giray, L. (2024). The Problem with False Positives: AI Detection Unfairly Accuses Scholars of AI Plagiarism. *The Serials Librarian*, *85*(5-6), 5–6, 181–189. https://www.researchgate.net/publication/386998010_The_Problem_with_False_Positives_AI_Detection_Unfairly_Accuses_Scholars_of_AI_Plagiarism. DOI: 10.1080/0361526X.2024.2433256

Glaveski, S. (2024). *Why English Dominates the World - it has nothing to do with 'white privilege'*. Medium. Available at: https://glaveski.medium.com/why-english-dominates-the-world-it-has-nothing-to-do-with-white-privilege-e9b401681273

Goh, K. L., Tan, S., & Chen, L. (2019). Multilingual Pedagogy in Higher Education: Adapting with Generative AI. *International Journal of Multilingual Education*, *1*(1), 65–78.

Gómez, M. J., Dabbah, J., & Benotti, L. (2025). A workshop on artificial intelligence biases and its effect on high school students' perceptions. *International Journal of Child-Computer Interaction*, *43*, 100710. DOI: 10.1016/j.ijcci.2024.100710

González, A. S., & Rampino, L. (2024). A design perspective on how to tackle gender biases when developing AI-driven systems. *AI and Ethics*, ●●●, 1–18.

González-Sendino, R., Serrano, E., Bajo, J., & Novais, P. (2023). A review of bias and fairness in artificial intelligence.

Goorney, S., Sarantinou, M., & Sherson, J. (2023). The open master: A new model of transnational higher education. *Distance Education, 44*(4), 765–776. DOI: 10.1080/01587919.2023.2280064

Gouseti, A. (2025). Emerging AI trends in higher education: Challenges and opportunities. *Ethics and Education, 20*(2), 101–118.

Gouseti, A. (2025). The ethics of using AI in K-12 education. *Ethics and Education, 20*(1), 1–15.

Grady, A. R., & Lewis, J. A. (2024). Perceptions of academic discrimination mediate the relationship between political minority status and self-censorship among US college students. *Discover Psychology, 4*(1), 191. Advance online publication. DOI: 10.1007/s44202-024-00308-1

Graham, R., & Misra, S. (2020). EdTech in the Global South: Challenges for teachers. *International Journal of Educational Development, 77*, 102234.

Gray, S. L., Edsall, D. G., & Parapadakis, D. (2025). AI-Based Digital Cheating At University, and the Case for New Ethical Pedagogies. *Journal of Academic Ethics, 23*(4), 2069–2086. Advance online publication. DOI: 10.1007/s10805-025-09642-y

Greco, C. M., & Tagarelli, A. (2023). Bringing order into the realm of Transformer-based language models for artificial intelligence and law. *Artificial Intelligence and Law, 32*(4), 863–1010. DOI: 10.1007/s10506-023-09374-7

Green, W. H. (2024). *Report to the President for year ended June 30, 2024.* MIT Energy Initiative.

Gripsy, J. V., Selvakumari, S. N., Sheeba, L., & Kumaran, B. S. (2025). Transforming Student Engagement Through AI, AR, VR, and Chatbots in Education. In Chatbots in Educational Leadership and Management (pp. 73-100). IGI Global Scientific Publishing.

Gruenhagen, J. H., Sinclair, P. M., Carroll, J. A., Baker, P. R., Wilson, A., & Demant, D. (2024). The rapid rise of generative AI and its implications for academic integrity: Students' perceptions and use of chatbots for assistance with assessments. *Computers and Education: Artificial Intelligence, 7*, 100273. DOI: 10.1016/j.caeai.2024.100273

Guler, N. (2021). Teaching culturally and linguistically diverse students: Exploring the challenges and perceptions of nursing faculty. *Nursing Education Perspectives, 43*(1), 11–13. DOI: 10.1097/01.NEP.0000000000000861

Guo, Y. (2025). *University Belongingness Among Professional Doctoral Alumni in the US Transnational Education in China: A Mixed Methods Case Study* (Doctoral dissertation, The University of Arizona).

Guo, S., & Ling, L. (2019). Toward transnational communities of practice: An inquiry into the experiences of transnational academic mobility. *Adult Education Quarterly, 70*(1), 26–43. DOI: 10.1177/0741713619867636

Guo, Y., & Wang, Y. (2024). Exploring the effects of artificial intelligence application on EFL students' academic engagement and emotional experiences: A mixed-methods study. *European Journal of Education, 60*(1), e12812. Advance online publication. DOI: 10.1111/ejed.12812

Gutowski, N., & Hurley, J. (2025). Forging Ahead or Proceeding with Caution; Developing Policy for Generative Artificial Intelligence in Legal Education. DOI: 10.2139/ssrn.5076598

Guzzo, T., Ferri, F., & Grifoni, P. (2023). Lessons Learned during COVID-19 and Future Perspectives for Emerging Technology. *Sustainability (Basel), 15*(14), 10747. DOI: 10.3390/su151410747

Haider, S. A., Ahmad, K. M., Akbar, J., Soni, M., Keshta, I., AlGhamdi, A., & Shahzadi, H. M. (2025, April). Generative AI as a Catalyst for Transforming Transnational Engineering Education: Opportunities, Challenges, and Future Directions. In *2025 IEEE Global Engineering Education Conference (EDUCON)* (pp. 1-8). IEEE. DOI: 10.1109/EDUCON62633.2025.11016469

Hajji, S. (2023). Educational sovereignty and artificial intelligence challenges: the case of Morocco. In *Artificial Intelligence in Higher Education and Scientific Research: Future Development* (pp. 101–116). Springer Nature Singapore. DOI: 10.1007/978-981-19-8641-3_8

Hall, S. (1990). Cultural identity and diaspora. In *Identity: Community, culture, difference* (pp. 222–237). Lawrence & Wishart.

Hamad, H. A., & Charles, T. (2024). The role of educational leaders in ensuring academic integrity with online assessments. *Open Journal of Leadership, 13*(2), 154–167. DOI: 10.4236/ojl.2024.132010

Han, S. (2024). Data and statecraft: Why and how states localize data. *Business and Politics, 26*(2), 263–288. DOI: 10.1017/bap.2023.41

Haoning Mah, G., Hu, X., & Yang, W. (2021). Digital technology use and early reading abilities among bilingual children in Singapore. *Policy Futures in Education, 19*(2), 242–258. DOI: 10.1177/1478210320980575

Hargittai, E., & Hsieh, Y. P. (2013). Digital inequality. In Dutton, W. (Ed.), *The Oxford handbook of internet studies* (pp. 129–150). Oxford University Press.

Hasegawa, T., Yamada, H., Nishimura, H., & Kobayashi, M. (2025). The Role of AI and Virtual Learning Environments in Enhancing STEM Education. [IJESTE]. *International Journal of Education, Science, Technology, and Engineering, 8*(1), 1–10. DOI: 10.36079/lamintang.ijeste-0801.746

Hatahet, T., Raouf Mohamed, A. A., Malekigorji, M., Clerkin, C., & Sandrey, L. (2024). Personal and engagement factors in remote learning contributing to high student achievement in a transnational education context: A quantitative study. *Advances in Online Education: A Peer-Reviewed Journal, 2*(4), 330-350.

Hattie, J., & Timperley, H. (2007). The power of feedback. *Review of Educational Research, 77*(1), 81–112. DOI: 10.3102/003465430298487

Hayes, N., & Introna, L. D. (2005). Cultural Values, Plagiarism, and Fairness: When Plagiarism Gets in the Way of Learning. *Ethics & Behavior, 15*(3), 213–231. DOI: 10.1207/s15327019eb1503_2

Hazzan-Bishara, A., Kol, O., & Levy, S. (2025). The factors affecting teachers' adoption of AI technologies: A unified model of external and internal determinants. *Education and Information Technologies, 30*(11), 15043–15069. DOI: 10.1007/s10639-025-13393-z

Healey, N. M. (2018). The challenges of managing transnational education partnerships: The views of "home-based" managers vs "in-country" managers. *International Journal of Educational Management, 32*(2), 241–256. DOI: 10.1108/IJEM-04-2017-0085

Healey, N. M. (2023). Transnational education: The importance of aligning stakeholders' motivations with the form of cross-border educational service delivery. *Higher Education Quarterly, 77*(1), 83–101. DOI: 10.1111/hequ.12371

Heffernan, A., Murphy, M. P. A., & Yearwood, D. (2022). Can active learning be asynchronous? Implementing online peer review assignments in undergraduate political science and international relations courses. *European Political Science, 21*(4), 537–549. DOI: 10.1057/s41304-022-00386-6

Heinrich, E. (2025). A Systematic-Narrative Review of Online Proctoring Systems and a Case for Open Standards [Review of A Systematic-Narrative Review of Online Proctoring Systems and a Case for Open Standards]. Open Praxis, 17(3). International Council for Open and Distance Education. DOI: 10.55982/openpraxis.17.3.836

Henderson, M., Bearman, M., Chung, J., Fawns, T., Buckingham Shum, S., Matthews, K. E., & de Mello Heredia, J. (2025). Comparing generative AI and teacher feedback: Student perceptions of usefulness and trustworthiness. *Assessment & Evaluation in Higher Education*, 1–16. Advance online publication. DOI: 10.1080/02602938.2025.2502582

Heradio, R., de la Torre, L., Galan, D., Cabrerizo, F. J., Herrera-Viedma, E., & Dormido, S. (2021). Virtual and remote labs in education: A 10-year review. *Computers & Education, 159*, 104002. DOI: 10.1016/j.compedu.2020.104002

Herodotou, C., Rienties, B., Verdin, B., & Boroowa, A. (2019). Predictive Learning Analytics "At Scale": Towards Guidelines to Successful Implementation in Higher Education Based on the Case of the Open University UK. *Journal of Learning Analytics, 6*(1), 85–95. DOI: 10.18608/jla.2019.61.5

He, S. (2023). The impact of new media and artificial intelligence technologies on ideological and political education in higher education institutions and countermeasures. *Proceedings of EAI International Conference*. DOI: 10.4108/eai.8-9-2023.2340095

He, X., & Burger-Helmchen, T. (2024). Evolving Knowledge Management: Artificial Intelligence and the Dynamics of Social Interactions. *IEEE Engineering Management Review*, •••, 1–30. DOI: 10.1109/EMR.2024.3519342

Higher Education Institutions. B.C. (2024) *Upcoming report: Sustainability of tne partnerships in Egypt, Qatar and the UAE, Upcoming report: sustainability of TNE partnerships in Egypt, Qatar and the UAE | British Council*. Available at: https://opportunities-insight.britishcouncil.org/features/upcoming-report-sustainability-of-tne-partnerships-egypt-qatar-and-uae (Accessed: 03 August 2025).

Hill, C. (2021). Evolving models of transnational education: new partnerships and reducing risk. Why are we so afraid of change? In *The Evolution of Transnational Education* (pp. 111–125). Routledge. DOI: 10.4324/9781003225386-12

Hinds, J., Williams, E. J., & Joinson, A. N. (2020). "It wouldn't happen to me": Privacy concerns and perspectives following the Cambridge Analytica scandal. *International Journal of Human-Computer Studies, 143*, 102498. DOI: 10.1016/j.ijhcs.2020.102498

Hiniker, A., Wang, A., Tran, J., Zhang, M. R., Radesky, J., Sobel, K., & Hong, S. R. (2021, June). Can conversational agents change the way children talk to people? In *Proceedings of the 20th Annual ACM Interaction Design and Children Conference* (pp. 338-349). DOI: 10.1145/3459990.3460695

His Highness Sheikh Mohammed bin Rashid Al Maktoum (2025) *UAE National Strategy for Artificial Intelligence 2031,* https://u.ae/. Available at: https://ai.gov.ae/wp-content/uploads/2021/07/UAE-National-Strategy-for-Artificial-Intelligence-2031.pdf (Accessed: 17 August 2025).

Höfrová, A., Balidemaj, V., & Small, M. A. (2024). A systematic literature review of education for Generation Alpha. *Discover Education, 3*(1), 125. DOI: 10.1007/s44217-024-00218-3

Hofstede, G. (2011). Dimensionalizing Cultures: The Hofstede Model in Context. *Online Readings in Psychology and Culture, 2*(1). Advance online publication. DOI: 10.9707/2307-0919.1014

Hofstein, A., & Lunetta, V. N. (2004). The laboratory in science education: Foundations for the twenty-first century. *Science Education, 88*(1), 28–54. DOI: 10.1002/sce.10106

Holden, C. (2018). Adapting Tinto's Framework: A Model of Success and Failure in a Middle Eastern Trans-national Setting. *Studies in Higher Education, 43*(6), 1002–1019. DOI: 10.1080/03075079.2016.1212004

Holmes, W., Bialik, M., & Fadel, C. (2019). *Artificial intelligence in education promises and implications for teaching and learning*. Center for Curriculum Redesign.

Holmes, W., Bialik, M., & Fadel, C. (2019). *Artificial intelligence in education: Promises and implications for teaching and learning*. Center for Curriculum Redesign.

Holmes, W., Bialik, M., & Fadel, C. (2022). *Artificial Intelligence in Education: Promises and Implications for Teaching and Learning*. Center for Curriculum Redesign.

Holmes, W., & Miao, F. (2023). *Guidance for generative AI in education and research.* UNESCO Publishing.

Holstein, K., McLaren, B. M., & Aleven, V. (2020). Designing for complementarity: Teacher and student needs for orchestration support in AI-enhanced classrooms. *British Journal of Educational Technology, 51*(6), 2115–2131. DOI: 10.1111/bjet.12908

Hopbach, A. (2022). *UNESCO-OECD guidelines for quality provision in cross-border higher education.* UNESCO. https://unesdoc.unesco.org/ark:/48223/pf0000389910

Hopfenbeck, T. N., Zhang, Z., Sun, S. Z., Robertson, P., & McGrane, J. A. (2023). Challenges and opportunities for classroom-based formative assessment and AI: A perspective article. *Frontiers in Education, 8*, 1270700. Advance online publication. DOI: 10.3389/feduc.2023.1270700

Huang, T. (2025). NetChoice, Regulatory Competition, and the Real Battle Behind Social Media Regulations. SSRN Electronic Journal. DOI: 10.2139/ssrn.5222236

Huang, R., Liu, D., Tlili, A., Yang, J., & Wang, H. (2022). AI-enhanced collaborative learning: Emerging trends and pedagogical practices. *Computers & Education, 190*, 104625. DOI: 10.1016/j.compedu.2022.104625

Hu, J., Lai, Y., & Yi, X. (2024). Effectiveness of social media-assisted course on learning self-efficacy. *Scientific Reports, 14*(1), 10112. DOI: 10.1038/s41598-024-60724-0

Hutchins, E. (2006). *Cognition in the wild* (8. pr). MIT Press.

Hutson, J., & Plate, D. (2024). The Algorithm of Fear: Unpacking Prejudice Against AI and the Mistrust of Technology. Journal of Innovation and Technology, 2024(1). DOI: 10.61453/joit.v2024no38

Hu, Y.-H. (2025). Advancing asynchronous pre-class learning in flipped classrooms: Generative AI companions in business ethics. *Education and Information Technologies, 30*(10), 14367–14391. Advance online publication. DOI: 10.1007/s10639-025-13379-x

Huy, D. P. M., Nguyen, G. N., & Le, D. (2025). A Combine Solution for Online Exams Cheating Detection, Prediction, and Prevention Using Artificial Intelligence. In *Lecture notes in networks and systems* (p. 665). Springer International Publishing., DOI: 10.1007/978-981-96-3381-4_51

IBM. (2024, May 14). *European School of Management and Business (EUDE) | IBM*. Ibm.com. https://www.ibm.com/case-studies/eude

Idrizi, E. (2024). Exploring the Role of Explainable Artificial Intelligence(XAI) in Adaptive learning systems. 100. DOI: 10.1145/3660853.3660877

Ifenthaler, D., Majumdar, R., Gorissen, P., Judge, M., Mishra, S., Raffaghelli, J. E., & Shimada, A. (2024). *Artificial Intelligence in Education: Implications for Policymakers, Researchers, and Practitioners*. Technology Knowledge and Learning., DOI: 10.1007/s10758-024-09747-0

Igbinenikaro, E., & Adewusi, O. A. (2024). Policy recommendations for integrating artificial intelligence into global trade agreements. *International Journal of Engineering Research Updates, 6*(01), 001-010.

IHE. (2023) *Inclusive Higher Education Conference Proceedings*. London: IHE.

Imohimi, E. O. (2025). Building Privacy and Preserving AI Models for Secure Student Data Management in Educational Technology Platforms. *Journal of Intelligent Learning Systems and Applications, 17*(3), 149–171. DOI: 10.4236/jilsa.2025.173011

International Telecommunication Union. (2023). *Measuring digital development: Facts and figures 2023*. https://www.itu.int/en/ITU-D/Statistics

Ioannou, A., & Makridou, E. (2018). Exploring the potentials of educational robotics in the development of computational thinking: A summary of current research and practical proposal for future work. *Education and Information Technologies, 23*(6), 2531–2544. DOI: 10.1007/s10639-018-9729-z

Iqbal, S., Asgarova, G., & Hashmi, M. (2025). Integrating Generative AI in Language Learning Curricula: Pedagogical and Ethical Implications. *Journal of Educational Computing Research*.

Isakov, A., Urozov, F., Abduzhapporov, S., & Isokova, M. (2024). Enhancing Cybersecurity: Protecting Data In The Digital Age. *Innovations in Science and Technologies, 1*(1), 40–49.

Islam, M. R., Liu, S., Wang, X., & Xu, G. (2020). Deep learning for misinformation detection on online social networks: A survey and new perspectives. *Social Network Analysis and Mining*, *10*(1), 82. DOI: 10.1007/s13278-020-00696-x

Islam, M. T. (2023). Bangladeshi students' family fertilization for pursuing higher education in Australia. In *Handbook of Research on Developments and Future Trends in Transnational Higher Education* (pp. 247–264). IGI Global Scientific Publishing. DOI: 10.4018/978-1-6684-5226-4.ch013

Ito, M., Gutiérrez, K., Livingstone, S., Penuel, B., Rhodes, J., Salen, K., & Watkins, S. C. (2013). *Connected learning: An agenda for research and design*. Digital Media and Learning Research Hub.

Jaadi, M. E., Haidi, T., & Bouabdallaoui, D. (2025). *IAES International Journal of Artificial Intelligence (IJ-AI)*. IAES International Journal of Artificial Intelligence., DOI: 10.11591/ijai

Jaakkola, E. (2020). Designing conceptual articles: Four approaches. *AMS Review*, *10*(1-2), 18–26. DOI: 10.1007/s13162-020-00161-0

Jackman, G.-A., Marshall, I. A., & Carrington, T. (2024). Opportunity or Threat: Investigating Faculty Readiness to Adopt Artificial Intelligence in Higher Education. *Caribbean Journal of Education and Development*, *1*(2), 47–70. DOI: 10.46425/cjed1201029055

Jefferies, P., & Grodzinsky, F. (2007). Developing on-line collaborative research across international boundaries: Exploring the potential of new technologies. *International Journal for the Scholarship of Teaching and Learning*, *1*(2), 6. Advance online publication. DOI: 10.20429/ijsotl.2007.010206

Jensen, L., & Konradsen, F. (2022). A review of the use of virtual reality head-mounted displays in education and training. *Education and Information Technologies*, *27*(4), 4615–4637. DOI: 10.1007/s10639-021-10704-4

Jha, A. K. (2020). Understanding generation alpha.

Jiang, S. (2021). The call of the homeland: Transnational education and the rising nationalism among Chinese overseas students. *Comparative Education Review*, *65*(1), 34–55. DOI: 10.1086/712053

Jin, Y., Yan, L., Echeverria, V., Gašević, D., & Martinez-Maldonado, R. (2025). Generative AI in higher education: A global perspective of institutional adoption policies and guidelines. *Computers and Education: Artificial Intelligence*, *8*, 100348. DOI: 10.1016/j.caeai.2024.100348

Jisc. (2023, September). *AI in tertiary education: A summary of the current state of play* (3rd ed.). Jisc.

Jisc. (2025, July 2). *Global education and technology: Digital challenges associated with the effective delivery of transnational education*. Jisc.

Jivet, I., Scheffel, M., Schmitz, M., Robbers, S., Specht, M., & Drachsler, H. (2020). From students with love: An empirical study on learner goals, self-regulated learning and sense-making of learning analytics in higher education. *The Internet and Higher Education*, *47*, 100758. DOI: 10.1016/j.iheduc.2020.100758

Jobin, A., Ienca, M., & Vayena, E. (2019). The global landscape of AI ethics guidelines. *Nature Machine Intelligence*, *1*(9), 389–399. DOI: 10.1038/s42256-019-0088-2

Johnson, M., Schuster, M., Le, Q. V., Krikun, M., Wu, Y., Chen, Z., . . . Dean, J. (2020). T2T: Tiny and Transferable. arXiv preprint arXiv:2002.04745.

Johnson, D. W., & Johnson, R. T. (1999). *Learning together and alone: Cooperative, competitive, and individualistic learning* (5th ed.). Allyn & Bacon.

Jonassen, D. H., & Jonassen, D. H. (with Internet Archive). (2003). *Learning to solve problems with technology: A constructivist perspective*. Upper Saddle River, N.J.: Merrill. http://archive.org/details/learningtosolvep00jona

Jones, B. (2025). Enhancing cross-cultural exchange with AI: ChatGPT's role in an international online student conference. 1(1), 2138. DOI: 10.29140/jct.v1n1.2138

Joosten-ten Brinke, D., & Beekman, K. (2025). Responsible AI in higher education assessment: Principles, policy & practice. *Assessment in Education*. https://think.taylorandfrancis.com/special_issues/responsible-ai-in-higher-education-assessment

Joshi, P., Ahmed, S., & Sridhar, V. (2020). Multilingual NLP: Challenges and future directions. In *Proceedings of the ACL 2020 Workshop on Multilinguality*.

Joshi, P., Santy, S., Budhiraja, A., Bali, K., & Choudhury, M. (2020). The state and fate of linguistic diversity and inclusion in the NLP world. In *Proceedings of ACL*. https://doi.org/DOI: 10.18653/v1/2020.acl-main.560

Joulin, A., Grave, E., Bojanowski, P., and Mikolov, T. (2016). Bag of Tricks for Efficient Text Classification. *ArXiv, abs/1607.01759.*

Kabilan, M. K., Kabilan, M. K., Ahmad, N., & Abidin, M. J. Z. (2010). Facebook: An online environment for learning of English in institutions of.... *The Internet and Higher Education*, *13*(4), 179–187. DOI: 10.1016/j.iheduc.2010.07.003

Kai, G., Purba, C. A., Syaifuddin, I., & Fadhl Al-Hosaini, F. (2024). Critically Reviewing the Integration of Knowledge Management (KM) and Artificial Intelligence (AI): Future Trends and Implications. *SSRN*. Advance online publication. DOI: 10.2139/ssrn.4857763

Kamali, J. (2024). AI ethics as a complex and multifaceted challenge. *Educational Technology Journal*, *15*(2), 45–58.

Kang, P. E. (2022). Academic Integrity and the Inclusion of East Asian International Students in Canadian Higher Education. In Handbook of Research on Teaching Strategies for Culturally and Linguistically Diverse International Students (pp. 188-200). IGI Global Scientific Publishing. DOI: 10.4018/978-1-7998-8921-2.ch010

Kanont, K., Pingmuang, P., Simasathien, T., Wisnuwong, S., Wiwatsiripong, B., Poonpirome, K., Songkram, N., & Khlaisang, J. (2024). Generative-AI, a learning assistant? Factors influencing higher-ed students' technology acceptance. *Electronic Journal of e-Learning*, *22*(6), 18–33. DOI: 10.34190/ejel.22.6.3196

Kaplan, A. M., & Haenlein, M. (2010). Users of the world, unite! The challenges and opportunities of Social Media. *Business Horizons*, *53*(1), 59–68. DOI: 10.1016/j.bushor.2009.09.003

Kaplan-Berkley, S. (2022). Digital tools and streaming media converge to inspire social interactions of generation alpha. *International Journal of Early Childhood, 54*(2), 185–201. DOI: 10.1007/s13158-021-00301-y

Karim-Abdallah, B., Darko, G. O., Gyabaah, O., Fening, L. O., Chimsi, I., Derkyi, M. A. A., & Yeboah-Kyereh, A. (2025). Innovations, Technologies and Challenges Associated with Transnational Education. *African Journal of Applied Research, 11*(1), 560–587. DOI: 10.26437/ajar.v11i1.870

Karimi, H., & Khawaja, S. (2023). The impact of artificial intelligence on higher education in England. *Creative Education, 14*(12), 2405–2415. DOI: 10.4236/ce.2023.1412154

Karim, K. H. (Ed.). (2003). *The media of diaspora*. Routledge. DOI: 10.4324/9780203380642

Kasapidis, V. (2025). AI and Data Literacy: Challenges and Opportunities for Education. *European Journal of Education.*

Kashefi, P., Kashefi, Y., & Mirsaraei, A. G. (2024). Shaping the future of AI: Balancing innovation and ethics in global regulation. *Uniform Law Review, 29*(3), 524–548. DOI: 10.1093/ulr/unae040

Kasneci, E., Seßler, K., Küchemann, S., Bannert, M., Dementieva, D., Fischer, F., Gasser, U., Groh, G., Günnemann, S., Hüllermeier, E., Krusche, S., Kutyniok, G., Michaeli, T., Nerdel, C., Pfeffer, J., Poquet, O., Sailer, M., Schmidt, A., Seidel, T., & Kasneci, G. (2023). ChatGPT for good? On opportunities and challenges of large language models for education. *Learning and Individual Differences, 103*, 102274. DOI: 10.1016/j.lindif.2023.102274

Kastberg, P., & Ditlevsen, M. G. (2021). Let's talk about how we talk about employees.: A critical examination of the discursive construction of the employee in the textbooks that shape the HR managers of tomorrow. Research Portal Denmark. https://local.forskningsportal.dk/local/dki-cgi/ws/cris-link?src=au&id=au-7eed7534-b4f3-447e-91b6-0c9b39e21819&ti=Let%2019s%20talk%20about%20how%20we%20talk%20about%20employees.%20%3A%20A%20critical%20examination%20of%20the%20discursive%20construction%20of%20the%20employee%20in%20the%20textbooks%20that%20shape%20the%20HR%20managers%20of%20tomorrow

Kayyali, R. (2024). AI and assessment in transnational education. In *AI in Global Higher Education.* Springer., https://link.springer.com/chapter/10.1007/978-3-031-66623-0_6

Kazantheos, L. (2022) *Literary sources for Shakespeare's plays & poetry. Qudos Academy.* Available at: https://qudosacademy.org/2022/01/10/literary-sources-for-shakespeares-plays-poetry/

Kelso, E., Soneji, A., Navid, S. Z.-U.-H., Soshitaishvili, Y., Rahaman, S., & Hasan, R. (2025). Investigating the Security & Privacy Risks from Unsanctioned Technology Use by Educators. DOI: 10.48550/ARXIV.2502.16739

Kemp, S. (2021). The ethics of data and AI in education. *Journal of Digital Ethics, 5*(2), 211–226.

Kendrick, D., Young, B., Mason-Jones, A. J., Ilyas, N., Achana, F. A., Cooper, N. J., Hubbard, S. J., Sutton, A. J., Smith, S., Wynn, P., Mulvaney, C., Watson, M. C., & Coupland, C. (2013). Home safety education and provision of safety equipment for injury prevention. *Evidence-Based Child Health: A Cochrane Review Journal, 8*(3), 761–939. DOI: 10.1002/ebch.1911

Kergel, D., & Heidkamp, B. (2021). The digital transformation of higher education: International perspectives. *Education Sciences*, *11*(3), 118. DOI: 10.3390/educsci11030118

Ketteringham, M. (2025). Developing a 2nd-year undergraduate engineering communications module in a UK/China transnational education engineering program. In *English for Academic and Specific Purposes in the Classroom* (pp. 50-71). Routledge.

Ketzl, A. D. (2025). Knowledge Censorship in 21st Century Academia: An Overview with Attention to the Trends of Wokeism and Cancel Culture. *Open Journal of Social Sciences*, *13*(3), 330–345. DOI: 10.4236/jss.2025.133023

Khadri, H. O. (2021). University academics' perceptions regarding the future use of telepresence robots to enhance virtual transnational education: An exploratory investigation in a developing country. *Smart Learning Environments*, *8*(1), 28. DOI: 10.1186/s40561-021-00173-8

Khairullah, S. A., Harris, S., Hadi, H. J., Sandhu, R., Ahmad, N., & Alshara, M. A. (2025). Implementing artificial intelligence in academic and administrative processes through responsible strategic leadership in the higher education institutions. *Frontiers in Education*, *10*, 1548104. Advance online publication. DOI: 10.3389/feduc.2025.1548104

Khalil, H., & Alsenaidi, S. (2024). Teachers' digital competencies for effective AI integration in higher education in Oman. *Journal of Education and e-learning Research*, *11*(4), 698–707. DOI: 10.20448/jeelr.v11i4.6097

Khan, S. M. (2024). AI-powered tools for teaching English as a second language (ESL) in TNE. In *Bridging Global Divides for Transnational Higher Education in the AI Era* (pp. 121–140). IGI Global. DOI: 10.4018/979-8-3693-7016-2.ch006

Khan, S., & Alfaz, M. (2025). Towards a ministry-led quality assurance framework for transnational higher education: A comparative UK–UAE study. *International Journal of Environmental Sciences*, *11*(23s). https://theaspd.com/index.php/ijes/article/download/8793/6358/18220

Khan, S., Mazhar, T., Shahzad, T., Khan, M. A., Rehman, A. U., Saeed, M. M., & Hamam, H. (2025). Harnessing AI for sustainable higher education: Ethical considerations, operational efficiency, and future directions. *Discover Sustainability*, *6*(1), 23. Advance online publication. DOI: 10.1007/s43621-025-00809-6

Khasawneh, M. A. S. (2023). The Potential Of Ai In Facilitating Cross-Cultural Communication *Through Translation. Journal of Namibian Studies: History Politics Culture*, *37*, 107–130. DOI: 10.59670/jns.v37i.4654

Khlaif, Z. N., Abuhassna, H., & Qouzah, R. (2024). University teachers' views on the adoption and integration of generative AI tools for student assessment. Computers & Education. *Artificial Intelligence*, *5*, 100–110.

Khlaif, Z. N., Alkouk, W. A., Salama, N., & Abu Eideh, B. (2025). Redesigning Assessments for AI-Enhanced Learning: A Framework for Educators in the Generative AI Era. *Education Sciences*, *15*(2), 174. DOI: 10.3390/educsci15020174

Khosravi, H., Shum, S. B., Chen, G., Conati, C., Tsai, Y.-S., Kay, J., Knight, S., Martinez-Maldonado, R., Sadiq, S., & Gašević, D. (2022). Explainable Artificial Intelligence in education. *Computers and Education: Artificial Intelligence*, *3*, 100074. DOI: 10.1016/j.caeai.2022.100074

Khurshid, S., Amin, F., Masoodi, N., & Khan, M. F. (2023). Factors influencing online learning on social media. *International Journal of Learning Technology*, *18*(1), 3–27. DOI: 10.1504/IJLT.2023.131309

Kim, H. (2024). Guidelines for culturally and linguistically responsive instruction in higher education. *TESOL Journal*, *15*(4), e807. Advance online publication. DOI: 10.1002/tesj.807

Kim, J., Lee, H., & Cho, Y. H. (2022). Learning design to support student-AI collaboration: Perspectives of leading teachers for AI in education. *Education and Information Technologies*, *27*(5), 6069–6104. DOI: 10.1007/s10639-021-10831-6

Kizilcec, R. F., Huber, E., Papanastasiou, E. C., Cram, A., Makridis, C. A., Smolansky, A., Zeivots, S., & Raduescu, C. (2024). Perceived impact of generative AI on assessments: Comparing educator and student perspectives in Australia, Cyprus, and the United States. *Computers and Education: Artificial Intelligence*, *7*, 100269. DOI: 10.1016/j.caeai.2024.100269

Kleibert, J. M. (2022). Transnational spaces of education as infrastructures of im/mobility. *Transactions of the Institute of British Geographers*, *47*(1), 92–107. DOI: 10.1111/tran.12475

Klein, P., Ivanjek, L., Dahlkemper, M. N., Jeličić, K., Geyer, M.-A., Küchemann, S., & Susac, A. (2021). Studying physics during the COVID-19 pandemic: Student assessments of learning achievement, perceived effectiveness of online recitations, and online laboratories. *Physical Review. Physics Education Research*, *17*(1), 010117. DOI: 10.1103/PhysRevPhysEducRes.17.010117

Klimova, B., & Chen, J. H. (2024). The Impact of AI on Enhancing Students' Intercultural Communication Competence at the University Level: *A Review Study. Language Teaching Research Quarterly*, *43*, 102–120. DOI: 10.32038/ltrq.2024.43.06

Knight, S., & Ferrell, G. (2022, March 2). *Principles of good assessment and feedback*. Jisc. https://beta.jisc.ac.uk/guides/principles-of-good-assessment-and-feedback

Knight, J. (2015). Transnational education remodeled. *Journal of Studies in International Education*, *20*(1), 34–47. DOI: 10.1177/1028315315602927

Koehn, P. (2020). *Neural machine translation*. Cambridge University Press. DOI: 10.1017/9781108608480

Kofinas, A. K., Tsay, C. H., & Pike, D. (2025). The impact of generative AI on academic integrity. *British Journal of Educational Technology*, *56*(6), 2522–2549. Advance online publication. DOI: 10.1111/bjet.13585

Kolb, D. A. (1984). *Experiential learning: Experience as the source of learning and development*. Prentice Hall.

Korff, D. (2023). The Indian Digital Personal Data Protection Act, 2023, viewed from a European Perspective. SSRN Electronic Journal. DOI: 10.2139/ssrn.4614984

Kovari, A. (2025). A systematic review of AI-powered collaborative learning in higher education: Trends and outcomes from the last decade. *Social Sciences & Humanities Open, 11*(1), 101335. DOI: 10.1016/j.ssaho.2025.101335

Krajcik, J., & Shin, N. (2014). Project-based learning. In Sawyer, R. K. (Ed.), *The Cambridge handbook of the learning sciences* (2nd ed., pp. 275–297). Cambridge University Press. DOI: 10.1017/CBO9781139519526.018

Krištofík, A. (2025). Bias in AI (Supported) Decision Making: Old Problems, New Technologies. *International Journal for Court Administration, 16*(1), 3. Advance online publication. DOI: 10.36745/ijca.598

Krupp, L., Steinert, S., Kiefer-Emmanouilidis, M., Avila, K. E., Lukowicz, P., Kühn, J., Küchemann, S., & Karolus, J. (2024).. . *Challenges and Opportunities of Moderating Usage of Large Language Models in Education., 249*, 249–254. Advance online publication. DOI: 10.1145/3701571.3701590

Kumar, M., Kumar, R., Arisham, D. K., Gupta, R. K., Naudiyal, P., Goutam, G., & Mavi, A. K. (2025). Emerging AI impact in the healthcare sector: A review [Review of Emerging AI impact in the healthcare sector: A review]. European Journal of Environment and Public Health, 9(1). Lectito Journals. DOI: 10.29333/ejeph/15905

Kumar, S., Talukder, M. B., & Tyagi, P. K. (2025). The Impact of Virtual Reality and Augmented Reality in TNE Learning. In *Motivating Engagement, Belonging, and Success in Higher Education Student Experience* (pp. 359-382). IGI Global Scientific Publishing. DOI: 10.4018/979-8-3693-8089-5.ch013

Kunjumuhammed, S. K. (2024). Artificial Intelligence in Addressing Educational Inequality Dimensions in Higher Education Institutions (HEIs): A Critical Review. *Risks and Challenges of AI-Driven Finance: Bias, Ethics, and Security*, 146-164.

Kunnan, A. J. (2018). *Evaluating language assessments*. Routledge.

Labadze, L., Grigolia, M., & Machaidze, L. (2023). Role of AI chatbots in education: Systematic literature review. *International Journal of Educational Technology in Higher Education, 20*(1), 56. DOI: 10.1186/s41239-023-00426-1

Ladson-Billings, G. (1995). Toward a theory of culturally relevant pedagogy. *American Educational Research Journal, 32*(3), 465–491. DOI: 10.3102/00028312032003465

Ladson-Billings, G. (2014). Culturally relevant pedagogy 2.0: A.k.a. the remix. *Harvard Educational Review, 84*(1), 74–84. DOI: 10.17763/haer.84.1.p2rj131485484751

LaFleur, D. (2019, January 1). Transnational Partnerships and Dual Degrees: Entrepreneurial Strategies for Internationalization. *Proceedings of the 2019 AERA Annual Meeting*. DOI: 10.3102/1439066

Lancaster, T., & Clarke, R. (2016). Contract Cheating: The Outsourcing of Assessed Student Work. In Bretag, T. (Ed.), *Handbook of Academic Integrity* (pp. 639–654). Springer Singapore., DOI: 10.1007/978-981-287-098-8_17

Lande, J. (2025). Responsible Realism About Artificial Intelligence: How AI is Shaping Legal and Dispute Resolution Practice, Education, and Scholarship. SSRN Electronic Journal. DOI: 10.2139/ssrn.5309439

Landers, R. N., & Behrend, T. S. (2023). Auditing the AI auditors: A framework for evaluating fairness and bias in high stakes AI predictive models. *The American Psychologist, 78*(1), 36–49. DOI: 10.1037/amp0000972

Larsen, B. C. (2022). Governing Artificial Intelligence : Lessons from the United States and China. Research Portal Denmark, 300. https://local.forskningsportal.dk/local/dki-cgi/ws/cris-link?src=cbs&id=cbs-48598543-6d06-4e04-82ac-07eea8605f9f&ti=Governing%20Artificial%20Intelligence%20%3A%20Lessons%20from%20the%20United%20States%20and%20China

Latif, Y., Harrison, N., Chu, H.-E., Malik, A., & Nguyen, M. (2024). Unleashing cultural diversity knowledge for improved knowledge sharing and integration: An in-depth qualitative analysis. *Journal of Knowledge Management, 29*(1), 1–24. DOI: 10.1108/JKM-08-2023-0755

Lau, J., Zimmerman, B., & Schaub, F. (2018). Alexa, are you listening? Privacy perceptions, concerns and privacy-seeking behaviors with smart speakers. *Proceedings of the ACM on human-computer interaction, 2*(CSCW), 1-31.

Lauricella, A. R., Aladé, F., Russo, M., Strevett, A., & Herdzina, J. (2022). Children's visual attention and comprehension from synchronous video book reading. *Computers & Education, 191*, 104628. DOI: 10.1016/j.compedu.2022.104628

Laurillard, D. (2012). *Teaching as a design science: Building pedagogical patterns for learning and technology*. Routledge., DOI: 10.4324/9780203125083

Le Corre, J. Y., Burger-Helmchen, T., Tang, M., & Zhao, J. (2025). Innovative Learning Ecosystems for Entrepreneurial Education. *Transcending Boundaries: For a Sustainable Future of Higher Education, 6*, 110–129. DOI: 10.1163/9789004740990_006

Leander, S. K. (2019, August 20). *ASU develops world's first adaptive-learning biology degree | ASU News*. News.asu.edu. https://news.asu.edu/20190820-solutions-asu-develops-world-first-adaptive-learning-biology-degree

Lee, S. J., & Chae, Y. G. (2012). Balancing participation and risks in children's internet use: The role of internet literacy and parental mediation. *Cyberpsychology, Behavior, and Social Networking, 15*(5), 257–262. DOI: 10.1089/cyber.2011.0552

Leon, C., Lipuma, J., & Oviedo-Torres, X. (2025, July). Artificial intelligence in STEM education: A transdisciplinary framework for engagement and innovation. In Frontiers in Education, 10 (2025), DOI: 10.3389/feduc.2025.1619888

Leoni, L., Gueli, G., Ardolino, M., Panizzon, M., & Gupta, S. (2024). AI-empowered KM processes for decision-making: Empirical evidence from worldwide organisations. *Journal of Knowledge Management, 28*(11), 320–347. DOI: 10.1108/JKM-03-2024-0262

Levy-Feldman, I., & Libman, Z. (2022). One size doesn't fit all educational assessment in a multicultural and intercultural world. *Intercultural Education, 33*(4), 380–390. DOI: 10.1080/14675986.2022.2090174

Lewis, D., Hogan, L., Filip, D., & Wall, P. J. (2020). Global challenges in the standardization of ethics for trustworthy AI. *Journal of ICT Standardisation, 8*(2), 123–150. DOI: 10.13052/jicts2245-800X.823

Lewis, D., & Moorkens, J. (2020). A rights-based approach to trustworthy AI in social media. *Social Media + Society*, *6*(3), 2056305120954672. DOI: 10.1177/2056305120954672

Li, M., Enkhtur, A., Cheng, F., & Yamamoto, B. A. (2023). Ethical implications of ChatGPT in higher education: A scoping review. arXiv preprint arXiv:2311.14378.

Li, S., Xia, L., & Beech, H. (2025). Digital Empowerment: Innovative Technology Training for Language Teachers in a Transnational EMI University. In *Innovative Approaches to Staff Development in Transnational Higher Education* (pp. 297-320). IGI Global Scientific Publishing.

Li, S., Xia, L., & Beech, H. (2025). Digital empowerment: innovative technology training for language teachers in a transnational EMI university. In *Innovative Approaches to Staff Development in Transnational Higher Education* (pp. 297–320). IGI Global Scientific Publishing. DOI: 10.4018/979-8-3693-9102-0.ch012

Li, Y., & Goel, S. (2024). Operationalizing AI Auditability Measures: An AI Audit Case Study of College Admissions System.

Li, Z. (2025). Generative AI for Teachers' Self-Directed Professional Development. TechTrends: Journal of Educational Technology.

Liang, X. (2024). Using icebreaker questions to improve Chinese students' engagement in transnational education–An action research. *European Journal of Education*, *59*(2), e12621. DOI: 10.1111/ejed.12621

Lim, C. T., Bong, C. H., Wong, W. S., & Lee, N. K. (2021). A comprehensive review of automated essay scoring (AES) research and development. *Pertanika Journal of Science & Technology*, *29*(3), 1875–1899. DOI: 10.47836/pjst.29.3.27

Lindsay, E. D., Zhang, M., Johri, A., & Bjerva, J. (2025). The responsible development of automated student feedback with generative AI. arXiv. https://arxiv.org/abs/2308.15334 DOI: 10.1109/EDUCON62633.2025.11016572

Li, S., & Lin, J. (2025). Enhancing academic engagement and needs satisfaction through AI: A mixed-methods study in Chinese EFL tertiary education context. *European Journal of Education*, *60*(2), e70110. Advance online publication. DOI: 10.1111/ejed.70110

Lissak, G. (2018). Adverse physiological and psychological effects of screen time on children and adolescents: Literature review and case study. *Environmental Research*, *164*, 149–157. DOI: 10.1016/j.envres.2018.01.015

Liu, D. (2025). BORDERLINE CONTENT AND PLATFORMISED SPEECH GOVERNANCE: MAPPING TIKTOK'S MODERATION CONTROVERSIES IN SOUTH AND SOUTHEAST ASIA. AoIR Selected Papers of Internet Research. DOI: 10.5210/spir.v2024i0.13988

Liu, Y., Ma, Y., Chen, M., Ludwig, M., & Schneider, J. (2019). Text-DavinciGAN: Text to Image Synthesis using Generative Adversarial Networks. arXiv preprint arXiv:1907.00208.

Liu, Y., Ott, M., Goyal, N., Du, J., Joshi, M., Chen, D., . . . Stoyanov, V. (2019). RoBERTa: A Robustly Optimised BERT Pretraining Approach. arXiv preprint arXiv:1907.11692.

Liu, C., Chai, K. K., & Chen, Y. (2025, April). The Transformative Role of Generative AI in Higher Education: Perspectives from Academia and Industry. In *2025 IEEE Global Engineering Education Conference (EDUCON)* (pp. 1-6). IEEE.

Liu, C., Chen, H., Cao, X., Sun, Y., Liu, C. Y., Wu, K., Liang, Y.-C., Hsu, S.-E., Huang, D.-H., & Chiou, W. K. (2022). Effects of mindfulness meditation on doctors' mindfulness, patient safety culture, patient safety competency and adverse event. *International Journal of Environmental Research and Public Health, 19*(6), 3282. DOI: 10.3390/ijerph19063282

Liu, C., Singh, A., & Chen, C. H. (2019). Adversarial training for community question answering: A dataset and baselines. In *Proceedings of the 42nd International ACM SIGIR Conference on Research and Development in Information Retrieval* (pp. 445-454).

Liu, M., & Luo, J. (2015). Relationship between peripheral blood dopamine level and internet addiction disorder in adolescents: A pilot study. *International Journal of Clinical and Experimental Medicine, E-Century Publishing Corporation, 8*(6), 9943.

Livingstone, S., Mascheroni, G., & Stoilova, M. (2023). The outcomes of gaining digital skills for young people's lives and wellbeing: A systematic evidence review. *New Media & Society, 25*(5), 1176–1202. DOI: 10.1177/14614448211043189

Li, X., Wang, Y., & Garcia, D. (2020). Advancements in Generative AI for Multilingual Teaching-Learning Material Creation. *Journal of Educational Technology & Society, 23*(4), 127–140.

Li, X., & Zhou, W. (2024). When infrastructures collide: Transnational higher education and Chinese international students'(im) mobility in the pandemic era. *Asian Education and Development Studies, 13*(3), 195–207. DOI: 10.1108/AEDS-10-2023-0150

Long, D., & Magerko, B. (2020). What is AI literacy? Competencies and design considerations. In *Proceedings of the 2020 CHI Conference on Human Factors in Computing Systems*. https://doi.org/DOI: 10.1145/3313831.3376727

Long, J., & Lin, J. (2022). An empirical study on cultivating college students' cross-cultural communicative competence based on the artificial-intelligence *English-teaching mode. Frontiers in Psychology, 13*, 976310. DOI: 10.3389/fpsyg.2022.976310

Longo, G., & Albano, S. (2025). Bridging creativity and technology: Integrating generative ai into architectural pedagogy through hybrid frameworks. *AHFE International, 160*. Advance online publication. DOI: 10.54941/ahfe1005837

López-Meza, E., Terán-Bustamante, A., & Leyva-Hernández, S. N. (2024). SECI model of knowledge management: A thematic analysis with emphasis on agricultural organizations. *Iberoamerican Journal of Science Measurement and Communication, 4*(2), 1–10. DOI: 10.47909/ijsmc.133

Lu, H. (2025). Action Research as Practice-Led Research for Professional Development: A Case of Using Excel to Motivate Students to Learn in Transnational Education. In *Exploring Practice-Led Research for Professional Development* (pp. 179-200). IGI Global Scientific Publishing.

Luckin, R. (2018). *Machine learning and human intelligence: The future of education for the 21st century*. UCL Institute of Education Press.

Luckin, R., Holmes, W., Griffiths, M., & Forcier, K. (2016). *Intelligence unleashed: An argument for AI in education*. Pearson.

Luckin, R., Holmes, W., Griffiths, M., & Forcier, L. B. (2024). *Intelligence unleashed: AI in education*. Routledge.

Lukin, R., Rudoph, J., Grunert, M., & Tan, S. (2024) Exploring the future of learning and the relationship between human intelligence and AI. An interview with professor Rose Lukin. *Journal of applied learning and teaching*. Vol.7 no.1. Available at: https://journals.sfu.ca/jalt/index.php/jalt/article/view/1659/767

Lund, B. D., Lee, T. H., Mannuru, N. R., & Arutla, N. (2025). AI and academic integrity: Exploring student perceptions and implications for higher education. *Journal of Academic Ethics, 23*(3), 1545–1565. Advance online publication. DOI: 10.1007/s10805-025-09613-3

Luo, J., Zheng, C., Yin, J., & Teo, H. H. (2025). Design and assessment of AI-based learning tools in higher education: A systematic review. *International Journal of Educational Technology in Higher Education, 22*(1), 42. Advance online publication. DOI: 10.1186/s41239-025-00540-2

Luo, M., Zhao, L., & Lyu, B. (2022). [Retracted] Exploring the Fuzzy Integrated Assessment of College Students' Education for Innovative Entrepreneurship under the Background of Internet+. *Security and Communication Networks, 2022*(1), 4339772.

Luo, Y., & Wang, D. (2024). Revolutionizing education with AI: The adaptive cognitive enhancement model (ACEM) for personalized cognitive development. In *Proceedings of the 2nd International Conference on Machine Learning and Automation* (Vol. 82, No. 1, pp. 71-76). DOI: 10.54254/2755-2721/82/20240929

Lytras, M. D., Alkhaldi, A., Malik, S., Serban, A. C., & Aldosemani, T. (2024). *The evolution of artificial intelligence in higher education*. Emerald Publishing. DOI: 10.1108/9781835494868

Ma'abo, A. (2023). Benefits and challenges of transnational education: Reflections from a sino-british joint venture university. *International Journal of Chinese Education, 12*(1), 2212585X221144903. Advance online publication. DOI: 10.1177/2212585X221144903

Machado, C., & Seifert, T. (2024). Using Flip and Facebook to Create Windows and Mirrors for Transnational Learning: A United States-Israel Scholarship of Teaching and Learning Project. In *Encouraging Transnational Learning Through Virtual Exchange in Global Teacher Education* (pp. 152-171). IGI Global Scientific Publishing. DOI: 10.4018/978-1-6684-7813-4.ch007

MacLean, A. (2025) *A warning to the young: Just say no to AI. Engelsberg Ideas*, Available at: https://engelsbergideas.com/essays/a-warning-to-the-young-just-say-no-to-ai/

Madge, C., Raghuram, P., & Noxolo, P. (2014). Conceptualizing international education. *Progress in Human Geography, 39*(6), 681–701. DOI: 10.1177/0309132514526442

Madhu, N. Y.MADHU N YLATHA P HSAVITHA N. (2024). Revolutionizing Education: Harnessing AI for Personalized Learning Pathways and Student Success. *International Journal For Multidisciplinary Research, 6*(5), 28371. Advance online publication. DOI: 10.36948/ijfmr.2024.v06i05.28371

Magdy, W., Mubarak, H. A., & Salminen, J. (2025). Who should set the Standards? Analysing Censored Arabic Content on Facebook during the Palestine-Israel Conflict. 1. DOI: 10.1145/3706598.3713150

Magesh, V., Surani, F., Dahl, M., Suzgun, M., Manning, C. D., & Ho, D. E. (2025). Hallucination-Free? Assessing the Reliability of Leading AI Legal Research Tools. *Journal of Empirical Legal Studies*, *22*(2), 216–242. DOI: 10.1111/jels.12413

Maghsudi, S., Lan, A., Xu, J., & van Der Schaar, M. (2021). Personalized education in the artificial intelligence era: What to expect next. *IEEE Signal Processing Magazine*, *38*(3), 37–50. DOI: 10.1109/MSP.2021.3055032

Maguire, J., English, R., Cao, Q., & Seow, C. K. (2025, January). Themes in the declared use of generative artificial intelligence in assessment. In *Proceedings of the 9th Conference on Computing Education Practice* (pp. 17-20). DOI: 10.1145/3702212.3702217

Mahajan, P. (2025). What is Ethical: AIHED Driving Humans or Human-Driven AIHED? A Conceptual Framework enabling the 'Ethos' of AI-driven. *Higher Education*. Advance online publication. DOI: 10.14293/PR2199.001510.v1

Mahy, T., & Li, H. (2024). Get PhD Ready: An Orientation Course for New PGR Students in a Transnational Education Setting. In *English for Academic Purposes in the EMI Context in Asia: XJTLU Impact* (pp. 259–285). Springer Nature Switzerland. DOI: 10.1007/978-3-031-63638-7_11

Makransky, G., Borre-Gude, S., & Mayer, R. E. (2019). Motivational and cognitive benefits of training in immersive virtual reality based on multiple assessments. *Journal of Computer Assisted Learning*, *35*(6), 691–707. DOI: 10.1111/jcal.12375

Ma, L., Lee, C. S., & Goh, D. H. L. (2013, July). Investigating influential factors influencing users to share news in social media: A diffusion of innovations perspective. In *Proceedings of the 13th ACM/IEEE-CS joint conference on Digital libraries* (pp. 403-404). DOI: 10.1145/2467696.2467749

Maleku, A., Phillips, R. J. N., Um, M. Y., Kagotho, N., Lee, G., & Coxe, K. (2021). The phenomenon of spiritual homelessness in transnational spaces among international students in the United States. *Population Space and Place*, *28*(2), e2470. Advance online publication. DOI: 10.1002/psp.2470

Manches, A., & Plowman, L. (2017). Computing education in children's early years: A call for debate. *British Journal of Educational Technology*, *48*(1), 191–201. DOI: 10.1111/bjet.12355

Mandinach, E. B., & Gummer, E. S. (2016). What does it mean for teachers to be data literate: Laying out the skills, knowledge, and dispositions. *Teaching and Teacher Education*, *60*, 366–376. DOI: 10.1016/j.tate.2016.07.011

Mania, K. (2022). Legal Technology: Assessment of the Legal Tech Industry's Potential. *Journal of the Knowledge Economy*, *14*(2), 595–619. DOI: 10.1007/s13132-022-00924-z

Ma, R., & Kou, Y. (2021). " How advertiser-friendly is my video?": YouTuber's Socioeconomic Interactions with Algorithmic Content Moderation. *Proceedings of the ACM on Human-Computer Interaction*, *5*(CSCW2), 1-25. DOI: 10.1145/3479573

Markey, K., Graham, M. M., Tuohy, D., McCarthy, J., O'Donnell, C., Hennessy, T., Fahy, A., & O'Brien, B. (2023). Navigating learning and teaching in expanding culturally diverse higher education settings. *Higher Education Pedagogies, 8*(1), 2165527. DOI: 10.1080/23752696.2023.2165527

Martin, F., Bacak, J., Polly, D., Wang, W., & Ahlgrim-Delzell, L. (2023). Teacher and school concerns and actions on elementary school children digital safety. *TechTrends, 67*(3), 561–571. DOI: 10.1007/s11528-022-00803-z

Mary, D., & Joyce, M. (2024). AI and education: Impact of AI on learning outcomes in higher education. *International Journal of Scientific Research in Engineering and Management, 8*(8), 1–16. DOI: 10.55041/IJSREM37145

Masic, B., Nesic, S., Nikolic, D., & Dzeletovic, M. (2017). Evolution of knowledge management. *Industry, 45*(2), 127–147. DOI: 10.5937/industrija45-13201

Masrifah, K., Ahsanudin, M., & Ainin, M. (2025). Higher education in the Arab world: e-learning and distance education: edited by Adnan Badran, Elias Baydoun, Sandra Hillman and Joelle Mesmar, Switzerland, Springer, 2023, 201 pp., 170.99(eBook), 160.40 (Hardcover Book), ISBN: 978-3-031-33570-9.

Mattar, M. Y. (2022). Combating academic corruption and enhancing academic integrity through international accreditation standards: The model of Qatar University. *Journal of Academic Ethics, 20*(2), 119–146. DOI: 10.1007/s10805-021-09392-7

Ma, W., Adesope, O. O., Nesbit, J. C., & Liu, Q. (2014). Intelligent tutoring systems and learning outcomes: A meta-analysis. *Journal of Educational Psychology, 106*(4), 901–918. DOI: 10.1037/a0037123

Mbah, G. O.Geraldine O Mbah. (2024). Data privacy in the era of AI: Navigating regulatory landscapes for global businesses. *International Journal of Science and Research Archive, 13*(2), 2040–2058. DOI: 10.30574/ijsra.2024.13.2.2396

McCarthy, J. (2007). From here to human-level AI. *Artificial Intelligence, 171*(18), 1174–1182. DOI: 10.1016/j.artint.2007.10.009

McElhaney, K., Smith, G., Rustagi, I., & Groth, O. J. (2023). *Responsible AI: Tackling Tech's Largest Corporate Governance Challenges*. The Berkeley-Haas Case Series. University of California, Berkeley. Haas School of Business.

McKinley, J., Rose, H., & Zhou, S. (2021). Transnational Universities and English Medium Instruction in China: How Admissions, Language Support and Language Use Differ in Chinese Universities. *RELC Journal, 52*(2), 236–252. DOI: 10.1177/00336882211020032

McMillan, J., & Schumacher, S. (2014). *Research in Education Evidence-Based Inquiry*. Pearson.

ME, L., G, S. D., Shuba, S., Sneha, K., & Sofiya, S. (2024). Adaptive Learning Management System. DOI: 10.59544/PQYL6304/ICRCCT24P39

Mehrabi, N., Morstatter, F., Saxena, N., Lerman, K., and Galstyan, A. (2019). A Survey on Bias and Fairness in Machine Learning. arXiv.

Meinel, C., Friedrichsen, M., Staubitz, T., Reinhard, S., & Köhler, D. (2024). Assessment Methods for Online Teaching.

Melgar-García[1], L., Troncoso-García[1], Á., Gutiérrez-Avilés, D., Torres[1], J. F., & Troncosol, A. (2023, August). Explainable Artificial Intelligence. In *International Joint Conference 16th International Conference on Computational Intelligence in Security for Information Systems (CISIS 2023) 14th International Conference on EUropean Transnational Education (ICEUTE 2023): Proceedings* (Vol. 748, p. 358). Springer Nature.

Melo, N. (2024). The Impact of AI-Powered Tutoring Platforms on Student Achievement in STEM Subjects: The Case of Cameroon. Available at *SSRN* 5249691.

Menon, S., Suresh, M., & Raghu Raman, R. (2022). Enablers facilitating industry-academia, transnational education and university-community partnering agility in higher education. *Higher Education. Skills and Work-Based Learning*, *12*(3), 604–626. DOI: 10.1108/HESWBL-04-2021-0067

Merikangas, K. R., He, J. P., Burstein, M., Swanson, S. A., Avenevoli, S., Cui, L., Benjet, C., Georgiades, K., & Swendsen, J. (2010). Lifetime prevalence of mental disorders in US adolescents: Results from the National Comorbidity Survey Replication–Adolescent Supplement (NCS-A). *Journal of the American Academy of Child and Adolescent Psychiatry*, *49*(10), 980–989. DOI: 10.1016/j.jaac.2010.05.017

Merino-Gomez[1], A., & Curiel-Herrera, L. E. (2024, November). A Comparison of AI-Enabled Techniques. In *International Joint Conferences: 17th International Conference on Computational Intelligence in Security for Information Systems (CISIS 2024) and 15th International Conference on European Transnational Education (ICEUTE 2024)* (Vol. 957, p. 227). Springer Nature.

Miani, M. (2023). Making sense of brainstorming in transnational education: The challenge of contextualization. In *Handbook of research on developments and future trends in transnational higher education* (pp. 21–38). IGI Global. DOI: 10.4018/978-1-6684-5226-4.ch002

Microsoft. (2021). *AI for Accessibility*. https://www.microsoft.com/en-us/ai/ai-for-accessibility

Mikecz Munday, Z. (2021). Adapting to transnational education: Students' experiences at an American university in the UAE. *Learning and Teaching in Higher Education: Gulf Perspectives*, *17*(2), 121–135. DOI: 10.1108/LTHE-08-2020-0017

Mikolov, T., Sutskever, I., Chen, K., Corrado, G., & Dean, J. (2013). Advances in Neural Information Processing Systems: Vol. 26. *Distributed Representations of Words and Phrases and their Compositionality*. [REMOVED HYPERLINK FIELD]

Milchior, R. (2024). Digital platforms, competition law, and regulation. Journal of Intellectual Property Law & Practice. DOI: 10.1093/jiplp/jpae074

Ministry of Higher Education, Research and Innovation. (2022). *Higher education statistics report*. Government of Oman.

MIS Consultants. (2025) *AI law in UAE: Data Protection is a legal anchor,* https://misconsultants.ae/. Available at: https://misconsultants.ae/article/the-legal-framework-governing-artificial-intelligence-in-the-uae-data-protection-as-a-legal-anchor (Accessed: 14 September 2025).

Mishra, N., Habtemariam, G. M., Aebissa, B., Nayak, R. K., & Tripathy, R. (2024). Assessing the Effectiveness of Transnational Leadership on the Performance of Ethiopian University Graduates in Computing Technology: A Case Study. In *Engaging Higher Education Teachers and Students With Transnational Leadership* (pp. 238-256). IGI Global Scientific Publishing. DOI: 10.4018/979-8-3693-6100-9.ch013

Mislevy, R. J., Steinberg, L. S., & Almond, R. G. (2017). On the structure of educational assessments. *Measurement: Interdisciplinary Research and Perspectives*, *15*(3-4), 55–66.

Mitchell, M., Wu, S., Zaldivar, A., Barnes, P., Vasserman, L., Hutchinson, B., & Gebru, T. (2019). Model cards for model reporting. In *Proceedings of the Conference on Fairness, Accountability, and Transparency* (pp. 220-229). [REMOVED HYPERLINK FIELD] DOI: 10.1145/3287560.3287596

Mnkandla, E., & Minnaar, A. (2017). The use of social media in e-learning: A metasynthesis. *International Review of Research in Open and Distance Learning*, *18*(5), 227–248. DOI: 10.19173/irrodl.v18i5.3014

Modi, H. (2023). Leveraging Natural Language Processing for Legal Research: Trends and Future Directions. SSRN Electronic Journal. DOI: 10.2139/ssrn.4514036

Mok, K. H., & Sawn Khai, T. (2024). Transnationalization of higher education in China and Asia: Quality assurance and students' learning experiences. *Asian Education and Development Studies*, *13*(3), 208–226. DOI: 10.1108/AEDS-01-2024-0004

Molina, J., Olivares, R., & Pardo, A. (2022). Social constructivism in online learning environments: Implications for international collaboration. *Computers & Education*, *184*, 104499. DOI: 10.1016/j.compedu.2022.104499

Monitor, I. C. E. F. (2024, December 11). Continued growth reported for UK transnational education enrolments. https://monitor.icef.com/

Morandín-Ahuerma, F. (2023). Ten UNESCO Recommendations on the Ethics of Artificial Intelligence.

Morawa, A. H. E. (2008). Transnationalization of Legal Education: A Swiss (and Comparative) Perspective. SSRN Electronic Journal. https://papers.ssrn.com/sol3/papers.cfm?abstract_id=1596091

Morris, G. R., & Kozuch, S. (Eds.). (2024). *Engaging higher education teachers and students with transnational leadership*. IGI Global. DOI: 10.4018/979-8-3693-6100-9

Mouta, A., Llorente, A. M. P., & Sánchez, E. M. T. (2023). Uncovering Blind Spots in Education Ethics: Insights from a Systematic Literature Review on Artificial Intelligence in Education. *International Journal of Artificial Intelligence in Education*. Advance online publication. DOI: 10.1007/s40593-023-00384-9

Mouta, A., Torrecilla-Sánchez, E. M., & Pinto-Llorente, A. M. (2024). Design of a future scenarios toolkit for an ethical implementation of artificial intelligence in education. *Education and Information Technologies*, *29*(9), 10473–10498. DOI: 10.1007/s10639-023-12229-y

Mulla, T., Munir, S., & Mohan, V. (2023). An exploratory study to understand faculty members' perceptions and challenges in online teaching. *International Review of Education*, *69*(1-2), 73–99. DOI: 10.1007/s11159-023-10002-4

Muñoz-Basols, J., Neville, C., Lafford, B. A., & Godev, C. (2023). Potentialities of applied translation for language learning in the era of artificial intelligence. Hispania, 106(2), 171-194. Gripsy, J., Selvakumari, S., Sheeba, L., & Kumaran, B. (2025). Transforming student engagement through AI, AR, VR, and chatbots in education., 73-100. DOI: 10.4018/979-8-3693-8734-4.ch004

Muralidhar, L. B., Sathyanarayana, N., Kumar, V., & Santhosh, Y. (2025). AI learning and talent strategies in transnational education. In *Advances in Higher Education and Professional Development* (pp. 245–276). IGI Global Scientific Publishing. DOI: 10.4018/979-8-3693-9102-0.ch010

Muralidhar, L. B., Sathyanarayana, N., Kumar, V. L., & Santhosh, Y. (2025). AI learning and talent strategies in transnational education: driving global leadership with agility. In *Innovative Approaches to Staff Development in Transnational Higher Education* (pp. 245–276). IGI Global Scientific Publishing.

Murray, G., & Doe, C. (2024). Embedding Indigenous Perspectives: A Consideration of Place in Local and Transnational Education.

Murtiningsih, S., & Sujito, A. (2024). Reimagining the future of education: Inclusive pedagogies, critical intergenerational justice, and technological disruption. *Policy Futures in Education*, *23*(5), 14782103251341406.

Mwasalwiba, E. (2010). Entrepreneurship education: A review of its objectives, teaching methods, and impact indicators. *Education + Training*, *52*(1), 20–47. DOI: 10.1108/00400911011017663

Myers, A. (2023) *AI detectors biased against non-native English writers, Stanford Human-Centered AI.* Available at https://hai.stanford.edu/news/ai-detectors-biased-against-non-native-english-writers

Nadeem, M. (2024). Distributed leadership in educational contexts: A catalyst for school improvement. *Social Sciences & Humanities Open*, *9*, 100835. DOI: 10.1016/j.ssaho.2024.100835

Naidoo, V., & Sibiya, M. (2019). Graduate experiences with transnational nursing education: A qualitative enquiry. *International Journal of Health Care Quality Assurance*, *32*(3), 562–573. DOI: 10.1108/IJHCQA-06-2018-0155

Nakamura, L. (2008). *Digitizing race: Visual cultures of the Internet.* University of Minnesota Press.

Nathanson, A. I. (2001). Mediation of children's television viewing: Working toward conceptual clarity and common understanding. *Annals of the International Communication Association*, *25*(1), 115–151. DOI: 10.1080/23808985.2001.11679002

Nature Index. (2021). *AI research output by region.* https://www.nature.com/nature-index

Navarro, C., Arias-Calderón, M., Henríquez, C. A., & Riquelme, P. (2024). Assessment of student and teacher perceptions on the use of virtual simulation in cell biology laboratory education. *Education Sciences*, *14*(3), 243. DOI: 10.3390/educsci14030243

Nawaz, T. (2018). Internationalisation strategy, faculty response and academic preparedness for transnational teaching. *Education + Training*, *60*(9), 1084–1096. DOI: 10.1108/ET-09-2017-0141

Nelson, L. J., Padilla-Walker, L. M., & McLean, R. D. (2021). Longitudinal predictors of helicopter parenting in emerging adulthood. *Emerging Adulthood*, *9*(3), 240–251. DOI: 10.1177/2167696820931980

Nemorin, S. (2024). Towards decolonising the ethics of AI in education. *Globalisation, Societies and Education*, •••, 1–13. DOI: 10.1080/14767724.2024.2333821

Nesi, J., & Prinstein, M. J. (2015). Using social media for social comparison and feedback-seeking: Gender and popularity moderate associations with depressive symptoms. *Journal of Abnormal Child Psychology*, *43*(8), 1427–1438. DOI: 10.1007/s10802-015-0020-0

Neve. (2024, July 12). *LLMs and a regression to the mean.* https://neve.com/llms-and-a-regression-to-the-mean

Ng, S. (2012). The challenges of attracting asian students to study higher education in hong kong. *Higher Education Quarterly*, *66*(3), 272–292. DOI: 10.1111/j.1468-2273.2012.00524.x

Nguyen, A., Ngo, H. N., Hong, Y., Dang, B., & Nguyen, B. P. T. (2023). Ethical principles for artificial intelligence in education. *Education and Information Technologies*, *28*(4), 4221–4241. DOI: 10.1007/s10639-022-11316-w

Nicol, D. J., & Macfarlane-Dick, D. (2006). Formative assessment and self-regulated learning: A model and seven principles of good feedback practice. *Studies in Higher Education*, *31*(2), 199–218. DOI: 10.1080/03075070600572090

Nieto, S. (2010). *The light in their eyes: Creating multicultural learning communities* (10th anniversary ed.). Teachers College Press.

Nightingale, F. (2024). *Developing undergraduate engineering students' soft skills with interdisciplinary personal development planning modules in Chinese transnational education: a case study* (Doctoral dissertation, Nottingham Trent University).

Nikolopoulou, K. (2024). Generative artificial intelligence in higher education: Exploring ways of harnessing pedagogical practices with the assistance of ChatGPT. *International Journal of Contemporary Education*, *1*(2), 103–111. DOI: 10.47852/bonviewIJCE42022489

Nissenbaum, H. (2001). How computer systems embody values. *Computer*, *34*(3), 120–119. DOI: 10.1109/2.910905

Noble, S. U. (2018). *Algorithms of oppression: How search engines reinforce racism.* New York University Press. DOI: 10.18574/nyu/9781479833641.001.0001

Noller, D. T., & Thimesch, A. E. (2025). Artificial Intelligence in Higher Education: Legal Accountability and Best Practices for Upholding Student Privacy and Nondiscrimination Rights. *The Journal of Physician Assistant Education : the Official Journal of the Physician Assistant Education Association*, *36*(3), e308–e311. Advance online publication. DOI: 10.1097/JPA.0000000000000688

Ntloedibe, T., Foko, T., & Segooa, M. A. (2024). Cloud leakage in higher education in South Africa: A case of University of Technology. *South African Journal of Information Management*, *26*(1), 1783. DOI: 10.4102/sajim.v26i1.1783

Nyaaba, M., Wright, A., & Choi, G. L. (2024). Generative AI and Digital Neocolonialism in Global Education: Towards an Equitable Framework. DOI: 10.48550/ARXIV.2406.02966

Nyaaba, M., Wright, A., & Choi, G. L. (2024). Generative AI and digital neocolonialism in global education: Towards an equitable framework. *Journal of Global Educational Futures*, *9*(2), 45–67. https://arxiv.org/abs/2406.02966

O'Neil, C. (2016). *Weapons of math destruction: How big data increases inequality and threatens democracy*. Crown.

OECD. (2005). *Guidelines for quality provision in cross-border higher education*. https://ehea.info/Upload/Topic%203%20Simon%20Roy.pdf

OECD. (2021). *AI and the future of skills: Capabilities and assessments*. https://www.oecd.org/education/ai-future-skills.htm

OECD. (2021). *OECD skills outlook 2021: Learning for life*. OECD Publishing., DOI: 10.1787/0ae365b4-

OECD. (2023). *AI in Education: Policy Brief*. Organisation for Economic Co-operation and Development.

OECD. (2023). *OECD learning compass 2030: Competencies for future-ready students*. OECD Publishing.

OECD. (2024). The potential impact of artificial intelligence on equity and inclusion in education. OECD Education Working Papers, No. 215.

Ohannessian, C. M., Fagle, T., & Salafia, C. (2021). Social media use and internalizing symptoms during early adolescence: The role of co-rumination. *Journal of Affective Disorders*, *280*, 85–88. DOI: 10.1016/j.jad.2020.10.079

Ohio State University. (2025). Ohio State launches bold AI Fluency initiative to redefine learning and innovation.

Oman Authority for Academic Accreditation and Quality Assurance of Education. (2021). *Institutional standards framework*. OAAAQA.

Oman Authority for Academic Accreditation and Quality Assurance of Education. (2022). *Standards for higher education*. https://www.oaaaqa.gov.om/

Oman Authority for Academic Accreditation and Quality Assurance of Education. (2024, February). *Institutional Standards Assessment Manual* (Version 2).

Oncioiu, I., & Bularca, A. R. (2025). Artificial Intelligence Governance in Higher Education: The Role of Knowledge-Based Strategies in Fostering Legal Awareness and Ethical Artificial Intelligence Literacy. *Societies (Basel, Switzerland)*, *15*(6), 144. DOI: 10.3390/soc15060144

Open, A. I. (2023). AI text classifier: Limitations and considerations. https://openai.com

Ou, A. W., Stöhr, C., & Malmström, H. (2024). Academic communication with AI-powered language tools in higher education: From a post-humanist perspective. *System*, *121*, 103225. DOI: 10.1016/j.system.2024.103225

Ouellette, L. L., Motomura, A., Reinecke, J., & Masur, J. S. (2025). Can AI Hold Office Hours? DOI: 10.2139/ssrn.5166938

Ouyang, F., & Jiao, P. (2021). Artificial intelligence in education: A review. *Educational Philosophy and Theory*, *53*(12), 1229–1245. DOI: 10.1080/00131857.2020.1821181

Owusu-Agyeman, Y., & Amoakohene, G. (2021). Student engagement and perceived gains in transnational education in Ghana. *International Journal of Comparative Education and Development*, *23*(4), 297–316. DOI: 10.1108/IJCED-11-2020-0085

Özmen, E. (2024). Academic freedom: Normative ideals, contemporary challenges. *Zeitschrift für Politikwissenschaft*, *34*(3), 379–385. DOI: 10.1007/s41358-024-00390-w

Paas, F., Renkl, A., & Sweller, J. (2003). Cognitive Load Theory and Instructional Design: Recent Developments. *Educational Psychologist*, *38*(1), 1–4. DOI: 10.1207/S15326985EP3801_1

Pacheco-Mendoza, S., Guevara, C., Albán, A. L. M., & Fernández-Escobar, J. E. (2023). Artificial Intelligence in Higher Education: A Predictive Model for Academic Performance. *Education Sciences*, *13*(10), 990. DOI: 10.3390/educsci13100990

Pagallo, U., Aurucci, P., Casanovas, P., Chatila, R., Chazerand, P., Dignum, V., ... & Valcke, P. (2019). On good AI governance: 14 priority actions, a SMART model of governance, and a regulatory toolbox.

Page, E., Meyers, G., & Billings, E. (2024). Theory to practice: an assessment framework for generative ai.. Intersection: A Journal at the Intersection of Assessment and Learning, 5(4). DOI: 10.61669/001c.124250

Pai, R. Y., Shetty, A., Shetty, A. D., Bhandary, R., Shetty, J., Nayak, S., Dinesh, T. K., & D'souza, K. J. (2022). Integrating artificial intelligence for knowledge management systems – synergy among people and technology: A systematic review of the evidence. *Ekonomska Istrazivanja*, *35*(1), 1–23. DOI: 10.1080/1331677X.2022.2058976

Paivio, A. (1990). *Mental Representations*. Oxford University Press., DOI: 10.1093/acprof:oso/9780195066661.001.0001

Palmer, A. (2021). Investigating staff views on plagiarism in transnational higher education. *Journal of Applied Learning and Teaching*, *4*(2), 13–27.

Palmer, N., & Chandir, H. (2024). Education Beyond Techno-global Rationality: Transnational Learning, Communicative Agency and the Neo-colonial Ethic. *Journal of Creative Communications*, *19*(1), 59–73. DOI: 10.1177/09732586231206651

Pane, J. F., Steiner, E. D., Baird, M. D., & Hamilton, L. S. (2015). *Continued Progress: Promising Evidence on Personalized Learning*. RAND Corporation., DOI: 10.7249/RR1365

Papert, S. (1993). *Mindstorms: Children, computers, and powerful ideas* (2nd ed.). Basic Books.

Paris, D. (2012). Culturally sustaining pedagogy: A needed change in stance, terminology, and practice. *Educational Researcher*, *41*(3), 93–97. DOI: 10.3102/0013189X12441244

Paris, D., & Alim, H. S. (Eds.). (2017). *Culturally sustaining pedagogies: Teaching and learning for justice in a changing world.* Teachers College Press.

Pariser, E. (2011). *The filter bubble: What the Internet is hiding from you.* Penguin UK.

Parsakia, K. (2023). The effect of chatbots and ai on the self-efficacy, self-esteem, problem-solving and critical thinking of students. *Health Nexus, 1*(1), 71–76. DOI: 10.61838/hn.1.1.14

Pasquale, F. (2015). *The black box society: The secret algorithms that control money and information.* Harvard University Press. DOI: 10.4159/harvard.9780674736061

Patil, L. (2023). Education governance and digitization: Inherent conflicts and potential safeguards for a new social contract. *Prospects, 54*(2), 323–329. DOI: 10.1007/s11125-023-09668-3

Patil, M. P., Mahgoub, Y. O. M., Salama, A. M., Tahoun, Z., Johnston, L., Hamza, N., & Al-Oufy, A. (2025). *Cultivating sustainable architecture and built environments through cross-cultural education.* Smart and Sustainable Built Environment. DOI: 10.1108/SASBE-03-2025-0108

Pattrawiwat, K., Nilrungratana, P., Deewai, A., & Tuntivivat, S. (2024). The measurement model of family strengths for generation alpha in the thai context. *Behavioral Sciences (Basel, Switzerland), 14*(10), 921. DOI: 10.3390/bs14100921

Pearson, N., Biddle, S. J., Griffiths, P., Johnston, J. P., & Haycraft, E. (2018). Clustering and correlates of screen-time and eating behaviours among young children. *BMC Public Health, 18*(1), 753. DOI: 10.1186/s12889-018-5698-9

Peláez-Sánchez, I. C., Velarde-Camaqui, D., & Glasserman-Morales, L. D. (2024). The impact of large language models on higher education: Exploring the connection between AI and Education 4.0. *Frontiers in Education, 9*, 1392091. DOI: 10.3389/feduc.2024.1392091

Peng, S. (2024). Supporting transnational teaching in Finnish education export: Possibilities and limitations of using ChatGPT as a virtual assistant during short-term teaching abroad. *Innovations in Education and Teaching International*, •••, 1–5.

Pennington, J., Socher, R., & Manning, C. (2014). GloVe: Global Vectors for Word Representation. *Proceedings of the 2014 conference on empirical methods in natural language processing (EMNLP).* DOI: 10.3115/v1/D14-1162

Pereira, F. D., Rodrigues, L., Henklain, M. H. O., Freitas, H., Oliveira, D. F., Cristea, A. I., Carvalho, L., Isotani, S., Benedict, A., Dorodchi, M., & de Oliveira, E. H. T. (2022). Toward Human–AI Collaboration: A Recommender System to Support CS1 Instructors to Select Problems for Assignments and Exams. *IEEE Transactions on Learning Technologies, 16*(3), 457–472. DOI: 10.1109/TLT.2022.3224121

Pérez, J. C., Muñoz, A., & Hernández, M. (2022). Inclusive education through AI: Bridging the language gap. *International Journal of Educational Technology, 19*(3), 210–225.

Peterkin-Rawls, J. D. (2024). AI as a tool for education equity: A review of recent developments. Journal of Race. *Gender and Education, 13*(1), 1–15.

Phillips, B. (2021). UK further education sector journey to compliance with the general data protection regulation and the data protection act 2018. *Computer Law & Security Review, 42*, 105586. DOI: 10.1016/j.clsr.2021.105586

Piccerillo, L., & Digennaro, S. (2025). Adolescent social media use and emotional intelligence: A systematic review. *Adolescent Research Review, 10*(2), 201–218. DOI: 10.1007/s40894-024-00245-z

Pimentel, J. V., Malaluan, K. D., Daluperi, F. N. M., Vera, J. L. S. D., Sunga, J. E. T. A., Marin, A. J. B., & Limos-Galay, J. A. (2024). Benefits of AI chatbots and engagement of senior high school students in Divine Word College of San Jose. *International Journal of Research Studies in Educational Technology*, *8*(4). Advance online publication. DOI: 10.5861/ijrset.2024.8036

Ping, H. (2023). *Understanding Experiences of Faculty From the Home Institution in China-US Transnational Education Programs: A Phenomenological Case Study* (Doctoral dissertation, Texas A&M University-Corpus Christi).

Plano Clark Vicki, L., & Vicki, L. Plano Clark, Creswell John W., & John W. Creswell. (2017). *Designing and Conducting Mixed Methods Research* (third edition). SAGE Publications, Inc. (US).

Popenici, S. A. D., & Kerr, S. (2025). AI and higher education: Opportunities and challenges. *Journal of Educational Technology & Society*, *28*(1), 1–15. DOI: 10.1007/s11528-025-01002-3

Popenici, S. A., & Kerr, S. (2017). Exploring the impact of artificial intelligence on teaching and learning in higher education. *Research and Practice in Technology Enhanced Learning*, *12*(1), 22. DOI: 10.1186/s41039-017-0062-8 PMID: 30595727

Portes, A., & Rumbaut, R. G. (2001). *Legacies: The story of the immigrant second generation*. University of California Press.

Potkonjak, V., Gardner, M., Callaghan, V., Mattila, P., Guetl, C., Petrović, V. M., & Jovanović, K. (2016). Virtual laboratories for education in science, technology, and engineering: A review. *Computers & Education*, *95*, 309–327. DOI: 10.1016/j.compedu.2016.02.002

Pratham. (2022). *Hybrid learning program*. https://www.pratham.org

Praveenkumar, S., Anute, N., Vaissnave, V., Ragupathi, T., Fardale, S., Selvakumar, P., & Manjunath, T. C. (2025). Risks of AI Bias and Inequities in Learning. In *Advances in computational intelligence and robotics book series* (p. 257). IGI Global., DOI: 10.4018/979-8-3373-2302-2.ch009

Prince-Tritto, P., & Pönce, H. (2025). Causal Artificial Intelligence in Legal Language Processing: A Systematic Review [Review of Causal Artificial Intelligence in Legal Language Processing: A Systematic Review]. Entropy, 27(4), 351. Multidisciplinary Digital Publishing Institute. DOI: 10.3390/e27040351

Pruss, D., Pullen-Blasnik, H., Stevens, N., Rahman, S., Belitz, C., Stapleton, L., Dharmaraj, M. G., Aizeki, M., Molnar, P., Pinch, A. C., Ryan, N., de Lima, T. W., Widder, D. G., Tiwari, A., Brown, L. F., Sexton, J. S., & Nunes, P. (2025). Prediction and Punishment: Critical Report on Carceral AI. DOI: 10.2139/ssrn.5017321

Przybylski, A. K., & Weinstein, N. (2017). A large-scale test of the goldilocks hypothesis: Quantifying the relations between digital-screen use and the mental well-being of adolescents. *Psychological Science*, *28*(2), 204–215. DOI: 10.1177/0956797616678438

Quality Assurance Agency for Higher Education. (2020a, December 21). *How UK higher education providers managed the shift to digital delivery during the COVID-19 pandemic*. QAA.

Quality Assurance Agency for Higher Education. (2020b, May 20). *Effective practice in UK transnational education during the COVID-19 pandemic*. QAA.

Quality Assurance Agency for Higher Education. (2023, January 30). *The rise of artificial intelligence software and potential risks for academic integrity: A briefing paper for higher education providers*. QAA.

Quality Assurance Agency for Higher Education. (2024). *UK Quality Code for higher education*. Author. https://www.qaa.ac.uk

Quality Assurance Agency. (2014) *Review of UK transnational education in United Arab Emirates: Overview,* https://www.qaa.ac.uk/. Available at: https://www.qaa.ac.uk/docs/qaa/international/review-transnational-education-uae-14.pdf?sfvrsn=1407f481_2 (Accessed: 11 August 2025).

Quality Compass. Navigating the complexities of the artificial intelligence era in higher education. (2024). *The Quality Assurance Agency for Higher Education.* https://www.qaa.ac.uk/docs/qaa/news/quality-compass-navigating-the-complexities-of-the-artificial-intelligence-era-in-higher-education.pdf?sfvrsn=8179b281_11

Quintián, H. Héctor/Corchado Quintián (Emili), & Lora, A. T. (2024). *International Joint Conferences.*

Qureshi, F., & Trotter, J. (2025). Leading a transnational university campus: An interview with James Trotter about academic leadership and working in multicultural higher education environments. *Journal of Applied Learning and Teaching*, *8*(1), 298–305.

Radianti, J., Majchrzak, T. A., Fromm, J., & Wohlgenannt, I. (2020). A systematic review of immersive virtual reality applications for higher education: Design elements, lessons learned, and research agenda. *Computers & Education*, *147*, 103778. DOI: 10.1016/j.compedu.2019.103778

Rahwan, I., Cebrian, M., Obradovich, N., Bongard, J., Bonnefon, J. F., Breazeal, C., & Lazer, D. (2019). Machine Behavior. *Nature*, *568*(7753), 477–486. DOI: 10.1038/s41586-019-1138-y

Ramesh, D., & Sanampudi, S. K. (2022). An automated essay scoring systems: A systematic literature review. *Artificial Intelligence Review*, *55*(3), 2495–2527. DOI: 10.1007/s10462-021-10068-2

Ramineni, C., & Williamson, D. M. (2013). Automated essay scoring: Psychometric guidelines and practices. *Assessing Writing*, *18*(1), 25–39. DOI: 10.1016/j.asw.2012.10.004

Rashid, A. (2024). Untitled. DOI: 10.55277/ResearchHub.vq5dnd6h

Rayimqul o'g'li, A. Y., & Ogunode, N. J. (2025). Modern Research in the Field of Translation in Foreign Countries. Spanish Journal of Innovation and Integrity, 43, 187-191.

Recommendation on the Ethics of Artificial Intelligence. (2022). https://unesdoc.unesco.org/ark:/48223/pf0000381137

Recommendation on the Ethics of Artificial Intelligence—UNESCO Digital Library. (n.d.). Retrieved 9 October 2025, from https://unesdoc.unesco.org/ark:/48223/pf0000380455

Rehman, S. U. (2025). Adaptive Learning Systems for Personalized Language Instruction in Transnational Higher Education. In Bridging Global Divides for Transnational Higher Education in the AI Era (pp. 165-190). IGI Global Scientific Publishing.

Rehman, T. U. (2025). The transformative impact and evolving landscape: A comprehensive exploration of the globalization of higher education in the 21st century. *Journal of Further and Higher Education, 49*(3), 346–361. DOI: 10.1080/0309877X.2025.2457537

Reis, C. S., & Sun, Y. (2025). An Innovative Approach to Integrating AI Into Learning and Teaching at a Transnational University in China. In *Training and Development in Transnational Higher Education* (pp. 331–346). IGI Global Scientific Publishing. DOI: 10.4018/979-8-3373-1897-4.ch016

Reisch, L. A., & Büchel, D. (2016). Consumer Rights 2.0: Consumers in the Digital World : Report of the Advisory Council for Consumer Affairs. In Research Portal Denmark (p. 74). Technical University of Denmark. https://local.forskningsportal.dk/local/dki-cgi/ws/cris-link?src=cbs&id=cbs-81996cb7-9b5a-474c-8e63-d16bcd74cbd8&ti=Consumer%20Rights%202.0%3A%20Consumers%20in%20the%20Digital%20World%20%3A%20Report%20of%20the%20Advisory%20Council%20for%20Consumer%20Affairs

Renick, T. M. (2020). Predictive analytics, academic advising, early alerts, and student success. *Big data on campus: Data analytics and decision making in higher education*, 177-197.

Reyes, R. L., Isleta, K. P., Regala, J. D., & Bialba, D. M. R. (2024). Enhancing experiential science learning with virtual labs: A narrative account of merits, challenges, and implementation strategies. *Journal of Computer Assisted Learning, 40*(6), 3167–3186. DOI: 10.1111/jcal.13061

Rezaei, M. (2025). Artificial intelligence in knowledge management: Identifying and addressing the key implementation challenges. *Technological Forecasting and Social Change, 217*, 124183. DOI: 10.1016/j.techfore.2025.124183

Rian, I. M. (2024, April). Transnational Education (TNE) in the Architecture of Digital Age: A Critical Evaluation of a Sino-British University. In *International Conference on Trends in Architecture and Construction* (pp. 1447-1457). Singapore: Springer Nature Singapore.

Rigos, J. C. (2022). *Applicant Reactions to Highly Automated Video-Interviews: Examining the Influence of Augmentation and Discrimination Experience*. Hofstra University.

Roe, J., O'Sullivan, D., Arumynathan, P., & Kappen, B. (2024). Paraphrase or plagiarism?: Exploring EAP students' use of source material in a transnational university context. *Journal of Applied Learning & Teaching, 7*(2), 232–245.

Rogoff, B. (2003). *The cultural nature of human development*. Oxford University Press.

Roll, I., & Wylie, R. (2016). Evolution and revolution in artificial intelligence in education. *International Journal of Artificial Intelligence in Education, 26*(2), 582–599. DOI: 10.1007/s40593-016-0110-3

Rong, X. L., & Preissle, J. (2009). *Educating immigrant students in the 21st century: What educators need to know*. Corwin Press.

Rosati, E. (2024). Infringing AI: Liability for AI-Generated Outputs under International, EU, and UK Copyright Law. *European Journal of Risk Regulation, 1*. Advance online publication. DOI: 10.1017/err.2024.72

Roshanaei, M., Olivares, H., & Lopez, R. R. (2023). Harnessing AI to foster equity in education: Opportunities, challenges, and emerging strategies. *Journal of Intelligent Learning Systems and Applications, 15*(04), 123–143. DOI: 10.4236/jilsa.2023.154009

Ross, J. (2025) *Students worry they learn nothing from AI – but want it anyway. Times Higher Education.* Available at: https://www.timeshighereducation.com/news/students-worry-they-learn-nothing-ai-want-it-anyway

Ross, S. M. (2014). *A First Course in Probability*. Pearson.

Rosunally, Y. (2024). Inclusive Learning Environment in Transnational Education: A Case Study of a First Year Software Engineering Programme. *Transnational Education Review, 2*(1), 1–19. DOI: 10.33182/ter.v2i1.3183

Rowley, M., & Skipper, Y. (2021). Student and staff expectations and experiences of a UK–China Transnational Education collaboration. *Journal of Applied Research in Higher Education, 13*(5), 1374–1387. DOI: 10.1108/JARHE-01-2020-0021

Roy, S. (2023). Quality assurance of transnational education (TNE). OECD. https://ehea.info/Upload/Topic%203%20Simon%20Roy.pdf

Royal Decree No. (2022). *6/2022 issuing the Personal Data Protection Law (PDPL).* Official Gazette of the Sultanate of Oman.

Royal Decree No. 6/2022 issuing the Personal Data Protection Law. (2022, February 9). *Official Gazette* (No. 1429). https://decree.om/2022/rd20220006/

Rozenshtein, A. Z., & Frazier, K. (2025). Large Language Scholarship: Generative AI in the Legal Academy. DOI: 10.2139/ssrn.5200768

Rozo-García, H., Alcantar-Nieblas, C., & Ramírez-Montoya, M. S. (2024). Scale to measure student perception in collaborative online international learning experiences: Design and validation. *Frontiers in Education, 9*, 1401295. DOI: 10.3389/feduc.2024.1401295

Ryan, R. M., & Deci, E. L. (2022). Self-Determination Theory. In Maggino, F. (Ed.), *Encyclopedia of Quality of Life and Well-Being Research* (pp. 1–7). Springer International Publishing., DOI: 10.1007/978-3-319-69909-7_2630-2

Saaida, M. B. (2023). AI-Driven transformations in higher education: Opportunities and challenges. *International Journal of Educational Research and Studies, 5*(1), 29–36.

Saliba, R. (2024). Transformation in transformative learning: A reversed experience of faculty members teaching in transnational higher education institutions in qatar. *Social Sciences & Humanities Open, 9*, 100823. DOI: 10.1016/j.ssaho.2024.100823

Saliya, C. A. (2025). AI as a Scaffold for Innovation, Equity, and Lifelong Learning: Education through the Lens of the Integrated Flexible Approach. *Equity, and Lifelong Learning: Education through the Lens of the Integrated Flexible Approach (July 22, 2025).*

Salloum, S. A. (2024). AI Perils in Education: Exploring Ethical Concerns. *Artificial Intelligence in Education: The Power and Dangers of ChatGPT in the Classroom*, 669-675.

Sánchez-Martín, C. (2021). Teachers' transnational identities as activity: Constructing mobility systems at the intersections of gender and language difference. *TESOL Quarterly*, *56*(2), 552–581. DOI: 10.1002/tesq.3066

Sanusi, I., & Olaleye, S. (2022). An insight into cultural competence and ethics in K–12 artificial intelligence education. *2022 IEEE Global Engineering Education Conference (EDUCON)*, 790–794. DOI: 10.1109/EDUCON52537.2022.9766818

Sarantinos, V. (2022). An Investigation of the Expansion and Influence of Western Paradigms in Transnational Education and the Impact for Small Businesses. In *Small Business Management and Control of the Uncertain External Environment* (pp. 69–84). Emerald Publishing Limited. DOI: 10.1108/978-1-83909-624-220211005

Sarwari, A. Q., Javed, M. N., Mohd Adnan, H., & Abdul Wahab, M. N. (2024). Assessment of the impacts of artificial intelligence (AI) on intercultural communication among postgraduate students in a multicultural university environment. *Scientific Reports*, *14*(1), 13849. DOI: 10.1038/s41598-024-63276-5

Sbaffi, L., & Zhao, X. (2022). Evaluating a pedagogical approach to promoting academic integrity in higher education: An online induction program. *Frontiers in Psychology*, *13*, 1009305. DOI: 10.3389/fpsyg.2022.1009305 PMID: 36275294

Scardamalia, M., & Bereiter, C. (2006). Knowledge building: Theory, pedagogy, and technology. In Sawyer, K. (Ed.), *Cambridge handbook of the learning sciences* (pp. 97–118). Cambridge University Press.

Schmidt, D. A., Alboloushi, B., Thomas, A., & Magalhaes, R. (2025). Integrating artificial intelligence in higher education: Perceptions, challenges, and strategies for academic innovation. *Computers and Education Open*, *9*, 100274. DOI: 10.1016/j.caeo.2025.100274

Schnieder, M., Williams, S., & Ghosh, S. (2022). Comparison of in-person and virtual labs/tutorials for engineering students using blended learning principles. *Education Sciences*, *12*(3), 153. DOI: 10.3390/educsci12030153

Schueller, J. (2023). Transnational education, labor market outcomes and graduate employability: A scoping review. *Career Development International*, *28*(2), 196–216. DOI: 10.1108/CDI-05-2022-0121

Schulze, M. P., & Kleibert, J. M. (2021). Transnational education for regional economic development? Understanding Malaysia's and Singapore's strategic coupling in global higher education. *International Journal of Training and Development*, *25*(4), 363–382. DOI: 10.1111/ijtd.12242

Sclater, N. (2017). *Learning analytics explained*. Routledge., DOI: 10.4324/9781315679563

Selwyn, N. (2011). *Education and technology: Key issues and debates*. Bloomsbury Publishing.

Selwyn, N. (2019). *Should robots replace teachers?* Polity Press.

Selwyn, N. (2021). *Should robots replace teachers? AI and the future of education*. Polity Press.

Selwyn, N. (2023). *Education in a Digital World*. Routledge.

Sen, A. (1999). *Development as freedom.* Oxford University Press.

Sequeira, S. L., McKone, K. M., Diab, E. M., Thomas, J. G., Wolff, J., & Nesi, J. (2025). Characterizing adolescent social media experiences and links to momentary affect. *Journal of Adolescence, 97*(7), 1722–1737. DOI: 10.1002/jad.12530

Serry, M., Knockel, J., & Greenstadt, R. (2025). An Analysis of Chinese Censorship Bias in LLMs. *Proceedings on Privacy Enhancing Technologies. Privacy Enhancing Technologies Symposium, 2025*(4), 112–129. DOI: 10.56553/popets-2025-0122

Sethi, P. C., & Behera, P. K. (2021, February). Effective online teaching learning during COVID-19 pandemic. [). IOP Publishing.]. *Journal of Physics: Conference Series, 1797*(1), 012068. DOI: 10.1088/1742-6596/1797/1/012068

Shade, L. R., & Singh, R. (2016). "Honestly, we're not spying on kids": School surveillance of young people's social media. *Social Media + Society, 2*(4), 2056305116680005. DOI: 10.1177/2056305116680005

Shafiq, M., & Parveen, K. (2023). Social media usage: Analyzing its effect on academic performance and engagement of higher education students. *International Journal of Educational Development, 98*, 102738. DOI: 10.1016/j.ijedudev.2023.102738

Shahid, F., Elswah, M., & Vashistha, A. (2025). Think Outside the Data. *Colonial Biases and Systemic Issues in Automated Moderation Pipelines for Low-Resource Languages., 8*(3), 2331–2344. DOI: 10.1609/aies.v8i3.36719

Shahzad, M. F., Xu, S., Lim, W. M., Yang, X., & Khan, Q. R. (2024). Artificial intelligence and social media on academic performance and mental well-being: Student perceptions of positive impact in the age of smart learning. *Heliyon, 10*(8), e29523. DOI: 10.1016/j.heliyon.2024.e29523

Shams, F., & Huisman, J. (2011). Managing offshore branch campuses. *Journal of Studies in International Education, 16*(2), 106–127. DOI: 10.1177/1028315311413470

Sharma, M., & Sharma, N. (2024). *The Rise AI-enabled E-Learning Platforms and MOOCs.*, DOI: 10.55938/wlp.v1i5.180

Sharma, V., Saini, U., Pareek, V., Sharma, L., & Kumar, S. (2023). Artificial intelligence (AI) integration in medical education: A pan-India cross-sectional observation of acceptance and understanding among students. *Scripta Medica, 54*(4), 343–352. DOI: 10.5937/scriptamed54-46267

Sharples, M., Adams, A., Ferguson, R., & Gaved, M. (2025). Networked learning for AI-enabled education: Cross-national perspectives. *Computers & Education, 192*, 104650.

Shata, A. (2025). "Opting Out of AI": Exploring perceptions, reasons, and concerns behind faculty resistance to generative AI. *Frontiers in Communication, 10*, 1614804. Advance online publication. DOI: 10.3389/fcomm.2025.1614804

Shea, P., & Bidjerano, T. (2010). Learning presence: Towards a theory of self-efficacy, self-regulation, and the development of a communities of inquiry in online and blended learning environments. *Computers & Education, 55*(4), 1721–1731. DOI: 10.1016/j.compedu.2010.07.017

Sheoran, P., & Kaur, M. J. (2024). Artificial intelligence (AI) enhanced co-operative learning. *Journal of Advanced Multidisciplinary Research Studies and Development, 3*(5), 1–7.

Shermis, M. D., & Burstein, J. C. (Eds.). (2013). *Handbook of automated essay evaluation: Current applications and new directions*. Routledge. DOI: 10.4324/9780203122761

Shin, Y., Song, K., & Kim, S. W. (2021). Exploring Prompt Engineering for Open-Domain Question Answering. arXiv preprint arXiv:2103.09417.

Shokri, R., Stronati, M., Song, C., & Shmatikov, V. (2017). Membership inference attacks against machine learning models. In *2017 IEEE Symposium on Security and Privacy (SP)* (pp. 3-18). DOI: 10.1109/SP.2017.41

Siemens, G. (2005). Connectivism: A learning theory for the digital age. *International Journal of Instructional Technology and Distance Learning, 2*(1), 3–10.

Siemens, G., & Baker, R. S. (2012). Learning analytics and educational data mining: Towards communication and collaboration. In *Proceedings of the 2nd International Conference on Learning Analytics and Knowledge* (pp. 252–254). DOI: 10.1145/2330601.2330661

Simpson, R. (1996, September). Neither clear nor present: The social construction of safety and danger. [). New York: Kluwer Academic Publishers-Plenum Publishers.]. *Sociological Forum, 11*(3), 549–562. DOI: 10.1007/BF02408392

Sirkeci, İ., & Lo, L. (2023). Editorial: Transformative impact of artificial intelligence on higher education. *Transnational Education Review, 1*(2), 65–67. DOI: 10.33182/ter.v1i2.3193

Slade, S., & Prinsloo, P. (2013). Learning analytics: Ethical issues and dilemmas. *The American Behavioral Scientist, 57*(10), 1509–1528. DOI: 10.1177/0002764213479366

Slavin, R. E. (1995). *Cooperative learning: Theory, research, and practice* (2nd ed.). Allyn & Bacon.

Slimi, Z., & Carballido, B. V. (2023). Navigating the Ethical Challenges of Artificial Intelligence in Higher Education: An Analysis of Seven Global AI Ethics Policies. *TEM Journal, 12*(2).

Smith, C. J., Choromides, C., Boyd, V., Proudfoot, L., Wright, M., & Stewart-Knight, F. (2023). Inclusive and Flexible Curriculum Design Framework in Work-based Learning: Providing High Impact Transnational Education Opportunities in Sub-Saharan Africa. In *High Impact Practices in Higher Education: International Perspectives* (pp. 149-167). Emerald Publishing Limited.

Smith, A., Lee, B., & Johnson, C. (2021). Enhancing Multilingual Academic Communication through Generative AI. *Journal of Multilingual Academic Communication, 9*(2), 142–157.

Solano-Flores, G. (2011). Assessing the cultural validity of assessment practices. In Basterra, M. R., Trumbull, E., & Solano-Flores, G. (Eds.), *Cultural validity in assessment: Addressing linguistic and cultural diversity* (pp. 3–14). Routledge.

Sperling, K. (2024). In search of AI literacy in teacher education: A scoping review. Computers & Education. *Artificial Intelligence*.

Šramová, B., & Pavelka, J. (2023). Generation Alpha media consumption during Covid-19 and teachers' standpoint. *Media and Communication, 11*(4), 227–238. DOI: 10.17645/mac.v11i4.7158

Srishti, R. (2025). Cultural immersion and experiential learning in sustainability education. Global Cultural Immersions in Learning for a Sustainable Future, 49-76. DOI: 10.4018/979-8-3373-2508-8.ch002

Steele, A. R., & Douglas, H. E. (2021). Investigating the educational experiences of transnational students: Differences in academic integration, social integration, and institutional and goal commitment. *The British Journal of Educational Psychology, 91*(4), 1414–1433. DOI: 10.1111/bjep.12424

Stewart, J. (2015). *Calculus*. Cengage Learning.

Stone, P., Brooks, R., Brynjolfsson, E., Calo, R., Etzioni, O., Hager, G., . . . Teller, A. (2022). Artificial intelligence and life in 2030: the one hundred year study on artificial intelligence. *arXiv preprint arXiv:2211.06318.*

Strang, G. (2006). *Linear Algebra and Its Applications.* Cengage Learning.

Strubell, E., Ganesh, A., & McCallum, A. (2020, April). Energy and policy considerations for modern deep learning research. *Proceedings of the AAAI Conference on Artificial Intelligence, 34*(09), 13693–13696. DOI: 10.1609/aaai.v34i09.7123

Strzelecki, A. (2023). Students' acceptance of ChatGPT in higher education: An extended unified theory of acceptance and use of technology. *Innovative Higher Education, 49*(2), 223–245. DOI: 10.1007/s10755-023-09686-1

Suárez-Díaz, J. L., Rodríguez-Barroso, N., & Gómez-Trenado, G. (2024, October). Interactive Telegram Bot as a Support Tool for Teaching in Higher Education. In *International Conference on EUropean Transnational Education* (pp. 352-361). Cham: Springer Nature Switzerland. DOI: 10.1007/978-3-031-75016-8_33

Suárez-Orozco, C., Suárez-Orozco, M. M., & Todorova, I. (2008). *Learning a new land: Immigrant students in American society*. Harvard University Press. DOI: 10.4159/9780674044111

Sudhir, V.VARIGANJI SUDHIR. (2024). The ethics of AI in the administration of higher education. *International Journal for Multidisciplinary Research, 6*(6), 30189. Advance online publication. DOI: 10.36948/ijfmr.2024.v06i06.30189

Suguku, D. (2023). Pillar of internationalization in higher education: The contribution of international collaborations and online delivery approaches to internationalization in HEIS. In *SHS web of conferences* (Vol. 156, p. 05004). EDP Sciences. DOI: 10.1051/shsconf/202315605004

Su, J., Ng, D. T. K., & Chu, S. K. W. (2023). Artificial intelligence (AI) literacy in early childhood education: The challenges and opportunities. *Computers and Education: Artificial Intelligence, 4*, 100124. DOI: 10.1016/j.caeai.2023.100124

Su, J., & Yang, W. (2023). Unlocking the power of ChatGPT: A framework for applying generative AI in education. *ECNU Review of Education, 6*(3), 355–366. DOI: 10.1177/20965311231168423

Su, J., Yang, W., Yim, I. H. Y., Li, H., & Hu, X. (2024). Early artificial intelligence education: Effects of cooperative play and direct instruction on kindergarteners' computational thinking, sequencing, self-regulation and theory of mind skills. *Journal of Computer Assisted Learning*, *40*(6), 2917–2925. DOI: 10.1111/jcal.13040

Su, J., & Zhong, Y. (2022). Artificial Intelligence (AI) in early childhood education: Curriculum design and future directions. *Computers and Education: Artificial Intelligence*, *3*, 100072. DOI: 10.1016/j.caeai.2022.100072

Sumner, J. A., Colich, N. L., Uddin, M., Armstrong, D., & McLaughlin, K. A. (2019). Early experiences of threat, but not deprivation, are associated with accelerated biological aging in children and adolescents. *Biological Psychiatry*, *85*(3), 268–278. DOI: 10.1016/j.biopsych.2018.09.008

Sun, Y. (2025). An Innovative Approach to Integrating AI Into Learning and Teaching at a Transnational. *Training and Development in Transnational Higher Education*, 331.

Sun, D., Cheng, G., Yu, P. L. H., Jia, J., Zheng, Z., & Chen, A. (2025). Personalized stem education empowered by artificial intelligence: A comprehensive review and content analysis. *Interactive Learning Environments*, *33*(7), 1–23. DOI: 10.1080/10494820.2025.2462156

Sun, K., Zou, Y., Radesky, J., Brooks, C., & Schaub, F. (2021). Child safety in the smart home: parents' perceptions, needs, and mitigation strategies. *Proceedings of the ACM on Human-Computer Interaction*, *5*(CSCW2), 1-41. DOI: 10.1145/3479858

Suntharalingam, P. (2024). Transnational Education in South/Southeast Asia: Thoughts and Reflections from a Higher Education Partner University in the United Kingdom. In *Critical Reflections on the Internationalisation of Higher Education in the Global South* (pp. 101-120). Emerald Publishing Limited.

Suntharalingam, P. (2025). Introduction to transnational higher education (TNE). In Bridging Global Divides for Transnational Higher Education in the AI Era (pp. 1-28). IGI Global Scientific Publishing.

Sun, Y., Li, N., Hao, J., Sarno, L., & Wang, L. (2022). Post-covid-19 development of transnational education in china: Challenges and opportunities. *Education Sciences*, *12*(6), 416. DOI: 10.3390/educsci12060416

Sutedjo, E., Liu, P., & Chowdhury, T. (2025). Advancing equity and inclusion in educational practices with AI. *British Journal of Educational Technology*, *56*(3), 1–15.

Sutedjo, E., Liu, P., & Chowdhury, T. (2025). Generative AI in Higher Education: A Cross-Institutional Study on Faculty Preparation and Resources. *Computers & Education*.

Syihabuddin, M., Suraj, N. A., Hyldgaard, S. E., & Kainth, N. (2025). Mini Review on Knowledge Management in Higher Education Challenges and Strategies for Effective Implementation. *Socio-Economic and Humanistic Aspects for Township and Industry*, *3*(1), 199–206. DOI: 10.59535/sehati.v3i1.466

Symons, K., Vanwesenbeeck, I., Walrave, M., Van Ouytsel, J., & Ponnet, K. (2020). Parents' concerns over internet use, their engagement in interaction restrictions, and adolescents' behavior on social networking sites. *Youth & Society*, *52*(8), 1569–1581. DOI: 10.1177/0044118X19834769

Taherdoost, H., & Madanchian, M. (2023). Artificial Intelligence and Knowledge Management: Impacts, Benefits, and Implementation. *Computers, 12*(4), 72. MDPI. https://doi.org/DOI: 10.3390/computers12040072

Takavarasha, S.Jr, Van Heerden, R., Thakur, S. C., & Jordaan, A. (2023). Cyber-security in the era of the COVID-19 pandemic: A developing countries' perspective. *International Journal of Industrial Engineering and Operations Management*, *5*(2), 77–85. DOI: 10.1108/IJIEOM-02-2023-0026

Tandon, S., Bennett, D., Mark Nataraja, R., & Pacilli, M. (2023). Outcome following the surgical management of varicocele in children and adolescents: A systematic review and meta-analysis. *Therapeutic Advances in Urology*, *15*, 17562872231206239. DOI: 10.1177/17562872231206239

Taneri, P., & Özbek, Ö. (2023). Promoting diversity and culturally responsive pedagogy in higher education. *Uluslararası Türk Eğitim Bilimleri Dergisi*, *2023*(21), 765–813. DOI: 10.46778/goputeb.1333036

Tan, X. (2024). Artificial intelligence in teacher professional development [Computers & Education: Artificial Intelligence.]. *Systematic Reviews*, •••, 2015–2024.

Tariq, M. U., & Abonamah, A. A. (2021). Proposed Strategic Framework for Effective Artificial Intelligence Adoption in UAE. *Academy of Strategic Management Journal, 20*(Special Issue 2), 1–14. https://www.abacademies.org/articles/proposed-strategic-framework-for-effective-artificial-intelligence-adoption-in-uae.pdf

Temper, M., Tjoa, S., & David, L. (2025). Higher Education Act for AI (HEAT-AI): A framework to regulate the usage of AI in higher education institutions. *Frontiers in Education*, *10*, 1505370. Advance online publication. DOI: 10.3389/feduc.2025.1505370

Thakur, R., Kaushik, S., Chopra, G., & Rohilla, H. (2025). TrueGradeAI: Retrieval-Augmented and Bias-Resistant AI for Transparent and Explainable Digital Assessments. DOI: 10.48550/ARXIV.2509.22516

The AI Fluency Lab. (2025). About The AI Fluency Lab.

The Assessment Network. (2025) *Assessment and AI – where are we now?* [Blog]. Cambridge Assessment. Published 27 May. Available at: https://www.cambridgeassessment.org.uk/blogs/Assessment-and-AI-where-are-we-now/ (Turnitin, 2025. *AI writing detection in the new, enhanced Similarity Report.* [online] Available at: https://guides.turnitin.com/hc/en-us/articles/22774058814093-AI-writing-detection-in-the-new-enhanced-Similarity-Report

The Study of Right to Freedom of Expression. (2025). The Study of Right to Freedom of Expression, Digital Media Laws and Demand for Innovation. *Law and World*, *11*(1), 114–124. DOI: 10.36475/11.1.9

Theopilus, Y., Al Mahmud, A., Davis, H., & Octavia, J. R. (2025). The role of parental mediation strategies and online behaviour on internet addiction in young Indonesian children: A parent survey study. *Behaviour & Information Technology*, •••, 1–24. DOI: 10.1080/0144929X.2025.2578709

Thoriquttyas, T., & Rohmawati, N. (2024). How far artificial intelligence influenced Mu'allim, Murabbi, and Mudarris? Transhumanism and diffusion of innovation theory's perspective. *Suhuf*, *36*(2). Advance online publication. DOI: 10.23917/suhuf.v36i2.6302

Throuvala, M. A., Griffiths, M. D., Rennoldson, M., & Kuss, D. J. (2019). School-based prevention for adolescent internet addiction: Prevention is the key. A systematic literature review. *Current Neuropharmacology*, *17*(6), 507–525. DOI: 10.2174/1570159X16666180813153806

Tikly, L. (2019). *Education for sustainable development in the postcolonial world: Towards a transformative agenda for Africa*. Routledge. DOI: 10.4324/9781315211343

Time. (2025). The AI industry is funding a massive AI training initiative for teachers.

Times of India. (2025). AI to be integrated across all engineering, BBA and BCA curricula: AICTE chief.

Timms, M. J. (2016). Technology and education: What's the connection? *Phi Delta Kappan*, *97*(8), 8–13.

Tirendi, D., & Gargiulo, L. (2024). Measuring the impacts of social media on daily life from millennials to generation alpha. *International Journal of Research in Humanities and Social Studies*, 26-33.

Touretzky, D. S., Gardner-McCune, C., Martin, F., & Seehorn, D. (2019). Envisioning AI for K–12: What should every child know about AI? *Proceedings of the AAAI Conference on Artificial Intelligence*, *33*(1), 9795–9799. DOI: 10.1609/aaai.v33i01.33019795

Trager, R., Harack, B., Reuel, A., Carnegie, A., Heim, L., Ho, L. L., Kreps, S., Lall, R., & Larter, O. hÉigeartaigh, S. Ó., Staffell, S., & Villalobos, J. J. (2023). International Governance of Civilian AI: A Jurisdictional Certification Approach. SSRN Electronic Journal. DOI: 10.2139/ssrn.4579899

Tran, N. H. N., Amado, C. A. D. E. F., & Santos, S. P. D. (2023). Challenges and success factors of transnational higher education: A systematic review. *Studies in Higher Education*, *48*(1), 113–136. DOI: 10.1080/03075079.2022.2121813

Trifiró, F. (2025). The global recognition challenge for transnational education. In *Transnational Education and the Recognition of Qualifications*. Routledge., https://www.taylorfrancis.com/chapters/edit/10.4324/9781003488316-8 DOI: 10.4324/9781003488316-8

Trilling, B., & Fadel, C. (2009). *21st century skills: Learning for life in our times*. John Wiley & Sons.

Tse, A. (2025). Teacher's Reflection on Character Education at a Transnational University: Character Education at the Tertiary Level. *Training and Development in Transnational Higher Education*, 219-238.

Tsolidis, G. (1997). *Foreigners, Family and the Nation: Greek–Australian Narratives of Belonging*. Oxford University Press.

Twenge, J. M., Haidt, J., Blake, A. B., McAllister, C., Lemon, H., & Le Roy, A. (2021). Worldwide increases in adolescent loneliness. *Journal of Adolescence*, *93*(1), 257–269. DOI: 10.1016/j.adolescence.2021.06.006

U.S. Department of Commerce. (2022). *Digital Equity Act programs*. https://www.ntia.gov/page/digital-equity-programs

UAE Government Portal. (2021) *UAE strategy for Artificial Intelligence: The Official Portal of the UAE government, UAE Strategy for Artificial Intelligence | The Official Portal of the UAE Government.* Available at: https://u.ae/en/about-the-uae/strategies-initiatives-and-awards/strategies-plans-and-visions/government-services-and-digital-transformation/uae-strategy-for-artificial-intelligence (Accessed: 10 August 2025).

UK Open University. (2021). *OU Analyse | Knowledge Media Institute | The Open University.* Open.ac.uk. https://analyse.kmi.open.ac.uk/

Ulven, J. B., & Wangen, G. (2021). A systematic review of cybersecurity risks in higher education. *Future Internet, 13*(2), 39. DOI: 10.3390/fi13020039

Umoke, C. C., Nwangbo, S. O., & Onwe, O. A. (2025). The governance of AI in education: Developing ethical policy frameworks for adaptive learning technologies. *International Journal of Advanced Scientific Management and Technology, 11*(2), 71–88. https://www.iiardjournals.org/get/IJASMT/VOL.%2011%20NO.%202%202025/The%20Governance%20of%20AI%20in%20Education%2071-88.pdf

UNESCO. (2020). *COVID-19: How are countries addressing the digital learning divide? A snapshot of policy measures.* https://unesdoc.unesco.org/ark:/48223/pf0000373307

UNESCO. (2021). *Recommendation on the ethics of artificial intelligence.* https://unesdoc.unesco.org/ark:/48223/pf0000381137

UNESCO. (2021). *Recommendation on the Ethics of Artificial Intelligence.* UNESCO Publishing. https://www.unesco.org/en/legal-affairs/recommendation-ethics-artificial-intelligence?utm_source

UNESCO. (2021a). *AI and education: Guidance for policymakers.* https://unesdoc.unesco.org

UNESCO. (2021b). *Recommendation on the ethics of artificial intelligence.* https://unesdoc.unesco.org/ark:/48223/pf0000379920

UNESCO. (2021c). *Global education monitoring report: Non-state actors in education.* https://unesdoc.unesco.org

UNESCO. (2021d). *National ICT policies in education: A comparative analysis.* https://unesdoc.unesco.org

UNESCO. (2022). *Reimagining our futures together: A new social contract for education.* UNESCO Publishing.

UNESCO. (2022). *State of the education report for teachers in India 2022.* https://unesdoc.unesco.org

UNESCO. (2023). *AI and Education: Guidance for Policy-Makers.* UNESCO Publishing.

UNESCO. (2023). Guidance for generative AI in education and research. https://unesdoc.unesco.org/ark:/48223/pf0000385861

UNESCO. (2024). AI Competency Framework for Teachers. Retrieved from UNESCO. (2024). Ethical principles for AI in education. UNESCO Policy Paper No. 45.

UNESCO. (n.d.). *Artificial Intelligence in Education: Ethical and Policy Frameworks.* UNESCO Digital Education Resources.

UNICEF. (2022). *Learning passport: AI in refugee education*. https://www.learningpassport.org

United Nations Educational, Scientific and Cultural Organization. (2021, November 23). *Recommendation on the ethics of artificial intelligence*. https://unesdoc.unesco.org/ark:/48223/pf0000377897

United Nations. (2022). *Our common agenda: Report of the Secretary-General.*

Universities UK. (2021, November 29). *Lessons from the pandemic: Making the most of technology in learning and teaching*. Universities UK.

University of Cambridge. (2023) 'The Discovery of DNA Structure – 70th Anniversary', *University of Cambridge*. Available at: https://www.cam.ac.uk/stories/DNA-structure-discovery-cambridge-70th-anniversary

University of Melbourne. (2024, July 26). *AI learning assistant*. Learning Management System. https://lms.unimelb.edu.au/learning-technologies/ai-learning-assistant

Upsher, R. (2025) Comment in *AI use in higher education* [presentation], UCFB CPD, 12/9/25, Wembley.

UUKi. (2023) *Transnational Education (TNE) data,* https://www.universitiesuk.ac.uk/. Available at: https://www.universitiesuk.ac.uk/what-we-do/policy-and-research/publications/features/uk-higher-education-data-international/transnational-education-tne-data (Accessed: 05 September 2025).

Vajjhala, N. R., & Strang, K. D. (2022). Impact of information communication technology strategies on learning effectiveness. [IJOPCD]. *International Journal of Online Pedagogy and Course Design, 12*(1), 1–14. DOI: 10.4018/IJOPCD.292026

Valkenburg, P. M., Meier, A., & Beyens, I. (2022). Social media use and its impact on adolescent mental health: An umbrella review of the evidence. *Current Opinion in Psychology*, *44*, 58–68. DOI: 10.1016/j.copsyc.2021.08.017

van den Berg, G. (2025). Teachers' experiences of using artificial intelligence from an open distance learning context: Successes, challenges, and strategies for success. *Discover Education*, *4*(1), 192. DOI: 10.1007/s44217-025-00596-2

Van Den Eijnden, R., Koning, I., Doornwaard, S., Van Gurp, F., & Ter Bogt, T. (2018). The impact of heavy and disordered use of games and social media on adolescents' psychological, social, and school functioning. *Journal of Behavioral Addictions*, *7*(3), 697–706. DOI: 10.1556/2006.7.2018.65

van der Ven, H., Corry, D., Elnur, R., Provost, V. J., & Syukron, M. (2024). Generative AI and social media may exacerbate the climate crisis. *Global Environmental Politics*, *24*(2), 9–18. DOI: 10.1162/glep_a_00747

Van Dijk, J. A. (2020). *The digital divide*. Polity Press.

van Leeuwen, A., Teasley, S. D., & Wise, A. F. (2022). Teacher and student-facing learning analytics. In C. Lang, G. Siemens, A. F. Wise, D. Gašević, & A. Merceron (Eds.), *Handbook of Learning Analytics* (2nd ed., pp. 129–140). SoLAR. DOI: 10.18608/hla22.013

VanLehn, K. (2011). The relative effectiveness of human tutoring, intelligent tutoring systems, and other tutoring systems. *Educational Psychologist*, *46*(4), 197–221. DOI: 10.1080/00461520.2011.611369

Vannucci, A., Flannery, K. M., & Ohannessian, C. M. (2017). Social media use and anxiety in emerging adults. *Journal of Affective Disorders, 207*, 163–166. DOI: 10.1016/j.jad.2016.08.040

Varona, D., & Suárez, J. L. (2022). Discrimination, bias, fairness, and trustworthy AI. *Applied Sciences (Basel, Switzerland), 12*(12), 5826. DOI: 10.3390/app12125826

Varsity (2025) 'Open(ing up about) AI', *Varsity Cambridge*. Available at: https://www.varsity.co.uk/comment/29600

Vartiainen, H., Tedre, M., & Valtonen, T. (2020). Learning machine learning with very young children: Who is teaching whom? *International Journal of Child-Computer Interaction, 25*, 100182. DOI: 10.1016/j.ijcci.2020.100182

Vaswani, A., Shazeer, N., Parmar, N., Uszkoreit, J., Jones, L., Gomez, A. N., Kaiser, Ł., & Polosukhin, I. (2017). Advances in neural information processing systems: Vol. 30. *Attention is all you need.* [REMOVED HYPERLINK FIELD]

Veale, M., & Binns, R. (2017). Fairer machine learning in the real world: Mitigating discrimination without collecting sensitive data. *Big Data & Society, 4*(2). Advance online publication. DOI: 10.1177/2053951717743530

Veale, M., Binns, R., & Edwards, L. (2018). Algorithms that remember: Model inversion attacks and data protection law. *Philosophical Transactions. Series A, Mathematical, Physical, and Engineering Sciences, 376*(2133), 20180083. DOI: 10.1098/rsta.2018.0083

Verdoodt, V., Lievens, E., & Chatzinikolaou, A. (2023). The EU Approach to Safeguard Children's Rights on Video-Sharing Platforms: Jigsaw or Maze? *Media and Communication, 11*(4). Advance online publication. DOI: 10.17645/mac.v11i4.7059

Vertovec, S. (2009). *Transnationalism.* Routledge. DOI: 10.4324/9780203927083

Viberg, O., Cukurova, M., Feldman-Maggor, Y., Alexandron, G., Shirai, S., Kanemune, S., & Kizilcec, R. F. (2024). What explains teachers' trust in AI in education across six countries? *International Journal of Artificial Intelligence in Education, 35*(3), 1–29.

Vieriu, A. M., & Petrea, G. (2025). The impact of AI on students' academic development. *Education Sciences, 15*(3), 343. DOI: 10.3390/educsci15030343

Vila Seoane, M. F. (2021). Data securitisation: The challenges of data sovereignty in India. *Third World Quarterly, 42*(8), 1733–1750. DOI: 10.1080/01436597.2021.1915122

von Schomberg, R. (2024). Towards a New Ethos of Science or a Reform of the Institution of Science? Merton Revisited and the Prospects of Institutionalizing the Research Values of Openness and Mutual Responsiveness. SSRN Electronic Journal. DOI: 10.2139/ssrn.4892603

Voogt, J., & Roblin, N. P. (2012). A comparative analysis of international frameworks for 21st century competences: Implications for national curriculum policies. *Journal of Curriculum Studies, 44*(3), 299–321. DOI: 10.1080/00220272.2012.668938

Voss, W. G. (2022). TRANSATLANTIC DATA TRANSFER COMPLIANCE (28 B.U. J. SCI. & TECH. L. 158 (2022)). HAL (Le Centre Pour La Communication Scientifique Directe). https://hal.archives-ouvertes.fr/hal-03793307

Voss, W. G. (2021). Airline Commercial Use of EU Personal Data in the Context of the GDPR, British Airways and Schrems II. *Colo. Tech. LJ*, *19*, 377.

Vygotsky, L. S. (1980). *Mind in Society: Development of Higher Psychological Processes* (Cole, M., Jolm-Steiner, V., Scribner, S., & Souberman, E., Eds.). Harvard University Press., DOI: 10.2307/j.ctvjf9vz4

Walan, S. (2025). Primary school students' perceptions of artificial intelligence–for good or bad. *International Journal of Technology and Design Education*, *35*(1), 25–40. DOI: 10.1007/s10798-024-09898-2

Wallace, M., & Dunn, L. (2013). *Teaching in transnational higher education.* Routledge. DOI: 10.4324/9780203930625

Wang, J., & Ling, S. (2024, August). Digitalization Empowers Cross-border Education in the Post-pandemic Era on the Basis of China-Africa Cultural Memory Project. In *2024 4th International Conference on Big Data Engineering and Education (BDEE)* (pp. 66-73). IEEE. DOI: 10.1109/BDEE63226.2024.00019

Wang, J., Zhang, S., & Zhang, C. (2015). A new adaptive educational testing approach based on data mining. In 2015 IEEE 15th International Conference on Advanced Learning Technologies (pp. 252-253).

Wang, L., & Wang, T. (2024) 'Integrating AI in academic research – Changing the paradigm', *University World News*, 2 May. Available at: https://www.universityworldnews.com/post.php?story=20240502160437 39

WANG. (2025). Artificial intelligence as a catalytic mechanism: A theoretical framework and practical pathways for reshaping the industry-education integration ecosystem. *Integration of Industry and Education Journal*, *4*(3), 1–9. DOI: 10.6914/iiej.040301

Wang, J. (2025). Triple-A transnational education (TNE): Addressing intercultural challenges. *Frontiers in Communication*, *10*, 1568138. DOI: 10.3389/fcomm.2025.1568138

Wang, S., Wang, F., Zhu, Z., Wang, J., Tran, T., & Du, Z. (2024). Artificial intelligence in education: A systematic literature review. *Expert Systems with Applications*, *252*, 124167.

Wang, T., Díaz, D. V., Brown, C., & Chen, Y. (2023). Exploring the Role of AI Assistants in Computer Science Education: Methods, Implications, and Instructor Perspectives. *2023 IEEE Symposium on Visual Languages and Human-Centric Computing (VL/HCC)*, 92–102. DOI: 10.1109/VL-HCC57772.2023.00018

Wang, T., Lund, B., Marengo, A., Pagano, A., Mannuru, N., Teel, Z., & Pange, J. (2023). Exploring the potential impact of artificial intelligence (AI) on international students in higher education: Generative AI, chatbots, analytics, and international student success. *Applied Sciences (Basel, Switzerland)*, *13*(11), 6716. DOI: 10.3390/app13116716

Wang, Y., Yu, T., & Cheng, W. (2023). Cross-cultural collaborative learning in AI-supported virtual environments. *Interactive Learning Environments*, *31*(5), 1047–1064. DOI: 10.1080/10494820.2022.2134567

Wang, Z. (2022). Chinese students at UK universities: Transnational education mobilities as a stepping-stone to adulthood. *Population Space and Place*, *28*(7), e2571. DOI: 10.1002/psp.2571

Wargo, K., & Anderson, B. (2024). Striking a balance: Navigating the ethical dilemmas of AI in higher education. *EDUCAUSE Review*. https://er.educause.edu/articles/2024/12/striking-a-balance-navigating-the-ethical-dilemmas-of-ai-in-higher-education

Warraich, M. K. S., Usman, H., Zakir, S., & Mehboob, M. (2025). Ethical Governance of artificial intelligence Hallucinations in legal practice. 4(2), 603. DOI: 10.71085/sss.04.02.297

Warren, S. J., Vogt, E. B., Tincher, B., & Yang, J. (2025). Enhancing quality assurance through strategic artificial intelligence integration: A framework for higher education digital transformation. *Quality Assurance in Education*. Advance online publication. DOI: 10.1108/QAE-09-2024-0183

Wasserman, L. (2013). *All of Statistics: A Concise Course in Statistical Inference*. Springer. [REMOVED HYPERLINK FIELD]

Wei, G. and Niemi, H. (2022). Ethical guidelines for artificial intelligence-based learning: a transnational study between china and finland. AI in Learning: Designing the Future, 265-282. DOI: 10.1007/978-3-031-09687-7_16

Wenger, E. (1998). *Communities of practice: Learning, meaning, and identity*. Cambridge University Press. DOI: 10.1017/CBO9780511803932

Wen, Y., Wang, Z., & Guo, X. (2025). Trends and applications of AI in immersive learning environments: A systematic review of empirical research. *Interactive Learning Environments*, •••, 1–19. DOI: 10.1080/10494820.2025.2524029

Wertsch, J. V. (1997). *Mind as Action*. Oxford University Press., DOI: 10.1093/acprof:oso/9780195117530.001.0001

Weuts, R., Bleher, J., Bleher, H., Flores, R. T., Xuanyang, G., Pujszo, P., & Almási, Z. (2025). AI Governance in Higher Education: A course design exploring regulatory, ethical and practical considerations. DOI: 10.48550/ARXIV.2509.06176

Wheeler, K. (2024). Global AI ethics: Bridging cultural divides in technology. *Technology Magazine*. https://technologymagazine.com/articles/global-ai-ethics-bridging-cultural-divides-in-technology

Whelan, E., Islam, A. N., & Brooks, S. (2020). Applying the SOBC paradigm to explain how social media overload affects academic performance. *Computers & Education*, *143*, 103692. DOI: 10.1016/j.compedu.2019.103692

White, J. D. (2023). Academic integrity in the age of AI. EDUCAUSE Review. https://er.educause.edu

Whittaker, M., Crawford, K., Dobbe, R., ... (2021). *The AI Now report: Racial bias and surveillance in AI systems*. AI Now Institute. https://ainowinstitute.org

Wieczorek, M., Hosseini, M., & Gordijn, B. (2025). Unpacking the ethics of using AI in primary and secondary education: A systematic literature review. *AI and Ethics*, *5*(5), 1–19. DOI: 10.1007/s43681-025-00770-0

Wilkins, S. (2017). Ethical issues in transnational higher education: The case of international branch campuses. *Studies in Higher Education*, *42*(8), 1385–1400. DOI: 10.1080/03075079.2015.1099624

Wilkins, S., & Balakrishnan, M. S. (2013). Assessing student satisfaction in TNE. *International Journal of Educational Management*, *27*(2), 143–156. DOI: 10.1108/09513541311297568

Williams, B. A., Brooks, C. F., & Shmargad, Y. (2018). How algorithms discriminate based on data they lack: Challenges, solutions, and policy implications. *Journal of Information Policy*, *8*, 78–115. DOI: 10.5325/jinfopoli.8.2018.0078

Williams, D., & Jowallah, R. (2025). The intersection of AI and cultural inclusion in higher education. In *AI and Inclusive Pedagogy*. Springer., https://link.springer.com/chapter/10.1007/978-3-031-93567-1_14

Williamson, B. (2024). The Social life of AI in Education. *International Journal of Artificial Intelligence in Education*, *34*(1), 97–104. DOI: 10.1007/s40593-023-00342-5

Williams, R., Kaputsos, S. P., & Breazeal, C. (2021). Teacher perspectives on how to train your robot: A middle school ai and ethics curriculum. *Proceedings of the AAAI Conference on Artificial Intelligence*, *35*(17), 15678–15686. DOI: 10.1609/aaai.v35i17.17847

Williams, R., Park, H. W., Oh, L., & Breazeal, C. (2019, July). Popbots: Designing an artificial intelligence curriculum for early childhood education. *Proceedings of the AAAI Conference on Artificial Intelligence*, *33*(01), 9729–9736. DOI: 10.1609/aaai.v33i01.33019729

Winner, L. (1980). Do artifacts have politics? *Daedalus*, *109*(1), 121–136.

Wise, A. F., Knight, S., & Ochoa, X. (2021). What makes learning analytics research matter. *Journal of Learning Analytics*, *8*(3), 1–9. DOI: 10.18608/jla.2021.7647

Wolff, J., & Atallah, N. (2021). Early GDPR penalties: Analysis of implementation and fines through May 2020. *Journal of Information Policy*, *11*, 63–103. DOI: 10.5325/jinfopoli.11.2021.0063

Women, U. N. (2021). *Gender snapshot 2021: Achieving the SDGs*. https://www.unwomen.org/en/digital-library/publications

Wood, D., Bruner, J. S., & Ross, G. (1976). The role of tutoring in problem-solving. *Journal of Child Psychology and Psychiatry, and Allied Disciplines*, *17*(2), 89–100. DOI: 10.1111/j.1469-7610.1976.tb00381.x

Woolf, B. P. (2009). *Building intelligent interactive tutors: Student-centered strategies for revolutionizing e-learning*. Morgan Kaufmann.

World Bank. (2021a). *Digital economy for Africa initiative: Broadband access and affordability in Africa*. https://www.worldbank.org/en/programs/all-africa-digital-transformation

World Bank. (2021b). Remote learning during [*Lessons from country experiences*. https://www.worldbank.org/en/topic/edutech]. *COVID*, *19*, •••.

World Bank. (2022). *World development report: Education and the digital economy*. https://www.worldbank.org

World Bank. (2023). *Digital technologies in education: A global outlook.* World Bank Group.

World Economic Forum. (2023). *Future of jobs report 2023.* World Economic Forum.

World Economic Forum. (2025). *Responsible AI in higher education: Skills, trust, integrity.* https://www.weforum.org/stories/2025/09/responsible-ai-in-higher-education-building-skills-trust-and-integrity

World Wide Web Consortium. (2024). *Web Content Accessibility Guidelines (WCAG) 2.2.* https://www.w3.org/TR/WCAG22/

Wright, A., Nyaaba, M., & Choi, G. L. (2021). A decolonial approach to AI in higher education teaching and learning: Strategies for undoing the ethics of digital neocolonialism. *International Journal of Critical Digital Pedagogy, 3*(1), 21–39. https://www.researchgate.net/publication/356554140

Wu, Z. (2024). A Double-Edged Sword: Reconsidering Education and Political Knowledge in Authoritarian Context. SSRN Electronic Journal. DOI: 10.2139/ssrn.4787180

Wu-Ross, A. L. J. (2024). *An Appreciative Inquiry Into Transnational Education University Strategies and Government Policies* (Doctoral dissertation, Auckland University of Technology).

Xia, Y., Shin, S. Y., & Kim, J. C. (2024). Cross-cultural intelligent language learning system (CILS): Leveraging AI to facilitate language learning strategies in cross-cultural communication. *Applied Sciences (Basel, Switzerland), 14*(13), 5651. DOI: 10.3390/app14135651

Xie, Z., Yu, Y., Zhang, J., & Chen, M. (2022). The searching artificial intelligence: Consumers show less aversion to algorithm-recommended search product. *Psychology and Marketing, 39*(10), 1902–1919. DOI: 10.1002/mar.21706

Xue, Y., Chinapah, V., & Zhu, C. (2025). A Comparative Analysis of AI Privacy Concerns in Higher Education: News Coverage in China and Western Countries. *Education Sciences, 15*(6), 650. DOI: 10.3390/educsci15060650

Yadav, N., Liu, J., Ortu, F., Ensafi, R., Jin, Z., & Mihalcea, R. (2025). Revealing Hidden Mechanisms of Cross-Country Content Moderation with Natural Language Processing. *Findings of the Association for Computational Linguistics: ACL, 2022*, 22434–22452. DOI: 10.18653/v1/2025.findings-acl.1153

Yang, Z., Qi, P., Zhang, S., Bengio, Y., Cohen, W. W., Salakhutdinov, R., & Manning, C. D. (2018). HotpotQA: A Dataset for Diverse, Explainable Multihop Question Answering. *ArXiv.*/abs/1809.09600

Yang, W., Ng, D. T. K., & Su, J. (2023). The impact of story-inspired programming on preschool children's computational thinking: A multi-group experiment. *Thinking Skills and Creativity, 47*, 101218. DOI: 10.1016/j.tsc.2022.101218

Yang, Y., Kim, M., Rondinelli, M., & Shao, K. (2025). Pensieve Grader: An AI-Powered, Ready-to-Use Platform for Effortless Handwritten STEM Grading. DOI: 10.48550/ARXIV.2507.01431

Yankova, D. (2024). Academic Integrity Policies in Higher Education Institutions Across Cultures. *English Studies at NBU, 10*(1), 5–20. DOI: 10.33919/esnbu.24.1.1

Yan, Y. (2025). A systematic review of AI ethics in education. Computers & Education. *Artificial Intelligence.*

Yan, Y., & Liu, H. (2024). Ethical framework for AI education based on large language models. *Education and Information Technologies*. Advance online publication. DOI: 10.1007/s10639-024-13241-6

Yan, Z. (2006). What influences children's and adolescents' understanding of the complexity of the Internet? *Developmental Psychology*, *42*(3), 418–428. DOI: 10.1037/0012-1649.42.3.418

Yao, C. W., & Collins, C. (2019). Perspectives from Graduate Students on Effective Teaching Methods: A Case Study from a Vietnamese Transnational University. *Journal of Further and Higher Education*, *43*(7), 959–974. DOI: 10.1080/0309877X.2018.1429583

Ye, J. (2025). Engaging Coachees and Measuring Success in Cross-Cultural Transnational Education: A Systematic Literature Review. *Innovative Approaches to Staff Development in Transnational Higher Education*, 363-388.

Yeo, M. A., & Newton, J. M. (2021). Inclusive Transnational Education Partnerships: A Case Study of a Master of Arts in TESOL Program. *RELC Journal*, *52*(2), 287–306. DOI: 10.1177/00336882211011275

Yeung, K., & Bygrave, L. A. (2022). Demystifying the modernized European data protection regime: Cross-disciplinary insights from legal and regulatory governance scholarship. *Regulation & Governance*, *16*(1), 137–155. DOI: 10.1111/rego.12401

Yoder-Himes, D. R., Asif, A., Kinney, K., Brandt, T. J., Cecil, R. E., Himes, P., Cashon, C. H., Hopp, R. M. P., & Ross, E. (2022). Racial, skin tone, and sex disparities in automated proctoring software. *Frontiers in Education*, *7*, 881449. Advance online publication. DOI: 10.3389/feduc.2022.881449

Yu, H., & Guo, Y. (2023, June). Generative artificial intelligence empowers educational reform: Current status, issues, and prospects. []). Frontiers Media SA.]. *Frontiers in Education*, *8*, 1183162. DOI: 10.3389/feduc.2023.1183162

Yusuf, A., Pervin, N., & Román-González, M. (2024). Generative AI and the future of higher education: A threat to academic integrity or reformation? Evidence from a multicultural perspective. *International Journal of Educational Technology in Higher Education*, *21*(1), 21. DOI: 10.1186/s41239-024-00453-6

Zamchalova, I. Y. (2023). Artificial intelligence: Risks and perspectives of culture. Intellect. Innovations. *Investments*, (5), 102–110. DOI: 10.25198/2077-7175-2023-5-102

Zawacki-Richter, O., Marín, V. I., Bond, M., & Gouverneur, F. (2019). Systematic review of research on artificial intelligence applications in higher education–where are the educators? *International Journal of Educational Technology in Higher Education*, *16*(1), 1–27. DOI: 10.1186/s41239-019-0171-0

Zawacki-Richter, O., Marín, V. I., Bond, M., & Gouverneur, F. (2024). Systematic review of research on AI in higher education. *International Journal of Educational Technology in Higher Education*, *21*(1), 1–36.

Zhai, C., Du, L., Qiao, H., Zhang, Y., Yuan, X., & Zhu, H. (2025). Research on artificial intelligence empowering innovation in traditional Chinese culture. *International Conference on Measurement, Communication, and Virtual Reality (MCVR 2024)*, 60. DOI: 10.1117/12.3069480

Zhang, C., Schießl, J., Plößl, L., Hofmann, F., & Gläser-Zikuda, M. (2023). Acceptance of artificial intelligence among pre-service teachers: A multigroup analysis. *International Journal of Educational Technology in Higher Education*, *20*(1), 49. DOI: 10.1186/s41239-023-00420-7

Zhang, J., & Zhang, Z. Y. (2024). AI in teacher education: Unlocking new dimensions in teaching support, inclusive learning, and digital literacy. *Journal of Computer Assisted Learning*, *40*(4), 1871–1885. DOI: 10.1111/jcal.12988

Zhang, Q., Mohammad Ismail, M. I. R., & Zakaria, A. R. B. (2025). Enhancing intercultural competence in technical higher education through AI-driven frameworks. *Scientific Reports*, *15*(1), 22019. DOI: 10.1038/s41598-025-03303-1

Zhang, W., Li, A. W., & Wu, C. (2025). University students' perceptions of using generative AI in translation practices. *Instructional Science*, *53*(4), 633–655. Advance online publication. DOI: 10.1007/s11251-025-09705-y

Zhao, Z., An, Q., & Liu, J. (2025). Exploring AI tool adoption in higher education: Evidence from a PLS-SEM model integrating multimodal literacy, self-efficacy, and university support. *Frontiers in Psychology*, *16*, 1619391. Advance online publication. DOI: 10.3389/fpsyg.2025.1619391

Zhao, Z., & Zhang, L. (2023). Design of artificial intelligence cultural creative industry based on machine learning. *Soft Computing*, •••, 1–12. DOI: 10.1007/s00500-023-08693-w

Zheng, C., & Ouyang, H. (2023). Factors influencing quality of transnational education: Evidence from a Sino-UK MA program. *Frontiers in Psychology*, *13*, 1099359. DOI: 10.3389/fpsyg.2022.1099359 PMID: 36698605

Zhou, X., & Schofield, L. (2024). Using social learning theories to explore the role of generative artificial intelligence (AI) in collaborative learning. *Journal of Learning Development in Higher Education*, (30). Advance online publication. DOI: 10.47408/jldhe.vi30.1031

Zhu, H. (2025). Identifying and mitigating ethical risks in AI for education: A systematic review. *Humanities & Social Sciences Communications*.

Zhu, H., Yan, Y., & Li, J. (2025). Ethics in AI for education: A systematic review. Computers & Education. *Artificial Intelligence*, *6*, 100–112.

Zhu, Y., Zhu, Z., Xu, W., & Zhu, Y. (2025). Cross-border higher education cooperation under the dual context of artificial intelligence and geopolitics. *Frontiers in Education*, *10*, 1656518. Advance online publication. DOI: 10.3389/feduc.2025.1656518

Zimmerman, B. J. (2002). Becoming a self-regulated learner: An overview. *Theory into Practice*, *41*(2), 64–70. DOI: 10.1207/s15430421tip4102_2

Zlotnikova, I., Hlomani, H., Mokgetse, T., & Bagai, K. (2025). Establishing ethical standards for GenAI in university education: A roadmap for academic integrity and fairness. Journal of Information. *Communication and Ethics in Society*, *23*(2), 188–216. DOI: 10.1108/JICES-07-2024-0104

Zviel Girshin, R., Rosenberg, N., & Kukliansky, I. (2024). Early childhood robotics: Children's beliefs and objective capabilities to read and write programs. *Journal of Research in Childhood Education*, *38*(2), 317–335. DOI: 10.1080/02568543.2023.2259946

Zwanikken, P., Peterhans, B., Dardis, L., & Scherpbier, A. (2013). Quality assurance in transnational higher education: A case study of the troped network. *BMC Medical Education*, *13*(1), 43. Advance online publication. DOI: 10.1186/1472-6920-13-43

About the Contributors

Mazhar Malik is Associate Director/Head of Artificial Intelligence department at UWE Bristol, with extensive expertise in cybersecurity, IoT, digital forensics, and computing education. He has held senior academic leadership roles in the UK and internationally, including at Head of Computing and IT at Global College of Engineering and Technology Oman. Dr. Malik actively contributes to global programme reviews, academic quality assurance, and professional accreditation. His research interests include network and IoT security, digital forensics, data analytics, and technology-enhanced learning. His research portfolio includes over 50 peer-reviewed publications on secure routing in IoT, smart cities, medical data analytics, and AI-enhanced cybersecurity. Notable works include contributions to Vehicular Communications, Computers, IEEE Access, PLOS ONE, and Scientific Reports.

Yasmine Z. Rosunally is a Senior Lecturer in Information Science at the University of the West of England, with over 18 years of experience in higher education. She specialises in Transnational Education (TNE), curriculum design, and international programme management, having led initiatives across China, Nepal, Vietnam, and Hong Kong. Yasmine is a recognised researcher in technology-enhanced learning, gamification, and AI in education, with numerous publications in high-impact journals. She holds a PhD in Applied Computing and is a Senior Fellow of the Higher Education Academy (SFHEA). Yasmine also serves as an external examiner and advisor for several UK universities.

Nuzhat Younis is a Lecturer and SFHEA with extensive experience. She is currently affiliated with UWE Bristol and EDA College, delivering undergraduate and postgraduate modules while supervising research projects across multiple domains, including cybersecurity and business analytics. Nuzhat has a diverse academic and technical background, with teaching and leadership roles across the UK, Middle East, and South Asia. She is pursuing a PhD in Management and IT, focusing on the impact of AI tools in higher education. Passionate about inclusive digital education, she actively contributes to curriculum development, quality assurance, and staff training initiatives.

***

Ashraf Alam currently holds the position of Research Faculty at the Centre of Excellence in Public Policy, Sustainability and ESG Research, housed within the Faculty of Law and Policy Studies at Alliance University, Bangalore. Renowned for his transdisciplinary acumen spanning education, technology, and policy studies, Dr. Ashraf has been distinguished as one of the World's Top 2% Scientists by Stanford University and Elsevier, an accolade that highlights the breadth and depth of his scholarly impact. His prolific academic output includes over fifty SCOPUS-indexed publications and more than one hundred conference presentations at esteemed national and international academic forums. His educational trajectory reflects both depth and versatility: a Ph.D. in Education from the Indian Institute of Technology (IIT) Kharagpur, an M.Ed. with a concentration in Mathematics Education, and a B.S. in Computer Science from the University of Delhi. He also holds postgraduate degrees in Public Administration (M.A.) and Mathematics (M.Sc.), supplemented by a suite of postgraduate diplomas in Higher Education, Guidance and Counselling, Educational Technology, Criminology and Police Administration, and Value Education. Dr. Ashraf is an active participant in global scholarly discourse. As Associate Editor of Frontiers in Education, he plays a pivotal role in curating and guiding intellectual contributions across the Educational, Pedagogical, and Learning Sciences. Concurrently, he serves as Founder and Director of Academic Chronicles Private Limited, where he orchestrates editorial board formation and develops strategic frameworks for peer-reviewed publishing in the Social, Behavioural, and Humanistic Sciences. His research has been disseminated through elite academic platforms, including Elsevier, Springer, Taylor & Francis, Wiley, Routledge, Sage, Emerald, and IEEE, and addresses a remarkably diverse array of topics such as pedagogical theories, educational administration, educational psychology, educational sociology, educational policy, technology-integrated learning, mathematics education, educational philosophy, educational technology, teacher education, and AI/ML in learning environments. Dr. Ashraf's scholarly rigor is further demonstrated by his success in qualifying multiple prestigious examinations including UGC-NET-JRF in both Education and Adult and Continuing Education, UGC- NET in Public Administration, and GATE in Humanities and Social Sciences. At the heart of Dr. Ashraf's intellectual ethos lies a steadfast belief in education as a catalytic and emancipatory force capable of engendering social justice, human flourishing, societal progress, and sustainable transformation. His recent explorations into 'Happiness Engineering' and holistic well- being in school ecosystems articulate a vision of education that transcends instrumentalist paradigms, prioritizing emotional intelligence, global consciousness, empathy, and psychosocial resilience among learners. His research agenda seeks to conceive educational praxis through the affordances of inclusive digital learning, gamified instructional design, and artificial intelligence (AIEd), thereby constructing robust, ethically grounded frameworks for 21st century education. At Alliance University, Dr. Ashraf remains committed to architecting pedagogical models that not only cultivate intellectual dexterity and cognitive excellence but also prepare learners for morally responsive leadership, intellectual nimbleness, and responsible global citizenship in an increasingly volatile, uncertain, complex, and ambiguous (VUCA) world.

Hajar Rashid Alkalbani is an Assistant Professor at Global College of Engineering and Technology (GCET), Oman, with extensive experience in computing education, cybersecurity, information systems, and applied IT practice. Her academic qualifications include a Master of Science in Information Systems from Sultan Qaboos University, complemented by certifications in cybersecurity, digital literacy, and networking. She has been actively involved in delivering modules across computational thinking, information systems, software development, creative technologies, web foundations, and security management. Her research and professional interests focus on cybersecurity practices, information systems, computing education, and technology-enhanced learning, with a recent publication on enhancing cybersecurity in logistics networks in Oman.

Swati Chauhan is Professor and Head of the Department of English at Manav Rachna International Institute of Research and Studies (Deemed to be University), Faridabad, Haryana. She holds an M.A. and Ph.D. in English Literature and was the university topper in her postgraduate studies. With over twenty-one years of teaching experience at undergraduate and postgraduate levels, she has previously served at

Lingayas University, MDU Rohtak, and MJPRU Bareilly. She has guided eight doctoral scholars, with four Ph.D. degrees already awarded under her supervision, and has mentored numerous postgraduate dissertations. Dr. Chauhan has published forty-one research papers in reputed national and international journals, including Scopus and Web of Science indexed ones, and has edited five academic books. She has presented thirty-five papers in conferences, organized faculty development programs and international seminars, and frequently delivers invited lectures. A member of multiple editorial boards, she has received several honors, including the SSPS Academic Excellence Award (2022) and the Karmsu Kaushlam–Best Faculty Award (2024) from Manav Rachna Educational Institutions.

Pooja Choudhary is a Ph.D. scholar associated with Symbiosis Centre for Management and Human Resource Development in Pune, India, under the affiliation of Symbiosis International (Deemed) University and currently working as assistant professor at Global Business School and Research Centre (GBSRC), Pune. Her research focuses on critical aspects of organizational behavior and management. She has co-authored papers on high-performance work systems, employee happiness, workplace bullying, family incivility, and psychological distress, which have been published in good journals. Pooja Choudhary's research demonstrates a keen interest in exploring dynamics contributing to sustainable organizational growth and well-being in the workplace.

Harleen Kaur Professor and HOD at School of Management CGC university Mohali has teaching and research experience of more than 16 years. She has actively participated in a great number of International & National Seminars, Conferences, FDPs and Workshops as Convener, Resource Person & Delegate etc. Her areas of interest and research are in industrial and organizational psychology, employee engagement, corporate social responsibility and consumer psychology. She has taught organizational behaviour, foundations of human resource management, labour legislations, organizational development and change management, organizational psychology, and cross cultural management. She has published papers in various national and international journals.

Chrissie Gallagher-Mundy is a senior lecturer and senior fellow at UCFB Wembley, specialising in physical activity, sport and the role of technology in learning. She began her career in the fitness industry, founding the London Academy of Personal Fitness (LAPF), one of the first providers of home based one-to-one personal training in the U.K. Alongside her entrepreneurial businesses, she has written extensively, publishing 13 books on health, fitness and recovery. Her current focus is on the challenges and opportunities of artificial intelligence in higher education, with particular interest in rethinking assessment, feedback and academic integrity. She combines practical teaching experience, curriculum innovation and a sustained writing career to advocate for inclusive and future-focused educational practice.

Rajiv Gurugopinath serves as an Assistant Professor of Law at Ramaiah College of Law, Bengaluru, and is also enrolled as an advocate with the Karnataka State Bar Council. He began his academic journey with a B.A. LL.B. degree from B.M.S. College of Law, Bengaluru, and went on to complete his Master of Laws (LL.M.) in Constitutional and Administrative Law from University Law College, Bangalore University, where he authored a thesis on “Constitutional Implications of the Appointment of Judges of the Higher Judiciary in India – A Critical Evaluation.” He further pursued a Master of Business Laws (M.B.L.) at the National Law School of India University, Bengaluru. Dr. Gurugopinath earned his doctorate from the School of Law, Vel Tech Rangarajan Dr. Sagunthala R&D Institute of Science and

Technology, Chennai, with his research focusing on "Right to Health – A Study on the Legal Framework and Its Implementation with Special Reference to Bangalore Urban District." An active academic and practitioner, he has presented and published widely in national and international conferences, delivered invited lectures, judged moot courts and legal events, and engaged as a resource person in diverse forums. His teaching and research interests span Constitutional Law, Administrative Law, Jurisprudence, Criminal Law, Business and Intellectual Property Law, as well as Health and Medical Laws. Drawing from both advocacy and academia, he emphasizes a balanced, practice-oriented approach to legal education.

Rohan Jowallah has worked in education for over twenty years. He has taught at various levels: elementary school, middle school, high school, and university. He currently works as an associate instructional designer at the University of Central Florida (UCF). Before joining UCF's Instructional Design Team, Rohan was employed as an Academic Program Planner by The University of The West Indies Open Campus. Rohan has presented at several international conferences and has had several peer-reviewed publications. He continues to develop work for publication. He has also been a reviewer of several international journals. Rohan also teaches online as an adjunct lecturer for two universities. Rohan's current research interests are teaching and learning in higher education, with particular emphasis on online learning and teaching, blended learning and inclusive practices in higher education.

Ro-Hanna Jowallah is a software engineer currently completing her final semester in the Master's program in Cybersecurity at the University of Central Florida (UCF).

Ramya Krishnappa is an accomplished legal academic and Assistant Professor of Law at Ramaiah College of Law, Bengaluru. A member of the Karnataka State Bar Council, she graduated with a B.A. LL.B. from B.M.S. College of Law, Bengaluru. She went on to pursue her Master of Laws (LL.M.) in Constitutional and Administrative Law at KLE's Law College, Bengaluru, where she was awarded a Gold Medal for academic excellence. Her doctoral research was undertaken at Christ University, Bengaluru, where she earned a Ph.D. in Law on the theme "Study on the Legal Framework and Working of Panchayat Institutions with Special Reference to Mandya District." Her scholarship reflects a deep commitment to grassroots governance and constitutional development. With over six years of combined teaching, research, and practice experience, Dr. Krishnappa has established herself as a dedicated educator who prioritizes interactive learning, critical analysis, and student engagement. She is passionate about mentoring young law students, advancing legal research, and contributing meaningfully to both academia and practice.

Nguyen Trung Ky, PhD, is a lecturer at the School of Computer Science and Engineering, International University, VNU-HCM. He teaches programming languages and Artificial Intelligence. His interests include natural language processing, generation and machine learning.

Patrick McCrudden holds a PhD in global value supply chains and specialises in international strategy, transnational education, and the integration of artificial intelligence in higher education. With extensive experience bridging academia and industry, the author's research focuses on how educational institutions navigate complex regulatory environments and adapt to technological transformation in global contexts. The author has published work examining the intersection of transnational education governance, AI policy frameworks, and institutional strategy, with a particular focus on UAE-UK educational partnerships. As the author of They're Not Artificial Anymore: Are We Ready?, the author explores the implications of agentic AI for educational institutions, human development, and organisational governance. Current research interests include the ethical governance of cognitive technologies in education, AI-driven student support systems, and the sustainability of transnational education models in contexts of regulatory divergence. The author brings practical experience in strategic communication, business development, and organisational change management to inform the analysis of how institutions navigate competing regulatory frameworks whilst maintaining academic quality and institutional legitimacy.

Pranay Pandey is a distinguished educator and researcher, currently serving as an Assistant Professor in the Department of Education at Bhatter College, Dantan (Autonomous), West Bengal, India. With an academic foundation in Computer Science, he completed his B.Sc. and M.Sc. before securing First Class First (Gold Medal) distinctions in B.Ed., M.Ed., and M.Phil. in Education from Ramakrishna Mission Sikshanamandira, Belur Math. Dr. Pandey also holds postgraduate degrees in Education and Psychology, a PG Diploma in Guidance and Counselling, and a Ph.D. in Education from Kazi Nazrul University. A prolific scholar, he has authored several books, published widely in reputed journals, developed twelve standardized psychological assessment scales, and holds eight registered copyrights. He serves on editorial boards of national and international journals and has delivered invited lectures across institutions worldwide.

Rozalin Routray is a researcher in the Faculty of Management at Symbiosis International (Deemed) University in Pune, specializing in Human Resource Management & Organizational Behavior. Her research interests revolve around the intersection of human resource practices and organizational development. Currently, her research focuses on exploring Skill Development, Training, Performance Appraisal and Artificial Intelligence within the context of human resource management and Higher Educations. Her PhD research encompasses an in-depth analysis of HRM practices and their impact on fostering diversity and inclusion in the workplace. For further communication, she can be reached at rozalinroutray2009@gmail.com.

Pancham Singh is working as an Assistant Professor in the Information Technology Department at AKGEC, Ghaziabad since 2007. He has over 17 years of teaching experience and one year of industry experience. He completed his B.Tech. in Computer Science & Engineering from Dr. A.P.J. Abdul Kalam Technical University (formerly UPTU), Lucknow, in 2005. He earned a Master's Degree in Information Technology from RTU, Kota, in 2013. Currently, he is pursuing a Ph.D. at Netaji Subhas University of Technology (NSUT), New Delhi, since January 2023. He has written and edited four books in Computer Science and Engineering. He has presented and published more than 45 papers in reputed Conferences and Journals. He has also reviewed more than 100 research papers in IEEE, Springer conferences and Journals. Mr. Singh has published 35 National and International Patents, 5 design grants and 1 Utility Grant. He was a session chair at the International Conference ICDT 2024. At AKGEC, he worked as a timetable in-charge for over 13 years (2010-2023) and a media in-charge for over 8 years (2015-2023). He has performed Flying Squad Duty for AKTU as an in-charge and team member four times. He has attended

Vinita Sinha is currently a Professor (OB&HR) at Symbiosis Center of Management & Human Resource Development, A constituent of Symbiosis International University, Pune, India. She is doctorate in Psychology. Having completed Master in Psychology with specialization in OB she also holds Post Graduate Diploma in Human Resource Management, Post Graduate Diploma in Health Psychology & Behavior Modification. Her areas of interest in teaching and research stretch out in Psychology, OB & HR, evolving trends in management and education, viz-- Social media, accreditation, psychological issues at work, quality aspects of work, psychological well-being, work stress, role stress, attrition trends, etc.

Janaki Sivakumar is an accomplished academic and researcher with extensive experience in computer science education, artificial intelligence, and data-driven innovation. She serves as the Programme Leader for two undergraduate programmes and Module Leader for six modules at the Global College of Engineering and Technology (GCET), Oman, where she has also held the position of Deputy Head of Department. Her teaching and research expertise span across artificial intelligence, cybersecurity, data visualization, and machine learning applications. Dr. Janaki has authored a book on Data Visualization and actively integrates innovative learning technologies into her modules, such as Machine Learning and Predictive Analytics and Programming for Data Science. She is also deeply engaged in academic enhancement and outreach. As the faculty in charge of the British Computer Society (BCS) Student Chapter at GCET, she leads several student engagement initiatives, including AI hackathons, smart device competitions, and school outreach workshops aimed at promoting AI literacy and innovation. Her current research interests focus on AI in cybersecurity, teaching and learning through AI, and cyber forensics. Dr. Janaki regularly conducts workshops and seminars on Design Thinking, Digital Pedagogy, and AI-Driven Teaching Innovation for both faculty and students. Through her academic leadership and commitment to quality education, Dr. Janaki continues to contribute to the advancement of transnational higher education in Oman, fostering a culture of creativity, employability, and technological excellence among learners.

Tuhina is a Senior Research Fellow (UGC), UGC-NET Qualified, and Ph.D. Scholar in the Department of English at Manav Rachna International Institute of Research and Studies, Faridabad, India. Her research explores the intersections of diaspora, transnational education, and digital culture, with a particular focus on the psychosocial and cultural well-being of diaspora youth. In her academic work, she examines how technological innovations such as Artificial Intelligence reshape learning, identity, and cultural continuity across borders. Her scholarship reflects a sustained engagement with the evolving dynamics of globalization, migration, and cultural belonging in the digital age.

Basanthy V M is an Assistant Professor at the Global College of Engineering and Technology (GCET), Muscat, Oman, where she serves in the Department of Mechanical Engineering. She holds an M.Tech in Computer-Aided Structural Analysis and Design and a Postgraduate Certificate in Education from Liverpool John Moores University, UK. She has over 14 years of teaching experience complemented by industry experience in the construction sector. Her research interests include sustainable construction practices, green building technologies, teaching and learning through AI and the integration of innovative approaches in engineering education.

Shivani Vashist is currently serving as Registrar at the Regional Centre for Biotechnology (RCB), Faridabad, Haryana, India. She has extensive administrative and academic experience in higher education, contributing to institutional development and governance. Her professional journey reflects a commitment to fostering academic excellence, research facilitation, and collaborative learning environments. Dr. Vashist continues to play a pivotal role in advancing interdisciplinary education and supporting innovation-driven academic initiatives at RCB.

Index

A

B

C

D

E

F

G

H

I

K

L

M

N

O

P

Q

S

T

U

V

www.ingramcontent.com/pod-product-compliance
Lightning Source LLC
LaVergne TN
LVHW060253011026
849161LV00011B/2704